MARRIAGE AND FAMILY
Coping with Change

MARRIAGE AND FAMILY
Coping with Change

LEONARD CARGAN
Wright State University

Wadsworth Publishing Company
Belmont, California
A Division of Wadsworth, Inc.

Sociology Editor: Sheryl Fullerton
Production: Mary Forkner, Publication Alternatives
Designer: Richard Kharibian
Copy Editor: Kathleen Engelberg
Cover Designer: Gary A. Head
Cover Photograph: Alan McEvoy

© 1985 by Wadsworth, Inc. All rights reserved. No part of this book may be reproduced, stored in a retrieval system, or transcribed, in any form or by any means, electronic, mechanical, photocopying, recording, or otherwise, without the prior written permission of the publisher, Wadsworth Publishing Company, Belmont, California 94002, a division of Wadsworth, Inc.

Printed in the United States of America

1 2 3 4 5 6 7 8 9 10—89 88 87 86 85

ISBN 0-534-04410-7

Library of Congress Cataloging in Publication Data

Cargan, Leonard.
    Marriage and family.

    Bibliography: p.
    1. Family life education—Addresses, essays, lectures. 2. Marriage—Addresses, essays, lectures. 3. Family—Addresses, essays, lectures. I. Title.
HQ10.C27   1985   306.8   84-21964
ISBN 0-534-04410-7

CONTENTS

PREFACE xi

Part One   INTRODUCTION: CHANGING VARIATIONS   1

I   THE CHANGING PICTURE   5

     1   *David R. Mace.* CONTEMPORARY ISSUES IN MARRIAGE   5
         Contemporary issues in marriage revolve around companionship, sex, parenthood, and stability.

     2   *Daniel Yankelovich.* THE NEW NORMS OF DOMESTIC LIFE   11
         The majority idealize a family life of the past but would not return to it if it meant going back to old rules.

     3   *Marvin B. Sussman.* THE FAMILY TODAY   17
         The family life of today reveals variety: the nuclear family, the single-career family, the dual-career family, the single-parent family, the remarried nuclear family, the kin family, and various forms of experimental families.

II   VARIATIONS: SUBCULTURAL DIFFERENCES   24

     4   *Evelyn L. Barbee.* FAMILIES OF ETHNIC PEOPLE OF COLOR: Issues in Social Organization and Pluralism   24
         Failure to accept the fact that the United States is composed of people from diverse ethnic and racial backgrounds leads to a lack of understanding of family life in America.

     5   *Jaime Sena-Rivera and Charlotte Moore.* LA FAMILIA CHICANA   30
         A picture of the Chicano family structure reveals that it is changing.

Part Two   GENDER AND SEXUALITY: INFLUENCES ON INTIMATE RELATIONSHIPS   41

III   ROLE CHANGES   47

     6   *Phyllis LaFarge.* THE NEW WOMAN   47
         The core message of the women's movement has been widely accepted and is leading to changes in values, relationships between men and women, housework, and child rearing, but not without inner conflict.

7   *Betty Friedan.* THEIR TURN: How Men Are Changing   56
   A well-known feminist claims that American men are at the edge of a tidal wave of change—a change in their very identity as men.

IV   SEXUAL EXPRESSION   63

8   *Ira L. Reiss.* SOME OBSERVATIONS ON IDEOLOGY AND SEXUALITY IN AMERICA   63
   Ideological beliefs and practices concerning human sexuality blind us to the reality of our sexual lives.

9   *Dennis Brissett and Lionel S. Lewis.* THE BIG TOE, ARMPITS, AND NATURAL PERFUME: Notes on the Production of Sexual Ecstasy   76
   A survey of sex manuals reveals that sex is being asked to provide that which heretofore had been provided by the family, organized religion, and the workplace combined.

10   *Philip Blumstein and Pepper Schwartz.* COUPLES: The American Way of Loving   88
   American beliefs are presented regarding kissing, loving, position during sex, compatibility, possessiveness, love, jealousy, working, monogamy, trust, cheating, faithfulness, children, and extramarital sex.

V   DEVELOPING INTIMACY   93

11   *David Knox and Kenneth Wilson.* DATING BEHAVIOR OF UNIVERSITY STUDENTS   93
   There are discrepancies in what men and women expect on dates.

12   *Lillian Africano.* DATING AND THE SINGLE PARENT   97
   Every parent knows that a good parent-child relationship can be enriched by every new shared experience. Dating, although a dilemma, is no exception.

13   *Davor Jedlicka.* FORMAL MATE SELECTION NETWORKS IN THE UNITED STATES   102
   Formal mate selection networks abound, since opportunities for meeting eligible persons are seldom available.

Part Three   TO MARRY OR NOT TO MARRY: THE QUESTION OF ALTERNATIVES   109

VI   SINGLES   112

14   *Leonard Cargan and Matthew Melko.* BEING SINGLE ON NOAH'S ARK   112
   An examination of what it's like to be single in the world of the marrieds shows that some beliefs about singles are myths and some are realities.

15   *Peter J. Stein.* MAJOR TASKS FACED BY SINGLE ADULTS   116
   Singles cope with the tasks of adult life using a variety of styles.

VII   COHABITATION   126

16   *Carl A. Ridley, Dan J. Peterman, and Arthur W. Avery.* COHABITATION: Does it make for a Better Marriage?   126
   The type of cohabitation relationship—Linus blanket, emancipation, convenience, or testing—reflects the needs, goals, motivations, and competence of the persons involved.

17 *Barton E. Bernstein.* SO PUT IT IN WRITING   134
 Couples contemplating cohabitation must explore, or at least be aware of, present and future legal perils.

VIII   ALTERNATIVE FORMS   139

18 *David L. Weis.* THE EMERGENCE OF NONEXCLUSIVE MODELS OF THE MARITAL RELATIONSHIP   139
 An overview of previous research is presented, along with a discussion of the social psychological factors that may influence nonexclusive marital sexual patterns.

19 *James Ramey.* EXPERIMENTAL FAMILY FORMS—THE FAMILY OF THE FUTURE   149
 Americans have trouble defining experimental family forms because they are unaware of the family pluralism existing in our society.

Part Four   BEING MARRIED   161

IX   MAKING IT   166

20 *Virginia Satir.* MARRIAGE AS A HUMAN-ACTUALIZING CONTRACT   166
 A well-known marriage counselor believes that in order to make changes in the marital relationship, it is necessary to make changes in the human beings who make the marriage.

21 *Nick Stinnett.* IN SEARCH OF STRONG FAMILIES   172
 An examination of strong families reveals their characteristics.

22 *Richard L. Mason.* FOURTEEN DAYS TO A RICHER MARRIAGE: A Do-It-Yourself Marriage Enrichment Program   176
 When a group experience is not available, it is possible to enrich your marriage by following this program.

23 *Chuck Hillig.* YOUR BELIEFS CAN SABOTAGE YOUR RELATIONSHIPS   182
 Myths about how people operate can lead to problems in interpersonal relationships.

24 *Marcia Lasswell and Norman M. Lobsenz.* THE INTIMACY THAT GOES BEYOND SEX   185
 Couples can improve their ability to share an intimate relationship by improving their understanding of the relationship and the barriers to achieving it.

X   THE QUESTION OF EQUALITY   190

25 *Dair L. Gillespie.* WHO HAS THE POWER? The Marital Struggle   190
 Despite the talk, it is still a caste/class system rationalizing the preponderance of the male sex.

26 *Barbara Chesser.* BUILDING FAMILY STRENGTHS IN DUAL-CAREER MARRIAGES   202
 Two-career families are probably a testing ground of things to come as changes occur in sex roles.

27 *Linda Haas.* ROLE-SHARING COUPLES: A Study of Egalitarian Marriages   207
 Role-sharing is a life-style that demands the wholehearted and enthusiastic willingness of both spouses to participate.

Part Five   THE FAMILY INSTITUTION   217

XI   THE FAMILY GROUP   223

28   *Margaret Duggan.* FAMILY: A Mini-Society   223
  The family is assembled primarily by sheer dumb luck, and yet it is expected to solve our deepest social problems.

29   *Murray A. Straus, Richard Gelles, and Herbert Yahraes.* PHYSICAL VIOLENCE IN FAMILIES   225
  Family violence is a learned behavior that can be prevented.

30   *Jerry Bergman.* LICENSING PARENTS: A New Age of Child-Rearing?   229
  Licensing might provide a means for minimizing the damage done by incompetent parents.

XII   TO PARENT?   236

31   *E. E. LeMasters and John DeFrain.* FOLKLORE ABOUT PARENTHOOD   236
  A rich ethos of romantic folklore has evolved to ensure that the needed role of parenthood is not avoided by most adults.

32   *Bernard Berelson.* THE VALUE OF CHILDREN: A Taxonomical Essay   248
  The reasons for wanting children are culturally imposed, institutionally reinforced, and psychologically welcome.

33   *Patricia Kain Knaub, Deanna Baxtor Eversoll, and Jacqueline Holm Voss.* IS PARENTHOOD A DESIRABLE ADULT ROLE? An Assessment of Attitudes Held by Contemporary Women   252
  Contemporary women will have children, but it will be a little later.

XIII   LIVING WITH CHILDREN   258

34   *Alison Clarke-Stewart.* THE FAMILY AS A CHILD-CARE ENVIRONMENT   258
  Some characteristics of the most adequate kinds of environmental care for young children are presented.

35   *John DeFrain.* ANDROGYNOUS PARENTS TELL US WHO THEY ARE AND WHAT THEY NEED   263
  Androgynous child rearing made easy may be a means of relieving the so-called inevitable decline in family-life satisfaction with the advent of children.

36   *Blaine R. Porter.* SINGLE-PARENT FAMILIES   270
  Adjustments and responsibilities of the single parent are discussed.

37   *Sharon K. Turnbull and James K. Turnbull.* TO DREAM THE IMPOSSIBLE DREAM: An Agenda for Discussion with Stepparents   274
  Some conflicts and stresses of stepparenting can be eased with these guidelines.

XIV   THE POST-PARENTAL PERIOD   278

38   *Polly Greenberg.* THE EMPTY NEST SYNDROME   278
  It's not just that the children are leaving, it's that an era is ending.

39   *Audrey C. Foote.* THE KIDS WHO WON'T LEAVE HOME   283
  The empty nest syndrome may not be a reality, but the return to the nest is.

40 *Victor Kassel.* POLYGYNY AFTER 60   287

Changing certain aspects of the structure of marriage could eliminate some of the social problems of the aged.

Part Six   TRANSITIONS   293

XV   DIVORCE AND WIDOWHOOD   297

41 *Stan L. Albrecht and Phillip R. Kunz.* THE DECISION TO DIVORCE: A Social Exchange Perspective   297

Even when marriages have gone bad, it is almost never easy for the individuals involved to make the decision to terminate their marriages.

42 *Paul Bohannan.* THE SIX STATIONS OF DIVORCE   310

The complexity of divorce is due to the fact that at least six things are happening at once.

43 *Carolyn Balkwell.* TRANSITION TO WIDOWHOOD: A Review of the Literature   312

Death of a spouse brings traumas, grief, and the necessity of restructuring one's life.

XVI   REMARRIAGE   323

44 *Ann Goetting.* THE SIX STATIONS OF REMARRIAGE: Developmental Tasks of Remarriage and Divorce   323

The situations that a person may expect to encounter upon entering and participating in remarried life can be part of a complex process.

45 *Andrew Cherlin.* REMARRIAGE AS AN INCOMPLETE INSTITUTION   333

The present remarriage situation approaches chaos—each family has to work out its own destiny without any realistic guidelines.

XVII   THE FUTURE   341

46 *David Knox.* TRENDS IN MARRIAGE AND THE FAMILY—THE 1980's   341

The latest trends in marriage and family have a behavioral implication for family educators and counselors—to stay informed.

47 *Rosabeth Moss Kanter.* THE NEW UTOPIAN VISION? Bringing Community to the Family   347

New family forms indicate a movement toward the "postbiological family."

APPENDICES: SOME GUIDES   355

A   *Sylvia Porter.* Why Budget?   356

B   *Consumer Reports.* What You Should Know about Divorce Today   365

PREFACE

An examination of textbooks in introductory sociology would reveal that society consists of various institutions designed to meet its basic needs. The major ones are economics, education, the family, politics, and religion. The most pervasive of these is considered to be the family because all persons are born into some form of family. Through its role of socializer of the young, the family transmits society's norms and values and thus becomes society's "traditional culture-bearer." This outcome of a family function makes it difficult to accept and adjust to social changes that are, in turn, affecting family relations. Thus, controversies abound in regard to gender roles, sexual behavior, alternatives to traditional marriage, family roles, child bearing, living with children, and even the future of the family. A resulting problem for the family is the difficulty in obtaining the necessary information for dealing with these controversies. The primary objective of this anthology is to provide this link for dealing with the issues brought about by change.

The first step in providing this framework for this text was the "identification of those issues considered to be the most important. As the cross-chapters list in the Instructor's Manual indicates, numerous marriage-and-family texts were examined. The result is that this text examines the important controversies listed above. The second step was an exhaustive search of the literature for materials dealing with these controversies. The result is a balance of articles in each section that are both interesting and highly readable. Finally, manuscript reviewers' comments were incorporated to make all aspects of the anthology relevant and useful. The resulting extensive introductions to each section of the anthology discuss the major themes of that topic section, noting how each article relates to these themes. The study questions immediately following the section introductions will help to guide you to important items in the readings. It is suggested that you try to answer these questions as you read the material.

Because the anthology is so comprehensive it can be used in several ways to aid in the instructional process—to expand the student's comprehension of main topics, to illustrate lecture materials, and to provide a basis for class discussion. Articles that deal with controversial issues can be used for debate or as the basis of small-group activities.

For the convenience of the instructor, the Instructor's Manual cross-lists chapters in major marriage-and-family texts with corresponding sections in this anthology. This list will facilitate the use of this text with almost all of the major marriage-and-family texts. The Instructor's Manual also contains an abstract of each article's major theme, findings, and conclusions; multiple-choice and essay questions for testing purposes; and a film list by subject matter.

I would like to thank the authors and publishers of the articles for their permission to use them in *Marriage and Family: Coping with Change*. Thanks also go to the reviewers—Betsy Bergen, Kansas State University; Peter Chroman, College of San Mateo; Nancy A. Greenwood, North Dakota State University; Carla B. Howery, American Sociological Association;

Mary Ann Lamanna, University of Nebraska, Omaha; Jack Thiessen, Messiah College; Peter Uhlenberg, University of North Carolina; Eugenia S. Wentworth, Portland Community College. Thanks is also offered to the departmental secretaries, Glena Buchholtz and Betty Snow, to the student aides who helped to assemble and type the material; to Mary Cargan for her many helpful suggestions; and to former student Donna Kothman for her excellent proofreading. To all I give a very large "thank you"!

Leonard Cargan

MARRIAGE AND FAMILY
Coping with Change

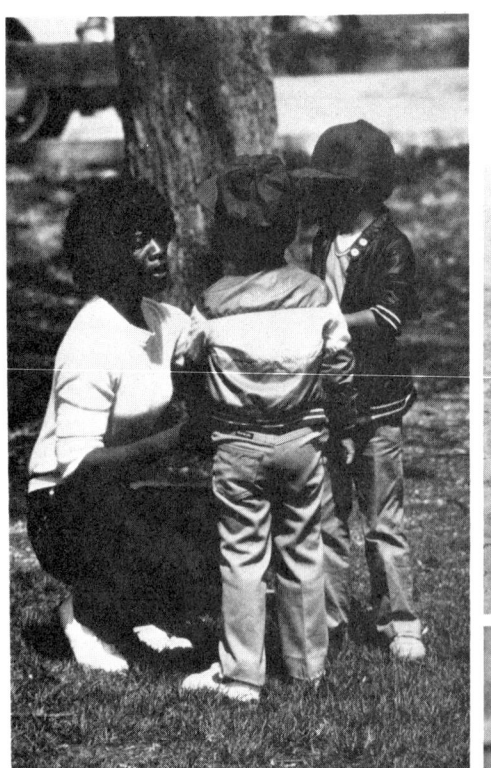

Photographs by Alan McEvoy

Part One

INTRODUCTION: CHANGING VARIATIONS

A glance at American history since the turn of the century reveals that the institution of marriage and family, like other social institutions, is not a static one. The structure and meaning of these twins of personal intimacy have undergone change, and they continue to do so.

For much of the first half of this century, tradition and family custom were an important part of family life. Family unity was usually a more important consideration than were personal needs or attitudes. Gender and age roles were clearly defined and limited, and individual liberty was sacrificed for the sake of continuity and security (Duggan, 1980, p. 261).

Seemingly in support of these values, the married portion of the population had increased throughout this period, with a sudden increase in marriages occurring in the 1950s—from 60 percent to 67 percent of the adult population (U.S. Department of Health, Education and Welfare, 1979, p. 11). With two thirds of its adult population married and the beginnings of a baby boom underway, the United States had become, much more than ever before, a marriage-and-family-oriented society. The fifties became known as the golden age of the family.

The mass circulation magazines emphasized the high value placed on marriage by criticizing the life-styles of what were then known as "bachelors" and "spinsters." Some representative titles include "When Being Single Stops Being Fun," "The Necessary Melancholy of Bachelors," and "There Is No Place in Heaven For Old Maids." They also promoted marriage directly with such titles as "How Come A Nice Girl Like You Isn't Married?" "129 Ways to Get a Husband," and "How to Be Marriageable" (Cargan and Melko, 1982, pp. 229–30). Social scientists added to this emphasis by focusing their research on dating behavior and on ways of achieving marital success and satisfaction. For example, a survey of various studies of marital adjustment indicated that being older and having more education were important predictors of a successful marriage. A marriage was also more likely to be successful if the couple knew each other for a longer period of time before marriage, if they had a good premarital relationship, if they were religious and of the same faith, if neither was previously divorced, if the woman was not pregnant before the marriage, and if both spouses' parents were happily married. In general, "the data seem to say that conventional people and conventional marriages stand the best chance for marital adjustment" (Stephens, 1968, pp. 113–33).

The social unrest of the mid-1960s—protests for social and civil rights and against the Vietnam conflict—revealed that the mood of solace and contentment in marriage was for many an illusionary one. A surface indicator of this discontent was the rising divorce rate. Within ten years of the high point in marriage euphoria, the divorce rate more than doubled, from 2.1 to 4.4 percent per 1000 females. This figure was even higher than that following the end of World War II, when many "quickie" marriages were terminated (U.S. Department of Health, Education and Welfare, 1979, p. 11). Other signs of disaffection with the institution of marriage were a declining marriage rate; movements to such alternative life-styles as remaining single, communal living, and cohabitation; changes in what was considered proper sexual conduct; and the movement for women's rights.

Even beliefs about the family were becoming suspect, with rising statistics on marital and child abuse, sexual molestation of children by their parents, and premarital pregnancy and abortion. A demystification of family life was underway.

The end of the conflict in Vietnam marked another change in attitudes toward marriage and the family. Just as the fifties, the golden age of the family, could be referred to as a "togetherness" decade and the sixties, with its idealistic social commitment, as an "us" decade, so the calculating seventies could be called a "me first" decade. The emphasis had shifted from a joining of partners in an apparently ideal state, to a shared protest of the inequalities of that state, to a preoccupation with one's own fulfillment. From such therapists as Abraham Maslow, Rollo May, Fritz Perls, and Carl Rogers came the ideas of self-fulfillment, self-liberation, self-actualization, and self-expression, (Chilman, 1983, p. 17). This emphasis encouraged a "me first" attitude that was suspect in the breakdown of the traditional family unit. For example, single-parent families began to increase more quickly than traditional two-parent families (Duggan, 1981).

So far, the eighties would seem to reflect both a continuation of the trends begun in the midsixties and seventies and a concern with the effects of those trends. However, the pace of change has slowed as society adjusts to the new patterns that have formed in recent years (Cherlin, 1983, p. 33). Nonetheless, questions and controversies abound: Is marriage a sacred and social obligation, or is it a means of personal fulfillment? Will traditional gender-role behavior or androgynous gender-role behavior be more fulfilling for the child? Should sex be traditional or expressive? What is the role of sex in or out of marriage? Should prospective marital roles be traditional, or should they involve equitable task sharing? It becomes apparent from these questions that a slowing pace of change is greatly needed.

These changes in our concepts of marriage and family are reflected in the first two chapters of this anthology. In the first article, David R. Mace discusses the relationships between marriage and companionship, sex, parenthood, and stability, and he concludes that marriage will continue as an institution because of its fulfillment of the functional outcome of these relationships. In the second article, Daniel Yankelovich also examines the changes that have occurred in marriage by comparing past and present family attitudes. By comparing several national polls, he finds that Americans increasingly accept working wives, smaller families, women who remain single, abortion up to three months of pregnancy, and dual-parent care for children. On the other hand, the use of drugs and extramarital affairs still command majority condemnation. Yankelovich concludes that a desire by the majority to return to the perceived image of family life in the fifties may be in contradiction to the currently accepted rules of domestic life.

This contradiction reflects the fact that social change is always accepted with ambivalence. Few would wish to restore the family's lost functions by closing schools, day-care centers, fast-food operations, and homes for the elderly; by eliminating educational and job opportunities for women; or, for that matter, by restricting the availability of sexual activity outside of marriage. Yet it is these very changes in functions that have led some people to speak of the "death of the family." This is due to the difference in the areas of change. When change occurs in technical areas, it is seen as progress. But when change occurs in such social institutions as the family, our own personal experiences are involved, and so our ability to be objective is limited.

Familiarity also leads to two other difficulties in understanding marriage and family behavior: the ethnocentric belief that our family cultural patterns are natural and thus superior, and a romanticizing of the past—a past that never was. For example, the extended family was no more prevalent in colonial society than it is today; more families have two parents alive today than in those days; yesterday's mothers probably devoted the same amount of time to their children as today's working mothers do, since they had to do housework without labor-saving devices; divorce is replacing death as the family disrupter, but with the advantage that most divorced people remarry (Bane, 1976).

Examples of these changes can be seen in the final article of the first chapter. Marvin Sussman summarizes the arguments in the "death of the family" debate by noting the changes that have occurred, why they have occurred, and the strengths of the resulting alternative family styles. As can be seen in this article, the meanings and functions of the family may change, but change can be considered an important indicator of energy in family life. When old rules and customary patterns of behavior are no longer applicable, their disappearance causes a loss not only of ease, but of "the constraints of traditional, taken-for-granted patterns of behavior (Skolnick, 1981).

Announcements of the family's death, then, are premature. So far as their actions indicate, Americans strongly favor marriage and a family existence. Thus, nine out of ten young adults will eventually marry, although somewhat later than their counterparts in the fifties and sixties (*Newsweek*, p. 26). The brisk rate of remarriage reaffirms the belief that Americans are losing neither their interest in marriage nor their desire for compatible marriages. However, it is difficult to evaluate the strength of the family, because changes in the family are emphasized by the increase in such "negative" indicators as family disruption and dissolution. This does not have to be the case. Rather than emphasizing the increase in one-parent families, "it could be said that 89 percent of the population were living in families," and that "81 percent of the families with children under 18 had both parents present" (Kitagawa, 1981, pp. 13–14). In sum, the majority of Americans marry, remain married, and have children. Thus, the family is functioning better than critics would have us believe, since it is still the prime source of intimacy and nurturing, albeit now in more recognizable and accepted variations.

The articles in chapter 2 remind us that there never has been a single model of love, marriage, and family organization in the United States. Beliefs of universality tend to obscure our recognition of "historical precedents for multiple legitimate family arrangements" (Skolnick, 1981). Pluralism is the best description of family structures in this country of ethnic, racial, and religious differences. In the first article in chapter 2, Evelyn L. Barbee describes two of these different family forms and notes that such forms may be functional for a particular cultural group. Native Americans see themselves foremost as members of kith and kin rather than as a unified nation sharing many traits and a common language. For them, the preexisting network of family and kinship has priority over other ties. Similarly, the Afro-American family is divided into three basic forms, which are subdivided into 12 other forms. The majority of these families are not, as the literature implies, female headed.

In the second article, Jaime Sena-Rivera and Charlotte Moore examine another erroneous belief, the belief in the extended family of the American Chicano. They note the development of pluralistic family forms with the movement of the Chicano to urban areas. We can thus see why it is necessary to step outside our own culture and "note the arbitrary and variable nature" of our beliefs; to recognize that our marriage and family creeds and mores are not inevitable or universal (Keller, 1971, p. 580).

STUDY QUESTIONS

Chapter I

Mace
1. Why has marriage existed throughout human history?
2. Do you agree that in the future men and women will seek to enter marriage more eagerly than in the past? Why?

Yankelovich
1. With which three of the normative changes would you agree? Why?
2. With which three of the normative changes would you disagree? Why?

Sussman
1. Indicate reasons why the family is obsolete and why it is viable.
2. What has brought about the pluralistic structure of families?

Chapter II

Barbee
1. What two features of the Native American family did you find most appealing? Why?
2. What has been the result of the focus on the negative aspects of the Afro-American family?

Sena-Rivera and Moore
1. Why do Sena-Rivera and Moore state that the trigenerational household is not the norm for Mexico or Mexican-Americans?
2. Indicate five features of the prototype *familia*.

REFERENCES FOR PART ONE

Bane, Mary Jo. 1976. *Here to stay: American families in the twentieth century.* New York: Basic Books.

Cargan, Leonard, and Matthew Melko. 1982. *Singles: Myths and realities.* Beverly Hills, Calif.: Sage.

Cherlin, Andrew. 1983. A clouded crystal ball. *Newsweek,* January 17, p. 33.

Chilman, Catherine S. 1983. Prologue: The 1970's and the American families (a comitragedy). (eds). In *Contemporary families and alternative life styles,* ed. by Eleanor Macklin and Roger H. Rubin. Beverly Hills, Calif.: Sage.

Duggan, Margaret. 1981. Violence in the family. In *Understanding the family,* ed. by Cathleen Getty and Winnifred Humphreys. (eds). New York: Appleton-Century-Crofts.

Keller, Suzanne. 1971. Does the family have a future? *The Journal of Comparative Family Studies,* Spring.

Kitagawa, Evelyn M. 1981. New life-styles: Marriage patterns, living arrangements, and fertility outside of marriage. *Annals,* January.

Newsweek. 1983. A clouded crystal ball. *Newsweek,* January 17, p. 26.

Skolnick, Arlene. 1981. The family and its discontents. *Society,* January/February.

Stephens, William. 1968. Predictors of marital adjustment. In *Reflections on marriage.* New York: Crowell.

U.S. Department of Health, Education and Welfare. 1979. *Monthly vital statistics report,* Vol. 27, No. 13. Washington, D.C.: Government Printing Office.

THE CHANGING PICTURE

1

CONTEMPORARY ISSUES IN MARRIAGE

David R. Mace

MARRIAGE IN THE PAST

The archaeologists now tell us that we have had at least a million years of man. They are not able to report with equal confidence that we have had a million years of marriage; but I strongly suspect that we have. We can be certain that, during those million years, the continuity of the race was provided for by the fact that women had babies. We know that they couldn't have had babies without first having had sexual intercourse with men. We know that the experience of motherhood makes a woman vulnerable, and in the grim struggle for existence we can assume that the woman whose man stayed with her and supported her through the experience of motherhood would have a better chance of survival than the woman left to fend for herself. The search for food and shelter and safety was probably most successfully carried out by small groups of people cooperating with one another; and the most natural nuclear grouping, in terms of mutual needs and mutual service, is a man, a woman, and their children. So it is a reasonable supposition that marriage of some sort has existed throughout the entire period of human history.

This was the view of Edward Westermarck, who wrote the classical three-volume *History of Human Marriage* nearly eighty years ago. One of his major conclusions was that marriage is a universal human institution and has been part of the social structure of all settled societies; but that it is also a very flexible institution, and has existed in many forms. He defined marriage as "a relation of one or more men to one or more women which is recognized by custom or law and involves certain rights and duties both in the case of the parties entering the union and in the case of the children born of it."

Another of the major findings of Westermarck was summarized in his famous dictum that "marriage is rooted in the family, and not the family in marriage." What he meant was that human survival depends upon providing the best possible conditions for the birth and upbringing of children, that experience has shown these conditions to be best provided in family life, and that therefore marriage must be controlled and safeguarded by the community in order to ensure the continuity of the family.

This concept of marriage as subsidiary to the family, and therefore subservient to it, has domi-

---

David R. Mace, "Contemporary Issues in Marriage." Address given at the annual meeting of the Southeastern Council of Family Relations, February 26, 1968, Charleston, South Carolina. Unpublished material printed by permission of the author.

nated human history and has never been seriously challenged until our own time. But we are living today through an era of tremendous cultural change, in which all our institutions are being severely shaken; and marriage is no exception. In fact, marriage is changing so much that it is literally being turned inside out. If you think this sounds like dramatic exaggeration, let me assure you that I mean it quite literally; and let me explain what I mean.

In the entire sweep of human history, there have been only two major changes in our way of life—changes so vast that I prefer to call them "social mutations." The first was when man stopped being a wandering hunter and food-gatherer, a puny pigmy fighting against the enormous forces of a hostile nature, and learned to cooperate with nature by growing his food and taming wild animals and enlisting them in his service. This was the change from the nomadic to the agricultural way of life. It led to a long period of relative prosperity, with people living on the land in comparative security. The family was the basic unit of society, and it was generally a large or "extended" family of one kind or another, in which the kinship groups were united in cooperating with one another for the common good. The family was a very rigid institution, resisting all change and dedicated to maintaining the *status quo* from generation to generation.

Then came what we call the Industrial Revolution, which led to the second major social mutation in human history. We are in the midst of this now, and there has never been anything like it before. It began in England with the building of the first factories, and the flocking of the people from the land to the cities. We know all about this change, because we are part of it. The enormous advances of science and technology have now given man power over nature, so that its great forces are more and more coming under his direct control. This is changing radically the entire pattern of human living. Because it is happening gradually, we are not aware how profound the change is. It is almost as if the human race were being transferred from one planet to another, and having to adapt to almost entirely new conditions.

What is important for us is that our new environment is breaking up all our traditional institutions and forcing us to create new ones of quite a different kind. Professor J. K. Whitehead, the English social philosopher, expressed this very well when he said that before the Industrial Revolution, an institution could survive only if it had rigidity and stability; whereas since the Industrial Revolution, the qualities needed for survival are the opposite, namely flexibility and adaptability. These were in fact qualities that the traditional type of marriage could not tolerate. Consequently, marriage and the family as we have known them in the past, throughout most of human history, are breaking down, and must break down. There is absolutely no possibility that they will survive in the new urban-industrial culture that is taking shape everywhere in the world today.

Many people take alarm at this, because they assume that marriage and the family are themselves breaking down. It is very important to stress the fact that this is not so. The disintegration of the old rigid patterns is not something unhealthy, but something healthy. It is the inevitable prelude to the establishment of new patterns that will be much more appropriate to our new way of life. The family is changing, not breaking down. And, as Clark Vincent pointed out in a speech at an N.C.F.R. Conference, the family is showing its fundamental health by proving, after long centuries of rigidity, that it is actually capable of considerable adaptation to our new environment.

In the process of this adaptation, marriage is being turned inside out. In the old days, the central goal in marriage was that it must fulfill certain social and familial obligations—the continuation of the family line, the family inheritance, the family tradition—while somewhere out on the periphery there was a pious hope that the couple might get along harmoniously together. But so long as the familial obligations were met, nobody cared very much whether the couple were happy or unhappy in their interpersonal life. That was quite secondary.

Today, however, the central goal in marriage is personal fulfillment in a creative relationship, and the traditional familial and social obligations have moved out to the periphery. The mood of today is that if your marriage doesn't turn out to be happy, you quit, because finding happiness in marriage is the fulfillment of its fundamental objective.

Some people consider this change of goal as a manifestation of selfishness and irresponsibility. But the change of goal actually corresponds with the change of environment. In the old rural-agricultural society, the major business of life was economic survival and physical safety, and marriage had to conform to these requirements. But in an affluent society, economic survival is taken for granted; and the police, though they have troubles, do their best to assure us of physical safety. In our urban-industrial society, many of the traditional functions of marriage and the family—education, economic production, recreation, and many others—have been taken over by the state. And now our deepest need is for *emotional* security, for the survival of our sense of personal worth and individual significance in a vast world of people in which the individual often doesn't seem to count for anything. By shifting its focus, marriage has now become the primary means by which this individual need for comfort and support and love and understanding can be met. Gibson Winter calls this the "quest for intimacy." In our study of the Soviet family, my wife and I found that in the days of Stalinist terror, marriage was sometimes the only means by which people could keep sane. Surrounded by insecurity, they found their security in the openness and the cathartic communication they could enjoy as husband and wife, when they were alone together. There is a sense in which this kind of need, though not in the same extreme sense, is pervading the whole of modern life. And if marriage can meet that need, it will simply be manifesting one of its dormant potentialities which was almost totally neglected in the past, but is highly relevant today.

MARRIAGE IN THE PRESENT

This brings us to the point at which we can look at contemporary issues in marriage. There are so many of these that it is hard to choose; but for this discussion I have selected four:

1. Marriage as Companionship. You will remember that Ernest Burgess, who might be called the father of family sociology, summarized the fundamental change that is taking place today in the title *Marriage: From Institution To Companionship*. So our focus today is upon marriage as a relationship. This is what we are concerned about, this is what more and more of what we are writing about marriage focuses upon, this is what marriage counselors are working with and trying to facilitate. So I would say that the primary issue in modern marriage is how we can make it a really creative relationship for husband and wife.

When we think of marriage in these terms, however, we begin to realize that husband and wife enter not into one relationship, but into two relationships, which coexist and interact, and yet can be clearly distinguished from each other. There is the relationship between two persons living together as partners, sharing life on an equal basis; and there is the relationship between a man and a woman, which is not equal at all, but reciprocal and complementary. In simple language, married couples have to contrive to be both good partners and good lovers. Failure in one of these areas will not compensate for success in the other. There must be a reasonable measure of satisfaction in both.

The concept of husband and wife as equal partners, sharing life in openness and intimacy, represents a radical break with tradition. Of course there have always been marriages in which good partnership was achieved; but there has never before been a time in which this was a primary criterion of success applied to *all* marriages. Indeed, traditional societies devised two means by which the concept of equal partnership, and of the two-vote marriage, was carefully avoided. First, a hierarchical distinction was made between husband and wife, the husband being acknowledged as having almost all the power, and the wife being compliant and obedient. Second, the spheres of influence of husband and wife were rigidly segregated, so that there was the minimum chance that they might compete or clash with one another. These devices were highly developed, and there is no doubt that they were based on the discovery that attempts to make marriage a relationship of close sharing led to explosive consequences that must be avoided in the interest of family stability.

But in our modern world we have deliberately given a central place to this concept of the shared life; and the explosive possibilities are very much with us! It would not be too much to say that interpersonal conflict, far from being an extraneous element in modern marriage, actually represents the raw material out of which an effective marital partnership has to be shaped. Unless we clearly recognize this, and deliberately teach young people to expect conflict in marriage, and to cope with it adequately, we simply doom large numbers of them to inevitable disillusionment and even disaster. Conflict in marriage is simply the emotional manifestation of disagreement, which is an inevitable consequence of difference. And difference cannot be avoided between two people who live in continuing intimacy, because it is unreasonable to imagine that two different people would always want to do the same thing in the same way at the same time. By insisting on homogamy as a primary condition for successful marriage, we have contrived to minimize interpersonal conflict. But I am not at all sure that the marriages of people with a minimum of difference are necessarily the best marriages. There are enormous potentials for creativity and growth in two people who begin with a good deal of difference, but have the maturity to resolve it and grow together.

When we consider the other relationship in marriage, that of husband and wife as lovers, we encounter at once the fascinating but baffling question of masculine-feminine interaction. For long centuries this has been rather naively interpreted in terms of dominance and submission, or even as superiority and inferiority. One of the somewhat bizarre side-effects of the emergence today of the idea of marriage as companionship is the open revolt of youth against the extreme stereotypes of masculinity as hairy-chested male aggressiveness on the one hand, and docile female compliance on the other. Modern youth has dramatized this protest in the long-haired boy who is not ashamed to identify himself with femininity by looking like a girl, and the modern girl who does not feel any loss of womanhood when she engages in activities that hitherto were reserved exclusively for men.

2. Marriage and Sex. There is an argument going on at the present time as to whether there is a sexual revolution or not. I am in no doubt whatever about this question. There is, emphatically, a sexual revolution. But the confusion is caused by the fact that people are arguing not about the revolution, but about the consequences of it. In my judgment, a revolution is by definition a complete change, a reversal of what previously was believed. But a revolution also, in my view, always takes place in the realm of ideas, and then is gradually translated into changed patterns of living. In these terms, we can say emphatically that the sexual revolution is not only here; it is now almost complete. It began about three-quarters of a century ago, and has resulted in a total change in the way we think about sex. Beginning with an attitude that considered sex essentially negatively, as unwholesome and regrettable though perhaps an unavoidable necessity, we have moved to an attitude which sees sex positively, as something essentially good and creative, though of course capable like everything else of misuse. If a change of this magnitude is not a revolution, I can think of no other radical change in human thinking that is worthy of the name.

However, this revolution has led to many consequences, and one of them concerns the relationship between sex and marriage. In the older cultures, where sex was officially recognized only as a means of procreation for married people, and unofficially as a clandestine pastime in which men exploited women with little regard for the interpersonal implications, a state of uneasy equilibrium could with a little difficulty be maintained. But our new attitude to sex has broken this up completely, and forced us to reevaluate the total situation.

What has precipitated the crisis is the change in our concepts of mate selection. So long as the parents or village elders chose your husband or wife for you, there was no need for boys and girls to be exposed to the risks of meeting socially and forming friendships. Indeed, Confucius insisted that after the age of seven a boy and girl must never even sit together in public! But once the principle was established that young people could choose each other, they naturally wanted to do so on a basis of personal compatibility, and personal compatibility has to be tested out in a period of friendship. Once this has been conceded in any culture, the flood gates are open to the free association of unmarried men and women. This means that it is henceforth impossible to confine sex to marriage by the appeal to force or fear, and sexual morality becomes a question of conscious and deliberate choice based on an acceptance of certain values, which all men and women will not necessarily accept.

Once a principle is established that a man and woman who are unmarried may respond to each other emotionally, and carry that response as far as they personally choose, it becomes impossible to exclude married people from the same privileges. Once premarital chastity has become a matter of conscious choice, marital fidelity follows suit. The consequences of infidelity for the married are of course generally more serious, and this introduces restraints, but we should not be realistic if we did not recognize that one of the major issues in marriage today, in an era where increasingly effective contraceptives are available, is the question of how far married couples generally will accept the principle of sexual exclusiveness, and what is likely to happen to marriage if they don't.

3. Marriage and Parenthood. We all recognize that there has been a radical change in our pattern of marriage, but we are not so ready to see that there has been a corresponding change in parenthood. The societies of the past were rigidly structured, and had little use for individualists who refused to accept the roles allocated to them. The son was expected to follow in his father's footsteps, or to go in whatever direction the family decided was appropriate for him. The task of families was therefore to bring up children to be obedient conformists, who would do what they were told without expressing individual preferences or asking awkward questions. Parenthood was therefore essentially a task of molding human beings to accept their lot without resistance or complaint.

Today, in our open society, obedient conformists become social misfits. In a world where the individual must stand on his own feet and shape his own destiny, qualities that are desirable are the opposite of those needed in the past—namely, autonomy and self-reliance, and the capacity to handle a degree of personal freedom seldom experienced in the past. To prepare children for living in this new world, parents have to accept completely new roles. Their task now is not to mold the child into conformity, but to cooperate with him flexibly in learning to use freedom with wisdom and restraint. This is a much more difficult task, and puts a heavy strain on modern families.

One aspect of this strain is the need for a child to see in his parents the effective exercise of freedom in good relationships and cooperation. We used to accept, without critical examination, the principle that one of the child's primary needs was to be brought up in a home where his father and mother were both present. But the question is now being asked, whether the mere presence of father and mother is enough, if their relationship is vitiated by destructive conflict. We would all agree with the principle that a warm, loving relationship between husband and wife creates the perfect emotional climate for the healthy development of the child. But we have been less willing to examine what the atmosphere created by a bad marriage does negatively to the emotional life of the child. In the close and confining atmosphere of the nuclear family, a continued state of unresolved marital conflict might well be a breeding-ground of psychopathology. In the old extended family, this was unlikely to happen, because there were always other family members in whom the child could find emotional compensation when his immediate parents caused him anxiety and distress.

4. Marriage and Stability. We have seen that in the past the continuity of the family was absolutely essential, and everything else had to be sacrificed to it. Today, our values are different. In the old days, the married couple were shut up in a box together and had to get on with the familial tasks that were committed to them, whether they were happy together or not. I once asked a group of Indians what an Indian wife could do if she found herself in an intolerable marital situation. Quite seriously, I was told that the correct solution for this problem was suicide! This was true throughout the Orient, and there are plenty of illustrations that it was resorted to on occasions. The stability of marriage was the primary value, and nothing else mattered in comparison.

Today the emphasis has shifted, and I believe the shift is permanent. We must face realistically the fact that in the future it will be impossible to hold marriages together by coercion from outside. They will only be held together by cohesion from within. What this means is that the principle that an unhappy marriage must be tolerated for the sake of the stability of the institution, which is an article of Catholic dogma, will be less and less readily accepted in the future. People who consider their marriages unhappy will get out of them, either to remarry or to abandon marriages as a way of life. I think we are moving to the point at which the primary value in marriage will no longer be stability, but creativity. We may not like this, or approve of it. But we can hardly suggest that the difference between stability and creativity in marriage can be equated to the difference between good and evil.

What seems to be clear from our discussion is that the case for a good marriage is overwhelming. A good marriage results in the kind of companionship that marriage is ideally fitted to provide in our modern world. A good marriage finds its own satisfactory solution of the sexual needs of the partners, and provides the atmosphere for happy and successful parenthood. But a bad marriage, or a poor marriage, or a mediocre marriage, poses problems for the persons involved, and for the society to which they belong, which can no longer be avoided or neglected.

What is clear is that marriage in contemporary culture raises all kinds of problems and questions which simply did not bother our ancestors. Those of us who are workers and specialists in this field have been facing these problems and questions. As I perceive the situation, there are three basic tasks that confront us. The first is study and research, so that we may identify the true nature and dimensions of the problems. The second is a massive program of education to enlighten people concerning what is happening to marriage today, and to give them some intelligent understanding of the task they assume when they get married. The third is to develop counseling services to tide married people through the crises that are inevitable in the close and intimate kind of relationship they are asking marriage to provide. The programs we have developed have been on the right lines, and we have made considerable headway with them. What we now need is the widespread support of the community, and the money to provide the services that are needed. This will come only when the community and the nation recognize that good marriages are their most precious asset, and that bad marriages lead to costly and destructive consequences.

MARRIAGE IN THE FUTURE

I have tried to indicate that the changes that are taking place in marriage are a healthy adaptation to the new functions marriage must serve in the altogether different environment in which our children and our children's children will have to live. In the vast, impersonal world of the future, technology will achieve miracles in ministering to human need. But what technology cannot do is to provide for that deep need in all of us that can only be met through intimate relationships in which we know ourselves to be loved and cherished, supported and sustained. There are many ways in which this need can be met, but none that can compare with the experience of a really happy marriage. None of us can predict what life will be like on this planet for distant future generations. But in the foreseeable future, I believe men and women will seek to enter marriage not less eagerly, but more eagerly, than in the past. And as our knowledge increases, and as we learn to make it available and assimilable through sound education and effective counseling, I think the chances are that people will become more mature and more creative, so that they are able to enter into the relationships in depth that make marriages truly happy and successful. In short, as I look into the future of marriage I feel rather optimistic. I do not share the gloomy forebodings that I often hear expressed by those around me. As I look ahead, my feeling is that the potentialities of marriage have not been exhausted. On the contrary, they have not yet begun to be fully developed. I think there is a good chance that what the children of today will see, in their lifetime, is not marriage sinking ignominiously into obsolescence, but blossoming and flourishing as it has never done before in human history.

2

THE NEW NORMS OF DOMESTIC LIFE

Daniel Yankelovich

Many observers have concluded from the news coverage of the past year—the Reagan sweep, the disarray of political liberalism, the tighter constraints of our economy, the emergence of fundamentalist groups opposed to the ERA, abortion, and sex education—that the United States is swinging back to the disciplined, self-sacrificing habits that ruled American life before the heyday of affluence. But that inference is incorrect.

When I asked young women in the 1950s why they cherished marriage, family, and children as their inevitable destiny, many were rendered tongue-tied. My question struck them as unanswerable, meaningless. Asked why she wanted to get married and have children, one woman replied, sarcastically, "Why do you put on your pants in the morning? Why do you walk with two feet instead of one?"

We all know that very little can be taken for granted any longer when it comes to Americans' attitudes toward sexual relations, marriage, family, and childrearing. Some of the changes that have taken place are so profound that we may not realize that they may yet be evolving into newer forms, forms that can now be only dimly discerned. However, to get a perspective on what may be happening, we need to appreciate the shifts of the past few decades.

A variety of surveys point to at least 20 major normative changes in American life in recent years. These 20 are not necessarily the most important changes; they simply are the ones that have been measured in surveys. (See the chart on p. 12.) But at least half of them have to do with domestic norms and portray the virtual abandonment of some of our most deeply entrenched beliefs about marriage and the family. (In some instances we have trend data going back to the 1930s; in others the comparisons go back only 10 or 20 years or even less; and, in a few instances, there are no previous measures, so we must infer from other evidence that a change has taken place.)

The study I conducted in the late 1950s among single and married women in their teens and early 20s demonstrated the strength of marriage norms. All the single women I interviewed assumed they would marry and have children. The married women who did not yet have children all stated that they planned to have them; most wanted three or four children or more. The mothers in the study were all married, and each pronounced herself thoroughly satisfied with being a mother. Although several of the young mothers admitted that they had become pregnant without intending to, none of them felt comfortable saying outright that she did not want to have a child.

These attitudes toward marriage and children were confirmed by a study conducted by the University of Michigan at about the same time. The

---

From Daniel Yankelovich, *New Rules: Searching for Self-Fulfillment in a World Turned Upside Down* (New York: Random House, 1981). Copyright © 1981 by Daniel Yankelovich. Reprinted by permission of the author. This article originally appeared in *Psychology Today,* April 1981.

Twenty Major Changes in the Norms Guiding American Life

1. Disapprove of a married woman earning money if she has a husband capable of supporting her.	1938	
	1978	
2A. Four or more children is the ideal number for a family to have.	1945	
	1980	
2B. Two children is the ideal.	1936	
	1980	
3. For a woman to remain unmarried she must be "sick," "neurotic," or "immoral."	1957	
	1978	
4. Would vote for a qualified woman nominee for President.	1937	
	1980	
5. Condemn premarital sex as morally wrong.	1967	
	1979	
6. Favor decision making abortion up to 3 months of pregnancy legal.	1973	
	1980	
7. Agree that both sexes have the responsibility to care for small children.	1970	
	1980	
8. Approve of husband and wife taking separate vacations.	1971	
	1980	
9. Agree that "hard work always pays off."	1969	
	1976	
10. Agree that "work is at the center of my life."	1970	
	1978	
11A. Men: Would go on working for pay even if they didn't have to.	1957	
	1976	
11B. Women: Would go on working for pay even if they didn't have to.		
	1976	
12. Increase in level of anxiety and worry among young Americans 21–39 years of age.	1957	
	1976	
13. Agree that "the people running the country don't care what happens to people like me."	1966	
	1977	
14. Agree that they "can trust the government in Washington to do what's right."		
	1976	
15. Experience a "hungering for community."	1973	
	1980	
16. Americans with a "sour grapes" outlook on life.	1970	
	1980	
17. Agree that it is morally acceptable to be single and have children.	1979	
18. Agree that interracial marriages are not morally wrong.	1977	
19. Agree that it is not morally wrong for couples to live together even if they are not married.	1978	
20. Agree that they would like to return to standards of the past relating to: sexual mores, "spic and span" housekeeping, women staying home and only men working outside the home.	1979	

Sources:
The Gallup Opinion Index—Nos. 1, 2, 4
NORC: The University of Chicago—No. 1
Institute for Social Research: University of Michigan—Nos. 3, 11, 12, 14
The Roper Organization: for Virginia Slims—No. 4
Yankelovich, Skelly, and White, Inc.—Nos. 5, 7, 8, 9, 10, 15, 16, 17, 18, 19, 20
Harris Survey (ABC/Harris)—Nos. 6, 13

study asked a national cross section of Americans what they thought of anyone, man or woman, who rejected the idea of marriage. An overwhelming majority—a full 80 percent—severely criticized those who preferred the single state, stigmatizing them as "sick" or "neurotic" or "immoral." The remaining 20 percent were neutral, neither condemnatory nor approving. Fewer than one percent had anything good to say about the unmarried state.

By the late 1970s the country's interpretation of the kind of person who would deliberately choose to remain unmarried had shifted strikingly. In another Michigan study, condemnatory attitudes shrunk from 80 percent to a mere 25 percent—from virtual consensus to minority standing. A three-fifths majority (61 percent) swung into the neutral column, and a significant number (14 percent) praised the choice of the unmarried state as a valid and positive way of life. In other words, in the late 1950s, 80 percent of all Americans held that being unmarried was an unnatural state for a man or woman: to be normal was to be married. By the late 1970s, a mere generation later, virtually the same proportion (75 percent) had changed their normative premise.

According to Elizabeth Douvan, a Michigan researcher associated with the study, "Norms about marriage and parenthood have changed dramatically over the past 20 years. Today marriage and parenthood are rarely viewed as necessary, and people who do not choose these roles are no longer considered social deviants."

Furthermore, and also in sharp contrast with the past, it has become normal to think of marriage as not being permanent. When an NBC/Associated Press poll asked Americans in 1978 whether they thought "most couples getting married today expect to remain married for the rest of their lives," a 60 percent majority said no. As Sheila M. Rothman writes in *Woman's Proper Place:* "In the 1950s as in the 1920s, diamonds were 'forever.' In the 1970s diamonds were for 'now'."

These shifts are not just a matter of our changing attitudes and values. Norms influence behavior. Single households (defined by the U.S. Census Bureau as men or women living alone or with an unrelated person) have had an explosive growth rate, increasing 66 percent from 1960 to 1980. During this same period, single-parent families (mainly women, but now including more than one and a half million men) also grew rapidly—from 9 percent of all households in 1960 to 14 percent now. Together, these two categories constitute nearly four out of 10 households. Marriage and traditional family life are growing less universal all the time.

Between 1960 and 1977 it is estimated that the number of unmarried couples living together more than doubled—from 439,000 to 957,000. *Time* magazine quotes one woman, a 27-year-old graduate student living in Kansas, describing her parents' reaction to the news that she was living with a man: "When I first told my parents I had a new roommate, they immediately knew what was going on. My mother's first words were, 'Don't do all the cooking and cleaning'." When Yankelovich, Skelly, and White asked in surveys for *Time* whether people thought it was "morally wrong for couples who are not married to live together," more than half (52 percent) answered no.

There has been a dramatic change in attitudes toward childbearing as well. From the once universally held norm that a childless woman was, by definition, barren and not a complete woman, we have moved to a widespread acceptance of childlessness without stigma. A study by my firm shows that virtually all Americans (83 percent) now believe it is acceptable to be married and not have children. A majority (59 percent) reject even the weaker version of that concept, that "people who do not have children are selfish." In the same tolerant spirit, three out of four Americans say it is now morally acceptable to be single and have children—an astonishing turnabout in mores when one recalls the scandal and disgrace formerly associated with having a child out of wedlock.

Here, too, changes in behavior parallel the shift in norms. In recent years the fertility of American women has followed a steady downward trend—from 118.3 births per 1,000 women of childbearing age in 1955, to 66.7 in 1975. In the period from 1955 to 1959, a woman in her childbearing years could expect to have 3.7 births; in 1965 to 1969, 2.6 births; in 1977, 1.8. In the 1950s married young women who did not want babies were reluctant to admit it. Now I often encounter the reverse situation in interviews: many young women deny any interest in having babies; they admit to harboring a "curiosity" about the experience of childbirth and mothering only if pressed.

So much has been written in recent years about changing sexual norms that we need not dwell on them at length. A few survey findings sum up the story. As recently as 1967, a Yankelovich, Skelly, and White survey for CBS News found that most parents of college-age youths (85 percent) condemned all premarital sex as morally wrong. Now, a majority (63 percent) condone it: "If two people love each other, there's nothing morally wrong with having sexual relations." Nearly the same majority (57 percent) reject the norm that a woman should be a virgin when she gets married. And most Americans now reject the old double standard: "If a husband plays around a little, that's excusable, but a wife never should."

In another form, the double standard lives on. Its existence can be documented in the mere 45 percent plurality of Americans who find male nudes in women's magazines acceptable, as compared with the nearly 60 percent who accept female nudes in men's periodicals. The divergence is merged again, however, in the nearly doubled acceptance of total nudity in films and plays in the last 10 years.

Another change: for the first time in American society, only minorities of adults report discomfort at "having friends who are homosexuals," and while slim majorities still feel that homosexual relations may be morally wrong, there is a declining willingness to restrict the sexual preferences of consenting adults by law; barely one-quarter of the population (21 percent) express a desire for a return to traditional standards in sexual relations.

Not surprisingly, normative changes relating to sexuality, childbearing, and marriage also affect sex roles: the male/female division of effort in the family. Changing norms of what a woman is "supposed to do" as wife and mother and what a man is "supposed to do" as husband and father are transforming the institutions of the workplace and the family. Probably no set of shifting norms carries greater significance for the culture.

Norms affecting whether a wife should work outside the home have reversed themselves within a single generation. It should be kept in mind that some women in America have always worked outside the home. In recent years the number of working women has increased, but the phenomenon is not novel. What is new is not the fact of women working, but its cultural meaning. In the 18th century, and particularly in the 19th, it was not unusual for the whole family—the husband, his wife, and his children—to work for pay outside the home. In the late 19th and early 20th century, as the nation industrialized and its wealth grew, it became a source of pride for a man to be so successful as a provider that his children and even his wife no longer had to work outside the home. In the early post-World War II years, the majority of women with children who worked were blue collar, not bluestocking. When middle-class women worked outside the home, couples spun elaborate rationalizations to ensure that the husband's position as chief bread-winner not be undermined, either in his own eyes or in the eyes of others. The social meaning of his wife's working was that the husband was incapable of providing for his family—he was less than a man.

This shared meaning, which equated manliness with earning power, persisted with great force until the late 1960s. One of my favorite survey questions asks people to define what they mean when they use the phrase "real man." Until the late 1960s, an 85 to 90 percent majority defined a real man as someone who is a good provider for his family. Other meanings—sexual potency, physical strength, being a responsible and caring human being, being handy around the house—always fell far behind this root cultural meaning. In recent years, however, the definition of a real man as a good provider declined from the No. 1 spot to the No. 3 position and slipped from 86 percent in 1968 to 67 percent a decade later. The cultural definition persists, but in attenuated form.

Even more strikingly, the change in the female work population reflects a marked shift in social meanings. Whereas in the past it was mainly blue-collar women who worked for pay, now it is the better educated, upper-middle-class women who increasingly work outside the home, seeking the satisfactions of paid employment that include the financial but are not limited to it.

The cultural meaning of a woman working outside the home has shifted subtly from an act that diminishes the manliness of the "head of household" to one that enhances the status of the woman without adversely affecting the man. As recently as 1970 only a minority of Americans (42 percent) wanted unstintingly to strengthen women's status in our society. By the end of that decade, a two-thirds majority in a Harris survey (64 percent) approved this goal, and work outside the home has become the key to achieving it.

Our research indicates that husbands and wives have different perceptions of the stresses caused by women working. A substantial 25 percent of working wives say their husbands are bothered by having them away from home so much; only one percent of the husbands admit to being so bothered. One out of five working wives claims her husband is disturbed that the home is not as neat and clean as it was before she went out to work, but virtually none of the husbands say that bothers them. Husbands, on the other hand, do admit to disliking pressure to help around the house and say their wives underestimate the discomfort to the whole family caused by the fact that they worked outside the home.

The dual-earner family is rapidly becoming the norm, now accounting for a majority of upper-income households. Economic need pushes many women to take paying jobs outside the home rather than do housekeeping or voluntary work, but it is not always easy to define economic need. In many families, both spouses work in order to maintain a standard of living that they have come to enjoy and expect, though they hardly "need" it, in a literal sense. Indeed, an impressive 67 percent of women who work say that they do so for reasons of self-fulfillment as well as for economic reasons. The majority of women today, including those who work for pay *and* those who stay at home, state that their ideal of the woman who is truly fulfilling herself is someone who can manage a career as well as a home.

As in the case with so many norms, the path of change proceeds along the lines of age and education. Most of the women over 55 feel comfortable with a sharp cleavage of responsibilities between men and women, while only a minority of those under 35 like rigid divisions. Similarly, the old roles are endorsed by a minority of those with some college education (37 percent) and by a majority (57 percent) of those with a high school education or less.

One of the most far-reaching changes in social norms relates to what parents believe they owe their children and what their children owe them. Nowhere are changes in the unwritten social contract more significant or agonizing.

The overall pattern is clear: today's parents expect to make fewer sacrifices for their children than parents did in the past, but they also demand less from their offspring in the form of future obligations than their parents demanded from them. Measures of these attitudes in previous eras do not exist, largely because no one thought of the parent-child bond as anything but permanent. But the data now available are unmistakable.

In a series of studies on the American family carried out by Yankelovich, Skelly, and White in the 1970s for General Mills, the following key findings came to light:

Nearly two-thirds of all American parents (63 percent) reject the idea that parents should stay together for the children's sake even if the parents are unhappy with each other.

A similar majority (66 percent) feel that "parents should be free to live their own lives even if it means spending less time with their children." And an almost equal number of parents (63 percent) endorse the view that they have the right to live well now and spend what they have earned "even if it means leaving less to the children."

On the other hand, most parents recognize that in the name of fairness, if they reduce their level of sacrifice for the children, then the children should not be burdened with future obligations to them. Sixty-seven percent believe that "children do not have an obligation to their parents regardless of what their parents have done for them."

I've saved for the end of this discussion of the new domestic norms one survey finding that encapsulates the ambivalence Americans feel about these changes. The sweeping normative changes in marriage, family life, and the relationship to children I have described fill many people with sadness and nostalgia. The changes create a sense of loss, almost of grief, and give rise to many inconsistencies and contradictions. The large two-thirds

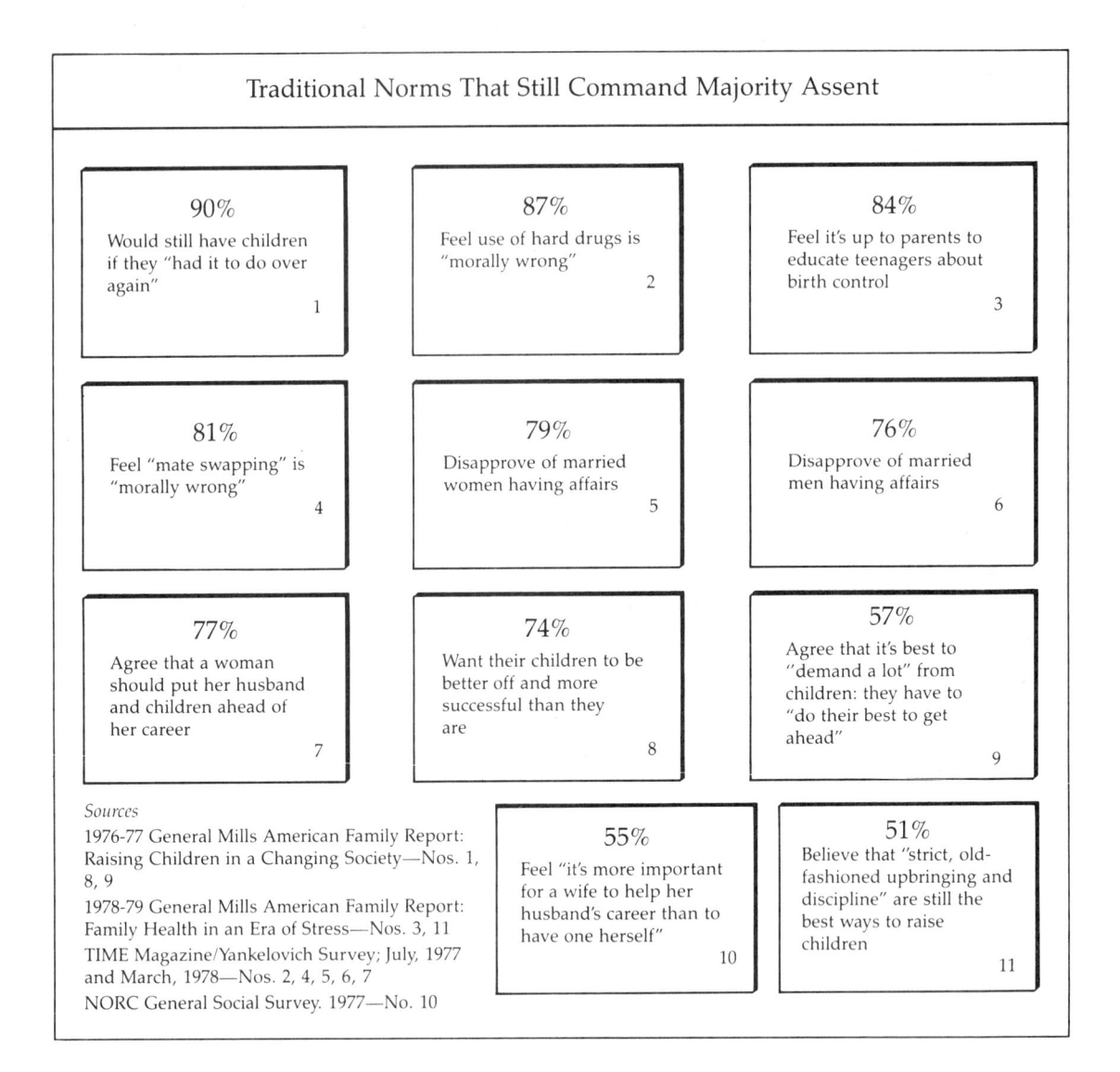

Traditional Norms That Still Command Majority Assent

90% Would still have children if they "had it to do over again" (1)	**87%** Feel use of hard drugs is "morally wrong" (2)	**84%** Feel it's up to parents to educate teenagers about birth control (3)
81% Feel "mate swapping" is "morally wrong" (4)	**79%** Disapprove of married women having affairs (5)	**76%** Disapprove of married men having affairs (6)
77% Agree that a woman should put her husband and children ahead of her career (7)	**74%** Want their children to be better off and more successful than they are (8)	**57%** Agree that it's best to "demand a lot" from children: they have to "do their best to get ahead" (9)
	55% Feel "it's more important for a wife to help her husband's career than to have one herself" (10)	**51%** Believe that "strict, old-fashioned upbringing and discipline" are still the best ways to raise children (11)

Sources
1976-77 General Mills American Family Report: Raising Children in a Changing Society—Nos. 1, 8, 9
1978-79 General Mills American Family Report: Family Health in an Era of Stress—Nos. 3, 11
TIME Magazine/Yankelovich Survey; July, 1977 and March, 1978—Nos. 2, 4, 5, 6, 7
NORC General Social Survey. 1977—No. 10

---

majority that express a reduced commitment of parents to children and children to parents also wish to see "a return to more traditional standards of family life and parental responsibility." (See the chart above for some of the traditional norms that retain widespread support.)

Why the contradiction? A related survey finding provides the key: majorities may claim, in the abstract, that they want to return to the family life of the past, but when it comes to specifics, only one out of five (21 percent) has any hankering to go back to traditional standards of sexual relations, to the spic-and-span housekeeping norms of the past, or to the male monopoly on working outside the home. Americans long for the warmth and closeness they associate with family life in earlier decades, but not if it means going back to the old rules.

How to preserve warmth and closeness while at the same time holding on to the new freedom to choose? That is the preeminent question about our domestic lives that is now confronting our culture.

3

THE FAMILY TODAY

Marvin B. Sussman

Is the family an endangered species? Future historians may label the 1970s as the decade of "The Great Family Debate." The question is: Can the traditional nuclear family created by the legal act of marriage survive? In discussing this concern I would like to examine what constitutes a family and consider the variety of family forms, including the dual working, single-parent and childless family, and their dealings with societal institutions and agencies. The debate over the family's future is by no means academic but one which has gripped all segments of the body politic.

Recently a member of the religious sect, Jehovah's Witnesses, came to my door with a pamphlet entitled "The Family—Can It Survive?" The booklet suggested that the existence of the family unit is threatened because we have a high divorce rate, increased inflation is forcing mothers to seek outside employment and thus give up their traditional parenting roles and violence in the family is increasing, as reflected by the higher incidence of battered wives and abused children. Increasingly, more and more families are no longer eating, working or praying together.

The group's position on these issues was that higher income would not solve these problems and that while education and counseling might offer some help, one should seek wise counsel in the Holy Bible, which provides answers to such questions as "What relationship should exist between a husband and wife for real happiness?; How can differences be resolved so that love is kept or restored?; What can help the generation gap between children and parents?; and How much discipline do children need and how should it be given?"

Such social scientists as Amitai Etzioni and Urie Bronfenbrenner, using more scientific arguments, have reached similar conclusions about the family's future. They assert that the family is becoming increasingly obsolete, with some of its essential and traditional functions under attack. They point to the availability of unlimited sex outside of marriage, the increase in singlehood with a consequent downgrading of the parenting role, the increasing dependence of people upon a complex and bureaucratized work system to meet such primary needs as shelter, food and maintenance and such secondary needs as education, leisure, work, social services and religion. The hamburger phenomenon of the 1970s—the growth of the fast food chains—threatens the traditional homemaker's role and there is increasing dependence on such specialized institutions as schools and social agencies in the socialization of children. Professor Etzioni predicts: ". . . if [the] increase in divorce and single households continues to accelerate as it did the last ten years, by mid-1990 not one American family will be left."[1]

Dr. Bronfenbrenner's posture is equally pessimistic. There is a touch of nostalgia to his stance. He recognizes the need for families to be formed

---

Marvin B. Sussman, "The Family Today: Is It An Endangered Species?" *Children Today*, March–April 1978. Washington, D.C.: U.S. Department of Health & Human Services, Office of Human Development Services.

and procreation to occur and that, in accordance with modern thought, it is necessary that couples have a relationship of shared partnership in regard to household and parenting tasks and responsibilities.

Not all behavioral scientists are taking the postures of Etzioni or Bronfenbrenner, however. Sociologist Mary Jo Bane, for example, believes that proponents of the family's demise have made selective use of demographic and historical data. The nuclear family consisting of husband, wife and offspring living in a separate household apart from either set of parents has existed side by side with extended households since historic American times. In 1870 the average household had 5.8 people, a very small family compared to the traditional extended family currently found in India and Pakistan, for instance, and in pre-World War II Japan.

Despite the alarming views presented by Etzioni, Bronfenbrenner and others, based on such parameters as the high divorce rate, we find that the rate of remarriage is equally high. This indicates that it is not marriage as an institution that is being rejected but only that specific marriage relationships are not all that people would like them to be and that the dictum that marriage is for life is no longer accepted. Most people want to be married but they do not want to stay in an unhappy marriage relationship.

The current concern regarding the increasing incidence of the single-parent family—16 percent of all households in the United States today—ignores the fact that there have always been single parents in the United States. The assumption that in early Colonial times nearly all children lived with both of their parents during their formative years is more myth than fact. High death rates and the mobility of the breadwinner, seeking an improved livelihood by westward migration, meant that more children in early America had fewer parental surrogates than today. Most children born in the 1970s have at least one parent living with them and there are no hard empirical data proving that two parents are better than one in performing the roles necessary for appropriate socialization of a child to help him or her become a vital, creative person.

FAMILY SURVIVAL

The years following the 1970 White House Conference on Children and Youth saw a growing recognition that the structure of the family varies extensively and that concern for the well-being of families should include consideration of both the traditional nuclear family—consisting of husband and wife created by the act of marriage and living with offspring in a residence apart from either set of parents—and other family forms—created by conditions in the larger society or by individual desire and motivation. The report of Forum Fourteen, "Changing Families in a Changing Society," in the *Report to the President: White House Conference on Children (1970)* highlighted the diversity in family structure and functions.

It begins: "Our pluralistic society of varying family forms and a multiplicity of cultures is a fact." Referring to the diversity of family forms in the United States, and the range of ethnic and racial variations within each one, it defines family functions:

"The family functions as a facilitating, mediating, adapting, and confronting system for its members who have differing aspirations, capabilities, and potentials. Families both adapt to, and simultaneously influence, the development, structure, and activities of today's complex urban and industrial institutions. But families differ in their adaptive capabilities largely because of variations in form, and they differ in their efforts to mitigate the demands of non-family groups and influence the behavior of outside organizations such as the school, welfare agency, or factory. *The primary tasks of families are to develop their capacities to socialize children, to enhance the competence of their members to cope with the demands of other organizations in which they must function, to utilize these organizations, and to provide the satisfactions and a mentally healthy environment intrinsic to the well-being of a family.*"

The report emphasized the need to recognize variations from the traditional ideal family form, the implications that such recognition has for parenting, socialization, mental and family health, public policy and legislation, and a need to examine policies and programs in order to see whether they support or constrain the behaviors of members of different family forms in maintaining and expressing themselves.

Since 1970 the Federal Government has provided increasing support for research and demonstration programs relating to family problems and issues. This indicates the seriousness of its concern over the family's current functioning and future. One expression of its interest is the proposed welfare reform legislation being developed by the Carter Administration. Another is that in 1977 the Office of Child Development (OCD) was replaced by the Administration for Children, Youth and Families, which administers all programs formerly in OCD as well as the Youth Development Bureau (formerly the Office of Youth Development) and the Title IV-B Child Welfare Services Program.

VARIANT FAMILY STRUCTURES

There are several ways to perceive the pluralistic structure of families in the United States. One major approach to developing a useful typology is to consider the strengths and weaknesses of different kinds of families, the issues and problems that must be solved by their members. Another way is to look at household distribution. One researcher, J. Ramey, compiled recent Bureau of Labor statistics and arrived at the pattern of household distribution shown in the accompanying chart.[2]

As shown, all but one percent of households have breadwinners and the number of nuclear families with two breadwinners (16%) is higher than the number with only one (13%). Childless households are in the plurality, reflecting the small-size family norm, zero population growth values and persistence of the pattern that after children are launched into college, jobs or marriage they establish households independent of the family in which they were reared. The single-headed households include an increasing number of individuals who are postponing or rejecting marriage or are between marriages or widowed. Even if early (teenage) marriage should once again become the predominant choice among young people, it is likely that the increasing number of widowed persons

DISTRIBUTION OF ADULT AMERICANS BY TYPE OF HOUSEHOLD

(Household Type)	(Percentage of all Households)
Heading single-parent families	16
Other single, separated, divorced or widowed	21
Living in child-free or post-childrearing marriages	23
Living in extended families	6
Living in experimental families or cohabiting	4
Living in dual-breadwinner nuclear families	16
Living in no wage-earner nuclear families	1
Living in single-breadwinner nuclear families	13

(whose life span is increasing) will sustain the percentage of this household form in future years.

A fundamental catalyst behind the development of pluralism in family forms is the movement toward a more equitous distribution of tasks within the household and parity in marital relationships, decision making, parenting, responsibilities for gainful employment and uses of income. In the pre-Revolutionary War period there were calls for egalitarianism in marriage and family life. Women of elite Colonial families such as Abigail Adams and Mercy Warren found a measure of equality with their spouses as they worked with them to rid the Colonies of an English crown and called upon their husbands and leaders of the Constitutional Assembly to consider the human rights of women. But along with all other Colonial women, they were subject to the common law of England, which was transported along with other baggage to the New World.

Inequality in marriage continued after the successful American Revolution and passage of a Declaration of Independence and Bill of Rights which provided unprecedented freedoms for the people of the new nation. Urbanization and industrialization had not reached the critical level of development necessary to provide education and occupational options for women of all social backgrounds.

The state marriage laws which came into existence followed the common law patterns. They denigrated the roles of women and perpetuated a chattel relationship between men and women by their emphasis upon marriage as a status rather than a contract. If marriage is viewed as a contract, it can be dissolved like any other contract when parties find it is not to their benefit and contractors do not live up to expectations. As a status, marriage is a matter of "public interest" to be dissolved only by the state, a procedure which contributed to continued male domination within the family. On the premise that women were incompetent, or at least incapable of providing for themselves, the adopted English common law, reinforced by numerous court decisions, stipulated the man's responsibility for providing for the family. In exchange, his wife carried out his wishes, bore and raised his children and followed him to wherever there was the best opportunity for a job.

Historians, family watchers and other experts will undoubtedly continue to debate the exact causes which have led to recent and continuing changes in gender roles. One explanation is that such situations and events as rapid urbanization and industrialization and two World Wars have made women's labor critical to the national effort and so gradually increased the base of economic and political power to include an increasing number of women.

More educational options for all members of society have led to less contentment with the status quo. The strong social movements of minority and youth groups in the 1950s and 1960s, legislation since the historic 1954 court decision on school desegregation and the development of mass communication networks have all helped push society toward gender role equality.

At the same time, changes in basic values have occurred within society as well as the family. The right to separate and file for divorce to dissolve a marriage is an accepted new value. Thirty-one states now have "breakdown of the marriage" and 13 others invoke separation—usually for one year—as a ground for divorce.[3] The fact that 44 of the 50 states have some version of a no-fault divorce law reduces the legal posture of divorce as an adversary process in which one partner must be found guilty and the other innocent.

Another critical value change has been the increased openness regarding human sexuality—and the distinctions made between sexual behavior for its intrinsic value and for procreation. As a result, there is widespread use of contraceptives, with voluntary sterilization now the most used and preferred technique for fertility control by couples who have been married more than 10 years or by those who have had all the children they want.

The current emphasis on the sharing of responsibilities and parity in couple relationships within the family has led to the emergence of the personal marriage contract.[4] Within the context of a society that supports partnership agreements or contracts and which has accepted the norm of zero population growth, there is also an increasing sense of individualism.[5] The family exists for the benefit of the individual, rather than the individual existing for the benefit of the family.

Concomitant with the emphasis on the individual is a view that parents as well as children have a right to live a full life and that attention should be given to the marital health of a couple.[6] There is a definite shift from viewing one's good work for future gains and rewards and to pass on a legacy to one's issue to viewing life in the present, in terms of one's own existence. Life should be experienced and activities and relationships judged for their intrinsic qualities—joy and satisfaction. It is in this changed time perspective—to consider the present rather than the past or the future—that human rights' movements, including the movement for sexual equality, have their ideological roots. The corollary is a reduction of faith in traditional family forms and institutions, together with an increased suspicion of authority.

Other shifts in values and perspectives result in less reliance for help, information and intimacy upon traditional organizations and institutions such as the church and school and more dependence upon one's peers for response and interest. As a consequence, ideologies and values long identified with established institutions are being rejected as sources of truth. The solution is to rely upon oneself, to take responsibility and do what is required, working with those few with whom it is possible to identify and communicate. Implicit is the assumption that an individual today can choose his or her own living pattern, pursuing the lifestyle and family form which promises the greatest self-actualization.

PROBLEMS AND ISSUES

Endemic to changes in family and household organization and intrafamily relationships are a diminished quality of parenting and increased unpleasantness in the way family members treat one another. Many studies suggest that the incidence of family violence—most often in the form of child abuse and wife-beating—is increasing. In reviewing the research on the extent of marital violence in the United States (and interpolating from three studies which used large samples of the population) S. Steinmetz reports that of the 47 million couples, possibly more than three million wives—and a quarter of a million husbands—experienced severe beatings from their spouses.[7]

The true incidence of child abuse and neglect is also difficult to determine. The National Center on Child Abuse and Neglect in the Children's Bureau, ACYF, estimates that it may be as high as one million cases a year. In one sample of intact families, a researcher discovered that in one of five families parents hit their children with some object as a routine aspect of childrearing and that more than four percent thrashed their children and over two percent threatened them with such bodily harm as stabbing or shooting. And these are "normal" families![8]

Unwanted births and teenage pregnancies are other pressing problems for families, agencies and society.

One development of the 1960s, the Forum Fourteen Report notes, "was the emergence of the client-centered society" and another critical problem is the conflict between the self-help efforts of family members in their roles as clients, patients, consumers, workers, pupils or victims and the organizational bureaucracies and professionals which provide services. Family-centered organizations are demanding reciprocity in their relationships with bureaucracies and are working to effect change in policies and allocation of resources. However, many efforts are being coopted by well- and some not so well-intentioned agencies and their staffs.[9] The professionals have resources and knowledge and the best that most families can do is develop competencies to use and deal with the bureaucratic procedures and workers in these human service agencies.

Battered spouses, abused children, unwanted pregnancies and individuals unprepared for handling the daily exigencies of survival are phenomena endemic to highly complex and differentiated societies; they occur among all family forms in varying degrees. A change in their incidence will only take place if basic modifications are made in our present social structures and in the allocation of economic resources and human services. This important issue cannot be treated in a short essay. What can be discussed here are some of the difficulties and some of the advantages encountered by individuals living in different types of households, as viewed by this family watcher. In so doing, I pass on to the reader responsibility to make an overall judgment of the strengths and weaknesses of American families.

My appraisal of the strengths and weaknesses of each of six different family forms, based on a review of empirical studies, clinical reports and my own research activity, follows.

The Single Career Family: intact nuclear family consisting of husband, wife and offspring living in a common household where one partner, usually the husband, is the provider. (Represents 13 percent of all households.)

Strengths

Maintains its position as the primary structure for potential socialization of members over the life cycle.

Is the primary unit for taking care of disabled, deviant and dependent members.

Is among the best adapted in terms of fitting the demands of the corporate economic structure.

Weaknesses

Is easily broken, with increasing intervention of organizations and expenditure of monies to maintain individuals of broken marriages and new family forms.

The single breadwinner of the working class is unable to provide adequately for its maintenance. Among the middle classes, there is difficulty in providing an expected quality of life.

The Dual Career Family: intact nuclear family consisting of husband, wife and offspring living in a common household where both partners work. (Represents 16 percent of all households.)

Strengths
Competent structure to provide maximal income for maintenance and to achieve quality of life aspirations.

Highly adequate form for effecting goals of gender equality. It provides work options for both marital partners and opportunity to share household tasks and marital responsibilities.

Weaknesses
Dependence on kin and institutional support systems for effective maintenance and functioning.

Developing but still non-institutionalized values and means to harmonize the career activities and ambitions of both partners and the roles concerned with marital relationships and parenting.

The Single Parent Household: with children under age 18. (Represents 16 percent of all households.)

Strengths
Many adults who can function as socialization models for children are potentially available. Adults other than parents may be more effective in teaching and socializing children.

If supported appropriately, the single parent can achieve greater self-expression than a married counterpart; accountability is limited to children.

For a significant number of single-parent families, which result as a consequence of separation and divorce, the removal or absence of a violent parent results in a nurturant and liveable family form.

Weaknesses
Need for support systems for parenting, economic and health maintenance and social relationships—often scarce or unavailable in particular communities.

The insufficiency of finances endemic to this family form often results in higher morbidity and expenditure of third party monies for maintenance and survival. Another consequence of economic deficiency is the pressure for some to remarry in order to obtain such support, with increased probability that the previous marriage experience will be repeated.

For some families, when the single parent is gainfully employed and substitute parents are unavailable or ineffective, the socialization is done by peers, and the behavior of children may be viewed as deviant and delinquent.

The Remarried Nuclear Family: husband, wife and offspring living in a common household. (Represents 11 percent of all households.)

Strengths
Previous marital experiences may result in an increased number (actual incidence unknown) of stable marriages.

Parenting, which may formerly have been the function of a single adult, may be shared with the new partner and his or her older children.

For some, there is improved economic status as a consequence of shared income.

Weaknesses
The difficulties in blending two formerly independent households into one functioning unit may result in extreme psychic stress for some members.

Formations consisting of two large-size families may require substantial economic help, counseling and other supports in order to survive.

Economic and social commitments to individuals of previous marriages may restrict the development of adequate, stable relationships in the new marriage.

The Kin Family: consisting of bilateral or intergenerational-linked members living in the same household. (Represents six percent of all households.)

Strengths

Maintenance of familial values and transmission of accumulated knowledge and skill are likely occurrences.

Multiple adults are available for socialization and shared household and work responsibilities.

Weaknesses

Demands for geographical mobility are not easily met.

From one perspective, the resistance to changes which threaten the maintenance of this family form can reduce the motivation of individuals to achieve in the society.

Experimental Families: individuals in multi-adult households (communes) or cohabiting. (Represents four percent of all households.)

Strengths

In communal forms, a large number of individuals are available to form a support system to meet individual needs, a situation especially important to individuals in transition from one family form to another, such as recently divorced women with small children.

Individuals not ready or unwilling to make a commitment to a long-term partnership can experience economic and social sharing, psychic growth and open communication and interpersonal relationships.

Weaknesses

Few of these forms have developed strategies, techniques or economic bases to sustain their activities or achieve their goals.

In a large number of experimental family forms, role responsibilities are not clearly delineated or articulated, with consequential difficulties in implementing parenting, economic, household and other functions.

NOTES

[1] A. Etzioni, "The Family: Is It Obsolete?", *Journal of Current Social Issues,* Vol. 14, No. 1, 1977.

[2] J. Ramey, "Experimental Family Forms—The Family of the Future," *Marriage and Family Review,* Jan./Feb. 1978.

[3] D. J. Freed, "Divorce Laws Coast to Coast," in *Family Law Reporter,* 4.1, text section #1, 1977.

[4] M. B. Sussman, Plenary Address, "Marriage Contracts: Social and Legal Consequences," 1975 International Workshop on Changing Sex Roles in Family and Society, Dubrovnik, Yugoslavia.

[5] J. Ramey, op. cit.

[6] C. E. Vincent, "Barriers to the Development of Marital Health as a Health Field," *Journal of Marriage and Family Counseling,* July 1977.

[7] S. Steinmetz, in a forthcoming article in *Marriage and Family Review,* 1978.

[8] M. A. Straus, "Violence in the Family: An Assessment of Knowledge and Research Needs," in *Child Abuse: Its Treatment and Prevention: Interdisciplinary Approach,* ed. Mary Van Stolk (Toronto; McClelland and Stewart, 1977).

[9] J. Lawton, "'Control' Is A Dominant Motif in Social Work Motivation," *Behavior Today,* Oct. 24, 1977.

II

VARIATIONS: SUBCULTURAL DIFFERENCES

4

FAMILIES OF ETHNIC PEOPLE OF COLOR: ISSUES IN SOCIAL ORGANIZATION AND PLURALISM

Evelyn L. Barbee

NATIVE AMERICANS

An important fact about attempting to force acculturation and eventual assimilation is that people cannot be swiftly remodeled to adapt to cultural patterns that are not in harmony with their ideals and aspirations. As a result of federal legislation that was ostensibly enacted in order to hasten the process of the assimilation of Native Americans, both the culture and the survival of Native Americans were placed in peril. For example, the General Allotment Act of 1887 (the Dawes Act) allowed the distribution of reservation land into individual allotments. Each family head was eligible for 80 acres of agricultural land or 160 acres of grazing land (Sorkin, 1978, p. 2). The underlying intent of this Act was to pressure the Native Americans into becoming individual farmers and thereby hasten their assimilation into white society. Since these farms were too small to generate an adequate income and because few Indians were interested in agriculture, most of the allotments were sold at low prices (Sorkin, 1978). As a result, by 1933 two-thirds of the Native American land base (91 million acres) passed into non-Native American hands.

Deloria (1969, p. 185) notes that culture is the expression of the essence of a people. This essence is composed of such things as language, knowledge, laws, and religious beliefs and generally refers to the customary ways of thinking and behaving that are characteristic of a particular people. How the essence of a Native American family is expressed in this pluralistic society depends upon the demographic, economic, and social setting in which one finds the family. In the United States there are members of more than 350 different tribes of Native Americans residing either in rural reservation communities or in urban areas.

In discussing contemporary plains reservation communities, Wax (1971, p. 75) points out that a reservation is not a unified nation composed of Native Americans speaking a common language and sharing many traits. The inhabitants of these rural settings see themselves first and foremost as mem-

---

Evelyn L. Barbee, "Families of Ethnic People of Color: Issues in Social Organization and Pluralism," in *Understanding the Family*, edited by Cathleen Getty and Winnifred Humphreys (New York: Appleton-Century-Crofts, 1981). Reprinted by permission.

bers of bands of kith and kin. *Kith* can generally be defined as acquaintances, friends, and neighbors living within the same locality who form a more or less cohesive group. *Kin* refers to affinal (by marriage) and consanguineal (by blood) relatives. Although their family organization has been described as extended, the networks of kith and kin more accurately refer to the groups that have been essential to the survival of Native Americans since, within the networks of kith and kin are found the processes of sharing, voluntary cooperation, equality, and solidarity (Wax, 1971, p. 76). Because the central problem of most reservation communities is economic, the real unit of survival is neither the nuclear nor the extended family, but a complex of families that are most often situated quite close to each other (Wax, 1971, p. 80).

The importance of kin and kith for the Native American closely parallels what Hsu (1971, pp. 69–70) refers to as "social baggage." In writing about the Chinese, Hsu points out that the preexisting network of family and kinship has priority over other human ties, and the individual is not as free to move away from it as his or her counterpart in other cultures. When a person does move away from these ties, he or she finds it difficult to form new associations without reference to the old ones. Thus, a Chinese person may be seen as facing the world with a large amount of social baggage. The Native American has a similar network of preexisting human ties with which she or he can relate. The ethnocentric reference point of the nuclear family has made it extremely difficult for reformers to understand Native American kith and kin organizations. Therefore, one of the main targets for reformers has been to break up the patterns of obligations and sharing that form the basis for Native American kith and kin groups (Wax, 1971, p. 76). The significance of this strategy can best be appreciated if one recognizes that in the Native American world, to be without relatives is to be really poor (Backup, 1979, p. 22).

Within Native American families, individual freedom and independence are two highly valued attributes. Wax and Thomas (1961, p. 311) refer to the Native American's belief in the right of self-determination as the "ethic of non-interference." All behavior, from gentle meddling to outright meddling is defined by Native Americans as outside the realm of proper action (Wax and Thomas, 1961, p. 310). In effect this means that interference in the behavior or actions of one person by another is neither allowed nor tolerated (Backup, 1979, p. 22). The ethic of noninterference holds even when an individual is engaging in behavior that may be destructive to self or others (Wax & Thomas, 1961, p. 309). As Good Tracks (1973, p. 30) notes, the extent to which a Native American adheres to this ethic depends upon the degree of acculturation and assimilation of the individual.

Backup (1979, p. 22), in discussing the importance of kith and kin to Native Americans, points out that the two most important groups in the family are grandparents and children. According to tradition, the very old and the very young "are safe within the universe and carefully watched by the Great Spirit." Native Americans view children as assets to the family. In the rural reservation communities, the primary socializing agent of the Native American child is her or his peer group (Wax, 1971, p. 84). Although the concept of parenting may be extended throughout the adults in the kith and kin network, many times children in the rural reservation communities are reared by their grandparents because their parents have migrated to urban areas (Wax, 1971, p. 71). In their socialization, Native American children are encouraged to be independent (there are no rigid schedules for eating and sleeping) and patient and to behave in an unassuming manner (Backup, 1979, p. 22). Furthermore, they are taught that the family and tribe are of foremost importance. Grandmothers are very important, and the aged in general are looked to for wisdom and counsel. The aged occupy the important position of relating traditions, beliefs, and customs through the role of storyteller (Backup, 1979, p. 22).

Although the popular image of the Native American is that of a rural Western reservation dweller, at least three-quarters of this population lives in urban areas and in the eastern portion of the country (Deloria, 1969, p. 251). Like previous migrants to the city, Native Americans tend to cluster together residentially and to elaborate distinctive institutions that are neither traditional nor urban middle-class. The question of survival in the urban areas has led to the formation of institutions such as Indian Centers. These centers provide a place where Native Americans can meet peer-group members. In addition, traditional activities, such as basket weaving and powwows, take place in the Indian Centers. Institutions like these enable Native Americans, as a community, to create a meaningful existence in the urban environment.

Although the nuclear family form can be found among some rural Native Americans, generally this form is more common among those who reside in urban areas. A recent study of Native Americans suggests that families at home in both the Native American and white world have a greater ability to survive and adapt to the city than those who are not. Using a bicultural model, these researchers point out that the urban Native American who learns both white and Native American ways is "best able to maintain a strong sense of self-esteem and thus make a satisfactory adjustment to the city" (Native American Research Group, 1975, p. 56). These researchers also found that urban Native Americans attempt to complement traditional peer group friendship patterns by frequenting centers, parks, and common meeting places for Native Americans.

A major issue that is being addressed by urban Native Americans today is that of identity. The migration of people from diverse tribes to the urban areas has promoted the rise of pan-Indianism. Concomitant with pan-Indianism has been the evolution of a tri-level sense of self: that of being a tribal person, a Native American, and an individual human being (Native American Research Group, 1975, p. 56). This issue of identity has been the impetus for a variety of courses designed to teach the Native American the skills to survive in white society while maintaining her or his own identity.

Not all Native Americans in urban areas use uniquely Native American institutions in their attempts to cope with urban life. Some have adopted the nuclear-family form. For others, the urban environment presents insurmountable obstacles to family life, and portions of the family may have to return to the rural reservation. A third group is likely to have preserved strong attachments to their kith and kin in the reservation communities. As a result, they may journey to the reservation frequently and may send their children there during vacations from school (Wax, 1971, p. 71).

The family form of Native Americans, with its emphasis on a wide network of kin and kith, has enabled many tribes to survive despite efforts to destroy them in the name of acculturation and eventual assimilation. In a pluralistic society, the concern should not only be with full cultural sharing but also with cultural diversity. In a situation of cultural diversity, the success of both individual and family in acting in accordance with expectations depends not only on the beliefs, values, and skills adopted for self, but also on an awareness of those with whom the individual interacts (Hannerz, 1971, p. 184). For the Native American, this cultural diversity can best be seen in the variability of family forms.

AFRO-AMERICANS

There has been a selective focus on the negative aspects of Afro-African family life because scholars do not seem to be interested in the Afro-American family as an institution in its own right (Billingsley, 1968, p. 197). In addition there seems to be little recognition that the study of these families can shed light upon American society in general. The essence of the general charge against the Afro-American family has been that the family is at least partially responsible for the economic, social, and personal problems faced by Afro-Americans in this society (Heiss, 1975, pp. 5–6). Since Billingsley brought attention to this selective focus on Afro-American family life, several works (Ladner, 1972; Staples, 1971; Hill, 1972) have been published in order to counteract the previous bias in the studies of these families.

Controversy remains as to whether Afro-Americans have their own unique culture and hence a distinctive family organization; some hold that the norms and values that Afro-Americans hold are simply a reflection of social class factors. For example, Glazer and Moynihan (1965, p. 33) state: "It is not possible for Negroes to view themselves as other ethnic groups viewed themselves because . . . the Negro is only an American and nothing else. He has no values and culture to guard and protect."[1] On the other hand, Herskovitz (1958) argues that many "Africanisms" survived slavery and are to be found in the present life-styles of Afro-Americans, including family structure, religion, music, dance, and the arts. A more balanced viewpoint is presented by Billingsley (1968, pp. 8–10) who, while noting that social class is a powerful dimension that helps to determine the condition of life for Afro-American families, also points out that the concept of ethnic subsociety helps to explain many of the commonalities of Afro-Americans in general.

The debate as to whether an Afro-American subculture exists has only relative importance. The position taken in this chapter is that Afro-American families should be viewed as forms of social organization with their own cultural dynamics. The social organization of these families adapts to economic and social changes in the American plural society. This position allows one to better understand the differences in Afro-American family form.

For the most part, the literature about Afro-American families has concentrated on the female-headed household. As a result, there has been an erroneous impression that the majority of Afro-American families are female-headed. In reality, publications like the *Moynihan Report* only deal with one-quarter of Afro-American families. Furthermore, these families have been characterized as "broken" and "unstable." For most social scientists, the term *stability* implies a situation where both husband and wife are present (Scanzoni, 1971, p. 3). The term *broken* usually refers to father absence in a family; *attenuated* would be a better term simply because it means that someone important to the family constellation is missing (Billingsley, 1968, p. 19). Thus, *attenuated* would refer to situations in which either of the biologic parents or parental surrogates is missing from the family.

In discussing the female-headed attenuated family, Hill (1972, p. 21) suggests that the self-reliance of Afro-American women as primary breadwinners exemplifies their adaptability in family roles. Unfortunately, this position comes perilously close to the stereotype of the Afro-American woman as a matriarch. As Ladner (1972, pp. 41–42) states:

In recent years the Black woman has almost become a romantic, legendary figure in this society because the vast conceptions of her as a person are largely dictated by these stereotypes. The idea that she is almost superhuman, capable of assuming all major responsibilities for sustaining herself and her family through harsh economic and social conditions has been projected in much of the popular as well as academic research.

Furthermore, the representation of single-parent families as "broken" and "unstable" tends to deal with these families as though they are "nonfamilies" (Herzog, 1966, p. 9). These negative views of the female-headed family lend support to the position that somebody should do something to make sure that all Afro-American children are put into families headed by males.

Few works point out the adaptability of Afro-American men in family roles. Billingsley (1968, p. 25) comments:

It is not at all uncommon for Negro men to engage in expressive functions with respect to the maintenance of family solidarity and to help with child rearing and household tasks. Researchers have found Negro men to be more helpful around the house than a sample of white men, *but they have chosen to give this fact a negative reading.*[Emphasis added.]

One can seriously question these negative interpretations. Perhaps these social scientists make these evaluations because they do not view the fulfillment of expressive functions in the family as a culturally legitimate role for males. To suggest that a family is inevitably stable and organized when the male is present is equally questionable.

Dichotomizing male- and female-headed families ignores the number of variations that exist among Afro-American families. Three basic forms of Afro-American family organization have been identified: nuclear, extended, and augmented (Billingsley, 1968, pp. 16–21). These are further subclassified into 12 basic forms that depend upon the presence or absence of either household head and other household members, including children, other relatives, and nonrelatives. Essentially, these adaptations can be viewed as responses to social and economic changes in the pluralistic society. Two forms of particular interest are the extended and the augmented.

Billingsley (1968, p. 20) describes four classes of relatives who may reside together in extended Afro-American families: (a) grandchildren, nieces, nephews, cousins, and young siblings under 18;

(b) peers of the parents, for example, siblings, cousins, and other adult relatives; (c) elders of the parents, for example, aunts and uncles; (d) parents of the family heads. The length of time that a relative may live with the family is variable and is often dependent on the reason that the individual came there. The authority structure of the family may shift considerably, depending on the status of the relative who moves in.

Martin and Martin (1978, p. 6) are two of the few social scientists to explore the social organization of the extended family. These authors suggest that the extended family has four defining characteristics: (a) It is comprised of four generations of relatives; (b) it is headed by a dominant family figure to whom the other members look for leadership in holding the family together; (c) it is interdependent in that relatives depend upon each other for emotional, social, and material support; (d) the dominant family figure always resides in the extended family's base household (this base is usually the center of extended-family activities).

From their study of Afro-American extended families, Martin and Martin (1978, p. 8) suggest that what may appear to be a nuclear family may in actuality be a subextension of an extended family base. Therefore, a family with a missing parent is not necessarily a "broken home" but may, in fact, be a vital part of a viable extended family (Martin & Martin, 1978, p. 9).

Although there has been little written about the extended-family form, even less reference has been made to augmented families. Essentially, augmented families are those that have unrelated individuals living with them as roomers, boarders, lodgers, or other relatively long-term guests. In 1970 there were 361,219 Afro-American families who had nonrelatives living with them (Department of Commerce, 1970b, p. 154). Often these unrelated persons exert major influence on the social organization of the family.

How the social organization of a family adapts to the social and economic changes in the plural society is closely related to the dynamics of the cultural group. For example, several authors (Stack, 1974; Hill, 1972; Billingsley, 1968) illustrate the kinship networks of Afro-Americans and how these are used, particularly in terms of crisis. The importance of kinship to Afro-Americans is exemplified by the number of fictive kin terms in an Afro-American community. Thus, one can find reference to a wide range of "play" relatives, for example, "play mother," "play sister," "play brother," etc. Each of these terms refers to a status and identifies the relationship between the speaker and the person being addressed. The classification of a friend as a kinsperson is accompanied by respect and responsibility (Stack, 1974).

These forms of Afro-American families can be seen as adaptations to changes in the plural society. It has been these adaptations to social organization that have allowed the Afro-Americans to survive as a group. In the face of oppression and sharply restricted economic and social support, the Afro-American family has proved to be a very resilient institution. As Martin and Martin (1978, p. 100) point out, the extended family is a powerful mechanism for meeting basic needs and providing its individual members with a sense of solidarity. As the dominant white majority in this plural society continues to deny opportunities for Afro-Americans to become full participants in its economy, the extended family remains a meaningful unit in sustaining its members. . . .

NOTE

[1] In the second edition of *Beyond the Melting Pot,* Glazer edits this passage to read "He bears no foreign values and cultures that he feels the need to guard from the surrounding environment" (1970, p. 53).

REFERENCES

Backup, R. 1979. Implementing quality care for the American Indian patient. *Washington State Journal of Nursing* (Special Suppl.), pp. 20–24.

Bennedict, B. 1962. Stratification in plural societies. *American Anthropologist* 64: 1235–46.

Billingsley, A. 1968. *Black families in white America.* Englewood Cliffs, N.J.: Prentice-Hall.

———. 1974. *Black families and the struggle for survival.* New York: Friendship.

Deloria, V. 1969. *Custer died for your sins.* New York: Avon.

Glazer, N., and D. P. Moynihan. 1965. *Beyond the melting pot.* Cambridge, Mass.: MIT Press.

Good Tracks, J. G. 1973. Native American non-interference. *Social Work* 18: 30–34.

Gordon, M. 1964. *Assimilation in American life.* New York: Oxford University Press.

Hall, E. T. 1969. *The hidden dimension.* Garden City, N.Y.: Anchor.

Hannerz, U. 1971. The study of Afro-American cultural dynamics. *South Western Journal of Anthropology* 27: 181–201.

Heiss, J. 1975. *The case of the black family: A sociological inquiry.* New York: Columbia University Press.

Herskovitz, M. 1958. *The myth of the Negro past.* Boston: Beacon Press.

Herzog, E. 1966. Is there a breakdown of the Negro family? *Social Work* 11: 3–10.

Hill, R. B. 1972. *The strengths of black families.* New York: Emerson Hall.

Hsu, F. L. K. 1971. *The challenge of the American dream: The Chinese in the United States.* Belmont: Wadsworth.

Ladner, J. A. 1972. *Tomorrow's tomorrow: The black woman.* Garden City, N.Y.: Anchor.

Martin, E. P. and J. M. Martin. 1978. *The extended black family.* Chicago: University of Chicago Press.

Native American Research Group. 1975. *Native American families in the city: Final report, American Indian socialization to urban life.* San Francisco: Institute for Scientific Analysis.

Scanozi, J. H. 1971. *The black family in modern society.* Boston: Allyn and Bacon.

Sorkin, A. 1978. *The urban Indian.* Lexington, Mass.: Heath.

Spencer, R. F., S. D. Sennings, et al. 1965. *The Native Americans.* New York: Harper & Row.

Stack, C. B. 1974. *All our kin: Strategies for survival in a black community.* New York: Harper & Row.

Staples, R. (ed.). 1971. *The black family: Essays and studies.* Belmont, Calif.: Wadsworth.

U.S. Department of Commerce. 1970a. *Census of the population: Characteristics of the population* (Vol. 1, Part 1). Washington, D.C.: Government Printing Office.

U.S. Department of Commerce. 1970b. *Census of population subject reports: Persons by family characteristics.* Washington, D.C.: Government Printing Office.

Wax, M. 1971. *Indian Americans: Unity and diversity.* Englewood Cliffs, N.J.: Prentice-Hall.

Wax, R. H. and R. K. Thomas. 1961. American Indians and white people. *Phylon* 22: 305–17.

Western Interstate Council for Higher Education in Nursing. 1976. Position paper: The phrase ethnic people of color.

5

LA FAMILIA CHICANA

Jaime Sena-Rivera and Charlotte Moore

FAMILIA IN THE KIN SYSTEM

Most family sociologists agree that the practice of mutual aid is basic to the functioning of the kin system. Jaime Sena-Rivera observed this practice as a young child. In a chapter he wrote for the new edition of *La Raza*, to be published soon as a textbook for use in courses on Latin American culture in the United States, he describes this family interaction as he remembers it from his childhood:

> It seemed that my father's brothers, and my father in turn, would go first to one another for loans of varying sizes (not always rapid) at various times instead of to banks or savings and loan associations. . . . ("Why go to strangers?" my father said. "And besides the Americans charge too much interest and they treat you like dirt when you don't know English so well. If you can't pay your brother back, there's no hard feelings. There are ways to make it up, always.") Also, each brother (and uncles and cousins) would see each other, especially if the other was older, as legitimate resources for finding work. . . . ("What is more decent," my father said, "than helping your brother or your friend to be independent, be a man, be a good husband or father or son? Besides, they put Mexicans off at The Unemployment.")

When still quite young, Sena-Rivera observed that many of the practices which he took for granted as a part of living were wrong in Anglo eyes. They might now be called *familism*, an impediment to individual mobility and the adoption of more varied role models. In a word, they were *dysfunctional*, according to his explanation in the same *La Raza* chapter, which says, in summary: "Family" is *supposed* to mean the nuclear family, not the extended network; residential proximity is considered extreme if many nuclear families, related by blood, live in the same unit or contiguous ones or even in the same neighborhood; nuclear families should be controlled in size; the practice of borrowing from one's kin creates an unnecessary burden rather than solidarity; economic and occupational interdependency impedes or prevents upward mobility; authority based on the eldest male criteria is arbitrary, paternalistic, and an impediment to individual mobility, and it keeps women overly repressed and submissive (in press).

Concerning the functions of the primary group structures of kin, neighbors, and friends in a technological society, Litwak points out the lack of human resources of the nuclear family group. Such a group, with only two adult members, often cannot handle acute emergencies alone and finds difficulty in managing tension arising from disputes among themselves. They are unable to diagnose incipient emotional troubles or be aware, by themselves, of better ways of handling childrearing, for instance. It appears that socialization learned through everyday activities, the value of neighborhood peer-group help in emergencies, the permanence and long-term ties of the kin, and the good feeling of friendship groups are complementary sources of strength to the nuclear family structure. The kin, neighbor, and friendship primary groups, then, provide resources

---

Jaime Sena-Rivera and Charlotte Moore, *"La Familia Chicana,"* in *Families Today*, edited for the U.S. Department of Health, Education and Welfare by Eunice Corfman (Washington, D.C.: Government Printing Office, 1979).

which complement those of the isolated nuclear family (1969).

It might be assumed that within the extended family, whether "classic" or "modified," the functions of these primary groups are largely "built-in" as valuable components of such a system. This seems to be true for the Chicanos. Indeed, the friendship group structure, which Litwak views as the weakest of the three components, seems quite strong in *la familia chicana.* First cousins, *los primos hermanos,* are commonly raised almost like brothers and sisters, and a particularly strong bond is forged among same-sex and same-age siblings and cousins. Even aunts and uncles are included, since many parents are ending their families at the same time the older children are beginning theirs. From his own experience, Sena-Rivera knows that this bond continues throughout the adult years, regardless of the divergent educational, social, or economic paths, even the attainments or failures, of the individual *familia* members.

Building the Hypothesis of La Familia Chicana

Sena-Rivera has reviewed the literature on Mexican-descent population in the United States and has concluded that many of those hypotheses concerning the Chicano extended family are misleading. He says (1976, p. 6): *"The tri-generational household has never been the norm for Mexico or for Mexicans in the United States or for other Chicanos, except at times of individual extended family or conjugal family stress, or periods of general societal disorganization."*

In short, the traditional Chicano extended family, as a grouping of independent nuclear households, forms a social organizational unit that might be called "kin-integrated." To prove the validity of this view, Sena-Rivera determined to seek out four extended families which had heads-of-households still living in the three older generations. Each family would be represented by one or more great-grandparents, a son or daughter, and a grandson or granddaughter with one or more children. His reasoning was that the carriers of the "old ways" are the immigrants of the 1910–1930 period and their descendants. From his previous research, he had concluded that proximity in time to the source of the Mexican extended family's traditions explained a more traditional behavior; his objective, therefore, was to determine the extent to which each generation tested the traditional culture in a largely alien setting and found it workable, for themselves as individuals, or for the family group. As members of the crowds of immigrants fleeing the Mexican Revolution of 1910 and the poverty and unrest of the two succeeding decades, the great-grandparents received their primary socialization in Mexico where they were born; the second and third generations of each extended kin group (except for a few in-laws of the families finally interviewed) were born in the United States and received their primary socialization here.

As Sena-Rivera puts it, "This particular social organization transcends many different historical periods." He decided to study this age group specifically because he "wanted a sense of history and some accountability, historically, as to why they came and how people coming at a certain period made it in the United States. Until recently, persons in that age group and their descendants were the largest segment of the Mexican population. That's changed now. We have no 'ideal type' anymore."

This observation was made in another way in a paper, "The Mexican American Family," presented at the Mexican American Seminars held in California at Stanford University in April 1970. Nathan Murillo contended: "The reality is that there is no Mexican-American family 'type.'" To support this claim, he pointed out that, like all other Americans, the thousands of Mexican-American families vary in: regional and socioeconomic factors, degree of assimilation and acculturation, historical and political differences, and in patterns of coping with each other and with their different environments. In some families, only Spanish is spoken; in others, Spanish is all but forgotten. Many trace their lineage to the Spanish, others to one or the other of the once-powerful Indian cultures. *Chicano,* a colloquial adaptation of the Spanish for *Mexican,* is a relatively recent term, used "with increasing frequency and with growing pride." Alternate labels throughout the years have been *Latino, Hispano, Spanish American,* or *American of Spanish descent* (1971, pp. 97–99). . . .

Prototype Familia

In many ways, this large, 141-member clan is highly typical of that aspect of Mexican-American culture known as *familia* at its most traditional, possibly because of its semirural, extraurban ambience. Close-knit and devoted—*unidos*—cousins, and aunts and uncles of the same age group, for that matter, interact like brothers and sisters. In-laws, especially females, are drawn into the intense relationship of the network. There is reflected here an emotional interdependence which, especially for the older members, satisfies most of the individuals' recreational and social needs, visits and larger gatherings being an important part of daily and weekly life. The sense of obligation to each other, to help in times of economic trouble or illness with small loans, household services, or child care, appears to stem not only from the sense of duty instilled in early childhood but from voluntary desire and strong emotional attachment. In general, most *familia* members hope to continue this involvement *along with* entry into the economic and social mainstream of their locality.

Their Faith

With the exception of one third-generation in-law, the *familia* members are Catholic. Their faith and their church are an integral and accepted part of daily and weekly life, although only routine ritual participation for some. Family bonds are strengthened further when godparents are chosen for christening, First Communion, and confirmation. Dr. Sena-Rivera says, though, that this custom is not as strong as it is nearer the border or in Mexico itself, where the "fictive" kinship, the practice of "claiming" relations through godparenting, is also still strong.

Marriage and Divorce

Familia A reflects, also, changes in patterns of marriage and divorce. A shift toward intermarriage with other groups is rather noticeable among them. From the one "out-marriage" out of eight marriages in the second generation, the daughter's second marriage to a Puerto Rican, to nine out of sixteen marriages in the third generation, eight to Anglos and one to a Cuban, the trend is striking. Striking, too, is the assimilation of most of these spouses into the warm interaction of the *familia*.

According to Sena-Rivera, *familias* in his study were in one respect not typical of many that he knows about: There were no common-law marriages among them. Only Sra. A's daughter had what was apparently a less than "formal" marriage. Serial marriage is quite acceptable, and divorce is no longer frowned on. As Sena-Rivera sees it, usually divorce "has meant that they haven't lost anything. In most cases, the children stay within the *familias*. It's an in-law, usually a male, who leaves. The divorce is not with the son, the blood line, so the daughter keeps the children. And apparently, when there is intermarriage or marriage with a divorced person, a man brings his own children, who are gladly accepted into the extended family."

Language and Assimilation

The grandson articulated a concern about a trend he has observed in *Familia A* and among his friends in the Michiana area when he expressed his regret that so many younger generation members know so little Spanish. In fact, the interviewers observed that given names in the fourth generation have been Anglicized when they are not actually non-Spanish.

Sena-Rivera has noticed change in his own group in northern New Mexico and southern Colorado. He adds, however, when speaking of both customs and language, that at present, with the huge numbers of Mexicans and other Latins coming in, there is still a good deal of language retention. Referring particularly to the Los Angeles area, he remarks: "They come across into LA now and work in small industries directly for Mexicans or at least for Mexican foremen, and shop in Mexican grocery stores. Even big super markets have Spanish clerks. . . . Now the burden is on shops and restaurants who serve these people rather than on the minority struggling to make their wishes known in English. This change has taken place in less than a generation. Now social services in LA have Spanish-speaking personnel and signs on buses and in public buildings are in Spanish; there are TV stations which are Mexican and there are other bilingual programs. Particularly the churches now have the masses and other services in Spanish, so there's not really a great deal of need to de-Mexicanize yourself.''

As Sena-Rivera reflected on this, he mentioned that some of the bilingual programs work but that many of them are simply devices for assimilation in a bilingual, bicultural civilization. Certainly it has been found among other groups who are making their way into the mainstream of American life that satisfaction is greater and alienation less among those who have achieved a bicultural balance, by retaining much of the old while assimilating much of the new. Sra. A's grandson sees this as a goal for his generation and his children's.

Grandson A sees other changes which should take place. While cherishing memories of the older generation and loving relationships with them, he feels that the younger generations of Mexican Americans should be more "independent" and less traditional. Friendship with Anglos should be fostered, he believes, and younger Chicanos should make an effort to participate in and enjoy things which their parents did not (or could not), such as travel and dating alone. Chief among the interests to be promoted is sports, the grandson's own personal delight.

The "Nonpersons"

A strange custom appeared during interviews. Usually, several interviews were necessary to fill out the branches on each family tree, and occasionally a few branches were not leafed out completely. "Somebody would crop up here and somebody there, and we'd try to straighten them out. What's a child doing over there in that household? He was born over here." And in the case of a couple of families, "all of a sudden you realize there's somebody who isn't even being talked about, and the person is declared almost a nonperson."

There was never any attempt to intrude or to probe more deeply than the family members wished to go. The interviewers were struck by the firm, quiet refusal to reveal information about a recent or imminent rupture in any couple. In the cases where someone had, seemingly, "disappeared," clues came only from comparing conversations and interviews among the various persons interviewed in the same *familia*. Females and their children involved in divorce had apparently rejoined their own extended families.

This kind of mystery first showed up in *Familia A* when Sra. A neglected to mention some of the daughter's children, and only later did the interviewers learn that the A grandparents had actually legally adopted this granddaughter. It was this same granddaughter who mentioned one uncle who did not visit with anyone because he has "set himself apart." Later, the interviewers realized that this was the individual who had refused to see them. The mystery remained closed.

Sena-Rivera said, "I didn't probe to find out exactly what these people had done that was so wrong that they were kicked out of the family. Since it was sensitive, the only way we found out was from a word here and a word there; then from different interviews we put the mystery together." He has observed that mental health practitioners who are not of or very close to this ethnic group are not likely to appreciate what being cut off in this way means, nor to understand how this diminishing of identity can destroy an individual and his sense of self. . . .

Las Chicanas

The remarkable women of *Familia B* epitomize, for Dr. Sena-Rivera at least, the strength of the countless women, Mexican and Mexican-American, who have borne children, prepared tamales, enchiladas, and all the rest for countless *familia* members, and worked side by side in the fields with their husbands and children. This kind of life has been the historical lot of these women on the estates of the *padrones* in Mexico and on the lands of Texas, New Mexico, California, or Midwest farmers. At the same time, apparently, most of them have managed to buttress within their *familias,* as an integral cornerstone of their culture, the image of male dominance, in spite of the low social and economic stature of their men. Quotations given below, from comments made by some of the B women to the interviewers, well illustrate their lives and their forceful personalities.

Sra. B, herself, exerted great influence on her family because of her strong maternal control and her fluency in English which, despite her illiteracy in both Spanish and English, aided her in dealing with an Anglo-dominated world. The help to her family in this one area alone was immeasurable and, further, she had no language barrier to separate her from third and fourth generation members. Her will was indomitable and her devotion tenaciously directed at saving her progeny from the poverty and unhappiness she knew in her childhood and from the deprivation of her early married years in Texas.

Her ambition for her family is reflected in her granddaughter, who said during her interview:

I think I'm better off than my brothers and sisters . . . and once in awhile I hear someone say, "Well, you've got money to do something." I do, but they forget that I work hard and save. I've been working since I was a freshman in high school. After high school, I went back to my counselor and he said, "Now, you don't want to go to college—you're just going to get married." You know. But I decided to go. First I got a job there (Indiana University, Bloomington), then I enrolled. Sometimes it was really hard—I didn't have any money. But I would never call my mother. I don't know if it was a sense of pride or because I didn't want to impose on her—she didn't have anything.

Loneliness brought together the six "Latinos" who were at the University at that time. This girl helped establish a Mexican-American program and is very proud of how well some of the members, including some women, have done. As she added, some of the women "even became lawyers."

She married at age 20, 3 years after her father died, and says of the early years of her marriage: "We started out with zero—nothing. We paid for our own wedding. We saved up for him to go to school because I wanted him to get a degree real bad—that meant a lot to me. We lived in furnished apartments and whatever. . . . He finished his degree in night school. . . ."

Now she is not certain about finishing the 2½ years she needs to get her own degree because of her commitment to her husband and child. But she wants it very much, "just to have it."

The granddaughter-in-law, too, shows the kind of support for her husband that has helped these Chicanos to "make it" in an alien culture and an unfriendly work environment.

I tell him to be a foreman, you know, or a big shot at the Mill—not just to stay down. Like before, he was an iron worker, and when it snowed, he was laid off. . . . Now he's in the Mill. It's less money than before when he was at the foundry, but there's always work whether there's rain or a storm or not and the benefits. . . . But he had to start at the bottom, in the labor. Two months ago, he took his exam to get into mechanics at the Mill. So, like, I would always build him up—you can do this, just try, you're not dumb. You've got to do that to your husband. If not, they don't think much of themselves—just so they're making money, they're happy. They should try to make more, and get up high, I think. . . .

Discrimination

Sra. B's poignant memories of her husband's work experiences are sadly typical of the experiences of all too many Mexican Americans and, for that matter, of most socioeconomically depressed newcomers to the United States work force. She described his struggles while working for the railroad in Texas:

All the Mexicans were assigned the hardest jobs, like digging, even if you could read and write—as he can—and were able to handle better work. Why? Because we were Mexican. They wouldn't give us a chance at nothing. There were many abuses. . . . Some of the foremen were very mean. They would see that you were marked down at the store for more than what you bought, and you always owed more than you made. That's not fair. . . .

In the memories of the great-grandparents of *Familia B,* discrimination extended beyond the work place. As Sra. B remembered it:

Life for the Mexican was pretty hard. . . . It was almost like for the colored. There was a lot (of) discrimination. They wouldn't allow you to eat at a table with a white—they would separate you. Once I went to meet my husband in another city. In the morning I went to a restaurant by the station to have breakfast. Now, I am pretty light and I can pass. They served me. When I returned to San Antonio with my husband, we stopped at the same restaurant. They saw my husband is Mexican. They wouldn't serve us up front. They wanted to serve us in the kitchen. . . .

Sra. B added that things had not been too different for Mexicans where they now live. She said that her husband had always had to work at the hardest jobs in the steel mills, under unhealthy conditions, and that he was never steadily employed or for many days a week. Sra. B then added, lest she make the one "white" interviewer feel uncomfortable, "I owe no grudges . . . I take things as they come—as God sends them."

Employment

In regard to the employment problems of the Mexican Americans, as with a study of illegal immigrants which he hopes to do, Sena-Rivera is afraid that his study, while good and valid, may be used against these people. "You can manipulate family associations, particularly emotive tendencies, to get at the various members and manipulate them even to hold down the work force," he explained. "Even these individual laborers say that. This person will stick with the job because he has greater responsibilities to a wide range of people. They can make greater demands on him than on another worker. I've seen that. I've heard 'white' employers speak in those terms: 'I'd rather have a Mexican worker because I know he'll be steady and work for less, because that money has to go to a lot of people.'"

While agreeing that many immigrant groups have met with similar difficulties, he added, "Our bad luck is that we came at the end of the Industrial Revolution, so that as a group we are locked into that stage of history that we can't get out of. . . . And even if we were able to move up, it's in categories that don't make that much difference. Like in academia . . . it's high prestige, but it's still a middle-class occupation in our society. . . . Each group has had to work its way in our country; that's true, but here, now, the average person has to work much, much harder."

Familia B in the third generation has a number of exceptions to the blue-collar caste of the older members. In addition to the police detective grandson-in-law and his clerical-worker wife, that generation includes a computer programmer, a musician, a telephone operator, a bilingual teacher, a secretary, a bank employee, and a salesperson. Among the other young, adult grandchildren, there are several college and university students. It is hard to say whether they are feeling at their age the constraints of their time and their ethnic group, of being "locked in," as Sena-Rivera describes it. Whether fuller entry into a bicultural world and emergence of more of the women out of the *casa* and into the working world will make a difference in *familia* life is a matter for further study.

Of this *familia,* the interviewers noted that they "did not receive any sense of being-at-the-bottom or depression from any member for living in this or similar neighborhoods and especially not from Sr. and Sra. B. At the same time, we do not wish to convey the impression that various members of *Familia B* are not desirous of, or not working toward raising, their present socioeconomic status."

Changes

The grandson's perceptions are interesting. In his interview, conducted in English with much Anglicization of Spanish surnames, he made distinctions among his relatives, calling anyone born and raised in Mexico "Mexican." To him, "Chicano" stands for those born in the States but who "think like a Mexican," and "Mexican American" means those of Mexican descent who "think like Americans."

The propinquity of most of these poor slum houses to their neighbors and the enforced propinquity of their numerous occupants to each other certainly do not epitomize the American Dream. They are not the Dream pictured in glossy magazines or on the ubiquitous television, whose aerials project from every tenement. But the always-room-for-one-more hospitality for other members of *familia* has been an assurance of the enduring qualities of the Chicano kin network. Will these qualities endure unchanged?

The Third Generation members of the *B Familia* who were interviewed indicate a possible drift. There is an embarrassment about inadequate space and enforced closeness which may interfere with the old hospitality-despite-inadequacies. The granddaughter, who wants to continue the large gatherings at Christmas, at least, like the all-*familia* party she went "all out" for the previous year, is looking for a larger house because "I don't have the room" to entertain adequately. The grandson indicates that he does not visit his siblings formally, or they him, except for calling on his next-older brother who has just bought a house where, the grandson feels, visits now will not be an imposition.

Transmission of Values

Familia B, throughout its generations, demonstrates well the transmission of values. The fathers in all of the *familias* in this study have been instrumental, in both precept and example, in teaching respect and obedience to one's elders and love and volition in helping all *familia* members. In addition to reinforcing these principles, the mothers have been largely responsible for teaching moral strictures and proper behavior to the young women of the *familias*. The B's granddaughter-in-law reported the lessons from her Mexican relatives, especially her own grandmother:

Not to take the pill! Take when God gives me a child, not to abort it, and to have as many children as he wants me to, you know. . . . Respect—respect for your elders, respect for your Mom.

I always had to respect my Mom and I did! She brought us up real strict, like the Mexican custom. Like my husband couldn't come into the house for the longest time while we were dating! She just didn't want him in the house "unless he wants to marry you—is going to ask for your hand." I'd say, "Well, Ma, we're not living like that any more," and she'd say, "While you're under this roof you are!" But then he proved himself, like there was no hanky-panky, and he didn't get me pregnant or anything so after 3 years, she let him come into the front (enclosed) porch! We had a little color TV there to watch together. We went together for about 5 years before we were married and he was finally allowed inside the house.

She said her husband, who told her later that he wouldn't have married her if she had been "easy" and that he was glad her mother had been strict with her, would be strict like that with his own daughters. His viewpoint does not entirely reflect the trend reported for some third-generation members, who are trying to adapt to different dating patterns, among other more "American" ways.

(Since the interviews, Senora B has died. The interviewers were of the opinion, when talking with the *familia*, that the group appeared to be at a crucial point in their cultural continuity. Senor B did not give the impression of stimulating enough emotional reaction alone or of having the material resources which might compensate for that lack. They feel, though, that the daughter who has been with her mother at the center of visits during the older lady's illness and the granddaughter who appears to want to continue the larger family gatherings may be able to carry on the role as the *familia* focal point.) . . .

Traditions and Changes

Except for their lack of male descent lineal heirs, *Familia C* exemplifies many of the attributes considered typical of this ethnic family group. There are the physical propinquity of three of the households, the interactions both emotional and dutiful, and the occupational assistance.

An additional evidence of interdependency is the drawing of the sons-in-law and so far, apparently, the grandsons-in-law, into the intensive, warm family interaction. This has occurred even though Sra. C has always believed firmly, so she indicated, that a woman's obligation must be first to her husband and children.

It remains to be seen whether the ties that bind this *familia* will hold after the great-grandparents die and the more affluent daughter and son-in-law leave the three-household enclave, as it is assumed that they will. Perhaps those ties will hold for a time, at least, because this is the daughter who, after the parents, appears to be the pivotal force in the lineal *familia*.

Spanish Language and the Chicano

This *familia* differs from the other three in the study in a highly significant detail, the transmission and retention of the mother tongue even to the fourth generation. Whether due substantially to the higher education of this particular great-grandmother, the extensive travels and ambition of the more affluent daughter and her husband, or the obvious advantage this ability has brought to the patrolman and his sister, it is hard to say. Perhaps each of these has been a factor. Certainly, the remembrance and frequent use of Spanish has facilitated communication among the generations, even though both great-grandparents do have some knowledge of English.

In "Growing Up Chicano," a chapter in one of his volumes of *Children of Crisis* (1978, pp. 353–354), Robert Coles describes the dependence of the Chicana mother on her own lanaguage: "Moreover, they have the Spanish language, a reminder that one is not hopelessly Anglo, that one has one's own words, one's way of putting things and regarding the world, and, not least, one's privacy and independence. No wonder many Chicana mothers, who can speak English easily, if not fluently, and who know full well that their children will be going to Anglo-run schools where English is the only or certainly the preferred language, choose to speak Spanish not just to their young children, but, it often seems, *at* them—as if the sound of the language offers the mother a sense of herself to fall back upon, a certain reserve that causes the child to feel comforted and loved. . . . The mothers, of course, are talking to themselves, reminding themselves that their children may well suffer in the future, but at the very least will not lose their language, their sense of a specific heritage: a religion, a nationality."

The Chicanos whom Coles observed and wrote about with such sympathetic perception live in Texas and other parts of the South and Southwest. Possibly those who migrated to the Midwest found a somewhat more egalitarian climate in which to raise their children and perceived less need for them to retain facility in their language. Perhaps this latter group envisioned a greater chance of upward mobility and thought that chance would be more possible with greater skill in English.

When more research studies of the Mexican in the United States are done, as Dr. Sena-Rivera hopes there will be, the use of Spanish only, English only, and of the two interchangeably should be investigated, with regard to region, socioeconomic class and mobility, and the institution of *familia* as a continuing and viable unit. It will be interesting to determine whether the younger generations of this ethnic group as a whole will find, as other groups apparently have, that the bilingual, bicultural mode is conducive to greater socioeconomic *and* emotional well-being. . . .

Predictions

"Forever and ever?" On the basis of a four-*familia* study, Dr. Sena-Rivera is hardly willing or able to make such a strong speculation. For one thing, there are other relevant factors to be tested, especially that of socioeconomic class. *Familia D* makes this circumstance evident since, although it is the most affluent and highest in status of the *familias* studied, it cannot be considered upper stratum.

Sena-Rivera does predict, however, that *familia,* as described in his study, will continue for at least one more full generation. Each generation, he says, tends to repeat with their children the patterns of socialization received in their own childhood. This cycle should carry, then, among the great-grandchildren as adults with their own households, into the 21st century—100 years of *la familia chicana.*

Changes Coming?

Familia D is typical in its intensity of *familia* involvement. It appears atypical, however, in the decline in ambition and economic achievement evident in the adult fourth-generation members. This apparent decline is reminiscent of the Anglo expression, "from shirtsleeves to shirtsleeves in three generations," not an unusual phenomenon. Perhaps the younger family members have the perception that Sena-Rivera articulated, that their group is "locked in" in the lower and middle class. Possibly, with their *familia* as buffer and refuge from the alienation and boredom endemic in many industrial jobs, plus the added cushion of their parents' relative prosperity, they see little need to put forth the effort necessary for advancement into other occupational fields. It is possible, of course, that they need only greater maturity.

Judging from the individual interviews, this family can be seen as happy, well-integrated, and more involved outside their own group than other *familias* in this study, who reported little activity outside of home, family, church, and work. The individuals who told about their community activity are proud of their engagement in the broader spectrum, but regret that it cuts into their time with the family, their first social group. Undoubtedly, this interaction with people of other cultures will make subtle changes in the Chicanos' perceptions of themselves and their own acculturation. Conversely, the perceptions which these "others" hold of persons of Mexican heritage will be altered as each becomes better acquainted with the other.

SUMMARY

In presenting the sociohistorical studies of four extended families of Mexican descent in the Michigan-Indiana-Illinois region, the researcher has investigated the contribution of the extended family structure and system to the individual's sense of well-being and to the *familia* as a social organization. He has explored this contribution, both subjective and material, within three lineal generations of each *familia* with objective and open-ended questions and limited direct observation. The findings have been charted on individual family trees, with each individual placed as a second-generation member and with each household, or *casa,* delineated within each *familia.*

Conclusions

This qualitative sample has revealed a few characteristics which appear to be constant for *these families* in *this* region:

> Migration from Mexico, largely to Texas, followed economic and political turmoil, repression of the Catholic Church, division of large landholdings, or fear for their lives or of induction into the armed forces.

> The immigrants arrived with some intention of returning to their homeland eventually, as, indeed, many of their relatives did.

> Migration from Texas occurred with news of better economic and working conditions in other parts of the United States and with the hope of finding greater equality and opportunity for themselves and their families.

> Catholicism is taken for granted as a part of the daily lives of these people. (Only one set of great-grandparents and, apparently, one in-law in the sample are non-Catholic.)

> Families are larger in the second generation than in the first because of better and more extensive health care. The norm appears to be holding for the third generation so far.

> The tendency toward out-marriages increases markedly with the generations, and some correlation between out-marriages and upward mobility has been noted. In this group, almost half of the marriages are with non-Mexican-descent spouses.

> The centripetal force of *familia* is notable even in the case of out-marriages since, almost universally, the non-Mexican-descent spouses have been drawn into the Mexican-descent *familias.*

> Upward mobility in both status and socioeconomic class has generally occurred unevenly within generations, depending somewhat on the urban or semirural locale of the *familias.*

> Socioeconomic class appears to work against *familia* integration only for the poorest.

> Dispersal to the suburbs or other more economically and socially favorable areas may, in time, lead to less intensive *familia* integration.

> The value of *familia* to the persons interviewed or to others indirectly observed cannot be overestimated, nor does it tend to diminish with the third generation. Different ways of interacting do occur with the passage of time and the involvement of individual members in work and community life, or with the use of the telephone rather than personal contact, but the intensive interaction goes on.

> *Familia* norms, learned from earliest childhood and practiced throughout life, are emphasized by the value of volunteerism supported by duty, blending desire for interdependence with love and a sense of disinterest.

> Individual *familia* members internalize their own self-fulfillment and self-worth as bound with those of their own *casa* and with the *casas* that have the same internalization of norms and values.

> *Familia* socialization is implanted mainly through example rather than instruction, through positive reinforcement rather than negative reinforcement or punishment.

> Age groups across generation lines in childhood and across status and class lines in adulthood ap-

pear to be the primary basis for peer associations in the formation of friendships.

Obedience and respect for one's elders, regardless of sex or remoteness of kinship, are integral in *familia* socialization, with the younger protected by the older. Adults are viewed according to their talents and learned skills, economic status and possessions, or masculine and feminine role qualities.

In general, those of the first generation think of themselves as Mexican, often literally in terms of citizenship as compared to cultural practices and affinity to the homeland; those of the second more often consider themselves Mexican-American, denoting a bicultural identity; the third generation has adopted the unhyphenated Mexican American, indicating cultural rather than nationalistic ties to the home country. Among younger members, the label Chicano indicates a rebirth of identification with Mexican cultural values which are considered less materialistic and individualistic than American values.

Each generation tends to repeat with its own children the *familia* socialization it received in childhood. . . .

REFERENCES

Coles, R. 1977. *Eskimos, Chicanos, Indians.* Vol. IV of *Children of crisis.* Boston: Little, Brown.

Litwak, E., and I. Szelenyi. 1969. Primary group structures and their functions: Kin, neighbors, and friends. *American Sociological Review* 34: 465–81.

Murillo, N. 1971. The Mexican American family. In N. N. Wagner and M. J. Hang (eds.), *Chicanos: Social and psychological perspectives,* pp. 97–108. St. Louis: C. V. Mosby Co.

Sena-Rivera, J. 1976. Casa and familia: The traditional Chicana extended family as functional in the U.S.A. today—Propositions and hypothesis toward further research. Paper presented at Annual Meeting of the American Sociological Association.

Photographs by Alan McEvoy

Part Two

GENDER AND SEXUALITY: INFLUENCES ON INTIMATE RELATIONSHIPS

Gender is a major factor affecting human behavior, both social and sexual. In this part we will examine the roles of gender and sexuality in intimate relationships, including dating, selecting a mate, marrying, raising a family, and remarrying. A belief commonly held in our society is that the child's gender at birth will determine the child's future gender behavior. That is to say, girls will grow up to act in a "feminine" way—dependent, emotional, expressive, gentle, nurturing, passive, and subjective, whereas boys will grow up to act in a "masculine" way—active, assertive, competitive, courageous, independent, rational, and self-confident (Guttentag and Bray, 1976).

Numerous studies have indicated that these gender-related beliefs are myths. In an examination of primitive behavior, it was found that there was no one, biologically "natural" set of male or female behaviors (Weisstein, 1971, p. 150). Societies have been found in which males and females do not behave in ways considered appropriate for males and females in Western society (Ford and Beach, 1981).

It is not, then, the infant's biological makeup—its sex chromosomes, glands, and organs—that determine its gender identity as a female or male. Rather, gender identity is the result of the child's "sex of assignment" and the learning of gender-related norms (Money and Ehrhardt, 1981, p. 12). Thus, males come to identify themselves as competent, intelligent, and motivated by power and personal accomplishment, whereas females see themselves as capable of warmth and desirous of friendly and harmonious relationships with others, but also as fearful and weak (Kagan, 1981, p. 41).

Research has found few differences between the sexes. Gender specific behavior continues because of the gender-typed structure and messages of our gender-typed environment. Thus, children are aided in their gender identity by the socializing agents of parents, peers, schools, and media. For example, parents treat male and female infants differently. They buy them clothing and toys in gender-specific colors, and they expect different behavior from them, aggressive for boys, docile for girls. They are also more gentle with girls than boys, cooing over the girls and roughhousing with the boys (Howe, 1972). It is these expectations and actions that bring about the very behavior that was anticipated. With increasing command of language, the child begins to sex-type itself and others according to the parental constructs. The result is that by two and one-half years of age, most children know clearly what sex they are and the "proper" feminine and masculine ways to behave (Albrecht and Bock, 1975).

Expectations also play a part in the school's differential treatment of boys and girls. There girls are expected to like reading and dislike math and science (Howe, 1972). The media, in the form of school books and television, reinforce these expectations by portraying women in traditional social roles, by underrepresenting women, by showing women as victims of jokes and insults, by portraying different modes of achievement for men and women, and by trivializing women and their concerns (Rickel and Grant, 1981).

There is a growing questioning of such "proper" gender behavior. Concern is increasing that traditional gender roles force both males and females into restrictive molds and keep them from realizing their full human potential. Thus, learning of the male gender role may result not in an inability to be expressive but in the belief by the male that he is not supposed to be expressive (Balwick and Peeks, 1981, p. 366).

This concern has led to the idea that children's socialization should include exposure to both feminine and masculine gender behavior: psychological androgyny "allows men and women to be both independent and tender, both assertive and yielding, both masculine and feminine." In other words, psychological androgyny expands the range of gender behavior for everyone (Bem, 1977, p. 319). For example, socialization practices that emphasize expressiveness and tenderness as well as instrumentality for men will bring about "a new kind of involvement of men with children" (Boulding, 1976, p. 117). Men and women replying to a radio talk station told of the benefits of being androgynous. The women referred to the "greater freedom they believe the men have in pursuing an occupation without being bound to home and children as their exclusive duty, and to the greater control and autonomy men seem to have." The men, on the other hand, said that "they would be relieved to be able to express their feelings of love, hurt, and anxiety as the women do" (Lasswell and Lasswell, 1982, p. 56).

As will be seen in chapter 13, however, the task of raising androgynous children is not an easy one, although the movement toward androgynous socialization is being aided by both the women's and men's liberation movements. The articles in chapter 3 echo this belief. In the first article, Phyllis LaFarge describes the impact of the feminist movement on women. Basically its effects include an expanded sense of identity and the belief that the humble work of maintenance and nurture is valuable and should be shared with men. In the second article, Betty Friedan concludes that American men are at the edge of a tidal wave of change that will affect their wholeness, their openness to feelings and to sharing on equal terms with women, and their very identity as men.

Unlike the changes in gender behavior, the changes in sexual behavior have been both rapid and widespread. Two time periods seem to stand out in the movement toward increased freedom in sexual behavior. The first is the period 1915–1920, a period that marked the "culmination of trends toward making the United States a modern industrial nation." The changing sexual picture was seemingly "part and parcel of an overall societal change occurring in all major social institutions." The second period of rapid social change was the period involving the change to a postindustrial society, 1965–1970.

The two periods can be distinguished by their relevant concerns. The postindustrial society was distinguished by its concern for the equitable distribution of rights and privileges, whereas the industrial society was primarily concerned with the production of goods and services (Reiss, 1973). In both periods doubts and questions were raised about societal values and morals. The result, as Ira Reiss notes in the first article of chapter 4, has been the delineation of areas of sexual controversy. These controversies have centered on genetic differences between the sexes, what constitutes sexual normality, the nature of exploitation and pornography, the acceptance and legality of abortion, and the development of a new mood in which sex is seen as play rather than as sin. He concludes that these controversies are the result of conflicting sexual scripts—a traditional-romantic ideology, in which sexuality is redeemed from guilt by love, versus a modern, naturalistic alternative, in which sexuality has as its goals physical pleasure and psychological intimacy.

As indicated above, one of the controversies that seemingly arose from this recent period of rapid social change concerned a new, permissive sexual mood and the acceptance of premarital sex. Actually, a glance at history reveals that premarital intercourse is not a new phenomenon. However, the rise of the middle class and the influences of Lutheranism and Calvinism led to a period in which the total moral fiber of the society was seen as weakened if sexual standards declined. In the industrial and postindustrial periods, this traditional morality has given way to a new morality in which physical sex is considered acceptable as long as it occurs after the establishment of friendship and love. Another, more amoral, idea has also gained ground—that the free expression of sexual desires has a positive effect on anxiety, frustration, and tension and adds to our happiness and life satisfaction (Farnsworth, 1977, p. 5). These changing moral beliefs have apparently caused an increase in the number of individuals engaging in premarital sex. A series of college surveys on female sexuality concludes that there has been "a significant increase in pre-marital coitus over the past twenty years" (Bell and Coughly, 1980, p. 354).

This growth in permissive sexuality has primarily affected females because of the double standard in which coitus was considered a need for men but not for women. A survey of sex manuals from the past 30 years reveals this change in the sex role of women, from a presumption of their being different and unequal, to humanistic sexuality, to sexual autonomy. Reflecting changing ideas of sexuality, the different-and-unequal model suggested that women can and should enjoy sex. However, sex for women was different than for men; it was more dormant and emotional and so needed to be awakened by the animalistic sexuality of the male. The humanistic version deinstitutionalized female sexuality by portraying it as a human quality present between two loving partners. Spurred by the feminist movement, a new model emerged in which women are portrayed as independent agents in charge of their own sexuality (Weinberg, Swenson, and Hammersmith, 1983).

These changing sexual ethics were seen as having different effects on women's liberation. Permissiveness is considered by some as essentially a premarital sex ethic giving females the same sexual rights and privileges enjoyed by men (Tomasson, 1970). Others believe that increasing sexual permissiveness has created "a new reservoir of available females . . . for traditional sexual exploitation, disarming women of even the little protection they had so painfully acquired" (Firestone, 1970). Regardless of which view is correct, awareness of the gender differences in sexual scripts improves our understanding of sexuality and its relationship to sex roles (Delameter, 1982).

Another outgrowth of the acceptance of premarital sex has been an explosive growth in teenage pregnancy. The Presidential Commission for a National Agenda (1980) has concluded that "there is perhaps no more serious health and welfare problem confronting the U.S. today than the high rate of adolescent pregnancy." It has been predicted that if present trends continue, at least one third of all girls now aged 14 will have had one pregnancy before they are 20 (Tietze, 1979). Yet, in the past few years there has been a substantial decline in adolescent pregnancy (Valentine, 1983).

One might wonder why there is so much growth in teenage pregnancy in a period when birth control is increasingly feasible. In a study of the sources and accuracy of sexual knowledge of adolescents, it was shown that the main source of sexual information is one's peers and that this source is the lowest in accuracy (Thornburg, 1981). Nor does this situation change very much with advanced formal education; inaccurate sexual information, along with beliefs in sexual myths, were also found to be common among college men and women (Mosher, 1979). In short, sexuality is seldom taught but is always learned. These findings lead to the conclusion that a "more systematic and accurate presentation of sexual concepts is needed among today's adolescents" due to their "earlier physical maturation, earlier peer involvement, increased early adolescent sexual involvement, and early learning of sex information" (Thornburg, 1981, p. 277).

It would appear that sex education should include access to contraception, since denial of access has not discouraged sexual activity among adolescents, and there is no reason to believe that access would encourage such activity (Cutright, 1972). However, the availability of contraceptives may not be the issue, since even when they are available they are not always used. In a study of women who had visited an abortion clinic, it was found that the question of whether or not to use contraceptives was "a weighting process between a series of fairly well-defined costs and benefits" (Luker, 1975, p. 36). The costs of using contraception included the acknowledgment that one is engaging in sexual intercourse; a limitation on romantic spontaneity; difficulties in trying to obtain and maintain effective contraception; male attitudes of indifference and opposition; and possible side effects. Potential benefits women gave for not using contraception—that is, for taking a chance on getting pregnant—included proving their womanhood; asserting their personal worth and providing someone to need and love them; discovering if they were fertile; forcing the male to redefine his commitment to the relationship; punishing their parents; being recognized as an adult; crying for help; and as a reward in itself (Lasswell and Lasswell, 1982, pp. 94–95). As can be seen, the problem of adolescent premarital pregnancy is a complicated one.

Chapter 4 concludes with a glance at the biophysical capacity of human beings for responsiveness. In sum, people are not naturally sexual. They must learn scripts that tell them how to have sex, who to have it with, and even the extent to which they are allowed to take advantage of their biophysical capacity for responsiveness. What then is one's biophysical capacity? According to an examination of sex manuals by Dennis Brissett and Lionel Lewis in the second article of this chapter, that capacity is limitless. The manuals espouse an openness and naturalness of sexual expression that will liberate sex for all; they also indicate how this may be accomplished. The authors conclude that sex is being asked to fulfill needs that were heretofore fulfilled by the family, organized religion, and the workplace, and that that is too heavy a burden. The final article of this chapter, by Philip Blumstein and Pepper Schwartz, describes the results of all these changes—the American way of loving. They note the role of kissing, position, and attitudes and satisfaction in regard to loving.

Another aspect of intimacy—dating—is discussed in chapter 5. We take the custom of dating for granted, but it is a relatively recent social phenomenon. Before World War I, most people lived and died in the same small community, a situation that meant that everyone knew everyone else and formal introductions were unnecessary (Hoult, Henze, and Hudson, 1978, p. 20). Dating or seeing a person on a regular basis occurred if the prospect was marriage, and then it occurred under the careful scrutiny of the parents.

Dating as we know it came with the changes brought about by rapid industrialization and urbanization. As people left small towns and used the telephone and automobile more, parental control decreased. Dating became more an aspect of recreation and adult role socialization than an aspect of mate selection, although it still functions as a significant element in this regard. Thus, the dating pattern shown in a study done in the 1950s revealed a sequence of five stages: group dating, random dating, pinning, engagement, and marriage (LeMasters, 1957). The mid-1960s brought about another change in the dating pattern, described by such terms as "getting together" and "going out" (Hoult, Henze, and Hudson, 1978, pp. 114–20). There was a move from the formality of dating to a more relaxed style of informal get-togethers and group activities, with the majority gradually evolving into pairs with less structured male and female roles (Murstein, 1980, p. 780).

The current dating scene as practiced by college students is described by David Knox and Kenneth Wilson in the first article of chapter 5. It would appear to be a combination of both types of dating described above, with sexual intimacy a major aspect. Dating is a "game in which individuals attempt to maximize their gains while minimizing their efforts" (Staples, 1978, p. 59), rather than a means to marriage. In sum, the motives for dating appear to be recreation, a means of learning about each other as individuals and as members of a group, a way of raising one's status, and a means of serious partner selection (Skipper and Nass, 1966).

The last two articles of chapter 5 deal with specific problems of dating. Dating for the newly separated is quite different from the former dating relationship. It includes a number of growth stages: in the first stage there is fear of social contact due to the long absence from the dating game; the "candy-factory stage" is an attempt to build one's ego by multiple dating or by having a number of short-term relationships; the "latching-on stage" involves entering into an immediate relationship in order to avoid the inevitable feelings of loss. When exploring the singles' world becomes lonely and empty, there comes a search for commitment and intimacy; the final stage involves risking again in a close and loving relationship (O'Phelan, 1983). In her article, Lillian Africano examines the problems of single parents reentering the dating scene, in which new rules are in effect. She concludes that every new shared experience is enriching for the parent-child relationship, and that dating is no exception if certain rules are followed.

As the article by Africano indicates, dating also exists for the noncollege and postcollege person, but without the college situation and atmosphere that help people meet each other. This has led to the development of computer match-ups, newspaper or magazine advertising for mates, singles' clubs and bars, and video-tape selections. In the last article of this part, Davor Jedlicka examines the formal mate selection networks in the United States, including newspaper networks, co-publisher networks, go-between networks, computer dating, and video-mate. Jedlicka notes that by joining formal mate selection networks, one reduces infringement on personality, minimizes the importance of appearance in initial encounters, and allows clear expression of what one desires in a relationship.

STUDY QUESTIONS

Chapter 3

LaFarge
1. What does LaFarge mean when she says that the feminist movement has expanded the identity of women?
2. How does the feminist movement view household duties and nurturing?

Friedan
1. Friedan notes ways that the feminist movement is affecting men. Think of other ways that men are changing, and note whether they are also a result of the feminist movement.
2. Friedan also notes several "payoffs" for men. What are some other "payoffs"?

Chapter 4

Reiss
1. What are the controversies surrounding the issues of genetic differences between the sexes and of sexual normality?
2. Compare the sexual scripts of the traditional-romantic ideology and the modern-naturalistic alternatives.

Brissett & Lewis
1. What do the sex manuals say about nature, performance, variety, anatomy, sexual equipment, sexual places, and sexual noises?
2. What does the term *liberated sex* imply?

Blumstein & Schwartz
1. Describe four of the findings that most surprised you.
2. What are the myths of extramarital sex?

Chapter 5

Knox & Wilson
1. How does one usually meet a date, and what usually happens?
2. What is the relationship between dating and intimacy?

Africano
1. How can a parent insure that his or her child is not feeling threatened by a date?
2. What should the relationship be between a date and the children?

Jedlicka
1. What is the difference between newspaper networks, co-publisher networks, and go-between networks?
2. What benefits accrue from membership in formal mate selection networks?

REFERENCES FOR PART TWO

Albrecht, Ruth E., and E. Wilbur Bock. 1975. *Encounter: Love, marriage, and family.* Boston: Holbrook.

Balswick, Jack D., and Charles W. Peek. 1971. The inexpressive male: A tragedy of American society. *The Family Coordinator,* October.

Bell, Robert R., and Kathleen Coughey. 1980. Premarital sexual experience among college females, 1958, 1968 and 1978. *Family Relations,* July.

Bem, Sandra L. 1977. Beyond androgyny: Some presumptuous prescriptions for a liberated sexual identity. In *Family in transition,* ed. by Arlene Skolnick and Jerome Skolnick, 2nd ed. Boston: Little, Brown.

Boulding, Elise. 1972. The family as an agent of social change. *The Futurist,* October.

Cutright, Phillip S. 1972. Historical and contemporary trends in illegitimacy. *Archives of Sexual Behavior.*

Delameter, John. 1982. Gender differences in sexual scripts. *Presented at Annual Conference of the American Sociological Association,* September.

Farnsworth, Dana L. 1965. Sexual morality and the dilemma of the colleges. *American Journal of Orthopsychiatry,* July.

Firestone, Shulamith. 1970. *The dialectic of sex.* New York: Morrow.

Ford, Clellan S., and Frank A. Beach. 1951. *Patterns of sexual behavior.* New York: Harper.

Guttentag, Marcia, and Helen Bray. 1976. *Undoing sex stereotypes.* New York: McGraw-Hill.

Hoult, Thomas, Laura F. Henze, and John W. Hudson. 1978. *Courtship and marriage in America.* Boston: Little, Brown.

Howe, Florence. 1971. Sexual stereotypes start early. *Saturday Review,* October 10.

Kagan, Jerome. 1969. Check one: Male/female. *Psychology Today,* July.

Lasswell, Marcia, and Thomas E. Lasswell. 1982. *Marriage and the family.* Lexington, Mass.: D. C. Heath.

LeMasters, E. E. 1970. *Parents in modern America.* Homewood, Ill.: Dorsey.

Luker, Kristin. 1975. *Taking chances.* Berkeley: University of California Press.

Money, John, and Anke Ehrhardt. 1972. *Man and woman, boy and girl.* New York: Mentor.

Mosher, Donald L. 1979. Sex guilt and sex myths in college men and women. *The Journal of Sex Research,* August, pp. 224–34.

Murstein, Bernard I. 1980. Mate selections in the 1970s. *Journal of Marriage and the Family,* November, pp. 777–92.

O'Phelan, Mary Louise. 1980. Once upon a time . . . again. *The Single Parent,* May.

Radlove, Shirley. 1983. Sexual response and gender roles. In *Changing boundaries,* ed. by Elizabeth Rice Augeier and Naomi B. McCormick, pp. 87–105. Palo Alto, Calif.: Mayfield.

Skipper, James K., Jr., and Gilbert Nass. 1966. Dating behavior: A framework for analysis and an illustration. *National Council on Family Relations.*

Staples, Robert, ed. 1978. *The black family: Essays and studies,* 2nd ed. Belmont, Calif.: Wadsworth.

Thornburg, Hershal D. 1981. Adolescent sources of information on sex. *The Journal of School Health,* April.

Tietze, Christopher. 1979. Adolescent pregnancy and childbirth. *Family Planning Perspectives,* July/August.

Tomasson, R. F. 1970. *Sweden: Prototype of modern society.* New York: Random House.

Valentine, Jeanette. 1983. The adolescent pregnancy problem. *Society for the Study of Social Problems,* August.

Weinberg, Martin S., Rochelle Ganz Swenson, and Sue Kiefer Hammersmith. 1983. Sexual autonomy and the status of women: Models of female sexuality in U.S. sex manuals from 1950 to 1980. *Social Problems,* February, pp. 312–24.

Weisstein, Naomi. 1971. Psychology constructs and female, or the fantasy life of the male psychologist. In *From feminism to liberation,* ed. by Edith Hoshind Altback. Cambridge, Mass.: Schenkman.

III

ROLE CHANGES

6

THE NEW WOMAN

Phyllis LaFarge

"I'm not alone any more," Freda Branch said when I asked her why she thought the women's movement had made her life better. Freda is 24 years old and a resident of University City, Missouri. Until pregnancy interrupted her studies, she had been preparing for a career as a dental technician while working at a tennis club, where she books court time. I asked her in what way she had felt alone. "Well," she replied, "when I was a kid people always said, 'Oh, you're not going to do that. That's something men do.' I always wanted to be a doctor, but at that time people thought that was something just for men."

Being a doctor was not Freda's only ambition when she was growing up: she wanted to be the statistician for her high school baseball team. "Boys had always done it," she recalled, "but I asked the coach and he said, 'Can you do it?' I said, 'You don't think I can, but I can,' and he gave me a chance. It was great. I got to travel with the team."

When Freda says she is no longer alone, she is acknowledging that she is part of a revolution that has swept over America—the revolution of the women's movement. Despite the clear changes this revolution has brought—the enormously increased numbers of women entering the professions, for instance—the women's movement is in many ways an intangible revolution. Although in recent years women have begun to feel differently about themselves and their place in the world, we are often not sure of just how they feel different and whether the difference is for better or worse.

To measure the impact of the women's movement, *Parents* sponsored a telephone poll of a national sample of women 21 to 35. The results confirmed that Freda is far from alone—and that her sisters are far from being the braless ideologues or briefcased executives often portrayed as feminist stereotypes.

WHAT IS THE WOMEN'S MOVEMENT TELLING US?

Before we look at the impact of the movement, however, let's look at its core messages. They concern identity. The women's movement supports an expanded identity for women. Giving a contemporary formulation to an age-old attitude, psychoanalyst Erik Erikson once postulated that woman's domain was the world of "inner space"—of

---

Phyllis LaFarge, "The New Woman," *Parents*, October 1983. Copyright © 1983 Parents Magazine Enterprises. Reprinted from *Parents* by permission.

childbearing, child rearing, and the intimate life of family. According to this formulation, men's domain was the less intimate, more public "outer" world beyond the home, often thought of as the world of work for pay or the "world of action." The women's movement has questioned the sex-linked nature of these distinctions and in doing so legitimized women who, like Freda, sensed that in order to be fully themselves, they must be free to find a place and play a role or roles in the "outer" world.

This expanded sense of identity is the aspect of the women's movement most reinforced by the media. But the movement carries another message as well, usually missed by the media but central to many feminists. This message concerns the special and enduring value of women's traditional role as maintainers of the fabric of daily life, including the fabric of intimate, daily relationships. According to this line of feminist thinking, women should not have to do this job alone—it should be shared with men—but whoever is doing it, the humble work of maintenance and nurturance should be valued as it historically never has been.

With the media tending to associate the women's movement with the expansion of women's identity, it's hard for many women to be alert to this alternative message, but some are. Cindy Keeling, for instance, of Rogers, Arkansas, is 27 years old and the mother of four children—Cliff, 8, Mandy, 4, and Carrie and Lindsey, 1-year-old twins. When I spoke with her, she had a job assembling B.B. guns at the Daisy Manufacturing Company, where her husband, Luther, also is employed, but she was working only because her family needed her paycheck. When asked what matters most to her, being a wife and mother or having a career outside the home, she answered, "I'm working, but it's more fulfilling being at home with my children." (Subsequently Cindy has been able to quit her job because her husband has taken over his father's part-time saw-sharpening business in order to supplement the family income.)

It would be easy to conclude from these statements that Cindy's life has been untouched by the women's movement, but this is not how she herself sees it. "The women's movement," she commented, "has made me a better wife and mother.

It has made me aware of things I wasn't aware of before." What kind of things? It was hard for Cindy to answer, but when she did, she said, "I feel that I'm more valuable than, say, a woman in the fifties would have felt. Being a wife and mother was what women then were expected to do. Today being a wife and mother is more like a career choice." It is the value the women's movement places on nurturance that helps Cindy feel the way she does.

But her words reflect another aspect of feminist thinking as well. Cindy feels she has a choice in life. The women's movement has helped women feel that they have the right to shape their own lives as well as a true possibility of doing so. This belief in a right to self-realization is a common thread in much contemporary psychological and political thinking and is not an exclusive attribute of the women's movement. But it is an especially potent message when applied to women.

Traditionally, women's destiny was molded not only by the same political and economic forces that shape men's lives but by the hazards and inevitability of childbearing and by a social "place" in society that reflected both the necessities of child rearing and the power of men. Technology has greatly changed all this—and very rapidly. Reliable birth control, better gynecological care, and easier home maintenance have liberated women so that nurturance and maintenance can be part of life rather than the whole. At the same time, technology has changed the nature of work and patterns of consumption, virtually necessitating the two-paycheck marriage. In the light of these changes, an expanded identity for women is an inevitability, and it's no coincidence that the women's movement has been a force for the last fifteen years: the movement provides ideological and emotional support for women seeking to find their way in a historically new situation.

THE ACCEPTANCE OF THE WOMEN'S MOVEMENT

With these changes in mind—and not forgetting Freda's attitudes or Cindy's—let's look at how widely accepted the movement is. At least among women under 35, it has gained wide acceptance: two-thirds of our poll respondents (67 percent) agree with its overall goals, and 42 percent believe that it has made their lives better. This conviction is not restricted to the upper middle class or to professional women: 46 percent of women with incomes under $15,000 a year, 40 percent of nonwhite women, and 38 percent of blue-collar women think they are leading better lives.

Women's thinking on a number of issues on which feminists have taken a stand is at least as revealing as their avowed allegiance to the movement itself: two-thirds feel that the Equal Rights Amendment should have been passed; 61 percent believe that advertising stressing women's sexual attractiveness is insulting to women; 56 percent think that homosexuals should be allowed to teach in the public schools; 82 percent think that stricter measures should be taken to reduce the amount of pornography available; 80 percent believe that job quotas to ensure equal opportunity are a good thing. Perhaps most astounding of all, 57 percent believe that abortions should be available to any woman who wants one.

HOW WOMEN SEE THE MOVEMENT

We'll return to these very liberal attitudes, but first let's consider how women see the movement. For the most part they see it in terms of support for an expanded identity: When asked to identify the goals of the women's movement, 76 percent mentioned the opening up of job opportunities for women and 73 percent an end to discrimination. This is corroborated by the fact that women are even more likely to agree with the goals of the movement and to believe they have benefited by it if they are well educated and in a managerial position—characteristics of individuals who are likely to want and enjoy expanded opportunities in their lives.

But to see women's acceptance of the women's movement only in terms of their desire for expanded opportunity in the outer world does not take into account the complexity of women's opinions and feelings. When asked what they regard as necessary for a fulfilling life, 76 percent say that love is necessary and 76 percent mention a good family life. Only 30 percent mention career as essential, although another 47 percent see it as important but not essential. How do these attitudes toward fulfillment dovetail with those they have toward the women's movement?

The answer is that although women today need and want opportunities in the "outer world" they have in no way let go of the values traditionally associated with the private "inner" world of family life. They are the adventurous, ambitious Freda, but they are the more traditional Cindy, too. A look at women's attitudes toward their own accomplishments and toward their work outside the home underlines the degree to which this is true. Sixty percent of our respondents regard their family life as their greatest accomplishment, and 66 percent believe that even when they are old they will still look on their family in this way. When asked which is most important to them, being a wife and mother or their work outside the home, 60 percent chose wife and mother, and only 18 percent chose work. (Eighteen percent refused to choose between the two options and said both were equally important, and this figure might have been higher if the question had not been worded to force a choice between a "career" and a "wife-mother" answer.) But at the same time, two-thirds work outside the home and most of those who are not employed at present expect to work in the future. Moreover, more report that they work because they enjoy it (32 percent) rather than because they need the money— 26 percent—although among nonwhite respondents the figure is 36 percent. Forty-two percent say they are motivated equally by enjoyment and need. Three-quarters of those working say they would continue working even if they could maintain their standard of living without doing so. Interestingly, the presence of young children scarcely affects this point of view: 71 percent of those with children under five would continue working even if they could maintain their standard of living without doing so.

Many women, however, even when they seek through work personal satisfaction and a measure of independence from their husband and family, are reluctant to give their ambitions or their work the same value as their husband's. Often they see their work in nurturant terms as "helping out" their husband and family. Thus Kathy Ramin, who works in Williamsport, Pennsylvania, assembling radar tubes, says, "I'd be bored if I didn't work, and I think when you don't work you feel your husband is doing you a favor giving you spending money. And the chores you do are insignificant." But in the next breath she commented, "When you work, you're helping your husband, helping him bring home the bread while you're taking care of your own needs for independence."

When you listen to a woman like Kathy, or a woman like Cindy, you realize the extent to which the ideas of the women's movement have penetrated the society: it's more than likely that fifteen years ago neither of them would have thought in the terms they do today.

It's equally clear, however, that the movement would never have achieved the measure of acceptance it has if it were its narrowest stereotype; that is, a relentless pursuit of economic equality with an implied contempt for traditional feminine roles and an implied belief that paid work is the only real and valuable work of the society. And to the degree that the women's movement is perceived as its stereotype, it may be even less accepted than it might be. This is suggested by the fact that women who are opposed to the movement tend to see it as pushing women in the direction of career at the expense of family, while those who identify strongly with its goals tend to see it as encouraging women to combine family life and work outside the home. In the light of what we know about women's enduring commitment to the values of the intimate world it is not surprising that they would reject any set of beliefs they perceived as asking them to turn their backs on their central course of fulfillment.

How can we characterize the women who have taken the goals of the women's movement to heart—but without surrendering traditional values? Mary Jo Bane, associate professor at Harvard's Kennedy School of Government, sees them as "a very special generation": "These are all baby-boom women. The oldest ones were born in 1947. That means their mothers produced the baby boom and subscribed to the ideology of children, family, and staying home. The older ones were in their twenties; and the younger, coming of age when feminist ideas came along. These women tend to be better educated than their mothers and more of them have worked before they married. Coming of age, they were the first generation in history for whom good birth control was available and acceptable. They realized, as their mothers were beginning to realize, that children and family are part of life but not the whole. Their attitudes are very liberal indeed, and what's so interesting is that these younger women have these very liberal attitudes at the same time that they are so devoted to children and family. The stereotype is that liberal social attitudes are associated with a lack of caring about home and family.

"It's not a trivial finding, either," Professor Bane continued, "that 26 percent of these women characterize themselves as 'very religious' and another 55 percent as 'somewhat religious.' That means that you don't have a bunch of crazies here but very mainstream people subscribing to very liberal attitudes."

WOMEN AND THEIR WORK

How is widespread acceptance of the goals of the women's movement changing women's lives? A solid majority (61 percent) of women see increased job opportunity as the principal effect of the movement and 83 percent feel they can expect equal pay for equal work—a somewhat surprising finding in the face of the fact that women still earn only 60 cents for every dollar earned by men.

Women in all lines of work believe that opportunity has increased. Carol Doran, an attorney with the Internal Revenue Service in Washington, D.C., commented, "Only in the last decade has my division hired women attorneys, but I think they've tried very hard to hire a lot of women."

Pat Stephens, who works in a central Oregon lumber mill, felt discrimination "is not near as bad" and that opportunity has increased. "Back in the sixties," she recalled, "three of us were working on a finger joint machine. We were all women and we'd been at the mill two years. We were making $2.65 an hour and they hired a boy just out of high school and paid him $3 to start. That wouldn't happen today."

But although discrimination "is not near as bad," it has not disappeared. "One thing I've noticed," Pat said, "is that lately they've been hiring all men. They are trying to phase out women, and they do seem to prefer the cutesy ones."

DISCRIMINATION: STILL WITH US

Only a minority of women (20 percent) feel that the women's movement has eliminated discrimination (whereas 73 percent believe that its elimination is a central message of the movement), and many have been touched by it in painful ways. Jacqueline Haloszka of Wheeling, West Virginia, for instance, is a single mother. After her divorce she looked for work as a bookkeeper with an accounting firm. Describing her feelings while job hunting, she said, "I was worried, because I'm a mother, too. So I told them right off what my situation was; I couldn't work nights and weekends during the tax season." Although she was promised that it wouldn't make any difference, she was the first to go when her firm merged with another.

Perhaps the most striking change with respect to the world of work that the women's movement has brought about is a kind of ferment of activity in women themselves: whatever obstacles women still encounter in the job market, they are continuing their education, starting their own businesses, and seeking advancement on the job. The bid system at the lumber mill allows Pat to try for a better job, and right now she is being trained for a position that will earn her nearly a dollar an hour more than she is making at present. Jacqueline Haloszka, who now works as comptroller for a construction company, is going to school to complete her training as an accountant—and is thinking of starting a business of her own. This ferment is not only a response to actual opportunity—which in some communities is not all that great—it's a response to the permission and encouragement to seek an expanded identity that is at the core of the women's movement. It is also evidence of women's greatly increased self-confidence—which women themselves tend to see as virtually as important a consequence of the women's movement as increased opportunity on the job. As Freda Branch puts it, "More women are venturing out and saying to heck with staying in their place. They're working, going to school, and having a good social life."

However, the advantage that numerous women are taking of new opportunities and new confidence, combined with the media's narrow definition of the women's movement—often emphasizing a "briefcase," "corporate success" image—can be undermining to women who are staying home to raise their children, even when they have made the choice to do so freely and are happy with the choice. "It makes you feel funny even if you are happy," commented Deanna Kimble of Wheeling, West Virginia. "If you have kids and you feel happy, you still feel odd." When a woman like this no longer feels "funny" or "odd"—and, be it said, when another sort of woman doesn't need to phrase a personal ad in the following manner: "Cute little neuroscientist looking for smart single men to knit socks for" (*New York Review of Books,* April 14, 1983)—the fullest, deepest messages of the movement will have been accepted by the society.

WOMEN AND MEN

It's much harder to tell how women feel the women's movement has changed their relationship with men than it is to tell what they feel it has done to their work opportunities. Only 20 percent feel that it has made it harder to hold marraiges together. Although more than 60 percent of the women had married by the time they were 22, only 26 percent thought a husband was necessary to a fulfilling life—as compared with the 76 percent who thought love and a good family life necessary. And 19 percent thought a husband was not at all related to fulfillment. The figure of 26 percent may be as low as it is, according to Mary Jo Bane, because respondents were asked if they considered a husband *absolutely* necessary, but even so it is striking and surprising and would undoubtedly have been higher for their mothers at a comparable age.

It is hard to be entirely clear how much these figures reflect changes brought about by the women's movement and how much they reflect a very broad change in the society of which the women's movement constitutes only a part.

Referring to this broader change, Dr. Peggy McIntosh, a program director at the Wellesley College Center for Research on Women, commented,

"Today I think people are aware that there are many forms of love you can experience in the course of your life. The definition of love has diffused in a healthy way. You can get love from friends, children, lovers, as well as husbands. Human warmth is necessary—women are sure of that—but the romantic twosome does not have an exclusive grip on women's imagination as it did for so many in the forties and fifties."

It may be, too, that the low figure of 26 percent represents a realistic attitude given the number of marriages that fail and the number of years a woman can expect to spend alone over the course of her life. (Ten percent of the women interviewed were divorced or separated and only 43 percent of these hope to remarry, although 22 percent characterize themselves as "unsure" with respect to remarriage.) The low figure of 43 percent reinforces the message of independence suggested by the attitudes toward marriage described above. It may also hint at pessimism about the possibilities of being one's own person within "a romantic twosome."

Many women are aware that, without actually leading to the breakup of a marriage, the expanded identity encouraged by the women's movement can cause difficulties in their relations with men. Margaret Wilkerson, director of the Center for the Study, Education and Advancement of Women at the University of California at Berkeley, commented, "I think one reason women are staying single is that they want more of a relationship than they can find."

For some very able women in the professions the situation can appear quite bleak. Attorney Carol Doran, who is not married, commented, "It's difficult, if not impossible, to combine marriage and a profession because of the difficulty of finding a sympathetic man. The attitudes of the men haven't caught up with women. Most men want someone who will stay home with kids and who will look up to them because they make a lot of money. If you're a professional, you're not what they're looking for."

Carol's position is a minority one, however; a substantial majority of women (70 percent) report that their husbands approve of their working. Nevertheless, this is a more positive response than women give when asked more impersonally if a wife and mother can expect her husband to feel threatened if she works. In reply to this more general question 26 percent think it very likely; and 56 percent, somewhat likely. Only 17 percent felt their husbands would not be threatened. It may be that women are much more ready to consider the possibility of being threatening in the abstract than they are in relation to their actual husbands. Perhaps this is all the more true because most women strongly believe that combining career and motherhood leads to greater self-esteem (72 percent feel that it is "very likely" that a woman will feel better about herself if she does so): it is hard to admit that what enhances your self-esteem may in fact be threatening to someone you love.

THE HOUSEWORK DILEMMA

Housework—or rather the sharing of housework—is another area in which the ideas of the women's movement have the potential to affect the relationship of husband and wife. In fewer than one in five marriages do couples share housework equally. Interestingly, the figures are not radically different among women who identify strongly with the women's movement. Only 24 percent of such women share housework equally with their husbands.

Why do men resist sharing housework—beyond the fact that anyone would avoid it if he or she could? The reason may lie in the fact that if a man shares housework or more than cursory child care, he assumes a new role—expands his identity. This may be far more threatening than perhaps continuing in an established role but experiencing it as somewhat diminished, as is the case when his wife works and he is no longer the sole provider. Sensing this, women may hold back from pushing their husbands to share housework and child care. The closer a change comes to intimate life and, particularly, to challenging the self-image of a loved one, the harder it may be for women to push for.

It would be wrong, however, to suggest that women do not think that men have been affected by the revolution in attitudes of which the women's movement is a part. Thirty percent of our respondents felt that a central message of the movement was the encouragement of men to be more expressive in ways usually associated with women—in other words to allow themselves to express feelings such as tenderness or vulnerability. And 20 percent thought the fact that men realized they could do so was a major consequence of the women's movement. These figures are not large, but they are of great interest given the fact that there is as yet little support among men themselves for change in this direction, and there is a lot for them to be threatened by in the women's movement.

Even women who are quite conservative may perceive that the women's movement has had an effect on their husbands. Deanna Kimble, for instance, is basically opposed to the women's movement. She feels that it has created unrealistic expectations among women, made the position of women more difficult, and made it harder to hold marriages together. Most of all, she believes that because the women's movement pressures women to work outside the home, children suffer. "When you come home at 5 you're tired and you don't get time to do anything special with the kids."

But a discussion of her husband's situation qualified her point of view. At the time Deanna was interviewed, her husband, Brian, had been laid off from his job in the shipping department of a tool company and Deanna had taken a part-time job in a fast-food restaurant to supplement the family income. She and Brian share the care of their four-year-old daughter. Deanna felt that the messages of the women's movement concerning men's roles made Brian's unemployed situation a little more tolerable for him. "It's easier with the women's movement for men to help out with housework and help with kids. I tease Brian about women's lib all the time in front of his friends, but they're doing the same thing. I think it's acceptable to him." Although Deanna states that the movement has made her life neither easier nor more difficult, it may in fact have made it easier by providing some societal support of the role temporarily forced on her husband.

FEMINIST CHILD REARING

The women's movement has profoundly influenced women's attitudes toward rearing children. Whereas the mothers and grandmothers of today's women would not have thought at all about the issue of innate biological differences between the sexes versus socialization—and, if pressed, would have favored biology—the ideas the women's movement has popularized about nurture versus nature have led 76 percent of our respondents to believe that social and behavioral differences between the sexes are the result of the way children are taught to behave. Only 9 percent think these differences are the result of biology, and only 12 percent think nature and nurture have an equal effect. By implication this belief in the power of socialization leads parents to believe they have a role and choice in their children's development that earlier generations would not have perceived in the same way.

How do women see themselves exercising this influence? Fifty-one percent would like to diminish the differences between boys and girls but not eliminate them altogether, and 30 percent would like to try for as few differences as possible. Thirty-nine percent of nonwhite respondents would like to try for as few differences as possible—a figure that Margaret Wilkerson finds "not surprising." "My hunch," she says, "is that it reflects a kind of historical egalitarianism that undergirds the black community. [Going back to slavery] both men and women worked in the fields and in the kitchen. More recently, both men and women have to work to support a family." Only 13 percent of our poll respondents would like to see the current range of differences continue in the next generation. This may be the most remarkable finding of the study. It suggests an extraordinary acceptance of a set of ideas that had hardly touched public consciousness twenty years ago as well as a very rationalist attitude toward human potential. And it's worth pointing out that these attitudes are shared even by those who see themselves as very religious or as political conservatives: only 14 percent of the very religious and only 17 percent of the politically conservative would like to see the socialization of children continue as now.

At the same time that the women's movement has changed attitudes toward the rearing of children, it has changed women's outlook on the place of children in their lives. Important as family life and children continue to be for them, the goal of an expanded identity has made it acceptable to women to consider postponing children while they build a base for themselves through work or study in the "outer world." When asked if a woman planning a career should start her career first and postpone children or vice versa, 60 percent of our respondents favored postponing children, and 29 percent were in favor of postponing career (11 percent were not sure). In fact, there are indications that these women are practicing what they preach, since of those who have children, less than 16 percent are 25 or under.

The same goal of an expanded identity leads women to believe that it is realistic to combine a career with motherhood: 77 percent of our respondents believe that it is possible to do so successfully—a point of view their mothers and grandmothers would not have shared to the same degree at all. However, when questioned on the more specific and sensitive issue of whether preschool children will thrive without the fulltime care of their mothers, only 59 percent thought they did not need their mothers' fulltime care, whereas 38 percent believed that preschoolers *do* require it. "You're still getting a lot of people who think it's a good thing to stay home when kids are young," Mary Jo Bane commented, "but these days 'young' gets defined as six or three, not eighteen."

A closer look at our sample reveals the way in which opportunity for an expanded identity influences these attitudes: 75 percent of those in management or professional positions feel that preschoolers can thrive without their mothers' fulltime care, whereas far fewer women feel this way if they have less opportunity in their lives: only 54 percent of women who had no more than a high school education felt this way. Moreover, the ideological character of these attitudes is suggested by the fact that 72 percent of those who identify strongly with the women's movement think that young children flourish without their mothers' fulltime care, but among women who identified themselves as political conservatives only a slim majority—53 percent—felt this way.

HIDDEN CONFLICTS

Although women want a role in the "outer world" while raising their children, pursuing it inevitably involves some degree of conflict—conflict that, given their commitment to balancing many roles, they may not always be entirely ready to admit to—at least in a telephone interview. When asked if they personally spent less time on family life than they liked because of work, only 13 percent said they did so frequently, although 38 percent said they did occasionally. Only 4 percent said they frequently left their children with child care they were less than entirely happy with while they went to work, and only 17 percent did so occasionally. However, when asked in much less direct and personal terms if a woman who combines career and motherhood will doubt that she is a good enough wife and mother, 25 percent of respondents said that it was very likely that she would do so; and 56 percent, somewhat likely. Moreover, 48 percent thought it somewhat likely that her children would get in trouble, and 26 percent thought it somewhat likely that the children would have emotional difficulties.

Traditionally women have tended to handle inner conflict over their sense of responsibility to their family by choosing work that is not too pressured or is in one way or another a good fit with family life. Implicitly if not explicitly, the "briefcase," "corporate success" stereotype of the message of women's movement discourages this approach in its attempt to help women better adapt to the world of work, particularly highly competitive work in the contemporary corporate setting. A profound aspect of women's nature and socialization is thus downplayed. "We women are trained to work for the decent survival of all," Peggy McIntosh comments. "That's the heritage we were raised with by virtue of our socialization, even if we're not aware of it."

Combining motherhood with most work situations is no threat to the "decent survival of all" as long as good child care is available, but a woman may feel it is an issue if she enters a highly competitive field and wishes to be outstanding. Our respondents' awareness of this problem was reflected in their answers to a hypothetical question concerning "Sara," a lawyer who would have to work 60 hours a week, as the men did in her firm, if she wished to become a partner. Fifty-eight percent of the sample thought she should give up the hope of being outstanding and settle for a lesser role in the firm so that she could spend time with her child; 26 percent thought she should devote herself to her career; and 15 percent were not sure what she should do. A commitment to the "decent survival of all" still has the majority voice, but the "briefcase," "corporate success" message of the women's movement has won at least theoretical concurrence from a quarter of the women.

Percentages, however, cannot suggest what it feels like for real women as opposed to the hypothetical Sara when they try to resolve conflicts between doing well by their family and fully pursuing their talents and ambitions. For many the solution—or the nearest thing to a solution—may be starting a family late and keeping it small. Carol Reagan, for instance, of Skokie, Illinois, is married and 30 years old. She works as a field representative for a county agency on aging and is meanwhile studying for a master's degree in public administration. So far she has not had a child. "I like my freedom and I don't think I should go into child rearing feeling that way," she said. "If I had one child," she continued, "it would be easier. I think perhaps I could manage one child with day care. If I had more than one child, I'd have to have a housekeeper." When asked if she thought her employer would be somewhat flexible to help her balance her job with mothering, she said, "My agency is flexible to a certain extent, but not my husband's company. And he certainly wouldn't get any paternity leave. And given the current economic situation I don't see that organizations are going to become more flexible. I think they're going to become more inflexible."

By implication Carol's remarks raise an important issue. As more women work outside the home the kind of family nurturance and maintenance provided preponderantly by women will have to be shared if families are not to live with a high degree of stress—particularly for children. Where is this support going to come from? From husbands? But they are not going to provide it unless they experience a wider, deeper change of consciousness than they now have—one profound enough to make them join women in insisting on modifications in the structure of the workplace. Or will it come from public-policy changes—but policy changes do not come unless people press for them—men as well as women—and it goes against the American grain to press for public solutions to what we tend to see as individual problems. Our American cult of the individual makes us think that families should solve their own problems—and to see help as intrusion or proof of weakness. The difficulty is that our very belief in opportunity for the individual, now that it has been extended to women, has created an unprecedented situation. We have created a "nurturance gap" in the society that cannot be filled without changes and solutions that go beyond what individual families can do. It is this nurturance gap that Carol Reagan, like many other women, struggles with when she thinks of having a child. Or, put more concretely, in the words of Margaret Wilkerson, "The findings of the *Parents* poll have strong implications for national child-care supports."

VOTING FOR CHANGE

It seems likely that awareness of the "nurturance gap" is an important part of the much publicized "gender gap"—the discrepancy between male and female voting patterns. Women want for themselves not only job opportunities and an end to discrimination but support for the values of nurturance and family life—and, in terms of the wider society beyond the family, help in assuring the "decent survival of all." This is what the political attitudes of the women in our sample suggest, particularly if one considers their views in the context of their values—their enduring commitment to family life, which a wish for an expanded identity has not changed. "Women in this age category," Margaret Wilkerson comments, "do not want to reject traditional roles but want to bring traditional values into the public arena."

Although the total sample characterized themselves as 23 percent conservative, 45 percent moderate, and 21 percent liberal, clear majorities endorsed federally guaranteed job opportunities (68 percent), job quotas to ensure equal opportunity for women (80 percent), and quotas for blacks and other minorities (73 percent). More striking, 73 percent thought that President Reagan's handling of issues especially important to women was fair or poor. Seventy-one percent thought that his handling of the economy was fair or poor—and this figure can be compared with 70 percent of women and 57 percent of men questioned in a national poll by NBC/Associated Press a month after *Parents'* poll was conducted in September, 1982 (but the NBC/AP poll sample included men and women of all ages, not just 21 to 35).

So far we have examined the ways in which the women's movement has changed women themselves and modified their attitudes toward work and their relationships within their families. But the question for the next decade may well be the impact of the women's movement on the society as a whole. As a remarkably liberal generation of women now in their twenties and thirties enter their prime and gain greater power, pressure is going to build for policies that guarantee "the decent survival of all."

7

THEIR TURN: HOW MEN ARE CHANGING

Betty Friedan

I believe that American men are at the edge of a tidal wave of change—a change in their very identity as men. It is a change not yet clearly visible, not really identified or understood by the experts and not even, or seldom, spoken about by men themselves. Yet this change will be as basic as the change created for women by the Women's Movement, even though it is nothing like the Women's Movement. Nobody is marching or making statements. There is no explosion of anger, no enemy to rage against, no list of grievances or demands for benefits and opportunities clearly valuable and previously denied, as with women.

This is a quiet movement, a shifting in direction, the saying of no to old patterns, a searching for new values, a struggling with basic questions that each man seems to be going through alone. At the same time, he continues the outward motions that always have defined men's lives, making it (or struggling to make it) at the office, the plant, the ball park . . . making it with women . . . getting married . . . having children . . . yet he senses that something is happening with men, something large and historic, and he wants to be part of it. He carries the baby in his backpack, shops at the supermarket on Saturdays, with a certain showing-off quality.

It started for many men almost unwillingly, in response to the Women's Movement. The outward stance of hostility and bristling defensiveness that the rhetoric of the first stage of the Women's Movement almost demanded of men obscured the reality of the first changes among them, the real reasons those changes were threatening to some men and the surprising relief, support—even envy—many men felt about the Women's Movement.

At first glance, all it looked like was endless arguments about his doing a fair share of the housework, the cooking and the cleaning; and his responsibility for helping with the children, getting them to bed, into snowsuits, to the park, to the pediatrician. Because now it wasn't *automatic* that her job was to take care of the house and all the other details of life while his job was to support

---

Betty Friedan, "Their Turn: How Men Are Changing," *Redbook*, May 1980. Copyright © by Betty Friedan. Reprinted by permission of Curtis Brown, Ltd.

everyone. Now she was working to support them too.

But then, even if she didn't have a job outside the home, she suddenly had to be treated as a person too, as he was. She had a right to her own life and interests; at night, on weekends, he could help with the children and the house.

He felt wronged, injured. He had been working his can off to support her and the children and now he was her "oppressor," a "male chauvinist pig," if he didn't scrub all the pots and pans to boot. "You make dinner," she said. "I'm going to my design class."

He felt scared when she walked out like that. If she didn't need him for her identity, her status, her sense of importance, if she was going to get all that for herself and have a life independent of him, wouldn't she stop loving him? Wouldn't she just leave? He was supposed to be the big male oppressor, yeah? How could he admit the big secret—that maybe he needed her more than she needed him? That he felt like a baby when he became afraid she would leave. That suddenly he didn't know what he felt, what he was *supposed* to feel—as a man.

I believe much of the hostility of men comes from their very dependence on our love, from those feelings of need that men aren't supposed to have—just as the excesses of our attacks on our male "oppressors" stemmed from our dependence on men. That old, excessive dependence (which was supposed to be natural in women) made us feel we had to be *more* independent than any man in order to be able to move at all. Our explosion of rage and our attacks on men masked our own timidity and fear at risking ourselves, in a complex and competitive world, in ways we never had had to before.

And the more a man was pretending to a dominant, cool, masculine superiority he didn't really feel—the more he was forced to carry the burden alone of supporting everyone against the rough odds of that grim, outside economic world—the more threatened and the more hostile he felt.

Sam, a foreman for an aerospace company in Seattle, Washington, believes that the period when his wife "tried to be just a housewife" was the worst time in his marriage. "If you decide you're going to say home and be taken care of," he says,

"and you have to depend for everything on this guy, you get afraid. *Can he do it?* It all depended on me, and I was in a constant panic, the way our business is now, but I'd say, 'Don't worry.'

"Susie was tired of her job anyhow," explains Sam. "It wasn't such a great job—neither is mine, if you want to know—but she had an excuse. She said she wanted to be home with the children. The pressure was on me. But it was crazy. Here I was, not knowing where the next paycheck was coming from after our Government contract ran out, suddenly supporting a wife and children all by myself.

"It's better now that she's working and bringing some money in," Sam insists. "And I don't just *help* with the kids. She has to be at work before I do, so I give them breakfast and get them off to school. The nights she works late, I make dinner, help with the homework and get everyone to bed. But I don't feel so panicky now—and she isn't attacking me anymore."

Phil Kessler, a young doctor who started out to be a surgeon, but who now has a small-town family practice in New Jersey talks to me as he makes pickles and his children run around underfoot in the country kitchen that is next to his office. "I was going to be a surgeon, super cool in my gleaming white uniform," he says "—the man I was supposed to be but knew I wasn't. So I married a nurse and she stayed home to raise our children, and she was supposed to fulfill herself through my career. It didn't work for either of us.

"I went through torture before every operation," Phil explains. "Then Ellen started turning against me. I always said the children needed her at home full time. Maybe because I was so scared inside. Maybe she didn't have the nerve to do her own thing professionally. All she seemed to want was revenge against me, as if she were locked into some kind of sexual battle against me, playing around, looking elsewhere for true love.

"When Ellen finally got up the nerve to do her own thing—she's a nurse-midwife now—it was a relief," says Phil. "The other stuff stopped. She could come back to being my wife. And I'm *redefining myself,* no longer in terms of success or failure as a doctor, though I still am a doctor, and not as superior or inferior to her. It was a blow to my ego, but what a relief to take off my surgical mask! I'm discovering my own value to the family.

"Now that I'm not so hurt and angry and afraid that she'll leave me, I can see that it's a hell of a fight for a woman to be seen as a person. I think she was afraid of trying to accomplish something on her own, so she made me the villain. But it's as hard for me to feel like a person as it is for her. We couldn't—either of us—get that from each other."

The new questions are harder for men because men have a harder time talking about their feelings than women do. That's part of the masculine mystique. And after all, since men have the power and the top-dog position in society that women are making all the fuss about, why should men want to change—unless women make them?

"Maybe men feel more need to pretend," says a sales engineer in Detroit, Michigan, who is struggling to take "equal responsibility" for the children and the house, now that his wife has gone to work in a department store. "I don't think men thought much about what it was to be a man," he explains, "until women suddenly were talking about what it was to be a woman—and men were left out of the equation.

"Now men are thinking about what it means to be a man. The Women's Movement forced us to start rethinking the way we relate to women and to our families. Now men are going to have to rethink the way they relate to their work. Our sense of who we are was always profoundly based on work, but men are going to begin to define themselves in ways other than work.

"In the '80s," this man says, "we're going to see more men dropping away from traditional male roles, partly because of the economy, partly because men are beginning to find other goodies at the table, like their children—areas where men were excluded before. Being a daddy has become very important to me. When I used to see a man on the street with his children on a weekday, I assumed that he was unemployed, a loser. Now it's so common—daddies with their children, at ease."

The truth is that many of the old bases for men's identity have become shaky. If being a man is defined, for example, as being *dominant, supe-* *rior*—as *not-being-a-woman*—the definition gets shaky when most of the important work of society no longer requires brute muscular force. The Vietnam war probably was the beginning of the end of the old caveman-hunter, gun-toting, he-man mystique. The men I have been interviewing around the country these past months are the men who fought in Vietnam or who went to graduate school to stay out of the war.

Vietnam was somehow a watershed. If men stop defining themselves by going to war or getting power from jobs women can't have, what is left? What does it mean to be a man, except *not-being-a-woman*—that is, physically superior and able to beat up everyone else? The fact is, when a man admits to those "messy feelings" that men as well as women have, he can't *play* the same kind of man any more.

Tony Kowalski, of the Outer Banks of North Carolina, was a pilot in Vietnam when it started for him. "I was a captain, coming up for major," he says. "I had all the medals, and I would have gone on for twenty years in the Air Force. Sitting up there over Nam, the commander, under heavy fire, the guys screaming into the mikes, the bombers and fighters moving in, me giving the orders, I was caught up in it, crazy-wild, excited. And then I woke up one day, coming out of Special Forces camp, and found myself clicking my empty gun at civilians. I knew I had to get out."

Tony can fly any piece of machinery. He took a job with an airline. "All I wanted was security," he says. "After one year I was furloughed because the company was having financial difficulties. There was no security. So I came back to this town where I grew up and took a job as a schoolteacher, working with seventh and eighth graders who were reading at the second-grade level. It was the 'reading lab,' the pits, the bottom—and traditionally a 'woman's job.' It's the hardest job I've ever done and it gets the least respect. Flying a three-hundred-and-twenty-three-thousand-pound Lockheed Starlifter can't compare." As a pilot Tony made $34,000 a year; as a teacher he makes $12,000.

"But maybe now," he says, "with the ladies moving in and picking up some of the financial slack—my wife works for a florist and as a waitress nights—a guy can say, 'I'm not going to get much of anywhere with the money anyhow. Why don't I do something really worthwhile from a human point of view?''

Another man, a West Point graduate of the class of '68, whose father and grandfather were Army men, insists that: ''Men can't be the same again after Vietnam. It always defined men, as against women, that we went to war. We learned it in the locker room, young. The worst insult was to be called all the four- and five-letter words for women's sex. Now that women are in the locker rooms at West Point, how can that work?

''Women have a powerful advantage,'' this man adds, ''because they aren't brought up to believe that if someone knocks you down, *he* has the courage, so you have to knock *him* down. Women aren't stuck with the notion that that kind of courage is necessary. It seems to me, ever since the Vietnam war, more and more men are reaching a turning point, so that if they don't get beyond these games, they start to die. Women will make a mistake if they reach that turning point and start to imitate men. Men can't be role models for women, not even in the Army. We badly need some new role models ourselves.''

At first it seems as if men and women are moving in exactly opposite directions. Women are moving out of the home and into the men's world of work and men are shifting toward a new definition of themselves *in* the home. As we move into the '80s social psychologist and public-opinion analyst Daniel Yankelovich is finding that a majority of adult men in the United States no longer are seeking or are satisfied by conventional job success. Only one in every five men now says that work means more to him than leisure.

''Men have come to feel that success on the job is not enough to satisfy their yearnings for self-fulfillment,'' says Yankelovich. ''They are reaching out for something more and for something different.''

Certain large signs of this movement are reported in the newspapers almost daily. Corporation heads complain that young executives refuse to accept transfers because of ''the family.'' Economists and government officials bewail increased absenteeism and declining productivity among workers. In the past ten years, more than half of West Point's graduates have resigned as Army career officers. College and graduate-school enrollments are dropping among men (as they continue to increase among women), and not just because it isn't necessary for men to evade the draft any more.

In the book *Breaktime,* a controversial study of men ''living without work in a nine-to-five world,'' Bernard Lefkowitz reports a 71-per-cent increase in the number of working-aged men who have left the labor force since 1968 and who are not looking for work. According to Lefkowitz, the ''stop-and-go pattern of work'' is becoming the predominant pattern, rather than the lifetime jobs and careers men used to pursue both for economic security and for their masculine identity.

''In the depression of the '30s,'' says Lefkowitz, ''men were anxious because they were not working. In the '70s men became anxious because their work was not paying off in the over-all economic security they had expected.''

Bob O'Malley, 33, quit his rising career in a big New York City bank to sell real estate on the tip of Long Island.

''I asked myself one day, if my career continued going well and I really made it up the corporate ladder, did I want to be there, fifteen years from now, with the headaches of the senior executives I saw being pushed off to smaller offices, their staffs, secretaries, status, taken away, or having heart attacks, strokes? Men who had been loyal to the company twenty-five years—it governed their whole lives—and to what end? I didn't want to live my life like that. I wanted to be more independent—maybe not making so much money but living more for myself.''

The trouble is that once men disengage themselves from the old patterns of masculinity and success, they are just as lost for role models as women are. Moreover, if a man tries to get out of his own bind by *reversing roles* with his wife—if he yearns for a superwoman to support him as she used to yearn for a strong man who would take care of her—it makes his wife uneasy.

''My husband wants me to have another child, and he says he'll quit his job and stay home to take care of the children,'' a woman in Vermont tells me. ''But why should that work for him when it didn't work for me? And maybe I don't want him to take over the family that much. Maybe I'd resent it—just working to support him."

It's a situation that didn't work when Dr. Phil Kessler, in the first flush of relief after dropping his surgical mask, tried reversing roles with his wife. In the first place, his wife couldn't make as much money as a nurse-midwife as he could make as a doctor. And somehow when she came home from work the house was never "clean enough," the meat loaf wasn't seasoned "right" and he'd also forgotten to put the potatoes on. So she would rush around, tired as she was, doing everything over, making him feel just as guilty as she had in the old days.

"Then I began to feel like a martyr," he says. "Nobody appreciated how hard I worked, taking care of the house and the children. Now that I'm doing my own work again—and bringing money in—I don't have to feel guilty if the house isn't all that clean. And now that they're treating her like a professional at the hospital, she doesn't notice the dust on the windowsills so much, either."

It takes trial and error, of course, to work out the practicalities, the real trade-offs, of the new equality between the sexes when both try to share home and work responsibilities. And it may be harder for men because the benefits of the trade-offs for them aren't that obvious at first. Women, after all, are fighting for an equal share in the activities and the power games that are rewarded in this society. What are men's rewards for giving up some of that power?

Jimmy Fox, a blue-collar worker in Brooklyn, New York, won't admit that there are any rewards for him in the trade-offs he's been "forced" to work out with his wife. "In our community," says Jimmy, "men don't freely accept women's equality. It's got to be slowly pushed down their throats. Men are the ones who go to the bar on the corner, drink, come home when the heck they want and expect supper to be on the table, waiting for them. When that starts changing, it scares them to death. It scared me.

"I didn't know what was going on," he says. "First thing I knew, my wife is going out to a women's organization, the National Congress of Neighborhood Women, and she wants to go do this, do that. She's learning, letting me know that things are wrong with our marriage. What am I supposed to do? It took five years before we got to the point where she went out to work and found her own role."

Today Jimmy makes $9,000 a year and his wife makes $9,000. "And when she's out working," says Jimmy, "I'm taking care of the baby. It's no picnic. Any man who wants to change places with his wife when his wife stays home and takes care of the house and children has got to be a maniac. Her job in the house was twice as hard as mine at the plant. I work ten, twelve hours. She works from when she gets up in the morning until she goes to bed."

When Linda Fox first started working, she says, "there were many, many battles between Jimmy and me. I wanted equality, which I thought meant that if he put three hours and twenty-two minutes into housework, then I would put in three hours and twenty-two minutes. I wanted a blow-by-blow division and I was fanatical about it. Jimmy was so happy to be relieved of some of the burden of being the only one with the paycheck that he was willing to do that, although I know he was teased by the guys at the bar."

The first payoff for men then, obviously, is economic survival. Unfortunately, few of the other big trade-offs of equality can be measured as mechanically as men's and women's making exactly the same amount of money (women on the average still earn only 59 cents to a man's $1) or their spending exactly the same amount of time on housework.

"What I've gained," says Avery Corman, who wrote the novel *Kramer versus Kramer,* on which the movie was based, from his own experience of taking over the children when his wife started a business, "is the joy—and it is a joy—of having my children really rely on me. I've gained this real participation in their upbringing because I've been active in it on a daily basis."

Unlike the Kramers, the Cormans remain happily married, and, he says, "what I've given up is being waited on myself. There are times when I'd really like to be the prince of patriarchs and sit around with my pipe and slippers with my wife and children tiptoeing around, but it sure isn't like that now and it never will be again. A secret part of me would sometimes like a less-equal marriage, would like to be catered to the way guys used to be.

"But the real payoff," he says, "is that men can begin to think about who they are *as men*. I can ask myself what I really want in life. With my wife out there earning, I don't have to be just a breadwinner."

Another big trade-off for men while women become more independent is more independence—more "space"—for them. An Atlanta cotton broker, now married at 30 to a woman with her own career, recalls his first marriage, to a woman who depended on him for everything.

"She made me feel suffocated," he says. "Living with a completely dependent woman is debilitating. You don't know why, but you just feel awful. She's breathing your air. She's passing her anxiety on to you. She's got no confidence in herself and she's looking to you for everything; but what she does is always put you down, make you feel you won't make it."

"She may be very sweet," he explains further. "She may be lovely, but all you know is that you don't have room to breathe. I never heard of any ruling class resigning, but as men realize that it's better to live with a nondependent woman the change will come about because the payoff is real—economic and emotional."

Paradoxically, part of the trade-off is that when women share the economic burden—and declare themselves equal persons in other ways—men are able to put a new value on personal qualities once considered the exclusive domain of women. It's the new American frontier for men, this exploration of their inner space, of the "messy feelings" we all have but that for too long were considered awesome and mysterious and forbidden territory for men.

When women share the work burden and relieve men of the need to pretend to false strengths, men can open up to feelings that give them a real sense of strength, especially when they share the daily chores of life that wives used to shield them from. "It grounds me—I have to admit it," says a man named Bernie, who for the first time, after 30 years of his mother's and wife's doing it for him, is cooking, shopping and washing clothes. "I like the relief from always thinking about my job, feeling like a disembodied head chained to a typewriter."

Or as a man named Lars Hendrix, of Oakland, California, expresses it: "It makes me feel alive. I don't have to pretend to be so strong because I feel good. I feel grounded. The silence that most men live with isolates them not only from women but also from other men. My wife's assault on my silence was at first extremely painful. She made me share my feelings with her. It brought an incredible sense of liberation, and maybe for the first time in my adult life a sense of reality, that I can *feel* my feelings and share them with her.

"But there'll still be a loneliness, for me and for other men," says Lars, "until we can share our feelings with each other. That's what I envy most about the Women's Movement—the way women share their feelings and the support they get from each other. Do you know how isolated and lonely and weak a man feels in that silence, never really making contact with another man?"

There is another, major problem. As men seek for themselves the liberation that began with the Women's Movement, both men and women have to confront the conflict between their human needs—for love, for family, for purpose in life—and the demands of the workplace.

A family therapist in Philadelphia, Pennsylvania, the father of a three-year-old son, talks about the conflict in terms of his own profession and personal needs. "I was working at one of the top family-training centers in the country," he says. "There was a constant theoretical discussion about getting the father back into the family, but the way the jobs were set up there, you had to work fifty, sixty hours a week. To really get anywhere you had to put in seventy hours and work nights, weekends. You didn't have time for your own family. I won't do that. My family is number one—my job is only to be a good therapist."

Recent managerial studies have shown that the long working hours and the corporate transfers that keep many men from strong daily involvements with their families or with other interests are not always necessary for the work of the company. But the long hours and the transfers do serve to keep a man *dependent* for his very identity, as well as his livelihood, on the corporation—dependent as a "company man."

Recently, at the National Assembly on the Future of the Family sponsored by the NOW Legal Defense and Education Fund, corporation heads and union leaders joined feminists and family experts in confronting the need for "practical and innovative" solutions to balancing the demands of the workplace and the family. The agenda for the '80s must include restructuring the institutions of work and home to make equality livable and workable—for women and men.

Women can't solve the problem alone by taking everything on themselves, by trying to be "superwomen." And women don't have the power to change the structure of the workplace by themselves. But while more and more men decide that they want some self-fulfillment beyond their jobs and some of the life-grounding that women always have had in the family—as much as women now need and want some voice and active power in the world—there will be a new, combined force for carrying out the second stage of liberation for us all.

It seems strange to suggest that there is a new American frontier, a new adventure for men, in the struggle for *wholeness,* for openness to feeling, for living and sharing life on equal terms with women. But it is a new frontier where both men's and women's needs converge. Men need new role models now as much as women do.

Men also need to share their new questions and feelings about work and family and self-fulfillment with other men. And Redbook invites them to do that, to share their questions and thoughts, in the pages of the magazine in coming months. To help each other. To begin to break out of their isolation and become role models for each other, as women are doing in the second stage of the struggle for liberation.

The dialogue has gone on too long in terms of women alone. Let men join women in the center of the second stage.

IV

SEXUAL EXPRESSION

8

SOME OBSERVATIONS ON IDEOLOGY AND SEXUALITY IN AMERICA

Ira L. Reiss

There is nothing new about the assertion that our ideologies severely limit our vision of the social world in which we live. Karl Marx popularized this notion by asserting that ideologies were the tools which capitalists utilized to rationalize their own economic interests. Marx's classic assertion was:

> The mode of production of material life conditions the social, political and intellectual life process in general. It is not the consciousness of men that determines their being, but on the contrary, their social being that determines their consciousness (Marx and Engels, 1962:363).

One may disagree with Marx's view of the singular power of economic interests but still believe in the power of ideologies to blind us to the realities of our social system. Surely most sociologists would accept such a general proposition and yet it has never been systematically applied to the area of human sexuality. My basic purpose in this paper will be to exhume some of the fundamental ideological beliefs in America concerning human sexuality and to show the value of a sociological approach to this area. Recent evidence indicates a new growth of ideological fervor in the area of sexuality during the last several years and thus this analysis is quite relevant to understanding our current milieu.

Ideologies are firmly held doctrines of particular philosophical groups. The doctrine of economic determinism held by Marxist philosophers and the doctrine of original sin held by fundamentalist Christian groups are such ideological beliefs. I will attempt to indicate some of the ideological underpinnings of our American sexual beliefs and practices and thereby show how they like all ideologies, blind us to various realities of our sexual lives. Of necessity, this investigation will have to rely on illustrative examples, current day events, and some speculation, as well as on more strongly established empirical data. But I will attempt to explicate the reasoning and evidence for each assertion. This article is an attempt to establish the value of this approach to sexuality and encourage further scientific investigation.

I will seek to derive and analyze our American sexual ideologies by means of an examination of five controversial substantive areas relevant to sexuality: (1) abortion, (2) genetic differences of

---

Ira L. Reiss, "Some Observations on Ideology and Sexuality in America," *Journal of Marriage and the Family,* May 1981, pp. 271–83. Copyrighted © 1981 by the National Council on Family Relations, 1219 University Avenue Southeast, Minneapolis, Minnesota 55414. Reprinted by permission.

the sexes, (3) exploitation and pornography, (4) sexual normality, and (5) sexual history. Surely, these areas do not completely cover human sexuality but they are central and will be used to show the value of this type of analysis.

ABORTION

In August of 1980, the CBS-*New York Times* poll gathered some rather interesting data on attitudes of American adults toward abortion. Two of their questions and the resulting marginals appear below:

Do you think there should be an amendment to the Constitution prohibiting abortions, or shouldn't there be such an amendment?

29% yes, 62% opposed, and 9% uncertain

Do you believe there should be an amendment to the Constitution protecting the life of the unborn child, or shouldn't there be such an amendment?

50% yes, 39% opposed, and 11% uncertain.

Clearly, if one were pro-choice, the question that would be more favorable to that position would be the first one; and if one were pro-life, the question most favorable to that perspective would be the second one. The public declarations of opposed groups on abortion indicate just such selective use of questions like those in the CBS poll.

To further show the complexity of our ideology regarding abortion, let us examine the results of the 1980 National Opinion Research Center poll (NORC) of 1,500 adults. The findings show that over half their sample *opposed* abortion *if* the question stated that abortion should be granted "for any reason the woman wants" or if "the woman doesn't want more children" or if "the woman is single." But less than 20 percent *opposed* abortion *if* the stipulation was that the pregnancy was due to rape or if child defects were suspected or if the mother's health was at risk (NORC, 1980: 142, 144, 164). A 1980 Gallup Poll shows that 25 percent of their respondents felt that abortion should be legal under all circumstances; 53 percent accepted abortion only under some conditions, and 18 percent said abortion should be illegal under all circumstances (*Minneapolis Tribune,* 1980). Thus, by choosing the precise question it is easy to show that the majority of people favor or oppose a particular position on abortion.

It is precisely in situations such as this that those with a strong ideological commitment on one side or the other of the abortion issue will tend to utilize the research findings to their own advantage. This is one example of how sexual ideologies can and do bias our utilization of data. Even more relevant is the conclusion that there is a need for sociological analysis of such data so that somewhere there is available a reasonably objective account of just what are American attitudes toward areas like abortion. Of course, this is not always easy to accomplish. Sociologists also have their ideological training in our culture and have strong peer-group feelings which pressure against publishing any results that could be used by an opposing ideology. Nevertheless, sociology can offer a refuge from politicized approaches to social reality if it becomes conscious of the need to do so. Of course, science has its own ideology concerning methods of discovering and organizing knowledge but that ideology is not necessarily attached to any private moral position concerning controversial issues like abortion. The scrutiny of published research by other scientists helps insure the avoidance of private moral biases in one's scientific work. In addition, research indicates that views on abortion are not isolated from our other values. Recent studies show that those who oppose abortion are more likely to be in favor of traditional male dominance and of traditional sexual views in other areas (Granberg and Granberg, 1980; Walfish and Myerson, 1980). Thus, the sociological study of abortion can increase our awareness of some broad ideological positions as well as increase our scientific knowledge of the abortion controversy.

GENETIC DIFFERENCES OF THE SEXES

Ideology often enters in to bias our approach to genetic differences. Those who favor equalitarian gender roles strive to minimize all known genetic differences between the sexes and those who wish to have segregated gender roles strive to enlarge the area of known genetic sex differences. From a sociological perspective, both groups labor in vain. Surely there are some hormonal differences like those attested to by writers such as Maccoby and Jacklin (1974). For example, males have several times the androgen levels of females. In numerous studies, and in primate research, such hormonal difference is predictive of aggressive differences. Maccoby and Jacklin conclude that this is true of humans and that males are inherently more aggressive than females. Androgen is also related to sexual motivation in that androgen is the common treatment for females who lack sexual interest. Are we to conclude from this that males are therefore inevitably more sexually motivated and more aggressive than females? Not at all.

What this means is that, on the average, males may have the potential to differ from females in the above fashion; but this is only a tendency, and many males and females overlap even in terms of tendency. Further, androgen levels are not predictive of sexual activity or interest in any straight-line fashion (Brown *et al.*, 1978; Schwartz *et al.*, 1980). More importantly, groups who wish to produce males and females who are equal on aggression or sexuality can do so by training. Clearly, human aggression and sexual interest vary tremendously *within* each sex and between the sexes in various cultures (Beach, 1977). In sum, then, genetic differences are just averages and tendencies and they can and are altered by training. They do not set immutable boundaries.

Relatedly, we know that females have more of the hormone called oxytocin and that this hormone can produce erect nipples and lactation at the sound of a crying infant, and yet most American mothers do not feel compelled to nurse their infants. Thus, training does and can alter our hormonal tendencies. Finally, even if we wanted to produce gender differences where there were no hormonal differences, we could do that, too. The debate about genetic differences then really has very little to do with unalterable gender-role differences or sexual-drive differences. Learning is so powerful a force in the human situation that such average tendencies do not necessarily predetermine very much at all. Our ideologies will determine our gender roles and our sexuality far more than our hormonal differences. It takes a sociologist and other social scientists to deliver this message to those who come prepared to do battle for their ideological position about genetic differences. The battle may still occur but at least we will have played out our role as scientists and made it possible for others to eventually grasp the situation in which they are involved.

EXPLOITATION AND PORNOGRAPHY

In today's public discussions of sexuality, one often hears the charges of sexual "exploitation." To what precisely does the term exploitation refer? Does a pornographic film exploit females in the film? Is pornography generally exploitive of females? There is no way to answer such questions unless we have a relatively clear definition of the term exploitation. However, the term is seldom defined in public dialogue because those who oppose pornographic films are convinced they are "bad" and, therefore, another "bad" term like exploitation is certainly appropriate. Relatedly, those who approve of pornographic films and literature are convinced that they are alright and, thus, they do not deserve the negative label of exploitation. One thing is clear, the term exploitation is used to apply to something thought to be negative but exactly what sort of negative thing is not clear.

The dictionary basically states that exploitation is to make use of someone for one's own advantage or to take more than one is giving. One way to define this is subjectively. We can ask persons if they think that they are using others for their own advantage and we can ask the potentially exploited person if they feel that they are being taken advantage of. If the answer is no, then even if we totally disapprove, we would have to agree that there is no exploitation occurring. But to my knowledge, few people have ever asked porno stars if they feel that in making a porno film they are getting as much as they are giving. They have not asked because most people are rushing to their own moral judgment and not asking how the persons involved feel. This judgment is made even though in other professions we use people's bodies for our pleasure and do not consider it exploitation, *e.g.*, professional football, nursing, and physical labor. It is an ideological and not a scientific conclusion that asserts that women in porno films *must* be exploited. This conclusion is based upon the premise that such use of our bodies is bad. I would suggest that it is our negative evaluation of body-centered sexuality that causes some Americans to label such sexuality in films as exploitive. The use of the body in these other professions is not sexual and thus is judged acceptable.

A second way that one can define exploitation is to state that it is an act against a particular moral code. In this case, the judgment could be made that if one's moral code says sexuality without affection (body-centered) is "bad," then such an act would, by definition, be exploitative, even if the actress involved protested that she did not feel exploited. This is compatible with Marx's notion of "false consciousness" wherein workers fail to see that they are "really" being exploited by the bourgeoise. Such an imposed definition of exploitation asserts that this act must "degrade" the actor and is therefore subject to such negative labels as exploitation. This is the more common usage and, clearly, it is quite vague and subject to meaning whatever the definer of the act thinks is "degrading."

I would contend that the strong ideological underpinnings that make one label pornography as exploitative are based upon the belief that sexuality which centers on the body and is without affection is wrong and, thus, there must be many negative consequences of such a wrong act. For example, consequences of pornography are at times asserted to be rape and violence against women. Here, too, the sociologist has an important role in trying to ascertain whether such consequences actually follow from pornography and, if so, in what way and for whom. One relevant research study in this area is that of Edward Donnerstein's (1980). Donnerstein has examined whether those subjects who viewed sexually violent films (rape) were more willing to administer shocks to other people than people who saw an erotic nonviolent film or a neutral film. The results indicate that those who saw violent-erotic films were more willing to administer electric shocks to women subjects in the study. But what can be objectively concluded from this? A great many pornographic films and magazines do not portray violent sexuality, that is, they do not show physical violence against females (Malamuth and Spinner, 1980). Further, the Donnerstein findings do not contradict the report of the Commission on Obscenity and Pornography (1970); rather, they extend and qualify those findings. The Commission has reported that pornographic materials do not promote sex offenses and that, in fact, sex offenders have been exposed to a *below* average amount of pornography. Donnerstein's work notes that it was predominantly from *violent* pornography that one gets results indicating an increase in violence towards females. Actually, mild forms of pornography (*Playboy* photos) have been found to *reduce* aggression towards females (Donnerstein et al., 1975). There is also the question of sensitivity to violent pornography. Certain types of males may be more ready than others to respond to such stimuli; therefore, the effects of increased violence may be quite selective. Donnerstein and others are interested in pursuing just this type of specification of their results in terms of facilitating and inhibiting factors and, thus, draw no overall conclusions at this time.

Often the public reaction to pornography is not based upon an understanding of the research evidence but upon the way that evidence appears once it has been filtered through their ideological positions. Some people have taken the Donnerstein findings as a basis for wanting to ban all pornography. Donnerstein himself does not accept such an interpretation of his study; for, as noted above, he does report that nonviolent pornography did not have the same effects as did violent pornography. Most pornography is not violent. Furthermore, the audience in a porno film often consists of 50-year-old males while rapists are usually young men (Chappell et al., 1977; Groth, 1979). Thus, any general unqualified causal connection between pornography and rape and violence is not called for by the evidence we possess today. As with the term exploitation, many would use the concept of "violence" broadly, *i.e.*, to be more than just physical abuse but to include "moral abuse." Such usage, of course, makes the term violence mean many different things and makes scientific conclusions difficult, since one would be free to label anything one didn't like as "violence."

American attitudes toward pornography are quite complex and contradictory. In the 1980 National Opinion Research Center national survey, it was found that most Americans view pornography as possibly leading to rape, but an even greater majority feel that sexual materials provided an outlet for bottled-up impulses. Further, most Americans do not want laws against such materials for adults (NORC, 1980). Clearly, social science analysis of this area could be helpful in furthering our understanding of causal connections and in the development of a typology of pornography and its users and an examination of its consequences.

Related to this issue of the consequences of pornography is the issue of body-centered sexuality in general. As noted above, those who oppose pornography generally oppose body-centered coitus or coitus that lacks affection or a personal quality and instead focuses on the bodily pleasures of sexuality. It may well be that opposition to pornography is, in good part, based upon opposition to body-centered coitus. So it is worthwhile to briefly look at this possible connection.

Every recorded civilization has had body-centered sexuality whether it be in the form of prostitution, orgiastic celebrations, or generally sanctioned body-centered sexuality. The physical body is a basic aspect of sexual attraction and it seems rather unlikely that any society could structure things to avoid this reality. Therefore, in any society, whatever body types are culturally decreed to be attractive will, at times, be sought not for love or romantic reasons but for themselves. What distinguishes cultures around the world, with very few exceptions, is not the absence or presence of body-centered sexuality but the evaluation of such sexuality. Some cultures, such as those in Polynesia, rate body-centered sexuality as good and desirable although not preferable to person-centered sexuality (Marshall and Suggs, 1971; Beach, 1977). Other cultures create a larger chasm between body and person-centered sexuality, although both are accepted. Western society is in the minority in its condemnation of body-centered sexuality as being below the acceptable level. I should note that there is a gender difference since most all societies accept body-centered sexuality for males, and it is predominately the strongly double-standard cultures which condemn such sexuality for females.

In part, the rejection of body-centered sexuality is rooted in an objection to the traditional view of women as exclusively sexual objects. Thus, some groups, in order to overcome this sexual-object view of females, wish to eliminate body-centered sexuality as evidenced in pornography and elsewhere. Whether this is right or wrong is beside the point—the point is that such a move is not likely to succeed. If changing the cultural image of females is desired, then *adding* other "favorable" female traits such as intelligence, sensitivity, and friendship to the common view of females will be much more effective in breaking down the existing stereotypes. It is notable that males do not often object to female admiration of the male body. This is most likely because males know that there are other things for which they are also valued. Thus, it would seem that the pathway to being treated as an equal is not by denying the undeniable physically attractive body, but rather by stressing the full range of human traits that is possessed by that group in addition to physical beauty. The dominant negative view of body-centered sexuality blinds many Americans to these other alternatives. Of course, there are groups who praise body-centered sexuality, but they are not as often heard from.

Another interesting aspect of our negative view of body-centered sexuality and pornography is that this criterion is almost never used in references to males. Who asks if male porno stars are exploited? Who asks if 16 and 17-year-old males are into prostitution? There is much less furor about such male activities because the concern for female body-centered sexuality is largely a part of the double standard. Therefore, in true double-standard fashion, we primarily talk about how female sexuality can be destructive while ignoring male sexuality. When we have strong ideological commitments, we often are unaware of just what we are overlooking. Many of those who oppose body-centered coitus also oppose the double standard. However, they fail to see how their views are congruent with male-domination viewpoints concerning the greater rights of males to practice body-centered sexuality.

Finally, the strong opposition in America to body-centered coitus is evidenced in our laws on pornography and obscenity. The legal definition is that any book or film which appeals predominantly to prurient interests is thereby pornographic and obscene. That means that if such a book or film is aimed at just giving us sexual excitation, it is illegal. This clearly shows our orientation to sexuality. Sexual pleasure is viewed as something to be condemned unless it is "purified" by love and affection in a person-centered relationship. Some of those who support this ideology against body-centered coitus do not realize the implication of such support for their overall view of sexuality.

SEXUAL NORMALITY

Probably the most obvious place to look for evidence of ideological blinders is in a culture's conception of what is "normal" and "abnormal" sexuality. Let me illustrate this by using the example of premature ejaculation. American males go to therapists for treatment of the "problem" of premature ejaculation. Now what does it mean to be a premature ejaculator? Premature for what? Since an orgasm does occur it is not a case of inability to achieve orgasm but rather achieving it too quickly in terms of some culturally imposed standard. The standard is the orgasm of the female partner—if orgasm occurs so quickly that the female has no opportunity to achieve orgasm in coitus, then the male orgasm is labelled premature. That this view is a specific cultural perspective should be apparent. In cultures that are more male dominant (*e.g.*, South American societies), a man who achieves an orgasm in 20 seconds after insertion might well be admired as virile and strong and no problem would be assumed. It is with the advent of equalitarian sexual ideas that premature ejaculation comes to be viewed as a problem. Thus, the "illness" is not a medical one in the strict sense; rather, it is one created by a particular cultural approach to human sexuality. The problem aspect in premature ejaculation is more analogous to the desire for cosmetic surgery than it is to the desire to treat kidney failure or a slipped disc. In this sense, what is defined as a sexual problem informs us about our cultural values concerning sexuality.

It is even more revealing to examine how premature ejaculation is treated by therapists in America. One very common technique is called the "squeeze technique." The objective is to have the female squeeze the penis to prevent orgasm and to thereby gradually teach the male how to control his orgasmic response. Given our focus on sexual intercourse as the major normal outlet for sexuality, such a technique is not surprising. However, if we think logically of what possibilities are available to deal with the desire not to leave the woman unsatisfied, we realize just how selective our therapy is. For example, one simple way to handle premature ejaculation is to instruct the male to bring the female to orgasm orally or manually. Why is this "solution" not typically utilized by therapists? I would suggest the reason is that our sexual ideology is coitally focused. We believe that coitus is the predominant way to express sexuality and that equal or preferable emphasis on other ways of achieving orgasm is not desirable. Some Freudian analysts still assert that to remove the emphasis from coitus is to encourage what they would label as "abnormal" or "disturbed" psychosexual development (Gadpaille, 1972). In part, this focus on coitus may be historically due to our traditional desire to produce more offspring who can serve as workers or warriors. In part, though, it also reflects a male-derived emphasis on a sexual act which is pleasurable.

Now let us go one step further and examine the nature of what we call sexual intercourse. Clearly, it is an act that is aimed at promoting male orgasm more than female orgasm. By definition sexual intercourse must entail contact with the penis and thereby make male orgasm very likely. Some dictionaries stress the "deposit of sperm" and thereby also point to male orgasm as central. There is no necessary contact in coitus with the female clitoris which would increase the likelihood of female orgasm. Given the types of physical contact involved in sexual intercourse, it is no wonder that females have had more orgasmic problems than males. In addition, sexual intercourse has been "stage directed" by the male. It is the male who is supposed to be the initiator, and at least on first coitus, it is he who decides what positions will be utilized and what sequence of sexual events will occur. Once again, then, the act is set up when the male is ready and to his specifications. Consequently, it is no wonder that more wives than husbands have "headaches." As this situation changes and females become more assertive sexually, I would predict that more husbands may well develop headaches!

But the important conclusion to draw from the above discussion of sexual intercourse is that the act which in Western cultures has become the ultimate sexual act is a male-controlled and male orgasm-oriented act and thus fits with the male dominance which is prevalent in the culture. Therefore, it is no surprise that our therapy is aimed at integrating male orgasm with female orgasm, especially in coitus, for that is the preferred sexual act. Once again, our cultural sexual ideology is writ large in the way we define problems and also in the way we seek to resolve them.

On this same topic of normality let us examine our attitudes toward homosexuality. In a 1980 poll (NORC, 1980), approximately 70 percent of adult Americans stated that homosexuality was "always wrong." Again, we can assert that our focus on heterosexual coitus is also involved in this judgment. A homosexual act clearly does not involve heterosexual coitus and in addition it involves two people of the same gender—a second violation of our sexual ideology. One can also discern here the American view of sexuality as being a very powerful force and one to be feared. This comes through in our view which seems to assert that homosexuality is virtually "infectious." If we have too much contact with a homosexual or allow a homosexual to talk to our children, then we may spread the homosexual's "ailment." This viewpoint not only displays our view of sexuality as overpowering but it also exhibits our lack of confidence in our commitment to heterosexuality. We are frightened that our heterosexuality can be changed if homosexuals are given any degree of public acceptance. The repeal of some equal treatment laws for homosexuals which has occurred in Florida and Minnnesota is testimony to precisely this sort of viewpoint.

Again, our view of normality seems based upon a view of heterosexual coitus as the prime "normal" state for adults. This is a view that Freud expressed in his emphasis upon the genital stage of development (Money and Musaph, 1977). Freud may well have been strongly influenced by Western culture just as we are today. However, when we examine our primate cousins, we find homosexuality to be quite common, although virtually never a preferred form of sexuality. The learned aspect of homosexuality in other primates can be seen in the recent findings that monkeys raised with siblings of only one sex display more homosexual behavior than monkeys raised with siblings of both sexes (IASR, 1980). Looking at other cultures, we find homosexuality frequently accepted. Thus, it is difficult for us to scientifically label such behavior as necessarily "disturbed" or "abnormal" (Beach, 1977). It would seem that such behavior is in our genetic line (other primates) and that it can be easily learned and accepted in other cultural settings. This should cause us to question the medical basis for calling it abnormal. However, there is an ideological basis for labelling homosexuality as abnormal. This basis involves our allegiance to heterosexual coitus as the standard for all to abide by, but this is hardly a medical basis. The moral position that homosexuality is abnormal is often passed off as being founded on sexual "health" notions, but as I have briefly noted above, there is no convincing scientific base for such a viewpoint (Bell and Weinberg, 1978; Reiss, 1980a). I should add here that there are many psychiatrists who would not view homosexuality as an abnormality but there are also many who do, and the public view, though somewhat more tolerant today, is still quite critical. The removal of homosexuality from the American Psychiatric Association's list of pathologies in 1973 should not be taken as proof that most all psychiatrists view homosexuality as a normal variation.

Our concepts of normality, health, and abnormality seem heavily influenced by our sexual ideology. Further sociological analysis can detail this state of affairs and afford us some additional perspective on ourselves that otherwise would be lacking. We should remember that in the 19th century many medical doctors were performing clitoridectomies on women who were "too" sexually responsive. This was done in the interests of "sexual health," as they then defined it (Comfort, 1967). We do not perform these operations today but there are scores of American wives who have recently undergone surgery, performed by a doctor in Dayton, Ohio, to redesign the coital area so that the clitoris is more easily contacted by the penis in the traditional male-above position (IASR, 1977). Here, again, we have dramatic evidence of the influence of our culture, not only on our mental concepts, but on our bodies also. The ideological dictates of a culture can pressure our bodies, as well as our acts and thoughts, toward conformity.

SEXUAL HISTORY

If our sexual ideology affects our conceptions of normality and reality in so many ways, then surely it must affect our conception of our sexual past. There is still in America a widespread belief that at sometime in our past we lived in a society in which most young people remained virginal until they married and then learned about sexuality in the marital bed and remained faithful to each other until death did part them. The Puritan period is often mentioned as one such time. But Arthur Calhoun's (1945) classic work indicates that nonvirginity was rather common during the end of the Puritan period in the 18th century. For example, in one church in Groton, Massachusetts, he reports that one third of the brides married confessed fornication to their minister. The nonvirginity rate was likely higher than this for it was predominantly pregnant brides who confessed fornication so that their babies might be accepted for baptism. Those nonvirgins who were not pregnant would not be under such pressure to confess. This sort of situation is not unusual historically. I have read the anthropological literature extensively in search for a culture in which males reach physical maturity (say, age 21) with the majority of them virginal. I have yet to find such a culture anywhere in the world at any time in history. Now, there may be a few such cultures that I have missed but surely they are quite rare.

The reasons for male nonvirginity are not difficult to discern. Males are normatively dominant in almost every society that has ever existed. This means that virtually all of our sexual codes are established by males. The reasons for this history of male dominance can only be speculated upon but it may be due to the fact that during our two million years on this planet we have been hunters and gatherers for all but the last 12,000 years. Male physical strength must have given males an advantage in such a setting and the tie to newborn infants via nursing must have weakened the competition from females. Such male dominance seems to have been strengthened in agricultural societies (Gough, 1971) but has been weakening in the industrial societies which began to appear approximately 200 years ago.

When a group in power sets up a code, it is set to their felt advantage. Accordingly, males set up a sexual code which allowed themselves to enjoy sexuality under a wide variety of conditions: premaritally, maritally, and extramaritally. But they also set up a provision that restricted their wives and daughters from much of the sexual enjoyment they decreed for themselves. This basic contradiction between male freedom and female restrictions is at the heart of the explanation of why human sexuality has been secretive and guilt ridden. If wives and daughters cannot engage in premarital or extramarital sexuality, then the majority of possible partners for males are eliminated. One source of female partners would be to violate some weaker group of males and take their wives and daughters or set up a class of prostitutes composed of females whose kinship ties have in some way been broken. But such patchwork solutions do not resolve the basic contradiction inherent in allowing males more sexual rights than females and there still are many males violating the restrictions on sexuality with in-group wives and daughters. This occurrence forces secrecy on sexuality and creates guilt feelings concerning the violation of the double-standard restrictions on wives and daughters. It is no wonder, then, that sexuality, particularly in the West, has come down to the 20th century with strong guilt, secrecy, and psychological qualms woven into its basic fabric.

Over the centuries, Western culture has worked out a modification of the traditional double standard by building up the cult of romantic love. Sexuality has indeed been viewed as negative behavior, but if it is done for the sake of a great love feeling, then perhaps the negative aspect in it can be exorcised by the goodness in love. Thus, love has become the great justifier and purifier of sexuality (Reiss, 1960; 1967). Of course, males have had cultural support for their sexuality so the love justification has been predominantly a female belief. For centuries sexuality which involves love has been viewed as more acceptable, even if not fully acceptable, for premarital couples. In fact, the Groton, Massachusetts data discussed above is testimony to the fact that 200 years ago couples were commonly engaging in sexual intercourse before marriage. What acceptance there was then of premarital coitus was in good measure a result of the fact that it occurred after a declaration of love and intention to marry.

We are still a double-standard culture (Reiss, 1980a). One illustration of this occurred in a sociologist's (Pepper Schwartz) class at the University of Washington. She asked her class a question about how many premarital sexual partners it was proper to have. Those who approved of premarital intercourse still allowed males to have many more sexual partners than they allowed for females. This is a modification of the traditional double standard, but there still are two codes: one to judge females and one to judge males, and that is the essence of any double standard.

Basically, then, our historical background, as far as actual behavior and operational norms go, is one of the double standard and not one of abstinence. Henry Kissinger was correct about the relation of power to sexuality. Power does have a way of legitimizing sexual rights and males have had greater power in virtually all societies. We can observe the relation of power to sexuality by noting that public opinion is much harsher when a black male rapes a white female than when a white male rapes a black female (LaFree, 1980). Equality in sexual rights for males and females will help achieve greater gender equality in other areas of life. Conversely, equality in overall gender roles is also very helpful in creating equality in sexual relations. We do not remove our social positions when we take off our clothes even though there are moments in sexual relations when our social positions are much less in focus than our physical position.

IDEOLOGIES: OLD AND NEW

The five areas I have briefly explored in this search for our basic sexual ideologies surely do not exhaust those that can be explored nor is the evidence fully in on even these five areas. The purpose of this paper is merely to open up such an exploration, not to complete it. I will now derive some basic ideological tenets from the above examination of ideologies and connect them with what I believe are the two major sexual ideologies of our day. I will first derive tenets that are part of what I shall call our Traditional-Romantic Ideology.

First and most fundamental to the Traditional-Romantic Ideology is the belief in the primacy and rightfulness of the double standard. Most explicitly, this expresses itself in the belief that gender roles should be segregated and distinct with the male role clearly being the dominant one. I would state this ideological tenet as:

1. Gender roles should be distinct and interdependent, with the male gender role as dominant.

This tenet underlies many of the traditional positions taken on the five controversial areas we have examined, but it is most central to our discussion of genetic sex differences.

A second tenet of the Traditional-Romantic Ideology is that body-centered sexuality is of lowest worth, particularly for females. This can be simply stated as:

2. Body-centered sexuality is to be avoided by females.

This tenet appeared most clearly in our earlier examination of sexual exploitation and pornography.

Sexuality as a very powerful emotion and one to be feared was a theme we mentioned in the discussion of sexual normality. Here, too, there is a double standard aspect since the belief usually asserts that males are more driven by such sexual forces and that females best be careful to avoid males when they are in such states of possession. The third tenet of the Traditional-Romantic Ideology then would be:

3. Sexuality is a very powerful emotion and one that should be particularly feared by females.

Also in our discussion of sexual normality we pointed out how coitally centered and male dominated our sexual ideology was. So our fourth tenet would be:

4. The major goal of sexuality is heterosexual coitus and that is where the man's focus should be placed.

Here, too, there is double-standard input because according to the Traditional-Romantic perspective such a goal is considered proper for males to feel and for females to accept.

The fifth and last tenet of the Traditional-Romantic Ideology concerns the relation of love and guilt to sexuality. Sexuality, because it violates the sexual prohibition for wives and daughters, entails guilt feelings. Females in particular have devised, as a partial justification for sexual behavior, the great power and value of romantic love. While men are viewed as driven by the power of lust, women are viewed as driven by the power of love. Love, at least in part, redeems and explains the female interest in sexuality. So the fifth tenet is:

5. Love redeems sexuality from its guilt, particularly for females.

We discussed the evidence for this tenet in our comments on historical views of sexuality.

The major theme running through all five of these ideological tenets of the Traditional-Romantic view of sexuality is the double standard. Male dominance is explicitly present in each tenet. These five tenets could be applied with reasonable accuracy to most cultures in the Western world although some modifications would need to be made for differences in the Mediterranean and Scandinavian subgroupings (Bourguignon, 1980; Reiss, 1980b). Many people in the Western world lack awareness of what adherence to these beliefs force them to include and exclude from their life styles. One purpose of this paper is to increase such awareness.

The 20th century has witnessed a challenge to these ideological beliefs. One of the reasons why it is now easier to become aware of the Traditional-Romantic Ideology in sexuality is that there is a new ideology that has set up opposing tenets. The new ideology is one I shall call the Modern-Naturalistic Ideology and it directly challenges each of the five tenets listed above.

In order to display the key differences, I will list below the five alternative tenets that the Modern-Naturalistic view would assert as part of its ideology:

1. Gender roles should be similar for males and females and should promote equalitarian participation in the society.
2. Body-centered sexuality is of less worth than person-centered sexuality, but it still has a positive value for both genders.
3. One's sexual emotions are strong but are manageable, by both males and females, in the same way as are other basic emotions.
4. The major goals of sexuality are physical pleasure and psychological intimacy in a variety of sexual acts and this is so of both genders.
5. A wide range of sexuality should be accepted without guilt by both genders providing it does not involve force or fraud.

The basic underlying principle in this newer ideology is the equalitarian relationship of males and females. There is relatedly a naturalistic view of sexuality and of its acceptability. The expression of sexuality is considered a good and proper part of much of human social life. Knowing what we know about equalitarian gender trends throughout this century, we as sociologists could have predicted that the Traditional-Romantic Ideology would be challenged by the Modern-Naturalistic Ideology. Let it be explicit that the newer ideology is based upon a fundamental way of thinking—most obviously, it eliminates the older ideological ways. Also, the newer ideology is based up on a fundamental moral view of the genders which assumes equality. One can easily deduce the different ways that an adherent of the Modern-Naturalistic Ideology and an adherent of the Traditional-Romantic Ideology would evaluate the issues of abortion, genetic differences, exploitation and pornography, sexual normality, and our sexual past. What we are witnessing in the 1980s in America in reference to sexual issues can be interpreted as fundamentally a clash of these two basic ideologies regarding human sexuality.

It should be clear that many people today are in transition and so they will adhere to elements of both the old and the new sexual ideologies. Furthermore, there are others who will display tenets which have not been explored in this paper. But many of the essentials of the two dominant ideologies have been outlined and this should be helpful in understanding our sexual customs.

Let us briefly look at the Bendix Corporation case involving the promotion of Mary Cunningham as one illustration of our sexual ideologies. Such a single case can only be illustrative, but I do believe it is instructive regarding our current ideology. I will not try to deal with the morality of the case or with the controversy about it. Rather, I will examine how the mass media handled this case and what that tells us about our sexual ideology. This story appeared in our mass media during October of 1980 and involved the suggested promotion in September, 1980 of Mary Cunningham to Vice President for Strategic Planning at Bendix. The promotion was put forth by her boss, Chief Executive William Agee. Rumors spread that Agee and Cunningham were sexually involved and that her promotion should therefore be denied. In October, 1980, she resigned from Bendix. From the ideological point of view several things are interesting in this case. First, almost all the news media coverage centered around the one question of whether Cunningham and Agee were sleeping together. The assumption appeared to be that if they were sexually involved then it was a foregone conclusion that her promotion should be denied. This popular view involves several tenets of the Traditional-Romantic sexual ideology. It stresses the all-powerful nature of the sexual emotion assuming that sexual relations will likely occur when a man and woman are together in business and, furthermore, such an emotion will dominate the evaluation of the woman for promotion. Also involved in many of the statements was the amazement that Cunningham could really be ready for such a promotion in just one year. Agee himself had been a "boy wonder" of Bendix and moved up in rank at a very fast pace without any questions being raised. Thus, the tenets concerning the separate treatment of each gender and the dominance of males also enter into the media coverage. Frequently a promotion in business is put forth by a man who is a close friend of the man up for promotion. Seldom is that situation judged as improper. Here, again, the powerful view of sexuality is much more distorting than friendship and the accepted dominance of males is visible in this interpretation of reality.

From a broader perspective one could have asked if Cunningham was qualified for promotion. The available evidence cited in the press indicated that she was thought to be qualified by those who examined her record. The conflict over her promotion could have been handled by having an outside impartial committee evaluate her qualifications for promotion. Such a routine procedure could avoid a favoritism charge in such cases. Yet no article that I read mentioned such a suggestion for future use in business or for this case. This was so, I believe, because in the popular press the focus was on the sexual aspects of the case. The key issue clearly seemed to be the sexual relations of Cunningham and Agee.

The Modern-Naturalistic Ideology asserts that sexual emotions are manageable, gender roles should be equal, and sexuality is generally acceptable, and it would have led to a different public treatment of the issue in the media. Of course, both ideologies express value judgments and neither is scientifically "better," but the point I am making here is that the predominance of the Traditional-Romantic Ideology in the public handling of the Cunningham case indicates that the newer ideology, although an increasingly popular one, is not the dominant position. The treatment of this case also shows how our ideology determines what we see as the "crucial issues" in any social situation involving sexuality. Of course, this is but one case, but the similarity in the mass media treatment was impressive. It would be valuable to do more careful analysis of a variety of such instances to develop a more considered judgment as to the relative use of our two major ideologies in the mass media.

CONCLUSIONS

The ways in which our sexual ideologies blind us to the totality of choices and interpretations has been the central topic of this paper. I have conceptualized the specific tenets of the two major ideologies as an aid to future conceptualization in this area. But the most important conclusion to be drawn from this analysis is that social science research can help us immensely in understanding the basic assumptions and values upon which we base our sexual life styles. Knowledge of such basic ideological elements will give us an excellent predictive base and will also provide clinicians and individuals with information that can help them in their work and in their personal lives.

In just the last several years, the evidence has mounted that the conservative forces in this country have organized to become an effective force, particularly in the religious and political spheres. Some have taken this as a sign that the society is moving to the "right." However, polls have consistently indicated very little change in the proportion of people who favor various positions on abortion, premarital sexuality, pornography, etc. (Reiss, 1980a). What has happened is that the conservative forces have organized more effectively and thereby increased their power if not their numbers. The signs are clear that the "left wing" forces are organizing more effectively now and that the 1980s will reverberate with the sounds of conservative-liberal battles over many sexual issues. It is precisely because of this recent organization that ideologies have become more prominent and the ability to obtain a nonideological view of human sexuality has accordingly decreased. This is precisely the time when a scientific perspective can add clarity and help define the issues.

Adherents to both major ideologies make claims to scientific support for specific aspects of the various positions they take. It is time that social scientists get off the sidelines and speak to the scientific issues involved in terms of what research has been done and in terms of our theoretical understanding of the situation. If we remain silent, then we will have given up our rightful claim to explain human social behavior even in areas as emotionally charged as sexuality. Of course, science cannot settle which ideology is "best" but it can deal with scientific questions such as genetic differences between the sexes, consequences of aborting or not aborting, meanings and uses of terms like normality and exploitation, and knowledge of our past sexual customs. Sociology and other social sciences offer a comprehensive perspective on the competing ideologies and an overview of the social scene that is not available elsewhere.

I have tried to show some ways in which sociology can address the issues raised in our ideologies. My attempt has been to encourage future work, for, admittedly, I have not fully explored all the issues raised nor has there always been full evidence available and, thus, some of my observations surely require additional examination. Finally, it should be clear that we will never have a society without ideologies, but we can have our ideologies tempered and examined by our social sciences.

Of course, as members of our society, we are also strongly emotionally committed to ideological positions of our own and this may make us hesitate to do anything that might weaken the successful outcomes of our private ideologies. Also, some may fear being attacked by those whose ideological beliefs are brought under scrutiny. But if the value of scientific inquiry is to prevail, then we need to pursue a scientific understanding of these private ideologies that we all possess. In this paper, I stress the value of following the *ideology* of science. Surely science, too, is based on ideological tenets regarding the nature of the world and the value of knowing it scientifically. Science, too, must be chosen on faith as one source for understanding the nature of the world. Nevertheless, in a time of ideological conflict, the ideology of science can serve as a predominant means of gaining understanding of our sexual ideologies and their place in our lives today. Social science can offer a perspective that is missing in the two dominant ideologies that are now grappling with each other on our national stage.

REFERENCES

Beach, F. A. (ed.)
    1977 *Human sexuality in four perspectives.* Baltimore: Johns Hopkins University Press.

Bell, A. P., and M. S. Weinberg
    1978 *Homosexualities.* New York: Simon and Schuster.

Bourguignon, E. (ed.)
- 1980 *A world of women.* New York: Praeger.

Brown, W. B., P. M. Monti, and D. P. Corrineau
- 1978 Serum testosterone and sexual activity and interest in men. *Archives of Sexual Behavior* 7 (March):97–103.

Calhoun, A. W.
- 1945 *A social history of the American family* (3 vols.). New York: Barnes and Noble Books.

CBS-New York Times
- 1980 August 1980 News Poll. Cited in Minneapolis Tribune. August 24, 1980, p. 9A.

Chappell, D., R. Geis, and G. Geis (eds.)
- 1977 *Forcible rape.* New York: Columbia University Press.

Commission on Obscenity and Pornography
- 1970 *The Report of the Commission on Obscenity and Pornography.* Washington, D.C.: Government Printing Office.

Donnerstein, E., M. Donnerstein, and R. Evans
- 1975 Erotic stimuli and aggression: Facilitation or Inhibition? *Journal of Personality and Social Psychology* 32:237–44.

Donnerstein, E.
- 1980 Aggressive erotica and violence against women. *Journal of Personality and Social Psychology* 39 (August):269–77.

Gadpaille, W. J.
- 1972 Research into the physiology of maleness and femaleness. *Archives of General Psychiatry* 26 (March):193–206.

Gough, K. E.
- 1971 The origins of the family. *Journal of Marriage and the Family* 33 (November):760–70.

Granberg, D., and B. W. Granberg
- 1980 Abortion attitudes: 1965–1980: Trends and determinants. *Family Planning Perspectives* 12 (September/October):250–61.

Groth, A.N.
- 1979 *Men who rape: The psychology of the offender.* New York: Plenum.

IASR, International Academy of Sex Researchers
- 1977 Paper presented by J. C. Burt at the Annual Meeting in Bloomington, Indiana.
- 1980 Paper presented by D. Goldfoot of the University of Wisconsin (Madison) at the Annual Meeting in Tucson, Arizona.

LaFree, G. D.
- 1980 The effect of sexual statification by race on official reactions to rape. *American Sociological Review* 45 (October):842–54.

Maccoby, E. E., and C. Jacklin
- 1974 *The psychology of sex differences.* Stanford: Stanford University Press.

Malamuth, N. M., and B. Spinner
- 1980 A longitudinal content analysis of sexual violence in the best-selling erotic magazines. *Journal of Sex Research* 16 (August):226–37.

Marshal, D. S., and R. C. Suggs
- 1971 *Human sexual behavior.* New York: Basic Books.

Marx, K., and F. Engels
- 1962 *Marx and Engels: Selected Works* (Vol. 1). Moscow: Foreign Languages Publishing House.

Minneapolis Tribune
- 1980 August 24, 1980, p. 9A.

Money, J., and A. Ehrhardt
- 1972 *Man and woman, boy and girl.* Baltimore: Johns Hopkins University Press.

Money, J., and H. Musaph (eds.)
- 1977 *Handbook of sexology.* New York: Elsevier Press.

National Opinion Research Center (NORC)
- 1980 *General social survey.* Chicago: University of Chicago Press.

Reiss, I. L.
- 1960 *Premarital sexual standards in America.* New York: Macmillan.
- 1967 *The social context of premarital sexual permissiveness.* New York: Holt, Rinehart and Winston.
- 1980a *Family systems in America,* 3d ed. New York: Holt, Rinehart and Winston.
- 1980b Sexual customs in Sweden and America: An analysis and interpretation." In *Research on the interweave of social roles: women and men,* ed. by H. Lopata. Greenwich, Conn.: JAI Press.

Schwartz, M. F., R. C. Kolodny, and W. H. Masters
- 1980 Plasma testosterone levels of sexually functional and dysfunctional men. *Archives of Sexual Behavior* 9 (October):355–66.

Walfish, S., and M. Myerson
- 1980 Sex role identity and attitudes toward sexuality. *Archives of Sexual Behavior* 9 (June):199–205.

9

THE BIG TOE, ARMPITS, AND NATURAL PERFUME: NOTES ON THE PRODUCTION OF SEXUAL ECSTASY

Dennis Brissett and Lionel S. Lewis

Ten years ago, we described how 15 popular marriage manuals published prior to 1966 characterized marital sex as work. We argued that marital sex, having already been transformed from a means of procreation to a form of recreation, was being depicted by the manuals in terms of a rather well-defined work ideology. Similar to many other forms of leisure, marital sex as a "play form" was justified by incorporating many principles and procedures of work. In this article, we examine 13 recently published manuals dealing with marriage and sex in order to see whether they reflect some of the presumed changes in the American character that are said to have occurred over the last decade.

Since at least the middle 1960s, it has been alleged that American society has undergone a kind of sexual revolution. Many forms of sexual behavior, which prior to the mid-1960s were either infrequent or well hidden, e.g., pornography, swinging, and the like, have become part of a growing number of recognized sexual variations in society. With these behavioral changes also has come a presumed change in the American mentality and attitude toward sexual behavior. This mentality can be characterized as an increased awareness, openness, toleration, and, perhaps, acceptance of the varied manifestations of sexuality, both in oneself and in others. Sexuality, like many other features of American life, has been subjected to what Theodore Roszak calls "the myth of objective consciousness." Sex has been rationalized, analyzed, and demystified; all of this being allegedly reflective of a more honest sexual attitude in which sex is no longer viewed as a source of innumerable problems, but, rather as a very natural source of human enjoyment.

A cultural development that has paralleled and, in fact, has encompassed this sexual revolution has been a growing emphasis on what Joseph Bensman and Arthur Vidich call the "consciousness of choice" among the middle classes in American society. Many Americans have come to assume that they have the possibility and, in fact, the right to choose their own style of living. Curiously, they feel a new self-reliance while exercising their options within the rather limited confines of the organizations and norms that constitute their social worlds. Part of this consciousness stems from the recognition that, although their choices of activity are often severely limited by other than self-imposed considerations, they usually can choose the style in which they wish to act. The choice is not life, but life style. A central tenet of this consciousness is the awareness that life style is both arbitrary and, perhaps, even capricious.

This type of consciousness appears to permeate the work of many people in society. The old

---

Published by permission of Transaction, Inc., from *Society*, Vol. 16, No. 2. Copyright © 1979 by Transaction, Inc.

ethic that people should work still prevails. What a person can choose, however, is, to a certain degree, the style of work, and to a much greater degree, the life style surrounding the work. It is our feeling that work style and life style have come to dominate most Americans' attitudes toward their work. Work itself, in fact, has become concealed by the work style and life style alternatives it makes possible. Unlike the era when persons had to justify their play as work, we now seem to be entering an age where work itself has to be justified as play. The disguise of play both creates and reaffirms the "consciousness of choice."

Stemming from, and perhaps reaffirming this "consciousness of choice" is a curious kind of individualism. Many people, recognizing the arbitrary nature of a society primarily concerned with style, have come to search for "reality" or an "absolute" within their own personal life space. What has resulted is an exaggerated preoccupation with the self. Tom Wolfe comments on what he calls the "alchemical dream" of the current society:

The old alchemical dream was changing base metals into gold. The new alchemical dream is: changing one's personality—remaking, remodeling, elevating and polishing one's very self . . . and observing, studying and doting on it. (ME!)

A very important part of this self-refurbishing project appears to involve an individual's sexual identity. One consequence of the sexual revolution has been a proliferation of sexual knowledge, attitudes, and activities to an ever-increasing proportion of the population. Both science, in its objective analysis of the physiology and psychology of sexual behavior, and pornography, in its explicit presentation of sexual variations, have tended to reduce sexual activity to the level of organismic response. Unfortunately, reductionistic characterizations of any facet of human life are hardly the stuff out of which human identities are constructed. While the sexual revolution certainly has involved a movement away (some would say, liberation) from the traditional repressions of sexual behavior, it has, at the same time, provided little in the way of human resources for people hoping to fashion a solid sense of sexual identity. Before the sexual revolution, sex for many people was mysterious, almost sacred. Currently, sex for most people is very understandable, almost secular. This is not to say that sex is not enjoyable, but only to say that it is nothing special—simply another aspect of one's everyday, commonplace, taken-for-granted world. We believe that people pursuing the "alchemical dream" are looking for something more. Although they may not be full-time participants in what Wolfe calls the "Third Great Awakening," they are seeking to dramatize what the sexual revolution has made mundane.

In light of these putative shifts in the nature of American life, we thought it appropriate to review some of the more recent sex manuals to see if they are reflective of these changes. On the basis of the sexual revolution, we would expect the manuals to reflect a more open, perhaps rational, view of sex with an emphasis on variation and a kind of physiological (naturalistic) honesty. Based on the growing emphasis on "consciousness of choice" and given our earlier characterization of sex as work, we would expect there to be more emphasis on both the life style context of sexual activity and the "stylistic aspects" of sexuality.

Given the modern penchant for self-improvement and development, we expect that the authors of the manuals will espouse, at the very least, an intense, righteous (reverent) and dramatic attitude regarding sexual matters. We suspect that they not only will promulgate the three basic values of the "new modern society"—communication, sharing, and relationship—but also emphasize a fourth, that of ecstasy, as a means of realizing an almost overwhelming sense of individualization.

LIBERATED SEXUALITY

Upon encountering the newer sex manuals, one quickly realizes that he or she is embarking on a large scale reinterpretation and redefinition of human sexuality. Although a work ethic is still apparent, the authors of the manuals make it quite clear that what they espouse is a new, clearer vision of sexuality than that to which the reader might traditionally be accustomed. In fact, sexual traditions are often equated with unrealistic sexual proscriptions:

Taboos and traditions: These are what we call rules and restrictions that have no practical foundation, but which are the result of custom or religious teaching. (Hegeler)

Usually, the past is viewed as a time of confusion and narrow-mindedness regarding sexual matters, as "for many years a veil of hypocrisy has surrounded everything associated with sex" (Copelan, *Woman*). The past is also used as a scapegoat for current problems of sexuality, particularly those suffered by women. Sometimes, the culprit is the distant past:

The sexual problems which plague modern women have their origins in the dark days of female slavery. . . . The result of this early crushing of the female spirit manifests its destructiveness in both the psychic and physical being of every woman. (Copelan, *Woman*)

Other times, it is merely the previous generation, as "most women who suffer from orgasmic impairment are innocent victims—good little girls who believed what their mothers told them" (Reuben). Most typically, the past is seen as producing a very inhibited, nonliberated view of sexuality.

The manuals promise something quite different. The question of the naturalness of certain sexual activities is addressed:

Nature and what is natural are far more diverse when it comes to sexual activity than the official cultural attitude and code of morals would have us believe. (Hegeler)

Even the necessity of sexual intercourse for an adequate sex life is questioned.

It took us generations, if not centuries, to be able to assert that sex wasn't only, or mainly, for procreation, but for pleasure. By the same token, just as procreation isn't necessary to sex, neither is intercourse. (Fellman)

Moreover, the monogamous nature of marriage is debated. In some cases, the virtues of extramarital sex are extolled. Sex outside of marriage is cited as a "potentially . . . important means for growth" (Lobell), or it may be "that there is some specific person you are just dying to go to bed with" (Lobell). In any case,

When the turn-off is total, well, we might as well say it bluntly: We believe there finally comes a time when sexual relations outside the marriage are right. (Magner)

The authors of one manual, in discussing the degree of sexual openness that parents should exhibit toward their children, extol the instance of one married couple's experiences with their three-year-old child, Icarus.

Sometimes he is in bed with Caleb and Joan when they make love. He runs over and tries to climb between his mother's legs when Caleb leaves. Recently Icarus has gotten into riding on Caleb's back while he is making love to Joan. One night after a particularly hectic week that strained all three of them, Icarus was hanging onto Caleb's back while he and Joan were making love. Icarus fell asleep, falling off onto the floor. Thunk. (Lobell)

The onus of incest is tempered through reductionistic analogy:

If we want to pass judgment on the question of 'incest' objectively, we should also bear in mind that incest is widely practiced by the breeders of agricultural animals in order to produce the finest and most desirable specimens possible. (Hegeler)

In short, the message is one of liberation. "Permissive sex is in" (Copelan, *Man*).

Although all authors do not agree on what particular liberated path the reader should follow (some authors still disdain extramarital or group sex), the matter of liberated sex is not deemed simply a human privilege, but a right; in fact, according to one author, a gift of God.

Liberated sex is yours from God. Perhaps the most meaningful single line for all sexual love from all of the Scripture is "Your body is the temple of the Holy Spirit." This means very simply that in the sexual action of your lives together every muscle and every curve, every pore and every nerve is sacred and precious and to be loved. (Magner)

In one author's opinion, the importance of uninhibited sex stems from the fact that sexual relations, particularly intercourse, reflect the character of people's entire lives:

Sex has a most direct way of sweeping aside surface phoniness, forcing us to see ourselves as we really are. It dramatically demonstrates to a woman what her man is and what his hang-ups are. It also lets him know what bothers her in a profound sense. Character traits show themselves. Tenderness flowers or is sadly lacking. Selfishness asserts itself, as does insecurity and lack of self-esteem. Cruelty, fear, guilt, sadism and masochism are all uncovered. A person's entire life is often capsuled in the course of copulation. (Copelan, *Woman*)

Besides,

it's fun. It keeps your weight down. It's good for your complexion. It keeps you young. It keeps you happy. It's good for your heart (if you do it regularly). And it keeps you worth living with! (Lobell)

But, more to the point, a truly satisfying (read liberated) sex life is alleged to be necessary for both men and women if they are to achieve anything better than a minimal life existence. As one author quotes another expert,

. . . the sexually happy man gets a better job, more money, and a better house—he enjoys life as a whole. (Masterton)

While,

a sexually satisfied woman is a healthier, livelier person. . . . Every part of the body works better when the sex organs function. The eyes are clearer. The face looks more rested and serene. Compulsive overeating often is diminished and a host of other changes take place. Many of the so-called tension diseases or psychosomatic ailments disappear or are alleviated. (Copelan, *Woman*)

DEMOCRACY OF LIBERATED SEXUALITY

Unlike most things in life, liberated sex is depicted as possible for everyone—whether an individual be young, elderly, impotent, frigid, physically or emotionally handicapped, or even just inhibited by inadequate socialization. Nowhere is this more evident than in the authors' discussion of sexual problems and their remedies. As one author puts it:

. . . the main point to bear in mind is that whatever your problems, *you are capable of becoming a truly memorable lover*—the kind of man a girl will never really forget all her life. (Masterton)

Sometimes the solution to one's problems requires exercise:

Fortunately, the problem of flaccid sexual muscles can be easily rectified. Once a woman accepts their existence and learns to strengthen their activity through exercise, sensation begins to develop where it never existed before. . . . In order to awaken them to their biological task, the muscles must be strengthened progressively by exercise. (Copelan, *Woman*)

Other problems might require a change of technique:

If the slight bitterness [when swallowing semen], rather than the whole idea, is what they dislike, it can easily be avoided by taking him really deeply. (Comfort)

Or a simple matter of breathing differently:

Sexual performance is greatly influenced by the way a person breathes. The inability to reach orgasm, for example, is directly connected with the withholding of the outgoing breath. Fear of letting go orgastic feeling makes people literally 'hold their breath'. . . . (Copelan, *Woman*)

As the following excerpt from a letter to, and response from, one of the authors illustrates, often the problem demands little more than a change of perspective.

Dear Sir:
Please give me some information about penis and scrotum size. . . . My penis when flaccid varies from 2'' to 4'' in length. During an erection it varies from 6'' to nearly 7'' when I have a full erection. At full erection it is approximately 4'' in circumference. . . . I know of no way to measure the size of my scrotum. Having spent much time at the beach this past summer, I was able to compare my penis size with that of my fellow males. I would say nearly 95% of the men I saw at the locker room possessed a penis and scrotum which was much larger and longer than mine. Their scrota were much fuller and larger than mine. Is my penis considered small, and will it cause me any difficulty? . . .

* * *

The penis of the man who wrote this letter is above average size, if anything. And yet he is concerned about it, feeling that it is, if anything, smaller than average. We find this to be true in many cases. The only explanation I have is that when a man glances down at his own penis, he sees it foreshortened, while looking at another man's organ he sees it full length. (Clark)

A more understanding sexual partner will sometimes make the difference.

Nothing will lessen this man's sexual capacity more certainly than a nagging wife. As we shall see shortly, the best possible therapy for impotence is a helpful, understanding sexual partner. (Clark)

If all else fails, persistence

. . . dogged persistence is necessary. Single-minded commitment to self improvement can lift any man out of mediocrity to superiority as a lover. . . . (Copelan, *Man*)

The realization that each individual is unique might provide a solution.

The big American myth is that every couple should be a perfect fit when they get into bed, physically and emotionally. I say, Hogwash. The truth is this: People should be different when they get into bed together (and men and women are quite different), and the goal should be to work out those differences for mutual satisfaction. The goal—and the fun.

And the ecstasy. (Fellman)

NATURE OF LIBERATED SEXUALITY

An implicit, but constant, theme running through the manuals is that although liberated sexuality is good, too much of a good thing is no good. Often, the analogy is to eating.

A large number of orgasms is not necessarily proof of a great degree of happiness. Twenty meals a day is no way to paradise either. But we should be enabled to satisfy our calorific as well as our sexual needs. (Hegeler)

However, the message of the manuals is certainly that it would be difficult to overindulge in liberated sexuality or to become overly uninhibited. For one thing, the intricacies and subtleties of sexual expression are said to be possibly infinite.

Sometimes we are asked if sex loses its mystery when it is faced so openly and experienced so fully. The very axis of the world spins on sexual energy. Its mystery is unfathomable. It has been the creative font of some of the world's greatest religions, mythologies, and civilizations. To think that the mystery of sex is so easily exhausted is pure conceit. And to fear exploring it is timid. (Lobell)

On the other hand, the rewards of a liberated sexuality almost seem worth any price. According to one author, "sex can be the most mind-blowing, bone-rattling, supercolossal experience any female ever had" (Reuben). It defies accurate description:

No biology lecture or book or song can ever define the wild orbit of your senses as climax claims you. For heavenly seconds that seem hours the spasms of the sexual crest snatch you from all reality. Small wonder, perhaps, that people tense to talk of it. (Magner)

Perhaps, most importantly, liberated sexuality is cast in that ancient theological principle of procuring self-fulfillment through the exercise of a supernatural gift:

There is a clear resemblance of emotions in sexual and religious passion. Sexual joy comes very near to certain types of religious joy. Notice how the emotions of faith in life and those of sex in life are often identically described. When you speak of "ecstasy" or "passion" or "rapture", you may be speaking of Paul halted on the road to Damascus by his encounter with God, or of two lovers halted at the coital crest by the paralysis of orgasm. (Magner)

Within this context:

The ultimate sexual liberation lies not in achieving some abstract uniform supersex ideal, but in being able to be yourself. Sexuality is ultimately a path to the *centeredness* of knowing and loving and accepting yourself. (Lobell)

SEXUAL PERFORMANCE

According to the newer manuals, sexual relations are not only organismic activities, but also human performances. Again, the analogy is often to eating, with satisfying sex being equated with feasting. One author, whose table of contents includes such chapter headings as "starters," "main courses," and "sauces and pickles," comments:

But still the main dish is living, unselfconscious intercourse—long, frequent, varied, ending with both parties satisfied, but not so full they can't face another light course, and another meal in a few hours. (Comfort)

The dramatic character of sex is addressed in a general way.

You are about to embark on the greatest adventure of your life—exploring your latent sexual potential. Think of yourself as being in charge of a new dramatic production. You are not only the drama's star, you are also the producer and director. The show is all yours—you can make it mediocre or magnificent. (Copelan, *Man*)

Its intricacies are highlighted.

. . . sexual intrigue is a subtle science, and sometimes you have to study every aspect in order to make your way through the camouflage laid out by your target. (Gray)

Sex is also described in the specific trappings of sexual games. One author suggests adding the following games (from expensive, through degrading, to total solipsism) to one's sexual repertoire:

The Rape Game
. . . literally rip her dress off, kiss her savagely . . . tear off her panties
The Prostitute Game
. . . undress her without any pleasantries, insult her; make her do really dirty things . . . tell her she's a lousy screw and slap down your money
The Humbert Humbert Game
Have her shave off her pubic hair; tie her hair in gingham ribbons . . . slide your fingers into her little cotton panties . . .
The Let's Do-All-Those-Bizarre-Things-We've-Heard-About Game
If, during this one afternoon, you want to masturbate into your girl friend's face, do it. (Masterton)

Often, sexual games are said to require costuming.

Dress up as Mata Hari—covered up to the neck, but with your breasts exposed, nipples tinted pink. Wear a plain, flannel nightie, with the back cut out so that the cheeks of your rear end are revealed. This get-up will so delight him, he'll no doubt nip your hind cheeks with his teeth or pinch them. . . . (Gray)

Conversely, one's workaday costuming should include a sense of the sexual.

The first thing in the morning, before taking a shower, he draws a clean cotton handkerchief across the underside of his scrotum. After dressing, he places the pheromone-saturated hanky in the breast pocket of his jacket and sallies forth to meet (or conquer) the world. (Reuben)

Droll understatements aside, the impression management inherent in sexual games can lead to confusion and uncertainty.

When women worry about hanging on to their husbands they often fake orgasm. These sad, frustrated, and neurotic wives get caught in a trap of sexual "role-playing." Like an actress, they "make believe" they reach an orgasm to keep their husbands by the old fireside. . . . When women put on a show of false feeling, they rationalize that they are doing so to protect the man's ego.

Does a women really fool a man about her sexual responsiveness? Well, to take off on a very old saying, *You can fool some of the men some of the time, but you can't fool all of the men all of the time.* . . . Sometimes, men will go along with the deception in order to avoid a confrontation with the woman's problem to which they themselves have no answer. Men may allow themselves to be fooled. (Copelan, *Woman*)

VARIETY OF SEXUAL EXPRESSION

According to the manuals, the particular ways in which human beings can and should express themselves sexually are almost unlimited. "Variety is as much the spice of sex as it is of life . . ." (Chartham). Notwithstanding their general attitude of liberation, the authors of the manuals document a far-reaching list of sexual practices, some tentatively explored in the earlier marriage manuals, others heretofore found only in other literature.

Beginning with the simple assumption that there "are six basic positions from which most others emanate: man on top; woman on top; man practicing cunnilingus; woman practicing fellatio; the familiar sixty-nine; rear vaginal entry" (Copelan, *Man*), a varigated agenda is outlined. The authors diligently document with infinite examples, the implications of the contention that people "are actually born with a multiplicity of possibilities of obtaining sexual satisfaction" (Hegeler).

Given the manuals' intense preoccupation with the range and variety of sexual expression, the discussions of straightforward intercourse are rather minimal. When the topic of intercourse is broached, it is usually the variations that are emphasized. One author, who discusses femoral, intermammary, and navel intercourse, outlines axillary intercourse as an occasional variation.

. . . Handle it as for intermammary intercourse . . . but with your penis under her right arm—well under, so that friction is on the shaft, not the glans, as in any other unlubricated area. Put her left arm round your neck and hold her right hand behind her with your right arm. She will get her sensations from the pressure against her breasts, helped by your big toe pressed to her clitoris if she wants it. (Comfort)

A "no hands" approach is also recommended:

Two naked people tied and put on a mattress together to make love fish-fashion, i.e. no hands. . . . (Comfort)

Although intercourse while standing is not.

Making love standing up kills your arches! Unless of course, the woman happens to be about four inches taller than the man. You may have more success than we've had. We happen to be a standard-size couple, male bigger than female, and whenever we try screwing upright I end up standing on my tiptoes for at least a half hour, and I am usually unable to walk for several days afterward because my feet just lock in that position. A stool isn't very much help; we've never found one the right height. Books piled up become a bit precarious. You have to clutch each other rather tightly to keep from toppling over backward, and you feel a little giddy in that position anyhow. Besides, Dick's cock keeps popping out at inappropriate moments which makes the whole thing totally unsatisfactory, despite what the marriage manuals say. However, I understand it's a marvelous exercise for those with flat feet. (McDonald)

Orality

Particular emphasis is put on the use of the tongue and mouth in sexual activity. Readers are cautioned:

If you haven't at least kissed her mouth, shoulders, neck, breasts, armpits, fingers, palms, toes, soles, navel, genitals, earlobes, you haven't really kissed her. . . . (Comfort)

Readers are chided about their reluctance to engage in uninhibited kissing, particularly of the genital area.

A great part of the anxiety over oral sex springs from failure to recognize that the human mouth is an important sexual organ.

. . . It's probably one of the busiest sexual organs of them all.

By contrast, the genitals themselves are bit players who only get onstage for the final scene of the last act. It all starts with an innocent kiss. (Reuben)

Often, something more than mere kissing is called for. One author simply advises:

Lick her all over.
Have her lick you all over. (Masterton)

Another, in describing the "tongue bath," is a bit more systematic:

. . . the rapid licking of the nipple with the tongue, exploration of the navel with the tip of the tongue, sucking or licking of the clitoris with lips and tongue. . . . (Chartham)

For those who believe that kissing the genitals is unsanitary, it is made clear that, "in effect, there is far more danger involved in a casual peck on the lips than in either fellatio or cunnilingus. But that never stopped anyone from snatching a kiss" (Reuben), (or, we might add, vice versa).

Masturbation

Masturbation, like oral sex, is deemed by the manuals to be an important element in one's sexual arsenal.

. . . Masturbation is one of the quite definitely commonest methods of satisfying one's sexual urges—in fact, if we want to count orgasms it is probably *the* most common—and always has been. Just as common and natural as eating when we are hungry. (Hegeler)

The necessity of masturbation for the male (or at least young males) is promoted:

Young men continue to masturbate even when they are dating girls and experiencing normal intercourse. The man who has reached maturity without ever having masturbated is a bit unusual, to say the least. . . . There would no doubt be many more sex crimes and violence, were it not for this safety valve. (Copelan, *Woman*)

This same author describes the masturbatory rights of the female.

Young women are demanding equal rights not only at the ballot booths, but in the bedroom.

Many young women claim that the use of devices, as well as manual manipulation, helps them to respond better when they are with a man. . . . *Masturbation that leads to improved heterosexual intercourse can only be considered as a positive conditioning force.* (Copelan, *Woman*)

Masturbation is also equated with between-meal snacks.

And in the same way that we may resort to a snack if we happen to get hungry, and enjoy it because it satisfies our craving for food perfectly. Well, we can also . . . let masturbation settle our sexual hunger and leave us free to think about other things again. (Hegeler)

Even the most sexually conservative manual allows for masturbation, but only under certain circumstances:

For many in love who must be separated from their lover by travel or by sickness, where sexual separation is extremely painful, masturbation is often helpful. . . . For those masturbation is not only to be permitted, it ought to be encouraged as perfectly normal.

. . . Masturbation can avoid unhappy sexual alliances or impetuous actions searching for a sexual sedative. It relieves tensions which can be agonizing. When wanted, the auto-erotic should be enjoyed, then put aside and forgotten. For a physiological parallel, consider the help many adults find in tears. More should. A different emotion, but the relief is similar. (Magner)

Another manual views a woman's ability to masturbate a man as a mark of an outstanding sexual partner.

A woman who has the divine gift of lechery and loves her partner will masturbate him well, and a woman who knows how to masturbate a man—subtly, unhurriedly and mercilessly—will almost always make a superlative partner. (Comfort)

Still another espouses a kind of masturbatory competition between marital partners.

Masturbate in front of her.
Have her masturbate in front of you.
Masturbate together and see who comes first (a prize to the winner). (Masterton)

Anatomical Odds and Ends

Coming in for special attention is a preoccupation with various parts of the anatomy not traditionally considered to be essential components of sexual activity. According to one author, "our whole bodies are one big hot spot. Yes, even noses!" (McDonald). Another author admonishes men that "as part of your training as a perfect lover, start thinking about your fingers, your mouth, your feet, and your body as sexual organs, as well as your penis" (Masterton). The use of armpits is described

They [armpit tufts] are there to brush the man's lips with; he can do the same more circumspectly. Kissing deeply in the armpits leaves a partner's perfume with you. (Comfort)

and promoted:

For some the greatest response is obtained if the tips of the underarm hair is brushed with the palm of the hand, while for others, quick dabs with the tip of the tongue in the centre of the armpit proves most exciting. (Chartham)

Other parts of the body, particularly when orally caressed, are said to be something worth exploring:

. . . while the back of her knees were only average—responsive to light strokes with the hand, if I use my tongue instead of my hands, she can't stand it for long. (Chartham)

The versatility of pubic hair is outlined.

Most lovers regard pubic hair as a resource. Try brushing it lightly, and learn to caress with it. It can be combed, twirled, kissed, held, even pulled. (Comfort)

In fact, ". . . in the woman it [pubic hair] can move the whole pubis, skillfully handled, to the point of orgasm" (Comfort).

The hair on one's head even has a place: "long hair or plaits can be rolled into a vagina, or the penis lassoed with a loop of it" (Comfort). Merely rubbing "your beard or stubble . . . [will] produce a dramatic response" (McDonald).

The part of the anatomy that is most redefined in terms of its sexual function is the foot. The soles of feet are mentioned as possible sites of sexual stimulation. However, the most important part of the foot for sexual purposes seems to be the big toe, as ". . . the big toe is a good penis substitute" (Comfort). It is also cited as an ideal instrument of mutual masturbation.

With a couple facing one another, they can stimulate each other with a high degree of response, the man gently caressing between the outer lips and in the general clitoral area, while the woman very gently strokes the perineum and scrotum of her partner. (Chartham)

Even

in a restaurant, in these days of tights, one can surreptitiously remove a shoe and sock, reach over, and keep her in almost continuous orgasm with all four hands fully in view of the table top and no sign of contact—a party trick which rates as really advanced sex. She has less scope, but can learn to masturbate him with her two big toes. (Comfort)

The big toe can be masturbated or fellated.

The stimulation [of the big toe] must be carried out by the partner and is most successful if the toe—which has obviously been washed spotlessly clean—is sucked. If the hand is used, the whole hand must clasp the toe and make the movements that are used by some men when masturbating. There are those who react to toe stimulation who find the sensation more intense if the mouth is used, of if some lubricant is used on the hand. (Chartham)

If not the big toe, than any toe:

A toe moving over your body feels very much like a finger, but the mental image and sensation it creates can be far more stimulating occasionally. Why? Simply because you know it's a toe. It's kinky. (McDonald)

VARIETY OF SEXUAL EQUIPMENT

The proliferation of sexual equipment cited by the manuals is quite impressive. While the authors of the older marriage manuals usually mentioned an assortment of sexual paraphernalia, the writers of the new sex manuals painstakingly point out the importance of various sexual aids. "Really enthusiastic sex usually involves at one time or another almost every piece of furniture in the house . . ." (Comfort).

A primary requisite of adequate sex is, naturally, one's bed, as ". . . in the selection of your bed the sleep comfort of the mattress is no more important than its lovemaking comfort" (Magner). Of course, ". . . one solution is to have two beds, one for sex and the other for sleeping . . ." (Comfort). However, "for some operations, especially bondage scenes if you like them, bedposts are essential, preferably tall ones . . .'' (Comfort).

The most conventional sexual equipment includes such items as a stool, mirror, chair without arms with a wide seat, a table, and pillows (Chartham). One author, who speaks to the importance of colored room lights, ropes, g-strings, leather, feathers, tape recorders, Land cameras, and honey, also features rings on one's penis and earrings on one's nipples, labia, and clitoris (Comfort). Another advises readers to ''. . . smother yourselves in scented oil, and make love like slippery seals'' (Masterton), or to utilize Siamese love beads.

> A centuries-old device which has only recently found its way on to the mass sex-aid market are Siamese love beads. These are a string of six or seven rubber ''peas'' which are pushed up the anus prior to lovemaking. At the moment of orgasm, they are pulled out, one by one. (Masterton)

The joys of dildoes (''some have bumps and feathers and ridges; others are plain pink or are artistically decorated with lifelike colored veins and arteries . . . one version has its own set of balls attached'' [McDonald]), wine and maraschino cherries are addressed (Gray). Also described are the intricacies of fellatio on ice.

> Put enough ice in your mouth to fill the small basin of the lower palate under your tongue. Take his penis in your mouth and let it rest in the coolness. Hold it there just long enough to give it a brisk shock, then swallow the melted ice and continue aggressively massaging his penis with your lips and teeth, roving nimbly over the top of his erection. Let your tongue deftly intrude into the orifice of his urethra. (Gray)

For those readers who are more mechanically inclined, probably the number one piece of equipment is the electric toothbrush. ''This little dispenser of dental hygiene offers an almost unlimited range of sexual sensations in the hands of an ingenious woman'' (Reuben).

Another instrument of oral hygiene, the home dental kit, can also have auxiliary uses. And ''the thing that makes it so exciting . . . is the way the water pulsates against [the] clitoris'' (Reuben).

If such equipment is not available, one can always turn to the vibrator, as even

> a small, battery-operated vibrator . . . can be used with a striking effect not only on the clitoral area, but the vaginal-rim, the nipples, under the breasts and the perineum in the woman, and the penis-head, penis shaft, nipples and perineum in the man. (Chartham)

Although most vibrators come in hand-held models, others are held by other parts of one's anatomy:

> There is . . . a kind of foam-rubber stretch stocking with a series of tiny vibrators built in that fits over the penis. When the gentleman flips a switch his penis is alternately squeezed and released about a hundred times a minute. (Reuben)

PROLIFERATION OF SEXUAL PLACES

Not only are readers of the manuals presented with an amazing array of sexual behaviors and techniques, they are also advised as to the broad spectrum of places in which and upon which one might engage in sexual expression:

> There are so many places to make love besides bed that you owe it to yourself to experiment a little. We can screw in exactly the same way, one night in bed and one night on a fur throw on the second story porch and experience different sensations and moods. The feel of the night wind on your bare breasts or cock, the night noises, the openness of the sky above you, and even the look of your skin in the darkness contribute to exciting sexual responses. If you live surrounded closely by neighbors, it adds fun and intrigue to make love above them while they're having an unsuspecting drink in their backyard below. (McDonald)

Sex is said to be enhanced if practiced in the shower or bathtub, on a desk, in a camper, in the kitchen, in a closet, in a deserted house (Comfort), in a limousine (Gray), at the foot of a tree (Chartham), in a garden or under a rug (Masterton), while dancing or on a swing (Comfort) on ''soft moss in the woods, a big piece of soft fake fur, cool leather in the summer, and long, soft grass'' (McDonald). For a quick tumble ''this might mean a chair, against a tree, in a washroom'' (Comfort).

Sometimes the utilization of special places raises special problems:

> Recently, a best selling how-to book proposed filling the bathtub with Jell-O and making love on top of it after it had hardened. Now this intrigued us, but being practical it immediately occurred to us that the family tub filled with Wild Cherry Jell-O might be a little tough to explain to our four very inquisitive children. You simply can't pull this off in the middle of the night and have all traces vanish with the dawn. How long does it take for 207 packages of Jell-O to harden? It may be fine for the dashing young bachelor with his own apartment who doesn't

care if he can't bathe for several days, but it's not the kind of thing that goes unnoticed in a family of six. (McDonald)

Lovemaking in or near water seems to hold a special fascination. Sometimes it heightens sexual pleasure:

. . . drawing the foreskin backwards and forwards, while the penis is held under water has a special arousal quality . . . and so has the cupping of the testicles in the hand and lightly moving them up and down under water. . . . (Chartham)

Other times it remedies a problem as "the girl who is too big . . . becomes light enough to handle, and one can prop her up at angles no acrobat could hold" (Comfort).

To be sure, having sex on the beach often enables the couple to take advantage of the natural rhythm of the sea.

They then go to the beach and lie on the sand, the woman face downwards. The husband goes into her from the rear and they couple as the incoming sea breaks over them in an uneven rhythm. Sometimes when it is raining and the wind is blowing and the waves are big, they couple in the sea, riding the waves, again in a rear-entry position. . . . (Chartham)

Yet some care is necessary:

You can have excellent straight intercourse lying in the surf if you can get a beach to yourselves, but sand is a problem, and keeps appearing for days afterwards. (Comfort)

One's sexual partner may "insist on fellatio" on the ski slopes (Gray) or in an airplane.

Strong, hard and active, he demands her attention and she acquiesces by burrowing under the afghan to suck him. Psychologically, the conditions under which airy Aries has chosen to satisfy her appetite has made your penis almost an inch longer than usual (at least it seems so to you), straining to be kissed and pummeled about in her hot mouth. . . . (Gray)

Or, one might try cunnilingus on a piano:

Do a "Helen Morgan" thing and sit on top of the baby grand. Standing in the curve of the piano he can achieve direct contact with your excited clitoris. Tonguing gently at first, then probing more and more insistently into your vagina makes for your climactic moment. (Gray)

No matter where one chooses to have sex, the important thing is to fill every moment with pleasure. This is true whether one is stationary as in a bathtub, since "foreplay can begin while the water is still being run," (Chartham) or, if one likes to move about in sexual activity.

He's a no-nonsense guy who, with one hand, can manipulate that pin on your dress, while his other hand is busy stroking your vulva. His fingers will explore your vagina as his thumb strokes your clitoris—all this from the armchair to the bed! (Gray)

SEXUAL NOISES

The authors of the manuals, as expected, devote considerable space to discussing the importance of good personal relationships as the proper context for sexual relations. Most of the manuals displayed a heightened sense of what we have formerly characterized as "mutual reciprocity," but of a somewhat different character.

A solid relationship is said to be built out of a mutual understanding and responsiveness between sexual partners before, during, and after the sexual encounter. What these manuals emphasize more than the earlier marriage manuals is a preoccupation with auditory communication during sexual relations. Sometimes inarticulate sounds seem to suffice—other times more seems necessary. One author, in discussing cries and loud moans, is "strongly of the opinion that sound—like sight—is a . . . successful aphrodisiac" (Chartham). Another recommends the male to: ". . . purr like a tomcat, growl deep in your throat like a giant Great Dane. With all of these sound effects, she'll know she's bringing much joy to you" (Gray). Sometimes, "loud sucking like a baby can work wonders" (Comfort). However, most of the authors emphasize talk as the appropriate medium of communication; sometimes to avoid problems.

Every step of the way we made sure that we were *both* comfortable, secure and happy. We continued to talk about all of our reactions to each experience and made sure that no fear or resentments were building up. It was only with this kind of bond between us that we were able to be more and more adventurous and to take greater risks. (Lobell)

Other times conversation keys one's partner to the proper stimulus:

We believe it is essential for two who are in love, who have dedicated their lives to be interwoven in marriage, to talk with absolute candor of stimulus desires. (Magner)

SEXUAL EXPRESSION

One author is particularly forceful in this respect, both in regard to sharing one's desires with one's partner ("[Tell her] that you want to get your prick in her cunt and fuck her. Be blunt, direct" [Gray]), and also in regard to keeping one's partner abreast of progress and giving instructions.

If you want her to take your penis in her mouth and suck it, tell her that you're removing your penis from within her and that you are finding your way over her downy, soft mound of venus, past her breasts then into her sucking mouth. Tell her to stroke up and down the shaft with her tongue. Instruct her to lap around the head of your penis, teething it lightly. You can tell her to move her mouth to the left testicle and devour it carefully and completely, then to the right testicle. (Gray)

Still other authors suggest communicating fantasies with each other. In general,

. . . uninhibited partners will tell each other about their fantasies. . . . Really communicating partners look for them and put them on the menu unannounced—there is no more complete communication. (Comfort)

More specifically,

when your wife is on top of you, riding your prick with her buttocks up in the air, ask her if she would like another man in bed so he could fuck her from behind while you are in her from the front. Reach around and fondle the lips of her vagina while describing to her what it would be like. A woman can do the same thing for her husband, describing what she and another woman or another man could do for his body. (Lobell)

DREARINESS TRANSCENDED?

It seems to us that the manuals examined here do indeed reflect certain changes in the American consciousness over the last decade. They convey a more rational-intellectual preoccupation with sexual variation. They emphasize the right of every individual to choose his or her own type of sexual activity, unfettered by the archaic conventions of an earlier age. They also make clear that sex is not a matter to be taken casually. Indeed sexual relations are extolled as the prototype of social relations, the microcosm of one's entire life.

Three-quarters of a century ago, Max Weber observed that in capitalism's "highest development," mechanistic, large, and complex institutions would come to dominate civilization, organizing our lives, affecting all aspects of behavior and thought. He predicted that in the last stage of cultural development, with the stranglehold of bureaucracy perfected, we would witness the ascent of "Specialists without spirit, Sensualists without heart." After taking inventory of the vast array of precepts for sex urged upon the readers of the manuals, we cannot help but wonder if, in fact, we are approaching that point with regard to human sexuality. One could not but be impressed with the intensity and specificity with which the authors of the manuals can describe analytically the mechanizations of sexual relations. Nor could one miss the reductionistic, mechanical imagery that is used to describe sexuality. Moreover, the authors appear to be particularly adroit in separating the sexual realm from other spheres of human existence. Sex becomes functionally autonomous in the pages of the manuals. As Joseph Epstein has remarked about sexologists in general, the authors of the manuals do not appear to be talking about human behavior at all, but rather, about the activity of the sexual apparatus that incidentally is found in humans. The sexual partners caricatured in the manuals seem strikingly akin to the "Lady of the Laboratory" described by Leslie Farber in his analysis of the Masters and Johnson research:

In a general way, her sexuality would have to be autonomous, separate from, and unaffected by, her ordinary world. . . . Her lust would lie at hand, ready to be invoked and consummated, in sickness or in health, in coitus or "automanipulation," in homosexuality or heterosexuality, in exasperation or calm, hesitancy or certainty, playfulness or despair.

Thus is sex removed from the context of distinctively human emotion and passion. One need not have spirit or feeling to be adept at sexual relations, only an adequate body and a lack of inhibitions. The "sex by choice" which is recommended seems little more than sex on demand, albeit mutually agreed upon demand. The attainment of a satisfactory sex life not only is viewed as everyone's right, but also as everyone's obligation.

With this liberation of sexuality comes also the exaltation of sexuality. The ministrations in the manuals grant sexual freedom a status as an ideological position. As Benjamin Zablocki and Rosabeth Moss Kanter have remarked, sexual freedom becomes the "basis for embryonic social movements and life style definition—and unconventional sexual preference [has gained] a rationale for becoming a badge of identity for some people." Sex without guilt becomes the *sine qua non* of one's life. Sexual ecstasy becomes a type of spiritual ecstasy; and sexual pleasure is described as the ultimate experience. The satisfaction of one's sexual urges is its own justification, while inadequate sexual relations become an unquestioned rationale for the dissolution of social relationships. In the area of sexuality, the fun morality of which Martha Wolfenstein spoke becomes curiously transformed into a kind of nonpuritan ethic. Instead of feeling guilty for having too much sexual pleasure, sexual partners now may very well experience anxiety for not having enough. Since almost everything is now permitted in the realm of sexuality, it is just possible that, as Epstein suggests, "nothing any longer is good enough."

It seems also possible, at least from a sociological perspective, that sex is being asked to carry too heavy a burden. It is being asked to provide that which heretofore the family, organized religion, and the workplace together afforded. There is the tacit promise that a well-developed sex life will help one transcend the dreariness and alienating experiences that are the lot of so many in contemporary society. It appears as likely that sex, as practiced according to the manuals, may very well do the opposite. We speak here not only of the chance that many individuals will not be able to live up to what some would consider the unrealistic expectations proffered by the manuals, but also to what many feel is a certain experiential reality of sexual relations. As Epstein puts it:

The relief . . . [sex] offers from the world is only as great as one's physical stamina, nothing is more sharply calculated to remind one of human limitations and the completion of no other act so quickly brings one back to reality;

hardly the stuff of sustained transcendence.

The authors of the manuals attempt to characterize much sexual activity as play; playing at seduction, playing at rape, playing as animals, playing with a variety of partners, experimenting in general as children do in games. Hopefully, this emphasis on play is obliterating a great deal of the grimness that has heretofore characterized so much sexual expression. The dictum that one should maximize sensations, that pleasure and gratification are the right of everyone, has probably moved American culture away from some of the problems associated with a more puritanical era. However, the implicit prescription that every man and woman must (or at least should) participate in sexual play is bothersome. So is the confusion in the manuals between play and games. Although the authors speak of sexual play, their descriptions usually border on sexual games. Unfortunately, most organized games, sexual or otherwise, seem to lose their playful character all too quickly. Actually, many of the playful escapades described in the manuals approximate the spontaneity and looseness that would characterize a refined interaction between Martin Heidegger's "das man" and George Mead's "generalized other"; perhaps pleasure, but very little, if any, fun. Unlike the previous sample of manuals we analyzed, the recent manuals do not define good sexual relations as merely a product of proper technique, diligent application, and mutual orgasm. However, the newer manuals almost seem obsessed with making sexual relations interesting through the stylization of its time, place, equipment, and manuevers. The emergent, spontaneous quality of human sexual interaction is lost in the linear exposition of the interesting sexual game.

A not unlikely hazard that inheres in all of this seems quite aptly characterized by Epstein's literary description of adultery.

On the forty-sixth floor of a luxurious building, commanding a splendid view of the city and of the lake, you committed adultery. The linen and towels were of the finest quality, and your partner in the escapade only slightly beneath them. She was experienced, complaisant, adept. To say that it was a casual encounter would be to make altogether too much of it.

REFERENCES

Chartham, Robert. 1970. *Sex for advanced lovers.* New York: New American Library.

Clark, LeMon. 1968. *101 intimate sexual problems answered.* New York: New American Library.

Comfort, Alex, ed. 1972. *The joy of sex.* New York: Simon and Schuster.

Copelan, Rachel. 1973. *The sexually fulfilled man.* New York: New American Library.

Copelan, Rachel. 1973. *The sexually fulfilled woman.* New York: New American Library.

Fellman, Sheldon, and Paul Neimark. 1977. *The virile man.* New York: Pocket Books.

Gray, Marlowe, and Urna Gray. 1974. *The lovers guide to sensuous astrology.* New York: New American Library.

Hegeler, Inge, and Sten Hegeler. 1974. *An ABZ of love.* New York: New American Library.

Lobell, John, and Mimi Lobell. 1975. *The complete handbook for a sexually free marriage.* Los Angeles: Pinnacle Books.

Magner, Ken, and Jeanadele Magner. 1977. *Liberated sex.* New York: Berkeley Medallion Books.

Masterton, Graham. 1975. *How to be the perfect lover.* New York: New American Library.

McDonald, Paula, and Dick McDonald. 1974. *Loving free.* New York: Balantine Books.

Reuben, David. *How to get more out of sex.* 1975. New York: Bantam Books.

10

COUPLES: THE AMERICAN WAY OF LOVING

Philip Blumstein and Pepper Schwartz

For American couples, the act of love is full of meaning. It always says something about the feelings of one partner for the other, the values they share and the purpose of their relationship.

To understand what sex means in the lives of our couples, we devised several measures. We tried to determine what each partner's expectations were and how well these expectations were being fulfilled. As sociologists we also looked at how couples use sex. Sex is an important resource partners have for influencing each other: They can use it to curry favor, to show displeasure, even to gain power in areas that have nothing to do with sex. And sex outside a relationship can also tell us a great deal about a couple and their expectations.

Sex, however, is not an isolated romantic haven. Money, religion, children—things that shape partners' behavior outside the bedroom also affected how they behave in bed. So we also weighed the impact of these external factors on our couples' sex lives.

Finally, we looked at the degree to which one partner worries about the other's having sex with someone else. Studying couples' views on monogamy tells us about the meaning of "loyalty" in couples and whether sexual variety can coexist with commitment.

Here, some of our findings.

DO PEOPLE KISS WHEN THEY MAKE LOVE?

Kissing may seem like the most innocent of sexual acts, but for some it is the height of intimacy. Many people told us that sex wouldn't seem as intimate if kissing were not part of it. This is particularly true for women. But some couples do not kiss every time they make love. We find that people kiss less during sex when they feel somewhat removed emotionally but still want a physical release. And couples who are feeling a lot of tension over mat-

---

Adapted from *American Couples* by Philip Blumstein, Ph.D., and Pepper Schwartz, Ph.D., as it appeared in *Redbook,* 1983, under the title "Couples: The American Way of Loving." Copyright © 1983 by Philip Blumstein and Pepper W. Schwartz. Reprinted by permission of William Morrow & Company.

ters that have nothing to do with sex or affection (money or work, for example) also kiss less often.

One wife described sadly how kissing had become a less regular part of having sex with her husband: "Kissing is equally important to both of us . . . but it's sort of becoming a lost art to us. . . . I think it's very erotic and I miss it. We kiss about fifty per cent of the time when we make love and it's always prior to the culmination of intercourse. . . . I think when you're in a marriage as long as I have been, you need to make an effort every four or five years to get back to kissing. We are trying to rediscover the art."

WHAT PART OF LOVEMAKING DO WOMEN ENJOY MOST?

Men have been accused of being obsessed with intercourse to the exclusion of all other sexual acts. Although it is true that most couples have intercourse when they have sex, and that men desire and initiate sex more often than women, intercourse is not always the way men most want to make love. When we look at what makes women and men happy with their sex life as well as satisfied with their entire relationship, we discover that intercourse is just one sexual act among others that men like—but a central ingredient in women's happiness.

Women prefer intercourse not because it is more physically satisfying but because of what it means to them. More than any other kind of lovemaking, intercourse requires the equal participation of both partners. So women feel an intimacy during intercourse they may not feel during other sexual acts.

Mitzi, a free-lance photographer, explained how she felt about having intercourse with her husband, Curt: "Intercourse is the emitting of emotion, and I think males only allow themselves to emit this emotion when they are in ecstasy. So for my husband, it is a real freedom. He's finally allowed to let go, to communicate, 'I'm happy. I'm having a good time. Oh, boy. Wow.' I think it's the best way he and I communicate."

Women may also feel that their male partners will not be as satisfied any other way. In their effort to please, women eventually measure the success of their sex lives by how often they and their husbands have intercourse. A woman may pick up on her partner's arousal and assume that his first and immediate desire is for intercourse. If he prefers to make love another way, she may feel slighted.

WHAT IS THE MOST COMMON POSITION?

The partner on top during intercourse has greater freedom of movement and is better able to direct the event. Both of these privileges may be thought of as traditionally male. Sometimes, of course, women do assume the superior position in lovemaking. But we found that this occurs more often when the man does not completely dominate the relationship and when the partners share power more equally. In these couples, the man does not always feel compelled to control the lovemaking, and his partner feels freer to try another position if she wants to.

As a woman acquires power in a relationship, her partner is more likely to respect her sexual preferences. When the woman does not always defer to the man's judgment, and when she has an equal say in the couple's decision-making, sex is more likely to include her being brought to orgasm by touch. She also feels more comfortable about telling him what she wants.

ARE WIVES GETTING WHAT THEY WANT?

When we asked people how sexually compatible they were, we found out that men feel their relationships are more compatible than women do. Because men are usually so much in control of the couple's sex life, this is not a surprise. Their female partners rated the very same relationships as less compatible. This is unfortunate because sexual compatibility is just as important to the wives as to the husbands.

WHICH SEX IS THE MOST POSSESSIVE?

When we asked people how troubled they would be if their partner had sex with someone else, we were surprised to learn that women are more possessive than men. This upsets many stereotypical notions: that men loathe being the "cuckold" and consider their women to be their "property"; that women forgive their men's wandering because it is a "natural" part of the male drive.

Instead, our findings show, women are more possessive than men because they are more vulnerable and dependent. Even after the gains of the women's movement, it is still harder for the average American woman to earn as much money as a man or to see herself as an independent force in the world. A woman still grows up believing she needs a man to take care of her and her children. We found possessiveness to be especially common among women with the most to lose—for example, those who are more committed to the relationship than their partner. They are frightened of what life would be like if their partner were to leave them.

WHICH SEX TAKES LOVE MORE SERIOUSLY?

How do people feel about sex without love? Wives are more likely to disapprove than husbands, perhaps because women have traditionally been taught to mistrust men who want to have sex before marriage. An unmarried woman may fear having sex without first being reassured of the man's love, or at least his respect. And a wife wants to believe that she and her husband were in love the first time they had sex. Now that they are married, she prefers to see their sexual relationship as sacred.

Gloria, a homemaker who has been married ten years, explained to us how sullied she would feel if her husband Pat were to have sex with someone else: "Before marriage we discussed monogamy and we both wholeheartedly agreed about how important it is. I don't believe in cheating and he doesn't believe in cheating. And it would make a mockery of marriage."

Married women feel that if their man is "different," then he can be trusted not to make sexual conquests. But this belief in their husbands' better nature also has its down side: If there is another woman, they assume the husband's interest cannot be casual or purely sexual. He's not that kind of man. No, the marriage must be in grave danger. An affair means the beginning of love for another and the end of love for her. No wonder wives are possessive!

Men, not surprisingly, feel different. They grow up learning that it is important to be sexually experienced before marriage. They may experiment with women whom they do not plan to marry in a context that is free from love or commitment. Neither their families nor their serious girl friends object to this, unless the men go overboard. When they marry it is assumed that they will put their sexual adventures behind them.

But most men continue believing that it is possible to have casual sex. As one husband, married for nine years, told us: "It's always been my belief that sex and love are two different things. For a man, sex is a physical thing and it can be as impersonal and as casual as shaking somebody's hand or eating a sandwich." Because men are so sure they can enjoy sex without romantic entanglement, many assume that if their wife was unfaithful, she too could put sex in its proper perspective and their relationship would not be endangered. Men are less possessive because they do not really expect women to look for outside sex and because they misjudge women's capacity to engage in sex without love.

But given what we have learned about women's sexual values, one thing seems clear: If a wife did have an affair, it would probably not be casual, and might well affect the future of their relationship.

HOW NORMAL IS JEALOUSY?

Couples sometimes take perverse delight in each other's possessiveness. They are making assumptions about what their partner's possessiveness says about emotional attachment. A very territorial partner is believed to be deeply in love and devoted to the relationship. A partner who shows no sign of jealousy is suspected of not really caring. Our data tell us that these feelings are misguided. Whatever causes some people to be more possessive than others, it is not their greater commitment to the relationship.

Testing a partner's feelings can be misleading. For example, a wife may flirt with another man at a party, hoping to get a rise from her spouse. If he seems jealous, she is pleased, believing he has demonstrated his commitment to her. But is it really his love that he's revealing? According to our data, what she may in fact be observing is his desire to display control of her actions.

What about the less possessive partner? Being unpossessive says little about a person's warmth, generosity or ability to love. Rather, the unpossessive partner is the one who has the upper hand—and knows it.

ARE WORKING WIVES TRUSTED LESS?

Couples, we find, fight less about sex outside their relationship—whether they are guilty of it or not—when the wife is a full-time homemaker. Husbands are less suspicious when they can account for their partner's whereabouts. But when their spouse is in an environment with workmates rather than mutual friends, they imagine the worst.

IS MONOGAMY OUT OF DATE?

In spite of all the worry about "infidelity," the personal standard that most people hold for themselves is monogamy. But what people believe and what they can live up to are two different things. More people told us they would like to be monogamous than have actually succeeded in doing so.

Fewer women have sex outside their relationship than men, and wives who have been non-monogamous usually have had only a few outside partners. Non-monogamous husbands have had more.

CAN YOU EVER BE SURE OF YOUR SPOUSE?

Ten years of monogamy does not mean the eleventh year is safe. Sex outside the relationship can occur at any point. Both new and well-established relationships are at risk.

In "young" marriages, husbands are less monogamous than wives. We cannot predict the future, but we think that about a third of the husbands and wives we surveyed will have extramarital sex sometime in the course of their marriage.

IF HE CHEATS ONCE, WILL HE DO IT AGAIN?

Our data indicate that extramarital sex may be an incident without becoming a habit. Most people fear that once a partner has stepped outside the relationship, he or she can never be trusted again. Or, if it is their own sexual involvement, they wonder whether they will be able to restrict themselves to their partner in the future.

We cannot predict what choices a specific individual may make, but many people do not go on to make a habit of non-monogamy. As one 26-year-old wife explains: "I was resisting the thought of being married—underline 'married.' I was restless. . . . I used having an affair as a way of expressing my worry about what I had committed myself to. . . . I consider it an unhealthy thing to have done and I selfishly put a lot on the line for very little. It won't happen again, I'm sure."

Many husbands have similar feelings, but there are more men than women for whom non-monogamy becomes a pattern rather than a one-time occurrence.

DOES LOVING YOUR HUSBAND KEEP HIM FAITHFUL?

Our findings show that the more powerful the man is in a relationship, the more non-monogamous he has been. Women are seldom the more powerful partner, but as they become more influential, they also become less monogamous.

Where does power come from? As we have seen, the less "needy" a person is, the more power he or she has. This was recognized over 40 years ago by the well-known sociologist Willard Waller, who wrote about the principle of less interest. According to this principle, the person who loves less in a relationship has the upper hand because the other person will work harder and suffer more rather than have the relationship break up. The partner's greater commitment hands power to the person who cares less.

In our study, we find that the partner who says, "I am more committed" is also more likely to be monogamous. He or she is too much in love and prizes the relationship too highly to look at other people.

DO CHILDREN MAKE MEN LESS FAITHFUL?

Having dependent children in the home has a big impact on marital relationships, particularly on husbands. Husbands with dependent children often told us that the presence of children interferes with sex. It is the quality, not the quantity, of sex they find wanting, since the couples' sexual frequency remains the same. Harold is a policeman, married ten years to Astrid, a homemaker. They are both in their early thirties. Harold explains how children get in the way: "We don't make love until the kids go to sleep. Then it's 'Be quiet,' or 'Don't make so much noise.' She actually put her hand over my mouth once. I was so pissed off, I just lost it."

Some husbands disagree with their wives about disciplining the children. Others think their wives give the kids too much affection. Herm, a graduate student in his late 20s, describes his wife Toni, 27, who has stopped working as a receptionist in order to take care of their new baby: "We are so tired, we just think of sex too late to do anything about it. And her body is still sore, she tells me. But I am afraid that she is also less interested. It's been four months and she puts so much into the kid that I feel she's more maternal than sexy. I am waiting because I do feel that it will get better."

Wives do not believe that the presence of children causes sexual problems. In our interviews they described child rearing as a temporary sexual inconvenience, or gave other explanations for sexual problems, such as fatigue or sexual incompatibility.

It may be that for mothers the rewards of children are so great that the costs are not recognized. Or the thought of children disrupting their sex lives may be so threatening to mothers that they will not consider it. We do not believe, however, that motherhood blinds women to the truth of what their husbands feel. Mothers simply accept the disruptions caused by children much more than fathers do.

ARE MEN WHO GO TO CHURCH MORE FAITHFUL?

We find that those who regularly attend church or synagogue are much more conservative in what they believe about sex. They feel that sex and love are inseparable, that pornography is bad and that homosexuals are not entitled to equal rights. But at the same time, there is very little difference between religious and non-religious couples when it comes to how they act. They have the same amount of sex. They are just as satisfied. They have no more and no fewer conflicts about sex. And, with few exceptions, religious people are as non-monogamous as anyone else. No matter how faithful people are to religious institutions, they are not insulated from the temptations of the flesh.

THE MYTHS OF EXTRAMARITAL SEX

It is widely believed that husbands and wives do not seek extramarital sex unless their marriages are unhappy. Another piece of folk wisdom is that spouses go outside for sex when there is too little of it at home. These are both misconceptions. We find that couples who are monogamous have neither more sex nor less than those who are not. However, some may say that it is not having a great deal of sex, but having very satisfying sex that keeps partners from straying. This also turns out to be untrue. Monogamous and non-monogamous husbands and wives are on the average equally pleased with their sex life at home. Another possibility exists: that spouses are non-monogamous because they are fundamentally unhappy with their relationship and are looking for a way out. Again, there is no evidence for this contention. Married people who have extramarital sex are, on the average, as happy with their relationship as monogamous couples. But they are not as certain that their relationship will last. These facts tell us two important things. First, most people are not propelled into extramarital situations by bad feelings about their marriage. Second, for most husbands and wives, infidelity is associated with less commitment to a future together.

V

DEVELOPING INTIMACY

11

DATING BEHAVIORS OF UNIVERSITY STUDENTS

David Knox and Kenneth Wilson

We stepped into the elevator on the way to our functional marriage course. Inside was a former student who said, "I really enjoyed that marriage class." We thanked her and asked what she liked about it. She replied, "I met my future husband."

If the number of women and men who go in their respective groups to campus movies is any indication, meeting partners of the opposite sex is a common problem among university students. "How do you meet people on this campus?" is a frequent question. As family life educators who talk about issues from bundling to test-tube conception we often have little data to answer some of the questions our students regard as most important. This study was designed to provide a series of answers to an array of questions including how to meet dating partners.

Previous studies on dating have focused on functions, types, desired characteristics of dating partners and premarital sexual behavior. Dating functions include recreation, companionship, socialization and mate selection (Winch, 1963; Skipper & Nass, 1966) whereas types of dating include playing the field, steady dating, and engagement (McDaniel, 1969). Specific dates may occur via the traditional method in which the man calls the woman or by meeting each other at a bar or party. The latter is referred to as "hanging around" (Libby, 1977).

What the partners look for in each other tends to be understanding, mutual affection, and emotional maturity (Melton & Thomas, 1976). Regarding their sexual behavior, depending on the study and the sample, between 50 and 80% of university students report engaging in intercourse during their premarital dating years (DeLamater & MacCorquodale, 1979; Bell & Coughey, 1980).

But this study focused on other aspects of dating. In addition to how students meet, we were concerned about where they go, what they talk about, and how much sex they expect how soon (or how late) in their dating experiences. We also asked about the degree to which their parents were involved in their dating relationships and how the students felt about such involvement.

David Knox and Kenneth Wilson, "Dating Behaviors of University Students," *Family Relations,* April 1981, pp. 255–58. Copyrighted © 1981 by the National Council on Family Relations, 1219 University Avenue Southeast, Minneapolis, Minnesota 55414. Reprinted by permission.

SAMPLE

Five hundred and fifty-five questionnaires were distributed to students at East Carolina University in 29 randomly selected classes. They were asked to complete the questionnaire at home and to return it at one of the next two class periods. Three hundred and thirty-four students (227 women, 107 men) completed the questionnaires (a 60% return rate).

The questionnaire included 21 close-ended questions about dating, sexual, and parental behaviors. These questions were developed from the responses to similar open-ended questions in a previous pilot study of 100 women and 100 men students at the same university. Chi-square was used to analyze the data.

TABLE 1
HOW 334 UNIVERSITY STUDENTS MET THEIR DATING PARTNER

Ways of Meeting	% Female n=227	% Male n=107
Through a friend	33	32
Party	22	13
At Work	12	5
Class	6	9
Other	27	41

MEETING/DATING EVENT/TALKING

How do university students meet the people they date? Most students reported that they came to know their current dating partner through a friend (Table 1). About a third met this way. Although other ways of meeting each other included "at a party," "at work" or "in class," no single way was mentioned as frequently as meeting someone through a friend. Those not meeting in these ways checked "other" which included "I grew up with him/her" and "we met on the school newspaper."

Going out to eat, to the football game (the data were collected during football season), to a party and back to his or her room was the typical agenda for an evening of dating. And for those who didn't do everything, eating out and going to his or her place seemed to be the most important.

But regardless of where they were, "our relationship" was the most frequent topic of conversation. About a third reported that this topic dominated what they talked about. Though less frequent, school and friends were other topics of conversation. Sex was discussed less than 5% of the time.

SEXUAL BEHAVIORS

The students revealed how many dates they felt they should have with a person before it would be appropriate to engage in kissing, petting, and intercourse (Table 2). Fourteen percent of both sexes felt that no dates were necessary for kissing to occur. Half of the women and 70% of the men felt that kissing on the first date was appropriate. And, by the fourth date, all but 3% of the women felt that kissing was o.k. Hence, kissing was viewed as appropriate within a short time.

But the responses about petting (hands anywhere) revealed more concern that this sexual behavior be delayed (Table 2). At least women felt that way. While over three fourths felt that petting should be delayed until after the fourth date, only one third of the men felt that way. Rather, almost one-third of the men felt that petting should occur on or before the *first* date.

Regarding intercourse, the tendency for men to want more sex quicker in the dating relationship than women was again evident. Almost half of the men felt that intercourse was appropriate by the fifth date in contrast to about 25 percent of the women.

SEXUAL VALUES

These women and men were aware of the discrepancies in how much sexual behavior how soon they and their partners wanted. Less than 15% of both sexes said that their dates always shared their understanding of how long people should wait before engaging in kissing, petting, and intercourse.

Since some of the students in the pilot study said that how much sex occurs how soon depends on the nature of the relationship and not on the number of dates, students in the present study were asked to specify the relationship conditions under which kissing, petting, and intercourse would be

TABLE 2
PERCENTAGE OF 227 WOMEN AND 107 MEN UNIVERSITY STUDENTS INDICATING
APPROPRIATENESS OF VARIOUS SEXUAL BEHAVIORS BY NUMBER OF DATES

Sexual Behaviors	0	1	2	3	4	5	6 or More
Kissing	W = 14%	W = 55%	W = 73%	W = 6%			
	M = 14%	M = 69%	M = 14%	M = 1%			
Petting	W = 3%	W = 4%	W = 5%	W = 9%	W = 3%	W = 15%	W = 58%
	M = 12%	M = 19%	M = 13%	M = 7%	M = 11%	M = 15%	M = 22%
Intercourse	W = 8%	W = 4%	W = 1%	W = 1%	W = 1%	W = 8%	W = 69%
	M = 8%	M = 11%	M = 9%	M = 8%	M = 2%	M = 10%	M = 52%

(Number of Dates)

appropriate. The various conditions included "feeling no particular affection," "feeling affection but not love," "being in love," "engaged," or "married." The results indicated that the more emotionally involved a person was in a relationship the more likely increasing levels of intimacy were regarded as appropriate. And, this was significantly ($p<.001$) more true for women than men. For example, intercourse with no particular affection was o.k. for about 1% of the women but for 10% of the men. That women are more concerned about the emotional context of a sexual relationship has been reported in earlier research (DeLamater & MacCorquodale, 1979; Reiss, 1967).

ENCOURAGING SEXUAL INTIMACY

What do university men and women do to encourage their partners to become more sexually intimate? Both say to be open about sex desires and expectations. "I get the sex issue up front," expressed one student; "I simply say that I want to make love." A quarter of the men and a third of the women encouraged sexual intimacy in this way. Other ways included "creating an atmosphere (music, candles, etc.)," "expressing love," "moving closer to," and "hinting." Women were more likely to use the latter two methods than men.

While alcohol and marijuana were not mentioned as being used on a frequent basis to encourage sexual intimacy, they were not uncommon on dates. Over half of the students said that they drank alcohol on their last date with fewer reporting use of marijuana. One-quarter of the men and 20% of the women said that they smoked marijuana on their last date.

DISCOURAGING SEXUAL INTIMACY

When partners disagree over whether or not to engage in increasing levels of sexual intimacy, the partner who does not want sex must do something to stop it. "Telling the partner to stop" is the way a third of the men and half of the women said that they discouraged sexual intimacy. "Ignoring sexual advances" and "keeping my distance" were also mentioned.

PARENTS AND DATING

Since our system of mate selection is "select your own" in contrast to arranged marriages in other cultures, the students were asked about their parents' involvement in their dating relationships. Women were significantly ($p<.01$) more likely than men to report that their parents tried to influence those they dated. Sixty percent of the women compared to 40 percent of the men said parental influence was involved. And, when asked, "To what degree have your parents interfered with your dating relationships?," the same pattern held—women were significantly ($p<.001$) more likely to say that their parents interfered.

Greater parental concern for the dating activities of the daughters over sons seemed to be what the respective sexes wanted. Women were much more likely to say that it was important to them that they dated the "kinds of people their parents would approve of." Twenty percent of the men said they didn't care what their parents thought in contrast to 10% of the women.

DISCUSSION AND IMPLICATIONS

Students often enroll in preparation for marriage classes to gain information they hope will be helpful in their own lives and relationships. One of their particular concerns is that they often have difficulty finding dating partners in a large university setting. Many look to parties, work, and classes as means of finding someone. But none of these ways (for these respondents) was as productive as meeting a partner through friends. Establishing relationships with *same* sex peers may be the best way to meet someone of the opposite sex. "When you don't have a date, go with a friend" is a suggestion family life educators might make to those seeking a partner.

Students might also be aware that (at least, on the basis of these data) discrepancies in what men and women expect on dates continues. Less than 15% felt that their dates always shared their understanding of how long they should wait before kissing, petting, and having intercourse. Men want to kiss, pet, and have intercourse in a shorter number of dates than women. And, since the result is potential conflict, students might be aware that other students encourage and discourage sexual intimacy in the same way—by being direct. To encourage sexual intimacy they tell their partner what they would like to do. Likewise, if they want to discourage sexual intimacy, they tell their partner to "stop."

Family life educators might help to prepare students for the potential conflict by making them aware of the discrepancies and encouraging in class communication exercises on such issues. One such teacher has developed such an exercise in which students verbalize what they expect from each other sexually.[1]

Differences also exist in reference to parental involvement in dating relationships. Parents exercise more influence/interference in the dating relationships of their daughters than sons (60 vs. 40%). Such parental involvement with the dating activities of their sons and daughters suggest that mate selection in America is not really "free." Individuals are not allowed to select their own partners. Rather, parents attempt to influence/interfere in the dating/mate selection of their offspring. Wanting their offspring to go with and marry "the right person with the right background" seems to be staple parental values in America. And in spite of the presumed "generation gap" most offspring regard their parents involvement in positive terms. Only about 25% report that they feel "very negative" or "negative" about their parents' involvement in their dating relationships. Family life educators/counselors may suggest to disillusioned parents that in spite of the resistance they may get from their offspring about their involvement in their dating activities, most students seem to feel good about limited parental involvement.

NOTE

[1] Britton, T. Personal communication. Lenoir Community College, Kinston, North Carolina, September, 1980.

REFERENCES

Bell, R. R., and K. Coughey. 1980. Premarital sexual experience among college females, 1958, 1968, and 1978. *Family Relations* 29: 353–57.

DeLamater, J., and P. MacCorquodale. 1979. *Premarital sexuality*. Madison: University of Wisconsin Press.

Libby, R. W. 1977. Creative singlehood as a sexual lifestyle: Beyond marriage as a rite of passage. In R. W. Libby and R. N. Whitehurst (eds.), *Marriage and alternatives: Exploring intimate relationships.* Glenview, Ill: Scott, Foresman.

McDaniel, C. O., Jr. 1969. Dating roles and reasons for dating. *Journal of Marriage and the Family* 31: 97–107.

Melton, W., and D. L. Thomas. 1976. Instrumental and expressive values in mate selection of black and white college students. *Journal of Marriage and the Family* 38: 509–17.

Reiss, I. L. 1967. *The social context of premarital sexual permissiveness.* New York: Holt, Rinehart & Winston.

Skipper, J. K., Jr., and G. Nass. 1966. Dating behavior: A framework for analysis and an illustration. *Journal of Marriage and the Family* 28: 412–20.

Winch, R. F. 1963. *The modern family.* New York: Holt, Rinehart & Winston.

12

DATING AND THE SINGLE PARENT

Lillian Africano

Back in the early fifties, I celebrated my sixteenth birthday and had my first real date. I died a thousand deaths as my parents inspected the young man to judge whether or not he was a fit companion for their precious daughter. Little did I dream then that some twenty years later I'd be playing out a similar scene as a recently separated mother of three.

This time my date faced a much rougher set of critics, a blue-ribbon panel consisting of my children: David, age twelve; nine-year-old Nina and five-year-old Arthur. None of them was prepared to like anyone I dated at that point, and the best I could hope for was an icy politeness—which is exactly what my gentleman caller got. As a matter of fact, the whole date was a little strained. I was as edgy as my children, and for good reason. We were all at the beginning of a new kind of experience for which we had no guidelines, no rules.

Many months later, when the dust, rubble and emotional fallout that accompanies any broken marriage had settled, we all became more comfortable in our skins again and more at ease in the new situations we faced together. But along the way, we struggled through any number of difficulties that have become increasingly commonplace in recent years. According to statistics, one child in six is being raised in a single parent home.

If life imitated television, every newly single parent would breeze through the new dating experience, and Saturday nights would be filled with the lighthearted banter familiar to viewers of *Eight Is Enough* and *One Day at a Time.* But in real life, flesh-and-blood children have complicated feelings about parents' dating—feelings that can't always be handled with a quip or an instant solution. And if the resingled parent doesn't recognize these feelings and respond to them, there may be problems that can cripple a family already troubled by death or divorce.

FIRST REACTIONS

Although each family has its own pulse and personality, younger children will generally be more tolerant and accepting of a parent's new adult friends. Teens and subteens, who are in the midst of discovering their own sexuality, will probably present stiffer resistance. But no matter how "liberal" a child's thinking seems, his initial reaction

---

Lillian Africano, "Dating and the Single Parent," *Woman's Day*, February 20, 1979, pp. 49–53. Reprinted by permission of *Woman's Day* Magazine. Copyright © 1979 by CBS Publications, the Consumer Publishing Division of CBS, Inc.

to Mom's or Dad's first date will usually be negative. "Mothers don't go out on dates," said my twelve-year-old son on that occasion—in the same no-nonsense tone he once used to inform me that mothers were "supposed" to play bridge. Both times he was raising questions about what a mother was "supposed" to be all about, and was letting me know that something I was doing (or not doing) required some explanation.

"After a death or divorce, the child expects and fears that the remaining parent is going to look for some adult company," says Dr. Donald J. Mayerson, a New York psychiatrist in private practice and on staff at both St. Vincent's and Lenox Hill hospitals. "The parent is entitled to this company, and the children don't have to suffer because of it. At the same time, the children need as much stability and security as the parent can provide. One way to give this is to begin a new social life in a thoughtful way and at a pace that will not make the child feel that his relationship with the remaining parent is being threatened.

"If a child is old enough, you can sit down and explain how much you cared for the deceased parent, or—if you're divorced—how much the marriage meant to you. Explain that you need friends of your own age, just as he does. But move slowly and with caution into the 'boyfriend-girlfriend' theme."

DATING TOO SOON

Well-meaning friends and relatives may urge the widowed or divorced parent to "get back into the swing of things," to "start living again." Children, however, rarely take such a sanguine and unselfish view of Mom's or Dad's playing boy-meets-girl with a perfect—or not-so-perfect—stranger, especially if the dating starts too soon after the marriage ends.

"There is no 'right time' for everyone," says Dr. Mayerson. "Children vary. Some eventually get tired of having all of Mom's or Dad's attention, and they're relieved when someone comes along to divert some of it. Others resist the idea for a long time. They may have fantasized having the parent all to themselves, and they will not welcome anyone who threatens that fantasy."

Probably few parents are immune from the problems of a transitional period, no matter how old the children are. I remember moments when it seemed that my children—especially my older son—were leading me, in none too subtle fashion, straight for a rocking chair built for one. At those moments I would feel martyred, resentful and full of arguments about parents rights and fair play. Fortunately I kept most of these to myself.

In time, when the grownup in me took over, I stopped worrying about my children's lack of understanding and tried to offer some of my own. I told them that they were the most important people in my life, that I would never do anything to hurt them—and then I tried to be patient. Gradually the resistance thawed, and the last holdout—my older son—let me know that we had turned a corner. One day we were shopping for school clothes, and the salesman was being very solicitous and charming. My son nudged me and whispered: "Hey, Mom, I think he wants to ask you for a date. Is he your type?" We both laughed, and that was the end of our "mothers don't date" period.

"WE DON'T NEED YOU—WHY DON'T YOU GO HOME?"

Children, like grownups, have different ways of handling situations that make them insecure or uncomfortable. Some withdraw; others come out swinging. A one-time neighbor of mine had one child, a little boy of ten who tried to play bouncer with any man who came to visit. "What time are you going home?" Joey would ask within minutes after a male guest's arrival. Sometimes if his mother wasn't in the room, he would go even further: "Why don't you go home—we don't need you here."

Other children have hit parents' dates with a wide range of rude and hard-to-ignore remarks, from "I don't like you" to "Mom's last boyfriend was much better-looking than you."

When this happens, a firm—but not punitive—response is needed. Children have to be told that although you understand what they are going through, there is no excuse for rude behavior to any guest or friend. Point out that they don't have to like all your friends in order to extend them common courtesy—just as you don't necessarily like all their friends but would not think of being unkind or hateful to them.

The same impulses that cause a child to become hostile can result instead in a fit of sulking every time Mom or Dad goes out. The silent sulk says, "Something's going on that I can't handle, and I don't seem to be able to do anything about it. But I'll be darned if I'll be cheerful and happy." Here again, a combination of patience and understanding is the most sensible response.

The child can be encouraged to talk about why he feels upset or threatened, and the parent can try to offer assurances to lay his fears at rest. Keeping the lines of communication open is important, even if it seems that no agreement is in sight. If you are pulling together and are busy building a satisfying life together, then acceptance on the dating issue will come in time.

MY CHILD THE MATCHMAKER

Occasionally children can be too agreeable, too "helpful" after they've accepted the dating procedure. They may fantasize a relationship between the parent and a favorite teacher, a scoutmaster or the Little League coach.

One fourth-grader, who very much missed the presence of a father or male friend in his life, was enchanted with his single and very popular male teacher. In Tommy's mind the teacher became a leading contender for Mom's hand. He tried to promote this match by involving his mother in all kinds of class trips and activities. Several times he embellished the teacher's general request for parent volunteers into personal invitations for his Mom alone. When nothing happened, Tommy asked his mother why she didn't invite Mr. Blank to dinner. At that point, Mom told Tommy that she appreciated his interest in her life and that she was glad he had found such a good friend in Mr. Blank. But, she added, friendships between people didn't happen just because someone wished they would, or because they seemed like a good idea. After all, she pointed out, Tommy couldn't stand the daughter of her best friend, no matter how much the two mothers wished they would get along.

A child's matchmaking efforts may not be subtle, but they shouldn't be laughed at. Though occasionally embarrassing, they can usually be gently discouraged.

WHO WANTS A MAN/WOMAN WITH CHILDREN?

After a death or divorce it's easy for the single parent to fall into a "Who will want me?" frame of mind. This is especially true in the case of single mothers.

One option is to adopt a "poor me" attitude. This will put into effect the Murphy's Law that says if you think of your children as a social liability, you will probably attract others who agree. At the same time, you will succeed in making your children feel pretty awful.

If, on the other hand, you can really appreciate the warmth, the sense of completeness that children give your home, then others will probably feel it too. While there is no guarantee that you will meet anyone who will accept you as you are, I have found it best to avoid—or drop quickly—anyone who acts as if the presence of my children is a high price to pay for a relationship with me.

MY CHILDREN ARE NO TROUBLE AT ALL

On the surface this attitude seems to be a positive one, but what it says, in effect is: "Yes, children are a drag, but mine are different." It tries to force children into best behavior and party manners, just to impress a stranger they would probably rather not have around anyway.

While I usually try to tone down the energy level of our three-children-plus-a-dog household for a first-time visit by anyone, sometimes fate steps in and gives a newcomer the full impact of our family circus. Once, a gentleman I *was* trying to impress paid a surprise call. As I opened the door, the dog bounded across the living room and leaped up to plant some very wet kisses on the man's face. My daughter was practicing gymnastic handstands, while my younger son played the "Cossack Dance" on the piano, and my older son cheered the television running of a horserace at Belmont Park. The gentleman did come back, and after that first encounter, we found it very easy to be ourselves.

Children obviously mean problems as well as joys, and the problems shouldn't be hidden. Says Dr. Mayerson; "I've seen awful second marriages take place because one of the partners has taken on the other's children without actually knowing what this involves. Sometimes the partner with the children tries to give the impression that life will be like *The Brady Bunch,* and when reality finally hits, it's like a nightmare."

WHEN CHILDREN DISAPPROVE

When children make negative comments about a newcomer, a single parent may take sides against his or her own children. But it may be unnecessary or unwise always to defend the person you date, especially if the defense makes the children think that you value a stranger more than you care about their feelings.

One man I dated made a serious blunder just minutes after he walked into my living room, where all the children were watching a hockey game. "I hate sports," said my date, without being asked. The three pairs of eyes turned on him, three sets of lips curled in scorn and three voices later pronounced him a sissy.

Since I, too, dislike sports, and since I have so far escaped my children's derision on that score, I assumed they were reacting to his patronizing attitude. I conceded that his manners could stand some improvement but said that I'd probably be spending an occasional evening with him.

The postscript to that evening was straight out of *The Odd Couple,* with my date as Felix Unger. Mr. X, it turned out, didn't like much of anything. He saw the world as a breeding ground for disease and disorder. On our second date, he announced he was allergic to dogs and refused to sit down anywhere in my house for fear of being blitzed by dog hairs. There was no third date.

Another instance wasn't so simple. In spite of the fact that they are being raised in New York City, my children have a fairly conservative, traditional set of values. They viewed with alarm my association with a man they described as a "hippie." Mr. Y had a steady job, but the children blanched at his long hair and his beard. What I had to do in this case was to show the children—in behavior as well as with verbal assurance—that I was not going to change simply because I associated with people who favored a different lifestyle. I tried not to defend Mr. Y too often, other than to point out that he was a kind, decent person. The children never did approve, but they did accept my right to see him.

"If children don't like your date, that may be perfectly natural," says Dr. Mayerson. "The problem comes if you feel caught in the middle. Then something is amiss. These situations are perfect setups for alliances—but they don't have to be. If you find yourself taking sides with your date, you might ask yourself if this pattern happened before. For example, when you were married, did you and your spouse line up against the children over certain issues?

"Playing us-against-them with a newcomer should be avoided. One way to do this is to make sure that the people you date don't try to impose their values or ideas on your children. I strongly feel that in a dating relationship, a newcomer should have little to say that affects the children. He should have nothing to say about their clothes, their behavior, their table manners. If there are problems he feels he must discuss, he should address his remarks to the parent."

DEFINING THE DATE'S ROLE

Just as there are people who behave as if your children are a natural disaster, there are others who will want to embrace them wholeheartedly, to create an instant family of their own. This may seem like a nice development, but it shouldn't be allowed to happen with casual dates. "Beware the date who wants to get involved with your children too quickly," says Dr. Mayerson. "You can create all kinds of problems if you allow children to become attached to someone and then have that person disappear. Letting this happen more than once can really be traumatic.

"If your date is genuinely motivated to spend some time with your children, there isn't any harm in an occasional movie, a trip to the museum or a shared day at the beach. The important thing is to identify the newcomer to your children. 'This is so-and-so. He is my friend.' He is *not* an 'uncle' or 'cousin' or anything else.''

BREAKING UP

Breaking up with someone your children have grown fond of can reinforce for them the very sad idea that people they like—especially adults—are apt to keep disappearing. That's why it's better to keep the child-date relationship from becoming "serious" unless you and your date are very serious.

If you and your date split up, you will have to help the child through this loss, just as you would help him through any other loss or disappointment. If the break-up is reasonably friendly, the former date can ease the child's sadness by keeping in touch for a while, by withdrawing gradually instead of cutting off all contact at once. One man who was willing to do this said: "I really liked that kid, and even though things didn't work out with his mother, I didn't want him to get hurt. It doesn't kill me to pick up the phone once in a while to say hello. When I have the time, I stop by at his Little League games, just as I used to do. I get a kick out of it, and I can see that it means a lot to him.''

ARE YOU GOING TO MARRY MOM? AND EVEN HARDER QUESTIONS

Since children are curious and frank by nature, a series of dates with the same person may lead to a question like "Are you going to marry my mom?" When that happens, the smoothest thing that Mom can do is to remain calm and reassure the child that he will be the first to know if and when a marriage is being considered.

A much harder question is: "Are you sleeping with Mr. Z?" There is no "right" answer for everyone, and no expert can give infallible advice that would apply to every family. Many newly single parents are right in the middle of their own crisis of values, trying to sort out just what it is they believe about their own sexuality and what they wish to teach their children.

In her book *Sex and the Single Parent* author Jane Adams presents the case for sexual frankness, arguing that there are "many situations more trauma-producing for a child than confrontation with parental sexual activity." My own feeling, however, is that a great deal of currently fashionable "honesty" merely dumps on a child all kinds of information he isn't equipped to handle. In most two-parent households sexuality remains a fairly private area, supported by fairly conventional values. If, when such a household breaks up, the remaining parent initiates a sexual revolution of his or her own, there may be unwelcome repercussions. Among these may be youthful imitation.

It's safe to assume that most single parents will not remain celibate for the rest of their lives. But as Charlotte Ford says in her soon-to-be-published book on modern manners: "I think it's important for your children not to meet your friends (lovers) at the breakfast table. Unless the children are very little, there's nothing casual about such a scene. A divorced person has every right to do whatever he or she wants, but until you are pretty secure in a relationship, I think it's best to keep the children out of it.''

Dr. Mayerson agrees: "If a widowed or divorced parent wants to have sex with someone he or she is dating, it should be on the outside—and it should be discreet. . . . When you create a sexual atmosphere around children, they may make all kinds of assumptions, may feel threatened or worried. I don't think they should have to deal with feelings like these unless the relationship is going to move from dating to something serious.''

Single parents have been around for a long time. But it's only recently that their numbers have dramatically increased—as has the probability that they will have a full and active social life. "What this means," says Dr. Mayerson, is "a new kind of personal contract between the parent and the children." After the loss of one parent, he explains, "you have a situation that calls for new rules and some of these involve dating. It's a situation that needs constant adjustment on both sides. . . . When parents begin to date again, it doesn't have to be a time only of problems; it can be part of the family's growth in a new direction.''

Every parent knows that a good parent-child

relationship can be enriched by every new shared experience. Dating is no exception, as long as Mom is really Mom when it counts. As long as you can communicate and discuss without becoming adversaries, it can be a time to learn together—about ends and beginnings and success and failure, about happiness and sadness, pleasure and responsibility, about new people and about one another.

13

FORMAL MATE SELECTION NETWORKS IN THE UNITED STATES

Davor Jedlicka

In recent years less conventional modes of mate selection have gained popularity in Western Europe (de Hoog & Jedlicka, 1978), Eastern Europe (Prokopec, 1974), and in the United States (Cameron, Oskamp & Sparks, 1977; Jedlicka, 1978; Strong, Wallace & Wilson, 1969). In addition to providing further evidence of this phenomenon in America, this study is also concerned with social psychological rationale that may account for it. Another purpose is to consider innovative modes of mate selection for clients who experience difficulties in conventional mate selection.

In the United States few values rank as high as romantic attachment. Yet, many people have little opportunity to meet suitable partners for sex and marriage. Some lack self confidence, and others have unacceptable traits for usual face-to-face relations, e. g., they are obese, very tall, very short, very old. Among these are some who, as a a result of their unawareness of an imbalance in the male-female ratio in their locality, mistakenly attribute their mate selection difficulties to personal inadequacies.

This paper suggests that at least some of these people could benefit from participation in selected formal mate selection networks including agencies, clubs, go-betweens, name-list brokers, and others who try to improve their clients' chances for contacts with the opposite sex. The word "network" captures the interdependence among brokers and agencies across the United States and abroad. The usual terminology—matrimony agency, computer dating, swinging clubs, etc., fails to encompass the variety of relationships that are sought and arranged. Clients may seek ephemeral or lasting relations with or without marriage. "Swingers" as well as the marriage minded are members of formal networks that cater to their diverse demands.

Counseling effectiveness may be improved by encouraging and aiding some clients to seek love, marriage, or companionship through less conventional means. Networks are particularly helpful when personal difficulties, social, demographic, or geographic barriers prevent easy initiation of intimate relationships.

BARRIERS TO MATE CHOICE AND EMERGENCE OF NETWORKS

Donald Neal, founder of one of the oldest correspondence clubs in America, assures his clients that,

---

Davor Jedlicka, "Formal Mate Selection Networks in the United States," *Family Relations,* Vol. 29 (1980), pp. 199–203. Copyrighted © 1980 by the National Council on Family Relations, 1219 University Avenue Southeast, Minneapolis, Minnesota 55414. Reprinted by permission.

"The ever-increasing ratio of men to women and women to men, in various age groups, makes the need and demand for correspondence clubs ever greater" (Neal, 1970, p. 10). The numerical disparity between the sexes in America is indeed an important barrier to successful mate selection through ordinary methods (Jedlicka, 1978). There is a considerable excess of single males under age 30. For example, in 1975 for every 100 never married females between the ages of 20 and 30, there were 193 unmarried males (U.S. Bureau of the Census, 1975). This ratio, however, declines progressively with age to reach 24 unmarried males per 100 unmarried females by age 75.

This enormous imbalance in the ratio of males to females occurs because younger females tend to marry older males even though females outlive males by about seven years on an average. Under such conditions, a certain proportion of young males will be unable to form enduring intimate relationships. Later in life, millions of aging women must remain widowed or divorced. Because opportunities for meeting eligible persons are seldom optimum, many join organized national networks in the hope of improving their chances of meeting the "right one."

Meeting the "right one" may be very difficult for those with narrow mate preferences. To illustrate, consider a 19-year-old girl who advertises in a matrimony magazine that she is searching for "love and marriage to a hip-looking, yet conservative partner." Judging from her age and picture there should be no shortage of suitors, but the combination of the "hip-looking and conservative" may be hard to come by in day-to-day life.

Personal advertisements expressing idiosyncratic desires are common among people seeking conventional or unconventional relationships. Consider the 21-year-old Mexican lesbian who describes herself as a "pretty, big breasted, petite type" and who seeks "permanent true love and sex with an extremely large, fat, white lesbian, up to 400 pounds." Such rare combinations of traits can best be matched through networks that extend beyond any one locality.

The desire of some Americans to marry out of their own race or ethnic group is another reason for the development of formal mate selection networks. As interracial marriages become more socially acceptable, many will feel freer to seek partners from different racial groups. But because of segregation and the unavailability of minority races in large parts of the continental United States, specialized networks bring Caucasians, Blacks, Hispanics and Orientals together.

Generally, when social, demographic or psychological conditions block formation of conventional or unconventional relationships, formal mate selection networks emerge. In the United States, these networks vary in discreteness, in the degree of third person involvement and in the sexual life styles of the members.

A NOTE ON METHODS

Most of the information in this study was obtained through content analysis of advertisements available to anyone for sale or inspection. When involvement in the networks was essential to determine how they operate, informants were used. There have been four informants, two of whom have searched for partners through networks on their own initiative. On two occasions unmarried people who were interested in dating through go-betweens and correspondence were recruited. Their membership-fees were paid in exchange for access to the solicited and unsolicited printed materials they received as a result of their memberships. They were also asked about their contacts with the go-betweens. No inquiry was made concerning any personal contacts or correspondence which resulted from their network memberships. Over the last five years these methods have been used to examine mate selection networks adapted for clientele of varied erotic desires. Some of these networks are discussed below.

NEWSPAPER NETWORKS

Bookstores, grocery stores and newstands across America distribute newspapers that carry personal advertisements for mate selection (Cameron, Oskamp & Sparks, 1977). A person who submits his advertisement for publication can be contacted only through the publisher who files all names and addresses and identifies each published ad by number and by the state of the advertiser's residence. An interested reader makes contact by writing letters in response to one or more advertisements. Each letter is sealed and identified by a number. These are then mailed to the publisher who, for a fee, addresses and forwards each letter. This procedure increases profit for the publisher and at the same time provides anonymity for the clients with a minimum of third person involvement.

Newspaper networks tend to develop separately for conventional and unconventional mate selection purposes. Conventional newspapers restrict advertisement to those who seek marriage. The unconventional cater to the "cheaters," "homosexuals," "swingers," "prostitutes," "bisexuals," etc. Each network reinforces the sexual standards of its members through editorial support. Thus, conventional and unconventional preferences can be expressed and chances for matches improved.

CO-PUBLISHERS NETWORKS

Co-publisher networks have operated in the United States for over 50 years. A co-publisher is a person who purchases matrimonial magazines from a publisher. The publisher profits from selling each issue of the magazine to as many co-publishers as he can recruit. Co-publishers advertise the magazine under their own names, recruit clients, and sell subscriptions or individual issues on request. They are known to their clients as matrimony agencies, friendship clubs, social clubs, etc. The publisher's identity is usually unknown to the clients.

Once a co-publisher and publisher enter into an agreement, the co-publisher places classified advertisements in popular magazines. When a client requests information, a magazine is forwarded with an application and further inducement to participate. On the first mailing, the co-publisher withholds the names and addresses, informing the client that these are available for a fee. The client is also told how to submit his own advertisements, and he is encouraged to subscribe to the magazine. If the client decides to advertise, he sends personal information and a picture to the co-publisher who retains a part of the fee and forwards the remainder to the publisher. The same procedure is followed by all other co-publishers in the network. Together they provide the publisher with enough new advertisers to keep the publication going.

These networks are not discreet. The pictures and information are widely distributed, and the names and addresses are made available to anyone who is interested. The people in these networks are invariably in search of conventional love and marriage. They often define their acceptable mates narrowly in terms of religion or other characteristics. Many have children and cannot date in the usual way. For them co-publisher networks expand the field of eligibles and provide contact opportunities that would not otherwise be available.

GO-BETWEEN NETWORKS

The use of informants was indispensible for discovering go-between mate selection networks. Through an inquiry from the "Headquarters" anyone may obtain information on how to join and what to expect from the network. That information was as follows:

> We have special confidential ways to provide identity protection. While we use modern electronic aids and retrieval methods, personal introductions require people. So every member is assigned to a membership coordinator and she handles all of the contact and referral details of your membership.

An informant who applied for this service verified that it operated as advertised. An application with a fee is mailed to the national "Headquarters," and from there it is forwarded to a local "membership coordinator." This person is a "go-between" in the traditional sense of the word. She contacts people by phone and makes arrangements for them to meet.

International go-between networks have been developed to introduce foreign girls to American males. American men are informed about these services through classified ads or small display ads in specialty male magazines. These advertisements indicate that agencies specialize in matching particular racial or ethnic combinations:

Guadalajara, centuries famous for its beautiful Spanish Mexican girls . . .
Blonde Swedish, lovely German girls, seek friends and husbands.

Chinese girls, exciting, attractive, loyal . . .
Japanese girls make wonderful wives.

On April 10, 1970, President Nixon signed into law a regulation whereby an engaged foreign girl can come to the U.S. to marry. This law made it easy for many Americans, even those with modest means, to seek and marry foreign girls. One agency boasts that "we usually can locate any age bracket that the client wishes, beautiful girls, good homemakers." That the agency can be successful is attributed to poor economic conditions. Young girls are said to be willing to come to America to escape the poverty in their countries.

Some agencies manage arrangements through their contacts and through their own bi-lingual staff visits to Latin America. Again the procedure is a network process which involves key managers abroad and in the United States. Through the network a client is able to overcome distance, language barrier and the cost that would be involved if he were to visit these countries on his own. Most networks, though, are not this involved and membership is not as expensive. Some agents never leave their offices. They collect photos and personal information from women abroad and pass them along to interested clients.

COMPUTER DATING AND VIDEO-MATE

"Computer Dating" is perhaps the best known method of managed mate selection (Strong, Wallace & Wilson, 1969). Computers are used to retrieve addresses of clients with matching characteristics. This matching is not accomplished through analytic methods such as a credit card company may employ in deciding whether or not a client is potentially a good credit risk. Computer matching is restricted to a few precoded categories of responses which are then sorted and matched in the manner that could be equally well accomplished through a punch-card sorter. The computer is an effective way for exchanging names and addresses of eligible people. However, as used today, it is among the least effective ways of matching idiosyncratic preferences.

Video-mate selection is a recent innovation. This service, unlike the others discussed here, is restricted to walk-in clients. A person videotapes a short self-description which is shown to other walk-in clients. Those who like the presentation purchase the address and phone number from the agent. This method minimizes third person involvement and appeals to those for whom identity protection is not important.

CONCLUSION

Due to current social and demographic conditions in America millions of people interested in sexual relations with or without marriage have difficulties achieving their goals through the ordinary face-to-face methods. Difficulties are compounded for those who fear failure, rejection or stigma. These people create a demand which maintains mate-selection networks in America.

Operations of such networks tend to specialize along two dimensions: the extent of the third person management and the extent to which the anonymity of clients is protected. Anonymity is crucial for clients whose sexual interests are illicit or who feel that unconventional mate selection methods are not socially acceptable. The third person involvement is greatest when it is direct as is the case with go-between networks. For example, matching very young girls in Latin America with older men in the United States requires considerable intervention. In other cases, go-between services are an option which some clients choose for expedience and discretion.

All networks discussed in this study may be classified according to these two dimensions:

Type of Third Person Involvement	Anonymity Yes	Anonymity No
Direct	Go-Between Networks	Traditional Arrangement
Indirect	Newspaper Networks	Computer, Video, Co-Publisher Networks

No national or international networks that provide direct personal service without regard to anonymity was found. This mode of mate selection seems to be restricted to traditional marriage arrangements in non-western societies (Freeman, 1968). In America such open personal service was widely practiced in the 1930's among Jews (Baber, 1939). Today, there is some unpublished evidence that Hindus in New York carry on this tradition. Generally, direct third person intervention is not acceptable in America even among those who abandon the conventional mate selection procedures.

Indirect third person involvement, such as management of mate selection networks, could be therapeutic for people suffering from mate selection anxieties. Through the networks a third person may be in the position to expand the field of eligibles, increase the number of choices and minimize the unpleasantness of the face-to-face rejections.

Counseling professionals may consider this alternative in addition to the usual "social skill training" (MacDonald, 1975). It is questionable whether "training and changing" are appropriate when personal characteristics which pose barriers in face-to-face matching count as assets in mate selection networks. For example, in networks, shyness, obesity, promiscuity, strong religiosity, and uncompromising standards of sexual behavior are openly sought and presented as individual variations that enrich the field of eligibles. In face-to-face situations, on the other hand, the same characteristics are likely to be interpreted as deviations or inadequacies.

In summary, the membership in formal mate selection networks reduces infringement on personality, minimizes the importance of appearance in initial encounters and allows clear expression of desired relationship commitment. These are network characteristics that lead to several hypotheses for further research:

1. People with idiosyncratic preferences or rare personal traits are more likely to feel self confident in formal mate selection networks than in face-to-face encounters.
2. The greater the imbalance in the male-female ratio in the client's community, the greater the chance of finding a match in a formal mate selection network as opposed to face-to-face encounters.
3. Widowed and divorced women with children are more likely to initiate affectionate, loving relationships through correspondence and network membership than through face-to-face encounters.
4. The consequences of initial rejection in a mate selection network are less intense than in face-to-face contacts.
5. The probability of forming lasting love and affection in mate selection networks is as great as in face-to-face contacts initiated by chance.

In the absence of data to support or refute these hypotheses, it might be argued that those involved in premarital counseling should maintain a neutral attitude toward the alternate mate selection procedures. Their clients when properly informed may wish to try some of the alternatives and open the opportunities for communion with others that otherwise might not be available.

REFERENCES

Baber, R. E. 1939. *Marriage and the family.* New York: McGraw-Hill.

Cameron, C., S. Oskamp, and W. Sparks. 1977. Courtship American style: Newspaper ads. *The Family Coordinator* 26: 27–30.

Freeman, L. C. 1968. Marriage without love: Mate selection in non-western societies. In R. F. Winch and L. W. Goodman (eds.), *Selected studies in marriage and the family,* 3rd ed. New York: Holt, Rinehart & Winston.

de Hoog, K., and D. Jedlicka. 1978. Partnerbemiddeling in Nederland en de Verenigde Staten. *Intermediair* 6: 15–19.

Jedlicka, D. 1978. Sex inequality, aging and innovation in preferential mate selection. *The Family Coordinator* 23: 137–40.

MacDonald, M. L., C. U. Lindquist, J. A. Kramer, R. A. McGrath, and L. D. Rhyne. 1975. Social skill training: Behavior rehearsal in groups and dating skills. *Journal of Counseling Psychology* 22: 224–30.

Neal, D. 1970. *Manual: How to operate correspondence clubs*. Vancouver, WA: Western Heart Club.

Prokopec, J. 1974. Knekterym problemum illdani zivotniho partnera pomoci samocinneho pocitace. *Demographie* 16: 23–31.

Strong, E., W. Wallace, and W. Wilson. 1969. Three-filter date selection by computer. *The Family Coordinator* 18: 166–71.

U.S. Bureau of the Census. 1975. Marital status and living arrangement: March 1975. *Current Population Reports* (Series p-20, No. 787), Washington, DC: Government Printing Office.

Photographs by Alan McEvoy

Part Three

TO MARRY OR NOT TO MARRY: THE QUESTION OF ALTERNATIVES

Despite the loss of various functions related to education, recreation, economics, and security, the family is still seen in our society as performing the important functions necessary for psychic well-being by providing love, stability, and loyalty (O'Brien, 1973, p. 51). It is also seen as the matrix for the development of personality (Ackerman, 1972, p. 16). It is little wonder, then, that the institution of marriage is thought of as part of the natural order of things. As a result, our value system has provided little social support for those who would prefer to remain single. Furthermore, we are socialized early to expect that we will eventually marry.

Such values have led to the belief that marriage is good and singleness is unfortunate, a bad state (Deegan, 1969, p. 9). Thus it is believed that people remain single because they are immature and unwilling to assume responsibility; or because they are unattractive ("real losers") or unhealthy either physically or mentally (latent homosexuals); or because they are socially inadequate (oddballs) and failed in the dating game; or because they were overconcerned with economics (self-centered); or because they were unlucky (Kuhn, 1955). In sum, "no matter how often it is called 'a positive, individual state,' the single life as . . . publicly drawn comes to this composite picture: the single is a poseur, a squanderer, a narcissist, a wastrel; he dances the hustle in the apartment house party room; loafs in his plastic sea horse in the . . . swimming pool; lives for lotions, balms and sprays; is a nonstop lover, drinker, laugher, and more (or less)'' (Rosenblatt, 1977, p. 14).

In the first article of chapter 6, Leonard Cargan and Matthew Melko examine these stereotypes and the retorts of the singles. It would appear that the "reality" of being single depends on one's marital status. Thus, singles could be considered deviant since they do not do as the majority does—get married. But, as the singles note, this does not ipso facto make them abnormal. Similarly, sexual behavior is considered normal only on a conjugal basis. But such beliefs ignore the long history and extent of behavior that would be called sexual deviancy, namely, premarital and extramarital sex.

In the second article, Peter Stein carries this examination a step further by noting who the singles are and what their needs are. As he indicates, the term *single* is becoming a label for a large and divergent category of people based on the one thing they have in common, their nonmarital status. The greatest need of these singles would appear to be a substitute network of social relationships to meet the needs of intimacy and companionship and to provide enduring bonds of social support. Otherwise, single life may become too lonely to be acceptable.

Fortunately for singles, numerous factors have emerged to make singlehood a more viable lifestyle. The processes of urbanization and industrialization have led to greater economic independence from the family, as well as fewer restrictions on behavior. A widening perception of rights has made it easier for individuals, especially women, to be independent. Also contributing to independence is the growth of such conveniences as frozen foods, fast-food restaurants, laundromats, and wash-and-wear clothes. Finally, the perception of singles as a market has led to the development of bars, clubs, and apartments for singles, special vacations and singles weekends at resort hotels, singles-only civic and church organizations, and even magazines and books for and about singles. These factors are all incentives to remain single. They provide the support needed for dealing with the pressures to seek the security and social benefits of marriage (Cargan and Melko, 1982, pp. 24–26). Added support is provided by the mass media, which exalt the free-floating single life, solitary but pleasurable and sexually fulfilling (Staples, 1978).

In sum, factors that make singlehood an attractive alternative to marriage include freedom from the restrictions of a binding relationship, self-sufficiency, increased opportunities for geographical mobility, and support groups (Kain, 1981, p. 3). There are, however, also many pressures that mitigate toward marriage, such as peer and parent socialization, cultural factors that idealize marriage, economic and social security, and desire for a family. The result of these mixed pressures is a delay in marriage, but the existence of the institution is not threatened. A nationwide survey revealed that Americans have a positive attitude towards marriage and that the vast majority of 18-year-olds planned to marry (Thornton and Freedman, 1983).

The desire for marriage or a marriagelike situation is seen in a study of college students' willingness to participate in traditional and alternative life-styles. Three of the four most popular choices were different types of marriage—egalitarian marriage, traditional sex-role segregated marriage, and five-year evaluation renewal of marriage. The fourth choice is the subject of chapter 7, cohabitation. Rejected by the students were such alternatives as spouse swapping, group marriage, and serial monogamy, while such alternatives as rural communes, children, marriage, and remaining single were reluctantly accepted (Strong, 1978).

This strong acceptance of cohabitation is reflected in the large increase in persons living together. According to the Census Bureau, from 1970 to 1980 their numbers increased from 523,000 to 1,560,000, and this figure probably underestimates the actual number of cohabitants (Glick and Spanier, 1980). The reasons for this growth include a more permissive attitude toward sex, improved methods and availability of birth control, the challenge to the double standard by the women's movement, and the relaxing of the *in loco parentis* role of the university.

The consequences of such growth can be viewed from the perspective of society or from that of the individual. Socially, cohabitation is not a threat to marriage since most people living together expect to marry eventually. However, it could delay marriage and so affect the birth rate. For the individual, the gains of cohabitation include companionship, sexual gratification, and economic savings (Newcomb, 1979). But, according to the first article in chapter 7, this explanation of the cohabiting relationship is too simple, since there are at least four patterns of living together, and each has its costs and benefits. The authors call them "Linus blanket," "emancipation," "convenience," and "testing."

The second article, by Barton Bernstein, deals with the problems that can arise if cohabitation lasts a long time and involves complete sharing, or if it ends up as an unplanned common-law marriage, or if the cohabitants decide to split up. Bernstein recommends a formal agreement be drawn up, covering the issues of real estate, personal property, insurance, and children, if any.

This section on alternatives is rounded out with discussions of alternative sexual relations within marriage and alternatives to monogamous marriage. One of the results of today's emphasis on self-growth is the belief by some that conventional marriage "imposes severe limitations on the personal growth of marital partners." The result is a dilemma between "the desire for personal growth and the restrictions imposed by "conventional marriage" (Myers, 1977, p. 35). Extramarital sex (EMS) could be self-enhancing when people value their marriage as the primary relationship and use EMS as a supplementary source of emotional or sexual gratification (Atwater, 1982).

In the first article of this chapter, David Weis concludes that such factors as the "isolation of the nuclear family, the growing egalitarianism of male/female relationships, the greater acceptability of premarital sex, the increasing mobility of American society, the advent of contraceptive technology" are all leading to increases in nonexclusive behavior. This behavior may include extramarital sexual relationships, swinging, sexually open marriages, intimate friendship networks, multilateral marriage relationships, and extramarital nonsexual relationships. In the second article of chapter 8, James Ramey carries these ideas a step further by noting the impact of various other changes on family forms. He indicates that such experimental family forms as group marriage and communes are developing due to our obsession with personal freedom, the effects of revolutions in demography, biology, economics, and communication, and the transformation of our sexual attitudes.

STUDY QUESTIONS

Chapter 6

Cargan and Melko
1. Describe three of the myths uncovered by this study.
2. Describe three of the realities demonstrated by the study.

Stein
1. What are the major tasks faced by singles?
2. Describe the coping styles of never-married adults.

Chapter 7

Ridley, Peterman, and Avery
1. Describe a benefit of each type of cohabitation.
2. Describe a cost of each type of cohabitation.

Bernstein
1. What are some of the benefits of having a prenuptial agreement?
2. What items should be included in a prenuptial agreement?

Chapter 8

Weis
1. Explain the basic social scripts for nonexclusivity.
2. Explain three of the different types of nonexclusivity.

Ramey
1. Indicate three areas of change and how they have affected experimental family forms.
2. Name several benefits of group marriage and communal living.

REFERENCES FOR PART THREE

Ackerman, Nathan W. 1972. In *Marriage: For and against*, ed. by Harold Hart. New York: Hart.

Atwater, Lynn. 1982. *The extramarital connection*. New York: Irvington.

Cargan, Leonard, and Matthew Melko. 1982. *Singles: Myths and realities*. Beverly Hills, Calif.: Sage.

Deegan, Dorothy Y. 1969. *The stereotype of the single woman in American novels: A social study with implications for the education of woman*. New York: Octagon.

Glick, Paul C., and Graham Spanier. 1980. Married and unmarried cohabitation in the United States. *Journal of Marriage and the Family*, February.

Kain, Edward L. 1981. Social determinants of the decision to remain never married. Annual Conference of the American Sociological Association, August.

Kuhn, Manfred. 1955. How mates are sorted. In *Family, marriage, and parenthood*, ed. by Howard Becker and Reuben Hill. Lexington, Mass.: D. C. Heath.

Myers, Lonny. 1977. A couple can also be two people. In *Marriage and alternatives: Exploring intimate relationships*, ed. by Roger W. Libby and Robert N. Whitehurst. Glenview, Ill.: Scott Foresman.

Newcomb, Paul Jr. 1979. Cohabitation in America: An assessment of consequences. *Journal of Marriage and the Family*, August.

O'Brien, Patricia. 1973. *The woman alone*. New York: Quadrangle.

Rosenblatt, Roger. 1977. The self as a sybarite. *Harpers*, March.

Staples, Robert. 1981. *The world of black singles: Changing patterns of male/female relationships*. Westport, Conn.: Greenwood.

Strong, Leslie D. 1978. Alternative marital and family forms: Their relative attractiveness to college students and correlates of willingness to participate in nontraditional forms. *Journal of Marriage and the Family*, August.

Thornton, Arlan, and Deborah Freedman. 1982. Marriage vs. single life. *ISR Newsletter*, August.

VI

SINGLES

14

BEING SINGLE ON NOAH'S ARK

Leonard Cargan and Matthew Melko

The world throughout history goes marching two by two. From Noah's Ark to the socialization process of today's society, two is the proper number, and in a world that counts by twos, the pressure to marry has been overwhelming.

THE GROWING SINGLES POPULATION

Whatever the social pressures, it is clear that singles have been growing as a percentage of the population in America. Since 1960, there has been a marked increase in the number of single households with a resultant decline in the number of nuclear families. Between 1960 and 1975, the number of adults between the ages of 20 and 34 who have never been married increased by 50 percent, while in the same period, the divorce rate doubled. The large increase in divorce is emphasized when it is noted that 39 percent of first marriages now end in divorce within 10 years, and 40 percent of second marriages end so within five years. In addition, the time interval between divorce and remarriage has increased, and so the number of those divorced but not remarried has doubled in the decade from 1963 to 1973. Thus, there has been a slowdown of marriage and remarriage versus a speed-up in the rate of divorce; the annual rate of first marriages has not been keeping pace with the growth of the prime age group for first marriages, and the divorce rate is now at the highest point in our history. The result is that there are now over 58 million single adults aged 18 and over (Stein, 1983, p. 27).

Why is the percentage of singles increasing? Consider first why we marry. Reasons given by marriage authorities include the bond of love or sex, mutual aid in the struggle for existence, and the desire for children (Ackerman, 1972, p. 12).

The changes that have occurred in the industrial age have undermined much of the logic behind these marriage imperatives of providing children, mutual aid, and love. The processes of urbanization and industrialization have reduced the percentage of people involved in farming occupations from more than 90 percent to fewer than 10 percent; more recent developments in organizational structure have meant a decline in the percentage of people engaged in family businesses;

Leonard Cargan and Matthew Melko, "Being Single on Noah's Ark," in *Singles: Myths and Realities* (Beverly Hills: Sage Publications, Inc., 1982). Reprinted by permission of the authors.

developments in medicine have reduced infant mortality. All of these factors have greatly reduced the importance of the child-bearing functions of the family. Then came the development of effective means of preventing conception: oral contraceptives and outpatient sterilization.

There have also been changes in the need for mutual aid in the struggle for existence. National highway systems and air transportation have greatly increased mobility, which in turn has contributed to the undermining of the extended family and therefore, for many people—married and single alike—a greater dependence on an extended community of friendships. Add to this a complicated change in attitudes that is partly independent of the change in family structure and partly reinforced by it: continued secularization of religion, a changing perception of the individual, and a widening perception of the rights of minorities, including women, blacks, the handicapped, and homosexuals.

For example, greater attention has been given to equal opportunity hiring practices, and this has provided women with greater opportunities for financial independence. It may also have reduced the perception of the single man as irresponsible and thus reduced pressure on him to marry or remain married.

Other factors that have emerged fortuitously have added to the independence of individuals from the need for marriage: the emergence of fast food restaurants, for instance, and, even more important, frozen foods, along with the development of laundromats, clothes that do not require ironing, and various convenience services. The increase in singles and a perception of them as a market have resulted in the development of bars and clubs for singles, packaged vacations for singles, small cars, new insurance policies, and various other benefits that, in turn, provide further incentive to people to remain single (Stein, 1976, p. 38). Also affecting the traditional appeal of marriage and family life for young people is the rising divorce rate and increasing criticism of this life-style by scholarly and mass media sources (Stein, 1978, p. 5).

In sum, there are many pressures which militate toward marriage, such as economic security, cultural pressures that idealize marriage, peer and parental socialization, and a desire for a family. However, there are also factors that make singlehood attractive in comparison to marriage, such as freedom from the restrictions of a binding relationship, self-sufficiency, increased opportunities for geographical mobility, and the existence of supportive groups (Kain, 1981, p. 3).

STEREOTYPES ABOUT SINGLES

Because there is a natural lag between the various steps of the scientific process, from awareness of an issue to the formation of hypotheses, it is not surprising that social scientists did not really begin to focus on the growth of singles until the 1970s. In the 1960s, family sociologists "either ignored singles or relegated them to boring out-of-date discussions of dating" (Libby, 1978, p. 164). Even in the seventies "they seem to deny that change was possible in family structure, the relations between the sexes, and parenthood" (Skolnick and Skolnick, 1977, p. 3). With the values of society strongly in favor of marriage and family (Ackerman, 1972; O'Brien, 1973) and little scientific knowledge of singles, singles were not perceived as a distinct social entity "that had its own characteristics, dynamics and unique features" (Adams, 1976, p. 10). Instead, singles were described with stereotypical images, usually negative, that implied they were carefree but incomplete, lonely, and undesirable. In addition, there was a change in the terminology being applied to the unmarried. The terms "bachelor" and "spinster" were replaced by the term "single" (Readers Guide). Although the concept was supposed to be specific to the never-married, it has been applied to all of the unmarried, thus blurring the distinctions between never-marrieds, divorced, redivorced, and widows. This has led to all unmarrieds being tainted with the same stereotypes and to ignoring their particular needs.

The stereotypes must be investigated because they may lead to serious and often unperceived discrimination. In order to deal with these stereotypes, a survey was made from a probability proportionate to size sample of 400 households from the Dayton metropolitan area—an area considered by George Gallup to be one of the ten typical areas of the nation *(Dayton Journal-Herald,* 1976, p. 1). Because it was not believed that all singles (or, for that matter, all marrieds) were alike, the sample data was subdivided into the categories of never-married, divorced, married, and remarried. Widows constituted too small a percentage of the respondents and were replaced via the sampling technique.

MYTHS AND REALITIES

It was believed at the beginning of the study that most of the stereotypes would prove to be myths and that singles would turn out to be similar to marrieds. However, as will be seen, stereotypes are indeed myths but others are or have become realities.

Myths

Singles Are Tied to Their Mother's Apron Strings. This stereotype is the belief that an attractive man or woman has not married due to an unresolved relationship with a parent. The data indicates that there is little difference between the never-married and married in their perceptions of relations with their parents. The divorced are not usually part of this image since they did, after all, get married.

Singles Are Selfish. The stereotype is that singles do not get married because they are too centered on themselves. But the selfish single does not emerge from the data. Singles were indeed more likely than marrieds to go nightclubbing (38 percent versus 16 percent) than to visit grandparents (19 percent versus 10 percent). So, even though likely to value success (36 percent versus 30 percent) and personal growth (56 percent versus 47 percent) whereas marrieds are more likely than singles to value love (63 percent versus 45 percent) and community service (28 percent versus 24 percent). Singles, however, are more likely than marrieds to value friends (56 percent versus 35 percent) and proved to be greater contributors to community service of two or more hours per week (19 percent versus 10 percent). So, even though marrieds are likely to value community service more, the singles deliver.

Singles Are Rich. Singles ought to be richer than marrieds—they have no spouses and children to support, they live in fancy condominiums or bachelor pads, and they are always out a'roaming. This "Joe Namath" image does not seem to be realized by most singles. Many are young, at the bottom of the economic ladder. Others are divorced, trying to support children and two households. On the whole, marrieds are better off economically than singles.

Singles Are Happier. Generally most people say they are happy most of the time. But on a number of specific questions about areas that would seem to contribute to happiness, the responses indicate there is more unhappiness than would be expected from the answer to the general question. On most of these responses, the indications are that singles are less happy than marrieds. For instance, on the loneliness questions singles were more likely than marrieds to be depressed when alone (24 percent versus 15 percent), much more often feel they have no one with whom they can really share (71 percent versus 44 percent) or discuss (66 percent versus 49 percent). Regarding health, singles are more likely to feel anxious (25 percent versus 17 percent), guilty (21 percent versus 11 percent), despondent (18 percent versus 10 percent), and worthless (19 percent versus 10 percent). Two possible signs of trying to compensate for unhappiness might be using pep pills and getting drunk often. Sure enough, singles are more likely than marrieds to use pep pills (11 percent versus 49 percent) and more likely to get drunk once a week or more (21 percent versus 7 percent). Finally, in total contemplated or attempted suicides, singles were again higher (55 percent versus 35 percent). All in all, there is very little here to support the idea that singles are happier than marrieds and much to suggest that they are, by several measurements, considerably less happy.

Singles Are Increasing in Numbers. This is true in America if we are considering numbers. But the percentage of singles in the population is lower today than it was at any time before World War II, and today's percentage appears to have peaked and to be approaching decline. It could be that even in numbers singles will be declining by the late eighties or early nineties. In sum, a demographic survey indicates that the growth of singles in the sixties and seventies was largely a function of the baby boom of the forties and fifties, and that even if the percentage of divorced population continues to increase, it is not likely to compensate for the decrease in the percentage of young adults.

Being Single Is Acceptable. This is a myth advocated but not accepted by singles. A review of titles in the *Readers Guide* throughout the century indicates that there has been little change in the preoccupation of singles with marriage. Titles about mate finding were as prevalent as ever in the seventies, and so were articles about making the best of it—implying that one must endure it if one cannot change it.

There Is Something Wrong with Singles. By measures of happiness or loneliness, singles may not be as well off as marrieds. However, there is nothing wrong with being lonely or sad some of the time. By measures of freedom singles may be better off than marrieds, but that does not make it wrong to marry. A married person may sometimes or often wish for freedom from the responsibilities of marriage, but on the balance she may consider it better to remain married. So may a single consider it on the balance to remain single, even if loneliness is a price to be paid. No, there is nothing wrong with being single.

Realities

Singles Are Deviant. It may seem incongruous to state that the image of something wrong with singles is a myth, but that singles are nonetheless deviant. But normality and deviance are defined by perceptions and the stereotype perceives marriage as normal. The label is usually applied to the singles who are in the 30–50 age bracket. Singles in this age bracket have been labeled deviant because they are not following the norm, not because their behavior can be demonstrated to be abnormal.

Singles Have More Time. This image has been posed in a different way. The marital image is that singles are free—they come and go as they please without worrying about baby sitters, they sleep nights without waking for children, and they go on vacation where they like. Focusing on time, it does appear that singles have more time than marrieds. More of them are likely to be spending more time visiting friends (66 percent versus 39 percent), and more are likely to be spending more time on hobbies (71 percent versus 56 percent). Singles are more likely than marrieds to go out socially twice a week (22 percent versus 16 percent) and much more likely to be out three or more times (30 percent versus 8 percent).

Singles Have More Fun. It may seem something of a contradiction to assert that although singles are less happy, they have more fun than marrieds, especially since they do not think so themselves (75 percent versus 83 percent). Then why say singles have more fun? Because in most specifics in which fun is imagined to be involved, singles are more involved. As just indicated, singles have more social outings. When they do go out, they are more likely than marrieds to go to movies, nightclubs, and theaters while the marrieds are going to social clubs, restaurants, or visiting relatives. When singles visit friends, they are three times as likely as marrieds to sit around smoking marijuana—a sharing, pleasurable experience—or getting drunk—which may be fun while you are doing it. In sum, it is possible that a person can go to dances and nightclubs, go out bicycling and camping more, and, in general, have high experiences but still on a day-to-day basis feel less happy.

Singles Are Swingers. From the standpoint of variety, singles have had more sex partners than marrieds at every level of involvement, 24 percent to 19 percent at 2–3 partners, 23 percent to 16 percent at 4–10 partners, and a decisive 19 percent to 6 percent at 11 or more partners.

Singles Are Lonely. It was expected that singles are neither happier nor lonelier than marrieds. The evidence from this study indicates that neither of these expectations were met. Thus, singles are more likely than marrieds to feel that they have no one to share with or discuss matters with. They are also more likely to feel that most people are alone. They are more likely to feel depressed just being alone and join social organizations because of loneliness. The answers on these specific kinds of activities reinforced the impression that singles are more lonely than marrieds.

Life for Singles Is Changing for the Better. Despite such continuities as a continued anticipation of marriage in the future, life and perceptions were qualitatively different for singles in the seventies and eighties from what they had been in previous decades of this century. The universal norm of marriage was being challenged for the first time in the seventies. There was an increase of articles in the sixties and seventies about single life, articles that took the lifestyle for granted and gave practical advice on the special problems of singleness. Another example seems to be the reduction of sexual frustration in the seventies. Though singles may not be as satisfied sexually as marrieds, the channels to satisfaction seem to be opening. There is also the changes involved with technology such as wash-and-wear clothing, laundromats, frozen foods, and fast-food restaurants. Finally, there is a perception of singles as a market and the accompanying development of items specifically for them such as apartments, vacation spots, and tours.

This examination of the myths and realities of being single allows for the dealing with the specific needs of singles. That is, by recognizing rather than ignoring such realities, singles can make a reality of that which earlier was referred to as a myth—being single is acceptable.

REFERENCES

Ackerman, Nathan W., in Harold Hart (ed). *Marriage for and Against*. New York: Hart, 1972.

Adams, Margaret. *Single Blessedness: Observations on the Single Status in Married Society*. New York: Basie, 1976.

Gallup, George. *Polster Visits Nation's Barometer. Dayton Journal-Herald,* June 22, 1976.

Kain, Edward L. Social determinants of the decision to remain never married. *American Sociological Association,* 1981.

Libby, Roger W. Creative singlehood as a sexual lifestyle: Beyond marriage as a rite of passage. In Bernard I. Murstein (ed). *Exploring Intimate Lifestyles*. New York: Springer, 1978.

O'Brien, Patricia. *The Woman Alone*. New York: Quadrangle, 1973.

Skolnick, Arlene and Jerome Skolnick (Eds). *Family in Transition*. Boston: Little, Brown, 1977.

Stein, Peter. The lifestyles and life changes of the never married. *Marriage and Family Review,* July/August 1978, 1–11.

Stein, Peter. Singlehood. In Eleanor Macklin and Roger H. Rubin (Eds). *Contemporary Families and Altnernative Lifestyles*. Beverly Hills, California: Sage, 1983.

Stein, Peter. *Singles*. Englewood Cliffs, New Jersey: Prentice-Hall, 1976.

15

MAJOR TASKS FACED BY SINGLE ADULTS

Peter J. Stein

Included among the major tasks faced by single adults are: achieving and maintaining friendships, intimacy, and fulfilling sexuality; maintaining emotional and physical well-being; making satisfactory living arrangements; seeking and finding productive work; becoming successful parents; and adjusting to aging. These issues are faced by all adults and they require decision making, the expenditure of physical and emotional energy, value and goal clarification, and resource allocation. The accomplishment of these tasks yields varying degrees of satisfaction, pleasure, discord, stress, and happiness. The discussion that follows is not meant

---

Peter J. Stein, "Singlehood," pp. 33–47 in *Contemporary Families and Alternative Lifestyles,* edited by Eleanor D. Macklin and Roger H. Rubins. Copyright © 1983 by Sage Publications, Inc. Reprinted by permission of Sage Publications, Inc.

to be exhaustive, but rather to highlight the major tasks and issues for single persons.

Friendship, Intimacy, and Sexuality

All humans need intimacy, yet the experiences of intimacy differ for single and married people, and among singles. Society today is undergoing a well-publicized revolution with regard to sexual attitudes and behaviors, and gender roles. One product of this is the growing acceptance of sexual relationships outside marriage, thus increasing the options available to single men and women (Libby, 1977).

Increased social and sexual availability presents both opportunities and problems. Personal enrichment, access to a variety of ideas and encounters, and the opportunity to select associates and activities consistent with one's own needs and goals are obvious advantages. Problems include limited access to the world of the married, the stress of juggling ever-shifting emotional commitments, the uncertainty of the commitment of others, and the lack of role clarity and social endorsement.

An important sexual outlet for singles, as well as for married people, is masturbation. Though there are no data regarding whether singles masturbate more or less than the general population, it can be assumed that its incidence is at least as high as the adult average, that is, 95 percent of men and 63 percent of women (Hunt, 1974).

Some single men and women choose celibacy (Brown, 1980), either as a long-term voluntary state, or as a temporary, perhaps difficult, state between relationships. Celibacy may be a religious requirement, may arise out of moral conviction, may be a means of conserving energy for creative endeavors, or may represent a flight from intimacy. The celibate person's degree of satisfaction with this lifestyle depends on the degree of motivation and on the freedom of choice.

Some singles have elected to be part of a new movement called the "New Celibacy." Its proponents argue that they are celibate by choice, not through default, often because of the disappointments, displeasures, and stresses of one-night stands. Some, such as Gabrielle Brown in *The New Celibacy* (1980), discuss the value of taking a vacation from sex. Critics argue that if celibate singles had a choice, they "would prefer a loving, sexual relationship with a partner" (Shostak, forthcoming). This debate will undoubtedly continue.

For many singles, sexual experimentation is a part of their single identity, enjoyed for itself or used as a stage leading to marriage or choice of a single sexual partner. Those who try a variety of relationships can learn much about the world and about themselves. They may avoid commitment in order to work on a career or on personal growth, or to recover from a painful past relationship. Some set up a hierarchy of relationships involving special obligations to a primary partner and lesser responsibilities to others. Personal enrichment is a possible benefit of this style of relationship, but the stress of managing conflicting commitments and a lack of clarity about one's role are potential problems (Clayton and Bokemeier, 1980).

There are two other sexual lifestyles that bear mention. Casual sexuality—whether heterosexual or homosexual—is more frequently practiced by single men than by single women. Many women find it difficult to be assertive enough to find a variety of partners, and women's commonly held ideas of love are more likely to be violated by this seeming promiscuity. "Relationship" sexuality is a more popular choice with women, whether as part of a monogamous or a sexual experimental lifestyle. A relationship is considered to be "leading somewhere" and sexual intercourse symbolizes a degree of caring between the partners (Laws and Schwartz, 1977).

Many singles believe that an individual cannot love more than one person at a time. Those who adhere to the Judeo-Christian ethic often prefer a monogomous relationship—a single sexual partner—even if it is without the obligations and daily responsibilities of marriage. As needs and desires change, these persons may move on to new partners, in a kind of serial monogamy.

Nonmarital cohabitation is a major source of intimacy for growing numbers of singles. Most cohabitors consider their relationship important, affectionate, supportive, and exclusive of other sexual involvements. Those who live together often claim to gain deeper self-understanding and emotional growth. Many homosexual as well as heterosexual couples choose cohabitation as a shorter- or longer-term alternative to marriage (Macklin, 1980).

Persons who elect a homosexual lifestyle often remain single because of legal constraints on gay marriage. Same-sex relationships may be just as diverse as heterosexual relationships. Some gay people prefer a permanent partner in a marriagelike arrangement, while others prefer living a single lifestyle. Public acceptance of homosexuality is an increasingly important issue for gays, as is active participation in the gay subculture. Political consciousness of the gay community is growing as are various gay and lesbian support systems (Vida, 1978; Levine, 1979).

Emotional and Physical Health

Historically, studies have shown that married people live longer than unmarrieds and that they use health care facilities less often. The complex cause-and-effect relationship between marital status and better health has been acknowledged, but more recent studies suggest that this relationship may no longer be as strong.

In a comprehensive review based on data from two national health surveys, Verbrugge (1979) writes that limiting chronic and work-disabling conditions are rather low for "noninstitutionalized single people." Among singles, the divorced and separated have the worst health status, followed by the widowed and the never married. Noninstitutionalized never marrieds "are the healthiest of all marital groups. . . . They take the least time off for health problems and have lowest utilization of physician and hospital services" (Verbrugge, 1979: 270). However, institutionalization rates for the never married are relatively high, and the total singles population is, in fact, less healthy than the total married population.

What happens to singles when they become ill? The lucky ones have a support group to which they can turn: family, neighbors, fellow communards, or roommates. Indeed, the crucial factor may not be marriage versus singlehood, but the strength of the support network. As the single state comes to be seen as less deviant, and more friends and groups become available to single adults, their general health and well-being should improve. Today, however, as single people grow older and their health deteriorates, they enter institutions more readily than do the married, having fewer opportunities for home care and fewer social responsibilities (Verbrugge, 1979).

A recent study of 400 single adults (Cargan and Melko, 1982) found no differences between marrieds and singles in terms of reported nightmares or crying spells, but did find that more singles worry and/or feel guilty, despondent, worthless, or lonely. However, it is the divorced that report feelings of despondency, worthlessness, sexual apathy, and loneliness more often than the never married. They note that if frequent contemplation of suicide is used as a measure, the figures are highest for the divorced (20 percent), followed by the never married (10 percent), and the married (7 percent).

In an important article examining the relationship between social class, marital status, life strains, and depression, Pearlin and Johnson (1981) reject the traditional interpretation that the poorer physical and mental health of singles reflects the unmet inner needs and emotional frustrations of never-married and formerly married people. Rather, this study examines the consequences of economic hardship, social isolation, and obligations of parents. These are three basic conditions of life to which unmarried people are both more exposed and more vulnerable. However, Pearlin and Johnson find that the greater life hardships of the unmarried only partly explain their greater incidence of depression. Even when hardships of married and unmarried persons are equally severe, the effects of these hardships are more devastating among the unmarried. "The combination most productive of psychological distress is to be simultaneously single, isolated, exposed to burdensome parental obligations, and most serious of all, poor." To what extent does marriage help fend off the psychological assaults of economic and social problems? Is its protective function the reason for the continued survival of marriage as an institution?

Living Arrangements

Among the important decisions single men and women face is where to live. This involves not only such fundamental matters as one's financial resources and the availability of housing, but also such questions as with whom to live, for what period of time, and what these decisions say to the world about oneself. Living arrangements are a central issue of single life, since each alternative involves many possibilities and limitations.

Shostak (forthcoming: 25) cites a recent MIT-Harvard Joint Center for Urban Studies report indicating that in the 1980s "only 50 percent of households will be headed by married couples compared with 80 percent in 1950. People will spend more years living alone or with roommates or partners. They will increasingly delay marriage, divorce more, remarry more slowly."

A single person may live alone, with friends or family, as head of a household, or as part of an unmarried couple. He or she may choose a commune, a single-family home, an apartment, or a dormitory. The most common trends in living arrangements for singles are the following.

Living Alone. In 1980 there were 17.8 million people living alone, an increase of 61 percent from the 10.9 million of 1970. Over those years the number of single residences maintained by persons under the age of 35 more than tripled, from 1.4 million to 4.8 million. A majority of these men and women are living in urban areas. New York City, Chicago, Los Angeles, Houston, and San Francisco are the most prominent. In each of these cities, and in others, there are areas that are occupied primarily by single adults living alone. But the greatest number of people living alone are not younger singles. Persons over the age of 45 constitute 65 percent of all those living alone, the largest group of which is elderly widows. Of all women living alone, more than half are widows over the age of 65.

While ideally single adults might choose living arrangements that reflect their needs and values, it is more likely that their household situations will reflect their economic status. For example, census data show that in 1977 the median income of women living alone was $3412, which means that half of these women actually received less than that figure. Since "housing choices will be somewhat limited, even for those with incomes up to $8000 . . . the wonder is not that so few aged parents share a home with an adult child, but that so many do not" (Hess and Markson, 1980).

Heading Households. About six out of ten single adult households are headed by single women. The number of single-parent households headed by women is now about 8.2 million, or 10.6 percent of the population, while only 1.6 million, or 2.1 percent of the population, are headed by men in the absence of a woman.

Cohabiting. Cohabitation is defined as a "more or less permanent relationship in which two unmarried persons of the opposite sex share a living facility without legal contract" (Cole, 1977: 67). Cohabitation has been around for a long time, but has become increasingly popular in the last ten years (Macklin, 1978, 1980). In 1980, some 3.2 percent of all "couple households" were unmarried men and women living together. In 1980 there were 1.56 million unmarried couples living together—three times as many as in 1970, when there were 523,000. Unmarried couples with no children represent about three-fourths of all unmarried couples. Some 63 percent of all unmarried couples were composed of two adults under the ages of 35. In 20 percent of all households, both partners were under age 25.

Why are so many singles choosing to live together as unmarried couples? The following factors are influential:

1. financial considerations such as the higher cost of living alone;
2. housing shortages in urban areas;
3. greater social tolerance of alternative living arrangements;
4. greater tolerance and support for cohabitation among undergraduates and graduate students and among postcollege adults;
5. greater acceptance of premarital sex;
6. changing gender role definitions; and
7. the sheer force of greater numbers of singles.

Paul Glick and Graham Spanier (1981) used data from the U.S. Bureau of the Census to estimate the prevalence of cohabitation in the United States. "Rarely does social change occur with such rapidity," they write. "Indeed, there have been few developments relating to marriage and family life which have been as dramatic as the rapid increase in unmarried cohabitation" (1981: 65). They mention the trend toward smaller families and the increase in age at which women begin childbearing as contributing to this phenomenon. They report that unmarried cohabitation is more common in large cities, more common among Blacks than among Whites, and most likely to end for any given couple within two years.

Work, Careers, and Occupations

Income and wealth derived from paid work is, for most of us, a central resource. Society places a high value on what we do for a living; so do the people we meet; so do we ourselves. Work provides the means for obtaining the goods and pursuing the activities that are the essence of the single lifestyle. Marketing experts recognize the impact of singles' consumption patterns in the marketplace and they create product lines and selling strategies to lure singles' dollars. From townhouses to sports cars, from tape decks to vacations in Mexico, goods are created and singles work to obtain the money to enjoy them.

Beyond the marketplace, work provides a crucial source of identity. Power, prestige, and privilege all flow from occupational involvement, as does a sense of self-worth. Single people are far more likely to place their career goals above interest in family. Some devote longer hours to work than their married colleagues, and many feel that they receive significant emotional support from their co-workers (Stein, 1976).

Though single women and men can make superior employees, some continue to receive lower wages than married colleagues and are sometimes passed over for promotion on the basis of their single status. A survey of fifty major corporations found that in 80 percent of the responding companies, the official corporate position was that marriage was not essential to upward mobility within the corporation. However, in a majority of these same companies, only 2 percent of their executives, including junior management levels, were single. Over 60 percent of the replies stated that single executives tend to make snap judgments, and 25 percent said that singles are "less stable" than married people (Jacoby, 1974). Discrimination may range from overt cases to more subtle ones involving the complex networks that exist in every institution: business-related friendships, luncheon conversations, and other informal contacts that affect job retention and promotion. Since race, sex, ethnic origin, and religion are also bases for discrimination, discrimination based on singleness is often difficult to isolate. Whatever its cause, such discrimination victimizes many men and women who hope to get ahead in their work, or hope just to get by.

The marital status and the socioeconomic status of women and their families are particularly influential in determining choices of occupation. Natalie Sokoloff's 1981 study of women college graduates showed that single and married women differed in their early career activities and in their occupational choices. The differences in career activities were due less to marital status than to socioeconomic status. Some of Sokoloff's findings were:

1. Almost all single women from all socioeconomic classes were employed, and 25 percent were involved in postbachelor's studies.
2. Married women were less likely to be employed or in school three years after graduation from college.
3. A larger percentage of women from lower socioeconomic status families remained single three years after graduation. This was true even when the women had children.
4. The largest percentage of single and married women were employed in professions traditionally considered "female."

For many women, obtaining a good education and entering a profession take priority over marrying and establishing a family, at least for a period of time. This is true of Black and White women from lower-middle-class families. Higginbotham's studies (1981, 1982) of middle- and lower-middle-class Black, college-educated women compared the relevant emphasis placed on marriage by the two groups. The upwardly mobile women from lower-middle-class backgrounds had parents who did not see future marriage prospects as assuring the desired mobility for their daughters. They therefore focused on educational success to the exclusion of other goals, including marriage. On the other hand, women from Black middle-class homes were expected to integrate careers with family life.

The problem of successfully integrating personal and professional life is compounded for many gay men. Keeping one's job often means hiding one's homosexuality. How this is accomplished, what happens when one is found out, and the extent of discrimination against gays throughout the working world are the focus of Martin Levine's "Employment Discrimination Against Gay Men" (1981). Public opinion polls report strong support for barring gays from high-status occupations; application forms are constructed to weed out gays; there is discrimination even in government licensing and security clearances. The struggle to conceal their sexual orientation from co-workers often leaves gay people feeling alienated and anxious, and if they fail to conceal it, the situation can be worse. Many companies enforce a policy of firing gays upon discovery. Others keep employees at a low level or transfer them to a "more suitable" job.

Parenting

Single parents may be separated, divorced, or widowed, or may never have been married at all. They tend to be older than most singles and their social lives are shaped by the daily responsibilities of child care. They may be independent and self-sufficient, but most are overburdened and financially strained (Benjamin, 1981).

There were 5.7 million one-parent families in 1978, an increase of 9 percent over 1977. More than 90 percent of these families are maintained by women. In 1980, 11.1 million children were living with their mothers alone, while about 1 million were living with their fathers alone. Overall, 19.7 percent of all children under 18 were living in one-parent families (U.S. Bureau of the Census, 1981).

Single parents experience three major worries: loneliness, children, and money. Their problems evolve over time. The first months after the breakup of a marriage are the most traumatic. The newly divorced person must deal with disputes over child support and custody as well as personal problems of depression, self-doubt, desire for revenge, and the need for new emotional involvements. Then come financial worries (Weiss, 1979). The median income in two-parent families is two to three times that of one-parent families. The economic hardships faced by single parents reflect the lower wages paid all women, particularly minority women, who make up 35 percent of all single mothers. Less than 30 percent of families headed by women report incomes as high as $10,000, compared with 70 percent of two-parent families. These single parents need skilled child care, part-time jobs with benefits, and easily available health care facilities (Stein, 1981).

The difficulties of providing for their own and their children's physical, social, and emotional needs often result in role overload and fatigue. It is difficult to develop and maintain a satisfying social/sexual life. Nonparents often consider single parents, with their attached responsibilities, less than "marriageable." Many single parents are reluctant to expose their children to dates who spend the night, and getting away for weekends or vacations requires child care arrangements. Not surprisingly, single mothers are somewhat less likely to remarry than other single women (Duberman, 1975).

How do women heading families feel about their situations? "Rarely is the concept put forward that the female-headed family is an acceptable family form or that, once divorced, it is all right for a mother to stay divorced," report Kohen, Brown and Feldberg (1981: 288). But presumptions in favor of the male-headed family have begun to be questioned as the advantages of singlehood emerge. When a couple divorces, the woman not only loses most of her right to the man's resources, but she also loses her personal dependence and obligations of service. For some women, the experience of heading a family may be more rewarding than were their marriages.

Rosenthal and Keshet (1981) found that young single fathers experience role conflicts between work and child care similar to conflicts experienced by single mothers. Moreover, full-time and half-time fathers averaged considerably less income than did men in intact marriages. Yet at home, men who learned to meet children's practical daily needs began to feel better about themselves and their relationship with their children. Bringing the criteria of work performance to the parenting role made them more at ease with their new obligations.

Aging

Only 12 percent of the 11 million single persons over the age of 65 have never married; 3 percent are separated, 77 percent widowed, and 7 percent divorced. There are dramatic differences in the statistics for men and women. Most notably 75 percent of men over the age of 65 are married and 14 percent are widowed, while only 37 percent of the women in this age group are married and 52 percent are widowed. The number of older never-married people is significant and their characteristics are varied.

What do we know about singles and aging? One of the few analyses done on the elderly never married tells us that they are not especially lonely in old age. They are similar to the married elderly in that both groups are more positive in outlook than the divorced or widowed elderly. Moreover, having never been married means that one avoids the desolation of bereavement following the death of one's spouse (Gubrium, 1975). A study of older women points out that the never marrieds had the best physical and psychological health and were the best able to cope in terms of facing up to problems and taking action. Experience with living alone appears to increase independence and autonomy and to have some beneficial effects for coping effectively (Wood, 1979). . . .

COPING STYLES OF NEVER-MARRIED ADULTS

Margaret Adams (1976), in a pioneering study of single women who had made successful life adjustments, cited three major factors responsible for making singleness a viable lifestyle for them: economic independence, social and psychological autonomy, and a clear intent to remain single by choice.

In his summary of the literature, Shostak (forthcoming) identifies six major coping mechanisms employed by singles. Three are traditional coping mechanisms for singles: permissive social attitudes, same-sex friendships, and marriage-deriding attitudes. The three more recent coping mechanisms are: assertive social attitudes, dating support systems, and prosinglehood options.

Citing a 1976–1977 Harris poll for *Playboy* of 684 never-married men, Shostak reports that "about twice as large a proportion of the never-married as the married males were designated 'innovators,' the most liberal of the four possibilities,[1] and less than half as many singles as married men were labeled conservative 'traditionalists' " (forthcoming: 19).

Single women have similar liberal attitudinal profiles, according to the 1980 Virginia Slims Poll. Though cautious about the incomplete data, Shostak indicates that single women and men "stand out . . . in their comparative permissiveness, liberality and acceptance of change" (forthcoming: 19).

Singles stress the importance of close, caring friendships, based on free choice and developing into a sense of mutuality. Stein (1976) interviewed sixty single men and women between the ages of 25 and 45, mostly college graduates employed and living in New York and Boston. In their departure from traditional family structures, they expressed a strong need for substitute networks of human relationships that provide the basic satisfactions of intimacy, sharing, and continuity.

Intimacy for these women and men came from both opposite or same-sex friendships. Groups of friends, formal or informal, are especially well suited to meeting the needs of single people, helping them to deal with life choices and to pursue personal growth. For many of the single people interviewed, friendships meant survival.

Marriage-deriding attitudes may be used to justify the unwed state. Some take a very critical stance with reference to marriage, feeling that "it is better to be single than caught in an unfulfilling marriage." There is a need among singles to develop a consistent and supportive world view.

Assertive social attitudes are apparent in the emergent ideology of positive singlehood, which is now documented in a number of magazines, journals, seminars, and the like. The positive aspects of singlehood are stressed in such titles as "Living Alone and Liking It," "Single Can Be Fun," and so on. The traditional appeal of marriage as a conveyor of respectability has been considerably weakened by the recent liberalizing of our social norms, and having children is no longer considered necessary for either full adulthood or for a full and happy marriage relationship (Burnley and Kurth, 1981; Cheung, 1982; Greenwood, 1978).

Dating support runs the gamut from singles' magazines and clubs catering to singles, to computer dating services, singles' bars, and vacation resorts. More formal structures are also emerging to provide intimacy and continuity among adults. They frequently take the form of group living arrangements, one type of "experimental family" (Cogswell and Sussman, 1972). While communal homes might include the socialization of children, they also focus on the needs for identity, intimacy, and interaction of adult members. Other structures include women's and men's groups, therapy and encounter groups, and organizations formed around specialized interests. Although not restricted to singles, they are particularly well adapted to meeting the needs of single people and were cited by the singles interviewed as examples of positive experiences in their lives (Stein, 1976). Such group interactions foster friendships and spur personal growth by providing a supportive context.

Shostak indicates the need to alter certain public policies that affect singles. "Nonmarried Americans need a fair hearing and positive changes in their roles as learners, as citizens, as renters, as cohabitors, as parents, as purchasers of 'singles only' services, and especially as the subjects of social science research" (forthcoming: 38). Shostak echoes the need for further research (see also Stein, 1978). For example:

1. What are the similarities and differences between voluntary and involuntary, temporary and stable singles (Shostak's ambivalents, wistfuls, resolveds, and regretfuls)?
2. How do women and men make decisions regarding preferred marital status and how committed are they to these choices?
3. To what extent are people "embedded" in their present married or single state?
4. How do singles opt for transitory versus long-term single life?
5. How does the experience of singlehood differ for men and women?
6. How do gender differences coupled with age intersect with work experiences, life arrangements, and social supports?
7. How much variation is there in the singlehood experiences of different ethnic, religious, and racial groups?
8. To what extent do existing social support systems provide help for singles, and what new forms of support are still needed?
9. What kinds of adults cope well and enjoy the single experience and who are those who are discontent? What social and psychological factors seem to account for these similarities and differences?
10. Have the stereotypes of single life changed to reflect its heterogeneity?
11. What are the work and career experiences of today's singles?

A crucial need also exists for a systemic comparison of cohorts of nonmarried and married men and women based on both aggregate and individual data that would lead to the development of concepts, typologies, and theories. Testable hypotheses must be generated and existing statistics need to be replicated. Interested social scientists will find many research opportunities; social practitioners and those concerned with social policy will find much to consider.

CONCLUSION

Singles are an important segment of the adult population. Their interests, their activities, and their lifestyles are often in the forefront of social trends. Singles take risks; they experiment; they consume; they set trends. Any one of us may some day belong to the singles population, if we are not now single. Statistics show that about one-third of young adults currently marrying will divorce; three out of four married women will become widows; many people will live together without marriage. There are many styles of adulthood in our society. Different people may choose different styles, or one person may adopt various styles in the course of a lifetime.

Although personal statements provide us with insight into single experiences, little has been done to provide a systematic examination of singlehood.

Singles have often been regarded as a somewhat deviant group, different from "normal" married adults, and until very recently they have been avoided as a subject of serious research. Recognition of the variations that exist within the singles population, and of the goals and concerns they hold in common with other people, such as meaningful work, friendship, financial security, health care, a comfortable and secure home, and self-esteem, is a result of recent research on this lifestyle. The interested researcher and practitioner will find many opportunities to do creative and constructive work.

NOTE

[1] The other three categories were traditionalist, conventional, and contemporary.

REFERENCES

Adams, M. 1976. *Single blessedness*. New York: Basic Books.

Benjamin, E. 1981. It's not easy being single after years of marriage: the social world of separated and divorced parents. Paper presented at the Annual Meetings of the SSSP.

Bloom, B., W. Hodges, R. Caldwell, L. Systra, and A. Cedrone. 1977. Marital separation: a community survey. *Journal of Divorce* 1 (Fall): 7–19.

Brown, G. 1980. *The new celibacy*. New York: McGraw-Hill.

Burnley, C. and S. Kurth. 1981. Never married women's perceptions of adult life transitions. Paper presented at the Annual Meetings of the SSSP.

Cargan, L. and M. Melko. 1982. Singles. Beverly Hills, Calif: Sage.

Cheung, L. M. 1982. Single Chinese-American women. Paper presented at the Annual Meetings of the Eastern Sociological Society.

Clayton, R. R. and J. L. Bokemeier. 1980. Premarital sex in the seventies. *Journal of Marriage and the Family* 42 (November): 759–75.

Cogswell, B. and M. Sussman. 1972. Changing family and marriage forms. *The Family Coordinator* 21 (September): 505–16.

Cole, C. L. 1977. Cohabitation in social context. In R. Libby and R. Whitehurst (eds.), *Marriage and alternatives*, pp. 62–79. Glenview, Ill: Scott, Foresman.

Duberman, L. 1975. *The reconstituted family*. Chicago: Nelson-Hall.

Glick, P. C. 1979. Future Americans. Washington COFO Memo 2 (Summer/Fall): 2–5.

——— and G. Spanier. 1981. Cohabitation in the U.S. In P. J. Stein (ed.), *Single life: Unmarried adults in social context*, pp. 194–209. New York: St. Martin's.

Greenwood, N. A. 1978. Safely single or wisely wed? A sociological analysis of singleness as a positive lifestyle. Master's thesis, California State University, Sacramento.

Gubrium, J. F. 1975. Being single in old age. *International Journal of Aging and Human Development* 6 (Fall): 29–41.

Hess, B. and E. Markson. 1980. *Aging and old age*. New York: Macmillan.

Higginbothan, E. 1982. Educated single Black women: marital options and limits. (unpublished).

———. 1981. Is marriage a priority? Class differences in marital options of educated black women. In P. J. Stein (ed.), *Singles life: Unmarried adults in social context*, pp. 259–67. New York: St. Martin's.

Hunt, M. 1974. *Sexual behavior in the 1970s*. Chicago: Playboy.

Jacoby, S. 1974. 49 million singles can't all be right. *New York Times Magazine* (February 17): 41–49.

Kohen, J., C. Brown, and R. Feldberg. 1981. Divorced mothers. In P. J. Stein (ed.), *Single life: Unmarried adults in social context*, pp. 288–305. New York: St. Martin's.

Laws, J. L. and P. Schwartz. 1977. *Sexual scripts: The social construction of female sexuality*. Hinsdale, Ill: Dryden.

Levine, M. 1981. Employment discrimination against gay men. In P. J. Stein (ed.) *Single life: Unmarried adults in social context*, pp. 268–73. New York: St. Martin's.

———, ed. 1979. *Gay men: The sociology of male homosexuality*. New York: Harper & Row.

Libby, R. 1977. Creative singlehood as a sexual lifestyle: beyond marriage as a rite of passage. In R. W. Libby and R. N. Whitehurst (eds.), *Marriage and alternatives*, pp. 37–61. Glenview, Ill.: Scott, Foresman.

Macklin, E. D. 1980. Nontraditional family forms: a decade of research. *Journal of Marriage and the Family* 42 (November): 905–22.

———. 1978. Nonmarital heterosexual cohabitation. *Marriage and Family Review* 1 (March/April): 1–12.

Pearlin, L. I. and J. S. Johnson. 1981. Marital status, life strains, and depression. In P. J. Stein (ed.), *Single life: Unmarried adults in social context,* pp. 165–78. New York: St. Martin's.

Rosenthal, K. and H. Keshet. 1981. Childcare responsibilities of part-time and single fathers. In P. J. Stein (ed.), *Single life: Unmarried adults in social context,* pp. 306–24. New York: St. Martin's.

Shostak, A. (Forthcoming.) Singlehood: the lives of never-married employed Americans. In M. Sussman and S. Steinmetz (eds.), *Handbook on marriage and the family.* New York: Plenum.

Sokoloff, N. 1981. Early work patterns of single and married women. In P. J. Stein (ed.), *Single life: Unmarried adults in social context,* pp. 238–59. New York: St. Martin's.

Stein, P. J., ed. 1981. *Single life: Unmarried adults in social context.* New York: St. Martin's.

———. 1976. *Single*. Englewood Cliffs, N.J.: Prentice-Hall.

U.S. Bureau of the Census. 1981. *Marital status and living arrangements: March 1980.* Current Population Reports, Series P-20, No. 365. Washington, D.C.: Government Printing Office.

Verbrugge, L. 1979. Marital status and health. *Journal of Marriage and the Family* 41 (May): 267–85.

Vida, V., ed. 1978. *Our right to love: A lesbian resource book.* Englewood Cliffs, N.J.: Prentice-Hall.

Weiss, R. 1979. *Going it alone.* New York: Basic Books.

———. 1975. *Marital separation.* New York: Basic Books.

Wood, V. 1979. Singles and aging. Paper presented to the Annual Meetings of the National Council on Family Relations.

VII

COHABITATION

16

COHABITATION: DOES IT MAKE FOR A BETTER MARRIAGE?

Carl A. Ridley, Dan J. Peterman, and Arthur W. Avery

In the classroom and in counseling, individuals persist in their desire to know if living with their boyfriend or girlfriend will prepare them better for a satisfying marital relationship in the future. In addition, a common question in counseling is: "My girlfriend/boyfriend and I have been dating for a while and . . . ah, well, we were wondering, what, ah, . . . you think about people living together before marriage?" As counselors and educators, our initial response to such an inquiry is to clarify the nature of the question and the feelings that underlie it. Beyond that, however, we often find ourselves saying, "Well, . . . sometimes living together before marriage can provide positive experiences that will better prepare you for marriage, whereas other times living together is simply a matter of convenience for the individuals involved and is not likely to provide a better foundation for marriage."

Carl A. Ridley, Dan J. Peterman, and Arthur W. Avery, "Cohabitation: Does It Make for a Better Marriage?" *The Family Coordinator,* April 1978, pp. 129–36. Copyrighted © 1978 by the National Council on Family Relations, 1219 University Avenue Southeast, Minneapolis, Minnesota 55414. Reprinted by permission.

No doubt all of us have witnessed cohabiting relationships which have proven particularly valuable for the individuals involved. The partners have learned to be more aware of their needs, more open and honest in their communication, more accepting of their own strengths and weaknesses and those of their partner, and perhaps more aware of the reciprocity necessary for maintaining satisfactory heterosexual relationships. Unfortunately, we have also seen situations where cohabiting relationships, not unlike some marital relationships, have been sources of constant misunderstanding, frustration, and resentment for the persons involved. Interactions of this type where one or both partners leave the relationship with a loss of self-esteem and a lack of self-confidence in their ability to maintain relationships with the opposite sex are not likely to encourage successful heterosexual relationships in the future.

Based on an understanding of our students and clients, then, we need to determine the likely benefits and costs of a cohabiting relationship. Unfortunately, as Blaine (1975) so aptly pointed out, "no scientifically valid survey has yet been made which shows the effect of living together beforehand upon marriage" (p. 32). As is frequently the problem, we are forced as counselors and teachers to advise individuals without having sufficient information on the issue at hand.

Despite the general lack of careful empirical study on the effects of living together before marriage on later marital success, it seems reasonable to conclude from the available evidence that not all cohabiting relationships have the same impact on individuals. In an initial attempt to describe the differential impact of cohabitation on the individuals involved, the authors focused their attention on a recent study by Peterman, Ridley, and Anderson (1974) that describes the background, personal, and interpersonal characteristics of cohabiting college students. It was apparent from a review of these findings that there is not a single type of cohabitation relationship, but rather several different types. In one type, both partners perceive themselves as well-adjusted and see the relationship as a positive learning experience. In another type, however, one or both partners see themselves as not well-adjusted and perceive the relationship as a source of dissatisfaction.

A basic assumption of this paper is that cohabiting relationships are not inherently good or bad for the persons involved, but rather they have the potential to be both depending on the goals, expectations, and skills of the cohabiting individuals. In the following section, several types of cohabiting relationships are discussed in the hope that by recognizing individual and relationship characteristics associated with positive cohabiting experiences and comparing those to characteristics associated with negative cohabiting experiences, we will be better able to assess the likely impact of a cohabiting experience on those who seek our counsel.

TYPES OF COHABITING RELATIONSHIPS

Four commonly observed types of cohabiting relationships are described in terms of their potential value as marriage preparation experiences for the individuals involved. The major objective of this typology is to identify and explain some of the general discernable themes of cohabiting relationships, not to describe numerous individual relationship variations. The typology is based on an integration of information from existing research on cohabitation (e.g., Henze & Hudson, 1974; Lyness, Note 1; Macklin, Note 2; Peterman, et al., 1974) as well as on clinical observations.

Each type of cohabiting relationship described ("Linus Blanket," "Emancipation," "Convenience," and "Testing") has outcomes that can be evaluated as providing positive and negative marriage preparation experience. In all types of cohabiting relationships, some learning takes place (e.g., increased knowledge base, increased self-awareness), but in some the potential loss of self-esteem mitigates many of the gains.

"Linus Blanket." The first type of cohabiting relationship described here, "Linus Blanket," is characterized by what appears to be an overwhelming need for one member of the pair to have a relationship with *someone*, with little apparent regard for whom, or under what conditions. To have someone to be with, even though he or she may treat you badly, is better than not having anyone at all. It seems that the need to feel secure through a relationship makes it virtually unimportant to evaluate the circumstances of relationship formation, the motivations of the partner, or the conditions surrounding relationship continuation. Thus, the primary goal of this relationship is one of emotional security. For example, the insecure partner (male or female) in this situation comes across as a clinging vine. When interacting with others, this individual typically stays physically close to the partner, depends on him/her to carry the conversation, and when the individual speaks, comments revolve primarily around the partner. So long as the more secure partner does not feel trapped in this situation and their behavior remains predictable, the insecure partner's basic needs are likely to be met. The fragility of this relationship seldom leads to the type of interaction between partners that increases the development of interpersonal skills important for maintaining heterosexual relationships. The insecure person attempts to elicit interaction with the secure partner which can be interpreted as self-confirming. Negative statements made to the insecure person (frequently in the form of criticisms) are often interpreted as a severe questioning of his or her self-worth. The result is that the more secure person perceives and/or acts as if

the partner is fragile ("can't take criticism") and that they cannot "rock the boat" without hurting their partner and the relationship.

Since it is through the constructive handling of disagreements that internal relationship changes take place (e.g., Raush, Barry, Hertel, & Swain, 1974), the more secure partner is often forced into accepting the relationship as it is or leaving it. If the relationship is maintained, open communication and successful problem solving do not take place and thus the experience does not serve as "practice" for improving the skills of the partners. Continued interaction is likely to be ritualized following traditional lines of male-female role behavior. In this case, the "Linus Blanket" relationship provides an opportunity to learn sex role stereotyped behaviors. When a "Linus Blanket" type relationship terminates, the insecure individual typically suffers a loss of self-esteem which neutralizes much of the potential gain of having lived with someone in an intimate relationship.

"Emancipation." Peterman, et al. (1974), found that more than 75 percent of the "repeating" cohabiting males and females (those with more than one cohabiting experience) reported that their longest cohabiting experience lasted less than six months. Two relatively distinct types of cohabiting relationships appeared typical of this group—"Emancipation" and "Convenience." Although the "Emancipation" type of cohabiting relationship was apparent for both males and females, perhaps the clearest example of this pattern was found among Catholic females who started cohabiting early in their college years and maintained a pattern of short duration but frequent cohabiting relationships (Peterman, et al., 1974). It was concluded that these females must be experiencing pulls, pushes, and resistances to becoming involved in cohabiting relationships. Such resistances may reside primarily in socialization to strict sexual standards from family and church which deny guilt-free participation in sexualized heterosexual relationships. The restrictions seem to be countered by internal pushes to loosen external controls and to demonstrate increased freedom by becoming sexually active. Peer pressures which typically support a liberalized set of sexual norms place the Catholic females in a potentially double binding situation. The double bind develops something like this: peer pressure and the desire for more self control result in her becoming involved in a cohabiting situation. The subtle guilt feeling of "doing something wrong," however, makes it difficult for her to become actively involved in the cohabiting situation and ultimately forces her exit. Once out of the relationship, the pulls and pushes reassert themselves and the cycle repeats itself. In an attempt to determine the effect of this type of cohabiting situation on the female, a general principle originating in Gestalt therapy provides an interesting perspective. Namely, when someone is carrying around extensive "unfinished business," it is difficult to function adequately in the here and now. The "unfinished business" in the "Emancipation" type of cohabiting relationship continues to encourage cohabiting relationships while a value system does not support it. Tenuous involvement in the cohabiting relationship does not allow for the type of practice necessary to improve interaction skills. When the pattern is left unchecked, reasons for exit from the relationship are rarely understood and result in confusion and self-doubt on the part of both partners. Should the cohabiting experiences serve the purpose of helping the person work through the value-behavior discrepancy, then the increased self-knowledge would be reflected in better preparation for future heterosexual relating.

"Convenience." A third type of cohabiting relationship, "Convenience," is perhaps best exemplified in the short duration cohabiting relationship of freshmen or sophomore males. This cohabiting situation allows the males to have regularized sexual contact and the luxuries of domestic living without the responsibilities of a committed relationship. The performance of many of the domestic tasks falls to the female simply because she is thought to be more skilled and/or has been socialized to perform them. His major task is to keep the female interested in the relationship when it appears that she is putting more into the relationship than he is. If he can maintain this type of relationship, and most do not, he is probably exhibiting a fairly high interpersonal skill level even though the inequity of the relationship may seem somewhat unjust. This type of cohabiting situation provides a rich opportunity for both the male and the female

to learn the idea of reciprocity—mutual giving and getting in a relationship. She can learn that unconditional giving can have limited long-range pay off and that assessments of what one is giving and getting are important in certain contexts. At times it appears that the female is trying to make the male so dependent on her that he would not think of leaving the relationship. At other times, it appears she is simply fitting into the culturally prescribed role for women. It appears that the male is getting much practice at strategic interaction by trying to maintain his freedom to interact with others (keeping his options open), but at the same time presenting to his partner a high level of involvement in the cohabiting relationship. Generally, he seems to learn a great deal about the day-to-day aspects of domestic life (role behavior) and at least some exchange skills. His guarded openness serves the purpose of preventing the type of involvement that escalates the relationship toward a premature commitment.

Although it may appear from the above description that the male is getting the better end of the deal, it should be noted that both the male and female are learning important aspects of "survival" within intimate relationships—even though this learning may be painful for one or both of them. Although the authors have found from their experience that this situation is most typical with the male in the convenience role, the situation is sometimes reversed with a more assertive female forming and maintaining the relationship primarily for its convenience qualities. Future research will be needed to determine if this type of heterosexual interaction early in the college years makes it more difficult to make permanent commitments later in life.

"Testing." Individuals who are in the "Testing" type of cohabiting relationship are typically well-adjusted people (lacking extensive past grievances or major individual problems) who exhibit a higher than average interpersonal skill level upon entrance into a cohabiting relationship. Macklin (1974) suggests that one of the most difficult tasks in a cohabiting relationship is to form a good intimate relationship while at the same time maintaining individuality and autonomy. The mutuality-autonomy issue seems to surface primarily when the individuals involved have met their security needs and are motivated to try out a quasi-committed relationship with the intent being to learn more about themselves and complex intimate relationships. When their basic needs have been met, they are then able to move outside their own skin and become interested in the well-being of their partner. This willingness to get to know one's partner facilitates deeper reciprocal levels of self-disclosure. In a sense, the partners seem to use the relationship to get to know more about themselves—their likes and dislikes, and to learn more about how intimate relationships of this type apparently lead to a deeper level of self-understanding for both individuals. However, when the relationship solidifies too quickly—prior to the development of individual interests and preferences—the partners feel overinvolved and dependent on the relationship with the accompanying sense of loss of identity (Macklin, Note 2).

The combination of perceived loss of identity and high relationship cohesiveness *without* commitment increases the probability that many "Testing" relationships will terminate at this juncture. If the mutuality-autonomy issue is handled successfully, the relationship may develop in one of three directions:

1. The relationship can terminate because the primary objectives for its formation (of which they may or may not have been aware) have been accomplished (increased self-understanding within a relationship context and increased knowledge of day-to-day intimate living).
2. The relationship can become an enduring cohabiting relationship similar to a marriage relationship, but without formal commitment and the ever-present possibility of terminating the relationship. The effects on the relationship of a lack of formal commitment and the availability of alternative sources of gratification is as yet unclear. It might be suggested that the persons involved would have to possess sufficient interpersonal skills to maintain this type of relationship without experiencing continuous crises through attempts to establish relationship predictability.

3. Another direction the relationship could take is for the goal to be extended from increasing self-understanding within the relationship context to developing a marital relationship which would involve further testing of compatibility and the ability to work together. If the cohabiting experience demonstrated to the couple that they could not work together, the relationship would likely terminate. If compatability testing were positive, escalation toward marriage would be likely.

The authors have taken a special interest in the termination of those "Testing" relationships which are less traumatic for the participants with the idea that much can be learned about the acquisition of interpersonal skills and marriage preparation under these conditions. Although it is unclear why some terminations are as easy as they are, some information is available that may help to explain it:

1. Most of the individuals in "Testing" relationships have had a rich dating history in which the outcome was a confirmation of their desirability to the opposite sex and a developed repertoire of interpersonal skills.
2. Cohabitation was a small step from their previous experiences in terms of the degree of involvement and complexity of the heterosexual relationship. Although frequently not at a conscious level, participants had ordered their experiences with increased complexity so that cohabitation was only different from previous involvements in degree, not type. Thus, they were largely prepared for what would be required of them in a complex cohabiting situation. It has been hypothesized that heterosexual relationship termination (including cohabitation termination) will be traumatic when the involvement that is being terminated is very different from the previous level of involvement. It is when this gap exists that the relationship is most "potent" in terms of its positive or negative impact on the participants. For example, termination of a cohabiting relationship would be more traumatic when the highest level of previous involvement had been "casual dating" than when the previous involvement had been "going steady."
3. Another factor which cushions the impact of termination is that "Testing" cohabitors typically have a fairly extensive network of like and opposite sex relationships (Peterman, et al., 1974) that provide friends at termination and a pool of possible eligibles for future involvement. Rather than being alone in their loss, they have friends to talk to and to become involved with and the known ability to start new heterosexual involvements when desired.
4. Lastly, they exhibit a high interpersonal skill level at termination by "closing the door" to the relationship. When termination was the result of unresolved problems, each partner knew what went wrong and how they contributed to the problem.

In short, the major potential advantage of a cohabiting relationship is its structural complexity. The potential extensive demands of a cohabiting relationship, in particular a "Testing" type of relationship, more closely approximate marital demands than any other courtship pattern. Thus, if individuals have experience in which gradual increments of interpersonal skills were learned, cohabitation can be an ideal situation for "trial marriage" and for learning the complexity of intimate relationship functioning. However, if preparatory experiences have not occurred, cohabitation tends to result in: (a) social isolation, and (b) solidification of non-adaptive interactional patterns within the cohabiting relationship.

IMPLICATIONS

It should be apparent at this point that a specific answer to the question of whether cohabitation makes for a better marriage is as yet unavailable. With a knowledge of the cohabitation typology presented here *and* an accurate understanding of the persons involved, however, it should be easier to assess the potential effects of cohabitation on the individuals. In order to do this effectively, several important factors must be considered, including: (a) partners' motivations for cohabiting, (b) partners' expectations for the cohabiting experience, (c) partners' personal and interpersonal needs and goals, (d) partners' interpersonal skill levels, (e) the present status of the relationship (e.g., level of commitment), (f) the effects of the partners' previous heterosexual experiences, and (g) the support structure of the partners' interpersonal networks.

Fortunately, much of this information can be obtained either through personal interaction or observation of the individuals involved. Although it is obvious that there are wide individual differences in these areas, as a general rule it appears that cohabiting relationships are likely to provide positive learning experiences and better preparation for marriage when the participants: (a) have as cohabitation goals, greater self-understanding within a heterosexual context and increased knowledge of day-to-day aspects of intimate living, (b) have realistic and mutually agreed upon expectations for the cohabiting experience, (c) do not have strong "deficiency" needs for emotional security (e.g., "Linus Blanket") or a residue of past grievances and/or unfinished business (e.g., "Emancipation"), (d) have higher interpersonal skill levels (e.g., the ability to openly and honestly express their feelings, the ability to understand and accept their partner, and the ability to mutually solve problems), (e) have had a relationship where the present degree of involvement closely approximates that of a cohabiting relationship (e.g., steady dating rather than casual dating), (f) have a rich dating history resulting in positive self-perceptions in terms of their desirability to the opposite sex, and (g) have a fairly extensive network of like and opposite sex relationships where important needs are being met.

Although the above guidelines outlining conditions under which cohabitation is likely to provide positive learning experiences and better preparation for marriage are critical, an equally important factor is how the counselor will obtain sufficient information from the couple to assess these relationship dimensions. One effective way is through a series of open questions, both indirect and direct, that will likely give the counselor and the couple enough information to make the above assessments about the cohabiting experience. A list of questions which the authors have found particularly useful in their counseling experience is presented in Table 1. Questions posed by the counselor to the couple are noted in the first column, while sev-

TABLE 1
SAMPLE COUNSELOR QUESTIONS FOR COUPLES CONTEMPLATING LIVING TOGETHER

Counselor Questions	"Good" signs and "Concern" signs
1. Could you talk a little bit about how each of you came to the decision to live together?	*Good signs:* Each partner has given considerable thought to the decision, including the advantages and disadvantages of living together. *Concern signs:* One or both partners have given little thought to the advantages and disadvantages of living together.
2. Perhaps each of you could discuss for a minute what you think you will get out of living together?	*Good signs:* Each individual is concerned about learning more about self and partner through intimate daily living. Both wish to obtain further information about each other's commitment to the relationship. *Concern signs:* One or both partners desire to live together for convenience only. They want to live together to show independence from parents or peers.
3. Could each of you discuss what you see as your role and your partner's role in the relationship (*e.g.*, responsibilities, expectations)?	*Good signs:* Each individual's expectations of self and partner are compatible with those of partner. *Concern signs:* One or both individuals have given little thought to the roles or expectations of self and/or partner. Individuals disagree in terms of their expectations.

TABLE 1 *(Continued)*

Counselor Questions	"Good" signs and "Concern" signs
4. Could each of you identify your partner's primary physical and emotional needs and the degree to which you believe that you are able to fulfill them?	*Good signs:* Each individual has a clear understanding of partner's needs and is motivated and able to meet most of them. *Concern signs:* One or both individuals are not fully aware of partner's needs. Individuals are not motivated or able to meet needs of partner.
5. Would each of you identify your primary physical and emotional needs in your relationship with your partner? To what degree have these needs been met in the past? To what extent are these needs likely to be met if the two of you were to live together?	*Good signs:* Each partner clearly understands his or her needs. Most of these needs are presently being met and are likely to continue to be met in a cohabiting relationship. *Concern signs:* One or both partners are not fully aware of their needs. Needs are not being met in the present relationship and/or are not likely to be met if the individuals live together.
6. Could each of you discuss what makes this relationship important to you? What are your feelings toward your partner?	*Good signs:* Partners care deeply for each other and view the relationship as a highly significant one. *Concern signs:* One or both individuals do not care deeply for their partner or do not view the relationship as a highly significant one. Partners have an emotional imbalance with one partner more involved in the relationship than the other.
9. Could each of you discuss your ability to openly and honestly share your feelings with your partner?	*Good signs:* Both individuals have had a rich dating history. Individuals have positive perceptions of self and opposite sex and are aware of what they learned from previous relationships. *Concern signs:* One or both partners have had minimal dating experience. Individuals have negative perceptions of self and/or of the opposite sex and do not seem aware of having learned from their prior relationships.
8. Perhaps each of you could talk for a minute about how your family and friends might react to the two of you living together?	*Good signs:* Each individual is aware of the potential repercussions of family and friends should they learn of the cohabiting relationship. Family and friends are supportive of the cohabiting relationship, or couple has considered how they will deal with opposition. *Concern signs:* One or both individuals are not fully aware of possible family and friends' reaction to their living together. Family and friends are not supportive of the cohabiting relationship.
9. Could each of you discuss your ability to openly and honestly share your feelings with your partner?	*Good signs:* Each individual is usually able to express feelings to partner without difficulty. *Concern signs:* One or both individuals have difficulty expressing feelings to partner or do not believe expressing feelings is important.
10. Could each of you discuss your partner's strengths and weaknesses? To what extent would you like to change your partner, relative to their strengths or weaknesses?	*Good signs:* Each individual is usually able to accept feelings of partner. Individuals are able to accept partner's strengths and weaknesses. *Concern signs:* One or both individuals are not able to understand and accept partner. Individuals have difficulty in accepting partner's strengths and weaknesses.

TABLE 1 (Continued)

Counselor Questions	"Good" signs and "Concern" signs
11. How do each of you handle relationship problems when they occur? Can you give some examples of difficult problems you have had and how you have dealt with them?	*Good signs:* Both individuals express feelings openly and are able to understand and accept partner's point of view. Individuals are able to mutually solve problems. *Concern signs:* One or both partners have difficulty expressing feelings openly or in accepting partner's point of view. Couple frequently avoids problems or fails to solve them mutually.

eral "good signs" (i.e., general indicators that the couple has at least adequately attended to the issues posed in the question) or "concern signs" (i.e., general indicators that additional attention needs to be devoted to the issues or that the couple's response calls into question the value of cohabitation for the couple) are shown in the second column. The questions are designed to help the counselor obtain information from couples on several important issues identified earlier as important for cohabiting couples (e.g., partners' motivations and expectations for cohabiting). These sample questions are not intended to be definitive or inclusive of all possible questions nor are they presented in any sequential order. A given counselor will of course want to select particular questions appropriate to his/her goals as well as the unique characteristics of the individuals involved. These questions, however, should give the counselor a general idea of one approach to assessing the effects of cohabitation as a marriage preparation experience.

SUMMARY AND CONCLUSIONS

The degree to which cohabiting experiences prepare individuals for marriage depends in part on the needs, goals, motivations, and competence of the persons involved. It would seem unfortunate to conclude that cohabitation is inherently good or bad preparation for marriage, but rather it should be viewed as having the potential for both, with the characteristics of the individuals and the relationship being of critical importance in determining the long-range effects of cohabitation.

Educators and counselors can discuss the concept of living together before marriage with the openness and objectivity with which they discuss other premarital heterosexual experiences. They can outline the personal skills and abilities which individuals typically require in order to function effectively in marriage as well as how certain types of cohabiting arrangements can facilitate growth in these areas. One such area where a cohabiting experience can prepare individuals for marriage involves sex roles and sex role expectations. With changing socialization patterns, sex role structures and expectations of husbands and wives are no longer as clearly defined as they once were. As Peterman (1975) noted:

Partners must now work out a role differentiation to suit their own unique personal and pair characteristics rather than simply following models handed down by tradition. To do so requires replacing romantic myth by a capacity to be more aware of one's own needs, learning habits of openness, practicing becoming accurately empathic, acquiring information and technique in human sexuality, ridding oneself of sexist attitudes, and so forth. (pp. 40–41)

Lee (1975) expressed another potential positive outcome of cohabitation: "The essence of marriage is commitment, the contract and the concern shared by the couple. If they express these mutual responsibilities as living together without formal marriage, it is likely that when the formal promises are made the marriage will have greater endurance" (p. 41). The authors have argued that living together before marriage may also result in unpredictable or clearly negative consequences: "If living together is undertaken as a trail of compatibility motivated by curiosity rather than by commitment, the results are likely to be as whimsical and unpredictable as the curiosity of the participants" (p. 41).

In summary, the guidelines presented in the previous section—linked to the cohabitation typology outlined earlier—hopefully will serve as a first step toward increasing our understanding of how cohabitation affects preparation for marriage. Future research is sorely needed, however, to further clarify the types of cohabiting relationships, the degree to which couples might move from one type to another, and to identify the person and relationship characteristics that play an important role in determining the long-range effects of living together before marriage.

NOTES

[1] J. F. Lyness, "Open marriage among former cohabitants: 'We have met the enemy: Is it us?'" (Manuscript submitted for publication, 1976.)

[2] E. D. Macklin, "Unmarried Heterosexual Cohabitation on the University Campus." (Unpublished manuscript, Cornell University, 1974.)

REFERENCES

Blaine, G. B. 1975. Does living together before marriage make for a better marriage? *Medical Aspects of Human Sexuality* 9:32–39.

Henze, L. F., and J. W. Hudson. 1974. Personal and family characteristics of cohabiting and noncohabiting college students. *Journal of Marriage and the Family* 36:722–27.

Lee, R. V. 1975. Does living together before marriage make for a better marriage? *Medical Aspects of Human Sexuality* 9:41–44.

Peterman, D. J. 1975. Does living together before marriage make for a better marriage? *Medical Aspects of Human Sexuality* 9:39–41.

Peterman, D. J., C. A. Ridley, and S. M. Anderson. 1974. A comparison of cohabiting and noncohabiting college students. *Journal of Marriage and the Family* 36:344–54.

Raush, H. L., W. A. Barry, R. K. Hertel, and M. A. Swain. 1974. *Communication, conflict and marriage.* New York: Jossey-Bass.

17

SO PUT IT IN WRITING

Barton E. Bernstein

Two consenting adults, a man and a woman, decide to live together. When children, money, property or lawyers become involved, the relationship suddenly changes. The new status becomes more meaningful. Uncertainty becomes a problem in itself. What may have started as a simple experiment in togetherness becomes a financial and legal as well as emotional entanglement. What are the actual and potential issues involved? How should they be approached and solved?

When a man and a woman live together it is called "cohabitation." This can be a short duration relationship or it can last years and involve complete sharing and total commitment. More and

Barton E. Bernstein, "So Put it in Writing," *The Family Coordinator,* October 1977, pp. 361–66. Copyrighted © 1977 by the National Council on Family Relations, 1219 University Avenue Southeast, Minneapolis, Minnesota 55414. Reprinted by permission.

more individuals find that they are not ready for marriage in the traditional sense, or that marriage would be a financial liability, as in the case of Social Security. They would rather live together initially either as an end in itself or as a prelude to marriage.

Occasionally parties who begin a relationship of cohabitation unwittingly end up in a common law marriage. In states which permit common law marriage three elements are generally required: the parties (a) agreed to be married, and after the agreement (b) they lived together in this state as husband and wife and (c) they are represented to others as married (Texas . . .). The statement concerning the principles of law would appear to be clear and unassailable. Applying the law to a given situation is a jury (fact) question and often depends on the makeup of the jury, the credibility of the witnesses, capacity of counsel or the whim of the judge. For example:

A wealthy man and a poor woman decide on a weekend trip. They register as Mr. and Mrs. in a hotel 6 p.m. one evening. The next morning he goes jogging and is killed by a truck. She testifies they agreed to be married, held themselves out to the hotel clerk as man and wife and lived together for an evening. He is dead. Are they married? Is she a stranger or a grieving widow entitled to an intestate share of his estate? A jury could decide either way.

Or

A man and woman purchase a house after they have cohabited three months. He has a terrible credit rating so it is purchased in the woman's name. They maintain separate business identities but since each has a child of a former marriage living with them they occasionally introduce each other to school officials as Mr. and Mrs. Friends consider them single. They have applied for credit on one occasion as Mr. and Mrs. to avoid embarrassment. The house was purchased for $30,000. A pool has been installed and the neighborhood has improved. House and improvements are now worth $70,000. They separate. Can he get a divorce and share the $40,000 equity in the house? Is he a husband or a tenant with conjugal rights entitled to nothing? A jury could decide either way.

If one is careful, common law marriage is avoided and cohabitation remains a relationship of two people of opposite sexes, terminable at will, which exists so long as both parties elect to maintain the relationship. No divorce is needed. The parties separate and the relationship has ended.

Although a casual relationship would appear to be free from legal problems, such may not be the case in the long run. Many factors are worth considering.

In marriage, the rules are easily defined. Traditions, cases, precedents, texts, and family codes of the various states abound with all the ground rules, both substantive and procedural.

Cohabitation has no such legal tradition, and for this reason requires more planning in its inception and detailed provisions for parting of the ways. Since the law governing cohabitation may vary, a contractual arrangement should be established to provide for ease in managing and dividing the ongoing day-to-day accumulations, as well as in the event of a sudden or gradual termination. Rarely is a person entering into cohabitation directed to an attorney in order to engage in this advance planning.

If cohabitation follows the pattern of complete sharing, there is a true community of interests, and the parties may be tenants in common (Black's, 1968) or joint tenants (Black's, 1968) in any property acquired by common or comingled funds. Usually both work, but if not, and only one works and contributes financially and the other contributes services around the home in the form of cooking, cleaning or other household chores, a more difficult problem evolves. Each makes a contribution. Each must be compensated. Each must be protected where there is a common bank account, joint savings account, a regular accumulation of realty or any other items which the parties acquire. What might be acquired? How might each party's interest be protected?

REAL ESTATE

Record title to a homestead or any real estate is evidence of ownership. Third parties may rely on the recorded title. Mortgage companies will lend money to single people on the basis of income as well as the mortgage loan value of the security. A peaceful parting would not cloud the title, as the recorded deed would govern.

However, suppose the parties purchased a house in a rapidly appreciating area and the $30,000 home is now a $75,000 home, or the $5,000 shack on the lake is now resort property worth $50,000.

Is it fair that the party named in the deed or record owner realize this unforeseen gain? Is there some greater equity which should prevail? Needless to say, the non-record owner would truly feel "had," if as a courtesy or perhaps to save embarrassment to the family the deed were received in the other party's name. If sufficiently agitated, the non-record owner would consult an attorney who would endeavor to impress either a partnership interest (Black's, 1968), a constructive (Black's, 1968) or resulting trust (Black's, 1968) or some other type of equitable ownership in the property. Litigation with all its bitterness and invective, would surely result. Some arrangement should be made to provide a release and clear deed for either party in the event the relationship terminates. There should be a balancing of the equities. If joint contributions have been made, provision must be made in cash or kind to compensate the non-record owner, so that both parties feel that upon parting they have been treated fairly.

PERSONAL PROPERTY

All couples accumulate jewelry, clothing, appliances, furniture, automobiles and perhaps, if the parties are planning for the future, even stocks and bonds and other securities. Automobiles have a record owner listed in the title certificate or registration in all states, and the title certificate would govern. Likewise, securities are issued in one or both parties' names, and the person in whose name the security was issued would be considered the record owner. Other items are different. The tracing of household goods after a few years of accumulation is impossible. A division in kind is possible, but this takes a genuine sense of fair play which may or may not be present should the division be hostile. Cohabitation, like marriage, may terminate in bitterness, frustration and anger.

A suggestion in this area would be to have a "yours" and "mine" list. Thus as items were purchased and placed into common use, they would be inserted on a current list which would serve as a contract on dissolution. Each list would indicate that the owner of the property on the list was one or the other, although both parties could share in the use of these items so long as they resided together.

Another method might be a clear understanding that various items would be purchased and bills of sale received in the name of one party or the other. In the event of a division, each party would receive that item for which he had a bill of sale. Other techniques might be available, as in a dissolution of a partnership (Bouvier's, 1974). Whatever the technique, it must be reduced to writing, signed, maintained current, and available for use in a courtroom in the event the division cannot be done peaceably.

INSURANCE

Few single couples have considered or taken out substantial life insurance on themselves or another party. Nevertheless, the problems are the same as in marriage. A true, lasting relationship requires the parties to consider insurance probabilities. Not all parties are covered by their employers for insurance, and major medical insurance will cover a "spouse" and dependents only, not girl friends and boy friends. Genuine care must be exercised in procuring insurance. The agent must guarantee that the surviving beneficiary has an insurable interest, and that the insurance contract is not subject to contest by a former spouse, children of a former marriage, parents or other family members. All parties should explore the usual major medical, income disability, retirement, and life insurance plans. One fact is almost certain. Should the survivor of a short-term or possibly long-term relationship of cohabitation be the beneficiary of a substantial policy, one can be sure the family of the deceased would seek some theory, in law or in equity, which would enable the family to share in the insurance bonanza. This is true especially if there are children of a former marriage. Certainly, should the designated beneficiary have been recently changed from a parent, child, or other family member to the new roommate, one can anticipate a suit immediately over the proceeds of the policy on the grounds of fraud or duress. The insurance company, not wanting to be involved, would tender the money into the registry of the court and let the interested parties fight it out. Thus if insurance is involved, both parties must make certain that all legal procedures have been followed so as to guarantee effective insurance coverage.

WILLS AND ESTATES

Individuals with any property at all should be encouraged to execute a professionally drawn will. This is universally true whether the parties cohabiting are single, or married.

Depending on the jurisdiction, a will may be holographic (handwritten) or typewritten, witnessed by two or three witnesses, and/or in some state notarized. A document executed without the statutory formalities is not a valid will and generally serves no useful purpose.

Although a lawyer is not absolutely necessary to draft and oversee the proper execution of a will, in the sense that one can draft and execute his own will, more often than not a non-professionally drawn will is a lawyer's bonanza and a probate nightmare.

Imagine parties cohabiting for an extensive period of time. They have accumulated a homestead, a lakehouse, income producing property and a farm together with the various mortgages attached to each. Or they have gradually assembled household goods, objects of art, jewelry, a stamp or coin collection, stocks in individual or joint names, a canoe, an automobile, a camera or cameras and a few years' acquisiton of films and photographs. Or they have joint charge accounts, debts, accounts receivable and payable, long- or short-term bank loans, or oil royalties. Some of the above, all of the above, or perhaps just one of the above. One party dies. There is no will, or if there is a will it is hopelessly out of date and does not at all reflect the new relationship. Suddenly the survivor has a new interest to deal with. An ex-wife, children, parents, brothers and sisters are all interested. What started out as togetherness between the primary individuals ends in a totally new relationship as new parties step in to fill the shoes of the former mate, armed with rights acquired legally under an old will or by virtue of state laws providing for rights of interstate succession.

What is the solution? Parties intending to cohabit where there will be any accumulation of property whatsoever should visit with a lawyer. First, an inventory should be prepared so that each can dispose of all previously accumulated property in accordance with that particular party's wishes. Second, the parties should project the possible property to be acquired and their testamentary desires. A will should be drafted reflecting these desires, properly executed and maintained in a safe place. Third, whenever a change occurs in the primary relationship, the surrounding family, the tax laws or the finances of the parties, the will should be reviewed with an attorney and updated. A current will which disposes of property in accordance with the testator's wishes will not solve all problems, but it will provide the maximum protection available.

CHILDREN

If children are born of any union, they must be nurtured, loved, supported and educated. Abortion and adoption are one answer. A father may voluntarily legitimate a child, pay child support and have rights of visitation. A mother may file a suit for paternity and seek child support from the biological father. Where the cohabitation continues until the child's majority, property rights can be protected by gifts, wills, insurance and contracts. Where the cohabitation ends and the parties love or feel obligated toward the child, the child may, by agreement, receive the benefits of a traditional household.

The real problem emerges when a party terminates cohabitation, leaving children or a pregnant woman behind. Paternity suits, although permitted by law, are costly. Paternity must first be established to the satisfaction of a judge or jury. Then child support must be established and enforced.

Mothers with custody and child support set for them in a divorce decree face endless and costly litigation in the enforcement of child support awards against recalcitrant former spouses. This is just as true in cases involving a mother with a child born out of wedlock where the father considers the former relationship a bad dream that he wishes would simply go away. Where a parent elects to get lost and not provide for his children, he will most likely be successful. The woman must consider this realistic probability. Where children are a possibility, though remote, a meeting of the minds must be established concerning the rights and the obligations of the parties.

CUSTODY

Juries are usually composed of individuals older than the general population, and they may be demanded in many jurisdictions. Judges cannot be counted upon as being in the vanguard of liberality.

When a person has custody of a child by a prior marriage and cohabits, there is a clear risk that the former spouse may successfully maintain an action to change custody. This is especially true if the former spouse is either remarried and now has a family in the traditional American mold, or if single and living an exemplary life. Attorneys wax eloquent in arguments concerning the sanctity of the home and motherhood as opposed to "living in sin against the law of God and man." Thus a mother or father with custody faces a clear and present danger of losing the children by living in cohabitation. This is by no means certain, but it is a fact to be faced squarely and considered. One step to the bond of matrimony eliminates the problem. Is it worth it?

CONCLUSION

Although law concerning the traditional marriage is well settled, the law concerning cohabitation is less clearly defined. Parties who enter into a relationship of cohabitation are beginning the same general pattern as a traditional marriage. They will accumulate. They will buy. They will sell, alter, improve, trade, and dispose of all manner of real and personal property. They will rear and visit children by former marriages. They ultimately will or might hope to live comfortably in retirement on the estate garnered during their life together.

Contract, partnership and family law apply to parts of the arrangement, but there is no consolidated body of law, nor is there likely to be, such as a family code governing cohabitation. Therefore, couples considering cohabitation must explore or at least be aware of present and future legal perils, with children and custody being an obvious and traumatic potential.

VIII

ALTERNATIVE FORMS

18

THE EMERGENCE OF NONEXCLUSIVE MODELS OF THE MARITAL RELATIONSHIP

David L. Weis

One of the better known alternative scripts is the concept of open marriage presented by Nena and George O'Neill (1972a, 1972b, 1974). In their view, an open marriage is characterized by: (1) living in the "here-and-now" with realistic expectations, (2) respect for personal privacy, (3) role flexibility, (4) open and honest communications, (5) open companionship (an openness to personal relationships outside the marriage that *may or may not* include an agreement to allow ES), (6) equality of power and responsibility, (7) pursuit of personal identity, and (8) mutual trust. In the only empirical study of the degree of "openness" in marriages, Wachowiak and Bragg (1980) report that marital openness is correlated with fewer children, less frequent church attendance, younger age, and higher marital adjustment for wives (as measured by the Locke-Wallace Scale). Strictly speaking, the O'Neill model is not necessarily a script for nonexclusivity. Although they do maintain that ES can be successfully incorporated into a marriage if it is mutually agreeable to a couple and although they do support the establishment of a network of intimate friends outside marriage, the clear focus of their approach is self-determination. The O'Neills urge couples to set their own mutually agreeable rules for marriage. They would be as disturbed by the suggestion that married persons should have ES as by the dictate that such behavior be avoided. Despite this, the term "open" marriage is frequently taken to imply a marriage in which there is an agreement for consensual ES, although this is a gross misuse of the term.

This has led to some confusion in the years since the model first appeared. One is never certain when an author uses the term open marriage whether he or she is referring to the concept presented by the O'Neills or to the more widely held notion that open marriage means "playing around." This has led some writers (Buunk, 1980b; Knapp, 1975, 1976; Knapp and Whitehurst, 1977; Watson, 1981) to use the term "sexually open marriage" to refer to those marriages with a consensual agreement permitting ES. Others (Cole and Spanier, 1974; Knapp, 1975; Libby, 1977; L. G. Smith and Smith, 1974; Ziskin and Ziskin, 1975) use the term "comarital sex" to refer to consensual ES.

While it is certainly important to distinguish

David L. Weis, "The Emergence of Nonexclusive Models of the Marital Relationship," pp. 199–209 in *Contemporary Families and Alternative Lifestyles*, edited by Eleanor D. Macklin and Roger H. Rubins. Copyright © 1983 by Sage Publications, Inc. Reprinted by permission of Sage Publications, Inc.

139

extramarital behavior that is acknowledged and approved of by the spouse from that which is not, one must also recognize that many different types of behavior and agreements are subsumed under the rubric of comarital experiences. As one example, not all couples agree to permit the same type of extramarital experiences. Some couples establish agreements to permit friendships outside of marriage as long as they are not sexual. Some agree to permit ES if the ES relationship is temporary (like a fling on a business trip) or nonintimate. Some agree to allow ES "as long as I don't know about it." In short, couples make agreements that permit and also rule out various kinds of nonexclusive behavior. Each of these various agreements represents a slightly different scripting for nonexclusivity. Discussions of and research on comarital agreements must recognize that these scripts can vary on dimensions such as the degree of sexual involvement desired, the degree of intimate involvement desired, the degree of openness with the spouse, and the amount of time spent with the extramarital partner (Buunk, 1980b; Sprenkle and Weis, 1978).

An example of a particular comarital script is the pattern Ramey (1972, 1975, 1976) calls "intimate friendship networks." The focus of Ramey's model is the creation of an interpersonal network of close, loving friends. Within this context, married persons might conceivably have sexual relations with another member of the network. However, sex per se is not the focus of the interaction; intimacy is. Many couples involved in an intimate friendship network would not accept casual ES with a person outside of that network—the very opposite of many consensual agreements.

A very different example of a comarital script is provided by the lifestyle known as swinging or mate sharing. Swinging is a pattern in which couples share sexual interaction with others in a social context defined by the participants as recreational play (Bartell, 1970, 1971; Gilmartin, 1974, 1977, 1978). Swinging is something married couples do together. The formation of an extramarital sexual relationship by either of the spouses alone is a violation of the script. Whereas intimate friendship networks are designed to allow sexual contact between intimate friends, swinging is specifically structured to prevent intimacy (Bartell, 1970, 1971). Some writers have used terms such as "utopian swinging" (Symonds, 1970) or "interpersonal swinging" (Varni, 1972, 1973) to describe types of mate sharing oriented toward interpersonal intimacy rather than recreation, but such intimate arrangements are more in line with Ramey's model than with what is typically called swinging.

Thus far, two basic social scripts for nonexclusivity have been identified: (1) nonconsensual extramarital experiences and (2) consensual extramarital experiences. Both of these scripts are part of a larger script that views monogamous marriage as the primary intimate relationship. The last social script to be considered here concerns relationships that are nonmonogamous as well as nonexclusive. In general, the scripting for such lifestyles is similar to that for other nonexclusive patterns with respect to such beliefs as the diffusion of love/intimacy, the negative evaluation of jealousy, the multilateral character of need meeting, and the view of multilateral intimacy as growth enhancing (Constantine and Constantine, 1973; Ramey, 1972; Rimmer, 1966, 1969a). According to Ramey (1972), the primary difference between group marriage and open marriage or intimate friendship networks is the degree of commitment required of individuals. Multilateral involvements also challenge the notion of primacy in intimate relationships.

A few notes of caution must be added to this scripting perspective. The social scripts depicted here reflect the opinions and beliefs of various writers. There is little, if any, empirical verification that individuals actually internalize scripts as outlined here. Future research will need to determine the specific factors that constitute the various scripts for nonexclusivity. The present framework may be appropriately viewed as a set of hypotheses to be tested. Another issue concerns the very nature of social scripts at a theoretical level. Scripts are cognitive organizations of behavior. They are not, however, the behaviors themselves. It is not necessarily the case that individuals will establish lifestyles consistent with their scripts. For example, it cannot be assumed that someone who exhibits swinging behavior ipso facto has a swinging script. This person may have been coerced. Scott's (1980a) study of man sharing is another example.

Man sharing is clearly a multilateral relationship, but apparently one that many Black women enter because of structural constraints rather than to express a multilateral script. In fact, it would be enlightening to see what types of scripts the various participants of man sharing have as they enter such relationships and how those scripts change as the relationship proceeds. Quite clearly, more attention needs to be directed at the relationship between nonexclusive scripts and nonexclusive behavior.

A SELECTIVE REVIEW OF RESEARCH ON NONEXCLUSIVITY

The previous section suggested that, while much has been written about the belief structures characterizing nonexclusive lifestyles, there has been little empirical investigation of how those belief structures are related to the actual experience of nonexclusive lifestyles. . . .

Extramarital Sexual Relationships

One major avenue of research on ES has been the assessment of attitudes toward ES. Results with a variety of samples have consistently indicated that approximately 70 percent of American adults continue to disapprove of ES (Blum, 1966; Bukstel et al., 1978; Glenn and Weaver, 1979; Levitt and Klassen, 1974; Reiss et al., 1980; Singh, 1976). Approval of ES has been found to be related to: (1) being male, (2) young age, (3) low religiosity, (4) high education, (5) gender egalitarianism, (6) political liberality, (7) unhappiness with marriage, and (8) premarital sexual permissiveness. The Reiss research group (1980) has presented a theoretical model of extramarital permissiveness (see Reiss et al., 1980) and, although much of it still needs to be tested, it represents a major step in thinking about nonexclusivity. Finally, Buunk (1980a) found with a Dutch sample that the intent to engage in ES is related to a need for intimacy, marital need deprivation, a facilitative social context, approval by the spouse, and gender egalitarianism. Unfortunately, because of the failure to assess attitudes toward specific types of ES, one cannot be certain that the relationships identified by previous research will also appear for specific types of ES.

Another major focus of research on ES has concerned the possible relationship between ES and marital happiness. Although several studies have found that ES involvement (usually assessed in terms of whether the respondent had ever had ES or not) is significantly related to marital unhappiness, these same studies indicate that many ES participants have happy marriages (Atwater, 1979; Bell et al., 1975; Cuber and Harroff, 1965; Edwards and Booth, 1976; Hunt, 1969, 1974; Johnson, 1970a, 1970b; Levin, 1975; Roebuck and Spray, 1967). Dissatisfaction with marriage is commonly thought to be a major motive for ES (Sprenkle and Weis, 1978). However, such variables as curiosity, desire for personal growth, and desire for new experience also appear to be motivating factors (Atwater, 1978, 1979; Buunk, 1980a; Ellis, 1969, 1972; Kinsey et al., 1948; Kinsey et al., 1953). Glass and Wright (1977) have provided evidence that the relationship between ES and marital satisfaction varies with the length of marriage and is different for men than it is for women.

Researchers have also explored the relationship between ES and structural variables,[1] equity (Walster et al., 1978), alienation (Whitehurst, 1969), and family violence (Whitehurst, 1971). Other topics of research have included extramarital sexual fantasy (Neubeck and Schletzer, 1962) and the formation of ES liaisons in a cocktail lounge (Roebuck and Spray, 1967).

Once again research on the behavioral aspects of ES has been weakened by the failure to distinguish types. Kinsey et al. (1948, 1953) reported that 50 percent of American men and 26 percent of American women experience ES at least once. It would appear that the rate for women has increased (Anthanasiou et al., 1970; Bell et al., 1975; Hunt, 1974; Levin, 1975; Maykovich, 1976) possibly because of the increased number of women working outside the home (Levin, 1975). It does appear that most ES is still of the nonconsensual and secretive variety and that it is more likely to be short term in nature (Hunt, 1974). However, few researchers have actually assessed such variables as length of the ES relationship or the degree of openness with the spouse.

Swinging. Of the various forms of consensual ES, the one that has received the most research attention is swinging. It has been estimated that 2 percent of the American population has participated in swinging (Athanasiou et al., 1970; Hunt, 1974). Comparisons of swingers with nonswingers reveal that swingers tend to be: (1) less religious, (2) overwhelmingly middle class, (3) predominantly White, and (4) quite "normal" except for their swinging behavior (Bartell, 1970, 1971; Breedlove and Breedlove, 1964; Denfeld and Gordon, 1970; Gilmartin, 1974, 1977, 1978; Twichell, 1974; Varni, 1972; Walshok, 1974). Bartell (1970, 1971) reported that the swingers in his study (from the midwest) tended to be politically conservative and were unlikely to have gone to college. Moreover, the wives in the Bartell study were unlikely to be employed outside the home. These findings stand in contrast to other studies, which have found swingers to be politically liberal and more likely to have gone to college, with the husbands likely to be employed in professional or white-collar positions and the wives employed outside the home (Denfeld and Gordon, 1970; Gilmartin, 1974, 1977; Twichell, 1974).

In a comparison of swinging and nonswinging couples, Gilmartin (1974, 1977, 1978) found that the swingers have less rewarding relationships with their parents; interact more frequently with their friends, but less with neighbors and relatives; are less attached to agents of social control like the church; gain heterosexual experiences at a younger age and with more partners; have sexual relations more frequently; marry younger; and are more likely to have been divorced in a previous marriage. The swinging couples did not significantly differ in marital happiness in comparison to the control couples, although they did report higher ratings than those control couples engaging in secretive ES (Gilmartin, 1977, 1978).

Husbands tend to initiate swinging behavior (Bartell, 1970, 1971; Henshel, 1973; Varni, 1972), and wives usually respond negatively to the suggestion (Varni, 1972). For those couples who overcome their initial anxieties, swinging can contribute positively to the marriage by increasing openness and sharing between the husband and wife (Bartell, 1971; Denfeld and Gordon, 1970; Varni, 1972). It must be noted, however, that this is a view expressed by active swingers. In a study of couples who had dropped out of swinging and gone to a marriage counselor, Denfeld (1974a, 1974b) found that such problems as jealousy, guilt, emotional attachments, boredom, and perceived threats to the marriage were common reasons for dropping out of swinging. Unfortunately, there has been no research identifying the factors that differentiate couples who are satisfied with swinging from those who are not.

Sexually Open Marriage (SOM). In contrast to swinging, which is a behavior shared by husbands and wives, some couples establish mutual agreements to allow each other to have openly acknowledged, independent sexual relationships with other partners (Macklin, 1980). There have been very few empirical investigations of such consensual agreements. Beltz (1969) reported that none of the five clinical couples he studied had been able to successfully incorporate ES into their marriages. Knapp (1976) and Whitehurst (Knapp and Whitehurst, 1977) found their White, middle-class samples to be highly individualistic, nonconformist, stimulated by complexity, and motivated by personal value systems. These couples reported such problems as: (1) jealousy, (2) loneliness, (3) complex negotiations, (4) lack of social support, and (5) conflict over free time. They also cited increased self-esteem and increased awareness of self and others as benefits derived from pursuing a sexually open marriage. Most were unwilling to return to a more traditional relationship. Knapp and Whitehurst (1977) suggested that this lifestyle required: (1) the desire to maintain the primacy of the marriage, (2) a high degree of affection between spouses and a mutual agreement over the choice of lifestyle, (3) the skills needed to manage complex relationships, and (4) the selection of extramarital partners who would not compete with the spouse.

Buunk (1980b) has studied the ground rules or strategies that SOM couples evolve to reduce potential threats to the marriage. Buunk identified five types of couple strategies: (1) primary value placed on maintaining the marriage, (2) limiting the intensity of the ES involvements, (3) keeping the spouse fully informed of ES relationships, (4) approving ES only if it involves mate exchange, and (5) tolerating ES if it is invisible to the spouse. Buunk's research represents an important step in our understanding of nonexclusivity. It would be enlightening to explore the relationship between type of strategy and the consequences of extramarital behavior.

The only longitudinal evidence of effect of SOM on marriage comes from a two-year study of persons who had experienced such a relationship (Watson, 1981), some of whom were divorced at time of first interview and some of whom were still in an ongoing SOM relationship. Those who were divorced indicated that the SOM experience had been motivated by an unfulfilling marriage, that their outside relationship had been more satisfying, and that they did not desire to return to an SOM relationship. After two years, members of the ongoing group were still married but, with one exception, had adopted an exclusive relationship although they still saw SOM as a possible future choice. Watson concludes that SOM may be a stage in a relationship rather than an ongoing lifestyle.

Intimate Friendship Networks (IFN). Ramey (1975, 1976) has studied 380 individuals participating in IFN. In general, these persons seem to have the same kinds of personal characteristics and experience similar costs/benefits as the couples studied by Knapp and Whitehurst. The overwhelming majority reported being satisfied with their primary relationship, but it must be noted that Ramey focused his investigation on persons participating in IFN for ten years. Ramey maintains that IFN develop from the practice of sexually open marriage over an extended period of time.

Multilateral Marriage/Relationships. Multilateral or group marriage has probably been the least studied of the lifestyles addressed in this chapter, and it is probably the least common as well. Joan and Larry Constantine's research (1973) on group marriages in the United States is virtually the only source of data on American groups, and their various publications constitute the bulk of the empirically grounded literature (Constantine, 1978; Constantine and Constantine, 1972, 1973, 1974, 1977; Constantine et al., 1972). The Constantines report that the typical multilateral marriage consists of four adults. Most persons enter a multilateral marriage with their spouse, and if the group dissolves, most of the original pair bonds survive. In fact, the original pair bonds appear to retain some semblance of primacy after the formation of the group, and this may be a factor working against the success of the group.

Scores on the various personality profiles employed by the Constantines indicate that participants tend to have a high need for change and autonomy and low need for order, guilt, and deference. Common motives for entering a group marriage include a desire for more companionship, sexual variety, love, and personal growth Few of the groups studied by the Constantines lasted more than a year. The major problems leading to a break-up seemed to be communication difficulties, jealousy, and interpersonal conflict.

Scott (1980a, 1980b) has studied the phenomenon of man sharing in contemporary Black American communities by interviewing eleven consensual and eleven legal wives. Man sharing is a pattern where two (or conceivably more) women living in separate dwellings each maintain an intimate relationship with one man. Scott refers to this pattern as a form of Black polygamy, although other writers (Allen and Agbasegbe, 1980; McAdoo, 1980) deny this claim largely on the basis that the lifestyle is not voluntarily chosen by women and is not socially legitimated. It would appear that the imbalanced sex ratio among Blacks and the economic deprivation of Blacks compel Black women to accept man-sharing arrangements (Allen and Agbasegbe, 1980; McAdoo, 1980; Scott, 1980b). Scott counters such criticisms by noting that Black women do consent to man sharing and that these relationships are socially recognized in the Black community. This study can be applauded for its focus on a group that is not representative of the white middle class usually studied by researchers of nonexclusivity.

Extramarital Nonsexual Relationships

As noted earlier, relatively little attention has been given to the nonsexual relationships established outside of marriage. Weis and Slosnerick (1981) report the results of a study of the attitudes of college students toward a range of male/female extramarital interactions. Approximately 80 percent of the students disapproved of ES. However, one-half of the students indicated approval of such activities as dancing or eating dinner when the spouse was absent, and nearly 80 percent approved of going to a movie. Approval of the various extramarital situations was related to: *(1)* disassociation of sex, love, and marriage, *(2)* premarital sexual permissiveness, and *(3)* being male. Approval was *not* related to marital status or length of marriage. These findings indicate that exclusivity is a multidimensional construct influencing scripting for nonsexual as well as sexual interactions. The fact that a majority of the students approved several of the nonsexual extramarital situations also suggests that researchers who have been interested in studying changing attitudes toward exclusivity may be focusing on the wrong end of the continuum. Because sexuality is viewed by Americans as the most intimate of behaviors, it seems likely that attitudes toward sexual exclusivity would be the last to change.

AN ASSESSMENT OF THE FUTURE

What can research to date tell us about future trends? Many writers argue that American society is about to experience a shift toward nonexclusive values, but few of these claims are substantiated by data. Glenn and Weaver (1979) maintain that the greater permissiveness of young, highly educated persons in a national study of ES attitudes may lead to an increased acceptance of ES in the future. However, other studies raise some doubts about this. Strong (1978) reported that consensual ES, spouse swapping, and group marriage were ranked as the least desirable of a group of twelve lifestyles in a study of 354 college students. They were also the only nonexclusive lifestyles included in the study. In a study comparing Black/White and Male/Female college students, Ericksen (1980) reported that White males were the group most likely to indicate they would participate in a marriage with consensual ES, but only 17 percent of them were willing to participate in such a marriage. Rao and Rao (1980) conducted a similar study of Black students' willingness to participate in various lifestyles. They found 13 percent willing to have consensual ES, 7 percent willing to swap spouses, 8 percent willing to participate in a group marriage, 7 percent in polyandry, and 14 percent in polygyny. None of these studies provides much evidence that nonexclusive lifestyles will be viewed as more acceptable in the foreseeable future.

This does not necessarily mean, however, that American society will continue to maintain the norm of exclusivity. Reiss (1980) notes that, with respect to premarital sexual norms, behavior changes preceded attitudinal changes. There are several factors that suggest that a similar shift may occur in extramarital experiences during the next several decades. The growth of technology and the growth of female participation in the labor force is already leading to an increase in male/female interactions involving married persons. While it is certainly not the case that all or even most of these interactions will result in a sexual exchange, it is certainly true that opportunities will develop. The growing divorce rate is resulting in increases in what is sometimes called serial monogamy. It could just as easily be called serial nonexclusivity. One result will be that increasing numbers of Americans will experience multiple (though not at the same time) intimate/sexual relationships, and they will be exposed to the benefits of multiple intimacy. The decreases in age of first intercourse will have similar impact on premarital experience by increasing the probability that young people have several intimate/sexual relationships before marriage.

Each of the above factors, plus the growth of singlehood as a lifestyle (Libby and Whitehurst, 1977), will mean that America will increasingly be characterized by what Farber (1964) calls permanent availability. The increased isolation of the nuclear family, the growing egalitarianism of male/female relationships, the greater acceptability of premarital sex, the increasing mobility of American society, the advent of contraceptive technology, and the increased alienation of contemporary society have all been offered as possible factors leading to increases in nonexclusive behavior. As these factors converge, more Americans are likely to have at least minimal experience with multiple intimacy and sexuality. In effect, it is being suggested here that there will be increases in nonexclusive behaviors over the next fifty years, even though most people today do not want those changes. As a consequence, it seems reasonable to predict that most nonexclusive behavior will continue to follow the secretive, nonconsensual mode for some time to come. It seems premature to make any predictions about the various consensual models discussed in this chapter. After all, those models have only recently emerged; they are still being "tested for suitability," and Americans are still a long way from acknowledging that many of us will not lead exclusive lives.

The prediction that there will be increases in nonexclusive behaviors in the next several decades must be viewed as highly speculative at best. Unfortunately, there has been little research on the factors cited here as likely to influence increases in nonexclusivity. This can be viewed as one of the major weaknesses of research on nonexclusive lifestyles. Sadly, little is known about the social factors that are related to nonexclusive lifestyles—the very type of knowledge we need to make precise predictions of future behavior. . . .

NOTE

[1] Given the length of this chapter, it is not possible to review that research here. In essence, results are similar to those with ES attitudes (for more detailed reviews of ES research, see Libby, 1977; Macklin, 1980; Reiss, 1980).

REFERENCES

Allen, W. R., and B. A. Agbasegbe. 1980. A comment on Scott's "Black polygamous family formation." *Alternative Lifestyles* 3, 4: 375–81.

Andelin, H. B. 1974. *Fascinating womanhood*. New York: Bantam.

Athanasiou, R., P. Shaver, and C. Tavris. 1970. Sex. *Psychology Today* 4 (July): 39–52.

Atwater, L. 1979. Getting involved: women's transition to first extramarital sex. *Alternative Lifestyles* 2, 1: 38–68.

———. 1978. *Women in extramarital relationships: A case study in socio-sexuality*. New York: Irvington.

Banasher, M. 1978. Infidelity: what it can and can't do for your love life. *Mademoiselle* (March): 210–19.

Bartell, G. D. 1971. *Group sex: A scientist's eyewitness report on the American way of swinging*. New York: Wyden.

———. 1970. Group sex among the mid-Americans. *Journal of Sex Research* 6: 113–30.

Bell, R. R., S. Turner, and L. Rosen. 1975. A multi-variate analysis of female extramarital coitus. *Journal of Marriage and the Family* 37, 2: 375–84.

Beltz, S. E. 1969. Five-year effects of altered marital contracts: a behavioral analysis of couples. In G. Neubeck (ed.), *Extramarital relations*, pp. 162–89. Englewood Cliffs, N.J.: Prentice-Hall.

Blum, S. 1966. When can adultery be justified or forgiven? *McCall's* (May).

Breedlove, W., and J. E. Breedlove. 1964. *Swap clubs: A study in contemporary sexual mores*. Sherbourne Press.

Bukstel, L. H., G. D. Roeder, P. R. Kilmann, J. Laughlin, and W. M. Sotile. 1978. Projected extramarital sexual involvement in unmarried college students. *Journal of Marriage and the Family* 40, 2: 337–40.

Buunk, B. 1980a. Extramarital sex in the Netherlands. *Alternative Lifestyles* 3, 1: 11–39.

———. 1980b. Sexually open marriages: ground rules for countering potential threats to marriage. *Alternative Lifestyles* 3, 3: 312–28.

Cadwallader, M. 1966. Marriage as a wretched institution. *Atlantic Monthly* (November): 62–66.

Cazenave, N. A. (ed.). 1980. *Black alternative lifestyles*. Special issue of *Alternative Lifestyles* 3 (November): 371–504.

———. 1979. Social structure and personal choice: effects on intimacy, marriage and the family alternative lifestyle research. *Alternative Lifestyles* 2 (November): 331–58.

Chesser, E. 1956. *The sexual, marital and family relationships of the English woman*. Watford, England: Hutchinson's Medical Publications.

Christensen, H. T. 1973. Attitudes toward infidelity: a nine-culture sampling of university student opinion. *Journal of Comparative Family Studies* 4 (Autumn): 197–214.

———. 1962. A cross-cultural comparison of attitudes toward marital infidelity. *International Journal of Comparative Sociology* 3: 124–37.

Clanton, G., and L. G. Smith (eds.). 1977. *Jealousy*. Englewood Cliffs, N.J.: Prentice-Hall.

Cole, C. L., and G. B. Spanier. 1974. Comarital mate-sharing and family stability, *Journal of Sex Research* 10: 21–31.

Constantine, L. L. 1978. Multilateral relations revisited: group marriage in extended perspective. In B. I. Murstein (ed.),

Exploring intimate life styles, pp. 131–47. New York: Springer.

———, and J. M. Constantine. 1977. Sexual aspects of group marriage. In R. W. Libby and R. N. Whitehurst (eds.), *Marriage and alternatives: Exploring intimate relationships,* pp. 186–94. Glenview, Ill.: Scott, Foresman.

———. 1974. Sexual aspects of multilateral relations. In J. R. Smith and L. G. Smith (eds.), *Beyond monogamy,* pp. 268–90. Baltimore: Johns Hopkins Press.

———. 1973. *Group marriage: A study of contemporary multilateral marriage.* New York: Macmillan.

———. 1972. Dissolution of marriage in a non-conventional context. *Family Coordinator* 21, 4: 457–62.

———, and S. K. Edelman. 1972. Counseling implications of comarital and multilateral relations. *Family Coordinator* 21 (July): 267–73.

Cooper, D. 1970. *The death of the family.* New York: Vintage.

Cuber, J. F. 1969. Adultery: reality versus stereotype. In G. Neubeck (ed.), *Extramarital relations,* pp. 190–196. Englewood Cliffs, N.J.: Prentice-Hall.

———, and P. B. Harroff. 1965. *Sex and the significant Americans.* Baltimore: Viking.

Decter, M. 1972. *The new chastity.* New York: Berkley Medallion.

DeLora, J. S., and J. R. DeLora (eds.). 1972. *Intimate life styles: Marriage and its alternatives.* Pacific Palisades, Calif.: Goodyear.

Denfeld, D. 1974a. Dropouts from swinging. *Family Coordinator* 23 (January): 45–59.

———. 1974b. Dropouts from swinging: the marriage counselor as informant. In J. R. Smith and L. G. Smith (eds.), *Beyond monogamy,* pp. 260–67. Baltimore: Johns Hopkins Press.

———, and M. Gordo. 1970. The sociology of mate swapping. *Journal of Sex Research* 6: 85–100.

Edwards, J. N., and A. Booth. 1976. Sexual behavior in and out of marriage: an assessment of correlates. *Journal of Marriage and the Family* 38, 1: 73–81.

Ellis, A. 1972. *The civilized couple's guide to extramarital adventure.* New York: Pinnacle.

———. 1969. Healthy and disturbed reasons for having extramarital relations. In G. Neubeck (ed.), *Extramarital relations,* pp. 153–61. Englewood Cliffs, N.J.: Prentice-Hall.

Ericksen, J. A. 1980. Race, sex, and alternate lifestyle choices. *Alternative Lifestyles* 3, 4: 405–24.

Farber, B. 1964. *Family: Organization and interaction.* San Francisco: Chandler.

Ford, C. S., and F. A. Beach. 1951. *Patterns of sexual behavior.* New York: Perennial.

Francoeur, A. K., and R. T. Francoeur. 1974. *Hot and cool sex.* New York: Harcourt, Brace, Jovanovich.

French Institute of Public Opinion. 1961. *Patterns of sex and love: A study of the French woman and her morals.* New York: Crown.

Gagnon, J. H., and C. S. Greenblat. 1978. *Life designs: Individuals, marriages, and families.* Glenview, Ill.: Scott, Foresman.

Gagnon, J. H., and W. Simon. 1973. *Sexual conduct: The social sources of human sexuality.* Chicago: Aldine.

Gecas, V., and R. Libby. 1976. Sexual behavior as symbolic interaction. *Journal of Sex Research* 12 (February): 33–49.

Gilmartin, B. G. 1978. The Gilmartin Report. Secaucus, N.J.: Citadel.

———. 1977. Swinging: who gets involved and how? In R. W. Libby and R. N. Whitehurst (eds.), *Marriage and alternatives: Exploring intimate relationships,* pp. 161–85. Glenview, Ill.: Scott, Foresman.

———. 1974. Sexual deviance and social networks: a study of social, family and marital interaction patterns among co-marital sex participants. In J. R. Smith and L. G. Smith (eds.), *Beyond monogamy,* pp. 291–323. Baltimore: Johns Hopkins Press.

Glass, S. P., and T. L. Wright. 1977. The relationship of extramarital sex, length of marriage, and sex differences on marital satisfaction and romanticism: Athanasiou's data reanalyzed. *Journal of Marriage and the Family* 39 (November): 691–703.

Glenn, N. D., and C. N. Weaver. 1979. Attitudes toward premarital, extramarital, and homosexual relations in the U.S. in the 1970's. *Journal of Sex Research* 15: 108–18.

Gordon, S., and R. W. Libby (eds.). 1976. *Sexuality today—and tomorrow.* North Scituate, Mass.: Duxbury.

Henshel, A. 1973. Swinging: a study of decision-making in marriage. *American Journal of Sociology* 78 (January): 885–91.

Hunt, M. 1974. *Sexual behavior in the 1970's.* New York: Dell.

———. 1969. *The affair.* New York: World.

Hymer, S. M., and A. M. Rubin. (Forthcoming.) Therapists' attitudes and clinical experiences with alternative lifestyle clients. *Small Group Behavior.*

Johnson, R. E. 1970a. Extramarital sexual intercourse: a methodological note. *Journal of Marriage and the Family* 32 (May): 279–82.

———. 1970b. Some correlates of extramarital coitus. *Journal of Marriage and the Family* 32 (August): 449–56.

Keller, S. 1971. Does the family have a future? *Journal of Comparative Family Studies* II (Spring): 1–14.

Kinsey, A. C., W. B. Pomeroy, and C. E. Martin. 1948. *Sexual behavior in the human male.* Philadelphia: Saunders.

Kinsey, A. C., W. B. Pomeroy, C. E. Martin, and P. A. Gebhard. 1953. *Sexual behavior in the human female.* Philadelphia: Saunders.

Knapp, J. J. 1976. An exploratory study of seventeen open marriages. *Journal of Sex Research* 12: 206–19.

———. 1975. Some non-monogamous marriage styles and related attitudes and practices of marriage counselors. *Family Coordinator* 24 (October): 505–14.

———, and R. N. Whitehurst. 1977. Sexual open marriage and relationships: issues and prospects. In R. W. Libby and R. N. Whitehurst (eds.), *Marriage and alternatives: Exploring intimate relationships,* pp. 147–60. Glenview, Ill.: Scott, Foresman.

Laws, J. L., and P. Schwartz. 1977. *Sexual scripts: The social construction of female sexuality.* Hinsdale, Ill.: Dryden.

Levin, R. J. 1975. The Redbook report on premarital and extramarital sex: the end of a double standard? *Redbook* (October): 38–44, 190–92.

Levitt, E. E., and A. D. Klassen. 1974. Public attitudes toward homosexuality: part of the 1970 national survey by the Institute for Sex Research. *Journal of Homosexuality* 1, 1: 29–43.

Libby, R. W. 1977. Extramarital and comarital sex: a critique of the literature. In R. W. Libby and R. N. Whitehurst (eds.), *Marriage and alternatives: Exploring intimate relationships,* pp. 80–111. Glenview, Ill.: Scott, Foresman.

———, and R. N. Whitehurst (eds.). 1977. *Marriage and alternatives: Exploring intimate relationships,* Glenview, Ill.: Scott, Foresman.

Lobell, J., and M. Lobell. 1972. *John and Mimi: A free marriage.* New York: St. Martin's.

Lopata, H. Z. 1971. *Occupation housewife.* New York: Oxford University Press.

Macklin, E. D. 1980. Nontraditional family forms: a decade of research. *Journal of Marriage and the Family* 42 (November): 905–22.

Maykovich, M. K. 1976. Attitude versus behavior in extramarital sexual relations. *Journal of Marriage and the Family* 38 (November): 693–99.

Mazur, R. 1973. *The new intimacy.* Boston: Beacon.

———. 1970. Beyond morality: toward the humanization of the sexes. Paper presented at the Annual Meetings of the National Council on Family Relations.

McAdoo, H. P. 1980. Commentary on Joseph Scott's "Black polygamous family formation." *Alternative Lifestyles* 3, 4: 383–88.

McMurty, J. 1977. Monogamy: a critique. In R. W. Libby and R. N. Whitehurst (eds.), *Marriage and alternatives: Exploring intimate relationships,* pp. 3–13. Glenview, Ill.: Scott, Foresman.

Melville, K. 1980. *Marriage and family today.* New York: Random House.

Morgan, M. 1973. *The total woman.* Old Tappan, N.J.: Revell.

Murdock, G. P. 1949. *Social structure.* New York: Macmillan.

Neubeck, G. (ed.). 1969. *Extramarital relations.* Englewood Cliffs, N.J.: Prentice-Hall.

Neubeck, G., and V. Schletzer. 1962. A study of extramarital relationships. *Marriage and Family Living* 24, 3: 279–81.

O'Neill, N. 1977. *The marriage premise.* New York: M. Evans.

———, and G. O.'Neill. 1974. Open marriage: a conceptual framework. In J. R. Smith and L. G. Smith (eds.), *Beyond monogamy,* pp. 56–67. Baltimore: Johns Hopkins Press.

———. 1972a. *Open marriage: A new life style for couples.* New York: M. Evans.

———. 1972b. Open marriage: a synergic model. *Family Coordinator* 21, 4: 403–09.

Otto, H. A. (ed.). 1970. *The family in search of a future,* New York: Appleton-Century-Crofts.

Ramey, J. W. 1976. *Intimate friendships.* Englewood Cliffs, N.J.: Prentice-Hall.

———. 1975. Intimate groups and networks: frequent consequences of sexually open marriage. *Family Coordinator* 24 (October): 515–30.

———. 1974. Communes, group marriage and the upper-middle class. In J. R. Smith and L. G. Smith (eds.), *Beyond monogamy,* pp. 214–29. Baltimore: Johns Hopkins Press.

———. 1972. Emerging patterns of innovative behavior in marriage. *Family Coordinator* 21, 4: 435–56.

Rao, V. V., and V. N. Rao. 1980. Alternatives in intimacy, marriage, and family lifestyles: preferences of Black college students. *Alternative Lifestyles* 3, 4: 485–98.

Reiss, I. L. 1980. *Family systems in America.* New York: Holt, Rinehart & Winston.

———, R. E. Anderson, and G. C. Sponaugle. 1980. A multivariate model of the determinants of extramarital sexual permissiveness. *Journal of Marriage and the Family* 42, 2: 395–411.

Rimmer, R. H. 1977. *Come live my life.* New York: Signet.

——— (ed.). 1973. *Adventures in loving.* New York: Signet.

———. 1972. *Thursday, my love.* New York: Signet.

———. 1971. *You and I . . . searching for tomorrow.* New York: Signet.

———. 1969a. *Proposition 31.* New York: Signet.

———. 1969b. *The Harrad letters.* New York: Signet.

———. 1966. *The Harrad experiment.* New York: Bantam.

———. 1964. *The rebellion of Yale Marratt.* New York: Avon.

Roebuck, J., and S. L. Spray. 1967. The cocktail lounge: a study of heterosexual relations in a public organization. *American Journal of Sociology* 72: 388–95.

Rosner, S., and L. Hobe. 1974. *The marriage gap.* New York: McGraw-Hill.

Roy, R., and D. Roy. 1977. Is monogamy outdated? In

R. W. Libby and R. N. Whitehurst (eds.), *Marriage and alternatives: Exploring intimate relationships,* pp. 22–34. Glenview, Ill.: Scott, Foresman.

———. 1968. *Honest sex.* New York: Signet.

Russell, B. 1929. *Marriage and morals.* New York: Liveright.

Ryals, K., and D. Foster. 1976. Open marriage: a question of ego development and marriage counseling. *Family Coordinator* 25, 3: 297–302.

Safilios-Rothschild, C. A. 1969. Attitudes of green spouses toward marital infidelity. In G. Neubeck (ed.), *Extramarital relations,* pp. 77–93. Englewood Cliffs, N.J.: Prentice-Hall.

Schnall, M. 1976. *Your marriage.* New York: Pyramid Books.

Schwartz, P. 1977. Female sexuality and monogamy. In R. W. Libby and R. N. Whitehurst (eds.), *Marriage and alternatives: Exploring intimate relationships,* pp. 229–40. Glenview, Ill.: Scott, Foresman.

Scott, J. W. 1980a. Black polygamous family formation: case studies of legal wives and consensual "wives." *Alternative Lifestyles* 3, 4: 41–64.

———. 1980b. Reprise: conceptualizing and researching American polygyny—and critics answered. *Alternative Lifestyles* 3, 4: 395–404.

Singh, B. K., B. L. Walton, and J. J. Williams. 1976. Extramarital sexual permissiveness: conditions and contingencies. *Journal of Marriage and the Family* 38, 4: 701–12.

Skolnick, A. J., and J. H. Skolnick (eds.). 1971. *Family in transition: Rethinking marriage, sexuality, child rearing, and family organization.* Boston: Little, Brown.

Smith, J. R., and L. G. Smith (eds.). 1974. *Beyond monogamy.* Baltimore: Johns Hopkins Press.

———. 1970. Co-marital sex and the sexual freedom movement. *Journal of Sex Research* 6: 131–42.

Smith, L. G., and J. R. Smith. 1974. Co-marital sex: the incorporation of extramarital sex into the marriage relationship. In J. R. Smith and L. G. Smith (eds.), *Beyond monogamy,* pp. 84–102. Baltimore: Johns Hopkins Press.

Sprenkle, D. H., and D. L. Weis. 1978. Extramarital sexuality: implications for marital therapists. *Journal of Sex and Marital Therapy* 4: 279–91.

Strong, L. 1978. Alternative marital and family forms: Their relative attractiveness to college students and correlates of willingness to participate in non-traditional forms. *Journal of Marriage and the Family* 40, 3: 493–503.

Sussman, M. B. (ed.). 1975. *The second experience: Variant family forms.* Special issue of *Family Coordinator* 24, 4.

——— (ed.). 1972. *Variant marriage styles and family forms.* Special issue of *Family Coordinator* 21, 4.

Symonds, C. 1970. The utopian aspects of sexual mate swapping: in theory and practice. Paper presented at Annual Meetings of the Society for the Study of Social Problems, Washington, DC.

Twichell, J. 1974. Sexually liberality and personality: a pilot study. In J. R. Smith and L. G. Smith (eds.), *Beyond monogamy,* pp. 230–45. Baltimore: Johns Hopkins Press.

Varni, C. A. 1973. Contexts of conversion: the case of swinging. In R. W. Libby and R. N. Whitehurst (eds.), *Renovating marriage,* pp. 166–81. Danville, Calif.: Consensus.

———. 1972. An exploratory study of spouse swapping. *Pacific Sociological Review* 15: 507–22.

Wachowiak, C., and H. Bragg. 1980. Open marriage and marital adjustment. *Journal of Marriage and the Family* 42, 1: 57–62.

Walshok, M. L.. 1974. The emergence of middle-class deviant subcultures: the case of swingers. In J. R. Smith and L. G. Smith (eds.), *Beyond monogamy,* pp. 159–69. Baltimore: Johns Hopkins Press.

Walster E., J. Traupmann, and G. W. Walster. 1978. Equity and extramarital sexuality. *Archives of Sexual Behavior* 7 (March): 127–42.

Walters, J. (ed.). 1977. *The family and the law.* Special issue of *Family Coordinator* 25, 4.

Watson, M. A. 1981. Sexually open marriage: three perspectives. *Alternative Lifestyles* 4, 1: 3–21.

Weis, D. L. 1979. Toward a theory of social scripting: the measurement of extramarital sexual scripts. Ph.D. dissertation, Purdue University.

———, and M. Slosnerick. 1981. Attitudes toward sexual and nonsexual extramarital involvement among a sample of college students. *Journal of Marriage and the Family* 43, 2: 349–58.

Whitehurst, R. N. 1977. Jealousy and American values. In G. Clanton and L. G. Smith (eds.), *Jealousy,* pp. 136–39. Englewood Cliffs, N.J.: Prentice-Hall.

———. 1971. Violence potential in extramarital sexual responses. *Journal of Marriage and the Family* 33: 683–91.

———. 1969. Extramarital sex: alienation or extension of normal behavior. In G. Neubeck (ed.), *Extramarital relations,* pp. 129–45. Englewood Cliffs, N.J.: Prentice-Hall.

Zetterberg, H. 1969. *On sexuallivet: Sverige.* Stockholm: SOV.

Ziskin, J., and M. Ziskin. 1975. Comarital sex agreements: an emerging issue in sexual counseling. *Counseling Psychologist* 5: 81–84.

19

EXPERIMENTAL FAMILY FORMS—THE FAMILY OF THE FUTURE

James Ramey

WHAT IS AN EXPERIMENTAL FAMILY FORM?

Americans have trouble defining experimental family forms, perhaps because they are unaware of the family pluralism in our society. The latest Bureau of Labor (March 1977, Note 1) figures indicate that in 1975, adults were distributed in United States households as follows:

Heading single-parent families	16%
Other single, widowed, separated, or divorced persons	21
Living in childfree or postchildrearing marriages	23
Living in dual-breadwinner nuclear families	16
Living in single-breadwinner nuclear families	13
Living in no-breadwinner nuclear families	1
Living in extended families	6
Living in experimental families or cohabiting	4
	100%

James Ramey, "Experimental Family Forms—The Family of the Future," *Marriage & Family Review*, January/February 1978, pp. 1–9. Reprinted by permission of The Haworth Press.

With the exception of the final category, these are variant family forms, not experimental family forms, although within them there may be some experimental forms, such as the single person who deliberately chooses to conceive and raise a child out of wedlock. Neither lay persons nor professionals avoid confusing the issue by lumping together those who actually change family structure with those who merely modify or redefine sex roles within the existing family structure—a process that occurs in almost every generation. Cogswell and Sussman explored this area in some depth in an article in 1972.

Bookshelves are crowded with titles on alternative marriage and family forms, including contract marriage, childfree marriage, trial marriage (cohabitation), homosexual marriage, sexually open marriage, family clusters, intimate groups and networks, multiadult households, consensual and nonconsensual adultery, single-parenting, swinging, communes, group marriage, and singlehood. We are now beginning to see a rash of information about yet another family form, one heretofore so taboo that it was mentioned only in whispers—the incestuous family. During the single month of April 1977, four major television programs were devoted to this subject.

How does one relate these seemingly disconnected and sometimes overlapping variations on interpersonal relating? How many people are they likely to attract? In a 1972 article, expanded in *Intimate Friendships* (1976), this author suggested a paradigm for establishing a complexity continuum on which they could be located. This continuum is anchored at one end in the absence of relationships—the celibate hermit—and then ranges through ever more complex nonprimary relationships, such as uncommitted dating, intimate groups and networks, or having a lover, to variations of primary relationships, such as cohabitation, contract marriage, traditional monogamous marriage, voluntary childfree marriage, or homosexual marriage. Even more complex are primary relationships plus nonprimary relationships, as in the case of consensual or nonconsensual adultery in marriage, sexually open marriage, or multiadult households. Mutiple primary relationships are found in group marriages. Finally, the most complex form is a combination of multiple primary relationships and nonprimary relationships. One example is a partner in a group marriage who is also a member of an intimate network with an outside lover.

There appears to be high association between the number of adherents to a particular lifestyle and its complexity; the more complex the lifestyle, the fewer practitioners. Constantine and Constantine (1973) estimate 1,000 group marriages or fewer in the United States. Zablocki (1977) estimates fewer than 50,000 individuals live in communes in the United States. The overwhelming majority of adults live in the least complex lifestyles, alone or with a single partner.

Despite these small numbers, communes and group marriages capture the imagination of behavioral scientists and popular writers. The vast outpouring of both serious and popular writing about experimental family forms has concentrated on such multiadult households or on such nonmonogamous relationships as swinging (couple-front consensual adultery) and sexually open marriage.

One clue to this preoccupation with complex lifestyles is revealed by the second part of the title of this review article—the future of the traditional nuclear family. What is considered to be the traditional nuclear family, a breadwinner-father, a housewife-mother, and two children under eighteen accounted for only 7 percent of the population in 1975 (Bureau of Labor Statistics, Note 1)! Etzioni, while not reporting the source of the data, declared, "the proportion of married households out of total households declined from 72.5% in 1965 to 64.9% in 1976. . . . While the average annual rate of decline was 33% for the first three years of this period, it tripled to 97% for the last three years" (1977, p. 487). He suggested that a generation from now, should this trend continue, there would not be a married household left. While this was not a prediction, he nevertheless said it sufficed to show that the family is an endangered species.

Those who predict the demise of the family fail to take into account that we have always had a plurality of family forms. It is unrealistic to use the monogamous nuclear family as the common starting point for all explorations of current experimental family forms, much less for an assessment of future family forms. Plural family forms have been the ideal in most cultures and times and are still preferred in some societies today, although even in these societies most people can only afford a dyadic marriage. Murdock (1949) stated that only 43 of the 238 societies he surveyed could be classified as monogamous, when preferential marriage form was used as the criterion. It is not the mere complexity of multiadult households that mitigates against them in our society.

In the United States, especially since the Civil War, we have idealized the nuclear family form even though we have not all lived in this type of family. Most individuals actually experience several family forms during their lives. Perhaps the reason we assume that we all live in a nuclear family is because we overwhelmingly tend to adopt dyadic primary relationships or none at all, despite the family form in which we live.

Much of the change in family form in the future can be expected to involve shifts in the number of individuals living in existing family forms. As the population ages there is an expansion in postchildrearing marriages. In the past five years, single-parent families have grown 11.5 times the rate of dual-parent families. Cohabitation now accounts for nearly 1 percent of all adults (Bureau of the Census, Note 2). Deliberately childfree couples account for almost 5 percent of all adults, yet the percentage of never-married individuals is not as high today as it was before World War I. The percentage of single parents is about the same as it was in 1910, and the percentage of childfree couples is less than one-fourth the percentage in the 1920s (Glick, 1977).

HISTORICAL CONTEXT

Three areas of change in our society are critically important to the current development of experimental family forms. The first of these is the American obsession with *personal freedom*. In the early days of the Republic this urge was expressed by striking out for the western frontier and carving oneself a place from the wilderness. As the physical frontier began to disappear, the Horatio Alger tradition began to emerge whereby one carved one's place out of the economic or technological frontier through the exercise of "Yankee ingenuity." That individualistic tradition has not abated in our society, but it has been reshaped in recent decades. While part of the population has remained steeped in the rugged individualist tradition of marriage, kids, a house, a boat, two cars, and a place in the country, others have responded to a new emphasis on individual growth and freedom that may include, but clearly transcends, the economic emphasis of rugged individualism. Maslow's vision of self-actualism has been stripped of its emphasis on responsibility and reduced to "do your own thing." More about this later.

The second area of change that must be considered in any realistic appraisal of experimental family forms is the impact of *four revolutions* that have occurred in this country over the past hundred years. The demographic revolution has wrought vast changes. In 1900, the average woman lived 47 years, 18 of them being childbearing years. By 1974, the average woman lived 74 years and only 8 involved childbearing (Francoeur, 1972). Today, the couple that remains married has better than one out of three chances to celebrate their 50th wedding anniversary. In fact they can expect to have over 30 years together after their children are grown and gone. 'Til death do us part takes on a very different meaning today than it did in 1900.

The biological revolution is of more recent vintage and is still occurring. Already the pill, which became generally available as recently as 1962, has been superseded by contraceptive sterilization as the most popular means of birth control among married couples. By 1973, contraceptive sterilization had tripled within three years even among the 15–24 age group (Westoff, 1976). In 1975, a survey of a sample of 3,403 married white men and women was conducted, the fourth in a series of National Fertility Studies. It was reported in 1975 that about 6.8 million couples chose surgical sterilization compared to 7.1 million wives using the pill to prevent an unwanted birth. Medical reasons accounted for 1.1 million additional sterilizations (*Sentinel,* 1977). Today in the United States, as in the rest of the world, sterilization is the preferred means of contraception. Women can at last control their own biology.

The economic revolution is also extremely relevant to our examination of change, for it has brought us to a point in history when for the first time the family is no longer the basic unit in society. Today the individual, male or female, can perform all the functions once reserved to the family—economic self-sufficiency, maintaining a household, meeting sexual needs, and raising children. The individual can now be the basic unit and in growing numbers is exercising this ability. Over a third of our adult population is single and living alone or with children. The individualistic tradition brought us first to the isolated nuclear family unit, with its instability and atomizing influence on the community, and now, because it is no longer possible to keep women "barefoot and pregnant," it is giving rise to a shift from family to individual units.

Finally there is the fourth revolution in communication. My father, grandfather, and great-grandfather grew up in essentially the same world. New ideas took decades and sometimes a generation to become part of general knowledge in their day—long enough to be processed, modified, accepted or rejected, and integrated into one's store of information. I have little more than a foothold in my father's world, and my children even less in mine, for the pace of change has been immeasurably speeded up, not alone by the acceleration of technological development but perhaps even more by instantaneous communication. We were armchair participants in the war in Vietnam. We all walked on the moon, and hundreds of millions of people all over the world simultaneously cheered a

14-year-old girl as she exhibited perfect form in the Olympic games in Montreal. Today we are innundated with information—more than we can process, much less integrate.

The change that is being wrought by these four revolutions is vast and cumulative, and most of it is yet to come. Already we have seen the flowering of the women's rights movement, a flowering that could not come about until women controlled their own economic and biologic futures. And this issue is very germaine to our examination of experimental family forms.

THE SEXUAL TRANSFORMATION

There is still one area of change that we must examine in order to understand the intellectual history underlying our current concern with experimental family forms—the transformation of our sexual attitudes. Sexual modernists (Robinson, 1976) contend that sexual experience neither threatens moral character nor drains vital energies, as the Victorians were wont to say. They practically denied women any sexual life, while the modernists contend that she is at least the sexual equal of the male. In addition, the modernists raise serious doubts about whether marriage and the family can or should be the only context for the expression of sexuality. Although European Romantic sexual doctrine also affirmed the essential worth of erotic experience, they also split with the modernists over the concept of sex for sex's sake, arguing that sex is of value only within the context of an intense psychological relationship, even if that relationship should occur outside marriage.

Havelock Ellis was a romantic, according to Robinson, who argued for broadening the spectrum of acceptable sexual behavior based on animal behavior and cultural relativism. He was an early spokesman for looking at homosexuality as variant rather than deviant and he defused the explosive issue of masturbation in young boys by pointing out that it was especially common in females. As an investigator of normal, rather than pathological sex, Ellis switched the traditional concern about the control of sexual activity in courtship to concern about sexual arousal as a potential problem. Ellis coined the term "trial marriage" for the preparenting stage of marriage many years before Margaret Mead advocated two-step marriage. He was in favor of divorce as an automatic right to either party so long as the children are taken care of. He believed in licensing parents rather than nonparents (Robinson, 1976, pp. 4–30).

According to Robinson, Ellis believed that men and women sought not just variety in sex but variety in romance and he hoped that the bonds of marriage could be loosened enough to accommodate this need. He felt that a number of simultaneous relationships were possible and that in an atmosphere of trust and truth about outside relationships there would be no jealousy. In other words, his stress was on psychological fidelity rather than sexual exclusivity (pp. 32–33).

Alfred Kinsey sought to undermine established categories of sexual wisdom rather than to create new ones. He concentrated on showing that sexual differences could be plotted on a curve or spectrum and avoided concern about the emotional aspects of sexuality by evaluating sexual experience in terms of counting orgasms without regard to how they occurred. He debunked the importance of marriage by showing that more than half of all orgasms were derived from sources outside intercourse between marriage partners, i.e., they were derived from socially disapproved and in large part illegal sources (Robinson, 1976, pp. 54–76).

Kinsey argued that while premarital sexual experience contributed to sexual success in marriage, once the knot was tied the problem of sexual outlet was largely resolved. Thus it was not until 1948 that he began asking his subjects about extramarital petting. However, in contrast to Ellis, he seemed to feel that extramarital sex should not be emotionally involved, lest it adversely affect the marriage. The idea that sex was permissible only when people loved each other was no less absurd to Kinsey than the belief that masturbation caused insanity. Only when repressed did sexual urges threaten emotional stability so that a rational society, in his view, would promote not only a positive but essentially a casual attitude toward sex, especially among the young.

Robinson feels that Masters and Johnson primarily differ from Kinsey in their antithetical sexual values and in their explicitly therapeutic intent.

He is particularly concerned about their bias toward female masturbators, exhibitionists, older individuals, upper-class subjects, and sexual inclinations.

> Their emphasis on the similarity of female and male response, their belittling of the penis and the lore associated with it, their campaign against the vaginal orgasm, and their inclination to judge sexual experience from an essentially marital, even monogamous, perspective all exemplify tendencies that are subtly supported by the bias of their sample. Their conservatism manifests itself in three broad areas of sexual inquiry. . . . They conceive of sexual life in terms of enduring, heterosexual relationships of substantial affection. They seem at times as much concerned with procreation as with pleasure. They betray an antibehavioral bias and a weakness for upbeat psychologizing in the manner of the neo-Freudians. On the other hand, they take genuinely progressive or even radical positions on women, on the elderly, and on masturbation. (pp. 140–41)

For Masters and Johnson an extramarital affair is a confession of marital failure and is itself a significant contributor to sexual inadequacy. A marriage should be saved no matter how emotionally bankrupt it may be.

Robinson concludes that the distinctive feature of contemporary culture is the casual and often brief extramarital alliances that are both known to and approved by the marriage partner and that this is the crux of the unresolved tensions of modern sexual tradition. We want to rid ourselves of the repressions of a romantic past but we fear emotional emptiness in a deromanticized future, even while we anticipate its greater freedom.

In review, there are three intertwined threads that establish the historical perspective for experimental family form evaluation; the press toward individual freedom and growth; the impact of the demographic, biologic, economic, and communications revolutions; and the unresolved conflict between sex as a physical need and sex as part of an elaborate emotional relationship.

CURRENT UNDERSTANDING OF EXPERIMENTAL FAMILY FORMS

Alice Rossi (1977) defends the monogamous nuclear family and takes issue with those who argue for sexual equality: "Sexual liberation seems to mean that increasing numbers of women are now following male initiatives in a more elaborate, multipartner sexual script [in which] to be faithful, possessive, exclusively heterosexual, and able to postpone gratification are signs of immaturity and oppression. . . . In the post-nuclear-family era, the adult can turn parenthood on and off and exchange children as well as sexual partners. It is not at all clear what the gains will be for either women or children in this version of human liberation. . . . recreational sex has contemporary ascendence over procreational sex (pp. 14–16)."

I have argued elsewhere that equity rather than equality should be the goal of human liberation (Ramey, 1976). Already we are seeing some women who have taken on male roles succumbing to typical male stress diseases, such as ulcers, heart disease, and loss of hair due to increased production of androgens. Much of Professor Rossi's critique is directed at the pop writers and propagandists for alternative lifestyles who have generated so much heat and so little light on the contemporary scene, rather than at those who are making a serious attempt to understand what is happening. The latter group, almost without exception, is convinced that most people will continue to live in familiar family forms.

What is required are hard facts about current behavior in experimental family forms and theory frameworks within which to assess these family forms, relate them to more conventional family forms, and predict the likelihood that they will persist, grow, or decline. We need to know what happens to practitioners of experimental family forms and to their relationships. Actual research data on experimental family forms is sparse and most of what exists is exploratory, descriptive, and based on opportunity samples.

Group Marriages

Larry and Joan Constantine have published the only study on group marriage or, as they call it, "multilateral marriage" (1973). (These are nonlegal marriages where three or more adults of both sexes live together as a family.) They found over a hundred groups, corresponded and met with more than 30, and intensively studied the 11 groups that form the basis for their book. Their in-depth study was considerably more thorough than most studies of the family ever attempted, involving multiple visits, separate interviews with each adult and child in the group as well as with the group as a whole, the use of both group and individual interview forms and questionnaires, and feedback sessions with both individuals and groups. In addition they secured psychological profiles, marital adjustment and satisfaction scores, and personality inventory scores on their 40 participants. They investigated their subjects' beliefs and values, their individual expectations and motives for forming a group marriage, and the disadvantages and problems they found. They examined the way the group related to significant others, to job, and to the community, and how they shared responsibilities, finances, and chores. They looked at the impact of the group on its children, if any, at the type of planning and structure they used in setting up the group, and at how they dissolved it.

Their results can best be summed up in their own words:

Multilateral marriage is, of course, an ideological extreme in which the traditional family boundary is completely eliminated, while a new, similar boundary is erected around the multilateral unit. But our research does not show this to be happening; internal boundaries are present, though highly diffuse; primary dyadic relationships are recognizable. . . . We do not expect that more than a small minority of families will be based on multilateral marriage. In many ways, it is the most difficult and extreme departure from previous models. Surprisingly, in its purest form its moral base is not at all distant from conventional morality. Sex and intimacy remain tied to marriage, and the boundaries of several of the intact groups in our knowledge are traditionally tight. Some couples have felt comfortable about cross-marital sex only after they regarded themselves as "engaged to be group married." (pp. 233, 235)

Communes

The most comprehensive study of communes so far undertaken in the United States is the Urban Communes Project, a three-year study, headed by Ben Zablocki. This project involves a sample of almost 700 men and women in 60 urban communes in Los Angeles, Houston, Atlanta, Minneapolis, Boston, and New York. In each city the study focused on religious, political, craft, music, art, and therapeutic groups. Some were intensely ideologic, while others were merely places where people chose to share economically. Some were highly structured, some were not. Some included children, but most did not. The overwhelming majority of the participants were single, and all groups included both sexes. These groups were found to constitute an important form of social support for some single individuals. Participants listed the following reasons for joining a commune, in rank order:

1. Economic
2. Order and regularity
3. Friendship and support from caring people in a noncaring world
4. As a way to leave home
5. To break with the past
6. In search of a viable alternative to things they had tried but did not like
7. Exploratory—a way of trying out a new lifestyle just for the sake of new experience
8. A way to live with a lover
9. A way to live in a single state in the company of others
10. A search for like-minded people
11. Companionship, or community

Participants indicated a number of activities made easier by communal living:

To be single	70%
To find out what you want in life	70
To be the kind of person you want to be	72
To meet financial emergencies	72
To find out who you are	74
To meet new people	77
To relate to people openly and spontaneously	80
To solve emotional problems	81
To be cared for when physically ill	82

Despite the wide variation in the types of communes studied, there was considerable uniformity regarding reported advantages. For some respondents joining was a hard decision, while others joined friends who were already there.

Communes located in Houston, Boston, and Los Angeles found it easier to find suitable housing. The average participant stays for two years. Some move on to another commune in the same town. Some attempt to change the structure of the commune and, if unsuccessful, move on to one more to their liking. Some leave to marry, often to persons they met while living communally, while others just drop out to return to their previous lifestyle. A significant proportion of the sample was steadily employed and led normal, rather than freaky lives, while pursuing undergraduate and graduate education or careers.

In contrast to the urban communes studied by Zablocki, most rural communes have involved a drop-out philosophy and few have survived for more than a season, with a few notable exceptions, such as Twin Oaks, The Farm, or the Hutterite communities. What these survivors have in common is discipline, structure, goals, rather than a "do your own thing" philosophy. The religious communes, such as the Hutterites, are the most highly structured and have the strongest, most centralized leadership. Such highly structured groups have much lower turnover than other types of communes, but this is achieved at the cost of isolation from the rest of the world.

For many people who have not yet experienced such a commitment or who do not wish to make such a choice, multiadult households, such as communes, represent a way of finding community and economic sharing without making a marriage or cohabitation commitment. For those who have already tried marriage or cohabitation and found such an arrangement too constricting—not providing sufficient freedom to grow and develop—multiadult households also promise a way to remain single, but within the structure of a strong support group. This is particularly relevant to divorced women with small children. There are also happily married or cohabitating couples who want to open up their relationships even more than would be the case if they were simply to practice sexually open relating, by actually sharing living quarters with other married and/or unmarried adults. Other studies of communes have found similar results (Kanter, Jaffe, & Weisberg, 1975; Alam, Note 3).

Swinging

Several descriptive studies of swinging have been published (Symonds, 1971; Bartell, 1971; Palson & Palson, 1972), but the most rigorous study to date has been Gilmartin's 1975 study in which 100 swinging couples were matched with 100 control couples on age, income, neighborhood, marital status, education, and children. Contrary to the stereotype of the swinger as portrayed by Bartell and others, this carefully conducted study found that swingers became romantically interested and involved earlier in life, began dating and courtship earlier, and appeared to have a greater need for social-heterosexual interaction than did the controls. In general they were more involved in the community than nonswingers, but were less religious. They reported much more frequent intercourse with their own spouses and were less bored with life than the controls. No divorces were reported to have occurred after the couple began swinging. Gilmartin concluded that "As far as any outsider can tell, swinging has not had any apparent negative effect on their marriages or lives" (p. 58).

In their forthcoming book on the Sexual Freedom Movement, James and Lynn Smith (Note 4), who followed a sample of 700 swingers over several years, report a progressive expansion of boundaries on the part of many married couples in their study. These couples first tested the feasibility of comarital sex, or couple-front swinging, in which the couple always participated together, either in the same room or at least at the same party in different rooms. If this proved comfortable, they then expanded their relationship boundary further, to allow individual rather than couple-front extramarital sex. If this was also found to be compatible, the boundary was further extended to allow for intimate friendships, i.e., friendships that include social, emotional, intellectual, family, and career intimacy as well as sexual intimacy. Such relationships tend to be long-term, rather than short-term ones. Their book, tentatively titled *Consenting Adults,* should add considerably to our understanding of swinging, which appears to involve about 4 percent of the adult population.

Sexually Open Marriage

To date, only three studies have been reported on sexually open marriage (Ramey, 1975, 1977; Knapp, 1976; Knapp & Whitehurst, 1977). The (1975) Ramey study of 380 participants in intimate groups and networks concentrated on those who had practiced sexual openness for at least ten years (15+ years was the average reported), since the focus was on the effect of sexual openness on the primary relationship. One-third of the respondents were single but 80 percent of the toal sample were in primary relationships. Knapp concentrated on those who were married and had only recently opened their relationship since her interest was in the transition to sexually open relating and its effect on the couple. The Whitehurst study included some of both types.

Respondents in all three studies were remarkably similar except in age. They were uniformly upper-middle class, with above-average education, income, and interest in community affairs. The women as well as the men tended to be in full-time careers in academic, professional, managerial, or creative arts areas, and the women tended to be "liberated," i.e., willing to initiate relationships with men. Respondents were strikingly secure in their primary relationships, and exhibited a strong sense of self. Most had established definite ground rules for relating to others, although these were sometimes more implicit than explicit.

Perhaps the most striking factor about these respondents was the very high percentage of first-borns. Knapp found 53 percent and Ramey 57 percent first-borns (Ramey, 1977). Kagan (1977) found that "The combination of a firm commitment to the standards of adults and an affinity for coherence, consistency, and order among standards leads first-borns to adopt more idealistic philosophical positions and to prefer single, unifying principles in both morality and science, in preference to ones that are pluralistic or expedient." This is consistent with the findings of these three studies that their subjects' personal philosophies were holistic and humanistic and unaccepting of a view of marriage that excluded meaningful intimacy with anyone else.

Knapp (Knapp & Whitehurst, 1977) reported that on the Myers-Briggs Type Indicator (MBTI), which measures personality differences that result from the way people perceive and the way they judge, "72% of the sample fell into one of three categories: the extravert-intuitive (39%), the introvert-intuitive (18%), and the introvert-feeling type (15%). While estimations place the number of intuitives in the general population at about 25%, they made up 80% of the sample, most closely resembling standardization groups of highly creative artists" (p. 155). The Ramey respondents appeared to fall largely into these same categories.

The composite characteristics of people who practice sexually open marriage or are otherwise involved in intimate groups or networks—many are single or cohabitating—as indicated by these samples suggest that a particular type of person is more likely to try sexually open relating. Such a person would be imaginative, a risk-taker, self-assured, unconcerned about convention, an opinion leader, an idealist, one who thinks for him or herself, a "mover and shaker" as they say in Philadelphia. Knapp concludes that "if current trends persist, such persons would be females more often than males" (p. 156). Knapp further suggests that sexually open marriages are the most viable experimental family form because "they have very low visibility, do not require special living arrangements, and are based upon intactness of the marital unit. . . . When it works well, participants combine the security and specialness of the marital commitment with the freedom and individuality required for self-actualization" (p. 159).

LOOKING TO THE FUTURE

In addition to the Ramey complexity continuum paradigm discussed above, there are two others which provide a framework for understanding more about experimental family forms. Libby (1977) describes a paradigm for understanding how people move from one type of relationship to another. He uses role, exchange, and symbolic interaction theory. The suggestion is that we should explore with research subjects the nature of their past as well as present relationships and work through the process of rewards and costs they associated with the transition decisions they made and are making as they consider and anticipate future relationships. He suggests that we use role models in reevaluating our relationships with significant others as crucial events occur in those relationships and that bonding or unbonding occurs as a result of these evaluations, thus leading the individual to move from one type of relationship to another, possibly, but not necessarily of the same type (pp. 50–57). Unfortunately Libby's paradigm is descriptive and tells us nothing about the likelihood that the individual will pick one or another lifestyle, and would involve extremely difficult and expensive research.

Whitehurst (1977) presents a "Fallout Model" as "a means of examining how alternative lifestyle choices occur in the process of leakage from the social controls that keep most people tracked into conventional marriage" (p. 319). Assuming the same independent variables for all people, Whitehurst suggests that those who search for alternatives will exhibit such intervening variables as

> High sense of personal security, high personal autonomy need, similarity of lifestyle, opportunity, and support system availability. Those who remain in conventional marriages will exhibit opposite intervening variables: Low sense of personal security, low need for personal autonomy, lack of perceived opportunity or support systems (or presence of conventional supports). (p. 321)

He assumes that only a few individuals will fit his model because the masses are scripted by their early socialization toward conventional marriage. He hypothesizes distribution of fallout from conventional to alternative systems somewhat analogous to Ramey's continuum of growing complexity. Whitehurst sees a future in which conventional marriages that include nonconsensual adultery will predominate, followed by modified open marriages (not sexually open), traditional monogamous marriages, postmarried singles, and variations on sexually open marriage, with multiadult households and triads or group marriages at the low end of the scale of probability (p. 324).

It is interesting to note that the Libby, Whitehurst, and Ramey paradigms are not competing but rather explain different aspects of the phenomenon of involvement in experimental family forms. The Ramey paradigm predicts the likelihood that a particular lifestyle will become popular by suggesting that there is an inverse relationship between the complexity of the lifestyle and the number of adherents it will have. The Libby paradigm suggests the actual mechanism by which individuals are likely to shift from one lifestyle to another, and the Whitehurst paradigm suggests the intervening variables that differentiate which individuals are most likely to shift to an alternative lifestyle.

ANALYSIS

What has not occurred in this field up until now, although many have ventured predictions about the future, is the use of available sophisticated techniques for prediction. The Delphi Method, for example, has been well researched and applied in many settings, as documented by Linstone and Turoff (1975) in a highly readable and comprehensive book. The Delphi Method involves getting individual opinions from a group of experts about when a particular event or innovation will occur, then feeding back the resultant information to the group, giving each a chance to refine and/or defend his contribution. After several iterations, the findings are then presented as the group consensus. The assumption is that this method will make possible utilization of the best known input to a set of common problems. It is interesting to note that Delphi predictions usually err on the conservative side. Application of this process might be of value in clarifying our understanding of where we are and where we are going as American families.

This review paper has sought to explain where we are and how we got here, vis a vis experimental family forms. It has identified the social imperative toward ever greater individualism; the biological, economic, demographic, and communication revolutions; and the indecision of the modernists' sexual doctrine as the reasons why we are today and will be increasingly in the future concerned about experimental family forms. In spite of our concern, very few studies have been published to date that provide hard data about experimental family forms. These were reviewed, together with several paradigms that have sought to explain various aspects of the phenomenon.

Much remains to be done. There has not yet been a single national probability sample research project funded in this area. Several have been proposed, but funding from federal agencies has been parsimonious. We need to study the connection between experimental family forms and the law. We need to relate the experimental family form to social change. We need to collect census data that clearly reflects the number of citizens living in multiadult households or cohabitating. We need to extend the preliminary work relating specific experimental family forms with specific personality types. So far, this work indicates some very interesting patterns but tells us nothing about causality.

We are in need of longitudinal studies of persons who have been identified as having participated in *any* experimental family form. Just as the same people show up at many different humanistic psychology programs such as encounter, est, primal therapy, and the like, it would appear that those who are interested in experimental family forms move from group to group until they find the right group, if indeed they ever do.

We need control studies of people practicing sexually open marriage, people practicing group marriage, and people living in multiadult households. A dollars-and-cents evaluation of the benefits of the multiadult household as compared to a control group with the same income would also be revealing. It is time to stop doing descriptive research and start working on the tough problems of comparing the efficacy of experimental family forms with the more common variations detailed in the first section of this review.

NOTES

[1] Bureau of Labor Statistics, *News release,* USDL 77-191 (March 8, 1977).

[2] Bureau of the Census, *Population characteristics* Series P-20, No. 306 (January 1977).

[3] S. F. Alam, "Middle class communities" (Paper presented at the annual meeting of the National Council on Family Relations, St. Louis, October 1974).

[4] J. Smith, and J. Smith, "Consenting adults: An exploratory study of the sexual freedom movement" (Book in preparation, 1977).

REFERENCES

Bartel, G. 1971. *Group sex.* New York: Wyden.

Cogswell, B. E., and M. B. Sussman. 1972. Changing family and marriage forms: Complications for human service systems. *Family Coordinator* 21 (4): 505–16.

Constantine, L. L., and J. M. Constantine. 1973. *Group marriage.* New York: Macmillan.

Etzioni, A. 1977. Science and the future of the family. *Science* 196 (4289): 487.

Francoeur, R. T. 1972. *Eve's new rib.* New York: Dell.

Gilmartin, B. G. 1975. That swinging couple down the block. *Psychology Today* 8 (9): 54–58.

Glick, P. C. 1977. Updating the life cycle of the family. *Journal of Marriage and the Family* 39 (1): 5–13.

Kagan, J. 1977. The child in the family. *Daedalus* 106 (2): 33–56.

Kanter, R., D. Jaffe, and K. Weisberg. 1975. Coupling, parenting, and the presence of others: Intimate relationships in communal households. *Family Coordinator* 24 (4): 433–52.

Knapp, J. 1976. An exploratory study of seventeen sexually open marriages. *Journal of Sex Research* 12 (3): 206–19.

Knapp, J., and R. Whitehurst. 1977. Sexually open marriage and relationships: Issues an prospects. In R. Libby and R. Whitehurst (eds.), *Marriage and alternatives,* pp. 147–60. Glenview, Ill.: Scott, Foresman.

Libby, R. 1977. Creative singlehood as a sexual lifestyle: Beyond marriage as a rite of passage. In R. Libby and R. Whitehurst (eds.), *Marriage and alternatives.* Glenview, Ill.: Scott, Foresman.

Linstone, H., and M. Turoff. 1975. *The Delphi method.* Reading, Mass.: Addison-Wesley.

Murdock, G. 1949. *Social structure.* New York: Macmillan.

Palson, C., and R. Palson. 1972. Swinging in wedlock. *Society* 9 (4): 28–37.

Ramey, J. 1972. Emerging patterns of innovative behavior in marriage. *Family Coordinator* 21 (4): 435–56.

Ramey, J. 1975. Intimate groups and networks: Frequent consequence of sexually open marriage. *Family Coordinator* 24 (4): 515–30.

Ramey, J. 1976. *Intimate friendships.* Englewood Cliffs, N.J.: Prentice-Hall.

Ramey, J. 1977. Sexual behavior and alternative life-styles. *Society* 14 (3).

Robinson, P. 1976. *The modernization of sex.* New York: Harper and Row.

Rossi, A. 1977. A biosocial perspective on parenting. *Daedalus* 106 (2): 1–32.

Symonds, C. 1971. Sexual mate swapping and the swingers. *Marriage Counseling Quarterly* 6: 1–12.

The Sentinel. (Winston-Salem, N.C.). 1977. July 22, p. 31.

Westoff, C. F. 1976. Trends in contraceptive practice: 1965–1973. *Family Planning Perspectives* 8 (2): 54–57.

Whitehurst, R. 1977. Changing ground rules and emerging life-styles. In R. Libby & R. Whitehurst (eds.), *Marriage and alternatives.* Glenview, Ill.: Scott, Foresman.

Zablocki, B. 1977. *Alienation and investment in the urban commune.* New York: Center for Policy Research.

Photographs by Alan McEvoy

Part Four

BEING MARRIED

Being married is both a public and a private condition, since the marriage contract is both a legal contract authorized by the state and a personal contract between two unique people.

The state has an interest and a role in the marriage contract since it desires to accomplish various functions via the marriage contract: safeguarding normal behavior by legitimizing sexual union; protecting the property rights of each individual as well as of the couple; protecting the individuals involved from spouse and child abuse and from exploitation in such forms as bigamy; determining legitimacy of the children for purposes of name, inheritance, and social and financial responsibility; safeguarding against prohibited relationships like incest; and guaranteeing the legality of the contract by providing licensing and eligibility standards for the marriage, as well as grounds for its dissolution (Albrecht and Boch, 1981).

As a means of protecting these interests, the state makes four role-based assumptions about the marriage relationship; in so doing, it ignores the personal part of the contract, the fact that it is made by two unique individuals. These assumptions are that the husband is the head of the family and is responsible for support, and that the wife is responsible for domestic services and child care (Weitzman, 1974). The first assumption is reflected in the woman's loss of an independent identity when she gives up her name, in her lack of a right to determine residence, and in her treatment by various credit groups. The second assumption is reflected most clearly at the time of separation or divorce. The wife is usually obligated to support the children if the husband is unable to do so, but she is never obligated to support the husband, whereas the husband must support the children and sometimes the wife. The third and fourth assumptions are also best demonstrated when a marriage is being dissolved. The courts seldom provide reimbursement to the wife for her services as a homemaker, and they usually assign any children to the mother because parenting is seen as her "natural and proper" role.

As indicated, these assumptions overlook the individuality of the component parts—the husband and the wife. Despite recent court rulings, such as the Equal Credit Opportunity Act and rulings on gender-specific support, which have mitigated the effect of some of these assumptions, the experience and desires of the couple are, in general, ignored. For this reason many couples are beginning to write their own marriage vows. These vows reflect their personal goals and expectations regarding their relationship, children, sexual relations with others, household arrangements, financial rights and obligations, and even the termination of the contract. Although not legally binding, a premarital contract does bring to light issues that will affect the continued happiness of the couple. For example, since both persons may be pursuing a career, it is important to note decisions regarding children and change of residence if a career advancement for one occurs. In effect, the move to a personal contract reflects a change in people's expectations of marriage. In the past, marriage was seen as a practical matter involving certain responsibilities for each spouse. Today, marital expectations involve such personal factors as mutual affection, companionship, and individual growth.

Writing a prenuptial agreement setting forth the nuances of individual marital expectations might seem calculating, a denial of romantic love. Actually, it suggests that the partners realize there is little connection between qualities that arouse feelings of romance and qualities that lead to comfort and fulfillment in a marriage (Alpert, 1981). In fact, "one of the reasons that the marriage institution does not live up to its expectations is because of the many myths and unrealistic expectations that individuals bring to marriage" (Olson, 1983). Many of these myths revolve around the connection between love and marriage, such as the idea that people marry because they are in love, or that all problems can be solved if people are really in love. The notion that one is marrying for love may cause one to ignore other, less romantic reasons for getting married. These may include holding false impressions of marriage as it is portrayed in tradition and in literature, meeting parental or societal expectations, alleviating loneliness, gaining economic help, and improving one's situation (Lederer and Jackson, 1968).

The myth of marriage as a panacea and the consequent widespread ignorance of the legal rights and responsibilities of marriage suggest another reason for making a prenuptial agreement. Writing their vows in the form of a legal contract would oblige the "potential partners to explore together in advance of marriage—and in writing—their motives for marrying, as well as the extent of their intended commitment with regard to children, property sharing, and future alimony, should the marriage fail." This is a way of making "the tough part of marriage getting in instead of getting out" (Sheresky and Mannes, 1972, p. 33).

Writing prenuptial agreements may overcome the state's lack of interest in preparing people for marriage; it may also force some people to reconsider their marriage vows as they balance the magic of courtship with the realities of marriage. But such contracts cannot solve all problems, since many prospective mates are deficient in the skills that make a marriage work and prefer to rely on love to conquer all. It is with this idea that the articles of part four are concerned.

In chapter 9 the factors involved in developing good marriages are examined. In the first article, Virginia Satir notes the steps that society can take toward making marriage a human-actualizing contract. She offers a variety of challenging ideas that would improve human existence and therefore the marital relationship, adding that "we have all the resources for the needed change but do not yet know how to use them." In the second article, Nick Stinnett carries this idea a step further by utilizing the material from a study of strong marriages. He indicates that the people involved in such marriages are appreciative of one another, like to spend time together, have good communication patterns, are committed to promoting each other's happiness and welfare, have a high degree of religious orientation, and deal with crises in a positive manner.

In the third article, Richard Mason turns to specific means by which a couple can strengthen their marriage. He notes that despite the efforts indicated, conflict is inevitable between intimates; nevertheless, conflict does not have to be destructive. In fact, it has been said that quarreling and making up help to stabilize the marriage and are the hallmark of true intimacy (Bach and Wyden, 1968, p. 11). The main point is that such conflict must be productive rather than destructive. Two factors are involved in turning belittling and punishing conflict into conflict that leads to a redefinition of the situation. First, the partners have to fight fairly, and second, they have to make communication more effective, since ineffective communication is probably the principle cause of marriage failure (Mace, 1975, p. 41).

Steps involved in fair fighting include the following: getting the problem out into the open rather than letting it fester; being specific about what one doesn't like and how one wants it changed; not overdramatizing or including side issues; avoiding references to relatives or others; attacking the problem and not each other; staying with it until the problem is resolved (for this step it helps to learn the art of compromise, to take some simple steps for improvement, and not to equate losing with a loss of self-esteem); and finally, giving each other cues, such as some humor, when tensions are eased (Douval and Hill, 1980, p. 286).

Good communication allows a couple to experience intimacy and security with each other and, like constructive conflict, involves active participation requiring concentration and feedback. That is, to ensure that individuals are hearing what is being said, it is necessary that they paraphrase what they hear and ask clarifying questions. Both participants can be honest and open by using "I" messages, which express one's own feelings, rather than "you" messages, which place blame and are likely to elicit a defensive reaction. Not only does this leveling express real feelings and show where each person stands, but it also allows the listener to express his or her empathy with the feelings and thoughts being expressed by the other. Finally, it should be realized that communication is more than the words themselves. In fact, only 7 percent of the impact of an emotional message is from the words, whereas 55 percent is from the speaker's facial expression and 38 percent is from the tone of voice (Mehrabian, 1972).

Putting effective communication together with fair fighting brings out some additional factors that can be included in the overall effort to make conflict productive. Except for feedback, the initiator of the complaint should be allowed to make remarks without any interfering comments, counterclaims, or other interruptions; the initiator should extend the same conditions to the respondent; and both should offer solutions relative to the issue. All of this should take place at an appropriate time and place (Bach and Wyden, 1960).

The last two articles in chapter 9 examine further the development of effective marriages. Chuck Hillig notes the effect of belief systems on conflict, claiming that what people believe about how others operate is the source of much conflict. He describes three myths that affect relationships: the myth that others can make one feel some emotion; the myth that one should always have good reasons for feeling the way one does; and the myth that one's partner should automatically know what one wants. Marcia Lasswell and Norman Lobsenz sum up many of the ideas expressed in this chapter by noting the factors involved in intimacy. Expressing and enhancing intimacy involves confiding in one's partner, sharing trivialities, realizing the importance of lighter actions, using verbal communication, expecting intimacy with each kind of sexual experience, and, last but most important, touching.

Another aspect of marital interaction involves the question of equality in the relationship. On the surface, this would appear to be a moot point, since our ideology stresses the equality of all citizens, especially, one would think, in a freely arranged marriage contract. However, as the discussion of the marital contract indicated, appearances are deceiving. Aside from the inequality implied by the state's gender-role assumptions, another element of inequality develops out of our custom of men marrying women who are slightly inferior to them. Studies reveal a marriage gradient, in which "older, more-educated, higher-salaried, higher-status husbands are regularly matched with younger, less-educated, lower-salaried, and lower-status wives" (Stiehm, 1975, p. 33). The author of this quote quite legitimately asks about "the consequences of pairings based on a mutually agreed-to unequal relationship." In the first article of chapter 10, Dair Gillespie indicates that such a relationship means a power balance tipped in favor of the male. She summarizes the elements of this inequality and concludes that "for a wife to gain a modicum of power, she must participate in the labor force, her education must be superior to his, and her participation in organizations must excel his."

The first part of this quest for equal power is already a reality for many wives: there has been a dramatic increase of women in the labor force. In 1980, 52 percent of women aged 16 or over were in the labor force, an increase of 28 percent since 1950 (Voydanoff, 1983). The results reveal that working wives do have more power than full-time housewives, especially in regard to spending the family income (Hoffman and Nye, 1974, p. 167). However, it should be recognized that wives have always worked and contributed to the family, not only through their unpaid domestic work, but through labor done in the home, such as taking in laundry or selling canned goods. The change is in the recognition of that work, as a substantial proportion of wives now earn their income away from the home (Aldous, 1981).

When Gillespie's first criterion is met, the question arises of what the benefits are for the working wife besides greater power in spending the household income. We also wonder what price she is paying for this greater power. In the second article in chapter 10, Barbara Chesser indicates that other benefits to wives include greater economic self-sufficiency, more money to deal with financial

163

demands, greater freedom to develop their potential, and an enhanced sense of identity. The potential for cohesion is also greater in two-income families, since there is additional motivation for empathy, companionship, and affection when the wife also performs economic duties and the husband also performs household duties, (Voydanoff, 1983). The penalties for working wives involve increased stress, both internal and external to the household. The internal stressors include the discontinuity between early gender-role socialization and the present life-style, the conflicting demands of family and work, and role overload from the considerably increased total volume of activities. The external stressors include cultural strain from lack of normative support, occupational inflexibility and demands for geographical mobility, and lack of time for social interaction with friends and relatives (Skinner, 1980). There is additional stress for the couple that is geographically separated. The commuter couple, a growing subgroup of the dual-career family, experiences even more personal and marital stress, due to the lack of day-to-day sharing, the continual state of transition, and loneliness (Gerstel and Gross, 1983).

Since the "social support structures have not changed in response to the increasing number of employed couples" (Aldous, 1981, p. 125), the question arises, How will dual-earner/dual-career couples cope with the stresses of their commitments? In the final article of this part, Linda Haas asserts that the answer will be role-sharing symmetry in the traditionally segregated family roles, including the breadwinner role, the decision-maker role, and the domestic role. Such sharing, she concludes, provides both individual and family benefits, but it requires the "wholehearted and enthusiastic willingness of both spouses to participate." Such a condition may be at hand, since 63 percent of a national sample of adults indicated that they "preferred an equal marriage of shared responsibilities in which the husband and wife cooperate on working, homemaking, and child-raising" (Scanzoni, 1982).

STUDY QUESTIONS

Chapter 9

Satir
1. Which three challenges excite you the most? Why?
2. What does Satir mean when she says, "We have all the resources for the needed change but do not yet know how to use them"?

Stinnett
1. Explain briefly the six strengths of a strong family.
2. Which of the five recommendations seems most plausible? Why?

Mason
1. Why does Mason advise couples to be free of distractions, share positive thoughts, stick with feelings, not analyze, use personal pronouns, and stay in the present?
2. Do you think the described program will actually help marriages? Why?

Hillig
1. Explain how the three myths can affect your relationships.
2. Why do people accept these myths?

Lasswell and Lobsenz
1. What is and what isn't intimacy?
2. Explain the three barriers to intimacy.

Chapter 10

Gillespie
1. Is marriage a free contract between equals? Give three reasons why it is or is not.
2. Give three reasons why Gillespie says, "For a wife to gain a modicum of power, she must participate in the labor force, her education must be superior to his, and her participation in organizations must excel his."

Chesser
1. Indicate five of the issues involved in dual-career marriages.
2. Indicate five of the advantages of dual-career marriages.

Haas
1. What are the individual benefits of role sharing?
2. What are the family benefits of role sharing?

REFERENCES FOR PART FOUR

Albrecht, Ruth E., and E. Wilbur Boch. 1975. *Encounter: Love, marriage and family.* Boston: Holbrook.

Aldous, Joan. 1981. "From dual-earner to dual-career and back again. *Journal of Family Issues,* June.

Alpert, Gerald. 1973. Needed a rebellion against romance. *Journal of Family Counseling.*

Bach, George R., and Peter Wyden. 1968. *The intimate enemy: How to fight fair in love and marriage.* New York: Morrow.

Douval, Evelyn M., and Reuben Hill. 1960. *Being married.* Lexington, Mass.: D. C. Heath.

Gerstel, Naomi, and Harriet Gross. 1983. Commuter marriage: Couples who live apart. In *Contemporary families and alternative lifestyles,* ed. by Eleanor D. Macklin and Roger H. Rubin. Beverly Hills, Calif.: Sage.

Hoffman, Lois, and F. Ivan Nye. 1974. *Working mothers.* San Francisco: Jossey-Bass.

Lederer, William J., and Don D. Jackson. 1968. *The mirages of marriage.* New York: Norton.

Mace, David R. 1975. The outlook for marriage: New needs and opportunities. *Foundation News,* November/December.

Mehrabian, Albert. 1972. *Nonverbal communication.* Chicago: Aldine-Atherton.

Olson, David H. 1972. Marriage of the future: Revolutionary or evolutionary change? *The Family Coordinator,* October.

Scanzoni, John. 1982. *Sexual bargaining.* Chicago: University of Chicago Press.

Sheresky, Norman, and Marya Mannes. 1972. A radical guide to wedlock. *Saturday Review,* July 29.

Skinner, Denise A. 1980. Dual-career family stress and coping: A literature review. *Family Relations,* October.

Stiehm, Judith. 1975. Equality between the sexes. *The New York Times,* July 2, p. 33.

Voydanoff, Patricia. 1983. *Work and family.* Palo Alto, Calif.: Mayfield.

IX

MAKING IT

20

MARRIAGE AS A HUMAN-ACTUALIZING CONTRACT

VIRGINIA SATIR

When I was asked to write this paper, the idea excited me. I have many thoughts about this subject. As I sit down now to write, I am overwhelmed at the enormity of their implications. My power of imagination fails me in visualizing how all these changes could be accomplished, given this world as it is today, with its vast numbers of people and the prevailing low image of a human being; this world, where love and trust are rarities and suspicion and hate are expected.

Person-person, male-female, and adult-child relations, as they exist today, seem pretty inhuman and many times even anti-human. The current legal and social structure frequently acts to aid and abet these inhuman contacts. Given the state of human relations today, it is not hard to understand current human behavior in marriage, the family, and other human transactions.

The effect of these inhuman and anti-human relations seems abundantly obvious in the widespread presence of mistrust and fear between human beings. If relationships are experienced as mistrust and fear, how can love and trust come about? Statistics on alcoholism, drug addiction, suicide, murder, mental illness, and crimes against persons or property are more specific indications of inhuman and anti-human treatment. Continuing wars between nations, racial strife, and poverty are global evidences of these same practices.

While these statistics do not include every person in our population, enough are included to make it more than just a random or accidental occurrence. This raises the basic question: *Is this how man really is inherently or is this the result of how he has been taught?* I would have to stop this paper right now if I believed that man's present behavior is the result of what he is, inherently. I believe man's behavior reflects what he has learned and I take hope in the fact that anything that has been learned can be unlearned and new learning can be introduced.

This, of course, raises another basic question: *What are these new learnings?* To talk about a change in the marriage relationship without talking about making changes in the human beings who make the marriage is, in my opinion, putting the

---

Virginia Satir, "Marriage as a Human-Actualizing Contract," in *The Family in Search of a Future: Alternate Models for Moderns,* edited by Herbert A. Otto, copyright © 1970, pp. 57–66. Reprinted by permission of Prentice-Hall, Inc., Englewood Cliffs, N.J.

cart before the horse. I would like to present some ideas which might go a long way toward moving us all a notch forward in our whole human existence and consequently in the marriage relationship.

What Would Happen If:

1. *Children were conceived only by mature adults?* If these parents felt prepared and knew, beyond few questions of doubt, that they had the skills to be wise, patient, and joyful teachers of human beings, of creative, loving, curious, real persons? Further, if this conception were an active mutual choice representing a welcome addition, instead of a potential deprivation or a substitute for a marital disappointment?

2. *Parenting were seen as probably the most crucial, challenging, and interesting job for each adult engaged in it?*

    a. The business and the working world would manage in such a way that young fathers would not be asked to be gone from Monday to Friday. Men are essential; their nonpresence hands child-rearing almost exclusively over to women. This skews the kind of parenting a child gets, which is reflected in his image of himself and others. An integrated person needs to have an intimate, real familiarity with both sexes. For many children, fathers are ghosts, benign or malevolent. If they are males, this leaves them with a hazy and incomplete model for themselves. If they are females, their relations and expectations of men evolve more from fantasy than reality. It seems to me that knowledge about, and familiarity with, the other sex in the growing-up years is a large factor in satisfaction in married life. Furthermore, male absence overdraws on the woman's resources, paving the way for all kinds of destructive results for herself, her children, and her husband. However we slice it, we come into the world with life equipment, but it remains for our experiences to teach the uses of it. After all, the husbands and fathers, the wives and mothers of today are the boys and girls of yesterday.

    b. Women who are mothers and men who are fathers could have auxiliary help without stigma in their parenting. Parenting for the first five years is a twenty-four-hour-a-day job. This gets pretty confining if there is no relief. Auxiliary help might go a long way toward breaking the possession aspect of parenthood and move it more toward the real responsibility of developing the child's humanity.

    c. There would be family financial allowances to people who needed them, not on the basis of being poor and just making survival possible, but because it was needed to facilitate optimum growth.

    d. Preparation for parenting would be seen as something to be actively learned instead of assuming that the experience of conception and birth automatically provided all the know-how one needed. Nobody calling himself an engineer would even be considered for an engineering job if all the preparation he had consisted of his wish to be one, and the knowledge he gained by watching his engineer father.

3. *The idea of developing human beings was considered so important and vital that each neighborhood had within walking distance a Family Growth Center which was a center for learning about being human, from birth to death.* These might well replace public welfare offices, among other institutions. In my opinion, this process, learning how to be human, will never end; I believe the human potential is infinite. We have barely scratched the surface.

4. *The literal context surrounding the birth event included full awareness for the woman giving birth, the active witnessing of the birth process by the father of the child and the rooming-in of all three for at least the first two weeks.* Everyone would get a chance to be in on the getting-acquainted process that necessarily takes place. In a first birth, the female would meet her husband in his father role for the first time; the male would meet his wife in

her mother role for the first time; each would meet a slightly new person. Many men and women feel like strangers to each other when they meet as fathers and mothers despite the fact that they have previously been husbands and wives.

The subsequent celebration following the birth could celebrate not only a birth of a new human being, but a birth of new roles for the adults as well. (The way some celebrations have gone would suggest immaculate conception.) Men often feel like useless appendages at this time. No wonder there are fears of replacement on their part. I wonder whether it would be as possible for men who are fathers to leave their families as readily as they now do if they were part of the literal birth proceedings, openly hailed and honored as being and having been essential, as are women. I wonder too, if this were done, whether the birth of a baby would create as much estrangement between husband and wife as it does.

5. *Child-rearing practices were changed.*
   a. The emphasis in child rearing would be on helping the child find out, crystal clearly, how he looked and sounded, how to tune in on how he felt and thought, how to find out how he experienced others and affected them, instead of only the admonishment to be good and find out how to please others.
   b. From the moment of birth he would be treated as a person with the capacity to hear, to see, to feel, to sense, and to think, different from the adult only in body development and, initially, in putting his sensory and thought experiences into words.
   c. He would have a predictable place in time and space.
   d. He would have real and openly welcomed opportunities to feel his power and his uniqueness, his sexuality and his competence as soon as his resources permitted it.
   e. He would be surrounded by people who openly and clearly enjoyed each other and him, who were straight and real with one another and with him, thus giving him a model for his own delight in interacting with people. Thus, the joy in relationships might overcome the grimly responsible outlook "becoming an adult" often has for a child.
   f. "Yes" and "no" would be clear, reliable, appropriate, and implemented.
   g. Realness would be valued over approval when there had to be a choice.
   h. At every point in time, regardless of age or label, he would always be treated as a whole person and never regarded as too young to be a person.
   i. Every child's feelings would be regarded with dignity and respect, listened to and understood; those around him would do the same with each other. There would be a basic difference between his awareness and expression of his feelings and thoughts, and the action he took in relation to them.
   j. Every child's actions would be considered separately from his expressions, instead of linking expressions of feeling with an automatic specific act. He would be taught that actions had to be subject to time, place, situation, other persons, and purpose, rather than being given a stereotyped "should" that applies universally.
   k. Difference from others would be seen clearly as an opportunity for learning, holding an important key to interest in living and real contact with others, instead of being seen primarily as something to be tolerated, or destroyed, or avoided.
   l. Every child would have continuing experience that human life is to be revered, his and that of all others.
   m. Every child would openly receive continuing knowledge of how he and all his parts work—his body, his mind, and his senses. He would receive encouragement for expressing, clarifying, and experimenting with his thoughts, his feelings, his words, his actions, and his body, in all its parts.
   n. He would look forward to each new step

in growth as an opportunity for discovery, encompassing pain, pleasure, knowledge, and adventure. Each phase of growth has special learnings that could be particularly planned for; evidence showing that a new growth step had been achieved would be openly and obviously validated, like celebrating with a party the onset of menstruation for girls and maybe a change of voice party for boys at the time of puberty. Further examples would be: parties for the first step, first tooth, first day at school, first overnight visit with nonfamilial members, first date, first sexual intercourse, and the first obvious and costly mistake. Mistakes are an inevitable part of risk taking, which is an essential part of growth, and needs to be so understood.

    o. He could see males and females as different, yet interesting and essential to each other, free to be separate instead of being implicit enemies or feeding on each other.

    p. He could get training in male-female relations, could prepare openly for mating and parenting in turn, which would be explained as desirable, and demonstrated as such.

    q. He would be openly let in on the experiences of adults in parenting, maritalling, and selfing.

6. *He could freely experience in an openly welcoming way the emergence of the sexual self.* This would require lifting the cover of secrecy on the genitals and all that it entails.

7. *The goal of being human was being real, loving, intimate, authentic, and alive as well as competent, productive, and responsible.*

We have never had people reared anything like this on a large enough scale to know how this would affect marriage, the family, and, in general, people-to-people relationships. We have never realized what impetus to a really better world and a socially more evolved people might be created for tackling the "insurmountable" problems of suicide, murder, alcoholism, illegitimacy, irresponsibility, incompetence, war, racial and national conflicts. I think this is worth trying.

In our society, marriage is the social and legal context in which new humans originate and are expected to grow into fully developed human beings. The very life of our society depends upon what happens as a result of marriage. Looking at the institution of marriage as it exists today raises real questions about its effectiveness.

The marriage contract in the Western Christian world has no provision for periodic review or socially acceptable means of termination. I would offer that this contract, as it stands, is potentially inhuman and anti-human, and works against the development of love, trust, and connectedness with other human beings. It is made with the apparent assumption that the conditions present at its inception will continue without change for eternity. This asks people to be wiser than they can possibly be. It is made at a time in the lives of the respective parties when they have the least preparation in fact with which to make this contract.

The contract exacts an explicit agreement that other intimate relationships with the same and the other sex shall cease and each partner shall be the sole resource of total comfort and gratification for the other. Implicitly, the current marriage contract abolishes individual autonomy and makes togetherness mandatory. Independent wishes and acts, or contradictory opinions are seen as threats to marriage.

If marriage partners hold on to their integrity and their individuality, their independent wishes and acts, or contradictory opinions, they may retain their integrity but lose the relationship. So, to preserve the marriage, one has to lose one's integrity if to manifest the integrity loses the marriage.

Almost any recent study of the sexual practices of married people reports that many marital partners do not live completely monogamously. Marital partners report from few to many extramarital sexual relationships, which are largely secret. Frequently-married persons practice a consecutive spousing which is a sort of polygamy done in parts. Mate-swapping, which is polygamy in the open, is becoming more frequent. The myth is monogamy; the fact is frequently polygamy. Evidently, the expectation that each mate should completely suffice the other is failing, and may, by its failure, demonstrate the unreality of this expectation.

Maybe with these facts we have to consider the possibility that human beings are not naturally monogamous.

Maybe monogamy is the most efficient and economic way to organize heterosexual relationships to permit child raising. If so, could monogamy as well as being efficient and economic also be creative, enjoyable, and growth-producing? Maybe this hinges on making possible individual autonomy as well as togetherness. Right now it looks all too often as though monogamy is experienced, after a relatively short time, as grim, lifeless, boring, depressing, disillusioning—a potential context for murder, suicide, mental human decay. Perhaps persons who had rearing of the kind I described would make marriage an exciting and alive experience, and then maybe monogamy could become the rich and fulfilling experience the poets describe.

The marriage contract with its implicit social expectation of chastity is based on the assumption that the expectation of an experience is the same as the actual experience. Chastity all too often disguises ignorance, naivete, and inhibition. These attitudes in too many cases contaminate the marital relationship rather than enhance it.

At this point, I can only fantasy how the sexual relationship in marriage would be changed if the marital partners had been brought up with openness, frankness, love, acceptance, and knowledge of their whole body and that of the other sex.

The current Western marriage contract has been derived from a chattel economic base, which stresses possessing. This frequently gets translated into duty and becomes emotional and sometimes literal blackmail. The quality of joy is lost in the game of scoreboard. "Who loses, who wins, and who is on top?" The result is the grimness I referred to earlier.

Obviously, only mature people can make workable contracts with some hope of achievement, not because they can predict the events, but because they have a workable, growth-producing, coping process to meet whatever comes along. Few people have had open access to the information and experience that could prepare them for being persons, let alone marriage partners.

From the time of puberty the underlying message is be careful of the other sex—the other sex is dangerous. The symbol of this is genital contact, namely intercourse. Many marriages are made by persons who secretly fear that the other sex is dangerous. Out of this is supposed to come intimacy, tenderness, and joining of efforts. How do potential enemies easily translate their relationship into one of intimacy and tenderness?

Maybe there needs to be something like an apprentice period which is socially approved, that precedes an actual marriage, in which potential partners have a chance to explore deeply and experiment with their relationship. This is not exactly a new idea.

In a period of living together, which was socially approved and considered desirable, each could experience the other and find out whether his fantasy matched the reality. Was it really possible through daily living to have a process enabling each to enhance the growth of the other while at the same time enhancing his own? What is it like to have to undertake joint ventures and being with each other every day? It would seem that in this socially approved context, the changes of greater and continuing realness and authenticity would be increased, and the relationship would deepen since it started on a reality base.

Right now such important learning is denied in an effort to preserve the fiction of chastity. It seems to me that this puts undue weight on something that is peripheral to the big goal—healthy, intimate, human relationships.

We have to have a socially accepted and desirable way to terminate a marriage when it appears that it no longer works. What if it could happen just by mutual consent and the only problem was how to plan for the continuing parenting of the children? I doubt that, between people who were authentic and real, this would be either so destructive or so frequent. Human beings with the best intentions and integrity make errors. There needs to be an honorable way to treat this most important error.

If we could truly see that the act of sexual intercourse has much to do with enriching self-esteem in the partners, and that it can represent the highest and most satisfying form of male-female contact, we would be more discriminating. Further, we would openly teach ways to make this possible. To accomplish this we must lift the cover of secrecy and ignorance. At the present time sexual contact is frequently seen as degrading, a form of war, merchandise, lust, a means of scalp-hunting, or as a scoreboard. In these circumstances, when conception results, the child is potentially doomed to the "psychiatric couch," to prison, to poverty, to premature death, or maybe worse yet, to conformity or boredom. How can one degrade or be destructive toward that which he considers openly, truly beautiful and part of his joy in existence?

If we were all to see the sexual act as the renewal value of the other and the increase of self-esteem in the self, if the decision to procreate was a voluntary, mutually-shared one entered into *after* the intimate, satisfying, renewing experience had been achieved by a male and female pair, what magnitude of revolution might we stimulate in a new model for person-to-person relations?

Anyone who has studied family process at all can see with one eye how (1) the sexual relationship is symbolic of the heterosexual interrelationship and this carries the significance of the person-to-person relationship, and (2) that the fate of the child hangs on this interrelationship.

Intercourse is a fact, not a symbol. Conception, pregnancy, and birth are also facts, not symbols. The child is a result of these facts, but his maturing is guided by the feelings that surround these facts.

I am implying three changes:

1. That the cover of secrecy be removed from the sexual part of the human being. With this cover off, ignorance can be removed.
2. That there be as much attention, care, and implementation, openly, creatively and confidently given to the care, maintenance, and use of the genitals as there is, for instance, to the teeth.
3. That a couple have a means to know when they have achieved intimacy in their relationship, which is based on their experience with, and awareness of, each other as real persons whom they value, enjoy, and feel connected with.

If we were taught from childhood on that our most important goal as human beings is to be real and in continuing touch with ourselves, this in turn would ensure a real connection with others. Were we taught that creativity, authenticity, health, aliveness, lovingness, and productivity were desirable goals, we would have a much greater sense of when this was achieved, and would also find it much easier to do so.

With the expectation of the age of marriage being around twenty and life expectancy being around seventy, close to fifty years of a person's life can be expected to be lived under the aegis of a marriage contract. If the contract does not permit an alive, dynamic experience with growth possible for both, the result is outrage, submission, destructiveness, withdrawal, premature death, or destructive termination. Maybe this type of marriage contract is impossible. If it is, then perhaps what we need to do is to find a way to conceive and bring up children that does not depend on a permanent relationship between the parents. The act of conception and birth could be entirely separated from the process of raising children. We could have child manufacturers and child raisers. We have much of this now except that is is socially stigmatizing. We work awfully hard to make adoption unsuccessful. "He is not my real child," or "She is not my real mother." Actually most of us know that the significance of the blood tie is mostly in our heads.

Maybe the most important thing is that new humans get born and then they are raised. Who does either or both may not be as important as that it is done and how it is done. Maybe if such a "division of labor" were effected, the energies of all the adults of the world would be more available for work and joy and less tied up with what they "should" be.

Procreation—coming about as it does, with little evidence that it will change much in the near future—guarantees that there will always be males and females around, and that they will be attracted to one another, in or out of marriage. Maybe this could be openly acknowledged and we could find ways to use it for our mutual benefit.

As for me, I think a relationship of trust, worth, and love between people is the highest and most satisfying way of experiencing one's humanity. I think this is where real spirituality takes place. Without it, humans become shrivelled, destructive, and desolate.

Right now, our current forms of human interaction, our fears, our suspicions, and our past are working against us. We have all the resources for the needed change, but we do not yet know how to use them. Our survival as a society may well depend upon finding these uses.

21

IN SEARCH OF STRONG FAMILIES

Nick Stinnett

A prominent family life educator, Dr. Richard Klemer, once remarked that if we had a nuclear war today, when the danger was past and it was safe for us to come out of hiding that the first thing most of us would do would be to look for our families. Or we would look for people who were very close to us and were like family to us. This statement impresses on me that our family life is more important to us than we may realize. As we look back in history we see that the quality of family life is very important to the strength of nations. There is a pattern in the rise and fall of great societies such as ancient Rome, Greece, and Egypt. When these societies were at the peak of their power and prosperity, the family was strong and highly valued. When family life became weak in these societies, when the family was not valued, when society became extremely individualistic, the society began to deteriorate and eventually fell.

We have considerable evidence that the quality of family life is extremely important to our emotional well-being, our happiness, and our mental health as individuals. We know that poor relationships within the family are very strongly related to many of the problems in society such as juvenile deliquency. Obviously, it is to our benefit to do what we can to strengthen family life and strengthening family life should be one of our nation's top priorities. Unfortunately, it has not been a top priority.

On the newsstand we see many books and magazine articles about what's wrong with families and the problems that families have. Many books predict that the family will disappear, that it is no longer meeting the needs of people. So much of what is written about families has focused on problems and pathology in family life.

Admittedly we need information about the problems, but we also need a balanced view. We need more information about positive family models and what strong families are like. We need to learn how to strengthen families. We don't learn how to do anything looking only at how it *shouldn't* be done. We learn most effectively by examining how to do something correctly and studying a positive model. We have not had this positive model as much as we need in the area of family life.

In this nation, we have many strong families. There has been little written about them because there has been very little research focusing on family strengths. It was with this in mind that we conducted the Family Strengths Research Project in Oklahoma. We are now doing this project on a na-

---

Reprinted from *Building Family Strengths: Blueprints for Action,* edited by Nick Stinnett, by permission of University of Nebraska Press. Copyright © 1979 by the University of Nebraska Press.

tionwide basis. Some of the findings from the Oklahoma study follow. We are continuing to find similar results. The things we have found are in agreement with what other researchers have found in other parts of the country. Our findings have implications for strengthening family life. . . .

THE SIX QUALITIES OF THE STRONG FAMILIES

Appreciation

The first quality of the strong families was certainly one of the most important qualities that we found. It emerged from many different questions and in many different ways that we were not expecting. The results were permeated by this characteristic. That quality is appreciation. These families expressed a great deal of appreciation for each other. They built each other up psychologically. They gave each other many positive psychological strokes, and made each other feel good about themselves.

Each of us likes to be with people who make us feel good about ourselves; we don't like to be with people who make us feel bad. One of the tasks of family counselors working with family members who make each other feel terrible is to get them out of that pattern of interaction and into a pattern where they can make one another feel good. William James, considered by many people to be the greatest psychologist our country has ever produced, wrote a book on human needs. Some years after that book was published he remarked that he had forgotten to include the most important need of all—the need to be appreciated. William James felt that one of the most basic needs that you and I have is to be appreciated. There are so many things that we do for which we receive no reward other than appreciation. So perhaps we all need to work on our ability to express appreciation. One difficulty that we have about expressing appreciation is that we sometimes fear that people will think we're not sincere or that it's empty flattery. This need not be a concern. We *can* be sincere. Every person has many good qualities, many strengths. All we have to do is look for them, and be aware of them.

There are many ways that we can develop the ability to express appreciation and thus make our human relationships better and certainly improve the quality of our family life. One of these techniques that is widely used is one that Dr. Herbert Otto, Chairman of the National Center for Exploration of Human Potential, has used and written about a great deal. It has also been a tool for many counselors and is now being used by families on their own. This is called the "strength bombardment" technique. It's very simple. Here is the way it operates. The entire family comes together. There may be a group leader or counselor or some member of the family can act as a leader. One person in the family is designated as the target person. For example, the mother may begin as target person. She is asked to list the strengths that she feels she has as a person. If she lists only two or three because she's modest, the leader can urge her to list others. After she has finished the list, her husband is asked to add to her list of strengths. Or he may elaborate on the strengths that she has already listed. When he has finished, each of the children is asked to add to mother's list of strengths. When this process is finished, the husband becomes the target person. The same procedure is repeated for him. Then each of the children becomes the target person.

The "strengths bombardment" technique is very simple, but the results have been amazing. When families do this exercise, they become more aware of each other's strengths, and more aware of their strengths as a family. They get into a pattern of looking for each other's good qualities and they also get into a habit of expressing appreciation to one another. The result of this with so many families is that it makes their interaction with each other more positive. Some follow-up studies done with families who have gone through this activity show that the increased positive level of interaction is maintained for a period of time after the exercise has been completed. Many families are now using this technique periodically on their own.

Spending Time Together

A second quality found among strong families is that they do a lot of things together. They spend a good deal of time together. It was not a "false" togetherness; it was not a "smothering" type of togetherness. They genuinely enjoyed being together. Another important point here is that these families structured their life styles so that they could spend time together. It did not "just happen." They made it happen. And this togetherness was in all areas of their lives—eating meals, recreation, and work.

3. Good Communication Patterns

The third quality was not a surprise. The strong families have very good communication patterns. They spend time talking with each other. This is closely related to the fact that they spend a lot of time together. It's hard for people to communicate if they do not spend time with each other. One of the big problems facing families today is not spending enough time together. Dr. Virginia Satir, a prominent family therapist, has stated that often families are so fragmented, so busy, and spend such little time together that they communicate with each other through rumor. Unfortunately, that is too often exactly what happens.

Another important aspect of communication is that these families also listen well. They reported that their family members were good listeners and that this was important to them. The fact that family members listen to one another communicates a very important message—that is respect. They are saying to one another, "You respect me enough to listen to what I have to say. I'm interested enough to listen too."

Another factor related to communication is that these families do fight. They get mad at each other, but they get conflict out in the open and they are able to talk it over, to discuss the problem. They share their feelings about alternative ways to deal with the problem and in selecting a solution that is best for everybody.

4. Commitment

A fourth quality characteristic of these strong families was a high degree of commitment. These families were deeply committed to promoting each others' happiness and welfare. They were also very committed to the family group as was reflected by the fact that they invested much of their time and energies into the family. We have not had very much research on commitment and perhaps in recent years it has not been fashionable to talk about commitment.

Some of the best research on commitment has been done in communes. Some communes have been successful; others have not been. One of the main differences found between the two groups is commitment. Those communes that are the most successful, that last the longest, that are the most satisfying in terms of the relationships are those in which there is a great deal of commitment—to each other and to the group. Again, commitment in the communes was reflected in the amount of time the members spent together. The same was true with the strong families.

All of us are busy and we sometimes feel like we have so many things to do that we are pulled in a thousand different directions at the same time. The strong families experience the same problem. One interesting action that these families expressed was that when life got too hectic—to the extent that they were not spending as much time with their families as they wanted—that they would sit down and make a list of the different activities in which they were involved. They would go over that list critically and inevitably there were some things that they really did not want to be doing, or that did not give much happiness, or that really were not very important to them. So they would scratch those activities and involvements off their lists. This would free time for their families, would relieve some of the pressure. As a result they were happier with their lives in general and more satisfied with their family relationships.

This sounds very simple, but how many of us do it? We too often get involved and it's not always because we want to be. We act so often as if we cannot change the situation. We do have a choice. An important point about these families is that they took the initiative in structuring their life style in a way that enhanced the quality of their family relationships and their satisfaction. They were on the "offensive." They did not just react; they made things happen. We may have talked too much about families in the context of families as simply reactors in society, being at the mercy of the environment. In fact, there is a great deal that families can do to make life more enjoyable. These strong families exercised that ability.

High Degree of Religious Orientation

The fifth quality that these families expressed was a high degree of religious orientation. This agrees with research from the past forty years, which shows a positive relationship of religion to marriage happiness and successful family relationships. Of course, we know that there are persons who are not religious who have very happy marriages and good family relationships. Nevertheless a positive relationship between religion and marriage happiness exists according to the research that we've had for many years. These strong families went to church together often and they participated in religious activities together. Most of them, although not all of them, were members of organized churches. All of them were very religious.

There are indications that this religious quality went deeper than going to church or participating in religious activities together. It could most appropriately be called a commitment to a spiritual life style. Words are inadequate to communicate this, but what many of these families said was that they had an awareness of God or a higher power that gave them a sense of purpose and gave their family a sense of support and strength. The awareness of this higher power in their lives helped them to be more patient with each other, more forgiving, quicker to get over anger, more positive, and more supportive in their relationships. Many of the values emphasized by religion when put into action can certainly enhance the quality of human relationships. Dr. Herbert Otto has observed we could spend more time looking at the spiritual aspects of developing human potential and perhaps we could benefit by exploring more about the spiritual aspects of developing family strengths. For these strong families, religion played a major role in their family strengths.

Ability to Deal with Crises in a Positive Manner

The final quality that these families had was the ability to deal with crises and problems in a positive way. Not that they enjoyed crises, but they were able to deal with them in a constructive way. They managed, even in the darkest of situations, to look at the situation and to see some positive element, no matter how tiny and to focus on it. It may have been, for example, that in a particular crisis they simply had to rely to a greater extent on each other and a developed trust that they had in each other. They were able to unite in dealing with the crisis instead of being fragmented by it. They dealt with the problem and were supportive of each other.

RECOMMENDATIONS

It is interesting that most of these qualities that we found to characterize strong families have been found to be lacking in families that are having severe relationship problems and in families broken by divorce. This fact supports the validity of the findings and suggests the importance of these qualities in building family strength. How can we translate this information into help to strengthen families? What kind of recommendations can we make? What can we do?

1. One recommendation is to help families develop some of these skills, such as the ability to express appreciation and good communication patterns. If we were able to do that relationships could be improved and the quality of family life could be made better.
2. A second recommendation that we could make is to have a comprehensive human relationships education program incorporated at the pre-school, elementary, secondary, and college levels. Isn't it amazing that we have not already done that? Good human relationships are basic and vital to our happiness, our well-being and our mental health.
3. Another recommendation that we could make to strengthen families is to conduct further research which identifies the characteristics of strong families. We've hardly begun. We need research on a national basis. We're in the process of doing that, but we need much more research on a national basis. We need to research family strength in alternate family

forms. We need research on the strengths of single-parent families, and on families in different ethnic groups.

4. Also, if we are truly serious about strengthening family life we might make more of a concerted effort to improve the image of family life. Perhaps we need to make commitment more fashionable. We are very much influenced by fashion. Some psychologists have stated that if we are really serious about strengthening family life, we are going to have to build much more prestige into being a family member, in being a good father, mother, wife, or husband. We are influenced tremendously by what we think we are rewarded for.

Perhaps we could improve the image of family life through some television spots like public service announcement. The Mormon Church, for example, has done an excellent job of this. They have some very effective television spots. These short announcements could communicate messages about the importance of expressing appreciation, or the importance of parents listening to their children, for example.

5. Finally, in terms of recommendations for strengthening family life, another thing that we are going to have to do is reorder our values and priorities. We will have to make family life and human relationships a top priority. We also will need to make family life and human relationships a top priority in terms of the way we spend our time and our energy.

Family life today can be strengthened and made much better. There is great potential and we can do it.

22

FOURTEEN DAYS TO A RICHER MARRIAGE: A DO-IT-YOURSELF MARRIAGE ENRICHMENT PROGRAM

Richard L. Mason

Marriage enrichment programs have become very popular in this country in recent years. They may be called by any of several names: marital enrichment, marriage encounter or pairing enrichment. All these names describe a basic process of deepening marital relationships.

Richard L. Mason, "Fourteen Days to a Richer Marriage: A Do-It-Yourself Marriage Enrichment Program." Printed by the USDA Cooperative Extension Service of N.Y. State University. Reprinted by permission of Richard L. Mason, Western Kentucky University.

The process usually involves meeting with other couples and going through certain activities under the direction of a group leader. Most experts feel that doing all or some of the activities in a group is the best way to enrich a marriage. However, such programs are not available everywhere. The purpose of this program is to provide directions for enriching your marriage when a group experience is not available.

One word of caution: Marriage enrichment is not the same as marriage counseling. Marriage enrichment is the process of making a good marriage better. Much as art and music are used to enrich a child's education beyond basics like math and science, marriage enrichment adds "icing on the (wedding) cake." Should you ever find that your marriage is in trouble, you are advised to seek marriage counseling. Professional help may be needed to get the foundation restored. Enrichment can come later.

A FOURTEEN-DAY PLAN

Enriching your marriage involves learning to share with each other at deeper levels. The idea is to become more intimate, through mutual self-disclosure and acceptance. The process is not a fast one. Learning to reveal more of yourself and to accept what your partner reveals to you takes time. Therefore, it is recommended that you agree together to do all fourteen activities, one each day for two weeks. Of course, you can do only some of the activities. Leaving out some will do you no harm. Some couples omit some activities because they sound hard to do or feel awkward. They may be the most important ones for that couple to do. Other couples start off well, but do not finish. Again, no harm done, but the best effects usually come from doing the whole program. A commitment on the part of both spouses to try the program for two weeks may keep you going when you get busy and are tempted to quit.

SOME HELPFUL HINTS

1. Pick a certain time each day to have your marital enrichment session—a time which will be relatively free of distractions.
2. Share positive thoughts and feelings only. This is not the time to complain or debate.
3. Share *feelings mostly*. This is not an exercise in reasoning. It is an exercise in sharing emotions like dreams, aspirations, love and concern.
4. Avoid evaluating and analyzing your partner's feelings. Work on *accepting* them.
5. Use personal pronouns. If you mean yourself, say so. Don't say "People appreciate others caring about them" when you mean "*I* appreciate *you* caring about *me*."
6. Stay mostly in the present. If you need to mention something in the past or future, give your present feelings about it.
7. Share only honest feelings. Avoid the temptation to say something your partner wants to hear when you really do not mean it.
8. Have a "time out" rule. Whenever either partner feels like he or she does not want to continue on a specific exercise, he may say "time out." The other partner then agrees to take a break or change the subject without asking why he does not wish to continue. Knowing this option is available will keep partners from feeling trapped into sharing something they are not ready to share. They can then approach it at their own speed. Or, they can decide to never approach it. People are often much more willing to try marriage enrichment if they know they have this option open to them.

LISTENING

One of the best ways to enrich a marriage is to improve communication between the partners. Today you will learn how to be a better listener. Tomorrow you will learn how to be a better talker.

Listening to what your partner is saying is one of the best ways to show him that you care. You need not only to listen, but also to show him that you are listening. You can do this by practicing what is called active listening or reflective listening.

In active listening the listener tries to understand what the speaker is saying. Then the listener puts his understanding of what the speaker said into his own words and says it back to the speaker to see if he got it right. He sends no message of his own at this point; he only feeds back what he thinks was said.

If the listener has not understood what the speaker meant, the speaker can then explain it further until the message that is sent is the message that is received. When these two messages agree, the listener can give his own response to the message. At this point the roles are reversed; the speaker now becomes the listener and the listener becomes the speaker. The process is repeated until clear communication is reached.

Example

Husband: "I sure am tired tonight."

Wife: "Sounds like you would rather stay home than go out tonight."

Husband: "Yes, I would. Do you mind?"

Wife: "No. That's fine with me."

Notice how this wife wisely checked the message out to make sure she understood what her husband really was saying before she responded to it.

Communication like this enriches a marriage because partners understand each other and because they feel like what they say is being heard.

Now, it's time for you to practice active listening.

Instructions

1. Decide which of you is to be the speaker and which is to be the listener.
2. The speaker sends a message.
3. In his own words, the listener feeds back what he hears the speaker say.
4. The speaker confirms the listener's response. (If his response is not what the speaker meant, steps 2 and 3 are repeated.)
5. Roles are reversed and the process is repeated.

Second Day

EXPRESSING FEELINGS

Most of the time when we want someone to do something we send them a "you" message. "Why don't you ever talk to me?", "Why do you do that?" and "(You) Stop that" are examples of "you" messages.

"You" messages are usually put-downs. All the responsibility for past and future behavior is put on the other person.

Naturally, put-downs invite other put-downs as in this example:

Wife: "Why don't you ever stay at home?"

Husband: "Why don't you ever shut up?"

It's usually better to send an "I" message when you want someone to do something. "I" messages are messages in which the speaker expresses his true feelings and takes responsibility for them. There is no putdown. Arguments are avoided. Issues can be discussed calmly.

Example

Wife: "I feel lonely here all alone. I need someone to talk to."

Husband: "I don't want you to be lonely. Maybe I can stay home more often."

Good "I" messages contain three elements: A feeling, a situation and a need. In the example above what was the feeling? The situation? The need?

Here is a good model for sending "I" messages: I feel _____ when (or if) _____ because I need _____. For example, "I feel all warm inside when you hug me because I need to be reminded of your love."

Of course, "I" messages are useful for effective complaining as in the second example. You are encouraged to use them for such purposes. However, during your marital enrichment time, you are to use them only for sharing positive feelings as in the third example.

Now let's practice some "I" messages.

Instructions

1. Pick a warm feeling you have toward your spouse.
2. Put it into the model for "I" messages: I feel _____ when (or if) _____ because I need _____.
3. Take turns sharing these feelings.
4. While your partner is sharing his warm feelings with you, practice active listening as in the exercise you did yesterday.

One final word about "I" and "You" messages. Whether a message is an "I" or a "You" message depends on more than just the use of the words "I" and "You". The attitude and manner in which it is said can make the difference between a "You" message and an "I" message. "I feel lonely here all alone" said in a nasty tone of voice is really a "You" message. It is saying "You make me lonely because *you* leave me here all alone."

Now you have two effective tools for communicating verbally with each other. You are encouraged to use them along with the other activities throughout the whole two weeks.

Tomorrow and on succeeding days you will be asked to write some things down. Before then buy two notebooks, one for each of you.

Third Day

WHAT I LIKE ABOUT THIS MARRIAGE

We all like positive feedback. Today's session is devoted simply to giving each other some.

Instructions

1. In your notebooks, write five things you like about your marriage. You may write about being married in general or about being married to your spouse in particular. You may want to use the "I" message model for phrasing them. For example, "I feel secure being married to you because I need someone to lean on at times and you are a good person to lean on."
2. Take turns reading these to each other and responding with active listening.

Fourth Day

LOVE LETTERS

Imagine that you and your spouse must be separated for a month or more. Perhaps the husband is in military service or must work out of town. Write a love letter to your spouse. Include only the usual components of a *love* letter. For example, you may write about how you miss your spouse, how you enjoyed the last time you were together, or what you plan to do when you see each other again. Omit the news parts like, "Johnny went to the dentist today." Write a real love letter.

Then put it in an envelope addressed to your spouse, put a stamp on it, and mail it. Finally, watch the mail box for the love letter addressed to you!

Fifth Day

LEVELS OF SUPPORT

There are at least three levels at which spouses support each other. At the highest level your partner feels as you do. He wants to join you. He backs you all the way. Another level is simply "being there." He is there to listen when you need to talk, to share what you have to share. The third level is "I don't approve, but I won't stand in your way." The bottom level is nonsupport. It says, "I don't approve and I won't help."

Each of the three levels of support may have a place in your marriage. The value of the first two are obvious. But even "I don't approve, but I won't stand in your way" often has value. It lets each partner be an individual and be accepted as such.

Write in your notebooks (1) a time when your spouse supported you all the way, (2) a time when he was there when you needed him, and (3) a time when he didn't really approve, but let you do your own thing anyway. Write how you feel about him doing each of these. Share these with each other.

Sixth Day

QUALITIES OF A SUCCESSFUL MARRIAGE

The well-known marriage counselor David Mace has listed eight qualities which he feels are necessary for a successful marriage:

1. The couple respect each other.
2. They meet crises successfully.
3. They are loyal and faithful to each other.
4. They reinforce and support each other.
5. They are truthful and open with each other.
6. They share the same basic values.
7. They are mutually affectionate.
8. They share the same goals.

Pick three or four of these qualities which are present in your marriage. In your notebook write specific ways in which your spouse exhibits these qualities. For example, in regard to number one, you might write, "You show that you respect me by listening carefully to my opinion when we must make a decision." Read these to each other.

Seventh Day

SYNERGY

A well-known love poem contains this line: "I love you not only for what you are, but for what I am when I am with you." In the same vein the O'Neill's based their best selling book *Open Marriage,* on "the idea of synergy—that one plus one equals more than two, that the sum of the parts working together is greater than the sum of the parts working separately."

In your notebook, write something that you are that you would not be if you had not married your spouse. For example, one husband wrote, "I am a better businessman because of you. Not that you taught me about business. It's just that I knew you were backing me emotionally and would still love me even if the business failed. This gave me the courage to try new things, to take risks."

Share these with each other.

Eighth Day

SHARING A PRIVATE THOUGHT

Your assignment for today is to share something with your spouse you have never shared before. It's not that this thought has been a secret; it's just that you've never thought to share it before or you were a little reluctant to share until now. It may be a dream, a feeling, a fantasy, a goal, an ambition, a desire, a meaningful poem, a new sex technique you want to try, or an idea for a new invention.

Write it in your notebook. Take turns reading them to each other.

Ninth Day

MARRIAGE EXPECTATIONS

People enter marriage with certain expectations of what married life will be like. When our expectations are not met we are unhappy and will likely say something about it. On the other hand, we may neglect to give positive feedback when our expectations are met. This exercise is designed to help us give such feedback.

In your notebook write three expectations you had of marriage or your spouse that have been met. Then write *how* they were met. For example, you might write, "I expected that marriage to you would provide me with emotional security. You have made me feel emotionally secure by showing me in many ways that you love me and want to spend your life with me. For example, I like the way you include me in your retirement plans."

Read these to each other.

Tenth Day

DISCOVERING COMMON INTERESTS

Each partner is to list ten or more things he or she (a) used to enjoy doing, (b) has always wanted to do, or (c) would like to do more often. Read your lists to each other. See how many things you both enjoy doing. See how many things your spouse likes to do that you did not know he/she liked to do. If possible, do one of the things on either list now.

Eleventh Day

THE STAGES OF MARRIAGE

In a sense you will have many marriages over your life time together. That is, your marriage will go through various stages. You will have a young marriage, a middle-age marriage and, hopefully an elderly marriage. Each new stage will have its own rewards, but it will also call for adjustments in the relationship. The purpose of this exercise is to reflect upon what you have meant to each other through these stages.

The first stage is the Honeymoon Stage. It lasts from the wedding to the arrival of children or until the thirties for couples who do not have children. The couple does almost everything together and has a lot of fun.

The second is the Childbearing Stage. It lasts from the arrival of the first child until the last child enters school. During this stage the husband and wife have less time and energy for each other. They also have less money and less privacy to use in building their relationship.

Next is the Childrearing Stage. At this time all the tasks and responsibilities of putting children through school must be met. The mother may go back to work. Life with teenagers must be adjusted. In the latter part of this stage middle-age must be faced. Wives go through menopause and husbands begin to see how far up the career ladder they are going to go.

The fourth stage is the Empty Nest Stage. The children are gone. Marriage, not parenthood, is again the primary relationship.

The fifth stage is Retirement. For the husband, especially, substitutes for job and career must be found.

Finally, Old Age is faced. Loss of independence and other changes must be adjusted to.

Instructions

1. Write down what your partner has meant to you at each stage through which you have already come.
2. Write down what he/she means to you at the stage you are now in.
3. Write down what you think he/she will mean to you in the stages to come.
4. Share these with your partner.

Twelfth Day

SEXUAL FEEDBACK

What sexual activity pleases you most? Specifically, what does your partner do that "turns you on"? Have you told him or her lately? He/she would probably be glad to hear it, even if he/she already knows it.

Write it in your notebook. Or, if you wish, you may write it on a separate piece of paper so that it may be destroyed after the session. Be specific.

Take turns reading these to each other, practicing active listening. You may be surprised to find that some seemingly insignificant thing you do is very meaningful to your partner.

Thirteenth Day

FLEXIBILITY

Think about those times when your spouse was very flexible in order to meet some of your needs. Perhaps she was willing to move to a far away city so you could accept a promotion. Perhaps he was willing to keep the children evenings or Saturdays so you could go to work or school. Maybe it was some small thing: He went to the movie you wanted to see or she watched the television program you wanted to watch.

Write in your notebook how you feel about him/her doing that for you.

Read these to each other.

Fourteenth Day

TEN AND TEN

This is your last exercise in the marital enrichment program. It has been left until last for a reason: You can continue to do it for as long as you wish.

Instructions

1. Each day take 10 minutes to write down some of your thoughts—thoughts about the day, about life, about your future, about anything.
2. Take 10 minutes to share these with your spouse.

MAKING IT

23

YOUR BELIEFS CAN SABOTAGE YOUR RELATIONSHIPS

Chuck Hillig

As a licensed marriage, family, and child counselor, I deal professionally with people who are having problems in their relationships. During my years in private practice, I have noticed that many couples entering therapy sincerely believe the same common myths about how people operate.

Myth #1 holds that other people, objects, or situations can, literally, *make* you feel some emotion. This single untruth probably helps to create more suffering, anger, and bitterness than the other myths combined.

For example, do you believe that other family members or friends are often responsible for your painful feelings? Before you answer that, think back to the times when you've accused others of having hurt you or of having made you angry. Sound familiar? I hear this from my clients every day.

Let's look at this closely. When you really believe that the cause of your emotional upset is somewhere *outside* of you, then you're implying that someone or something else is in charge of your painful experience. For example, if you believe that your spouse is, somehow, *forcing* you to react painfully, then you're admitting that you really have no other choice except to feel hurt and upset. When you believe that others are *making* you feel an emotion, then you are giving away your ability to *choose* your own responses.

This whole idea of choice is important because it is only through your choices that you are able to truly experience your own personal power. If you believe that you don't have any *choice* as to how you react, then you really have no *control* over the situation.

If you don't have any control, then it follows that you're not the one who is *responsible* for your painful experience. And if you're not responsible, then guess who ends up getting the blame?

Acting on the belief that "they" are "doing this terrible thing to me," it is easy then to *justify* your own behavior in response to them. "Since *they* have hurt me," you reason, "then *they* are also responsible for my negative reactions to them." For example, if I can point at my wife and say, "She made me get drunk because she made me angry," then I'm off the responsibility hook for my own actions.

It's all downhill from there. Once you've made that original decision that you're not responsible for your own discomfort, then you can give yourself permission to "get even" with those people who are "causing" you the emotional pain. But while you are justifying your own negative behavior, your mate is probably doing the very same thing to you. I have seen many couples who have be-

---

Chuck Hillig, M.A., M.F.C.C., "Your Beliefs Can Sabotage Your Relationship," *The Single Parent*, October 1980. Copyright © 1980 by Chuck Hillig. Reprinted by permission of the author.

lieved this myth all of their lives and have created for themselves a relationship filled with resentment, bitterness, and isolation.

Many couples resist giving up this belief because they just don't want to accept the responsibility for creating their own pain in the relationship. If they openly admitted to themselves that they alone were the source of their own discomfort, then they might feel pressured into doing something different. But since changes can be scary, many people simply choose to continue living with their pain but to hold their mates responsible for it. They each can take the pressure off themselves to change their behavior by directing their energies into making the other person not-OK and deserving of punishment.

Myth #1 is so widespread because its philosophy is continually reinforced on TV, in movies, in books, and in our popular songs. For example, millions of us firmly accept without question that rainy days can *make* us sad or that wearing old clothes can *make* us embarrassed. The truth is that situations and inanimate objects cannot *make* us feel anything any more than other people can *make* us feel anything. We all create our own feelings. Period.

How did we ever get to accept this myth in the first place? Probably 99 percent of us were indirectly conditioned as pre-schoolers to begin believing that we could control other people's feelings. For example, when our parents would say, "Don't tell Aunt Sue that you don't like her present because *you'll hurt her feelings*," it implied that we had the power to *force* Aunt Sue into feeling bad. Indirectly, though, it also implied that Aunt Sue and others could force *us* into feeling bad, too.

The simple truth is that we humans just do not have that much power to literally *force* each other into feeling some emotion. Significant others, of course, can make it much *easier* for us to *choose* one feeling over another, but the final choice of what and how we are going to feel is entirely ours. To give up our responsibility as the creator and the source of our own feelings is to experience only half of our power.

Myth #2 holds that you should always have *good reasons* why you are feeling anxious or upset about something and yet were just not able to figure out why. It seems that many of us have gotten programmed into believing that we should *always* be able to understand and explain our feelings to ourselves and to others. We can probably all remember times when our parents would ask us *why* we were feeling some way. Most of the time we knew, but there were always situations when we simply were not aware of the causes behind our feelings.

If I believe that I must always have *good reasons* for feeling the way I do, then what happens when I'm not able to come up with an explanation? What we all too often do with feelings that we can't understand or justify is to try to deny them and keep them inside of us. But this, in turn, only works to limit our experience of ourselves by keeping us defensive and out of touch with our own momentary reality.

The truth is that, sooner or later, we will likely create for ourselves all of the potential feelings that we as humans are capable of experiencing.

Although we might have a desire to commit murder, suicide, incest, etc., we are never required to *act* on those feelings. If we all did exactly what we momentarily felt like doing, our social structure would collapse around us. Since we have a free will which can determine our choices, we can learn to simply acknowledge and own these feelings as they arise from our unconscious.

We can best do this by giving ourselves complete permission to have these feelings, no matter how outrageous, as our truth for that moment. I often tell my clients to remember the acronym J-U-D-E in order to help remind them that they don't have to Justify, Understand, Defend or Explain their feelings to either themselves or to others.

For example, a man begins to feel jealous of his mate's financial success. Although he has an excellent job himself, he feels threatened at some deep level. If he believes that he needs to first have a "good reason" to be threatened and is unable to come up with one, he will likely repress the jealousy that is arising in him. But since he needs to do *something* with that "jealous energy," he may transform it into anger, resistance, and withdrawal.

Because he will not give himself permission to have such an "unreasonable" feeling as jealousy as his truth for that moment, he denies what he's feeling. When he does not create a space in his own personal "myth" about himself that can include the possibility that he, too, has the potential of creating an experience of "unreasonable jealousy," then he's stuck with the negative energy. This in turn only creates distance between him and his mate because the *actual* feeling—the "unreasonable jealousy"—has neither been acknowledged nor shared.

It is far healthier for the relationship to learn how to stop judging your own feelings and those of your partner. A feeling is a feeling is a feeling. The feeling doesn't hassle us nearly as much as the relationship that we set up in our own heads between the feeling itself and what we believe that we *should* be experiencing instead.

Learning to accept our feelings as they arise is really learning to say "yes" to our own experience of ourselves from moment to moment.

Myth #3 holds that my partner should automatically know what I want without me having to share this information with him or her. At some level, many people still want to believe in magic. Their reasoning is often, "Since my family loves me, they *should* know by now what I want and expect from them." However, this is a dangerous position because then it seems to follow that, if my partner doesn't automatically give me what I want, then he or she must *not* love me. Once these rejection mechanisms get triggered inside us, they create a fertile space for grudges, resentments, and hostility to grow.

The desire to have our wishes "divined" by our loved ones, probably has its origins in our unconscious memory as infants. Most of us had parents who fed us, changed our diapers, and generally attended to our needs. At a deep level, we probably became addicted to having our basic wishes satisfied consistently by some benevolent protector. Most importantly, this "all-powerful" guardian was miraculously able to predict what we wanted and to have it there for us. Although our needs were primitive and obvious at that age, many people still expect this kind of "magic" from their partners.

When we relieve ourselves of the responsibility of clearly communicating our needs to those around us, we unfairly place upon them the impossible burden of reading our minds. When they fail to pick up our signals or if they misinterpret our wants, it becomes easy for us to justify feeling hurt and angry.

Demanding that your mate automatically understand and fulfill your needs in the same way as your parents did when you were an infant is an unreasonable expectation. Clinging to such a belief is only setting yourself up to feel disappointed and betrayed.

The problem is, of course, that we don't easily see that we are holding these myths as infallible truths. They are *not truths;* they are only *belief systems*. Although these beliefs are often unconscious, we can become aware of them by observing our own behavior and by asking ourselves these questions: (1) Do I believe that someone or something else is responsible for my own painful feelings, or do I accept that I am always creating my own emotional experience? (2) Do I believe that I need to justify, understand, defend, or explain my feelings, or do I just allow myself to feel them? (3) Do I believe that the people who love me should magically know what I want and expect of them, or do I clearly inform them of my needs and desires?

By honestly answering these questions, we can begin to become more conscious of how our own belief systems are likely to work in our relationships.

24

THE INTIMACY THAT GOES BEYOND SEX

Marcia Lasswell and Norman M. Lobsenz

A man and woman may be close to each other in every physical way, yet remain emotional strangers. To lock away one's thoughts and feelings inside the strongbox of the mind is to deprive a partner of the most significant gift one can offer—the intimacy that goes beyond all others. Even the dictionary recognizes this. "Sexual intercourse" is the secondary definition of the word "intimacy." Its primary meaning is the "close personal relationship" that springs from the "inmost self." Thus, intimacy between husband and wife cuts across the totality of a marriage not just its sexual aspect. It is, perhaps, what we really mean (but do not realize we mean) by "love."

This intimacy that goes beyond sex presents difficulties for many couples. We all need it, we all want it. But not all of us know how to find it, nor are able to give it. Intimacy can be one of the knottiest areas to deal with, since differences in our ability to give and receive intimacy often stem from deep psychological causes. A marriage empty of intimacy, for whatever reason, is likely to intensify doubt about our own worth and adequacy—a doubt that gets translated into a further retreat from intimacy and sets up a cycle of isolation.

But couples can make a beginning, at least, at improving their ability truly to share an intimate relationship by better understanding the levels of intimacy; by learning to recognize some of the barriers to it; and by developing the skill to overcome these barriers.

WHAT INTIMACY IS, AND ISN'T

There's been a good deal of foolishness put forth about intimacy. Some would have you believe that while it is a bonus in marriage its absence is not fatal, that a couple can find sufficient satisfaction in a "colleague" relationship where both persons function independently but get on well together. Others hold intimacy to be the only essential element of a good marriage. In the reality of wedlock, the truth would seem to fall somewhere between these extremes.

We don't expect any couple would score 100 percent on an "intimacy rating," if there were such a scale. Nor should they. Each individual rightly reserves close-held emotional space for private thoughts and feelings. Couples who assume that there is always *complete* intimacy in a good marriage thus naturally feel, from time to time, that something is wrong in their relationship. They have set a standard for themselves (or had it set by outsiders) that is impossible to achieve. Moreover, intimacy manifests itself in many forms: a smile across a room, a shared joke, a family ritual, a kiss, a touch, sex, even in a certain inflection of the voice. How intimate a couple are, and what forms their intimacy takes, depends on how they "negotiate" the difference between their individual desires for it. Intimacy cannot be a one-way proposition. Ob-

---

Excerpt from "Sex and Other Intimacies" in *No-Fault Marriage* by Marcia Lasswell and Norman Lobsenz. Copyright © 1976 by Marcia Lasswell and Norman Lobsenz. Reprinted by permission of Doubleday & Company, Inc.

viously, a marriage between an emotionally giving (or needy) person married to a very private person will have a hard time achieving a degree of intimacy acceptable to both; for them all the emotional flow will be going in one direction.

As a practical matter, the level of intimacy between husband and wife is constantly changing. Moments of intense closeness intersperse with periods of varying emotional distance. Try this experiment. Draw two circles on a sheet of paper. One represents you, the other your spouse. Where they intersect and overlap represents your area of intimacy. For example, during a particularly good sexual experience the circles may overlap almost completely, like this:

But there also may be times when intercourse, though still satisfying, is not quite such an intense merging experience. One of you may be worried, or tired, or just not as interested as the other. The circles in that case might look this way:

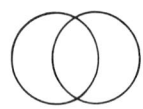

Yet the next evening, at a large noisy party—or just across a quiet living room—you may each look up from what you are doing and meet each other's eyes in a spontaneous exchange of silent affection. At that instant the circles will again be virtually superimposed—

and you are just as intimately linked as you were in that earlier act of sex.

During much of the twenty-four hours, as a couple go about the routines of living, their circles may barely touch:

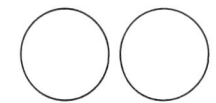

After a bitter argument, they may be widely separated:

And the silent sharing of a mood can bring them close again. Some years ago a writer friend described what he called "one of the most intimate moments of my married life." He and his wife were reading the papers on a lazy Sunday morning over second cups of coffee while the FM radio played in the background. "Suddenly," he said, "the music of Mozart flooded the room. Without exchanging a word or even a glance my wife and I simultaneously got up from our chairs, moved to the middle of the room, bowed to each other, and began to improvise the steps of a minuet. It all happened as if we had been one person. I shall never forget how close we felt."

In short, the circles constantly shift as each person gives and receives, withholds and blocks out.

BARRIERS TO INTIMACY

It may seem strange that anyone should want to avoid intimacy in marriage. Yet many people not only seek to avoid it but secretly fear it. Therapists believe the main reason is that intimacy, like trust, inevitably implies *vulnerability*. They are two sides of the same coin. Emotional sharing requires self-disclosure, and for many of us the idea of opening up our inmost centers is a scary prospect. Suppose we get hurt? Suppose we are rejected? Suppose we open up to find and to reveal to our partner that there is little or nothing inside?

Schopenhauer's parable about the porcupines which drew together for warmth but separated when their quills pricked each other illustrates the pull-and-push interplay of intimacy and vulnerability. Pained, the animals move apart; then, feeling the chill of the air they move close again, only to be hurt once more in the act of sharing warmth. We are often told that hate is the opposite of love, remoteness the reverse of intimacy. But it appears the real antagonist of both is the fear of being vulnerable to hurt, rejection or disillusionment.

One protection against vulnerability—and thus

a secondary barrier to intimacy—is to avoid the risk of self-disclosure by masking your true self. That's why some people can be comfortable emotionally so long as they can play the "role" of husband and wife. Doing the conventional and saying the expected things, we are saved from having to deal with the real feelings of real people. Sadly, it's all too easy to get on life's treadmill and keep running so steadily or so fast that we can find no time for intimacy. For men and women who have a poor opinion of themselves to begin with, the marital "role" is a convenient cloak to hide insecurities and weak self-images.

The retreat into role-playing is often an outgrowth of the artifices some couples adopt in their dating days. Ideally, courtship should be the time when men and women reveal themselves to each other with increasing intimacy. But even today—when so many courting conventions have gone by the boards and young couples dissemble less and level more—even now they still tend to conceal realities that might threaten their relationship. And when the *part* one plays succeeds in attracting and holding the person one wants, it gets progressively harder to step out of that character. But by dodging true intimacy in courtship we make it harder to achieve in marriage.

Even sexual intercourse defies intimacy when two people become actors in bed. A wife who for years faked orgasm so her husband would not feel a failure as a lover said, "Now I am trapped. I would like to be honest with him because that would be a start at solving our difficulty. But it would mean admitting I deceived him all this time." Like all other kinds of intimacy, sexual intimacy depends on maximum *mutual* openness.

INTIMACY AND SEX

A pathetic paradox of these sexually "free" times is that Americans are making love more but enjoying it less.

William Masters and Virginia Johnson estimate that half the married couples in the United States have sexual problems. Much sexual unhappiness grows directly out of the fear of intimacy. In fact, some couples develop sexual problems as a result of the stress one or both partners feel about being emotionally committed to an intimate relationship. For these people, sex may be good before and early in marriage. But when the realization hits that a good marriage demands ever-higher degrees of intimacy, there may be a retreat from sex.

While sexual distancing is almost always a sign of intimacy problems, sexual contact is not always a sign of emotional closeness. That is another paradox couples need to bear in mind. For example, there are marriages in which sex is the only good thing the couple share, and is sufficiently rewarding to hold together a relationship that lacks most other assets. Even men and women who are separated or divorced may still be drawn together sexually. For other couples, intercourse may represent the search for an antidote to loneliness, the "skin hunger" that desperately needs assuaging by human touch. It may offer reassurance that one is still vigorous and desirable. Or it may be a frantic effort to prove one still actually *exists*. Widows and widowers are often shocked to find that quite soon after a spouse's death they want—or form—a new sexual liaison. Similarly, there's an upsurge of sexual activity after major disasters. In both instances people are denying death, expressing the life force, saying with their bodies: "*I* am still here."

Withholding sex—being "too tired" or having a "headache"—is a standard method for turning an intimate act into a power struggle. Spoiling sex—being passive or brusque, repressing a climax or ejaculating too quickly—are somewhat crueler refinements of the technique. One woman drove her husband to fury by making casual remarks about the day's events during intercourse.

Sometimes couples quarrel in order to feel sexy. Making up in bed after a fight is a common marital pattern. It is reassuring when the bond of intimacy survives an argument. But if it is often done deliberately one needs to ask *why* quarreling is a turn-on. Marital therapist Laura Singer has observed that "it may be a way for a couple to distance themselves from each other to avoid true merging. . . . Or the act may be an extension of the fight. People may perceive a fight as firing their libido, but what it really fires is their hostility."

All these "uses" or "mis-uses" of sex distort its function as the most intimate link in marriage. Even more startling, however, is the use of sex as an outright *substitute* for intimacy. A person who is so alienated as to fear any close relationship may turn to sex as the only nonthreatening way to be with another person. When there routinely is physical contact with no emotional attachments, the act of love becomes the *denial* of intimacy.

EXPRESSING INTIMACY

Some husbands and wives are genuinely puzzled by the suggestion that they try to raise the intimacy level of their marriage. They agree with the theory but they do not know how to put it into practice. They seem to assume that a talent for sharing feelings is an inborn skill which can't be learned. Or that it takes "too much time" to cultivate. Or that their responsibilities keep them too much on the go, or too far apart, to be able to create a basis for true intimacy.

But there are any number of ways every couple can find to enhance and to express their mutual intimacy:

1. Confiding in your spouse is an aspect of intimacy. Think back and ask yourself whether you often tell a friend or neighbor something you feel you cannot or do not want to tell your wife or husband. If you do, perhaps you should ask whether you are being emotionally fair to your partner—and why you are shutting him or her out, or shutting yourself away.
2. Sharing "trivialities" is a way of increasing intimacy. Some people feel it's "boring" to tell a spouse all the little things that occur during the day. But marriage is essentially made up of these small details; they are the "nut and bolts" of living together. True, they are usually routine. But it you wait for some major event to happen you may wait quite a while.
3. Intimate behavior does not have to involve only grand passion or high drama. Intimacy is built as well (if not more soundly) on lighter, slighter actions: reading aloud; putting a loving note in a lunch box; giving a small but unexpected present; doing a chore the other person hates (without being asked); telling the other person when you have had a warm thought about him or her.
4. Verbal communication is an important part of intimacy because unless we can put feelings into words our partners may never know we have them. Even an argument can contribute to marital intimacy. If a couple can have an honest fight without letting it deteriorate into aggression or anger, it often leaves them feeling closer when it's over. As one couple said after a furious battle: "You can get mad and know it's *because you care* about each other." Conversely, poor communication can handicap a couple's efforts to be close.
5. While sex is the peak physical expression of intimacy, it's essential to remember that there can be many kinds of marital sex. There can be an intense spiritual or emotional merging. There can be sex that makes you feel like the most desirable man or woman in the world. There is casual love-making, playful "seduction," intercourse for the release of tension, reluctant sex, or sex on the purely physical "let's do it" level. One brings a different expectation of intimacy to each kind of sexual experience, and it is important for both partners to know what kind of expectation the other has for each particular experience.

   The emphasis on sexual technique in recent years has cut many couples off from true intimacy. They get so caught up in mechanics and methods that they lose sight of the need for feelings and concerns. Good physical sex is obviously important—but no two persons' cycle of desire coincides exactly all the time. Not even the perfect orgasm is any guarantee of interpersonal intimacy. Orgasmic sex can make a good marriage better; but a good marriage, with a high level of emotional intimacy, can also make for more or better orgasms.
6. Many men and women find pleasure in varying degrees of physical intimacy short of sexual intercourse. That's why touching is such a key factor in conveying intimate feelings. Americans avoid touching. They tend to think of body contact not in terms of comfort and affection, but in terms of sex or combat—both of which are prickly with cultural and psychological taboos. Thus a wife may come to resent a husband's touch if she thinks all it means is that he wants sex. Likewise, she hesitates

to touch him for fear *he* will think *she* wants sex.

Yet touching is the most natural act in the world. A touch can calm anxiety, ease pain, soothe fear, provide emotional security.

If you have hesitated to express or receive intimacy through touching but would like to experiment with it, try these steps:

1. Discuss the idea first with your partner. Nothing is more disconcerting than when one person suddenly and without explanation becomes a "toucher."
2. Begin with simple physical contacts that are customary in many families: a good-morning and good-night kiss, a hug in greeting or farewell.
3. Become more aware of your spouse's physical presence. Many couples become so familiar with each other's bodies that, paradoxically, they forget how those bodies *really* look and feel.
4. Touch yourself more often to develop a sense of body awareness. We do it automatically while drying after a bath, shaving, putting on makeup. But we should learn to do it consciously on occasion.

Touching should never be an implied demand to be touched in return, or a camouflage for clinging to another person.

Learn to be sensitive to when the other person wants—or does not want—to be touched. The important thing is to respect each other's feelings about it.

Is it better to experience intimacy at the risk of some hurt, or to avoid it in order to feel safe?

That is what economists call a "cost-reward equation." As with all such questions, the answer lies in the balance between how much it costs to get the reward we desire. To a vulnerable person it always *seems* safer to keep feelings at arm's length. But retreating from intimacy is no guarantee that you will not be hurt by someone, somehow, anyway. In the long run, reaching out and opening up is not only more rewarding but also less risky.

X

THE QUESTION OF EQUALITY

25

WHO HAS THE POWER? THE MARITAL STRUGGLE

Dair L. Gillespie

THE CHANGING POWER STRUCTURE

Modern theorists of the family agree that the American family has evolved from a paternalistic to a much more democratic form. Before the Civil War married women had many duties, few rights. They were not permitted to control their property, even when it was theirs by inheritance or dower, or to make a will. To all intents and purposes they did not own property. The husband had the right to collect and use the wife's wages, to decide upon the education and religion of the children, and to punish his wife if she displeased him. The right to will children, even unborn, to other guardians was retained by the husband. In the case of divorce, when granted at all, the husband had the right to determine the control of the children. To a married woman, her husband was her superior, her companion, her master. In every sector of the social arena, women were in a subordinate position. The church was one of the most potent forces for maintaining them in this position. Within the church, women were segregated from men, were not allowed to sing, preach or take public action. There were no high schools for girls, and no college in the world admitted women. Unpropertied males, slaves, and all women were not allowed into the political process at all.

Today, as the textbooks never tire of telling us, couples are more free to choose partners than formerly, they are able to separate more easily, the differences in age and culture between husband and wife are less marked than formerly, the husband recognizes more willingly the independence of his wife's demands, they may share housekeeping and diversions, and the wife may even work. In fact, sociologists claim that the modern husband and wife are so nearly equal in power that marriage today can be termed "democratic," "equalitarian," or "egalitarian."

These changes in the form of marriage are generally attributed to the entrance of women into the economic structure and to the extension of an equalitarian ideology to cover women. This type of explanation is careful to emphasize socioeconomic conditions of the past and the "rise of

---

Dair L. Gillespie, "Who Has the Power? The Marital Struggle," *Journal of Marriage and the Family,* August 1971, pp. 445–66. Copyrighted © 1971 by the National Council on Family Relations, 1219 University Avenue Southeast, Minneapolis, Minnesota 55414. Reprinted by permission.

women" in the American economy. However, socioeconomic conditions of the present are no longer examined, for it is assumed that women have won their rights in all social arenas, and if they haven't—well, ideology takes a while to filter down to the masses. New egalitarian ideals, they tell us, will bring about further socioeconomic changes and a better position for women.

In a major research project on the modern American family, Blood and Wolfe state:

> Under former historical circumstances, the husband's economic and social role almost automatically gave him pre-eminence. Under modern conditions, the roles of men and women have changed so much that husbands and wives are potential equals—with the balance of power tipped sometimes one way, sometimes the other. It is no longer possible to assume that just because a man is a man, he is the boss. Once upon a time, the function of culture was to rationalize the predominance of the male sex. Today the function of culture is to develop a philosophy of equal rights under which the saying goes, "May the best man win!"—and the best man is sometimes a woman. The role of culture has shifted from sanctioning a competent sex over an incompetent sex to sanctioning the competent marriage partner over the incompetent one, regardless of sex (1960, pp. 29–30).

There is good evidence, however, that the balance of power is tipped the same way it always was, and that the best man is very seldom a woman. I am arguing, then, against the *personal* resource theory and am positing that, in fact, this is still a caste/class sytem rationalizing the preponderance of the male sex. . . .

SOURCES OF MARITAL POWER

Socialization

Men and women are differentially socialized. By the time women reach marriageable age, we have already been damaged by the socialization process. We have been systematically trained to accept second best, not to strive, and to accept the "fact" that we are unworthy of more. Naomi Weisstein's "Kinde, Kuche, Kirche as Scientific Law" states this process clearly:

> How are women characterized in our culture, and in psychology? They are inconsistent, emotionally unstable, lacking in strong conscience or superego, weaker, "nurturant" rather than productive, "intuitive" rather than intelligent, and if they are at all "normal," suited to the home and family. In short, the list adds up to a typical minority group stereotype of inferiority; if they know their place, which is in the home, they are really quite loveable, happy, childlike, loving creatures. In a review of the intellectual differences between little boys and little girls, Eleanor Maccoby has shown that there are no intellectual differences until about high school, or if there are, girls are slightly ahead of boys. At high school, the achievement of women now measured in terms of productivity and accomplishment, drops off even more rapidly. There are a number of other, non-intellectual tests which show sex differences; I chose the intellectual differences since it is seen clearly that women start becoming inferior. It is no use to talk about women being different but equal; all of the tests I can think of have a "good" outcome and a "bad" outcome. Women usually end up at the "bad" outcome. In light of social expectations about women, what is surprising is not that women end up where society expects they will; what is surprising is that little girls don't get the message that they are supposed to be stupid until high school, and what is even more remarkable is that some women resist this message even after high school, college, and graduate school (1969, p. 7).

Thus, women begin at a psychological disadvantage when we sign the marriage contract, for we have differential training and expectations.

Marriage: A Free Contract Between Equals

Sociologists universally fail to discuss legal differences in power when the marriage contract is signed.[1] Marriage is ordinarily considered a contract freely entered into by both partners, and the partners are assumed to stand on common footing of equal rights and duties. Sheila Cronan (1969, pp. 2–4) examined this "free" contract between equals and found a few unlisted terms.

Sex. She found that the husband can legally force his wife to have sexual intercourse with him against her will, an act which if committed against any other woman would constitute the crime of rape. By definition, a husband cannot be guilty of raping his own wife, for "the crime (of rape) is ordinarily that of forcing intercourse on someone other than the wife of the person accused" (Gallen 1967, p. 6). Women are well aware of the "right" of the husband to "insist" and the "duty" of the wife to submit to sexual intercourse. The compulsory nature of sex in marriage operates to the advantage of the male, for though the husband theoretically has the duty to have intercourse with his wife, this normally cannot occur against his will. (Both partners are protected in that a marriage can be annulled by either party if the marriage has not been consummated.)

Other Marital Responsibilities. Women believe that we are voluntarily giving our household services, but the courts hold that the husband is legally entitled to his wife's services, and further, that *she cannot be paid for her work.* In *Your Marriage and the Law,* Pilpel and Zavin state:

> As part of the rights of consortium, the husband is entitled to the services of his wife. If the wife works outside the home for strangers, she is usually entitled to her own earnings. But domestic services or assistances which she gives her husband are generally considered part of her wifely duties. The wife's services and society are so essential a part of what the law considers the husband is entitled to as part of the marriage that it will not recognize any agreement between spouses which provides that the husband is to pay for such services or society.
>
> In a Texas case David promised his wife, Fannie, that he would give her $5000 if she would stay with him while he lived and continue taking care of the house and farm accounts, selling his butter and doing all the other tasks which she had done since their marriage. After David's death, Fannie sued his estate for the money which had been promised her. The court held that the contract was unenforceable since Fannie had agreed to do nothing which she was not already legally and morally bound to do as David's wife (1967, p. 65).

The legal responsibilities of a wife are to live in the home established by her husband, to perform the domestic chores (cleaning, cooking, washing, etc.) necessary to help maintain that home, and to care for her husband and children (Gallen 1967, p. 4). The husband, in return, is obligated to provide her with basic maintenance which includes "necessities" such as food, clothing, medical care, and a place to live, in accordance with his income. She has no legal right to any part of his cash income, nor any legal voice in spending it ("Know Your Rights," Women's Bureau, Department of Labor, 1965, p. 1). Were he to employ a live-in servant in place of a wife, he would have to pay the servant a salary, provide her with her own room (as opposed to "bed"), food, and the necessary equipment for doing her job. She would get at least one day a week off and probably would be required to do considerably less work than a wife and would not be required to provide sexual services.

Thus, being a wife is a full-time job for which one is not entitled to pay. (Chase Manhattan Bank estimates a woman's overall work week at 99.6 hours.) Furthermore, the wife is not entitled to freedom of movement. The husband has the right to decide where the family will live. If he decides to move, his wife is obliged to go with him. If she refuses, he can charge her with desertion. This has been upheld by the courts even in cases where the wife could be required to change her citizenship. In states where desertion is grounds for divorce (47 states plus the District of Columbia), the wife would be the "guilty party" and would therefore be entitled to no monetary settlement (Gallen 1967, p. 6).

A Married Woman's Name. Leo Kanowitz in *Women and the Law* found that the change in a woman's name upon marriage is not only consistent with social custom; it also appears to be generally required by law.

> The probable effects of this unilateral name change upon the relations between the sexes, though subtle in character, are profound. In a very real sense, the loss of a woman's surname represents the destruction of an important part of her personality and its submersion in that of her husband. . . . This name change is consistent with the characterization of coverture as "the old common-law fiction that the husband and wife are one . . . [which] has worked out in reality to mean that the one is the husband (1969, p. 41).

The Law of Support. The universal rule is that it is the primary obligation of the husband to provide financial support for the family. Kanowitz explored some of the legal ramifications of this general rule.

> The effects of the basic rule upon the marital relationship itself are complex. In common law marital property jurisdictions, the husband's legal obligation to support the family is not an unmixed blessing for the wife. That obligation has been cited, for example, as justifying his right to choose the family home. It has no doubt also played an important part in solidifying his legal role as head and master of the family. For in according the husband this position within the family, the law often seems to be applying on a grand scale the modest principle that "he who pays the piper calls the tune." However, even in the community property states, in which a wife's services in the home are theoretically viewed as being equal to or exceeding in monetary value the husband's earnings outside of the home, husbands have generally been given the rights to manage and control the community property, along with other superior rights and interests in it (1969, p. 69).

Thus, it is clear that husbands have access to legal advantages which wives do not have. True, the wife does gain legal protection against capricious action by the male, but in exchange, she becomes his vassal. He is the economic head of the joint household, and hence, represents it in view of society. She takes his name and belongs to his class. She follows where his work calls to determine their place of residence. Their lives are geared to the daily, weekly, annual rhythms of his life. She gives him her person and her private labor, but he wants more.

The "White Man's Burden." In today's "love match," the husband does not merely require an obedient and efficient worker, he wants something more. He wants his wife to love him, that is, to freely choose over and over again to be subjected to the control of the other, to make his welfare the center of her being.[2] This very demand is the crux of what husbands term their "oppression" as Simone de Beauvoir has so clearly observed:

> Her very devotion seems annoying, importunate; it is transformed for the husband into a tyranny from which he tries to escape; and yet he it is who imposes it upon his wife as her supreme, her unique justification. In marrying her, he obliges her to give herself entirely to him; but he does not assume the corresponding obligation, which is to accept this gift and all its consequences.
>
> It is the duplicity of the husband that dooms his wife to a misfortune of which he complains that he is himself the victim. Just as he wants her to be at once warm and cool in bed, he requires her to be wholly his and yet no burden; he wishes her to establish him in a fixed place on earth and to leave him free; to assume the monotonous daily round and not to bore him; to be always at hand and never importunate; he wants to have her all to himself and not to belong to her, to live as one of a couple, and to remain alone. Thus she is betrayed from the day he marries her. Her life through, she measures the extent of that betrayal (1968, p. H51).

Throughout their lives together, she attempts to wrest back from him, some measure of her independence. Surely, it is not entirely an accident that divorce rates are highest at this early phase of the marriage cycle and drop with the birth of children, when women are most dependent upon the husband economically and emotionally.

Economic Sources of Power

It is clear that an economic base of power is important in marriage, for the higher the husband on the social scale, the greater his decision-making in the family. Using three indices of success in the community, Blood and Wolfe found that all three affected power differentials in the family.

1. The higher the husband's occupational prestige, the greater his voice in marital decisions.
2. Income was an even more sensitive indicator of power than his occupation. The higher the husband's income, the greater his power.
3. The higher the husband's status (based on occupation, income, education, and ethnic background), the more power he had to make decisions.

The major break in power fell between white-collar occupations and blue-collar occupations, the middle-class husbands having much more power than working-class husbands. The increment to power by income was steady. By social status, there is a curvilinear relationship to power. The low-blue collar workers had more power than high blue-collar workers, and power for the husband increased again at the low white-collar level and the high white-collar level. Middle class husbands, then, are generally more powerful than blue-collar husbands, but in the blue-collar marriages, the low blue-collar worker has more power than the high blue-collar worker. I will discuss some of the possible causes of this in the section on education.

The material bases of power were operant despite the fact that middle-class husbands espouse a more egalitarian ideology than do working-class husbands. William Goode commented on this tension between the ideal and the real distributions of power.

> Since at present this philosophy [of equalitarianism in the family] is most strongly held among better educated segments of the population, and among women more than among men, two interesting tensions may be seen: Lower-class men concede fewer rights *ideologically* than their women in fact *obtain*, and the more educated men are more likely to concede *more* rights ideologically than they in fact grant (1963, p. 21).

He then supplies us with an excellent example of how ideology may be modified to justify the current distribution of power:

> One partial resolution of the latter tension is to be found in the frequent assertion from families of professional men that they should not make demands which would interfere with his *work:*

He takes preference as a *professional*, not as a family head or as a male; nevertheless, the precedence is his. By contrast, lower-class men demand deference as *men*, as heads of families.

As we can see, marital power is a function of income to a large extent, and egalitarian philosophies have very little impact on the actual distribution of power. It seems clear that the authority of the male is used as a justification of power where it is useful (working-class), and new justification will arise as they are useful, as in the case of professional men who demand deference because of their work, thus enabling them to accept the doctrine of equality while at the same time undermining it for their own benefit as males. If this is the effect of that much touted egalitarian ideology which will bring about better conditions for women and racial and ethnic minorities as soon as it filters down to the masses, it seems we will have a long, long wait for cosmic justice.

Blood and Wolfe claim that this superior power of high-status husbands is not due to coercion, but to the recognition by both partners that the husband is the one eminently qualified to make the decisions in the family. This argument is reminiscent of arguments in labor relations. The labor contract is assumed to be freely entered into by both partners. The power conferred on the one party by the difference in class position—the real economic position of both—is not taken into account. That economic relations compel the worker to surrender even the last semblance of equal rights is of no concern. Coercion (however subtle) based on economic power is still coercion, whether it involves wife-beating or not.

As further evidence that individual competence and resourcefulness (regardless of sex) are not the real issues, we must examine Blood and Wolfe's discussion of the *deviant* case—wife dominance. In these cases, they claim that wives who have superior power acquire it, not because they have access to pragmatic sources of power or because they are more competent than their husbands (heaven forbid!), but by default.

We will find throughout this study dissatisfaction associated with wife-dominance. This is not, however, simply a reflection of the breaking of social rules. Rather, the circumstances which lead to the wife's dominance involve corresponding inadequacies on the husband's part. An inadequate husband is by definition unable to make a satisfactory marriage partner. So the dominant wife is not exultant over her "victory" but exercises power regretfully by default of her "no good" or incapacitated husband (p. 45).

For Blood and Wolfe, wives can never gain dominance legitimately; it falls in our unhappy laps and is accepted only unwillingly and with much bitterness.

Despite the superior power gained by the husband because of his economic position, there are conditions under which wives do erode that power to some extent. Not surprisingly, the wife's participation in the work force is an important variable. Women who work have more power vis-a-vis their husbands than do non-working wives, regardless of race or class. The number of years the wife has worked also affects the balance of power—the longer she has worked, the more power she is able to obtain. This, to some extent, explains why blue-collar wives have more power than white-collar wives (in comparison to their husbands), since their participation in the work force is much higher than for the wives of high-status, high-income husbands (Blood and Wolfe, 1960, pp. 40–41).

Organizational Participation

Organizational participation, too, is a factor which affects marital decision making as shown by Blood and Wolfe's data. Women with much more organizational participation than their husbands alter the balance of power in the wife's direction. In those cases where the participation is equal or in which the husband is superior (by far the most frequent), the balance of power increases in the husband's direction (p. 39).

Education

Education was also influential in the distribution of power. The more education the husband has, the greater his power. High white-collar husbands continue to gain power if they exceed their wives' education (and chances are good that they do, in fact, exceed), and they lose it if they fall short of the wife. The same trend holds within the low white-collar and high blue-collar groups, leaving a low blue-collar reversal, i.e., low blue-collar husbands have more power even when their wives have superior educations (pp. 28, 38).

Mirra Komarovsky in *Blue Collar Marriage* has drawn attention to the fact that education is a much more important variable when the husband's income and social status are relatively low. In working-class families, the less educated and unskilled husbands have more power than do those with higher incomes. She attempted to explain some of the causes of this power anomaly. First, patriarchal attitudes are more prevalent among the less educated and hence, a source of power in some families. High school graduates, because of a social milieu which does not sanction patriarchal authority (though it does sanction male privilege), tend to lose power. Second, among the less-educated, the husband is more likely to excel in personal resources for the exercise of influence, and this margin of male superiority narrows among the high school graduates. Among the less-educated, the husband has wider contacts in the community than his wife. He represents the world to his family, and he is the family's "secretary of state." In contrast, a few of the more educated wives enjoy wider contacts and higher status outside the home than their husbands. Third, the education of the spouses was found to affect their degrees of power because of mating patterns. The effect of educational inequality appears to explain the lower power of skilled workers in comparison with the semiskilled. The skilled worker is more likely than the semi-skilled worker to marry a high school graduate. By virtue of their relatively high earnings, skilled workers may be able to marry better-educated women, but by marrying "upward" they lose the degree of power enjoyed by the semi-skilled over their less-educated wives. Fourth, male prestige or social rank was a source of power in low blue-collar families (1967, pp. 226–29).

Physical Coercion

Komarovsky is one of the few sociologists who has mentioned physical coercion as a source of power in the family. In her discussion of the low blue-collar family, she found that the use of physical violence was a source of masculine power. However, not only the use of physical violence, but its *threat* can be an effective form of control. She reports that one woman said of her husband: "He is a big man and terribly strong. One time when he got sore at me, he pulled off the banister and he ripped up three steps." With the evidence of this damage in view, this woman realized, as she put it, what her husband could do to her if he should decide to strike her (1967, p. 227).

Lynn O'Connor has suggested that threats of violence (in gestures of dominance) are not limited to any particular class, but are a universal source of male power and control. After discussing dominance gestures in primates, she states:

Although there have been no systematic studies of the gestures of dominance and submission in human groups, the most casual observation will show their crucial role in the day to day mechanics of oppression. An example should clarify.

A husband and wife are at a party. The wife says something that the husband does not want her to say (perhaps it reveals something about him that might threaten his ranking with other men). He quickly tightens the muscles around his jaw and gives her a rapid but intense direct stare. Outsiders don't notice the interaction, though they may have a vaguely uncomfortable feeling that they are intruding on something private. The wife, who is acutely sensitive to the gestures of the man on whom she is dependent, immediately stops the conversation, lowers or turns her head slightly, averts her eyes, or gives off some other gestures of submission which communicate acquiescence to her husband and reduce his aggression. Peace is restored; the wife has been put in her place. If the wife does not respond with submission, she can expect to be punished. When gestures of dominance fail, the dominant animal usually resorts to violence. We all know stories about husbands beating up their wives after the party when they have reached the privacy of their home. Many of us have experienced at least a few blows from husbands or lovers when we refuse to submit to them. It is difficult to assess the frequency of physical attacks within so called love relationships, because women rarely tell even one another when they have taken place. By developing a complicated ethic of loyalty (described above in terms of privacy), men have protected themselves from such reports leaking out and becoming public information. Having already been punished for stepping out of role, the woman is more than a little reluctant to tell anyone of the punishment because it would mean violating the loyalty code, which is an even worse infraction of the rules and most likely would result in further and perhaps more severe punishment (1970, p. 9).

That violence or the threat of violence may be more widespread than is currently admitted is also suggested by complaints made by wives in divorce. Goode in *Women in Divorce* found that almost one-third (32 percent) of the wives reported "authority-cruelty" as the reason for divorce. Authority problems are defined as being disagreements concerning permissible degree of dominance over wife and include cruelty, beating, jealousy, and "wanted to have own way" (1956, pp. 120, 123). Since Goode did not code cruelty or beating separately, we have no definite evidence as to the frequency of such behavior, but there is evidence that problems with male dominance are widespread in the population. Goode comments:

> . . . In different strata and groups, the husband may be permitted different control techniques. For example, the middle-class male will very likely be censured more if he uses force to control his wife than if he uses techniques of nagging, jealousy, or sulking. On the other hand, there is a strong reservoir of attitude on the part of the American male generally, that he has a *right* to tell his wife what to do. This attitude is given more overt expression, and is more frequently backed by force, in the lower strata. It is not so much that beating and cruelty are viewed as an obvious male right in marriage, but only that this is one of the techniques used from time to time, and with little or no subsequent guilt, for keeping control of the wife. . . . In our society, the husband who successfully asserts his dominance does enjoy some approval and even a modicum of envy from other males. Male dominance is to some extent actually approved (1956, p. 122).

Suburbanization

Blood and Wolfe also found that families living in the suburbs were more husband-dominant than those which live in the central city. This directly contradicts the popular image of suburban life as being dominated by women and therefore, oriented toward the satisfaction of women's needs. The data showed that suburban families were more husband-dominant at every status level than their urban peers (p. 36). They then speculated that suburban husbands were more powerful "because suburban wives feel more indebted to their husbands for providing them with a place to live which is more attractive than the industrial city of Detroit. If so, this fits the theory that power accrues to those husbands who are able to provide for their wives especially well" (p. 36).

In a recent study on the working class in suburbia, Tallman has suggested that other factors than the wife's gratitude might be working to build up the husband's power. He constructed a profile of the working-class marriage which indicated consistently that wives tend to maintain close ties with relatives and old girl friends while husbands continue their premarital peer group associations. Social and psychological support emanates, then, not from marriage partners, but from same-sex friends, and kin from long standing and tight-knit social networks. As a consequence, there is a relatively high degree of conjugal role segmentation which is characterized in part by a lack of communication between the spouses. In general the experiences of working class women are more localized and circumscribed than their male counterparts. Since their security and identity depend upon their position vis-a-vis a small group of intimates, their opinions and beliefs are both dependent upon and in accord with this group. Blue-collar women have minimal experience in the external world and tend to view it fearfully. Men, on the other hand, have more frequent social contacts, in part for occupational reasons, but also because they have been socialized into male roles which define them as family representatives to the outside world.

Tallman concluded that suburban women are more isolated because of disruptions in the primary group relations. The disruption of friendship and kinship ties are not only personally disintegrating for the wife but also demand fundamental changes in the role allocations in the family. Suburban wives are more dependent upon their husbands for a variety of services previously provided by members of tight-knit networks. In brief, he found that moving to the suburbs was experienced as a disintegrative force in the lives of many working class women, leading to a greater isolation and dependence upon the husband (1969, pp. 66–69). This partial explanation of the husband's increased power in the suburbs as being due to the wife's increased isolation and dependence seems eminently more reasonable than Blood and Wolfe's explanation that it is due to gratitude on the part of the wife. Tallman's data also indicates that the wife frequently regrets the move to the suburbs, despite more pleasant living conditions, because of its disruption of the kinship and friendship network.

Race

Blood and Wolfe report very little on black families, except to say that Negro husbands have unusually low power. Their data show that white husbands are always more powerful than their Negro status equals and that this is true within each occupational stratum, each income bracket, and each social level.[3] They concede that "the label 'black' is almost a synonym for low status in our society—and Detroit Negroes are no exception in having less education, lower incomes, inferior jobs, and lower prestige generally than whites. Since low status white husbands make relatively few decisions, we would expect Negro husbands to exercise little power, too" (p. 34).

What they fail to take into account (among other things) is that black women, too, are discriminated against in this society. They, too, have less education, lower incomes, inferior jobs, and lower prestige generally than whites. The fact that blacks are discriminated against does not explain power differentials within black families. To explain power differentials in black families, just as for white families, the sources of power for black men and black women must be examined and compared. Blood and Wolfe fail to do this.

Their primary purpose seems to be to demonstrate gross differences between black and white families, without bothering to report differences within black families. Andrew Billingsley in *Black Families in White America* has criticized just this approach used in sociological studies. He draws attention to the fact that class variables are as important in black families as in white families. "Negro families are not only Negroes to be compared and contrasted with white families, they may also be upper-class (10 percent), middle-class (40 percent), or lower-class (50 percent), with urban or rural moorings, with southern or northern residence, and most importantly, they may be meaningfully compared and contrasted with each other" (1968, p. 8).

Billingsley accounts to some extent for what may be part of the white/black differentials in overall power. He notes that Negro samples are dominated by low-income families and points out that even where income levels between whites and blacks are similar, the groups are not truly comparable, for the Negro group reflects not only its income level but its experience with prejudice and subjugation as well.

Because both black husbands and black wives are discriminated against in this society, it is absurd to explain power differentials between them as being due to race (as Blood and Wolfe do), unless there are mitigating factors brought about by racial discrimination which operate in favor of one sex's access to sources of marital power. Since data on the black family are so sadly inadequate, I can at this point only examine some demographic data which have possible implications for power distributions in black families.

Black women comprised 40 percent of all black workers in 1960. They earned considerably less than black men. The median earnings of full-time year round black women in 1959 was two-fifths that of black men.[4] (In 1964, it was 64.2 percent.)[5] The unemployment rate for black women is higher than for black men. In 1967, for Negro men aged 20–64, the unemployment rate was 3.7. For Negro women it was 6.0. The unemployment rates for black women under 20 were also higher than for Negro men.[6] Clearly, then, black women are not superior to black men in income.

In occupational status, we find that Negro women are most frequently in service jobs while Negro men are predominantly blue-collar workers. However, relatively more Negro women than men had professional or technical jobs, this being due primarily to their extensive employment as teachers and nurses. Of all full-time year round Negro workers in 1960, Negro women constituted nearly all the private household workers. They were more than half the number of Negroes employed as professional workers (61 percent) and other service workers (51 percent). Except for the clerical group in which the numbers were about equal, the remaining occupational groups (sales, managers, operatives, crafts, laborers, and farmers) had fewer Negro women than men.[7]

Negro women in general had a higher median education than Negro men. (This is also true in the white population.) The median educational level of nonwhite women was 8.5 years in 1960, but for men it was 7.9. However, at the top of the educational ladder, just as for the white population, men are more numerous.[8]

Though there are differences, we find that the relations *between the sexes* for both Negroes and whites are similar. Obviously, black men have suffered from discrimination in this society. This is evident in the figures of income, occupation, and education. However, it is also evident that Negro women have suffered discrimination, not only because of race, but also because of their sex. Thus, they are doubly oppressed. This, too, is evident in figures of income, occupation, and education.

Jesse Bernard in *Marriage and Family Among Negroes* has suggested still another variable which must be taken into account in Negro family patterns. She reports that there is an extraordinarily low sex ratio (number of males per 100 females) among urban Negroes as compared to whites. The ratio is especially low (88.4) in the critical years of marriageability. Bernard conjectures that the low sex ratio means that Negro women are competing for a relatively scarce "good" when they look forward to marriage, being buyers in a sellers' market (1966:69). While this is certainly not the cause of power distributions in the black family, it does suggest a source of male power.[9] Delores Mack, in a study of black and white families, supports this contention (1969).

What these findings suggest is that researchers have not carefully evaluated the logic of the assumptions of their hypotheses. They have looked at the white community; there they have observed that education, occupation, and income are important sources of power. . . . They have ignored the possibility that the sources of power in the Black community may be different from that in the white community. In fact, they have ignored one of the most potent forms of power in any marriage, but particularly sex power in Black marriages. Certainly researchers have noted the preoccupation of the Black male with sex. Some have viewed this preoccupation with sex as a form of escapism, failing to realize that this concentration on sexual activities may be a main source of power. The Black male is well aware, as Eldridge Cleaver notes, that he is the desired sex object for both the white and the Black female. He may use this power in his marriage, much as the white male uses his education and earning power as a lever in his marriage.

The threat or use of physical violence (as discussed above) is another factor which must be taken into account to explain power distributions in black as well as in white families. Obviously, a great deal of research on the differences within black families is needed, as Billingsley has suggested.

Life Cycle

The stages of the family life cycle also affect the marital power distribution. In the early (childless) stage of marriage, the wife is frequently working, but the pressure of social discrimination against women is already beginning to be exerted. Women are unable to procure anything but low paying, low status jobs as compared with their husbands. Already status background and autonomous experiences are being eroded. Though the married childless woman maintains some sort of independent social and economic status if she works, it is below that of her husband. During this period, the power of the husband is moderate.

With the birth of children, there is a substantial jump in power differentials, the husband universally gaining (Blood and Wolfe, 1960, pp. 41–44). There is more than a little truth in the old saw that the best way to control a woman is to "keep her barefoot and pregnant," for there is evidence that the power of the wife declines as the number of children grows (Heer, 1958, pp. 341–347). At this period after the first child is born, but before the oldest child is in school, the power of the husband reaches its maximum. Many women stop working during this stage and in doing so, become isolated and almost totally socially, economically, and emotionally dependent upon their husbands, further eroding any strength they may have gained due to earning power or participation in organizations. She loses her position, cannot keep up with developments in her field, does not build up seniority. Further, she loses that precious "organizational" experience, the growth of competence and resources in the outside world, the community positions which contribute to power in the marriage. The boundaries of her world contract, the possibilities of growth diminish. If she returns to work, and most women do, she must begin again at a low status job and she stays there—underemployed and underpaid. As her children grow up, she gradually regains some power in the family.

These data again call into question the theory of individual resources as the source of power in marriage. As David Heer pointed out, there is no reason, according to Blood and Wolfe's theory, for the power of the wife to be greater before she has borne children than when her children are pre-school age. Surely the wife with pre-school children is contributing more resources to the marriage than she did before their children were born (1963:138).

Power, then, is clearly not the result of individual contributions and resources in the marriage, but is related to questions of social worth; and the value of women and women's work, as viewed by society, is obviously very low. The contributions of women in the home are of little concern and are consequently little valued, as Margaret Benston explained in "The Political Economy of Women's Liberation" (1969, pp. 3-4).

In sheer quantity, household labor, including child care, constitutes a huge amount of socially necessary production. Nevertheless, in a society based on commodity production, it is not usually considered "real work" since it is outside of trade and market place. It is pre-capitalist in a very real sense. The assignment of household work as the function of a special category "women" meant that this group *does* stand in a different relation to the production than the group "men." We will tentatively define women, then, as that group of people who are responsible for the production of simple use-values in those activities associated with the home and the family.

Since men carry no responsibility for such production, the difference between the two groups lies here. Notice that women are not excluded from commodity production. Their participation in wage labor occurs, but as a group, they have no structural responsibility in this area and such participation is ordinarily regarded as transient. Men, on the other hand, are responsible for commodity production; they are not, in principle, given any role in household labor. . . . The material basis for the inferior status of women is to be found in just this definition of women. In a society in which money determines value, women are a group who work outside the money economy. Their work is not worth money, is therefore valueless, is therefore not even real work. And women themselves, who do this valueless work, can hardly be expected to be worth as much as men, who work for money. In structural terms, the closest thing to the condition of women is the condition of others who are or were outside of commodity production, i.e., peasants or serfs.

THE HUSBAND: MOST LIKELY TO SUCCEED

Thus, it is clear that for a wife to gain even a modicum of power in the marital relationship, she must obtain it from external sources, i.e., she must participate in the work force, her education must be superior to that of her husband, and her participation in organizations must excel his. Equality of resources leaves the power in the hands of the husband. Access to these sources of power are structurally blocked for women, however.

In the general population, women are unable to procure anything but low-status, low-paying, dead end jobs as compared with their husbands, be it factory or university.[10] Partly as a result of unequal pay for the same work, partly as a consequence of channeling women into low-paying jobs, the median income of women is far less than that of men workers. Black women tend to fare slightly better in relation to black men, but make only two-thirds as much as white women.

MEDIAN INCOME OF YEAR-ROUND FULL TIME WORKERS BY SEX AND COLOR, 1964

	Men	Women	Women as % of Men
White	$6,497	$3,859	59.4
Nonwhite	4,285	2,674	62.2

SOURCE: Fact Sheet on the Relative Position of Women and Men Workers in the Economy, U.S. Department of Labor, Women's Bureau, 1965, p. 3.

In higher socioeconomic classes, the husband is more likely to excel his wife in formal education than he is among blue-collar workers. Men predominate among college graduates, regardless of race, but adult women have a higher median of education (12.1 for women, 12.0 for men in 1964).[11] We have already seen that the educational attainment of the non-white population is lower [8.5 for women, 7.9 for men], reflecting discrimination on the basis of race.)

All of these areas are sources of power in the marital relationship, and in all of these areas women are structurally blocked from realizing our capacities. It is not because of individual resources or personal competence, then, that husbands obtain power in marriage, but because of the discrimination against women in the larger society. Men gain resources as a class, not as individuals, and women are blocked as a class, not as individuals.

In our mutual mobility bet the woman (as a class) always loses in the fight for power within the marital relationship. We live in a system of institutionalized male supremacy, and the cards are systematically stacked against women in all areas—occupational, political, educational, legal, as well as within the institution of the family. As long as the structure of society remains the same, as long as categorical discrimination against women is carried out, there is relatively little chance for the woman to gain autonomy, *regardless* of how much good will there is on the part of her husband.

The equalitarian marriage as a norm is a myth. Under some conditions, women can gain power vis-a-vis their husbands, i.e., working women, women with higher educations than their husbands have more power than housewives or women with lesser or identical education as their husbands, but more power is not equal power. Equal power we will never get so long as the present socioeconomic system remains.

NOTES

[1] It should be made clear that legality is not necessarily a basis for decision making. It merely reflects the position of society as to how the power is to be distributed when such distributions are contested in the courts. This normally occurs upon dissolution of marriage and not in an ongoing relationship.

[2] Conversation with Ann Leffler, 1969.

[3] Blood and Wolfe's report of the data is so skimpy that it makes interpretation difficult. For example, they say that the 35 high income husbands (over $4000) have lower mean power (4.09) than their 68 less affluent colleagues (4.56). This is possibly analogous to the distribution in the white blue-collar class, where low blue-collar husbands have more power than the high blue-collar husbands. Comparisons are difficult because, for the general population, income was broken into five groups, while for black families they used only two—over $4000 and below $4000. They reported that "the generalization that the husband's power is correlated with occupational status also holds within the Negro race" (4.31, 4.60, no cases, and 5.00 respectively). The only mention of Negro husbands and social status was that the few white husbands in the lowest status groups differ sharply from their powerless negro counterparts (no figure reported).

[4] Negro Women Workers, Women's Bureau, Department of Labor, 1964:23–25.

[5] Fact Sheet on the Relative Position of Women and Men Workers in the Economy, U.S. Department of Labor, Women's Bureau, 1965, p. 3.

[6] U.S. Department of Labor, Bureau of Labor Statistics, Employment and Earnings, Vol. 16, No. 7, January 1970, Table A-1 (Data under Negro heading is for "Negro and Other Races").

[7] Negro Women Workers, pp. 23–25.

[8] Negro Women Workers, pp. 13–14.

[9] This has also been suggested in several articles in *The Black Woman*, edited by Toni Cade (1970), particularly "Dear Black Man," Fran Sanders; "Who Will Revere the Black Woman?," Abbey Lincoln; "The Black Woman as Woman," Kay Lindsey; "Double Jeopardy: To Be Black and Female," Frances Beale; "On the Issue of Roles," Toni Cade; "Black Man, My Man, Listen!," Gail Stokes; "Is the Black Man Castrated?," Jean Carey Bond and Pat Peery.

[10] Handbook on Women Workers, U.S. Department of Labor, Woman's Bureau, 1965, pp. 34–35.

[11] Handbook on Women Workers, 1965, p. 172.

REFERENCES

deBeauvoir, Simone
   1968   *The second sex.* New York: Bantam Books.
Benston, Margaret
   1969   The political economy of women's liberation. *Monthly Review,* September.
Bernard, Jesse
   1966   *Marriage and family among negroes.* Englewood Cliffs, N.J.: Prentice-Hall.
Billingsley, Andrew, and Amy Tate Billingsley
   1968   *Black families in white America.* Englewood Cliffs, N.J.: Prentice-Hall.
Blood, Robert O., Jr., and Donald M. Wolfe
   1960   *Husbands and wives, the dynamics of married living.* New York: Free Press.
Cade, Toni
   1970   *The black woman, an anthology.* New York: New American Library.
Cronan, Sheila
   1969   Marriage. *The Feminist.* New York.
Gallen, Richard T.
   1967   *Wives' legal rights.* New York: Dell Publishing Co.

Goode, William
- 1956 *Women in divorce.* New York: The Free Press.
- 1963 *World revolution and family patterns.* New York: The Free Press.
- 1964 *The family.* Englewood Cliffs, N.J.: Prentice-Hall.

Heer, David M.
- 1958 Dominance and the working wife. *Social Forces* 36 (May): 341–347.
- 1963 The measurement and bases of family power: An overview. *Marriage and Family Living* 25 (May): 133–139.

Kanowitz, Leo
- 1969 *Women and the law, the unfinished revolution.* Albuquerque: The University of New Mexico Press.

Komarovsky, Mirra
- 1967 *Blue collar marriage.* New York: Vintage Books.

Mack, Delores
- 1969 *The husband-wife power relationship in black families and white families.* Ph. D. Dissertation, Stanford University.

O'Connor, Lynn
- 1970 Male dominance, the nitty-gritty of oppression. *It Ain't Me, Babe,* Vol. 1, No. 8, June 11–July 1: 9–11.

Pilpel, Harriet F., and Theodora Zavin
- 1964 *Your marriage and the law.* New York: Collier Books.

Safilios-Rothschild, Constantia
- 1969 Family sociology or wives' family sociology? A cross-cultural examination of decision making. *Journal of Marriage and the Family* 31, 2 (May):290–301.

Tallman, Irving
- 1969 Working class wives in suburbia: Fulfillment or crisis? *Journal of Marriage and the Family* 31, 1 (February): 65–72.

Weisstein, Naomi
- 1969 *Kinde, Kuche, Kirche as scientific law: Psychology constructs the female.* Boston: New England Free Press.

GOVERNMENT PUBLICATIONS

U.S. Department of Labor, Bureau of Statistics
- 1970 *Employment and earnings,* Vol. 16, No. 7, January.

U.S. Department of Labor, Women's Bureau
- 1965 *Fact sheet on the relative position of women and men workers in the economy.*
- 1965 *Handbook on women workers.*
- 1965 *Know your rights: What a working wife should know about her legal rights.*
- n.d. *Negro women workers in 1960.*

26

BUILDING FAMILY STRENGTHS IN DUAL-CAREER MARRIAGES

Barbara Chesser

INTRODUCTION

"Is a woman's place in the home?" Over 40 million women who work outside the home have said "No" to this question. Many of these women are the sole breadwinners for their families. They have no choice but to work outside the home. However, in all the families with a husband and wife present, 42% of the husbands and wives both work outside the home as compared to 29% in 1960. If projections are accurate, there will be an even greater increase of dual-career families in the future.

Because of the increasing number of dual-career families, all family life education efforts should deal with issues arising in dual-career families. Whether the efforts are preventive, enrichment, or interventional in nature, the marriages of the participants will be strengthened as they become more aware of the issues that arise in dual-career marriages. An increased awareness of these issues and possible ways to handle them constructively will increase the couple's coping skills and problem-solving abilities, thereby building family strengths.

Dual-career family as used in this paper means both husband and wife are pursuing careers and maintaining a family together. The word "career" usually refers to a job which requires a high degree of commitment and a fairly continuous developmental life. A career is different from a job or work, for work may involve any kind of gainful employment. Work may be full-time, part-time, and periodic over the years so that it can be easily changed to accommodate marital and childrearing responsibilities. Obviously the line of demarcation between a career and a job is not always clear. A career might be placed at one end of a continuum with higher levels of commitment, responsibilities, educational and emotional investment, whereas a job is at the other end of the continuum with lower levels of all these characteristics. The closer one comes to the career end of the continuum, the more likely the issues discussed in this paper will indeed be problematic within the marriage because of the higher level of commitment characteristic of a career as opposed to a job. The closer one approaches the job end of the continuum, the easier, relatively speaking, the issues will be to resolve because of less commitment and investment.

As family life educators share information about these issues, they should also assist their students in translating this information into new insights and problem-solving skills. By providing information and skills, a couple's array of alternatives for problem-solving is greater. Knowledge can add strength to a dual-career family.

In addition, advantages of dual-career families will be briefly examined. Recommendations for

---

Reprinted from *Building Family Strengths: Blueprints for Action*, edited by Nick Stinnett, by permission of University of Nebraska Press. Copyright © 1979 by the University of Nebraska Press.

building strengths in dual-career families will be offered.

ISSUES

To work or not to work outside the home may be an issue arising before the couple is married. Many variables will feed into this decision, but for the decision for the wife to work outside the home to be successfully carried out, the wife must really want or need to work. *Want* and *need* may be difficult to differentiate for some persons. For the two million women who head families, there is no choice: they *need* to work. Because of inflation, some wives with working husbands may also feel that they have to work to help pay the rent, buy groceries, and to rear their children. For other women, working may be a way to raise the family's standard of living. Others may work mostly to be with other people. In a society that often measures human worth by how much money you can make or what you do, many women want to feel better about themselves.

A couple's knowing why the wife works may be important to her being able to work outside the home and manage a marriage. Traditionally, man's work was his commitment. Woman's work was for extras: extra money, extra fulfillment, and extra interests. Being able to sort out why each works may seem too trivial or too philosophical to be practical. But many of the practical decisions in a two-career marriage often rest on why each partner works. Why a farmer's wife works during a drought year may be quite different from why a wife who is a college professor works year after year. Issues and problems may develop on the homefront for each of these couples. And each may require different solutions to keep the marriage on an even keel.

But most couples describe common problems regardless of why they say the wife works. Extra demands on time and energy seem to plague every two-career marriage. The wife may try to do all the housework as well as meet the rigorous demands of a job or career. The husband traditionally views housework as female's work and may have trouble helping with it. He may feel clumsy, or housework may make him feel unmanly, or he may be exhausted from his career. His wife may not want him to help her. She may doubt her own value if he can do "her" work.

Another issue many dual-career couples grapple with is whether or not to have children. An increasing percentage are opting for a childfree marriage, but many career couples merely are postponing the birth of their first child. And most career families have fewer children than couples which include a non-working wife.

Determination of the "best" time for having a child rests on considerations such as educational plans and establishment of a career and the effects of time-off on these two considerations. Also the availability of maternity leaves may determine the "best" time.

For dual-career couples who have a child, childcare becomes a concern. Adequate childcare facilities are still not widely available. Finding a reliable babysitter to stay in the home may be a challenge. The financial cost of childcare is usually another concern. When the child is older and in school most of the day, childcare may not be such a problem. Problems may come when a child does not follow the usual schedule, for example, when he or she is sick. Who stays home? Who takes the child to the doctor? To the dentist? Who leaves work to go to the parent-teacher conference? To the Christmas play? To weekly music lessons? In a traditional marriage, the decision is easy: the mother's job always gives in to the demands of the children. As women increasingly express commitment to their careers, couples are compelled to establish new criteria for decisions regarding childcare.

Obviously these criteria are increasingly complicated if a child requires extra care and supervision because of a health problem or a handicap of some kind. Working out satisfactory childcare and supervision may also be complicated if the careers of one or both of the partners in a dual-career marriage require travel.

How to handle career relocation if one spouse is offered a promotion which requires moving is another issue confronting some couples at one time or another in their careers. Decision-making in this situation may be extra perplexing if it is the wife being offered the promotion. Our culture supports relocations made on the basis of the husband's promotion, not the wife's.

The issue of how to spend the combined earnings of a dual-career marriage confronts most couples. Should the discretionary income be spent on luxuries or travel, or should it be saved or invested? Dual-career families come face to face with this question. Other couples may find that there is no discretionary income. Taxes may take an extraordinary portion of their combined earnings. Transportation expenses for two careers eat up an unreasonable mount of money. Wardrobe demands may gnaw insidiously at the combined earnings. Childcare may take its unfair portion. Eating meals out or the purchase of convenience foods may require an undue portion of the paychecks. This is when the couple must scrutinize the value of two careers in one marriage, or they may be challenged to search for desirable ways to economize.

Survival of a two-career family may depend upon the ability of husband and wife to make decisions satisfying to both. Some marriages thrive on the husband making all the major decisions and others depend upon the wife to make them. But partners in most dual-career marriages have to work at learning how to make decisions together. Traditionally, the man made the money, therefore he had the authority to make the decisions. If both husband and wife work to make the money, both have the right to make decisions. Deciding *who* is going to decide and *how* the decisions are made is often more critical than the decisions. Couples able to decide mutually with occasional compromise seem to survive two-career marriages.

Some male egos may be too fragile to survive a two-career marriage. A working wife may signal his failure to make enough money to be considered "successful." Or a wife who makes more money than the husband may threaten a weak male ego. Husband and wife in similar careers may compete too keenly. A wife may occasionally put her husband in a double bind. She may pressure him to succeed in his job while pressuring him to be a terrific husband and father.

Some women may be uncomfortable out of a traditional homemaker role. Society still judges a man by his job and a woman by her homemaking, as a companion, mother, and hostess. Some women may be frustrated if they do better in the work world than their husbands. All husbands and wives it seems are pressured to do more and to do it better. Tensions may really mount in dual-career families if these issues are not dealt with realistically and constructively.

If two-career marriages survive these first few hurdles, they still have not completed the obstacle course. Careers make rugged demands on a husband's and wife's time and energy. So do the children's schedules. Little time and energy remain for friends or recreation. Most couples cannot maintain friendships with all they would like to. So they must make choices—a few friends from his acquaintances, a few from hers, or maybe a few from church, or from parents of their children's friends. Couples need skills in learning to say no to some activities so they can say yes to those they want to do.

Individual partners need to know what they expect of themselves as well as from their mates. They need to examine what they expect of the marriage itself. Couples must communicate these expectations to each other. One husband whose first two-career marriage ended in divorce but who was managing well in a second one shared: "You gotta have lots of heart-to-heart talks of what you want out of marriage and what you are willing to do to accomplish what you want." He explained that not only husband and wife but the kids must have a good understanding of what everyone wants out of the family and the responsibilities each is willing to assume. "Otherwise," he went on, "the family becomes like an explosion in a mattress factory: they never get it all together."

Marriage may be unsafe at any speed, but having unrealistic and unreasonable expectations may be the speed that kills. If this were true for the traditional marriage in which the husband is the breadwinner and the wife is the hearth-warmer, then it certainly is truer for the two-career marriage. Other survival tactics may help, but realistic expectations of self and partner are essential, as one college professor with three young children pointed out:

You have to be realistic in what you expect of yourself and your marriage partner. It's impossible for one person to be terrific on the job, a terrific husband, a terrific father, and to keep the grass mowed all the time.

An enormous obstacle to two-career couples is the paucity of models of successful two-career marriages. And each two-career couple works though these issues in fairly unique ways that seem best for them. Their solution for a particular problem may not work for another couple.

Another complication is that many couples think other couples have solved most of these problems. Flashes of a superwoman haunt most women. This superwoman who knits marriage, career, and motherhood into a satisfying life without dropping a stitch is overwhelming and gives others miserable feelings of failure.

The foregoing discussion of some of the issues confronting most dual-career marriages may create a foreboding, ominous aura about the dual-career marriage. The marriages of those who do not work successfully through these issues, in fact, may be threatened. However, those who do at least to some extent successfully resolve some of the issues may enjoy some tangible benefits or advantages. Professionals should clearly outline these just as they teach about the issues that usually arise in a dual-career family.

ADVANTAGES

Some of the advantages which dual-career families may enjoy are briefly outlined as follows:

1. Dual-career families may enjoy some financial advantages. They may enjoy a higher standard of living. They may be able to accumulate savings. They may be able to provide financial security against possible disasters.
2. The wife may enjoy greater levels of creativity, self-expression, achievement, and recognition. She may enjoy being herself, not an appendage to her husband. This may help her be a better mother and wife.
3. Dual-career marriages provide a greater range of role models for children of both sexes.
4. The husband may be relieved of some of the pressures to succeed and to make money. Thus, he will be able to function more effectively as a husband and/or father.
5. The husband may enjoy his wife more since she will have outside activities and interests to share.
6. Sexual interest in the marriage may heighten in an unstereotyped, dual-career marriage.
7. Parent responsibilities can be shared. Husbands can enjoy their children more, and children can profit from having an available father.
8. Children may learn to be more responsible and more resourceful when their mothers work outside the home. This may reinforce their feelings of achievement, pride, and self-esteem.
9. Children may learn to respect their parents more, especially their mothers, as individuals.
10. The empty-nest syndrome which affects some in later years may be avoided somewhat if the wife is engaged in a meaningful career outside the home.
11. Coping with widowhood may be somewhat easier for the woman who has had a meaningful career in addition to her marriage career.
12. Increased empathy with the demands of the roles of each other may foster mutual respect and facilitate communication.
13. The increased sharing of roles may create feelings of equality, thus strengthening the family.

RECOMMENDATIONS

. . . [There] are other general recommendations that all could work on which would strengthen the American family. Some of these are as follows:

1. There should be increased knowledge throughout the educational career about role flexibility and/or change. In other words, rigid or stereotyped sex roles should be avoided in textbooks and other learning materials.
2. Mass media should avoid perpetuating stereotypes.
3. Stereotypic assumptions about sex roles should be avoided (for example, "women are absent more from work").
4. Better parent education should be available for all people.

5. There should be more high-quality childcare for working parents. Perhaps more neighborhood childcare provisions as well as industrial childcare should be explored.
6. Business and government could provide more flexible working conditions, including more flexible working hours, sharing of positions, and more part-time positions without discrimination of benefits, promotions, etc. Increased flexibility would reduce conflict between the demands of parents' employment and the needs of their families. Flexible working hours would also help in battling the war against the traditional 8 to 5 schedule that is based on the assumption that the wife is at home and free to take care of business matters within this time frame.
7. More equitable provisions should be provided for taking time off for childbearing and childcare.
8. An integrated network of family services should be developed more fully. All families need easily available preventive services.
9. Marriage and family counseling should continually be developed into a more effective resource for helping members of two-career marriages cope with their stresses and strains.
10. More research is needed on the effects of two-career families. For example, the effects of long-distance marriages on the partners and the children might be explored.

Two-career families are probably a testing ground of things to come as sex roles become more flexible and interchangeable, as inflation continues, and as more careers are open to women. Professionals who are directly involved in activities to help build strengths in families must energetically carry out all of the foregoing suggested recommendations, and they must continue to be supportive and empathic in whatever ways will help strengthen two-career families. And we as professionals need to cherish our own family relationships to provide a model of ways to build strengths in the two-career family.

REFERENCES

Austin, H. S. 1969. *The woman doctorate in America: Origins, career, and family.* New York: Russell Sage Foundation.

Bailyn, L. 1970. Career and family orientation of husbands and wives in relation to marital happiness. *Human Relations* 23:97–113.

Bebbington, A. C. 1973. The function of stress in the establishment of the dual-career family. *Journal of Marriage and the Family* 35 (August): 530–37.

Bem, S. L., and D. J. Bem. 1972. Training the woman to know her place. In L. K. Home (ed.), *The future of the family.* New York: Simon and Schuster.

Bernard, J. 1966. *Academic women.* New York: World.

Callahan, S. C. 1971. *The working mother.* New York: Macmillan.

Gannon, M. J., and D. H. Henrickson. 1973. Career orientations and job satisfaction among working wives. *Journal of Applied Psychology* 57:339–40.

Hall, D. T., and F. E. Gordon. 1973. Career choices of married women: Effects on conflict, role, behavior, and satisfaction. *Journal of Applied Psychology* 58:42–48.

Heckman, J. J. 1974. Effects of child care programs on women's work effort. *Journal of Political Economy* 82:S136–S163.

Holmstrom, L. L. 1973. *The two-career family.* Cambridge, Mass.: Schenkman.

Keniston, K., and The Carnegie Council on Children. 1972. *All our children: The American family under pressure.* New York: Harcourt Brace.

Slater, P. E. 1970. *The pursuit of loneliness: American culture at the breaking point.* Boston: Beacon Press.

Willett, R. S. 1971. Working in "a man's world": The woman executive. In V. Gornick and B. K. Moran (eds.), *Woman in sexist society.* New York: Basic Books.

Yarrow, M., et al. 1973. Child-rearing in families of working and non-working mothers. In M. E. Lasswell and T. E. Lasswell (eds.), *Love, marriage, family, a developmental approach.* Glenview, Ill.: Scott, Foresman.

27

ROLE-SHARING COUPLES: A STUDY OF EGALITARIAN MARRIAGES

Linda Haas

Many observers of changes in family roles have discussed the completely egalitarian or role-sharing arrangement as a theoretical possibility (Bailyn, 1978; Bernard, 1973; Bott, 1971; Garland, 1972; Nye, 1976; Scanzoni, 1972; Young & Willmont, 1973). The purpose of this paper is to report some results of a detailed empirical study of couples who have attempted role-sharing and generally succeeded in putting it into practice. The goals of the study were to discover the reasons couples adopted this alternative family lifestyle, the problems they had adjusting to it, and the solutions they developed to combat the problems encountered.

A marriage style based on the equal sharing of traditionally sex-segregated roles is very rarely found in practice and subsequently has been generally unstudied by social scientists. There have been several studies of dual-career families, but these families generally do not practice role-sharing. While the wife is committed to a career, her basic family responsibilities typically remain intact and her husband's career has precedence over hers (Bryson, Bryson & Johnson, 1978; Holmstrom, 1973; Poloma & Garland, 1971; Rapoport & Rapoport, 1977). Studies have also been done on American parents who shared the childcare role (DeFrain, 1975; 1979) and Norwegian couples where both spouses chose part-time work (Grønseth, 1976; 1978). Yet even in these studies, the role-sharing arrangement was only partly in evidence: DeFrain's androgynous parents did not share housework or breadwinning equally and Grønseth's work-sharing couples did not share housework or childcare evenly. Sociologists have also paid some attention to discovering the actual division of labor and its determinants in the general population (e.g., Nye, 1976), but their samples have not been large enough to incorporate many role-sharing families, and thus have given us little insight into the role-sharing lifestyle.

As distinct from the partial steps toward sex-role equality discussed above, fully developed role-sharing can be defined as the sharing by husband and wife of each of the traditionally segregated family roles, including:

The breadwinner role. The husband and wife are equally responsible for earning family income; the wife's employment is not considered more optional or less desirable than the husband's. Consequently, the spouses' occupations are equally important and receive equal status, or at least the occupation which has more status is not determined by notions of the intrinsic supremacy of one sex over the other.

The domestic role. The husband and wife are equally responsible for performing housekeeping

---

Linda Haas, "Role-Sharing Couples: A Study of Egalitarian Marriages," *Family Relations*, Vol. 29 (1980), pp. 289–94. Copyrighted © 1980 by the National Council on Family Relations, 1219 University Avenue Southeast, Minneapolis, Minnesota 55414. Reprinted by permission.

chores such as cooking, cleaning, and laundry.

The handyman role. The husband and wife are equally responsible for performing traditionally masculine tasks such as yardwork and repairs.

The kinship role. The husband and wife are equally responsible for meeting kinship obligations, like buying gifts and writing letters, which have traditionally been the wife's responsibility.

The childcare role. The husband and wife are equally responsible for doing routine childcare tasks and for rearing and disciplining of children.

The major/minor decision-maker roles. The spouses have generally equal influence on the making of major decisions which males have traditionally dominated and the minor decisions traditionally delegated to the female.

Specialization within any of these roles (e.g., husband cooks, wife launders) would be compatible with role-sharing, as long as specific tasks are not assigned to a spouse on the basis of sex (i.e., because they are deemed more appropriate for someone of his/her gender) and as long as the overall responsibility for the duties of each role is evenly shared.

STUDY DESIGN

Since past studies of the family imply that role-sharing couples make up a very tiny proportion of the general population, a random sampling design could not be employed in this study without a great amount of expense and time. Therefore, a type of purposive or strategic sampling technique was employed (cf. Glaser & Strauss, 1967). In the liberal university community of Madison, Wisconsin, 154 couples were identified who had been referred by others or by themselves as sharing fairly evenly the responsibilities of breadwinning, housekeeping, childcare, and decision-making. Their names were obtained through contacts in various local institutions and associations (e.g., a daycare center, a chapter of the National Organization for Women, a liberal religious group, university organizations) and through announcements published in local newsletters and newspapers.

Each of these couples was contacted by telephone during January, 1976. Whoever answered the phone was asked several questions designed to ascertain in a rough fashion whether or not his or her relationship was characterized by role-sharing, as reputed. To be included for further study, both spouses had to be engaged in, looking for, or preparing for work and spending roughly the same number of hours per week on work or school-related pursuits. The wife's employment could not be seen as something less permanent than the husband's, and an unequivocally affirmative answer had to be given to the question, "Would you say that each of you has roughly the same amount of influence over family decisions?" When asked, "What percent of all the housework that's done in your household do you think you do?", the answer had to be in the 40–60% range, as did the answer to a similar question about childcare.

In the group of couples who were initially contacted by phone and willing to be interviewed, nearly half turned out not really to practice role-sharing in their marriages, according to the rough preliminary measures. Among the remaining couples who were tentatively labeled as role-sharers, some types were not included in the study. One type consisted of couples who hired outside help for housecleaning. Since being able to afford cleaning help is not available to all economic classes and I was primarily interested in studying the factors which promise to increase role-sharing among couples on a widespread basis, a decision was made to exclude those having housecleaning help. Another group of role-sharing couples not picked for further study were those not legally married since they might have unique arrangements that I was not prepared to study in detail. Several other couples were eliminated for miscellaneous reasons, such as living too far out of town for convenient interviewing.

After eliminating couples on such grounds, there were 31 remaining who qualified on the various criteria and were willing to participate in the study. The sample was fairly homogeneous, despite efforts to recruit a variety of types for the study. For the most part, the people in the sample were training themselves for or engaged in jobs in professional fields, usually in social service or the humanities. The sample couples tended to be young, with a majority of them being 26 to 30 years old. The mean number of years they had been married was six. Nearly half of them had children, most of which were not yet old enough to go to school.

Both the husband and wife in each of the 31 couples were interviewed three times from January through June of 1976. Averaging 1½ hours each, these interviews usually took place in the couples' homes and were tape-recorded. The spouses were interviewed separately during most of the questioning. After the interviews, written forms were left with the individuals to be filled out and returned by mail. These included a time-budget and an attitudinal questionnaire.

The great majority of the 31 couples were later found to be generally as egalitarian as the preliminary phone measures suggested, when the extent and ways in which couples shared breadwinning, housekeeping, childcare, kinship obligations, and handyman chores were investigated. The family power structure was also studied by obtaining information on the process and outcome of several recent and hypothetical decision-making activities. Any departures from equality, were spread out, with no couples falling short on more than a small proportion of the numerous and fairly stringent standards for meeting an ideal of total role-sharing. Even those who failed to meet every last one of these standards showed themselves to be aspiring towards an ideal of marital equality not strived for by the general population or even by most dual-career couples. (See Haas, 1977, for a full description of all the indicators for role-sharing and specifics on how these couples measured up.)

RESULTS AND DISCUSSION

Motivations for Role-Sharing Behavior

In replies to open-ended questions about why they shared the responsibilities of breadwinning, decision-making, and domestic chores, each couple gave several motives for role-sharing. In the results which follow, couples are listed as giving a certain reason if either spouse reported it, but spouses usually answered the same way. Almost all of the couples in the sample revealed that they adopted role-sharing not as a result of an ideological commitment to sexual equality, but rather as a practical way of obtaining certain benefits which they perceived could not be realized in a traditional marriage with segregated husband-wife roles. The vast majority of couples said they became pessimistic about traditional marriage roles after trying a traditional pattern in their marriage in its early years. Over one-third of the individuals said they were also predisposed to attempt a non-traditional role pattern because they felt their parents had been constrained by the traditional familial division of labor. Finally, a handful of the respondents had been married previously and complained that conflict over sex-role expectations had been a major factor in their divorces.

The benefits attainable through role-sharing usually occurred to the wife first and more often aided her than the husband. However, a considerable part of the motivation to try a non-traditional pattern also involved a desire to liberate the husband from the confines of his traditional family role.

Benefits for the individual. One anticipated benefit for both spouses was a greater opportunity to develop their abilities and pursue personal interests without being limited by traditional role expectations. Over four-fifths of the sample adopted role-sharing so the wife could satisfy her desire to work outside the home for personal fulfillment. One-fifth of the couples reported picking the role-sharing lifestyle so that each spouse would have the freedom to quit outside employment for a time and pursue other interests.

Another motive for role-sharing was relief from the stress and overwork that results from having primary responsibility for a broad area of family life. Almost three-fourths of the couples wanted to eliminate the overload dilemmas faced by working women who remain primarily responsible for housework and childcare. This benefit of role-sharing did seem to have been realized, according to time-budget data collected in individual diaries for a week between the first and second interviews. Wives in the sample averaged 16.0 hours per week at housework, while men averaged 16.2.

Mothers in the study averaged 12.2 hours per week at specific childcare tasks, while fathers spent 10.4. The general equality of the workload was also evident in the finding that the women spent 26.8 hours per week at hobbies, watching television, socializing, organizational meetings, etc., compared to the men's average of 26.2 hours of leisure activities. In contrast, time-budget studies of the general population show employed husbands averaging almost 6½ more hours of free-time activities a week than employed wives (Szalai, 1972).

Over half of the couples mentioned that the role-sharing lifestyle was adopted so that the husband would not be burdened more than the wife with the provider responsibility and its concomitant anxiety and stress. While this benefit was fully achieved by the majority of couples in the study, at least one partner in one-third (10) of the couples (usually the male) reported a little difficulty in completely letting go of the traditional idea that the man is more responsible for earning income than the wife, or that the wife was less obligated to work to provide family income. In most of these cases, it was the wife's newer or lesser interest in a career that was used as an explanation for the partial retention of this traditional sex-role expectation for men. These 10 couples said, however, that this was an idea they no longer wanted to believe in and certainly would not act on.

Another major motive for role-sharing cited by these couples was greater independence of the husband and wife. While the role-sharers in the study neither desired nor actually led completely independent lives within marriage, over one-fourth of them initiated role-sharing to avoid the economic dependence wives traditionally have had on husbands, while one-sixth wanted to avoid the dependence most husbands experience when it comes to getting domestic chores done—e.g., cooking, laundry, mending.

Benefits for the family. Several people who were happier because of new opportunities for self-fulfillment and relief from one-sided burdens reported themselves to be better marriage partners as a side benefit, however there were other ways in which couples tried to improve their family life directly through role-sharing. For instance, almost two-thirds of the couples cited a desire to cut down on the resentment and conflict that they saw resulting from husbands having more power in marriage. Generally, a shared decision-making pattern was the first aspect of role-sharing to be tried, and the one aspect that was relatively easy to establish. Several individuals commented that a positive but unanticipated consequence of a shared decision-making pattern was that it called for a considerable amount of discussion and this communicating in turn brought greater intimacy between husband and wife.

Another way couples thought role-sharing would improve husband-wife relations, reported by one-fifth of the couples, was in giving them more in common—with both spouses working and both having domestic responsibilities. Several individuals reported that having so much in common caused them to appreciate and sympathize with each other more. Each could appreciate problems the other had at work or school because they came up against the same things, and they were less likely to nag at each other if a task went undone because they personally knew how hard it was to get around to doing an undesirable chore. Several people also said the role-sharing gave them the opportunity to do more things together, increasing interaction and thus enhancing husband-wife closeness. A few couples were in the same occupational field, so they could profitably discuss their work and occasionally work on projects together. The spouses also had occasion to be together while domestic chores were being performed. Since the work hours of husbands and wives were approximately even and their work schedules were often similar, the couples had occasion to spend a lot of their free time together.

Besides an improvement in husband-wife relations, another major benefit of role-sharing cited for the family was improvement in parent-child relations. This was not a factor in the initial decision to adopt role-sharing, but it became a reason for continuing the arrangement. Five of the twelve women with children at home felt they had become better mothers because they worked outside the home and shared childcare with their husbands. They felt they were less bored, less hassled with managing two roles, and not resentful about shouldering the entire burden of childcare. Three of the 24 parents mentioned that sharing childcare meant that the children got to know their father better than they would in a traditional family, and three parents thought children benefited by being exposed to more than just the mother's outlook on things.

The final major benefit for the family that couples wanted to achieve with role-sharing was greater financial security. One-fourth of the couples said they chose a dual-earner arrangement to provide the family with more income on a permanent basis. Incidentally, the vast majority of couples pooled their incomes, and in all of the couples the wife's income was not saved for extras but was used for family expenses as much as was the husband's.

Problems with Role-Sharing

While these couples' efforts to implement role-sharing brought the benefits they anticipated, several difficulties with this arrangement were reported in responses to questions about problems with role-sharing. Some of these problems appeared to result from certain personal obstacles related to vestiges of traditional sex roles in the family. Others seemed to come from trying to transcend sex roles within family units in the context of a larger more traditional society. Still other problems seemed to be inherent in the role-sharing lifestyle itself.

Problems sharing the domestic role. Of all the areas of role-sharing, couples reported problems most often in the establishment of an egalitarian division of domestic chores. These problems can be grouped into four types, listed here in order of their frequency: disinclination to do non-traditional tasks, discrepancies in housekeeping standards, wife's reluctance to delegate domestic responsibility, and lack of non-traditional domestic skills.

The most common type of problem in sharing domestic chores, reported by over half of the couples, was that one or both spouses lacked the inclination to do some non-traditional tasks for which they had skills or for which no special skill was required. About one-third of the couples with this problem mentioned that it was hard to break with the traditional pattern they had observed in their parents' households. Over one-third claimed that it often seemed more efficient to let the traditional spouse perform the chore in the face of the other partner's inexperience, busy schedule, or laziness.

Couples had different solutions for this problem. Most often, the spouse who felt over-worked (usually the wife) complained and threatened to stop doing the chore or some other task until the lazy spouse resolved to do better. Sometimes a temporary system of rotation was agreed upon to get the recalcitrant spouse into the right habit. Occasionally the lazy spouse would develop more of a liking or tolerance for the chore or become so experienced at it that the problem would be solved. Some couples ended up agreeing to some specialization in order to avoid further conflict, especially if each spouse wanted to avoid certain non-traditional chores that the other spouse did not mind doing.

Another frequent problem in overcoming the traditional chore pattern involved the standards spouses had for housekeeping. Over half of the couples reported that at an earlier time in their marriage the wives had generally advocated a much higher standard of orderliness and cleanliness in the household than their husbands. This did not produce any conflict as long as the woman was in charge of getting the chores done, but when the decision to share responsibility for chores was reached, wives pushed for chores to be done as often as they wanted to see them done and in the manner they preferred. They fretted about the condition of the house all the time and experienced embarrassment if someone dropped in unexpectedly. Husbands, on the other hand, wanted to do the chores according to their own ideas on how often they needed to be done and in the manner (often unconventional) that appealed most to them. Husbands consistently felt wives were too finicky and wives regarded husbands as too sloppy.

Most of the couples coped with this discrepancy in standards by simultaneously having wives lower their expectations and husbands raise theirs. This change was usually precipitated by wives being busy with their jobs or schoolwork and it was accompanied by many heated discussions and practical experiments. Both spouses generally professed to be happier with the new standard, but the wives still tended to believe in a somewhat higher standard than their husbands. When asked, "Do you think that housework is done as often and as well as you want it to be?" almost one-half of the wives (but less than one-third of the husbands) expressed discontent with the level or orderliness and cleanliness of their homes. Wives were also more likely to mention spontaneously that they would like to hire outside help, while most of their husbands opposed hiring an outsider to do domestic chores.

Since both the husband and wife were busy with jobs or schoolwork, it is not surprising that many individuals felt anxious about their housekeeping standard. On the other hand, there was little evidence that their homes were in fact being neglected, for their homes generally seemed neat and clean to the interviewers. The actual number of hours spent at traditional housekeeping tasks (around 20 hours a week per couple) was still rather high, though not in the 30–40 hour range for working couples or the 50–70 range for housewives found in other studies (Robinson & Converse, cited in Babcock, 1975; Walker, 1970). Either the role-sharing couples were correct in their belief that they had a low housekeeping standard, in ways not apparent to a casual visitor, or they skipped a lot of unnecessary housework and kept house more efficiently than traditional couples.

A third problem, mentioned by half the couples, was the wife's reluctance to give up her traditional authority over many domestic chores. For all but one of these couples, this problem had been overcome by the time of the study. One-third of the women in the study reported that they expected to do all the traditionally female domestic chores when they got married because of socialization—their mothers had done them and they had learned it was the woman's duty to do those chores. Some of the women in the sample mentioned that they had actually enjoyed the challenge of trying to be simultaneously a great housewife and a successful professional.

The change to a more even sharing of domestic chores was not easy. Not only did the wives have to contend with the husband's disinclination to do chores, they also had to cope with guilt feelings about abandoning their traditional role and with the mixed feelings they had seeing their husbands do nontraditional tasks. As their strong interest in a profession consumed more and more of their mental and physical energy over the years, however, housework seemed increasingly tedious rather than challenging. In addition, the women's movement led them to believe that doing double work is unfair and made them feel better about sharing domestic chores with their husbands.

The last type of problem couples had in sharing domestic chores was a lack of skills on the part of one or the other of the spouses. Over one-third of the couples cited this as an impediment to the realization of equality. For half of these couples it was the husband's lack of expertise in areas such as cooking or sewing which had caused problems, and in the other half of the cases it was the wife's inability to do things like make repairs or handle the car which had inhibited an equal sharing of responsibility.

Couples sought to cope with this type of problem by having the more knowledgeable spouse teach the other one the new skill, or by having the incapable spouse develop the necessary ability on his or her own. This solution often failed to work out, for the spouse without a certain skill often lacked a desire to persist through the frustration and disappointment accompanying the learning experience. Other individuals claimed they were too busy with their careers or hesitated giving up valuable leisure time to learn a new skill and it seemed more efficient to let the expert spouse do the task. Many tasks also came up only in a crisis (stopped-up drain, faulty car brakes, popped-off button) and many individuals felt that this was not a good time to learn. Normalcy would be restored quicker if the expert fixed things up. Finally, in cases such as wives trying to learn car maintenance and home repairs, they had to interact with skeptical and hostile outsiders in the pursuit of these skills (e.g., hardware store personnel, garage mechanics). As a result, wives tended to shrink away from this type of contact and avoid learning the task.

Wives were generally less successful at acquiring the skills required for the husband's traditional chores than vice versa. Husbands on the average spent the same amount of hours doing traditionally feminine domestic chores as wives but wives spent less time on the average than husbands on "male" chores such as interior home repairs and yardwork (1.3 hours per week vs. 2.9, according to time-budget data). The figures are small, but they do suggest that the wives, who typically were the instigators of role-sharing, hadn't put much effort into sharing all of the husband's traditional family responsibilities. Interestingly, most of the couples did not perceive this difference to be a problem, perhaps because masculine domestic chores take up so little time compared to other types of domestic chores.

A few couples had succeeded in getting one spouse to pick up a skill once possessed only by the other. Husbands learning how to mend was the situation most often cited. In these cases it seemed that learning was aided by the wife restraining herself from nagging the husband to learn, and by her giving him positive verbal reinforcement of non-condescending type.

Conflicts Involving Jobs. Besides problems in sharing domestic responsibilities, couples also described several difficulties associated with having two jobs in the sample family. One serious problem was conflict between the spouses' jobs or studies. All but three of the couples felt that conflicts between jobs could be a problem in the future, when asked about a hypothetical situation where one spouse would be offered a job in a city different from that in which his or her spouse already worked. Most couples had already settled on strategies for dealing with this situation. A strategy most of them planned to employ was to give the spouse who had the *less* marketable skills or the poorer job opportunities their choice when a conflict arose. (Husbands' jobs were not any more likely to be given priority in the total sample than were wives'.) The next most common plan was establishing a long-distance marriage—that is, both spouses accepting their job offers, living in different cities, and visiting each other regularly. This possibility was mentioned by over half of the couples, most of whom did not yet have children. For the most part, couples did not like the idea of separating but were willing to consider it as a way to maintain a dual-career marriage. Another solution mentioned by some couples was for husband and wife to take turns holding the job of their choice. Finally, a few couples mentioned that one spouse's job offer in another city might be regarded as an opportunity for the other to do free-lance work, engage in independent research, or start a business. Several couples hoped to avoid making a decision about job priority by only looking for jobs at the same time in the same geographic area. This solution was only available to couples in which the husband and wife were at comparable stages in their careers, which was not common, since husbands tended to be older than wives.

Another common problem was conflict between jobs and family responsibilities. This was reported by over half of the total sample, by husbands a little more often than wives (in contrast to typical dual-career couples, where the wife usually reports job-family conflicts). Most of those individuals reporting job-family conflicts mentioned that their jobs interfered with family responsibilities in various ways: housework didn't get done, they lacked energy and patience to interact well with their children, or they did not have enough leisure time to spend with their families. About one-third of those reporting conflicts mentioned that family duties interfered with their job performance: they had to cut down on over-time work, had trouble doing job-related work at home, had to rearrange their schedules when children became ill, or had little time to attend job-related meetings in the evenings and on weekends.

The couples' strategies for dealing with job-family conflicts usually involved adjusting housework. The most common strategy, employed by over one-third of the couples, was to cut down on housework or at least to give it a very low priority—after meeting job or school responsibilities and after spending free time with family members. Next most common was for couples to maintain a regular schedule of housekeeping so it never got out of hand. Several couples mentioned that almost daily they engaged in negotiation and discussion regarding who would assume responsibility for the various family chores that would come up that day. By careful planning they were able to save considerable time while also assuring that chores got done. The two couples with the oldest children had encouraged their offspring to take care of themselves to a great extent (e.g., wash their own clothes) and to assume regular responsibility for some household chores.

Several couples mentioned that they tried to cut down on their jobs' interference with family life by segregating the two as much as possible. Both husbands and wives tried not bring work home and tried to reserve weekends and evenings for family activities. It was not clear whether role-sharing put these individuals at a real career disadvantage, although some observers have suggested that it would (Hunt & Hunt, 1977). Many of the role-sharers in the study were noticeably productive in their fields, so perhaps a role-sharing lifestyle contains some compensations that allow an individual to do well at a career (e.g., interaction with spouse on professional matters, more efficient time-use).

CONCLUSION

The problems and pitfalls experienced by the role-sharers in this study suggest that role-sharing is a lifestyle demanding the wholeheartedly and enthusiastic willingness of both spouses to participate. Both partners have to take into account each other's job and leisure activities when planning things that impinge on each other. For these couples, this kind of commitment to role-sharing seemed to derive from the expectation that the arrangement would produce benefits for both spouses which would outweigh the costs of implementing a new style of marriage.

REFERENCES

Babcock, B., A. Freedman, E. Norton, and S. Ross. 1975. *Sex discrimination and the law—causes and remedies.* Boston: Little, Brown.

Bailyn, L. 1978. Accommodation of work to family. In R. Rapoport and R. Rapoport (eds.), *Working couples.* New York: Harper and Row.

Bernard, J. 1973. *The future of marriage.* New York: Bantam.

Bott, E. 1971. *Family and social network.* New York: Free Press.

Bryson, R., J. Bryson, and M. Johnson. 1978. Family size, satisfaction, and productivity in dual-career couples. *Psychology of Women Quarterly* 3:66–77.

DeFrain, J. 1975. *The nature and meaning of parenthood.* Unpublished doctoral dissertation, University of Wisconsin-Madison.

———. 1979. Androgynous parents tell who they are and what they need. *The Family Coordinator* 28:237–43.

Garland, T. N. 1972. The better half? The male in the dual profession family. In C. Safillos-Rothschild (ed.), *Toward a sociology of women.* Lexington, Mass.: Xerox.

Glaser, B. G., and A. L. Strauss. 1967. *The discovery of grounded theory: Strategies for qualitative research.* Chicago: Aldine.

Grønseth, E. 1976. Work-sharing families. In A. G. Kharchev and M. B. Sussman (eds.), *Liberation of women, changing sex roles, family structure and dynamics.* New York.

———. 1978. Work sharing: A Norwegian example. In R. Rapoport and R. Rapoport (eds.), *Working couples.* New York: Harper & Row.

Haas, L. 1977. *Sexual equality in the family: A study of role-sharing couples.* Unpublished doctoral dissertation, University of Wisconsin-Madison.

Holstrom, L. 1973. *The two-career family.* Cambridge, Mass.: Schenkman.

Hunt, J., and L. Hunt. 1977. Dilemmas and contradictions of status: The case of the dual-career family. *Social Problems* 24, 404–16.

Nye, F. 1976. *Role structure and analysis of the family.* Beverly Hills: Sage.

Poloma, M., and T. N. Garland. 1971. The myth of the egalitarian family: Familiar roles and the professionally employed wife. In A. Theodore (ed.), *The professional woman.* Cambridge, Mass.: Schenkman.

Rapoport, R., and R. Rapoport. 1977. *Dual career families reexamined.* New York: Harper & Row.

Scanzonl, J. 1972. *Sexual bargaining.* Englewood Cliffs, N.J.: Prentice-Hall.

Szalal, A. 1972. *The use of time.* Paris: Mouton.

Walker, K. 1970. Time-use patterns for household work related to homemakers' employment. U.S. Department of Agriculture, Agricultural Research Service.

Young, M., and P. Willmont. 1973. *The symmetrical family.* New York: Pantheon.

Photographs by Alan McEvoy

Part Five

THE FAMILY INSTITUTION

A dozen years ago it would have been unnecessary to define the term *family*. An idealized image of the family prevailed—a permanently married couple with at least two children, the husband as wage earner and the wife as homemaker. Alternative lifestyles, such as cohabitation, single parenthood, childless marriages, working mothers, and communal living, were all seen as deviant or pathological. Today we are relatively used to these alternatives (Chilman, 1983), and the result is that the topic of family life includes a broad range of issues covering the entire family cycle. For example, one of the subjects covered in this part is whether or not one should become a parent. This is a relatively new idea in this pronatalist society, one made possible by advances in contraception and by changing values. In the past, the sage advice of Dr. Spock was all that seemed to be needed to solve the problems of parenthood, but new findings, a trend toward egalitarian gender roles, and large increases in both single-parent and stepparent families have complicated the matter. Longer life expectancies mean that parents will have more time without children, but the implications of the "empty nest" are still unknown.

A surprising theme arising in discussions of the family is luck. In the first article in chapter 11, Margaret Duggan states it succinctly by noting that this "crucial social unit, the family, is assembled primarily by sheer dumb luck.'' Duggan contends that society expects the family to produce well-educated, healthy, law-abiding citizens, and yet it does not require parents to undergo any training for their role.

The effects of this neglect are seen in the startling statistics on family violence: 72 percent of families studied resorted to physical aggression to resolve sibling conflict, 69 percent to resolve parent-child conflict, and 30 percent to resolve conflict between spouses (Steinmetz, 1977). Although all of these areas of family violence have had a long history, they have only recently become recognized as social problems. For example, a glance at history would reveal that child abuse has evolved from infanticide and abandonment in early history, to the notion that the child was full of evil and needed purging during the medieval period, to the current idea that the child needs continuous socialization to become civilized (DeMause, 1975). The result is that parent-child violence is the most prevalent and accepted form of violence in the family. Since a positive relationship exists between corporal punishment and other forms of family violence, it would appear to be important to remove the general acceptance of physical punishment as a means of disciplining children (Steinmetz, 1977).

This is the theme of the second article in chapter 11. Other helpful factors in eliminating violence are recognizing that conflict is normal, realizing that conflicts can be settled by negotiation and compromise, deciding that violence is never acceptable, and eliminating the husband as the "head of the house." We could also change our current method of dealing with family violence, which is based on a tradition of noninterference in private family affairs and which means that we respond only after the fact, and only to prevent further abuse (Miller, 1981).

Although important, these suggestions deal just with the visible part of child abuse, the physical aggression. Many parents, however, are deficient in basic childrearing skills, having no training in general nutrition, developmental psychology, or the legal rights of children, according to Jerry Bergman in the final article of chapter 11. A national survey of courts revealed ten times as many cases of neglect as of abuse, and 60 percent of the cases involved deprivation of necessities (Leishman, 1982). For this reason, the White House Conference on Families recommended that the government acknowledge that education in family life can play an important role in strengthening families. Such areas could be covered as human development, marriage and the family, parenting education and child-care skills, interpersonal relationships, communication and decision making, and human sexuality (Alexander, 1982). Child welfare could thus be moved from the secondary stage of preventing further maltreatment to the primary stage of preventing abuse in the first place.

Bergman carries this recommendation a step further by suggesting that people be required to take such a course of study in order to obtain a license to parent. In this way, Bergman claims, all prospective parents would know some of the basic, accepted principles of raising children. The implication is that it is possible to teach the skills of parenthood.

As chapter 11 indicates, raising children is a difficult task and requires training. This may be a reason why some people have chosen to remain childless despite various pressures to have children. However, an examination of the literature reveals that the difficulty of the task is not a main factor in the decision to remain childless. The two reasons mentioned most often involve a concern with health and a concern with population growth, both of which could be considered unselfish factors. Two other reasons—a fear of pregnancy and a dislike of children—could be seen as involving personal "hang-ups." The remaining reasons tend to fit in with the societal image of childless couples as selfish: career commitment, economic desires, more opportunities, freer life-style, and fear of overload with both job and children (Gustavus and Henley, 1971). Other stereotypes about the deliberately childless are that they must be maladjusted, immature, unhappy, unfulfilled, lonely, immoral, or unhappily married (Veevers, 1979, p. 77).

These beliefs, however, are not supported by the findings on childless couples. Such couples are found to be significantly more cohesive as a result of doing more things together more frequently, such as talking and working on projects. They report a higher level of marital satisfaction and express a stronger determination to continue the marital relationship (Houseknecht, 1979). In fact, many studies have found that the presence of children in the family lowers the marital happiness or satisfaction of the parents (Glenn and McLanahan, 1982, p. 63). Children mean less flexibility in balancing work and family life, less sex and spontaneity, arguments over the big issue of childrearing, and vacations that are more trouble than they are worth (Korpivaara and Sweet, 1982). Nonetheless, various studies indicate that about 80 percent of parents enjoy their children and would become parents if they had it to do over again (Chilman, 1983). In sum, it appears that marriage can be well adjusted without children and that married couples can find sources of fulfillment other than children.

Despite these difficulties, most people will have children. Some see it as a natural activity that needs no further justification. Perhaps this is true, or perhaps these people are unconsciously responding to cultural pressures in the service of society's basic need to reproduce itself. Encouragement to have children comes from tax exemptions and various government support programs, according to E. E. LeMasters and John DeFrain in the first article of chapter 12. The mass media also promote the joys of parenthood with such themes as "rearing children is fun"; "children are sweet and cute"; "all married couples should have children"; "children improve a marriage"; "childrearing is easier today because of modern medicine, modern appliances, and child psychology"; and so on. Other factors in choosing parenthood, as noted by Bernard Berelson in the second article, involve providing oneself with power over children or a mate; proving one's virility or fecundity and one's competence in raising children; adding to one's status; achieving immortality by carrying on the family line and by creating a physical and psychological extension of oneself; enjoying the challenge and creativity of shaping another human; experiencing the pleasures of having, caring for, and loving children. The authors of the final article in chapter 12 summarize these positive and negative reasons as they explore the question of whether parenthood is a desirable role.

Some people believe that this question will soon be moot due to economic factors and technological change. Fewer couples will have children, as the average cost of bringing up a middle-class child rises to between $50,000 and $100,000. New forms of birth control and increased stress and environmental factors from the changing technology are also bringing down the birth rate. Additional factors include women's increasing economic independence, liberalized views toward working and childless women, a decline in religious authority, and an expansion of education for women (McFalls, 1981).

Moving from the question of whether to have children to the actuality of living with children is the next step in this examination of family development. The issue appears to be twofold. First we will look at the tasks of parenthood and how best to cope with them. Then we will examine one-parent and stepparent families in order to note the particular needs of these two rapidly growing segments of the family complex.

Parenting requires five major tasks: (1) providing for the child's physical well-being, its shelter, nutrition, and medical care; (2) promoting emotional well-being and normal personality development by helping the child to develop a sense of belonging and self-esteem and by making the child feel loved, wanted, and valued; (3) encouraging optimum intellectual and creative growth by understanding the relationship between such potential and the child's physical and emotional environment; (4) helping the child develop acceptable social relations by learning about adult roles and interaction with the opposite sex, as well as about such concepts as money, success, work, and future goals; (5) teaching the child moral values, that is, society's "rules" (Golanty and Harris, 1982).

Several parental styles have emerged as a means of dealing with these tasks. A long-term study covering almost 20 years revealed three overall style types: authoritarian, authoritative, and permissive (Yahraes and Baumrind, 1980). Authoritarian parents were strict observers of the rules, which contained restrictions on the child's independence and demands for obedience. Authoritative parents were somewhat more lenient in regard to opinions and decision making. Permissive parents allowed almost complete freedom to try to help the child reach its full potential.

Within these styles can be found five more common models: the martyr, the buddy or pal, the police officer or drill sergeant, the teacher-counselor, and the athletic coach (LeMasters, 1977). The martyr parents would sacrifice anything for the child. The buddy or pal parents try to avoid the generation-gap conflict by letting the children set up their own goals, rules, and limits. The police officer or drill sergeant parents are autocratic disciplinarians and insist on obedience to the rules at all times. The teacher-counselor parents are the reference experts in developing the child's full potential. The athletic coach parents use the idea of leading the children to do their best and be part of the family team.

Each of these parental types reflects the belief systems of the parents and is not necessarily the best way to be an effective parent. The task of describing this role has fallen to such "experts" as Spock and Gordon. For example, *The Effective Parent* reveals that the basic tenets for effective parenting are similar to those for effective communication and conflict resolution: "active listening" and "no-lose problem solving" (Gordon, 1980). Unfortunately, parents are often too busy lecturing, judging, blaming, and warning to listen to what the child is saying. Real problem solving means that neither party loses, and so it cannot be part of the authoritarian or permissive style types. In *The Effective Parent,* Gordon concludes that if parents want their children to adopt particular values, they should model the values themselves and share feelings with the children.

In the first article of chapter 13, Alison Clarke-Stewart adds to this advice on childrearing by turning to the very important early stages. She offers suggestions that will allow for easing the stress of parenting, preventing unnecessary family breakup, and letting parents of young children have a choice of raising children together or apart.

An important factor in helping a child develop its full potential involves encouraging "psychological androgyny," but, as with good communication skills and conflict-solving techniques, help is needed for people to undertake androgynous parenting. In the second article of chapter 13, John DeFrain states that we need social and political reforms, as well as educational and counseling services, if children are to be allowed to fulfill their potential.

In sum, there has been a "shift from encouraging parents to rear children to conform with anticipated adult life styles to rearing children to become self-actualizing individuals" (Bigner, 1972).

The difficulties of parenting are compounded in the single-parent and stepparent families, since they lack institutional guidelines and support. Single parents must provide a stable environment for their children while shouldering the added responsibility of making major decisions and coping with financial needs alone. In addition, they must deal with conflicting home and job responsibilities, inadequate child-care facilities, the lack of time and privacy for a separate social life, and loneliness. For the single father, there is also the lack of experience in parental and housekeeping roles (Phillips, 1981). It is little wonder, then, that single parents feel like the proverbial "fifth wheel" of society.

In the third article, Blaine Porter summarizes the challenges of being a single parent under the two broad headings of personal adjustments and parenting responsibilities. She concludes that the important question to ask is not why we are here or how we got in this situation, but where we go from here. Yet families headed by these second-class citizens—single parents—have increased so rapidly that they have become part of the mainstream; that is, they have become a viable, legitimate "family form in contemporary American society." However, lack of institutional support has led to a picture of single parenthood as "pathological." Research has shown that this is an inaccurate belief and that "single-parent family systems are not inherently disorganized nor detrimental to individual members" (Thompson and Gongla, 1983).

Like the single-parent family, the stepparent family is a rapidly growing alternative family form. And like the single-parent family, the stepparent family lacks institutional support. The resulting inconsistent cultural expectations of the stepparent role give rise to role ambiguity and role conflict, as well as negative associations with the stepmother or stepfather (Kompara, 1980). Stepparents also face problems of adjustment regarding finances, division of labor, ex-spouses, in-laws, food preferences, expectations for sexual intimacy, and personal space (Anderson, 1981).

There is a need for more understanding of the problems faced by stepparents and "a need to develop ways to integrate and institutionalize stepfamilies into the mainstream of society" (Kompara, 1980). In the final article of this chapter, Sharon Turnbull and James Turnbull indicate a number of steps that stepparents can take to ease their difficulties; provide neutral territory, set limits on behavior and enforce them, don't try to fit a preconceived role, don't expect instant love, and maintain the primacy of the marital relationship.

As was indicated in chapter 12, part of the proparenthood belief is that children add to a marriage. It follows from such beliefs that marital happiness must decline after the departure of the last child from the home. The "empty nest syndrome," as it is called, is part of this ideology. In the first article of chapter 14, Polly Greenberg explains the empty nest syndrome as a sudden change of ruts and a rather abrupt cessation of emotional transactions—in short, the end of an era. It is harder for women, she believes, because they are "encouraged to put all of [their] eggs in one basket, in one nest." They are then left trying to balance all their hard earned skills of submerging themselves for the family with no one at home to worry about. However, with more women involved in dual careers, the empty nest syndrome may be more of a problem for current mothers than for mothers in the future. Furthermore, the effects of the loss do not lead to an enduring decline in the psychological well-being of the middle-aged mother, and a positive result is seen in an increase in marital happiness (Glenn, 1980).

Due to economic factors and a change of attitudes regarding children living at home after reaching adulthood, the empty nest may be an alternating phase in the family cycle. As Audrey Foote states in the second article, postgraduate children come back to camp in their old bedrooms as a means of saving money and because the modern home offers a set of conveniences "and only a manageable number of hassles." The question, then, may not be how to adjust to an empty nest but how to empty the nest.

Another changing aspect of the postparental period involves the rapidly growing number of elderly and their problems in living independently. Their desire to be independent is often hindered by children who are not available to help deal with their health and household problems due to their geographic mobility. Similarly, daughters are now more likely to be working and so are also unavailable to help. The only alternative for the elderly is to turn to the total dependency of the nursing home (Streib, 1981).

Solutions other than this extreme are viable if people can overcome the cultural mores opposing alternative arrangements. One proposed alternative is the multiadult household of nonrelated senior adults sharing their home and expenses. Another alternative is that proposed by Victor Kassel in the final article of this chapter, the polygynous family structure. This type of household would provide such benefits as improved living conditions through shared friends, better opportunities for group health insurance, possible solutions for some sexual problems, interest in better grooming, and the opportunity to establish a meaningful family group.

STUDY QUESTIONS

Chapter 11

Duggan
1. In what ways is the family different from other units in our society?
2. Why does Duggan say that the family unit is assembled primarily by "sheer dumb luck"?

Straus, Gelles, and Yahraes
1. Indicate several factors that might account for the high level of family violence.
2. Explain three ways to prevent family violence.

Bergman
1. What reasons does Bergman give for licensing parents?
2. What would be accomplished by licensing parents?

Chapter 12

Lemasters and DeFrain
1. Which three of the myths did you find most plausible? Why?
2. What is the result of believing these myths?

Berelson
1. What are the cultural, political, and economic reasons for wanting children?
2. Explain five personal reasons for wanting children.

Knaub, Eversoll, and Voss
1. Why do the authors say that the effects of parenthood for the male are confused?
2. The authors note that preparation for being a parent is limited. Why?

Chapter 13

Clarke-Stewart
1. Explain four characteristics of adequate environments for caring for young children.
2. What does the author suggest for helping to prevent family breakup?

DeFrain
1. Indicate four of the reasons of sharing child care.
2. Describe four of the challenges facing androgynous families.

Porter
1. Explain several of the challenges of being a single parent.
2. Describe four of the unique characteristics of single-parent families.

Turnbull and Turnbull
1. Explain five of the do's and don't's of stepparenting.
2. Why does the author say there is a need for more understanding of the problems faced by stepparents?

Chapter 14

Greenberg
1. The author claims that the empty nest syndrome is more a question of society's values and pressures than a psychological problem. Why?
2. What does the author mean when she says an era is ending?

Foote
1. What is the new "life-style" of the 1970s?
2. Why are children returning to the nest?

Kassel
1. What are some of the problems of the aged?
2. How would polygyny after 60 resolve these problems?

REFERENCES FOR PART FIVE

Alexander, Sharon T. 1981. Implications of the White House conference on families for family life education. *Family Relations,* October.

Bigner, Jerry J. 1972. Parent education in popular literature: 1950–1970. *The Family Coordinator,* July, pp. 313–19.

DeMause, Lloyd. 1975. Our forebears made childhood a nightmare. *Psychology Today,* April, pp. 85–88.

Druley, Dawn. 1980. Thomas Gordon, the effective parent. *Parents,* December.

Glenn, Norval D. 1975. Psychological well-being in the postparental stage: Some evidence from national surveys. *Marriage and Family,* February.

Glenn, Norval D., and Sara McLanahan. 1982. Children and marital happiness: A further specification of the relationship. *Journal of Marriage and the Family,* February, pp. 63–72.

Golanty, Eric, and Barbara B. Harris. 1982. *Marriage and family life.* Boston: Houghton Mifflin.

Gustavus, Susan D., and James L. Henley, Jr. 1971. Correlates of voluntary childlessness in a select population. *Social Biology,* September, pp. 277–84.

Houseknecht, Sharon K. 1979. Childlessness and marital adjustment. *Journal of Marriage and Family,* May, pp. 259–65.

Kompara, Diane Reinhardt. 1980. Difficulties in the socialization process of stepparenting. *Family Relations,* January, pp. 69–73.

Korpivaara, Ari, and Ellen Sweet. 1982. Is there marriage after children? *Ms,* January, pp. 81–82.

LeMasters, E. E. 1957. Parenthood as crisis. *Marriage and Family Living,* pp. 352–55.

McFalls, Joseph A., Jr. 1981. Where have all the children gone? *USA Today,* March, pp. 116–18.

Miller, Carolyn Clark. 1981. Primary prevention of child mistreatment: Meeting a national need. *Child Welfare,* January.

Phillips, Robert A., Jr. 1981. Clinical issues in alternative lifestyles. *Groves Conference on Marriage and the Family.*

Steinmetz, Suzanne. 1977. The use of force for resolving family conflict: The training ground for abuse. *The Family Coordinator,* January, pp. 19–26.

Strieb, Gordon F. 1978. An alternative family form for older persons: Need and social context. *The Family Coordinator,* October, pp. 413–20.

Thompson, Edward, and Patricia Gongla. 1983. Single-parent families: In the mainstream of American society. In *Contemporary Families and Alternative Lifestyles,* ed. by Eleanor D. Macklin and Roger H. Rubin. Beverly Hills, Calif.: Sage.

Veevers, Jean E. 1979. Voluntary childlessness: A review of issues and evidence. *Marriage and Family Review,* Summer, pp. 1,3–24.

Yahraes, Herbert, and David Baumrind. 1980. Parents as leaders: The role of control and discipline. *National Institute of Mental Health Science Monographs,* pp. 289–97.

XI

THE FAMILY GROUP

28

FAMILY: A MINI-SOCIETY

Margaret Duggan

In the movie *Wizard of Oz,* Dorothy clicks the heels of her magic ruby slippers, repeating, "There's no place like home; there's no place like home...." What is there about the family that makes it different from other units in our society? People may establish membership in many different groups during the course of a lifetime. Certainly, there are pressures and stresses in any task-oriented group, and in many social groups as well. It is common knowledge that power struggles go on every day in large corporations. Aggressiveness and drive are the name of the game in the climb to the top of the corporate heap. Yet, we rarely read about "free-for-alls" in the board rooms. If violence in the family has become common enough to be considered routine, as mentioned earlier (Straus, 1976), then what makes the family as a group so different?

There are several factors that are unique to the family (Straus, 1976). For instance, the way in which it is organized distinguishes it from other groups. Families are composed of members of different sex- and age-groupings, and these differences are conducive to both gender and generational conflict. What the children value is frequently at odds with what the parents value. A husband may see the family income-tax refund as a chance to buy a power saw, while his wife has entertained visions of a new dishwasher. The wide range of activities and interests shared by family members provides more areas for possible disagreement. There is also a more intense involvement of the members as compared with the intensity of involvement in groups whose membership is elective. For instance, if Johnny gets into trouble with the law, the parent usually feels a personal sense of responsibility coupled with the right and duty to influence the child's behavior. The neighbors expect this; the police expect it; the entire community expects it. The message is, "He's your child; you'd better straighten him out." Implied, of course, is the understanding that the parent, as responsible party, will resort to whatever means are necessary. The methods or degree of influence are never really spelled out. Results count.

America is action-oriented. The community at large continually sends out signals reinforcing the old notion that "a man's home is his castle." The police refrain from intervening in domestic squab-

---

From Margaret Duggan, "Violence in the Family," in *Understanding the Family,* edited by Cathleen Getty and Winnifred Humphreys (New York: Appleton-Century-Crofts, 1981). Reprinted by permission.

bles, not only because of the danger to themselves, but also because of their reluctance to interfere in "private family matters." This attitude has been deeply ingrained in American culture and stems historically from the old frontier notion of the family as an island in the savage wilderness. Long before any sense of organized law and order of community developed, the family stood alone and solved its problems. Along these lines, when a group of Pennsylvania State University students were tested to determine their reactions to fights between men and women, according to how they perceived the relationship, 65 percent of the students tried to help when they believed that strangers were fighting each other, but only 19 percent did so when they thought the parties were married (*Psychology Today,* 1977). The frontier notion persists.

Since membership is not an elective matter, escape is not always feasible; this limitation is another source of intrafamilial conflict. Where is a 5-year-old child going to go? For that matter, a wife with no special skills, money, or training has a similar problem, especially if she has dependent children. Free day-care centers are still about as rare as dinosaur saddles.

Members must cope with the stresses inherent in an intrafamilial living situation, day after day, over a span of years. The usual course of events includes a series of maturational and situational changes that can be crisis producing for one or all members. This series includes births, marriages, deaths, job losses or changes, accidents (both major and minor), and illnesses. What other group in our culture faces as wide a range of stresses as does the family?

This social unit is expected to clothe, house, nurture, and educate its children, regardless of the resources at its disposal or of the extreme economic factors over which it has little or no control. Society expects the family to produce well-educated, healthy, law-abiding citizens. Many families face these enormous expectations with severe instrumental deficiencies. Basic intellectual endowment may be limited; finances for survival (let alone education) are often lacking; and the only nearby recreation area for many poor urban families is a garbage-strewn alleyway or a playground that is run by the street gang that happens to be in power at the moment.

The family is recognized as primary educator of the young. If the family is a battleground, the children learn battle tactics. To a child, love can be inextricably linked with violence in that those to whom she or he is closest also punish. If a child sees parents managing stressful situations by striking out, then a specific script for such actions has been provided (Bandura, 1973). Often the child learns violence only too well and later her- or himself becomes an abusive parent or spouse. It has been found that parents most likely to injure a small child are those who themselves were severely punished as children (Kempe & Helfer, 1972).

America has reached a stage of illusion regarding sexual equality. Whenever the media pay particular attention to a subject, people begin to feel that the accompanying issues have been resolved, or that they are at least in the process of resolution. Census documents, insurance forms, and many legal papers still reserve the first line for the "head of the household," with a second line for "wife." Significant salary differences between men and women persist despite the write-ups about the salary gains of the few women who have become corporate executives.

For the family, this period of transition toward a more egalitarian relationship between the sexes is a source of much overt and even greater covert friction. There have been no role models for men and women in transition. Roles have to be redefined, reinvented. Men moving away from traditional tasks and sharing in household chores are moving into areas previously defined as "women's work." Even if the man initially supported his wife's move into the job market, for example, resentment over the additional burden placed on him, or any threats to his masculinity, can produce anger and a sense of losing control. Hostility, if indeed he feels he must mask it, often erupts over trivial matters, such as deciding which partner is more tired at the end of the day or who is to take out the garbage, or he may use emotional withdrawal as a subtle, and even deadlier, form of sabotage. Violence, in one form or another, can then become a final, desperate expression, a kind of last resort. Rollo May (1972) has described violence as an expression of powerlessness—of impotence.

The interplay of cultural and emotional factors provides fertile ground for battle. These factors include notions of the sanctity of family privacy, of the husband as head of the household, and of economic inequality of the sexes, as well as the frustrations inherent in role transitions related to gender identity. Of importance, too, are society's expectations of the family and the general societal trend toward narcissistic gratification. In families with immature parents whose understanding of both the parenting role and the normal process of development in children is impaired, or parents to whom violence has become an acceptable response to life's problems, internal resources are severely limited. While contemporary families have gained mobility, they have suffered the loss of crucial external support systems. Not only are they deprived of a network of relatives, but also of that special sense of historically belonging in one place over generations. In 1938, Thornton Wilder described this notion in his play, *Our Town*. Goodbye, Grover's Corners!

The crucial social unit, the family, is assembled primarily by sheer dumb luck, in most cases with little or no preparation. It harbors our most intense emotions and is expected to solve our deepest social problems. . . .

REFERENCES

Bandura, A. 1973. *Aggression: A social learning analysis.* Englewood Cliffs, N.J.: Prentice-Hall.

Kempe, C., and R. Helfer (eds.). 1972. *Helping the battered child and his family.* Philadelphia: Lippincott.

May, R. 1972. *Power and innocence.* New York: Norton.

Psychology Today. 1977. Newsline. The bystanders' creed: Don't meddle in family fights. February, 10 (9), p. 29.

Straus, M. A. 1976. Sexual inequality, cultural norms and wife beating. *Victimology* 1 (Spring): 54–76.

29

PHYSICAL VIOLENCE IN FAMILIES

Murray A. Straus, Richard Gelles, and Herbert Yahraes

A ROOT CAUSE OF VIOLENCE: HOW CHILDREN ARE RAISED

Among the basic causes of wifebeating and husbandbeating, according to Straus, are the child-rearing patterns of American parents. Typically, these include the use of physical punishment and thus instill in the child the idea that violence is acceptable and even necessary.

When physical punishment is used, as it is in nearly all American households, Straus says, several outcomes can be expected. "First and most obviously, is learning to do or not do whatever the punishment" is expected to correct. Less obvious but equally or more important are three other lessons which are so deeply learned that they become an integral part of one's personality and world view. The first is the association of love with violence. The child learns that those who love him or her the most are also those who hit. The second is that

---

Murray A. Straus, Richard Gelles, and Herbert Yahraes, "Physical Violence in Families," in *Families Today*, edited by the U.S. Department of Health, Education and Welfare by Eunice Corfman (Washington, D.C.: Government Printing Office, 1979).

practice of physical punishment gradually establishes "the moral rightness of hitting other family members." Finally, the child also learns that "when something is really important, it justifies the use of physical force." The investigator adds: "These indirect lessons are not confined to providing a model for later treatment of one's own children. Rather, they become such a fundamental part of the individual's personality and world view that they are generalized to other social relationships, and especially to the relationship which is closest to that of parent and child: that of husband and wife."

Citing studies by other investigators, Straus points out that parents who abuse their children are often people who were severely punished physically themselves as children.

Both the national survey and research by a Straus colleague, Steinmetz, add another link to the chain of circumstances making for family violence. Husbands and wives who treat each other violently, Steinmetz found, punish their children physically more often than other couples. Moreover, their children act violently against brothers and sisters more often than do the children of other couples.

Another basic cause of family conflict, Gelles and Straus explain, is that family members spend so much time interacting with one another. And these interactions cover a broad range of subjects. For example, shall the stereo be used for Bach or for rock?; shall we go bowling or attend a movie?; who gets to use the bathroom first? Moreover, the degree of injury felt under certain circumstances is likely to be greater by far than if the same problem were to arise with an outsider. "The failure of a work colleague to spell or to eat properly may be mildly annoying. . . . But if the bad spelling or table manners are those of one's child or spouse, the pain experienced is often excruciating."

Among other reasons for the high level of family violence, the investigator cites these:

Dissatisfaction over undesirable behavior is exacerbated by parental attempts to change it.

Generational and sex differences in culture and outlook make the family "an arena of culture conflict."

Family statuses and roles are usually assigned on the basis of age and sex rather than on the basis of interest and competence. Further, "not all husbands have the competence needed to fulfill the culturally prescribed leadership role," so they assert themselves violently.

The family continuously undergoes major changes in structure because of such potentially stressful events as "the birth of children, maturation of children, aging, and retirement."

To protect, train, and control a child, "parents are permitted . . . to use a level of physical force . . . that is denied even prison authorities in relation to training and controlling inmates."

OTHER FACTORS MAKING FOR VIOLENCE

The national survey finds a correlation between the use of alcohol and the occurrence of violence in the home. Straus and his fellow-workers believe this is partly because some people get drunk as an unconscious excuse to beat up someone.

The educational level of the parents apparently does not affect family violence one way or the other. But income and occupation definitely do: the higher the income level and the higher the occupational status, the lower the amount of violence.

Families isolated from relatives and friends show higher rates of violence than do other families, probably because people with relatives and friends can turn to them for help, Straus believes, and also because relatives and friends can intervene if the situation deteriorates too far.

Also more likely to use violence are persons judged to have what Straus describes as *mean* personalities and persons with little social competence. The latter group turns to the use of force to compensate for a lack of ability to get along with people.

On the basis of earlier research by Steinmetz and others, Straus points out that violence in the family seems to lead to violence outside the family. "For example," he says, "almost all the political assassins came from homes where they had been much beaten." The national survey also corroborates earlier findings that the beaten child is the one most likely to become a childbeating adult.

Among other causes of family violence, Straus lists the characteristics of the species, the neurobiological makeup of specific persons, and personality development. In most cases, he and his colleagues believe, there is probably a complex interaction among all these factors.

THREE THEORIES OF VIOLENCE

The researchers also investigated three theories often used to explain interfamily violence.

The first is *conflict theory,* which holds that when individuals, groups, and organizations are faced with a problem, they do not seek consensus or compromise. Instead, each person or group seeks to further its own interests and views conflict as natural. "Violence is likely to occur in the family as an outcome of these conflicts," Straus says, "because violence is a powerful mode of advancing one's interest when other modes fail"; indeed, in some families, violence is the mode of first choice. At issue is not the presence of conflict, which is almost universal in this society, but the ways of resolving it.

Another proffered explanation is *resource theory,* which states that violence and threats of violence are fundamental to the organization of any social system, including the family. However, violence is used as a resource in the family only when other resources are lacking. For instance, a man who wants to be dominant in his family but has been poorly educated, holds a low-prestige job, and lacks skill in getting along with people may resort to violence to maintain his position in the family. Moreover, underdog family members may turn to violence to redress grievances when other resources are inadequate.

A third explanation is *structural theory,* in which violence is seen as an outcome or expression of social expectations, or the pattern of life, or the situation in which a person lives, all structural determinants of behavior.

Straus prefers this last theory and reports that the national survey confirms that it is the most important. However, the other two theories also contribute to the explanation of family violence.

HOW TO HAVE A FAMILY THAT DOES NOT USE FORCE

Suppose a person is about to get married, or has just recently married, and would like some specific ideas on how to avoid violence in the new family. What would Straus say?

Perhaps the first thing, he replies, is to recognize that conflict is a part of life, including family life. Having recognized that, one should realize that conflicts within the family can and should be settled nonviolently, just as they usually are outside the family. The chief means are negotiation and compromise, give and take. "One of the main principles to keep in mind is that you want things from other people but that they also want things from you, and it's possible to do a trade. There's a sort of reciprocity: If I do things that please you, you tend to do things that please me."

Another basic need, Straus continues, is to recognize that most people at the back of their minds have a rule which says that it's OK to hit someone if he or she is being unreasonable. Then the married couple must say, "The rule in this family is *no violence.*" "If they don't say that and mean it," Straus adds, "the other rule comes into play."

Of course, there has to be some means of getting justice; everybody has gripes. "You have to say what's bugging you, and the other person has to say what's bugging him. Then the two of you have to work it out. You can call the process *intellectualization,* or *reasoning,* or even *confrontation*—but confrontation in the sense of getting the issues out and discussing them, and trying to arrive at some settlement, without being abusive."

When a man comes home at night grouchy and complaining, and his wife tells him, "You're just bringing your conflicts home from the outside world and taking them out on me"—is the wife behaving acceptably?

"Yes, that's perfectly legitimate," answers Straus. "She's giving you her complaint, getting it out on the table, telling you what she thinks is wrong. That's OK. But if she said: 'You damn mean bastard, why do you deliberately do these things to torture me? What was wrong with your father and mother?' And other stuff like that. That's verbal violence, and it is wrong. It is *not* getting the issue out and discussing it."

Straus' research and observations convince him that a sizeable amount of physical violence *is* brought in from outside. "You beat up your wife because you couldn't beat up your boss. You're not *allowed* to beat up your boss but you *are* allowed to beat up your wife. Those are the rules of the game as it's been played thus far. Here again we have social structure theory at work."

Another fundamental step to forestall or eliminate family violence, Straus maintains, is to eliminate physical punishment, "because physical punishment provides the most fundamental training in the use of violence."

Physical punishment starts with infants. An infant crawling on the floor picks up something dirty and puts it in his or her mouth, so you tell the child not to do that. The child, of course, doesn't really understand, puts the thing in his mouth, and mommy or daddy slaps his hand. Now that's something done for the child's own good, but it's also something that teaches the child that love and violence go together, that those who love you are also those who hit you. And that's so indelibly fixed in the growing child's mind that most people think that it's a biological link rather than something that's just learned from earliest infancy on. In addition, the child learns it is morally right that the parents punish him physically, because, after all, it's for the child's own good. And that's the basic origin, I think, of the rule that it's okay to hit other family members if they're being unreasonable.

We've had lots of people say, "Yes, I was running around with that other man, so I deserved it when he threw the pot of hot coffee at me." That's going back to the little child. I don't mean that she's right running around with other men, but I mean that no matter what you do, no one has the right to throw a pot of hot coffee at you, or even to slap you, or push you. Even in prisons, we don't permit physical punishment any more.

Finally, there is one other way to prevent or eliminate family violence, Straus adds. That is to "eliminate the husband as 'head of the family' from its continuing presence in the law, in religion, in administrative procedure, and as a taken-for-granted aspect of family life." Straus makes this suggestion because he believes that probably the most basic factors leading to wifebeating are "those connected with the sexist structure of the family and society."

But however deeply rooted, violence is not a necessary or biologically inevitable fact of life. It is learned. It is an expedient or resort employed at the individual level and reflected at other levels. At the level of nations, violence is often sanctioned as a patriotic duty. At the level of a government's relations with individual citizens, it is sometimes forbidden and usually controlled. At the level of individuals' social relations with each other, it is almost always proscribed except for specified mitigating circumstances.

From level to level, from culture to culture, from age to age, the rules of conduct governing the use and expectation of physical violence have varied and also been related. But it is at the level of the family where most of us learn our initial lessons in violence, first in how we are treated and eventually in how we treat others.

REFERENCES

Gelles, R. J. 1976. Abused wives: Why do they stay? *Journal of Marriage and the Family* 38(4):659–68.

———. 1978. Violence towards children in the United States. *American Journal of Orthopsychiatry* 48(4):580–92.

Owens, D. J., and M. A. Straus. 1975. The social structure of violence in childhood and approval of violence as an adult. *Aggressive Behavior* 1:193–211.

Straus, M. A. 1974. Leveling, civility, and violence in the family. *Journal of Marriage and the Family* 36:13–30.

———. 1977. A sociological perspective on the prevention and treatment of wifebeating. In M. Roy (ed.), *Battered women*, pp. 195–239. New York: Van Nostrand Reinhold.

———. 1977. Societal morphogenesis and intrafamily violence in cross-cultural perspective. *Annuals of the New York Academy of Sciences* 285:717–70.

———. 1977–78. Wife beating: How common and why? *Victimology* 2:443–58.

———. 1978. Family Patterns and Child Abuse in a Nationally Representative American Sample. Paper presented to the Second International Congress on Child Abuse and Neglect, London, Sept. To be published in *Child Abuse and Neglect*.

———, R. J. Gelles, and S. K. Steinmetz. In press. *Behind closed doors: Violence in the American family*. New York: Doubleday/Anchor.

30

LICENSING PARENTS: A NEW AGE OF CHILD-REARING?

Jerry Bergman

Teachers, child psychologists, members of the clergy, and others have recently begun to talk about a system that would require a person to have a license before becoming a parent. They reason that "parenting" is such an important determinant of a child's development that society should make a much more concerted effort to minimize the damage done by incompetent parents.

Almost all the professions that deal with a person's physical or mental health require extensive training. A license to practice as a lawyer, doctor, registered nurse, social worker, or teacher is given only after at least four years of college. Yet to become a parent—the person most responsible for a child's development—presently requires no training, license, or experience. Society demands that a person obtain a license before pursuing such relatively simple tasks as driving a car, operating a ham radio, wiring a house, or prescribing a pair of glasses. Yet to do the job of a parent—one much more complex and crucial to the lives of so many—requires no license at all.

Those who work extensively with families have often noted that many parents are deficient in basic child-raising skills. An important reason for this is that most parents have virtually no training in general nutrition, developmental psychology, or the legal rights of children. Most people would never expect someone to perform a job as comparably complex as that of being a parent without substantial instruction. It would be like placing a third-grader in an atomic energy lab and expecting him to carry on research.

One example of the problems a lack of information can cause is seen in a case reported by pediatrician Margaret A. Ribble. She writes of a woman who came to a clinic complaining that her baby would rock violently back and forth with his arms tightly clasped around the end of a blanket. Observations showed that this behavior occurred regularly. During an interview, the baby's mother repeatedly stressed that she "had never played with him, that he had never been rocked or jiggled and had always been left in his own bed in the nursery to go to sleep by himself." She insisted that "the nursery was perfectly quiet and entirely isolated from the rest of the house." When it was suggested that she spend more time holding and playing with the child, she was horrified and said that she had been especially careful "not even to let the child's father see him late in the afternoon when he came home from business lest the baby become excited."

Treatment consisted primarily of helping the mother understand the need that children have for tactile, physical, and kinesthetic stimulation. When the mother applied what she was learning, her son

---

Jerry Bergman, "Licensing Parents: A New Age of Child-Rearing?" *The Futurist,* vol. 12, no. 6 (December 1978). Copyright © 1978 by the World Future Society. Reprinted by permission.

showed marked improvement. The woman was concerned about the child's behavior, but the problem was really with her own. Applying the same concern with correct information would do much to help her properly raise her child.

Many studies of parents who abuse their children have found that the parents' behavior is often caused simply by their ignorance of proper child-rearing practices. The parents were abused themselves as children, so they assume that abuse is the correct way to discipline their own children.

In these cases, simple instructions often almost totally halt the child abuse. The parents realize what they are doing, usually appreciate the help, and, although it takes time for them to overcome their habits, most eventually do. But first the necessary help must be given to the parents—and some would add, even if the parents are resistant to outside help.

If the state is able to step in and try to stop the short-term abuse that results in battered children, why shouldn't it have the same control over long-term abuse? Most people would get upset if they saw a parent abusing a child to the point of serious physical damage. But is not psychologically abusing a child just as harmful? Whereas bruises, lacerations, and broken bones will usually completely heal, psychological abuse may last until the child dies. Granted, long-term abuse is harder to detect, but our concern should be focused on the end result just as much as on the paths taken to get there.

THE RIGHTS OF CHILDREN

The social problems that swell from the ranks of the young are both obvious and growing fast. One out of every nine boys runs "afoul" of the law before his 18th birthday; from 10 to 30% of America's children clearly need some kind of psychological help. The problems are so rampant that people often pass them off as just "growing pains." But these growing pains cause suicides (the second leading cause of death among adolescents) and contribute to the rampant pessimism that marks society today.

Extensive research supports the contention that the way children cope with society is largely determined by the way their parents treat them during the first five years of their lives. Poor performance in school, mental retardation, crime, alcoholism, various sexual "deviations," and virtually all other social problems can be traced back, with varying degrees of evidence, to the family and the family structure.

All of society's efforts to ease these problems—spending billions for correctional institutions, prisons, mental hospitals, reformatories, Alcoholics Anonymous programs, etc.—are attempts to change the child *after the fact*. Even if these programs were effective, the present stream of maladjusted children that well-meaning but poorly trained parents continue to turn out is more than our system can handle.

We are not going to make serious inroads into the problems of crime, health, poverty, and poor school performance until we attack social problems directly at their source. By making sure that every parent at least knows the basics of child-rearing, we could do much to guarantee that many of the social problems that grip society today would diminish in years to come.

Any proposal to license parents would necessarily fall under attack by those proclaiming the "rights" of parents to have children. But what about the rights of children? Do not they also have a right to the pursuit of happiness? Unfortunately, a child's happiness depends largely upon his parents, a factor over which the child has no control.

The issue of licensing parents forms only part of a movement that is pressing for the recognition of children's rights. Books such as *Are Parents Bad For Children?* by Graham Blaine, *Birth Rights* by Richard Farson, *The Children's Rights Movement* edited by Beatrice and Ronald Gross, and *Children's Liberation* by David Gottlieb are leading the crusade. The fundamental argument of the many anti-abortion groups is that even fetuses have a right to life.

Children constitute probably one of the last groups against which American society still grossly discriminates. Most minority groups have fought for and won, at least on the law books, many of their rights. This is not so for children today.

However, the courts have recently begun to conclude that children do have some rights, including the right to receive an education and the right not to be sexually, physically, psychologically, or economically abused. Children's interests are starting to become sufficiently recognized for lawmakers and others to begin to enter the parental domain. And although signs of resistance by parents have recently appeared, protection for children is being extended in more and more areas.

CONTROLLING CONCEPTION

Licensing parents is actually just one more step in a process that for centuries has been giving human beings more and more control over conception. At one time people believed that conception depended on factors that today seem completely unrelated. But when people noticed that women have certain cycles of fertility, mankind gained some control over the process of birth. Later, mechanical and biochemical contraception further increased people's ability to control conception.

Today licensing parents has become feasible because of the increasing effectiveness of and knowledge about birth control methods, especially pill contraceptives, which have made it possible to decide who will be fertile and when. Of course, current contraceptives are not yet foolproof. Sterilization methods can't be used for licensing because such methods are generally irreversible. Scientists must develop the technology both to prevent conception before a license is obtained and then to restore fertility once a license is granted.

Such a technology now seems to lie only a few years away. The World Health Organization is experimenting in London with a "once a year pill" which has already been tested by 6,000 women in West Germany. Doctors claim that the pill is as safe as birth control pills taken daily. It consists of a 1½-inch tube containing the hormone progesterone which is implanted in the womb.

Researchers led by Sheldon Segal at the Rockefeller University Bio-Medical Division have also developed a contraceptive capsule implant that has passed clinical tests. The capsule is inserted under a woman's skin by a hypodermic needle and leaks a steady supply of progestin, a female hormone that prevents pregnancy by simulating pregnancy. Researchers have already perfected a three-year capsule, and work is under way to fashion a fairly permanent capsule. Reversal would require only removing the capsule. Men, too, could someday choose infertility if researchers develop contraceptives which render a man's sperm largely inoperative.

But even though present methods of birth control are not yet totally effective, people now still have little excuse for conceiving an unwanted child (and thus little excuse for abortion, since abortion is merely a belated means of birth control). Thanks to the contraceptives now available, parents can choose if and when to have a child. As a result, parents often wait until they reach certain personal or economic goals before having a child. Each child is thus planned, expected, and desired, so each child receives adequate care. From the perspective of history, it is only one more step for the government to help prospective parents decide on the best time to have a child.

If science establishes a procedure that would render males or females reversibly sterile, the question would automatically arise, Under what conditions should fertility be restored? These conditions could range all the way from those of personal choice to those of a strict licensing program. But some standard will be adopted. Now is the time to be concerned about developing the criteria. When the technology is suddenly upon us, we may have to act without proper experience and research.

The institutions that prospective parents could use in the future to gain the information needed for any kind of license are already available and plentiful. As more and more high schools offer child-rearing courses, more and more students could probably meet the requirements for a license without additional training. Thus the majority of young people could easily be prepared for licensing requirements well before any plan was begun. Then it would simply be a matter of slowly increasing the requirements to a realistic, but high level.

Already three regional television networks in West Germany have broadcasted an instructional course leading to a "parent certificate." If people who participate in the course can answer 32 out of 46 questions correctly, they receive a document which acknowledges that they have understood the material presented. Although West Germany does not require this course for parenthood, its existence points out the need parents have for certain basic skills.

If a general course of study were made the requirement for obtaining a license to become a parent, all prospective parents would know some of the basic, accepted principles of raising children. Of course, differences of opinion enliven virtually any subject area, and the teaching of parenting would be no exception. But the parent-to-be would not necessarily have to accept everything taught, and the class could discuss and debate points of contention. Then parents would at least know both sides—clearly a better situation than knowing neither side.

If schools develop educational programs such as this, presumably very few people would not be able to eventually qualify for a license. And for those that cannot, most people would probably agree that they should not have children anyway. This pool would include the severely retarded, those with brain damage, and the very young or very old. Many of these people already cannot have children for physical reasons.

A few of the basic areas with which prospective parents should be familiar are nutrition, anatomy, physiology, hygiene, child development, first aid, physical fitness, learning, and the psychological concepts of modeling, imitation, reinforcement, and discipline. Skills in the areas of child care, tolerance, control, and concern would also be of value.

Aside from having up-to-date knowledge about feeding formulas, bathing, changing diapers, taking care of diaper rashes, and the other nuances of child care, parents must understand the importance of showing concern for the child by fondling, carressing, rocking, singing, and speaking to the baby. Pediatrician Ribble has stated that a mother must be taught "that the handling and fondling which she gives are by no means casual expressions of sentiment but are biologically necessary for the healthy mental development of the baby."

True, having the proper knowledge does not guarantee that a person will be a good parent, but it is a step in the right direction. If parents were at least taught the basics of child-rearing, then work on the next step—insuring that those basics were effectively applied—could begin. We cannot assume that adults have the necessary awareness just because they are of age to be legally married and have children.

To pass drivers' education, states require both book knowledge and road experience. Likewise it may become feasible to require that parents not only have "the book work," but "the road work" as well. This would entail a parents' training program designed to make sure that parents learn how to effectively work with children.

THE PROBLEMS AND POSSIBILITIES OF LICENSING

Becoming a parent now requires only finding a mate. This task demands qualifications such as appearance, sociability, and availability, which are largely irrelevant to parenting. The choice depends primarily on a person's fussiness in selection. Nowhere in the process is any concern given to the children likely to be born from the union.

Yet the very mention of licensing parents raises fears of "1984"—of a world where courtship and marriage are completely subjugated to procreation. Of course, such extreme abuse is unlikely, and just because something can be abused does not argue against that thing—it argues rather for controlling or preventing the abuse. The prohibition fiasco is a good example of how society should not try to completely outlaw something that potentially can be abused; in the case of alcohol, society is much better off just trying to prevent the abuse.

Any proposal to license parents will probably elicit a barrage of protests that such a system limits the individual's freedom of choice and equal opportunity. "If I want to have a child," some will argue, "I have a right to have one." But the U.S. Constitution gives citizens no such right. It does give Americans the right "to the pursuit of happiness," but this guarantee could be used to argue for almost any desire. Also, neither the Hebrew nor Greek scriptures, nor even the Koran, support the contention that the right to have children is "God's law."

Even now, not every parent has the "right" to have a child. If a couple, for example, wants to adopt a child, they must undergo a fairly complex procedure to do so. Also, the retarded, criminals, and people below a certain age are barred from adopting children.

Some of these screening procedures may be open to criticism, but few people would argue that there should not be any screening. If we feel a need to screen the second set of parents, is there not just as great a need to screen the original set? Perhaps if the original set were screened, a second set would not be needed so often.

It is possible that a licensing agency could become a tool for people with selfish political or social ends in mind. However, any licensing board would wield only a limited amount of power. Once guidelines were set up, the board would have to follow existing rules. True, the head of a licensing board could influence the procedure according to his own personality, desires, goals, or political feelings, but strict guidelines would minimize this possibility.

Discrimination on the basis of social class could be another problem. Those most able to afford the schooling needed for a license, and those most intellectually capable, will probably be from the higher socioeconomic classes, resulting in favorable discrimination towards this group. Thus some people could see a licensing program as a racist attempt to wipe out certain ethnic groups that often have a difficult time in school.

A licensing program *would* inevitably bring a bias against certain groups of people. But if the primary requirement were passing a valid test, the bias would fall only against those who did not have the information needed to pass the test, regardless of why they lacked the information. Furthermore, even though the lower classes often show more affection for their children than the middle and upper socioeconomic classes, the higher classes are often the most financially and intellectually capable of raising children. A licensing system could reverse the current situation, where reproduction rates are negatively related to education and income (i.e., the more income and education one has, the smaller the family one has).

Another argument against any licensing requirement stems from the common belief that child psychologists disagree among themselves on how to raise a child. But a survey of the leading books on child rearing finds the advice fairly consistent. The tone and stress may differ, but there are generally few major disagreements in the advice given.

The mandatory sterilization part of licensing would probably cause the most severe problems. Those with religious objections, including the Christian Scientists, some evangelical Christians, and most Catholics, would strongly object. This religious factor alone may cause a significant proportion of Americans to fight licensing. According to a recent Gallup poll, almost half of Americans consider themselves "evangelical Christians," and Catholics constitute 24% of the population.

Those with honest religious objections to a program of temporary sterilization must be considered separately. The program planners could easily isolate this group and not require them to submit to the program's regulations. As with the conscientious objectors, a few people would strongly oppose the program, and it will not be that difficult to determine the sincerity of their belief.

All of these problems facing the implementation of a licensing program must be considered before any steps are taken. With this careful examination, programs could be developed to insure that problems do not and cannot materialize. Obviously, the immediate imposition of a wholesale licensing program would be foolish; it must rather be phased in gradually, probably over several generations. Even if a full-scale program were effective, it might do more harm than good. We must be sure of the advantages before we intrude further on the lives of individuals.

ALTERNATIVES AND INEVITABILITIES

Let us look at some alternatives to licensing parents. One is to improve the child guidance clinics, juvenile courts, family service clinics, and other agencies that try to deal with the problems of youth. Unfortunately, parents usually do not confront situations and use these agencies until the problem becomes severe, and thus it is usually too late. Even if correction at this point is possible, it is extremely inefficient. Parents may be able to turn on to the correct road if they have clear directions well ahead of time, but once past their turn it is difficult to find their way back. Compared to curative programs, preventive programs are much more humane, cost less, and are undoubtedly much more effective.

Another method of giving a child high quality parents, which makes use of an institution called the kibbutz, has been tried in Israel. On a kibbutz, the responsibility for raising the children is invested in a few highly qualified people. Such a program is even more drastic than licensing parents. Taking children away from their natural parents and putting them in an institution staffed by highly qualified people may prove successful, but it is extremely expensive and clearly more radical than the alternative considered in this article.

The potential for improvement in the current system of child-rearing awaits our action. If society continues to muddle through without somehow beginning to influence the quality of parents a child has, the social problems that afflict the U.S. will undoubtedly prove very difficult to subdue.

The feeling held by the public that people have a "right" to have children, regardless of their financial or intellectual capacities, sanctions almost any parental behavior short of obvious bodily disfigurement. However, in American society, rights are generally abridged if exercising them harms someone else. And the child raised by inept parents has not only been harmed himself but will probably go on to harm society as a whole through the medical, criminal, or simple psychological burden he places upon it.

Thus, considering both the rights of the child and of society, governments have the authority to control parents if their actions transgress upon those rights. Even now, if parents are sufficiently incompetent, the government will step in. Therefore, society already has a limited right to screen potential parents. Licensing parents would simply be an extension of this right to more fully recognize the damage a bad parent can do.

Screening and selecting potential parents will by no means guarantee that a child will have ideal parents, but screening will weed out most of the more grossly unqualified individuals. Even if the procedure is only partly successful, the requirements will undoubtedly prove better than no standards. Furthermore, since licensing will help determine what factors make for good parents, a licensing system can later be improved.

This self-correcting aspect of a licensing system could be one of its greatest benefits. Because a licensing agency presumably would have the power to rescind as well as grant a license, the agency could both insure high standards of child care and carry on the extensive research needed to understand the variables of raising children. Even under the present system, children that are abused can be taken away from their parents. A licensing system would not be drastically different.

Just as there were strong objections to licensing doctors and lawyers nearly a generation ago, likewise people will have many objections to licensing parents. However, few would argue that a person's right to practice medicine is more important than society's right to be free of quacks, charlatans, and incompetent physicians. Today, the licensing of physicians is generally accepted, and the push is for stronger licensing in the field. Qualified physicians stand only to gain by licensing changes that upgrade their profession and eliminate physicians who not only harm patients but harm the reputation of medicine as a whole.

The present system of letting people produce children and rear them until the parents are proven incapable is no more sensible than letting a doctor practice for a while to see if he can cure anyone. When he mistakes a spleen for an appendix, he can no longer practice. Unfortunately, in the case of children, the damage done is often just as irreparable. Presently society cannot declare parents incompetent until the damage is clear and obvious. Only by identifying bad parents before they become so can irreversible damage be avoided. And this means looking at a couple *before* they become parents. By the time it shows up in the child, it is often too late.

The licensing of parents will probably arrive slowly through a series of court cases. As permanent birth control spreads, someone such as a convicted child abuser will most likely seek a court decision allowing his wife to become refertile. But the court will not want to grant permission without first insuring that the man will be able to raise a child without abuse. Once that step is taken, it is only one step further to control the reproduction of other groups not suited for parenthood—and then to gradually extend this control until everyone in society is included.

In time, the optimal ways of raising children, controlling for the many important variables often present, will be developed. An accurate knowledge of what works could then generate higher standards and more functional licensing requirements.

Probably the main benefit of licensing parents is that it will teach parents just how serious is the business of raising children by forcing them to think about the problems they will likely confront as parents. The tragedies caused by neglect, ignorance, and inability will not be eliminated, but they will undoubtedly be reduced. Even a small reduction would probably justify a licensing program, for even a small reduction, once achieved, would allow us to restructure future programs in an attempt to guarantee good parents for everyone.

XII

TO PARENT?

31

FOLKLORE ABOUT PARENTHOOD

E. E. LeMasters and John DeFrain

Some years ago Thurman Arnold wrote a very interesting and provocative book called *The Folklore of Capitalism*.[1] In this study Arnold analyzed folk beliefs or myths about the American economy. His thesis was that capitalism in the United States had changed so drastically in the last century that hardly any of the traditional theories about it were relevant any more—and yet they were constantly being quoted by persons who opposed any change in the government's economic policies.

In later years John Kenneth Galbraith has taken up where Arnold left off and uses the term *conventional wisdom* to describe beliefs about American society that he regards as erroneous.[2]

The clinical psychologist Albert Ellis has also used this approach in analyzing American attitudes and beliefs about sex.[3]

In a previous book about the American courtship and marriage systems the first author made extensive use of the concept of folklore.[4]

The reception of the Arnold and Galbraith books leads one to believe that this type of analysis is interesting and worthwhile.

In this chapter an attempt will be made to analyze folk beliefs about parenthood. In any civilization there is always a large body of folk belief about anything very important. As the term *folklore* or *folk belief* is used here, it means widely held beliefs that are not supported by the facts. Usually, these beliefs tend to romanticize the truth, although in some cases the reverse might be true. Reality might not be as bad as the folk belief would imply.

It is the writers' contention that persons living in modern civilizations are apt to think they do not believe in folklore, whereas in actual fact they do. Thus, they are apt to think their behavior is based on sound rational principles when in reality it is not.

The approach will be to state the folk belief and then to subject it and its implications to systematic analysis.

Rearing Children is Fun. No one can teach high school or college courses on the family without being impressed by this belief that rearing children is fun. It derives from the notion that "children are cute" (to be analyzed later). Young people are often heard to say: "Oh I just cannot wait to have children." The odd thing is that parents do not talk that way. This leads one to the conclusion that this belief reflects folklore and has no substantial basis in reality.

From E. E. LeMasters and John DeFrain, *Parents in Contemporary America,* 4th ed. (Homewood, Ill.: The Dorsey Press, 1983), pp. 21–38. Reprinted by permission.

The truth is—as every parent knows—that rearing children is probably the hardest, and most thankless, job in the world. No intelligent father or mother would deny that it is *exciting* as well as interesting, but to call it fun is a serious error. The idea of something being fun implies that you can take it or leave it, whereas parents do not have this choice. Fathers and mothers must stay with the child and keep trying, whether it is fun, or whether they are enjoying it or not. Any comparison to bowling, listening to jazz records, or sex is strictly coincidental.

In the words of Dorothy Rodgers, the wife of the composer Richard Rodgers: "It's true, I think, as a wise friend told me, that parenthood is a one-way river: parents give and children take. The love of a parent for a child is often the most generous, giving and unselfish love there is."[5]

And, in the wry words of family therapist Frank Farrelly, the child's response is "Gimmie! Lemmie! Iwanna!"[6]

We do not mean to deny that a great many parents enjoy their work and that they derive satisfaction from it. But to describe what parents do as fun is to miss the point. It would be like describing the sweat and tears involved in the artist's creation as fun. The life of Thomas Wolfe or that of almost any serious artist will convey the point.[7]

Brooke Hayward has an interesting way of helping us make our point: "One sleepless night when I was 13 or 14 . . . I finally accepted the idea that being a parent might be worse than being a child."[8]

Now that his military service is well in the past, the first author of this book can truthfully say that he enjoyed his years in the U.S. Naval Air Corps and that he would not have wanted to miss the experience. But it is also true that on almost any day of those three years he would have accepted his immediate discharge had it been offered. This feeling is very common to the millions of men who served in the armed forces during World War II (or any other war, for that matter). We think the sentiment also describes very accurately the feelings of millions of fathers and mothers.

The truth is somewhat as follows: Rearing children is hard work; it is often nerve-racking work; it involves tremendous responsibility; it takes all the ability one has (and more); and once you have begun you cannot quit when you feel like it. It would be helpful to young parents if they could be made to realize all of this before they enlist—or before they are drafted; as the case may be.

In pursuing the analogy between military service and parenthood, the writers have often heard parents refer to married couples who have no children as draft dodgers. The sentiment is similar to that which veterans of the armed forces have toward able-bodied men who somehow escaped military service in the last war (any last war will do.). The veteran feels that military service is a rough experience but that it has to be endured for the sake of the country; his feeling toward men who did not have this experience is ambivalent. In a sense he resents their escaping what he had to go through, but in another sense he recognizes that there may have been valid reasons why they were not in the armed forces.

This does not mean, however, that most parents regret having had children any more than it means that veterans regret having served their country. Of course, we do not hear much from the men who were killed or maimed in the wars, and we also do not hear too much from parents who have suffered much the same fate rearing their children.

Kenneth Kenniston says it so well:

. . . The parent today is usually a coordinator without voice or authority, a maestro trying to conduct an orchestra of players who have never met and who play from a multitude of different scores, each in notation the conductor cannot read. If parents are frustrated, it is no wonder: for although they have the responsibility for their children's lives, they hardly ever have the voice, or the power to make others listen to them.[9]

Children Are Sweet and Cute. When young people see small children they are apt to remark: "Your children are so cute!" It is true, of course, that small children *are* cute (at times), but this hardly exhausts the subject—or the adjectives parents use to describe their children when they are *not* being cute. Think back on the other adjectives you have heard used commonly to describe children, some endearing, some impairing.

Several years ago the first author published the results of a study of young parents entitled "Parenthood as Crisis."[10] This report stated that parents in our society have a romantic complex about child rearing and that they tend to suffer from a process of disenchantment after they become parents. When this study was summarized in the *New York Times,* a flood of mail descended on the writer from parents, with the vast bulk of it agreeing with the findings of the study. The response to this paper led the writer to feel that he had struck a responsive chord in the collective bosom of American fathers and mothers.[11]

Children Will Turn Out Well if They Have "Good" Parents. Logically, this should be so, and one would certainly like to believe that it is so. For that matter, it probably is *usually* a correct statement—but not always. Almost everyone knows of at least one nice family with a black sheep in the fold. It seems to be a rare family, indeed, that has not had some tragic experience with at least one child (assuming the family consists of several children).

It would be comforting to think that parents can guarantee happiness and success (the twin gods of our civilization), but the sad truth is that they cannot. Children are so complex and so different, and our society is so complicated, that fathers and mothers simply do not have the quality control one finds in industrial production. Parents with skill and ability, of course, probably have a better batting average than those of us with more modest talent—but even the good parents do not bat a thousand.

Someone has observed that marriage is perhaps the only game of chance at which both players can lose.[12] It might be that rearing children should be added to this list.

It would be fascinating and interesting (and perhaps frightening) to know what the actual success and failure rate is in rearing children in modern America. The writers have seen no respectable research (including their own) which would answer this question, and in a certain sense it cannot be answered because the terms are so hard to define.[13] When has a parent been successful with any given child? At what age do we judge the product—adolescence, early adulthood, middle age, or the life span? Do we include material success, physical health, mental health, spiritual health, or what?

One strategy for answering these difficult questions bears repeating though. Nick Stinnett, Greg Sanders, John DeFrain, and Karen Strand carefully studied more than 300 families nationwide who perceived their marriage and parent-child relationships to be positive. These strong families volunteered to a request in newspapers across the country, and when asked what qualities made for a strong family commonly responded with the following:

1. Appreciation.
2. Communication.
3. Commitment.
4. Spending time together.
5. Religion.
6. Positive coping with stress and crisis.

To see what percentage of parents in the United States perceive they have strong parent-child relationships, in essence, that they are successful in parenting, researchers could compare a random sample of American parents with the 300 families in our strong family study. This would be a laborious task, but useful.[14]

In an extremely unscientific manner, the first writer has surveyed a few families, with very sobering results. Winston Churchill and his wife, for example, appear to have been successful with only two of their children, yet both of these parents were remarkably successful in the other areas of life.[15] Franklin D. and Eleanor Roosevelt, certainly two of the most loved and revered Americans of the modern era, seem to have been only moderately successful in rearing their children—and this appraisal comes from Democrats, not Republicans.[16]

It is true that such families have most unusual family stresses because of the heavy burden carried by the father and mother in discharging their many public responsibilities, but the writers have also studied some families at very modest social levels with somewhat similar results. We know many people who feel they have completely failed as parents. Others report partial failure: some of their children are okay, others are hopeless. But in all cases, we counsel caution; it is best to reserve judgment. Progress comes slowly in the world, and it may be a while before a child comes around. The second author's seventh-grade science teacher years ago was Henry Goebel, and dear old Mr. Goebel has the best advice of all.

Goebel retired a few years ago after teaching more than 40 years. He worked with literally thousands of youngsters and hundreds of their parents.

"Mr. Goebel, Mr. Goebel, we just don't know what to do with Johnny," anxious parents would say to the wise old educator.

"Wait a year," he would reply without flinching. Ninety percent of the problems would disappear in a year's time (or be replaced by new problems), and only 10 percent of the parents would dutifully report to Mr. Goebel for further advice.

"Mr. Goebel, Mr. Goebel, we waited a year like you said and we still don't know what to do with Johnny."

"Wait another," Henry Goebel would say with quiet determination.

Children Improve Marriage. It would be nice to think so, but the research available does not support the belief. In his study of divorced women, Goode did not find that children had improved these marriages.[17] In a study of 852 middle- and upper-class parents, Rollins and Feldman found that only 18 percent of the husbands and wives reported higher levels of marital satisfaction after parenthood.[18] In an extensive review of the research on this belief, Charles Figley concludes: "A dramatic decrease in marital adjustment and marital communication occurs during the child-rearing period."[19] Norval Glenn and Sara McLanahan studied the effects of the presence of children on their parents' marital happiness with data from six U.S. national surveys. The researchers, in addition, looked at a number of important subpopulations of parents in these surveys: blacks and whites; males and females; highly educated people versus people with low levels of education; Catholics versus non-Catholics; women employed full time outside the home versus other women; and people who ideally wanted a lot of children versus people who wanted few children. The researchers found no evidence for positive average effects of children on the marriages of any of these subpopulations. "On the average children adversely affect marital quality," the researchers concluded.[20] In his study of fatherhood Leonard Benson decided that: "There is no evidence to suggest that having children improves or enhances a couple's ability to handle marriage problems."[21] Jessie Bernard is quoted as having said: "Children rarely make for added happiness between husband and wife."[22] As S. M. Miller, the behavioral scientist, said: ". . . We had amazing naiveté about the impact of having children—a naiveté, incidentally, that I see today having a similarly devastating effect on many young parents. We just had no idea how much time and emotion children captured, how they simply changed a couple's lives. . . ."[23]

If You Rear Them Right, They Will Stay Right. This may have been true in an earlier period of American history but it seems dubious today. Forrest S. Tennant, a doctoral student in the School of Public Health at UCLA, studied 5,000 American service men in Europe in 1971 in an attempt to determine whether being a Boy Scout, and honor student, or an athlete in earlier years had any relationship to later addiction to alcohol or drugs. He was disillusioned with his findings. "I was hoping to come up with some recipes for parents," he said, "but it didn't turn out that way."[24] A lot of parents would agree with him.

A mother said to the first author: "I am a devout Roman Catholic. I took my four children to church every week for 15 years and not one of them is a good Catholic today." In another interview a father said: "My wife and I have never used alcohol and have never served it in our home. We thought that if we set a good example, our children wouldn't drink. Now, all four of them go to taverns and bars and our oldest son has been diagnosed as an alcoholic. How do you explain that?"

The Nature of the Child Being Reared Is Really Not Very Important—Good Parents Can Manage Any Child. Three psychiatrists, after careful research, have concluded that this is a myth. In their book, *Your Child Is a Person*, Stella Chess, Alexander Thomas, and Herbert Birch report that the temperament of the particular child is one of the crucial factors in successful or unsuccessful parental role performance. It is interesting that the subtitle of this book is: "A Psychological Approach to Parenthood without Guilt."[25]

Julius Segal and Herbert Yahraes argue that Wordsworth's observation that the child is father to the man should be a caution to modern parents.

In their article "Bringing Up Mother" they point out that babies, with their extremely different temperaments, often train parents as much as parents shape them. In fact, we'd love to see, for example, a study of the relationship between colic and child abuse. It is a grisly experience to hear an anguished parent's descriptions of the emotions which wrench one when an infant cries uncontrollably for three, four, even five hours at a time.[26]

Truly, think of all the other special children in the world and how their needs can change the lives of parents. Lynn Wikler, for example, does an excellent job outlining the "Chronic Stress of Families of Mentally Retarded Children." It is almost impossible to imagine what it must feel like to be faced with the probability that one will be involved in very basic level parenting tasks for the rest of his or her life.[27]

Today's Parents Are Not as Good as Those of Yesterday. It is impossible to prove or disprove this sort of belief, of course, but it does seem to be prevalent. The truth is, as shown elsewhere in this study,[28] that standards applied to parents today have been raised, and it is also true that the laboratory in which parents have to operate (the modern world) has become infinitely more complex. All this tends to create the impression that parents as a group have deteriorated since the good old days of the 18th or 19th century. This sort of argument is usually clinched (at least to the satisfaction of the critic) by reference to the family of John Adams or Thomas Jefferson. Actually, nobody knows what most parents were like in the old days, but if we can compare them to what doctors and other practitioners of the era were like, it seems possible that they were not supermen or superwomen, but just plain fathers and mothers sweating out every child.

There is always a tendency to romanticize the past, and this seems to have done a very real disservice to modern parents.[29] Thumbing through books on life on the plains and prairies a century ago can be instructive. Invariably there will be a picture or two of a sod house in Kansas, Nebraska, or the Dakotas. The soddie will have a garden, mostly weeds, growing on the dirt roof; a cow may be up there on top munching away, too. The surroundings are unimaginably bleak. No trees or water; just dirt, dust, wind, and sun. The captions under the pictures are usually pretty predictable: "The Jones family on their farm in 1878: Jacob, his wife Emma, their 14 children, their cow Bessie, and a hired man." The children back in the days before planned parenthood are too numerous to name. Everyone in the picture is grim faced; each has "tombstones in his eyes." Winter is coming soon, and all 17 will be cooped up in the one-room dwelling for the better part of four or five months. Could anyone today sincerely believe that child abuse rates back then were less than now?

Childless Couples Are Frustrated and Unhappy. This may have been true in the 19th century or the early decades of the 20th century when fertility was more or less a cultural neurosis—but if it was true then, it is certainly not true now. Actually, the very early studies of marital satisfaction by Ernest Burgess and Leonard Cottrell, also by Burgess and Paul Wallin, failed to support this belief: some of the highest scores on the marital satisfaction scales used in these studies were made by childless couples.[30]

Parenthood in the 1980s is at last becoming a matter of choice—a man doesn't have to become a father today to prove his virility and a woman doesn't have to become a mother to prove her humanity. It seems to us that this is a step in the right direction.[31]

You Shouldn't Stop with Just One. Folk wisdom dictates that only children are lonely and spoiled. Ellen Peck writes in *The Joy of the Only Child* that contrary to these beliefs, only children are brighter, get along better with their peers, and are less spoiled.[32]

Judith Blake examined family size and the quality of children. For the purposes of her research, she defined quality as educational attainment among adults and college plans among youngsters. She found that her research supports the so-called dilution model (in the average family, the more children means the lower quality of each child in terms of educational attainment and college plans). Further, she found that children do not suffer in this realm of quality from the lack of siblings, and that last-borns are not handicapped by a "teaching deficit."[33]

Sharryl Hawke and David Knox take a balanced view of the situation. They studied only children and their parents and found both advantages and disadvantages to such a family style. The advantages include less financial expense and emotional demands on the parents, and more possessions, opportunities, and parental attention for the children. The disadvantages include parents' feelings of giving too much attention and protection to the child, and the child's feelings of loneliness and need for more companionship.[34]

There Are No Bad Children—Only Bad Parents. This, in the opinion of the writers, is one of the most destructive bits of folklore relating to parenthood. As Max Lerner points out, parents have become the bad guys in modern America, while children and teachers and other custodians and child-shapers (such as the television station owners) have become the good guys.[35] And, just as on television, the bad guys always lose.

Actually, Orville Brim has analyzed a rather lengthy list of factors other than parents which affect the destinies of children.[36] These include genetic factors; siblings; members of the extended family, such as grandparents; schoolteachers; playmates; the youth peer group; and so on. He concludes that parents have been held unduly responsible for shaping the destiny of their offspring.

Lerner takes the position that parental critics tend to be "child worshippers"—the child can do no wrong, all children are potentially perfect (or near perfect), and parents should be able to rear *any* child successfully if they only knew enough and tried hard enough.[37]

The writers are inclined to the view that some children are doomed almost from the point of birth: Try as they will, their parents seem destined to fail in their efforts to solve the various problems that arise during the child-rearing process. In an earlier America this was conceptualized as fate, but in contemporary America there is no such thing as fate; fate is just another word for poor parental role performance. It seems to us that this is folklore or mythology. It is also very unfair to parents who have made valiant efforts to help their children attain a decent and productive life.

We believe that it is most illogical to view children as good while indicting their parents as bad. In our work with abusive or neglectful parents, we have yet to meet someone currently doing a poor job as a parent who did not as a child have parents who did a poor job rearing them. Rather than blame parents for their failures, we find it much more useful to help them learn new ways to success. One middle-aged black woman comes to mind here: "Two of the kids turned out pretty good," she summarized for us, after telling a long tale of a hard, hard life for her which began in the worked-out farmlands of southern Mississippi in the Depression and was ending up in a lower-class neighborhood in a northern city. She had endured poverty, racism, hunger, and lack of education. "And," she added, "two of the kids just aren't amounting to nothing."

Was it her fault? Did she fail as a parent? we asked intensely, leaning toward her.

"I don't know. Maybe. But I always tried. And always did the best I knew how."

That, to us, is not failure.

Parents Are Adults. This bit of folklore might depend on the definition of the word *adult,* but the fact is that more than 22 percent of teenage girls in the United States bear a child before their 20th birthday.[38]

One teenage mother said to us: "My husband and I are just kids. We're growing up with the baby." This experiment may turn out well, but it frightens most child-development specialists.

Children Today Really Appreciate All the Advantages Their Parents Are Able to Give Them. Oddly enough, the reverse seems to be true: Children today are less appreciative and not more so. Numerous observers of the American family have come to this conclusion.[39]

College students are very frank about this: They regard what they have received as their *right* and not as something to be thankful for.[40]

In a sense, this same sort of psychology is characteristic of all of us living in the modern world; we take for granted inside toilets, painless dentistry, and religious freedom and simply complain when the system fails to deliver what we have come to consider our birthright. Thus, parents derive very little satisfaction from giving children all the modern advantages—they only feel guilty when they *cannot* deliver the goods.

The Hard Work of Rearing Children Is Justified by the Fact That the Children Will Make a

Better World. This is a consoling thought, and one that most parents need desperately to believe, but there is very little evidence to sustain it. It has more to do with hope than reality. Whether one looks at crime or alcoholism rates or the prospects of peace in the modern world, the picture is not encouraging.

One can always hope, of course, that the new generation will be braver, wiser, and happier than their parents have been. It is dubious, however, that this will prove to be true.[41]

The Sex Education Myth: Children Will Not Get into Trouble If They Have Been Told the Facts of Life. One mother said to us: "I do not see how such a thing (premarital pregnancy) could have happened to our daughter. She has known where babies come from since she was six years old."

This indicates how naïve some parents in our society are about the mystical power of sex education, which, at best, usually covers only the physiology of reproduction. Nothing is said about passion or seduction or the role of unconscious factors in heterosexual interaction. It seems to be assumed by such parents that sex is always a cold calculating act—as if Freud had never written a word to the contrary.[42]

The truth is that much (if not most) human sexual behavior is nonrational and only partly subject to continuous intellectual control. If this were not the case, illegitimate pregnancies in our society would be much fewer than they are and research data on adultery would be less massive.[43]

A great many human societies, such as the Latin culture, have always assumed that sex was too powerful for most humans to control, and they therefore arranged that persons for whom sexual relations were taboo were never left alone together.[44] Our society is relatively unique in that we have adopted just the opposite policy—at least for single persons: They are permitted (and even expected) to spend hundreds of hours alone without ever having sex relations until they marry. Research tells us, of course, that considerable proportions of them do have sexual relations before marriage, but only relatively few ever get pregnant. Or if they get pregnant, they marry before the birth of the child.[45]

The writers believe in sex education and think it belongs in every school and college curriculum, also in every family. But one should not expect too much of sexual knowledge. Attitudes, values, passion, and a host of factors determine the sexual behavior of any person at any given time with a particular partner. It could well be that the art of seduction has as much to do with premarital sexual relations as sex education does. Certainly the subconscious and unconscious factors analyzed by Freudians have to be taken into account in understanding why people behave the way they do sexually.

Parenthood Receives Top Priority in Our Society. This is a choice bit of folklore. Ask any employee if the company gives priority to his role as parent when they need a person in another branch in a different city. As a matter of fact, parenthood in American society has always had to defer to military and industrial needs, to say nothing about other community needs. Millions of fathers and mothers have to sandwich their parental role into niches between their other roles in the society.

The wife of a famous authority on the family once said to the first author: "My husband would have made a wonderful father, but he was never home when the children were young. He was always away making speeches on how people should solve their marital problems or rear their children. I took care of the children myself."

A divorced mother with three children put it this way: "My employer couldn't care less about my duties as a mother. The state requires me to be at work at 7:45 which means that I have to leave home an hour before the children go to school. Then I have to work until 4:30, so that the children are out of school over an hour before I get home. And when the schools are closed, I usually have to work because they won't give me time off. Don't tell me parenthood comes first in our society."

Love Is Enough To Guarantee Good Parental Performance. Bruno Bettelheim, one of the authorities on child rearing, says that love is not enough.[46] His main point is that love has to be guided by knowledge and insight and also tempered with self-control on the part of the parent.

It is quite possible, however, that the reverse proposition is true: that no amount of scientific or professional knowledge about child development will do parents (or their children) any good unless it is mixed with love for the child and acceptance of the parental role.

For example, the second author and his wife Nikki managed with their first daughter Amie's consent to get the child potty trained by age 31 months. Neither John nor Nikki at the time had any particular training in child rearing and picked up tips on a hit-or-miss basis. Seven years later, when second daughter Alyssa was born, the couple was loaded for bear: John was now armed with four years of experience in early childhood education and a Ph.D. in family studies, focusing on parent education and child development; Nikki had completed her training in early childhood education and had a bachelor's degree in human development. The DeFrains concentrated about $30,000 worth of education on the task of potty training Alyssa, and by age 28 months Alyssa succumbed.

In sum, it cost the DeFrains $30,000 to save changing diapers for three months. That's roughly $500 per diaper.

By the time daughter number three, Erica, came around, the DeFrains had completely given up. "Don't push the river," as the book title notes. Erica followed her big sister Alyssa around like a puppy most of the time. By the time Erica was 24 months old, four-year-old Alyssa had taught Erica how to use the toilet.

In a speech at the University of Iowa the first author argued that in his opinion most parents who fail as parents actually love their children—they fail in spite of their love.[47]

The One-Parent Family Is Pathogenic. No one would deny that it is helpful to have both a father and a mother in the home when children are growing up—this assumes, however, that the two parents are compatible and share the same philosophy of child rearing. In view of the rate of marital failure in our society, this statement is a large assumption.

But has it been proven that children cannot grow up properly in a one-parent family? In a careful review of hundreds of studies of children, Kadushin reached this conclusion: "The association between single-parent familyhood and psychosocial pathology is neither strong nor invariable."[48] Kadushin's main finding was that our society is not properly organized for the one-parent family—our social institutions were designed for the two-parent family system.

In a study of Head Start children, Aldous did not find significant differences in perception of adult male and female roles between the father-present and the father-absent children when race and social class variables were controlled.[49]

It does seem well established, however, that the chances of a child being in the so-called poverty group are significantly higher in our society when the father is absent.[50]

Parenthood Ends When Children Leave Home. It doesn't, of course. The out-of-sight, out-of-mind phenomenon does tend to help though; if you don't know that the kids are out late at night at a rock 'n' roll concert and that they're probably drinking or stoned, you can probably sleep better. Getting the young adults out of the nest certainly helps in this regard. But they still usually keep coming back: for money, to have their clothes washed, for advice and consolation, and so on. Parents are still giving more, and children are still receiving more for a long, long time after the nest empties.

To complicate matters, we have what some now are calling the reverse empty-nest syndrome. The children, after a stint in the real world, make a beeline for home. They come home after suffering a divorce; or they come home after college and spend several months hunting up a job while living off mom and dad again; or they get that job and get laid off and they're back again.

This leads to problems. The parents are getting adjusted to the freedom of childlessness. They can sleep through the night soundly, not half-expecting a call like one mother got:

"Mom?"

"Yeah, I guess it's me. But I can't tell for sure this late at night. What's the matter?"

"I got hit by a freight train."

"Oh. . . ."

It seems the young adult went through a railroad crossing a bit thoughtlessly and was broadsided by a 113-car coal train. Somehow he managed to climb free unscathed from his demolished clunker.

A popular writer was in Lincoln recently discussing the possibility of writing a book with the second author on the reverse empty nest. It seems she had just experienced it and was interested in exploring the issues with other parents. She happened to sit down with a very famous politician's wife during a conference and noted she was thinking of doing the book.

"Oh, Lord," the woman moaned. "Our boy just got a divorce and moved back home with us in Washington, and we're going crazy trying to cope!"

The Empty-Nest Syndrome Plagues Many Parents. Psychiatrists coined this delicious term to describe parents, usually mothers, who suffer from the debilitating sadness of losing the little birds to the world. It is certainly true that some parents despair over losing their young and wonder what they will now do besides rearing children to bring meaning into their lives. But researchers in family studies have modified this picture for us. As we mentioned earlier in this chapter, family life satisfaction does drop off rapidly with the advent of children. Researchers who follow parents longer into their middle and later years find that the satisfaction curve on the average rises after the children leave home. The pain of losing the young to the world for most parents apparently is more than adequately offset by the newfound freedom from responsibility. And as parents progress into the retirement years and become grandparents, satisfaction increases even more so. When our students study the results of these investigations they often wonder out loud if they should have children at all.[51]

Our reply: most people don't regret it in the long run. But don't go into this job starry-eyed.

And, Finally, Parents Alone Should Rear the Young. Actually, we believe the responsibility is far too great for two people or, increasingly, one person. If we do not have a legal mandate for community responsibility for children, we certainly have an ethical one.

We obviously are not advocating that all the children be shipped off immediately to a huge collective farm and daycare center somewhere out beyond the Salt Flats of Utah next to an MX missile site. But, in an important sense, we are all "our brothers' and sisters' keepers." It is healthy to have our children have contact with many other people: grandparents, friends, church people, and many more.

Margaret Mead put it so well shortly before she died. She argued that good care for children is unlikely to be given by adults "who find no meaning to life beyond the purchase of equity in a suburban house from which their children will move away, leaving their lives, once narrowly devoted to their own children alone, empty and meaningless."

If we are to change the situation, she argued, society will have to be restructured into communities in which the childless also have a responsibility for children and where parents see beyond the needs of their own biological or adopted children.

Today, she said,

There is a proliferation of zoned, closed communities in which families with large numbers of children are excluded in various ways because, owing to the way in which school taxes are collected, poor families with children represent a burden to the childless affluent.

The very necessary campaign in favor of zero population growth has carried with it—in many contexts—a rejection of parenthood and a rejection of children themselves; unwanted children have been classified as a kind of pollution.

All adults must take the responsibility for children, she argued.

Children seen at a distance are at best only wards or stepchildren—provided for out of guilt or sentimentality requiring no genuine personal effort.

Only by involving adults, all adults—adults who have never had children and adults whose children have grown up—can we hope to combine reform in the care of specific groups of children—deaf children, crippled children, orphaned children, abandoned children—with a genuine attempt to rethink the ways our towns and cities are built and the way our lives are lived.[52]

So be it.

This completes our discussion of the folk beliefs surrounding parenthood in American society. The list could be expanded almost indefinitely but perhaps enough has been said to make the point.

RESEARCH ON PARENTHOOD FOLKLORE

In 1972 Leslie Johnson of San Diego State College administered a questionnaire on myths (or folk beliefs) to 193 expectant parents (114 women and 79 men).[53] Three of the findings struck us as interesting: 68 percent of the respondents agreed with the statement: "Man has an inborn desire to have children"; 69 percent agreed with the statement: "Children are not born with problems, parents create them"; and 78 percent agreed with the statement: "If a parent prepares his child for the future, then the child will have the necessary resources to cope effectively with most eventualities." We submit that the respondents who agreed with these statements have been brainwashed—they are victims of folklore and mythology.

THE SOCIAL FUNCTION OF FOLKLORE ABOUT PARENTHOOD

It is a truism in sociology that one of the functional imperatives of any society (or social group) is that of replacement: the production and training of the people who will make tomorrow possible.[54] Along with defense of the group from attack, the replacement function is indispensable.

It follows that every society makes sure that reproduction (parenthood) will take place. Most societies, in addition, try to make sure that persons will only reproduce in some approved fashion—usually through some system of marriage. According to George Murdock, random reproduction is approved or permitted in very few human societies.[55]

When a societal function is relatively rigorous, as parenthood seems to be in our society, a rich ethos or romantic folklore evolves to assure that the role is not avoided by most adults. This can be seen in relationship to military service: The tremendous burden of bearing arms is made more palatable to people by the parades, the bands, the speeches about "serving your country," and the culture complex associated with patriotism. In the 1960s all of this was not enough to get many young men to volunteer to go to Vietnam, and the society has experienced a crisis as the result.

The main point here is that parenthood is so surrounded by myth and folklore that most parents do not actually know what they are getting into until they are already fathers and mothers. This creates many problems when the role proves to be more frustrating than they had expected. The lowered birth rate of the 1970s and 1980s seems to indicate that the mystique surrounding parenthood is not working as well as it did in earlier decades.

SUMMARY AND CONCLUSION

In this chapter we have been considering some of the folk beliefs (or myths) that cluster about parenthood in our society. It is not difficult to understand why these beliefs should exist. They tend to sustain parents in what is at best a very difficult and often discouraging job; furthermore, they explain (or seek to explain) many of the mysteries that the experts have not been able to explain to the satisfaction of most parents. These beliefs in some instances represent tradition, while in other instances they represent so-called scientific fact.

Given the inadequate state of knowledge about parenthood and child rearing in our society, it is not surprising that otherwise intelligent fathers and mothers are found harboring folk beliefs and scientific fallacies about parenthood and child rearing. The fact remains, however, that some of these beliefs can be harmful at times and can damage the morale of conscientious parents.

NOTES

[1] Thurman Arnold, *The Folklore of Capitalism* (New Haven: Yale University Press, 1937).

[2] John Kenneth Galbraith, *The Affluent Society* (Boston: Houghton Mifflin, 1958). For another treatment of folklore, see William J. Lederer and Don D. Jackson, *The Mirages of Marriage* (New York: W. W. Norton, 1968).

[3] Albert Ellis, *The Folklore of Sex* (New York: Charles Boni, 1951).

[4] E. E. LeMasters, *Modern Courtship and Marriage* (New York: Macmillan, 1957).

[5] Dorothy Rodgers, *A Personal Book* (New York: Harper & Row, 1977), p. 175.

[6] Frank's remarks come from a dialogue the second author and his graduate students had via teleconference call with Farrelly in the spring of 1979. Farrelly lives and works in Madison, Wisconsin, and is the co-author of *Provocative Therapy,* a refreshing approach to counseling.

[7] Persons who think it is fun to be a great writer should read *O'Neill* by Arthur and Barbara Gelb (New York: Harper & Bros., 1962). This is the story of the tormented life of the great playwright. Or take a look at any one of numerous biographies of John Steinbeck, another Nobel Prize winning author of *The Grapes of Wrath, Tortilla Flat,* and many other stunning novels.

[8] Brooke Hayward, *Haywire* (New York: Alfred A. Knopf, 1977), p. 200.

[9] Kenneth Keniston, *All Our Children* (New York: Harcourt Brace Jovanovich, 1977), p. 18.

[10] E. E. LeMasters, "Parenthood as Crisis," *Marriage and Family Living* 19 (1957), pp. 325–55.

[11] A more recent study of new parents came to different conclusions; see Daniel F. Hobbs, Jr., "Transition to Parenthood: A Replication and an Extension," *Marriage and the Family* 30 (August 1968), pp. 413–17. Although Hobbs refers to his study as a replication of the earlier study by LeMasters, an important difference is that the LeMasters sample was limited to middle-class parents. This does not appear to be true of the Hobbs sample.

[12] Someone else commented to the first author that marriage may also be the only game of chance in which both players *can win*.

[13] In their study of married couples in Detroit, Blood and Wolfe report that only 3 percent of the sample said they would not want any children if they had their life to live over again; see Robert O. Blood, Jr., and Donald M. Wolfe, *Husbands and Wives* (New York: Free Press, 1960), p. 137. It is interesting to note that of the 909 spouses interviewed for this study not one was a male.

[14] See Nick Stinnett, "In Search of Strong Families," in *Building Family Strengths: Blueprints for Action,* ed. Nick Stinnett, Barbara Chesser and John DeFrain (Lincoln: University of Nebraska Press, 1979), pp. 23–30; and Nick Stinnett, Greg Sanders, and John DeFrain, "Strong Families: A National Study," in *Family Strengths 3: Roots of Well-Being,* ed. Nick Stinnett, John DeFrain, Kay King, Patricia Knaub, and George Rowe (Lincoln: University of Nebraska Press, 1981), pp. 33–41.

[15] On the difficulties of child rearing in the Churchill family, see Jack Fishman, *My Darling Clementine* (New York: David McKay, 1963). This is the story of Mrs. Winston Churchill and her married life. See also Randolph Churchill, *Twenty-one Years* (Boston: Houghton Mifflin, 1965), the story of his childhood; and his *Winston S. Churchill* (New York: Houghton Mifflin, 1966). The latter volume details how seldom Winston Churchill saw his upper-upper-class parents when he was a child.

[16] At various times, almost all of the Roosevelt children seem to have had fairly serious problems when they were growing up; see Joseph P. Lash, *Franklin and Eleanor* (New York: W. W. Norton, 1971).

[17] William J. Goode, *After Divorce* (New York: Free Press, 1956).

[18] Boyd C. Rollins and Harold Feldman, "Marital Satisfaction over the Life Cycle," *Journal of Marriage and the Family* 32 (1970), pp. 20–28.

[19] Charles R. Figley, "Children and Marriage," *Journal of Marriage and the Family* 35 (1973), pp. 272–82.

[20] Norval D. Glenn and Sara McLanahan, "Children and Marital Happiness: A Further Specification of the Relationship," *Journal of Marriage and the Family,* February 1982, pp. 63–72.

[21] Leonard Benson, *Fatherhood: A Sociological Perspective* (New York: Random House, 1968), p. 114.

[22] Jessie Bernard interview quoted in the *Milwaukee Journal,* June 18, 1972. See also her study, *The Future of Marriage* (New York: World Publishing, 1972).

[23] S. M. Miller, "On Men: The Making of a Confused Middle-Class Husband," in *Family in Transition,* ed. Arlene and Jerome Skolnick, 2d ed. (Boston: Little, Brown, 1977), p. 244.

[24] Interview reported in the *Milwaukee Journal,* September 23, 1974. This study was a doctoral thesis.

[25] See Stella Chess, Alexander Thomas, and Herbert Birch, *Your Child Is a Person* (New York: Viking Press, 1965).

[26] See Julius Segal and Herbert Yahraes, "Bringing Up Mother," *Psychology Today,* November 1979, pp. 90–96. Alexander Thomas and Stella Chess expand on these ideas in *Temperament and Development* (New York: Brunner/Mazel, 1977).

[27] Lynn Wikler, "Chronic Stresses of Families of Mentally Retarded Children," *Family Relations* 30 (1981), pp. 281–88.

[28] See Chapter 4, "Role Analysis of Parenthood."

[29] A well-known family sociologist, William J. Goode, takes the position that we have no reliable history of the American family; see his paper, "The Sociology of the Family," in *Sociology Today,* ed. Robert K. Merton et al. (New York: Basic Books, 1959), p. 195. Even today we believe we are yet to see one.

[30] In the pioneer study of marital adjustment and its prediction, the conclusion was reached that couples with no children or one child rate their marriages significantly higher than couples with two or more children; see Ernest W. Burgess and Leonard S. Cottrell, Jr., *Predicting Success or Failure in Marriage* (New York: Prentice-Hall, 1939), pp. 258–59; see also a later study, Ernest W. Burgess and Paul Wallin, *Engagement and Marriage* (Philadelphia: J. B. Lippincott, 1953), pp. 712–13.

[31] For an extensive discussion of the nonparent movement in the United States, see Ellen Peck and Judith Senderowitz, eds., *Pronatalism: The Myth of Mom & Apple Pie* (New York: Thomas

Y. Crowell, 1974); also Jessie Bernard, *The Future of Motherhood* (New York: Dial Press, 1974). A good recent study is by Sharon K. Houseknecht, "Childlessness and Marital Adjustment," *Journal of Marriage and the Family*, May 1979, pp. 259–68.

[32] Ellen Peck, *The Joy of the Only Child* (New York: Delacorte, 1977).

[33] Judith Blake, "Family Size and the Quality of Children," *Demography* 18, no. 4 (1981), pp. 421–42.

[34] Sharryl Hawke and David Knox, *One Child By Choice* (Englewood Cliffs, N.J.: Prentice-Hall, 1977).

[35] Lerner, *America as a Civilization*, pp. 560–70.

[36] See Orville G. Brim, Jr., "The Influence of a Parent on Child," *Education for Child Rearing* (New York: Russell Sage Foundation, 1959), chap. 2.

[37] This discussion is in the section cited previously.

[38] Arthur A. Campbell, "Trends in Teenage Childbearing in the United States," in *Adolescent Pregnancy and Childbearing: Findings from Research*, ed. Catherine S. Chilman (Washington, D.C.: U.S. Department of Health and Human Services, NIH Publication No. 81-2077, December 1980), p. 5.

[39] See David Riesman et al., "From Morality to Morale: Changes in the Agents of Character Formation," *The Lonely Crowd*, rev. ed., (New Haven: Yale University Press, 1961), chap. 2. See also Lerner, "Children and Parents," *America as a Civilization*, pp. 560–70.

[40] This statement is based on an unpublished study of college seniors done by the first author at Beloit College, Beloit, Wisconsin, in 1958.

[41] One of the most penetrating analyses of the new American generation that we have seen is Kenneth Keniston, *Youth and Dissent* (New York: Harcourt Brace Jovanovich, 1971).

[42] See Sigmund Freud, *Sexuality and the Psychology of Love* (New York: Collier Books, 1963); almost any page will do.

[43] Each year the United States records roughly half a million births to unwed mothers. See John Stewart Dacey, *Adolescents Today* (Santa Monica, Calif.: Goodyear, 1979), pp. 226–29. Kinsey reported a significant amount of adultery by both wives and husbands in his sample—but considerably higher rates for husbands than for wives; see Alfred C. Kinsey et al., *Sexual Behavior and the Human Female* (Philadelphia: W. B. Saunders, 1953), pp. 409–45. In this second volume, Kinsey summarizes the data on men from the first volume and compares them with data on women. Morton Hunt followed up on Kinsey's research in the 1970s and found that at least half of the younger American men interviewed would probably engage in extramarital intercourse at some time during their marriage. Possibly more than a third of the women would eventually have sex with a man other than their husband. See Morton Hunt, *Sexual Behavior in the 1970s* (Chicago: Playboy, 1974), pp. 258, 261.

[44] For the Italian view of sex as too overpowering for individuals to control, see Luigi Barzini, *The Italians* (New York: Atheneum Press, 1964); also Irving R. Levine, *Main Street, Italy* (New York: Doubleday, 1963).

[45] In the 1940s a study in Indiana concluded that 20 percent of all first births in that state were conceived before marriage; see Harold T. Christensen, *Marriage Analysis* (New York: Ronald Press, 1950), p. 153. A 1970 survey by the Department of Health, Education and Welfare estimated the premature conceptions at closer to one third of all first births.

[46] See Bruno Bettelheim, *Love Is Not Enough* (New York: Free Press, 1950).

[47] See the *Proceedings* of a conference on *The Single-Parent Family* held February 11–14, 1976, at the University of Iowa.

[48] See Alfred Kadushin, "Single-Parent Adoptions: An Overview and Some Relevant Research," *The Social Service Review* 44 (1970), pp. 263–74.

[49] Joan Aldous, "Children's Perceptions of Adult Role Assignment," *Journal of Marriage and the Family* 34 (1972), pp. 55–65.

[50] See Alvin L. Schorr, *Poor Kids* (New York: Basic Books, 1966).

[51] For a discussion of these issues, and some alternatives from parents who are trying a new lifestyle in which fathers are more involved in parenting and mothers have added a job or career to their lives, see John DeFrain, "Androgynous Parents Outline Their Needs," *The Family Coordinator*, April 1979, pp. 237–43.

[52] William R. Wineke, "Margaret Mead: All Adults Responsible for Young." *Wisconsin State Journal*, June 2, 1979, section 4, p. 2.

[53] The first author was a participant in this study and received the results in a personal communication. The study was conducted in June 1972.

[54] Strictly speaking, we are referring to two separate functions here: that of reproduction or replacement, and that of socialization or training for adult roles; see Kingsley Davis, *Human Society* (New York: Macmillan, 1949).

[55] George Peter Murdock, *Social Structure* (New York: Macmillan, 1949).

32

THE VALUE OF CHILDREN: A TAXONOMICAL ESSAY

Bernard Berelson

Why do people want children? It is a simple question to ask, perhaps an impossible one to answer.

Throughout most of human history, the question never seemed to need a reply. These years, however, the question has a new tone. It is being asked in a nonrhetorical way because of three revolutions in thought and behavior that characterize the latter decades of the twentieth century: the vital revolution in which lower death rates have given rise to the population problem and raise new issues about human fertility; the sexual revolution in which sex is being liberalized, secularized, and divorced from reproduction; and the women's revolution in which childbearing and -rearing are no longer being accepted as the only or even the primary roles of half the human race. Accordingly, for about the first time, the question of why people want children can now be asked, so to speak, with a straight face.

"Why" questions of this kind, with simple surfaces but profound depths, are not answered or settled: they are ventilated, explicated, clarified. Anything as complex as the motives for having children can be classified in various ways so any such taxonomy has an arbitrary character to it. This one starts with chemistry and proceeds to spirit.

Bernard Berelson, "The Value of Children: A Taxonomical Essay," The *Population Council Annual Report—1972*, pp. 19–27. Reprinted by permission of the author.

TAXONOMY

The Biological

Do people innately want children for some built-in reason of physiology? Is there anything to maternal instinct, or parental instinct? Or is biology satisfied with the sex instinct as the way to assure continuity?

In psychoanalytic thought there is talk of the "child-wish," the "instinctual drive of physiological cause," "the innate femaleness of the girl direct(ing) her development toward motherhood," and the wanting of children as "the essence of her self-realization," indicating normality. From the experimental literature, there is some evidence that man, like other animals, is innately attracted to the quality of "babyishness."

If the young and adults of several species are compared for differences in bodily and facial features, it will be seen readily that the nature of the differences is apparently the same almost throughout the phylogenetic scale. Limbs are shorter and much heavier in proportion to the torso in babies than in adults. Also, the head is proportionately much larger in relation to the body than is the case with adults. On the face itself, the forehead is more prominent and bulbous; the eyes large and perhaps located as far down as below the middle of the face, because of the large forehead. In addition, the cheeks may be round and protruding. In many species there is also a greater degree of overall fatness in contrast to normal adult bodies. . . . In man, as in other animals, social prescriptions and customs are not the sole or even primary factors that guarantee the rearing and protection of babies. This seems to indicate that the biologically rooted releaser of babyishness may have promoted infant care in primitive man before societies were ever formed, just as it appears to do in many animal species. Thus this releaser may have a high survival value for the species of man.[1]

In the human species the question of social and personal motivation distinctively arises, but that does not necessarily mean that the biology is completely obliterated. In animals the instinct to reproduce appears to be all; in humans is it something?

The Cultural

Whatever the biological answer, people do not want all the children they can physically have—no society, hardly any woman. Everywhere social traditions and social pressures enforce a certain conformity to the approved childbearing pattern, whether large numbers of children in Africa or small numbers in Eastern Europe. People want children because that is "the thing to do"—culturally sanctioned and institutionally supported, hence about as natural as any social behavior can be.

Such social expectations, expressed by everyone toward everyone, are extremely strong in influencing behavior even on such an important element in life as childbearing, and whether the outcome is two children or six. In most human societies, the thing to do gets done, for social rewards and punishments are among the most powerful. Whether they produce lots of children or few and whether the matter is fully conscious or not, the cultural norms are all the more effective if, as often, they are rationalized as the will of God or the hand of fate.

The Political

The cultural shades off into political considerations: reproduction for the purposes of a higher authority. In a way, the human responsibility to perpetuate the species is the grandest such expression—the human family pitted politically against fauna and flora—and there may always be people who partly rationalize their own childbearing as a contribution to that lofty end. Beneath that, however, there are political units for whom collective childbearing is or has been explicitly encouraged as a demographic duty—countries concerned with national glory or competitive political position; governments concerned with the supply of workers and soldiers; churches concerned with propagation of the faith or their relative strength; ethnic minorities concerned with their political power; linguistic communities competing for position; clans and tribes concerned over their relative status within a larger setting. In ancient Rome, according to the Oxford English Dictionary, the proletariat—from the root *proles,* for progeny—were "the lowest class of the community, regarded as contributing nothing to the state but offspring"; and a proletaire was "one who served the state not with his property but only with his offspring." The world has changed since then, but not all the way.

The Economic

As the "new home economics" is reminding us in its current attention to the microeconomics of fertility, children are economically valuable. Not that that would come as a surprise to the poor peasant who consciously acts on the premise, but it is clear that some people want children or not for economic reasons.

Start with the obvious case of economic returns from children that appears to be characteristic of the rural poor. To some extent, that accounts for their generally higher fertility than their urban and wealthier counterparts: labor in the fields; hunting, fishing, animal care; help in the home and with the younger children; dowry and "bridewealth"; support in later life (the individualized system of social security).

The economics of the case carries through on the negative side as well. It is not publicly comfortable to think of children as another consumer durable but sometimes that is precisely the way parents do think of them, before conception: another child or a trip to Europe; a birth deferred in favor of a new car; the *n*th child requiring more expenditure on education or housing. But observe the special characteristics of children viewed as consumer durables; they come only in whole units; they are not rentable or returnable or exchangeable or available on trial; they cannot be evaluated quickly; they do not come in several competing brands or products; their quality cannot be pretested before delivery; they are not usually available for appraisal in large numbers in one's personal experience; they themselves participate actively in the household's decisions. And in the broad view, both societies and families tend to choose standard of living over number of children when the opportunity presents itself.

The Familial

In some societies people want children for what might be called familial reasons: to extend the family line or the family name; to propitiate the ancestors; to enable the proper functioning of religious rituals involving the family (e.g., the Hindu son needed to light the father's funeral pyre, the Jewish son needed to say Kaddish for the dead father). Such reasons may seem thin in the modern, secularized society but they have been and are powerful indeed in other places.

In addition, one class of family reasons shares a border with the category below, namely, having children in order to maintain or improve a marriage: to hold the husband or occupy the wife; to repair or rejuvenate the marriage; to increase the number of children on the assumption that family happiness lies that way. This point is underlined by its converse: in some societies the failure to bear children (or males) is a threat to the marriage and a real cause for divorce.

Beyond all that is the profound significance of children to the very institution of the family itself. To many people, husband and wife alone do not seem a proper family—they need children to enrich the circle, to validate its family character, to gather the redemptive influence of offspring. Children need the family, but the family seems also to need children, as the social institution uniquely available, at least in principle, for security, comfort, assurance, and direction in a changing, often hostile, world. To most people, such a home base, in the literal sense, needs more than one person for sustenance, and in generational extension.

The Personal

Up to here the reasons for wanting children primarily refer to instrumental benefits. Now we come to a variety of reasons for wanting children that are supposed to bring direct personal benefits.

Personal Power. As noted, having children sometimes gives one parent power over the other. More than that, it gives the parents power over the child(ren)—in many cases, perhaps most, about as much effective power as they will ever have the opportunity to exercising on an individual basis. They are looked up to by the child(ren), literally and figuratively, and rarely does that happen otherwise. Beyond that, having children is involved in a wider circle of power:

> In most simple societies the lines of kinship are the lines of political power, social prestige and economic aggrandizement. The more children a man has, the more successful marriage alliances he can arrange, increasing his own power and influence by linking himself to men of greater power or to men who will be his supporters. . . . In primitive and peasant societies, the man with few children is the man of minor influence and the childless man is virtually a social non-entity.[2]

Personal Competence. Becoming a parent demonstrates competence in an essential human role. Men and women who are closed off from other demonstrations of competence, through lack of talent or educational opportunity or social status, still have this central one. For males, parenthood is thought to show virility, potency, *machismo*. For females it demonstrates fecundity, itself so critical to an acceptable life in many societies.

Personal Status. Everywhere parenthood confers status. It is an accomplishment open to all, or virtually all, and realized by the overwhelming majority of adult humankind. Indeed, achieving parenthood must surely be one of the two most significant events in one's life—that and being born in the first place. In many societies, then and only then is one considered a real man or a real woman.

Childbearing is one of the few ways in which the poor can compete with the rich. Life cannot make the poor man prosperous in material goods and services but it can easily make him rich with children. He cannot have as much of anything else worth having, except sex, which itself typically means children in such societies. Even so, the poor still deprived by the arithmetic: they have only two or three times as many children as the rich whereas the rich have at least 40 times the income as the poor.

Personal Extension. Beyond the family line, wanting children is a way to reach for personal immortality—for most people, the only way available. It is a way to extend oneself indefinitely into the future. And short of that, there is simply the physical and psychological extension of oneself in the children, here and now—a kind of narcissism: there they are and they are mine (or like me).

> Look in thy glass and tell the face thou viewest,
> Now is the time that face should form another; . . .
> But if thou live, remember'd not to be,
> Die single, and thine image dies with thee.
> Shakespeare's Sonnets, III

Personal Experience. Among all the activities of life, parenthood is a unique experience. It is part of life, of personal growth, that simply cannot be experienced in any other way, and hence is literally an indispensable element of the full life. The experience has many profound facets: the deep curiosity as to how the child will turn out; the renewal of self in the second chance; the reliving of one's own childhood; the redemptive opportunity; the challenge to shape another human being; the sheer creativity and self-realization involved. For a large proportion of the world's women, there was and probably still is nothing else for the grown female to do with her time and energy, as society defines her role. And for many women, it may be the most emotional and spiritual experience they ever have, and perhaps the most gratifying as well.

Personal Pleasure. Last, but one hopes not least, in the list of reasons for wanting children is the altruistic pleasure of having them, caring for them, watching them grow, shaping them, being with them, enjoying them. This reason comes last on the list but it is typically the first one mentioned to the casual inquiry: "because I like children." Even this reason has its dark side, as with parents who live through their children, often to the latter's distaste and disadvantage. But that should not obscure a fundamental reason for wanting children: love.

There are, in short, many reasons for wanting children. Taken together, they must be among the most compelling motivations in human behavior: culturally imposed, institutionally reinforced, psychologically welcome. . . .

NOTES

[1] Eckhard H. Hess, "Ethology and Developmental Psychology," in Paul H. Musser, ed., *Carmichael's Manual of Child Psychology,* vol. 1 (New York: Wiley, 1970), pp. 20–21.

[2] Burton Benedict, "Population Regulation In Primitive Societies," in Anthony Allison, ed., *Population Control* (London: Penguin, 1970), pp. 176–77.

33

IS PARENTHOOD A DESIRABLE ADULT ROLE? AN ASSESSMENT OF ATTITUDES HELD BY CONTEMPORARY WOMEN

Patricia Kain Knaub, Deanna Baxter Eversoll, and Jacqueline Holm Voss

It was assumed in earlier decades that children were the natural and normal outcome of marriage, and a large family was deemed more appropriate than a small family. Since children were considered essential for family "togetherness" and, many believed, to women's sense of fulfillment, beginning a family early in marriage was the ideal. Women who did not have children early in their marriages were pitied for their incomplete, unfulfilled lives (Bernard, 1975; Hartley, 1977). This attitude was widely held not only by the public but also by the academic community of family scholars (Eversoll, Knaub, & Voss, 1979).

It is often suggested that we are living in a freedom-of-choice era regarding adult work roles, adult relationships and living arrangements, and parenting (separately and in combination). Although behavioral changes indicating liberalization in some life-style choices have been documented (Hawke & Knox, 1977; Libbey & Whitehurst, 1977; Rapoport & Rapoport, 1971), the one role for which behavior continues to be astoundingly homogeneous is women's participation in motherhood.

Most women have in the past and will continue to become mothers (Bernard, 1974, 1975; Blake, 1979; Frieze, Parsons, Johnson, Ruble, & Zellman, 1978). That females are socialized from babyhood onward to want and need to become mothers is well documented (Bernard, 1975; Bem & Bem, 1976; Hoffman, 1977; Walum, 1977). Further recent research suggests that (a) the proportion of women expecting or preferring to be permanently childless remains small (2.5% in 1976, according to *Fertility of American Women,* 1977), and (b) women continue to express a high level of consensus that parenthood is an advantage (Blake, 1979). Together these bodies of literature seem to predict a future in which most women will become parents.

Although the role of motherhood remains a surprisingly consistent choice for women, questions remain regarding attitudes toward the timing of parenthood. For example, only a decade ago research indicated the existence of attitudes that constituted a prevasive societal pressure toward having children early in marriage (Maxwell & Montgomery, 1969). On the other hand, there is the recent suggestion that women are waiting longer after marriage to have their first child (*Fertility of American Women,* 1977). It has been argued that a relationship exists between the delay of parenthood and such variables as educational level (Maxwell & Montgomery, 1969; Bernard, 1975), career orientation (Bernard, 1975), and feminist ideology

---

Patricia Kain Knaub, Deanna Baxter Eversoll, and Jacqueline Holm Voss, "Is Parenthood a Desirable Adult Role? An Assessment of Attitudes Held by Contemporary Women," *Sex Roles,* Vol. 9, No. 3 (1983), pp. 355–62. Copyright © 1983 Plenum Publishing Corporation. Reprinted by permission.

(Lott, 1973). What, then, are the attitudes of young women today toward the timing of parenthood? The present study was designed to determine young women's attitudes toward the timing of parenthood, the perceived effect of parenthood on males as well as females, the perceived contribution of children to the marital relationship, and the sample's perceived adequacy of their preparation to parent.

SAMPLE

A nonprobability, purposive sampling technique was used. The sample consisted of undergraduate, female students at a large midwestern university enrolled in sophomore, junior, and senior family or women's studies courses. A total population of 213 students was obtained, all enrolled in one of four undergraduate courses (i.e., Marriage and the Family, Preparation for Parenthood, Social-Psychology of Family Interaction, and Women in Contemporary Society). The respondents were primarily Anglo-American (99%), between the ages of 18–23 (89.6%), unmarried (81.6%), without children (93.6%), and from intact (92.9%) middle-class families, determined by the Hollingshead Two-Factor Index of Social Position. Fifty-three percent of the subjects' mothers were employed outside the home. As for the size of their family of orientation, 46.5% were from families of three or fewer children and 53.5% were from families of four or more children (mean number of children was 3.9).

INSTRUMENTATION AND STATISTICAL TREATMENT

The Attitudes Toward Timing for Parenthood Scale (ATOP), developed by Maxwell and Montgomery (1969) to measure attitudes toward parenthood, was administered the first day of spring semester classes to obtain data for the present study. The 11 items in the Likert-type scale were characterized by five responses, ranging from Strongly Agree to Strongly Disagree. Responses favoring early parenthood were given the highest score (5 points) and those favoring delayed parenthood were given the lowest score (1 point). The possible score range was from 10–50. An item analysis conducted by Maxwell and Montgomery indicated that each of the 10 scale items discriminated significantly between upper and lower quartile groups at the .001 level of significance. An additional item to measure perceived preparation for parenthood was constructed for the present study, based on Rossi's (1968) conclusion that "American mothers approach maternity with no previous child-care experience beyond sporadic baby-sitting, perhaps a course in child psychology, or occasional care of the younger siblings" (p. 35). The wording of this item was selected with the intent of eliciting a more specific reflective response to the notion of what being "prepared" to be a parent means. Separate questions were developed to obtain necessary demographic information.

The data analysis was comprised first of a frequency count for the sample as a whole; then an analysis of variance was employed to establish the existence of any significant variation among the groups (designated by course enrollment). The Student-Newman-Keuls procedure was implemented to identify the source of the group variation in statistically significant comparisons.

RESULTS

The data obtained in the present study indicate that young women (94.6%) expect parenthood to be one of their adult roles. However, the scale items (see Table 1) indicate that although women expect to become parents, they are largely in favor of delayed rather than early parenthood. Only 4.3% of the sample agreed that married couples with a mature love will be eager to have children as soon as possible (item 8). In fact, only 7.5% agreed that the best time to add children was the first two years of marriage (item 1). A majority of the sample (78.8%) felt it was important to enjoy one's social life first and have children later in the marriage (item 2). Further support for this attitude is provided by the fact that only 14.6% agreed that couples who do not have children are left out of social circles (item 9). These findings indicate that this group of young women no longer view parenthood as a necessary requirement for initiating or maintaining adult friendships. Furthermore, only 15.6% of the sample agree that people should have children while

TABLE 1
SCALE ITEMS BY PERCENT OF RESPONDENTS AGREEING AND DISAGREEING[a]

Item	Agree	Disagree	Undecided
1. The best time to begin having children is usually within the first two years of marriage.	7.5	86.8	5.7
2. It is important for a young couple to enjoy their social life first and to have children later in the marriage.	78.8	10.8	11.3
3. A marriage relationship is strengthened if children are born in the early years of marriage.	6.6	76.9	16.5
4. Women are generally happier if they have children early in the marriage.	5.2	72.7	22.1
5. Men are generally tied closer to the marriage when there are children in the home.	34.9	44.8	20.3
6. Most young married women lack self-fulfillment until they have a child.	8.9	81.7	9.4
7. Young couples who do not have children are usually unable to do so.	2.8	93.9	2.8
8. Married couples who have mature love for each other will be eager to have a child as soon as possible.	4.3	84.4	11.3
9. Couples who do not have children cannot share in the major interests of their friends who are parents, and are therefore left out of most social circles.	14.6	77.8	7.5
10. Children enjoy their parents more when the parents are nearer their own age; therefore, parents should have children while they are still young.	15.6	71.2	13.2
11. In general, research indicates that the majority of couples approaching parenthood for the first time have had little or no previous child care experience beyond sporadic babysitting, a course in child psychology, or occasional care of younger siblings. Considering your own background preparation for parenthood, would you judge that you are well prepared for the parenting experience?	34.7	53.1	12.2

[a] The percentages strongly agreeing and agreeing were combined, and the percentages strongly disagreeing and disagreeing were combined. Items 1-10 are from the Attitudes Toward Timing of Parenthood Scale (Maxwell & Montgomery, 1969). Item 11 was an additional item constructed to determine perceived degree of preparation for parenthood.

they are still young in order to ensure parent/child friendship (item 10).

The data in this study seem to support the contention that women may no longer need parenthood to feel fulfilled, for only 8.9% of the respondents agreed that young married women lack self-fulfillment until they have a child (item 6). The present sample was largely (72.7%) in disagreement with the notion that women are generally happier if they have children early in the marriage (item 4); however, this item elicited the largest undecided response (22.1%) of the 10 items.

The perceived influence that children exert on the male introduced the only ambiguity in an otherwise consistent attitude toward parenthood. The overall attitude of these young women reflected less emphasis on parenthood as an essential component of adult life. However, this consistent and decisive pattern is not evident in their response to item 5; while 34.9% of the sample agreed that children tie the male closer to the marriage, 44.8% disagreed and 20.3% were undecided.

The total scale score of each individual was used as a measure of the general perceived desira-

TABLE 2
MEAN SCORES FOR SCALE ITEMS (ATOP)

	Marriage and the Family	Preparation for Parenting	Social-Psychology of Family	Womens Studies
1. The best time to begin having children is usually within the first two years of marriage.	1.92	2.16	2.03	1.56[a]
2. It is important for a young couple to enjoy their social life first and to have children later in the marriage.	2.21	2.43	2.08	1.81[a]
3. A marriage relationship is strengthened if children are born in the early years of marriage.	2.26	2.13	2.00	1.50[a]
4. Women are generally happier if they have children early in their marriage.	2.30	2.21	2.09	1.92
5. Men are generally tied closer to the marriage when there are children in the home.	2.93	2.97	2.85	2.47
6. Most young married women lack self-fulfillment until they have a child.	1.97	2.21	2.04	1.81
7. Young couples who do not have children are usually unable to do so.	1.63	1.75	1.60	1.57
8. Married couples who have mature love for each other will be eager to have a child as soon as possible.	1.96	2.10	1.95	1.73
9. Couples who do not have children cannot share in the major interests of their friends who are parents, and are therefore left out of most social circles.	2.14	2.21	2.27	2.15
10. Children enjoy their parents more when the parents are nearer their own age; therefore, parents should have children while they are still young.	2.46	2.29	2.22	1.97
ATOP item sum 1–10 (total)	21.80	22.51	21.18	18.50[a]
11. In general, research indicates that the majority of couples approaching parenthood for the first time have had little or no previous child care experience beyond sporadic babysitting, a course in child psychology, or occasional care of younger siblings. Considering your own background preparation for parenthood, would you judge that you are well prepared for the parenting experience?	2.60	2.78	3.26	2.26

[a] Significant at .05 level.
[b] Items 1–10 are from the Attitudes Toward Timing of Parenthood Scale (Maxwell & Montgomery, 1969). Item 11 was an additional item constructed to determine perceived degree of preparation for parenthood.

bility of having children early in marriage. On the basis of these total score results, delayed parenthood appeared to be favored.

Although the data indicate that women expect to become mothers, more than half (53.1%) did not feel that they were well prepared to take on the parent role (item 11); 12.2% were undecided about their preparation, and 34.7% felt well prepared. When asked what they considered the ideal family size to be, the strongest support (46.5%) was indicated for the two-child family. The childless choice was selected by 3.3% of the subjects, with 2.8% desiring one child, 23.5% desiring three children, 22.0% desiring four or more, and 1.9%

undecided, on a continuum from "0" to "more than 5." If the subjects indicated that their ideal family included a child or children, they were asked to denote the sex preference of the first child. Strong preference for a male firstborn (61%) was identified, while 9.9% preferred female firstborns and 23.9% indicated no sex preference. A reversal occurred when the respondents were asked their sex preference of the second child, with 54.5% favoring a female child, 13.6% preferring a male, and 23.9% indicating no sex preference.

Statistically significant differences were observed between the women's studies group and the family course groups on the total score, on the first three items of the scale, and on the item measuring perceived preparation for parenthood (see Table 2). Although all student groups responded in the direction favoring delayed parenthood, the women's studies group was significantly more in favor of delay on items 1, 2, and 3 (see Table 2). The total score also reflects this general delayed directionality, only significantly stronger among the women's studies group than among all other student groups. In addition, the item that measured perceived preparation for parenthood indicated that the women's studies students perceived themselves as less well prepared to function as parents.

SUMMARY AND DISCUSSION

The results of this study clearly support the contention that women continue to view parenthood as a desirable role. This finding is hardly a surprise, given the strong enculturation process to which women are exposed regarding the desirability of parenthood. However, the attitudes concerning the timing of parenthood demonstrated by this sample represent a considerable shift. Research conducted in 1969 by Maxwell and Montgomery (surveying 100 female undergraduates) suggested that early parenthood was perceived as desirable, but the present sample (surveying 213 female undergraduates) was strongly supportive of delayed parenthood. Such a trend toward delaying parenthood, particularly among educated women, was forecast in 1974 by Bernard.

In the former study (Maxwell & Montgomery, 1969), 100% of the subjects indicated the ideal time for the birth of the first child would be within the first two years of marriage. The shift in attitude is noted in the present study, with only 7.5% agreeing that the best time to begin having children is usually within the first two years of marriage (see Table 1). If, as Bernard (1974) contends, it is the "societal vanguard" (affluent, young and well educated) that one must look for friends, then the finding of a shift toward delayed parenthood within this group would suggest a similar prediction for the general population. The authors acknowledge that the current sample represents a select group of undergraduates and direct comparisons cannot be made to all undergraduate females, but the prediction of a general trend seems justified.

Related to the general support for delayed parenthood was a strong rejection of the notions that (1) children are necessary to a woman's sense of fulfillment or happiness, (2) children are a requirement for maintaining friendships with other adults who have children, and (3) children represent an expression of mature love. Perhaps these rejections indicate that the women's movement has sensitized young women to the idea that adult happiness and fulfillment are results of self-growth, rather than conferred by the motherhood role.

The conflicting societal messages regarding parenthood and its impact on men and women's lives were demonstrated by the ambiguous responses to the item dealing directly with the male role. As a group, the sample appeared to be confused whether children tie a male closer to the marriage. Perhaps this attitude is reflective of the current divorce rate, which may suggest to them that even among couples with children, the males are not necessarily "tied" to the marriage. Another possibility may be that as women, the sample was more aware of the impositions and commitment required of motherhood in a patriarchal society and less certain of the binding effects of fatherhood.

In addition, the mixed societal messages seem to be evidenced in the fact that although the majority (94.6%) of the sample expect to become parents, over half (53.1%) felt inadequately prepared to function as mothers. Additional inquiry is needed to determine "why" they feel so unprepared for a role the majority indicate they will choose. Certainly, the potential for disillusionment and disappointment would seem to exist. Further research is warranted on this issue, particularly using a longitudinal design which would compare a sample's perceived attitudes with its actual decisions and experience regarding parenthood.

REFERENCES

Bem, S. L., and D. J. Bem. 1976. Case study of a nonconscious ideology: Training the woman to know her place. In S. Cox (ed.), *Female psychology: The emerging self*. Chicago: Science Research Associates.

Bernard, J. 1974. *The future of motherhood*. New York: Dial Press.

———. 1975. *Women, wives and mothers*. Chicago: Aldine.

Blake, J. 1979. Is zero preferred? American attitudes toward childlessness in the 1970's. *Journal of Marriage and the Family* 41(2):245–57.

Eversoll, D. B., P. K. Knaub, and J. H. Voss. 1979. Family strength: Are children a contributing factor? Paper presented at the 2nd Annual Symposium on Building Family Strengths. University of Nebraska, May.

Fertility of American women: June 1976. 1977. (Current Population Reports, Series P-20, No. 308). Washington, D.C.: Government Printing Office.

Frieze, I. H., J. E. Parsons, P. B. Johnson, D. N. Ruble, and G. L. Zellman. 1978. *Women and sex roles*. New York: Norton.

Hartley, R. E. 1977. Some implications of current changes in sex role patterns. In J. M. Bardwick (ed.), *Readings on the psychology of women*. New York: Harper and Row.

Hawke, S., and D. Knox. 1977. *One child by choice*. Englewood Cliffs, N.J.: Prentice-Hall.

Hoffman, L. W. 1977. Changes in family roles, socialization, and sex differences. *American Psychologist*, August, pp. 644–55.

Libbey, R. W., and R. N. Whitehurst (eds.). 1977. *Marriage and alternatives: Exploring intimate relationships*. Glenview, Ill.: Scott, Foresman.

Lott, B. E. 1973. Who wants the children? *American Psychologist*, July, pp. 546–51.

Maxwell, J. W., and J. E. Montgomery. 1969. Societal pressures toward early parenthood. *Family Coordinator* 18(4):340–44.

Rapoport, R., and R. Rapoport. 1971. *Dual-career families*. Baltimore: Penguin.

Rossi, A. S. 1968. Transition to parenthood. *Journal of Marriage and the Family* 30(1):26–39.

Walum, L. R. 1977. *The dynamics of sex and gender: A sociological perspective*. Chicago: Rand McNally.

XIII

LIVING WITH CHILDREN

34

THE FAMILY AS A CHILD-CARE ENVIRONMENT

Alison Clarke-Stewart

The following set of policy propositions derived from our review of research on child development is most directly linked to the focus of that review—namely, *the family*. Before going into these propositions, a few words of caution or clarification are necessary. There is a danger that some readers will interpret the propositions as a conservative plea to save the nuclear family at all costs since this is the optimal environment for rearing children. That is *not* the intention of the proposition. In fact, we have not examined literature that could lead to that inference. The research that was reviewed merely identified some characteristics of the most adequate kinds of environment and care for young children. However, it does seem true that at *present in our society* these conditions are most *likely* to occur within families. The "families" may be biological, adoptive, or self-chosen, but are small groups of people committed to the long-term care of their children. We are not claiming anything magical about "the family," but merely noting that in our society it is the most likely environment in which people will be decent and committed to each other and thus provide adequate child care. Research does suggest, however, that when outside pressures and environmental stresses act on the family this has an effect not only on children directly but also on the quality of child care that is provided. Research also shows that the number of families affected by these stressful circumstances—divorce, illegitimacy, urbanization, isolation, fragmentation, working mothers—is increasing from year to year (cf. Bronfenbrenner, 1975). Consequently, our propositions about the family take as their general theme urging, suggesting, and justifying services to provide supports that will help parents raise their children and give them satisfactory care.

A CHILD SHOULD BE HELPED TO DEVELOP A SECURE ATTACHMENT TO HIS OR HER PARENTS, AND THEN, INCREASINGLY, BE GIVEN OPPORTUNITIES TO INTERACT WITH OTHER ADULTS AND CHILDREN

During the infant's first year of life forming a *secure* "attachment" relation with another person—

Alison Clarke-Stewart, "The Family as a Child-Care Environment," in *Child Care in the Family: A Review of Research and Some Propositions for Policy* (Orlando, Fla.: Academic Press, Inc., 1977), pp. 93–106. Copyright © 1977 by Carnegie Corporation of New York. Reprinted by permission of Academic Press, Inc. and the author.

usually the mother—is important for development. The child's need for such a relationship has several implications for policy. First, we know that a necessary condition for the development of such an attachment is adequate positive, active interaction with a caregiver. We cannot yet specify precisely the limits of what is "adequate"—this would vary from baby to baby and caregiver to caregiver—but within the limits observed in normal families, the relation seems to be that the *more* interaction engaged in with *more* affection and *more* responsiveness the better. This suggests that the person who has primary responsibility for the infant's care (typically, the parent or foster parent) should be encouraged to interact with the infant warmly and frequently, particularly when the baby expresses a social or physical need.

There is also evidence that attachment develops more easily if there are *few* caregivers and if the same ones *continue* for a substantial period of time. This is a situation that in our society is most often provided by parents in a stable family. Children who have been observed by researchers developed attachments in the first year most successfully in the environment provided by a small family which had enough time for frequent, regular, consistent, and positive interaction among family members. If parents behaved negatively and unresponsively to the child or if they were seldom available for interaction, secure attachments did not develop. Under the latter circumstances, when family care in the first year is not adequate or available, other arrangements for child care should be made. When an alternative child-care arrangement is used at this age, however, parents should be especially sensitive to the quality of their—limited—interaction with the child and to the quality of the care provided by the substitute caregiver. Because the quality of interaction more than the quantity affects the attachment relation, it is possible that even brief, regular, interactions with parents, as long as they are positive and responsive, may be sufficient for the development of the infant's attachment to the parents. This issue requires further research.

Although it is true that having too many different caregivers is detrimental to the development of optimal attachment, this does not mean that a child is best raised by one person alone. In fact, after a primary attachment relation has been established, it is necessary for further development that the child separate from that person and form other social relations. This is best achieved when the child interacts often with a variety of people. Therefore, after the child has developed a primary attachment in the first year, parents should be encouraged to share the child's care with other adults, to offer the child opportunities to interact with other adults and, later, with other children. Supportive services for families that are socially isolated might well include supplementary part-time child care—babysitters, parents' helpers, family day care, center day care, nursery school, or play groups.

As we have noted, when a strong relationship with the mother or other caregiver has developed, children often react negatively to separations from that person or to strangers who approach the child intrusively or when alone. Whenever separation from the mother is necessary (for example, if she has to work or be hospitalized, or if the child needs to be hospitalized), measures should be taken to minimize the painful effect on the child. This is especially important from about seven months to three years, when effects of such separation are most pronounced. Such measures to alleviate separation distress might include providing adequate substitute care, preferably in the child's own home so he or she is in at least familiar surroundings; introducing separation gradually so the child learns that the mother will return; allowing the child to visit the mother in the hospital or vice versa; and not leaving the child alone with a stranger (i.e., the substitute caregiver or babysitter) but having mother stay with them until the child gets to know the other person.

Although most research on the development of attachment has focused on mothers, there is evidence that children also form attachments to their fathers in the first year. There are clear advantages for a child in having two strong social relationships—particularly when circumstances necessitate the mother's absence, as in the reasons listed above. To foster children's attachment to their fathers, therefore, fathers also should be encouraged to participate actively and frequently in positive interaction with their infants.

POLICY SHOULD ALSO PROMOTE THE PARENTS' ATTACHMENT TO THE BABY FROM THE BEGINNING

Adults, as well as infants, develop strong emotional attachments—one of particular significance being that of a mother to her baby. It is this attachment that allows mothers to tolerate the burdens of child rearing and to provide the loving care essential to children's development. Research suggests that the development of this attachment is associated with the birth, initial contact, and early care of the infant; the reciprocally interactive mother-child system clearly begins at the moment of birth, if not before. This has implications for at least three areas of policy: hospital maternity procedures, day-care arrangements, and employment practices.

To foster mutual mother-infant interaction and attachment, a "rooming-in" arrangement in the hospital, in which the newborn baby stays with the mother and is cared for by her rather than staying in a nursery, is supported by the data and is recommended as hospital policy unless there are prohibiting factors such as ill health or prematurity. The rooming-in arrangements should begin immediately after the birth. To facilitate a strong father-child relationship—and possibly to strengthen the mother-father tie at the same time—we might also propose that fathers "room-in" too. If rooming-in for fathers is unfeasible, hospital visiting hours could provide the father with free access to mother and infant at any time of day or night (family-centered maternity care), whereas visiting by others than those likely to be significantly involved in the child's life would be strictly limited. Not only should mother and father be given free access to the newborn, however, they should also—at least with their first infant—be given some guidance in infant care by the medical staff. Since having mothers care for their infants would relieve nurses of some of their nursery chores, the nursing staff might have more time in a family-centered ward to counsel parents who wanted it.

An alternative to the rooming-in scheme, and one which might have economic advantages for parents, would be to provide supportive services for having babies delivered at home. These deliveries could be performed by professional midwives associated with hospitals. In that way, emergency medical services would be available if needed. Another supportive service might be the provision of inexpensive but trained "mother's helpers" who would aid (but not supplant) mothers during the first few days or weeks postpartum, thus permitting an earlier return home from the hospital and an easier recovery for the mother.

Research on parental attachment has also clear and important implications for parents' use of nonparental day care for their infants. Although the quality and continuity of caregiving in the first three months is not as critical for the *infant's* psychological development as care from then on (i.e., the effects of early deprivation are often reversible), this period may be more critical for the development of the *parent's* attachment to the infant. Consequently, full-time day care in the first three months would not ordinarily be advisable.

Finally, the research on early parent-child attachment has implications for employment practices. In particular, it suggests the value for family relations of maternity and paternity leaves. Leaves from work for both mothers and fathers would, ideally, occur at the same time, following the infant's birth, and last for at least three months for both parents and for at least three months for the parent who was to be the primary caregiver. By this time, the parent would surely be "hooked," and the development of strong bonds between parents and infant well established.

SERVICES SHOULD BE PROVIDED TO HELP PARENTS PLAN THEIR FAMILIES AND RAISE THEIR CHILDREN

No one family structure is "ideal" for children's development. But it is possible to discuss the likely pros or cons for children in different family structures. The small, intact nuclear family of two parents and two to four children represents the present modal American family. This structure gives children the opportunity to develop an attachment to one or two adults; it gives parents the opportunity to interact often with each child; it allows each parent some help with child care from another adult; and it provides a buffer for unstable or deviant care from one parent, since there is another parent to take over or to provide a balancing influence. The larger extended family, however, has the advantage of providing parents with additional help and guidance with child care, and of providing children with ready access to a variety of different people. Since most families in the United States today are small and without the support of resident relatives, one policy suggestion is that these nuclear families be provided with the additional services ordinarily offered by larger extended families, for instance, supplementary care and social contacts, and, for poor families, "hand-me-down" toys, books, and clothes.

Another suggestion related to family size and structure is that information about and resources for family planning be made more readily accessible to parents and potential parents. Such information could include not only medical advice about birth control, but also information about the *costs* of having children—monetary, practical, and psychological—as well as about the rewards and joy that children can provide. Guidelines for counseling on family size and composition might be derived from research showing that a small family with spacing of at least 3 or 4 years between children may be most encouraging to children's development, because of possible withdrawal, lack of, or competition for parental attention in a large family of closely spaced siblings; or even from research suggesting the advantages of boy-girl sibling combinations for the development of both children's nonstereotyped sex roles. Such counseling naturally would be done on an individual basis, taking into account the clients' personal and cultural values and goals. It would include examination of the clients' motivation for having children, and provision of information that would let them realistically appraise the costs and benefits of having children, so they could make an intelligent and informed decision about having children, when, and how many. Such a counseling service could be particularly valuable for young adults.

There is also research on the *parental* structure of families, which seems to suggest that for children's development, family functioning and climate are more important than the number of parents *per se*. The *lack* of a father (or mother) is not as bad as *having* a father (or mother) is good. However, in our society, two-parent families generally have advantages over one-parent families in terms of status, monetary resources, and division of labor. Moreover, when a single parent has to be both caretaker and breadwinner, this presents great difficulties that can be alleviated only by services to assist him or her either financially or with child care. In line with the suggestion that we propose multiple solutions to such complex problems, here, we might suggest *both* strategies: income support for single parents in any income redistribution scheme, and "homemaker services" to assist single parents with cleaning, housekeeping, laundry, and cooking, thus relieving the physical burdens of parenting. Many single parents, especially those who are divorced or, until very recently at least, unmarried, also face problems of reduction in social status and activities. They must struggle against resentment of the opposite sex, the ex-spouse, or the child. They must overcome isolation, self-doubt, and overprotection or overpermissiveness toward the child. Supportive services for "parents without partners," therefore, might include: psychological or psychiatric counseling to counteract hurt or rejection, social activities (parties, discussions, group activities, etc.) to alleviate loneliness, consciousness-raising activities with other parents without partners, and counseling or help (parent aides) directly oriented toward child care. If the single parent can share the burden of child care with another adult—who is not necessarily a spouse or even of the opposite sex—it will benefit both parent and child. For the parent, it provides relief from the tedium of child care and consultation about child-related problems; for the child, it may break a too-intense bond with the parent, and it provides another role model—another adult to interact with.

As we have just suggested, there are difficulties for parents and children associated with the single parent family. Raising children is a difficult and consuming task—and more so for one person than for two. Problems are more common in one-parent families and more difficult to overcome; such families need extra support. As well as proposing services to assist single parents, therefore, we should also think of ways of preventing families from breaking up unnecessarily, of supporting families in crisis. More ready access for parents to marital counseling services may be one way. This could be accomplished by making marital counseling a tax-deductible expense, by including it in the coverage of insurance or health plans, or by giving or increasing government subsidies to marital therapy clinics (for example, in Community Mental Health Centers). Another preventive measure would be to revise or avoid welfare regulations that make it more profitable for a family to live apart—or to fake living apart. A third strategy would be to give priority to parents with young children or parents in conflict when measures to relieve environmental stresses are recommended or enacted. These measures might include job training and job satisfaction programs, guaranteed income programs, promotion systems, and housing programs. Finally, we might increase public awareness about birth control, abortion, and adoption options for married as well as unmarried parents.

The intention of the proposition and these suggestions about family counseling and family support, it must be stressed once more, is not to "preserve the institution of marriage" and "save the nuclear family," but rather to provide a variety of services to ease the stresses of parenting, prevent unnecessary family breakups, and allow parents of young children to *choose* whether to rear their children together or apart. Our primary goal, here, and elsewhere, is the provision of the best environments for the care of young children. . . .

REFERENCES

Bronfenbrenner, U. 1974. *Is early intervention effective? A report on longitudinal evaluations of preschool programs.* [DHEW Publication No. (OHD) 74–25]. Washington, D.C.: Department of Health, Education and Welfare.

———. 1975. The challenge of social change to public policy and developmental research. Paper presented at biennial meetings of the Society for Research in Child Development, Denver, April.

Horowitz, F. D., and L. Y. Paden. 1973. The effectiveness of environmental intervention programs. In B. M. Caldwell and H. N. Ricciuti (eds.), *Review of child development research,* Vol. 3, pp. 331–402. Chicago: University of Chicago Press.

35

ANDROGYNOUS PARENTS TELL WHO THEY ARE AND WHAT THEY NEED

John DeFrain

"Who shall rear the children?" This may be the crucial question young parents today are asking. In the past the question rarely came up; now, however, the subject is open and cause for legitimate debate.

For an apparently increasing number of parents, the answer is, in effect, "We both shall rear the children!" From birth on, these androgynous parents have set out to share "the joys and sorrows of parenthood." In this paper, I would like to give the reader some idea of who these parents are, and to outline their needs as they have reported them in our survey of their family patterns. The parents have described the educational and counseling services, and social and political reforms which would be helpful to them in their quest for a viable alternative family form.

METHODS

We set out to survey as many androgynous parents in our vicinity (Lancaster County, Nebraska) as possible. An androgynous couple was defined as two parents who share childcare relatively equally; operationally speaking, neither spouse taking more than 60% of the total time devoted to childcare in the family. Androgyny, in popular usage, refers to the human capacity for members of both sexes to be masculine and feminine in their behaviors—both dominant and submissive, active and passive, tough and tender. Earlier studies of androgynous parenthood (DeFrain, Note 1, Note 2) had noted the futility of randomly sampling parents in an area to gain a large sample of androgynous parents. Instead, snowball sampling techniques were used— androgynous parents referred us to other parents who were interviewed to determine whether or not they were appropriate for the study. This six-page interview was administered over the telephone to the parent who answered. Of 122 androgynous parents telephoned, all but two agreed to participate in the study. After the 20 to 30 minute telephone interview, 11-page questionnaires were mailed separately to both parents who were instructed to fill them out independently. One hundred completed questionnaires were returned, yielding an 83% response rate. The non-respondents were contacted to ascertain their reasons for not replying. All noted lack of time, making it difficult to determine whether their responses would have skewed the study results in a consistent direction.

FINDINGS

In this sample, the parents ranged in ages from the early twenties to early forties. The mean age was in the early thirties (mothers' mean age was 30.18; fathers' mean age was 31.60). They had been mar-

---

John DeFrain, "Androgynous Parents Tell Who They Are and What They Need," *The Family Coordinator*, April 1979, pp. 237–43. Copyright © 1979 by the National Council on Family Relations, 1219 University Avenue Southeast, Minneapolis, Minnesota 55414. Reprinted by permission.

ried an average of almost nine years (8.96). Fifty couples had a total of 84 children ($M = 1.68$). The average child was of kindergarten age ($M = 5.69$).

Level of education ranged from high school to the doctorate. The average level was a college degree plus some graduate work. A third of the parents have graduate degrees (25% had attained a Master's degree; 8% more had gone on for doctorates).

In terms of occupations, 57% of the androgynous parents considered themselves to be in the professional category, such as teachers, accountants, attorneys, bankers, professors, real estate brokers; 8% described themselves as proprietors, managers, or officials, such as farmers, wholesale or retail dealers, or in other managerial postitions; 3% were skilled workers or foremen, such as carpenters, printers, or electricians; 5% were semi-skilled or unskilled, such as delivery persons, laborers, or apprentices; 10% were office clerks, typists, or in the secretary category, and 14% were students. All were dual-career or dual-job families.

In earlier studies of androgynous parents (DeFrain, Note 1, Note 2), it was found that a large proportion (68%) described their jobs as relatively flexible in terms of the number of hours they work and the specific times they put in those hours. In this study, the same pattern held: 67% of the parents described their work as being flexible or very flexible in these terms; 22% described their jobs as being inflexible; and 5% described the work as being very inflexible.

Seventy-seven percent were of the Catholic, Jewish, or Protestant faiths; 11% were of another faith; and 10% had no religious preference.

In political terms, 1% described themselves as revolutionaries, 1% as radicals, 30% as liberals, 47% as moderates, and 15% as conservatives. In terms of their level of interest in feminism and human liberation, 16% described themselves as being active or very active supporters, 65% described themselves as being inactive but in agreement, and 15% (about half men and half women) were in disagreement with the movement.

What exactly were the work assignments in these families? To reiterate, by the operational definition to the study, neither partner could take more than 60% of the childcare duties. As a group, mothers had 54% of the childcare duties in sheer numbers of contact hours and fathers had 46%. In the job/career/educational sphere, these percentages were reversed: fathers did 54% of these labors and mothers 46%. Housework was divided on more traditional grounds, in general: the mothers did 77% of the cooking, 68% of the dishwashing, 73% of the cleaning, 68% of the grocery shopping, 74% of the laundry, and 87% of the ironing. Fathers did 79% of the servicing of the car, 77% of the lawn work, 85% of the household repairs, and took out the garbage 71% of the time.

Parents shared childcare in their homes for many reasons: (a) the wife believed it would be beneficial to the children if the husband were equally involved in their care; (b) the husband believed it would be beneficial to the children if he were equally involved in their care; (c) for financial reasons the wife had been working from the beginning of the marriage and wished to continue; (d) the wife was dissatisfied with her life as a homemaker and decided to pursue a career outside the home and the husband's help was necessary if this were to be possible; (e) the husband believed the wife was more interesting when she was working; (f) the husband loved his wife and wanted to relieve her of the burden of childcare; and (g) the wife was needed to assist in the family business, so the husband was needed to help rear the children.

In the exploratory work on androgynous parenting done in 1974, a common story was that of the career-oriented woman who quit to rear the children. This worked out fine until the children reached age two or three when they began going their own directions more regularly and the mother wished to do so also. She expressed her dissatisfaction to her husband, sometimes calmly, sometimes not so calmly. Over a period of months or years a pattern suitable to both began to evolve.

In the present study—three years later—we find a somewhat different trend which may reflect the effects of the feminist movement. Few of these women really became full-time homemakers for a lengthy period of time (18%). Fully 82% of the couples reported they have been sharing childcare relatively equally from the time the first child was born. This, of course, is open to question; but the fact that they believe this is a powerful case for the notion that any evidence of maternal guilt as seen in the sample of androgynous mothers in 1974 may be fast-disappearing among the 1977 cohorts. The world may be changing more quickly than we believed possible. This is a notion that bears close scrutiny by researchers in the future.

Almost all of the parents found the decision to share role responsibilities easy to make (98.5%). It appeared that they did not grapple with any burning philosophical issues, but, rather, simply continued the sharing mode set in the beginning of the dyadic relationship. Only one couple had devised any type of marital contract; and only 18% had any type of written schedule for work assignments in the family, indicating a relaxed and flexible approach.

The androgynous parents were asked what factors in their childhood or adult life, if any, prepared them for role sharing. Role models in the home in which they grew up, primarily their parents, rated most highly. These were both positive and negative role models. For example, an androgynous father said after watching his father's chauvinistic antics in refusing to help around the house, he was certain his home would be different. Fifty-eight percent rated this type of factor first, second, or third in importance. Other factors, in order of importance, were: experience in the working world outside the home before marriage (40% rated this first, second, or third); experience caring for children before the respondent had children of his/her own (28%); the women's liberation movement (22%); and earlier experience running a household (16%).

The majority of androgynous parents came from traditional families in terms of sex-role orientation. Almost a third (32%) of the androgynous mothers rated their parents as having adopted very traditional childrearing patterns, with the mother being almost totally responsible for the children; another 56% rated their parents as traditional; and only 12% rated their parents as non-traditional. None describe their parents as very non-traditional. Similarly, the androgynous fathers reported that almost a fourth of their parents were very traditional (24.5%); an additional 59.2% were rated as traditional; 12.2% as non-traditional; and 4.1% as very non-traditional.

Furthermore, three-fourths of the androgynous couples' mothers (71.4% for the men; 78% for the women) never worked outside the home while any of their children were of preschool age; and half of the androgynous couples' mothers (49% for the men; 50% for the women) never worked outside the home while any of her children were in kindergarten through the twelfth grade. These couples' models for child-rearing certainly did not come from their parents.

Adopting an androgynous parenting style is a great thing to do, according to these parents. Written responses to the questionnaire include glowing reports of the benefits of such a system. Quantitative data to support such reports, however, are harder to glean from the survey, because there is not an adequate baseline for comparative purposes. One measure would be to look at personal happiness and the strength of family relationships before and after the couple began sharing childrearing responsibilities. But, in this sample of parents, 82% report they have done this all along, so there is nothing to which to compare their present situation. The other 18% of the parents, who began sharing when the first child was older (on the average of age two to three) can be surveyed in the above manner; all 18 of these parents report their personal happiness and family relationships strength to be as high as before they began sharing (two-thirds of the eighteen parents rate their personal happiness and family relationships even higher).

Another way of evaluating the childrearing pattern would be to look at life satisfaction, and chart it in the traditional manner of family sociology. This method suffers, also, because most of the parents have shared childrearing throughout their relationships. But, Figures 1 and 2 illustrate the results of this method; though their validity may be questioned, they are most interesting. The family life satisfaction level, as evidenced by the mothers' and fathers' graphs, stays at a high level across the stages into the teen-age years. It is interesting to compare these graphs to the U-shaped marriage gradient reported by many other researchers. Although this method may be invalid for reasons of possible individual and cohort differences, it leads me to speculate that an androgynous childrearing mode may be a means of relieving the so-called

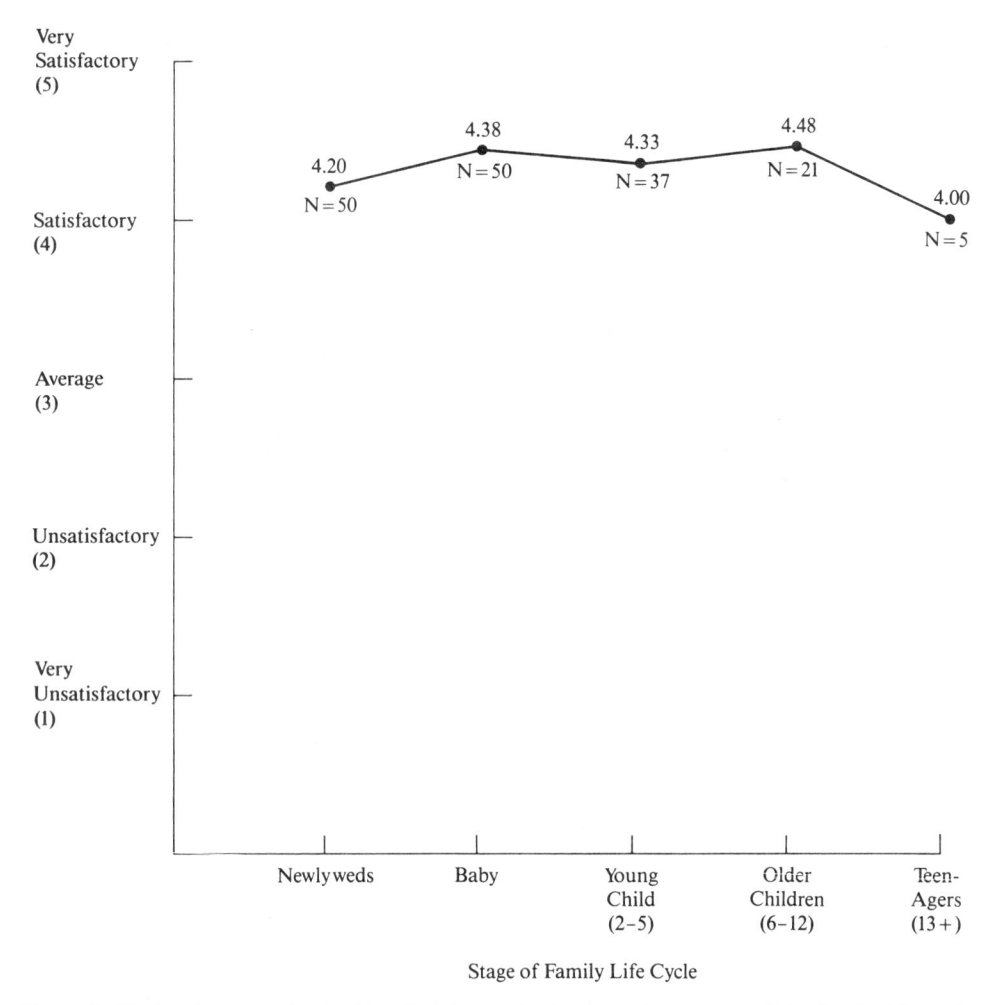

Figure 1. Mothers' average level of family life satisfaction in various stages of the family life cycle.

inevitable decline in family life satisfaction with the advent of children. The study has produced meager evidence for this contention; the direction of causality is far from being determined. There is much work to be done to clarify these issues.

And this, finally, leads to the question: What social support systems would these androgynous parents find helpful in maintaining and strengthening their family styles? In interviews and questionnaires administered over four years, parents have reported countless times of better family relationships (between parents, and among parents and children) and greater personal happiness because of adopting this style of parenting.

What, then, can be done to nurture such a family style? One father reported, "I can think of nothing that our society does to help families who want to try something new." Our culture he maintained, is oriented to the family with mother at home and father at work.

In this survey of androgynous parents, we asked them to list the difficulties they had in structuring their lives in this way. These difficulties are outlined in Table 1. If one arbitrarily defines a major difficulty as one in which at least a third of the parents have cited it, then difficulties in the social/political/economic realm greatly dominate difficulties in the inter-personal/familial realm.

Jobs, in short, are the biggest problem. They are inflexible in terms of the time the work is to be done and the amount of time one is to work. Forty-four percent of the couples have troubles matching

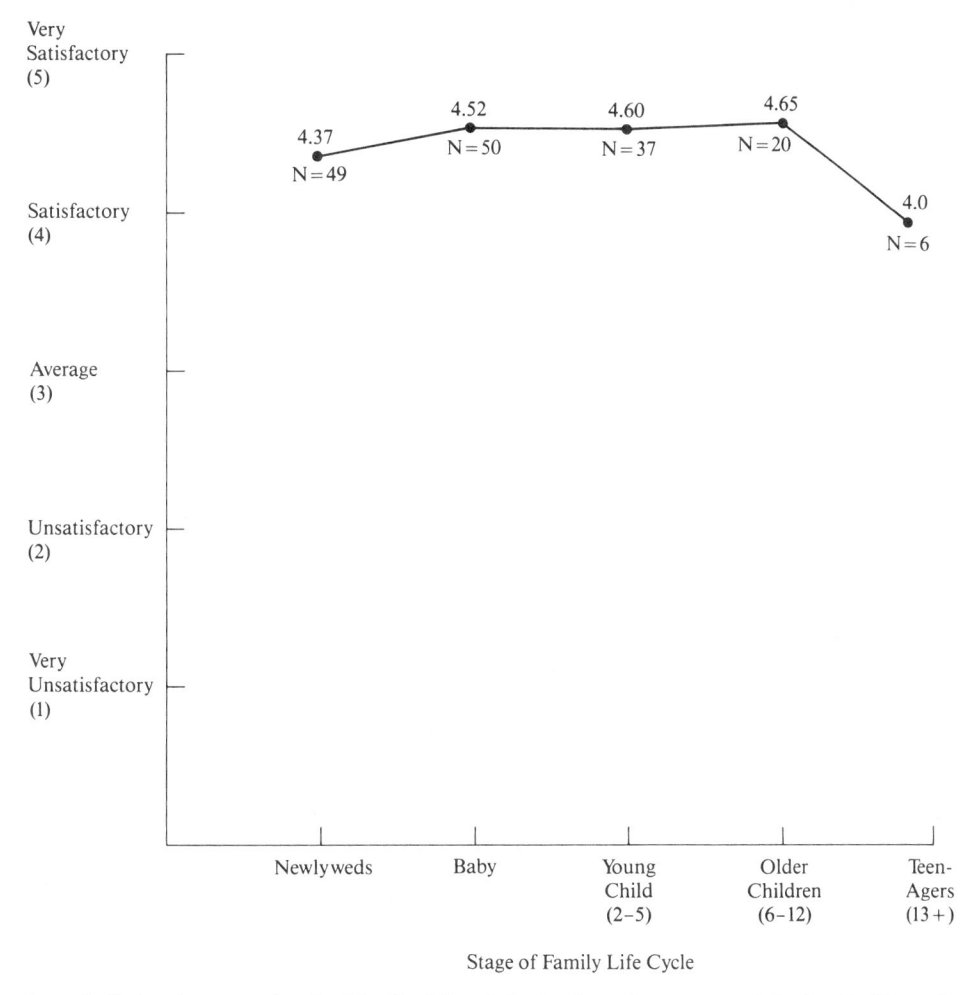

Figure 2. Fathers' average level of family life satisfaction in various stages of the family life cycle.

the husband's work schedule with the wife's; 44% say jobs are inflexible in terms of the number of hours of work per week, also. Finding adequate day care for the children is also a major difficulty. The only interpersonal/familial difficulty cited by more than a third of the couples is the spouses' differing views on housekeeping standards. Only 6% of the wives think husbands lack adequate parenting skills, yet 38% of the wives' views differ with those of their husbands on housekeeping standards. Housework may be one of the last major functions in our society to integrate. These percentages may not seem particularly high; but, we must remember that the majority of the androgynous parents describe their jobs as being relatively flexible compared to the average job. They have relatively good jobs in these terms, and, yet, their major problems are still job inflexibility. In an earlier study including blue-collar and lower-middle-class parents (DeFrain, 1975), it was concluded that this class of parents is somewhat interested in further integrating sex roles. In fact, they already are really not as sex-role stereotyped as it is often assumed of this class of people. Sixty-eight percent of the androgynous parents in this earlier sample described their jobs as being relatively flexible, while only 12% of the blue-collar and lower-middle-class parents described their jobs as flexible. It would appear that jobs have a tremendous influence on family lifestyles and behaviors—that they often lead families into directions they would not choose.

What, then, can society do to accommodate

TABLE 1
DIFFICULTIES CONFRONTING THE COUPLE SHARING CHILDREARING TASKS

	% of Mothers Citing This Difficulty	% of Fathers Citing This Difficulty
Job scheduling problems—matching husband's work schedule with wife's	44%	38%
Job inflexibility in terms of number of work hours per week	44%	28%
Spouses' differing views on housekeeping standards	38%	32%
Day care for children	32%	26%
Job inflexibility in terms of when work is to be done	30%	26%
Have no difficulties	22%	26%
Lack of support from other segments of society besides relatives	16%	8%
Lack of peer support	14%	4%
Lack of support from relatives	14%	6%
Spouses' differing views on childcare standards	14%	12%
Husband thought by wife to be lacking in housekeeping skills	12%	4%
Husband thought by wife to be lacking in parenting skills	6%	4%
Problems with the public schools	4%	4%

couples who wish to share childrearing? A look at the parents' answers, tabulated in Table 2, provides useful guidelines for professionals. Almost two-thirds of the androgynous parents endorse more flexible work schedules. Flexi-time proposals sprouting up around the country fit their needs beautifully. Besides benefits for those who wish to integrate family roles, flexi-time has also been used as a way to alleviate traffic problems in high-density areas, lower pollution levels, and make shopping and business-related activities easier for full-time workers who usually get off work when everything is closed up. In a flexi-time system, some workers would come early and go home early; others would come late and go home late. Flexi-time began in Europe in the late 1960's and according to Asher (1975) "has spread like an epidemic." In West Germany, 50% of the white collar work force benefits from it; in France, 30% of the total work force is on flexi-time and in Switzerland, 40% of the total work force. Recent estimates in the U.S. are that only 2% have flexi-time opportunities.

Better paying part-time jobs is a need of nearly two-thirds of the androgynous parents in this study. Currently, we have instituted system-wide discrimination against part-time workers by refusing them fringe benefits and giving them low pay. As far as I am concerned this is *de facto* sex discrimination, for women take the bulk of the part-time work. Sooner or later, a wise judge will find the reasoning underlying this discriminatory practice fallacious and unconstitutional. When this happens, it will be possible for both parents to work half-time and survive financially. As it stands today though, one half-time income plus one half-time income does not equal one full-time income.

Related to the demand for better paying part-time jobs is the need for more job-sharing opportunities. Two people would, thus, share the work, salary, and fringe benefits of one full-time job. I have talked with literally hundreds of workers in the past five years on whether half-time workers are productive in relation to their full-time counterparts. Only a handful believed full-timers are more efficient in their work, and only a handful believed most jobs could not be split down the middle if employers and employees alike were really willing to think creatively. Part-timers are eager to support this view.

Many androgynous parents also endorse day care programs for children in or near the buildings in which the parents work. Coffee breaks and lunches then could be spent with the children, and parents could be spared transportation problems.

TABLE 2
CHANGES SOCIETY CAN MAKE TO ACCOMMODATE COUPLES WHO SHARE OR WISH TO SHARE CHILDREARING AND OTHER FAMILY RESPONSIBILITIES

Change	% of Mothers Endorsing This Change	% of Fathers Endorsing This Change
More flexible work schedules—the employee having more control over work hours	66%	64%
Better-paying part-time jobs	64%	58%
Day care programs in locations nearby or in building where parents work	54%	52%
More part-time jobs	52%	36%
A four-day work week	50%	64%
Job sharing—two people sharing one full-time job	46%	28%
Increased fringe benefits for part-time workers	38%	42%
Public school financing of day care programs	28%	36%

Also, more than half want a four-day work week, and public financing of day care.

Especially interesting to professionals in family studies is the parents' perceptions of what we can do to help institute these changes. A third of the parents believe research could be useful (32% of the men and 34% of the women). Almost half believe articles and books in this area could contribute (40% of the men and 50% of the women). More than half believe counseling could be helpful to those parents who share childrearing and other family role responsibilities (46% of the men and 60% of the women). And, more than a third support social and economic changes in the political arena (44% of the men and 36% of the women).

These are concerned, highly-educated parents speaking. They have molded what they believe to be highly satisfactory family lives for themselves and their children. Perhaps their proposals warrant greater attention among those who are making a genuine effort to develop a society that is truly cognizant and committed to the needs of families.

NOTES

[1] DeFrain, J. D. "New meaning for parenthood" (Paper read at the Sixth Banff International Conference on Behavior Modification, Banff, Alberta, Canada, 1974).

[2] DeFrain, J. D. "Socioeconomic and personal influences on androgynous and conventional parenting modes" (Paper read at the Third Biennial Meeting of the International Society for the Study of Behavioural Development, University of Surrey, Guildford, England, 1975).

REFERENCE

Asher, J. 1975. Flexi-time, four-day weeks thrive despite recession. *APA Monitor* 6 (4):5.

36

SINGLE-PARENT FAMILIES

Blaine R. Porter

INTRODUCTION

Incidence of Single-Parent Families

The fastest growing family form in America today is the single-parent family. More than 11.7 million U.S. children under the age of 18 now live with only one parent. Another 2.5 million are not living with either parent. Approximately 95% of these children living in one-parent family situations are in female-headed families. Heads of households who were female and single (widowed, divorced, unwed mothers) increased 33.8% in the six-year period between 1970 and 1976. The rapidity of this growth and the number of children involved are both demonstrated in the following statistics:

1. In 1974, one child in eight under age 18 was living in a one-parent family.
2. In 1975, one child in seven under age 18 was living in a one-parent family.
3. In 1976, one child in six under age 18 was living in a one-parent family.

These data reveal only the incidence of this phenomenon. They do not reveal the trauma and hardships that many single parents and their children face daily. . . .

Reprinted from *Building Family Strengths: Blueprints for Action*, edited by Nick Stinnett, by permission of University of Nebraska Press. Copyright © 1979 by the University of Nebraska Press.

CHALLENGES OF THE SINGLE PARENT

Personal Adjustments

One is confronted with many adjustments upon returning to the single state after having been married. Although there are many differences between graduating from high school or college, or taking a new job, and that of being widowed, divorced or separated under other circumstances, there are some similarities. Both situations involve leaving behind certain familiarities and securities. Both are shaded with fears of the new and the unknown. Both provide opportunities for exploring, growing, becoming something new and even better.

Most formerly married persons whom I have interviewed responded that they feel like second-class citizens. This is especially true of those who have been divorced or who are unwed parents. They claim that society has put them in a classification which denies them the status and sense of belonging they would like to enjoy.

If children are involved in a family that has been broken, then the remaining spouse (in the case of bereavement) and the spouse granted custody of children (in the case of divorce) have greater responsibility. At the same time, for those who are divorced, approximately one-half of single parents (those who don't have custody) are usually deprived of a close association with their children. The task of parenting in any one of these situations will be dealt with later in this paper, but the point here is that these are required of the individual, personal adjustments that are usually new and frequently difficult.

Not only is one deprived of the more acceptable status in our society, but the companionship that was once there is missing. Regardless of the unpleasant times that may have been involved where couples have separated by choice, there are still memories of times spent together that were good and that are missed. It is sometimes difficult to maintain a healthy level of self-esteem as one reflects upon being abandoned or having failed or having been faced with a situation which did not seem to provide any attractive alternatives. In such a situation, one often faces a future of uncertainty and asks, "What is ahead for me now?" Unfortunately, the social supports that exist for intact families are frequently missing for the single parent.

Another of the personal adjustments required of the individual returning to the single state is dealing with the hurt of death or divorce. Others may try to sympathize and to offer assistance, but in most cases one has to cope with this challenge in his/her own unique way.

As one proceeds to try to carry on a meaningful and full and reasonably normal life after having returned to the single state, he/she often is faced with the reality that there are new restrictions placed on relationships with other adults. For example, a divorced woman, or even a widow, often discovers that her former female married friends view her as a threat now and are very jealous about her relationship with their husbands. Married men, in turn, are often afraid or uncomfortable in relationships with a divorced or widowed woman because of how their wives may react. The relationship becomes strained on both sides. Some men are on the make believing that single or divorced women are an easy mark, and the newly divorced or widowed woman may discover that she is faced with overtures and approaches that she has not had to deal with for quite some time—if ever. Probably one of the greatest personal adjustments in this regard is learning how to put up with being misunderstood, for both actions and words are frequently misinterpreted. A net result is that often, if not usually, the single parent must establish ties with new social groups and establish new personal relationships. Previous relationships usually change, even though one may not wish it so.

There is a danger of focusing too much on one's miseries and problems and, therefore, not engaging in activities that help one seek and find healthy solutions. We often share our feelings with others and occasionally derive strength from meeting with others who have common situations. However, it is important to avoid reinforcing self-defeating behaviors. Such persons often talk too much—especially about their problems. It is like talking about physical illness in a hospital—it is common and natural, but not healthy or productive.

Single parents often feel that others are watching more closely and that they are quick to criticize, often in a condescending way. For example, one may be confronted with a statement such as: "It is hard for you isn't it, Jane, when your son behaves that way, since you don't have a husband to help you out?" Her son's behavior may not be materially different from that of his age mates coming from intact families, but single parents are seldom given the benefit of the doubt.

One of the challenges facing new single parents is having feelings of discouragement and being overwhelmed with responsibilities and not having one with whom to share them. Sometimes the single parent may feel that he/she is making headway and then have an event, statement, picture, song or some other stimuli bring back memories and feelings that one thought had been processed and handled.

Coping effectively or ineffectively with personal adjustments will determine the single parent's potential success in dealing effectively with the parenting responsibilities which he/she will face. It is important to make reasonable progress in resolving personal problems, otherwise it is difficult if not impossible to be an effective parent. The task of parenting is a challenging one, even under the *best* of circumstances.

Parenting Responsibilities

The basic principles of effective parenting are the same whether or not the marriage dyad is complete or broken. I will not spend time discussing those here, but it is important to remember that a father and a mother may decide they will no longer remain together as husband and wife, but they must realize that they will be parents forever.

There are certain features or characteristics that seem to be unique to one-parent families. Let me now share with you some observations and experiences that are referred to most frequently by single parents. These are not inclusive but merely illustrative.

1. Many single parents identify a feeling of being incomplete. A vital feature seems to be missing. They are faced with the dilemma of whether to try to fulfill two roles or one. Of course, it is not realistic for one person to fill the roles of father *and* mother. Professionals need to help single parents not feel guilt about not being able to be all things to their children. Singleness may necessitate modification of tasks (cooking, shopping, breadwinning, etc.) but the role should be kept clear in the eyes of the parent and children.
2. Children in single-parent families are most often deprived of a consistent, present sex-role model for the absent parent. It is difficult to provide this role model on a substitute basis with regularity and consistency. Since 95% of children in single-parent families are living with a female head of household, it means that several million children are primarily receiving their male model as it is interpreted through the eyes of their mother. In some cases this, no doubt, has serious consequences.
3. Single parents are faced with the challenge of explaining death/divorce to children. This may be especially difficult for some, especially if the parent's feelings are still unclear or if he/she is not sure how much information to give.
4. There is often a temptation to place too much responsibility too early on children. A mother, for example, may say to a 10- or 12-year-old boy: "You have to be the man of the family now." That is too heavy a burden for a 10- or 12-year-old boy.
5. Parents also face the challenge of helping children cope with the stigma of being different—especially the divorced. Children, like their parents, sometimes feel like second-class citizens at school, church, or in the community. I recall the pathetic situation of one youngster who was invited to attend a party. As he cautiously rounded the corner into a room where considerable activity was taking place, he shyly inquired, "Is this the party for divorced kids?" But we need to remember that some children are better off being with one parent who is relatively happy and well adjusted than being in a situation where parents are constantly bickering, arguing and fighting. Some children seem to be rather indifferent and cope effectively, and others experience serious emotional trauma and sometimes require psychiatric treatment.
6. Unfortunately, battles often continue after a divorce. Some divorced couples fall into the trap of confronting each other in marriage and end up in a win/lose or lose/lose battle long after the divorce. They do not realize that the idea of "winning" a conflict is an illusion and that one person's victory inevitably turns into a loss for both of them, and even more seriously, if children are involved, it turns into a loss for the children also. In such a situation, everybody loses. . . .

SUMMARY

A parent without a partner is faced with:

1. The usual challenge of life and its responsibilities.
2. The task of adjusting to a usually hurting and/or traumatic experience of death or divorce or separation.
3. The responsibilities of parenthood—alone—which are often complicated by:
   a. Financial problems
   b. Children suffering from low self-esteem
   c. Children suffering from guilt, thinking that they are the cause of the divorce
   d. An uncooperative and difficult ex-spouse
   e. The temptation to use children as "sympathetic ears"
   f. The temptation to use children as "spies"
   g. The struggle of two parents trying to "win" children's approval, applying tactics that are known in legal circles as "the lollipop game"

    h. Children playing one parent against the other
4. Living in a society that provides very few social supports for his/her particular situation.
5. The overcoming of added burdens often imposed by "friends," relatives and social institutions
6. The difficulty of trying to finance two households instead of one (sometimes)
7. Uncertainty about the future
8. The dilemma of remarriage (sometimes)
9. The challenge of learning to know oneself, gaining control over one's life and future. This future is more bright with greater opportunities for women than ever before.
10. Not settling for less than one can achieve. We all have choices to make in given situations. I firmly believe that some individuals do not perform at as high a level as they are capable because they are unwilling to try the experience of pain, to take risks. We have discovered that many individuals have survived experiences they thought they could not endure: illness; accident; being lost in the mountains, desert, or wilderness; plane crashes; humiliating and torturing experiences in concentration camps. Usually these experiences were endured and individuals survived because they had no other choice or easy escape. Many times when we do have a choice we take what appears to be the easiest, least painful way rather than carefully analyzing the course of action that would be best in terms of long-range consequences.

We desperately need more research. The picture, circumstance, attitude and opportunities for single parents are changing rapidly. Very little empirical research is available about that and most of what we have deals with the affective dimensions of single-parent families. In the absence of the research we need I have shared with you my observations and experiences.

It is possible that the single parent feels as thousands of others have felt, namely, that he/she has been picked on, that fate has dealt him/her an unfair blow, that he/she does not deserve to be in the situation in which he/she finds himself/herself. Most of us have had things come our way that we did not deserve—both good and bad. The important considerations are not why we are here or how we got in this situation, but where we go from here.

May I share with you an account of a friend of mine as he recuperated in a New York room following surgery for cancer in his throat. He entered with fear; faced pain, risk, and an uncertain future. Loss was experienced; suffering occurred. He relived much of his past. He survived. He conquered. He achieved peace. He closed with the following:

> Some days have passed. Last night I had a full night of sleep without any medication. How glorious! The pigeons are cooing more pleasantly this morning. The Central Park birds are singing more lustily. Pain, the ugly, sadistic companion of the past three weeks, has moved out to give place first to the mild-mannered gentleman Distress, which in turn has now given way to the friendly person Comfort. And with Comfort comes Peace, and with Peace a return of memory of a certain Time, the Time with which I was formerly acquainted. The Time which has now rubbed its eyes, taken a deep breath, saluted, clicked its heels, and comes marching its way back into the normal sixty-second minutes and sixty-minute hours and twenty-four-hour days.
> TIME has been resurrected, peace restored, and life is good again![1]

I believe that a parent without a partner, through self-evaluation, goal-setting, determination, and discovering and building upon the strengths which he/she possesses, can have Peace restored and reach greater heights of achievement than have yet been experienced. Unfortunately, hundreds of thousands of single parents do not have the personal skills and resources to accomplish these alone. It is the task of professional persons to play a major role in providing help, leadership and influencing public policy so that more single-parent families can be effective, fully functioning ones.

Hasten the day!

NOTES

[1] Spencer W. Kimball, *One silent, sleepless night.* Salt Lake City, Utah: Deseret Book Company.

37

TO DREAM THE IMPOSSIBLE DREAM: AN AGENDA FOR DISCUSSION WITH STEPPARENTS

Sharon K. Turnbull and James M. Turnbull

Only recently have those who counsel families become aware of their need to become more sensitive to the emotional complexities faced by the stepparent. By and large, stepparents are an invisible group who are often reluctant to seek help or even to discuss the unique adjustment problems they face. There has been a recent increase in interest in the problems of stepfamilies, and a number of popular books such as the one by Noble and Noble (1977), are now available to assist the stepparent.

In a perceptive paper published in 1972, Shulman identified two important characteristics which distinguish stepfamilies from "ordinary" families: (1) fantasies and hopes play a much larger role in the family member's interactions; and (2) the stepparent expects more gratitude and acknowledgment from the stepchild. Research on stepparenting remains scanty. Following a survey of over 2,000 stepfamilies, Bowerman and Irish (1962) concluded that stepchildren experienced "greater levels of uncertainty of feelings and insecurity of position" and noted a "tendency of the parent to see the child as the source of all tension." Messinger (1976) reported the frequent presence of "guilt feelings about the lack of positive emotions or, frequently, negative feelings toward their partner's children. Similarly, the children who were required to respond to the parent's new mate as though they were the child's 'real' parents often reacted with feelings of guilt, hostility, rebellion, or withdrawal" (p. 196).

According to Visher and Visher (1979):

Stepparents' expectations of themselves are usually unrealistically high; since they may not be able to live up to these expectations, they often consider that there is something wrong with their feelings and with themselves. . . . So there is anger, guilt, and low self-esteem—and a need to conceal these feelings. (pp. 11–12)

Counselors and therapists, however, often express dismay at the seemingly trivial complaints of the stepparent who is painfully striving to achieve a "real" family. On the surface, their problems sound identical to those that arise, without undue trauma, in the daily lives of all parents. But the issues, however mundane, are imbued with extra meanings for the stepparent who is striving for perfection.

There is a need for more understanding of the problems faced by these families, and perhaps more importantly, for the provision of support and encouragement for the stepparent as he or she faces the difficult task of developing a role for which few

---

Sharon K. Turnbull and James M. Turnbull, "To Dream the Impossible Dream: An Agenda for Discussion with Stepparents," *Family Relations*, Vol. 32 (1983), pp. 227–30. Copyrighted © 1983 by the National Council on Family Relations, 1219 University Avenue Southeast, Minneapolis, Minnesota 55414. Reprinted by permission.

realistic guidelines exist. Regardless of the therapeutic approach which is used, the most critical element for success in counseling the stepparent is the development of a relationship of warmth and understanding. The "Ten Commandments of Stepparenting" which follow were developed to facilitate a familiarity with, and appreciation for, some of the conflicts and stresses commonly faced by the stepparent. They have been used by the authors as a stimulus for discussion with stepparents in individual, family, and group therapy situations. While they obviously do not represent a comprehensive catalogue of the problems faced by the stepparenting family, they provide a useful starting point for discussion.

THE TEN COMMANDMENTS OF STEPPARENTING

The natural family presents hazards enough to peaceful coexistence. Add one or two stepparents, and perhaps a set of ready-made brothers and sisters, and a return to the law of the jungle is virtually ensured. Some guidelines for survival include the following advice for stepparents:

1. *Provide neutral territory.* Just as the Romans had gods that lived in the house and protected it, stepchildren have a strong sense of ownership. The questions: "Whose house is it? Whose spirit presides here?" are central issues. Even the very young child recognizes that the prior occupation of a territory confers a certain power. When two sets of children are brought together one regards itself as the "main family" and the other as a subfamily . . . and the determining factor is whose house gets to be the family home. One school of thought suggests that when a couple remarries they should move to a new house, even if it means selling the family heirlooms. If it is impossible to finance a move to neutral territory, it is important to provide a special, inviolate place which belongs to each child individually.

2. *Don't try to fit a preconceived role.* When dealing with children the best course is to be straight right from the start. Each parent is an individual with all his or her faults, peculiarities and emotions, and the children are just going to have to get used to this parent. Certainly a stepparent should make every effort to be kind, intelligent and a good sport, but that does not mean being saccharine sweet. Children have excellent radar for detecting phoniness, and are quick to lose respect for any adult who will let them walk all over him or her.

3. *Set limits and enforce them.* One of the most difficult areas for a natural parent and stepparent living together is to decide on disciplinary measures. The natural parent has a tendency to feel that the stepparent is being unreasonable in demands that the children behave in a certain way. If the parents fight between themselves about discipline, the children will quickly force a wedge between them. It is important that the parents themselves work out the rules in advance and support one another when the rules need to be enforced. The rules need to be relatively minimal in the beginning but should attend to issues such as meal time, bed time, what to do about fighting, and getting ready for school in the morning.

4. *Allow an outlet for feelings by the children for natural parent.* It is often difficult for the stepparent to accept that his or her stepchildren will maintain a natural affection for their natural parent who is no longer living in the household. The stepparent may take this as a personal rejection. Children need to be allowed to express feelings about the natural parent who is absent. This needs to be supported in a neutral way so that the children do not feel disloyal.

5. *Expect ambivalence.* Stepparents are often alarmed when children appear on successive days or successive hours to show both emotions of strong love and strong hate toward them. Ambivalence is normal in all human relationships, but no where is it more accentuated than in the feelings of the stepchild towards their stepparent.

6. *Avoid mealtime misery.* For many stepfamilies meals are an excruciating experience. This, after all, is the time when the dreams of bliss-

ful family life confront reality. Most individuals cling to a belief in the power of food to make people happy. There is enormous satisfaction in having one's food enjoyed, and it is not coincidence that in fairy tales the food that the wicked stepmother offered was often poisoned. Since it is the stepmother who is most often charged with serving the emotionally laden daily bread, she often leaves the table feeling thoroughly rejected. If the status quo becomes totally unbearable, it is forgivable to decide that peace is more important and turn a blind eye, at least temporarily, to nutrition. Some suggested strategies include: daily vitamins, ridding the house of all "junk" foods, let the children fix their own meals, eat out a lot, and/or let father do some of the cooking so he can share in the rejection. Stepfathers tend to be less concerned about food refusal but more concerned about table manners. Obviously, constant fighting at the dinner table is not conducive to good digestion; but children can master the prerequisite etiquette with reasonable speed when both parents reinforce the message that table manners are expected.

7. *Don't expect instant love.* One of the problems facing a new stepparent is the expectation of feeling love for the child and for that love to be returned. It takes time for emotional bonds to be forged, and sometimes this never occurs. All stepparents must acknowledge that eventuality.

Alternately, nonacceptance by the children is often a major problem. Some children make it very clear that "You are not *my* mother or father!" This can be very painful or anger provoking, especially if it is the stepparent who is doing the cooking and laundry, and giving allowances. Most children under three have little problem adapting with relative ease. Children over five have more difficulty. Some children are initially devoted in their excitement at having a "new" mother or father, but later find that the words "I hate you" are potent weapons. This discovery frequently coincides with puberty. A thick skin certainly helps!

8. *Don't take all the responsibility. The child has some too.* Ultimately, how well the stepparent gets along with the stepchild depends in part upon the kind of child he or she is. Children, like adults, come in all types and sizes. Some are simply more lovable than others. If the new stepmother has envisioned herself as the mother of a cuddly little tot and finds herself with a sullen, vindictive twelve year old who regards her with considerable suspicion, she is likely to experience considerable disappointment. Like it or not, the stepparent has to take what he or she gets. But that doesn't mean taking all the guilt for a less than perfect relationship.

9. *Be patient.* The words to remember here are "things take time." The first few months and often years have many difficult periods. The support and encouragement of other parents who have had other similar experiences can be an invaluable aid.

10. *Maintain the primacy of the marital relationship.* It has been our experience that most stepparenting relationships have resulted from divorce by one or both members of the couple. There is a certain amount of guilt left over about the breakup of the previous relationship which may spill over into the present relationship and create difficulties when there are arguments. The couple needs to remember that their relationship is primary in the family. The children need to be shown that the parents get along together, can settle disputes, and most of all will not be divided by the children. While parenting may be a central element in the couple's relationship, both partners need to commit time and energy to the development of a strong couple relationship; this bond includes, but is greater than, their parental responsibilities.

REFERENCES

Bowerman, C., and D. Irish. 1962. Some relationships of stepchildren to their parents. *Marriage and Family Living* 24:113–31.

Messinger, L. 1976. Remarriage between divorced people with children from previous marriages: A proposal for preparation for remarriage. *Journal of Marriage and Family Counseling* 2:193–200.

Noble, J., and W. Noble. 1977. *How to live with other peoples' children*. New York: Hawthorne Books.

Schulman, G. 1972. Myths that intrude on the adaptation of the stepfamily. *Social Casework* 49:131–39.

Visher, E., and J. Visher. 1979. *Stepfamilies: A guide to working with stepparents and stepchildren*. New York: Brunner/Mazel.

XIV

THE POST-PARENTAL PERIOD

38

THE EMPTY NEST SYNDROME

Polly Greenberg

"When Susan, the second of my two children, left for college, I cried for two hours. For weeks, on and off, I felt blue, down in the dumps, discouraged," my friend Rebecca remembers.

"It's weird you would feel that way," I said, "You, of all people, you were always superwoman."

"Well, I suppose that's just the point," she said. "Suddenly there was no Little League, varsity team, car pool, job, sick child, dinner date, daughter's date, housework, etc. to mix, match, shuffle and deal with; life lost its challenge. When everything was easy, and there wasn't anything to juggle, I lost my sense of power."

"Permanently?"

"For about six weeks, pretty much of the time. Especially if I was doing anything that reminded me of family life, that is, until I got used to it, until I filled my time back up again to the comfort level with busy-ness, until juggling through the day was a laughing struggle again." Rebecca makes fun of herself, but she's right. Each person needs to feel personally powerful in one arena or another.

Furthermore, people are creatures of habit.

Even as we complain about the ruts we're in, we plop our feet in the comforting little tracks we made yesterday, and tend to our cozy little daily trivia.

In terms of the major and minor relationships we've spun around us, this is yet more true. The longer we live, the more we are used to the external and emotional routines and interactions that have invisibly evolved and ensnared us.

The sudden changing of our ruts and abrupt cessation of the emotional transactions that tie us in intricate ways to one another (not to mention the loss of a best friend from the household) is certainly a shock to the unsuspecting psyche.

"It's nurture loss. First my husband, then my children. Who will I nurture now?" Rebecca asks.

"Take in temporary foster kids. Call the social services under your city or county listings, every county has hordes of kids needing temporary nurturing. Volunteer in a hospital or a school one day a week. Everybody needs to nurture, and plenty of people are desperate for nurturing," Mary responds vehemently. "Women should learn to live alone and love it, just like men should learn they don't have to be "successful" on the treadmill to love themselves and their lives."

Everyone who's well-adjusted unconsciously shapes and fills the daily schedule so it feels just right—not too boring or lonely, not too rushed and

---

Polly Greenberg, "The Empty Nest Syndrome," *The Single Parent*, July/August 1983, pp. 17–23. Copyright © Polly Greenberg. Reprinted by permission of the author.

overwhelming, not too crowded with intimates, not too devoid of them. Some succeed better than others in achieving this balance. Rebecca's right: A stunning change in who's at home will leave you gasping, or, rather, gapping, until the waters of life have slowly flowed in.

Everyone has a *style* that's comfortable. Rebecca has always worked. But she's never had an interesting career. She takes pride in her abilities in home administration. She isn't only a juggler, she's a wizard. She likes the tension, excitement and feeling of achievement she gets from juggling, struggling and winning. Whatever our preferred style and comfort level, a huge change in it hurts.

A loss of power may be more of a problem for mothers losing their children to adulthood now than it will be for mothers in the future. The new generation of mothers has not been trained to consider mothering its main job. These women have more eggs in their baskets. When their children are grown, they may feel less "left" than some mothers in our generation. They'll have much more in which they're already involved to turn to. Doubtless, "empty nest syndrome" is more a situation in which society's values and pressures have pushed us than a fundamental psychological problem nestled in the heart of all women.

Even if your method of creating a comfortable climate for yourself to live in seems strange to others, it's painful to suddenly be without it. Maria's friends laughed at her for missing a son who trod all over her. Two months after her 19 year old had headed for the big snows of Alaska, Maria wept, "But I like being self-sacrificing."

Don't we each have a right to a few innocent psychological quirks? "Mine is feeling guilty," Sunny confides. "When I could no longer feel guilty about my son's problems, my mother's problems, my former husband's problems, I had to focus on *my* problem—what did I want out of the rest of my life. Oh, it was horrid."

My friend Tess sums up what research long ago proved: "Any major change in your life is a major stress. Many people react to stress by being depressed. For me, mothering was my main job. Duke paid alimony and child support, so I only worked part time at little jobs. When I had no nightly meals to fix and kids' friends' phone calls to answer, I felt like a person who's just lost his job. On top of that, I felt like I'd gotten divorced again, I'd lost another loved one. It was very stressful. I was very depressed—for about a week."

When the children leave home, a chapter of a woman's life has ended. It may have been a chapter much longer than the 18 years it usually takes one young person to grow up and grow out. When the last child leaves home, a woman must face the future. She must plan what to do next. This forces her to take a personal inventory. Many questions about priorities and values must be examined. What are my strengths? Weaknesses? My likes and dislikes? How can I make adjustments in my life creatively to fit these facts into a custom-made pattern for myself to grow in?

The first phase of adulthood is leaving the family. Leaving one's parents at around 18 and establishing a new home base is a time for discovery, a time to stretch one's newly feathered-for-flight independence, to test one's wings in terms of career success and to develop one's talents. Until recently, all this has been quite curtailed for women compared to men. Most women clipped their own wings for what they thought was expected—marriage and motherhood. As many women are well aware, there is substantial evidence that the majority of women leave a dependent status with their parents for a dependent status with their husbands. This may appeal to the woman who wants to duck responsibility for her own life, but as modern times move us along, this way of life appears attractive to fewer and fewer women.

Our society gives many women a message. We are encouraged to put all of our eggs in one basket, in one nest, that is. We put a great deal of energy into encouraging and tending to the lives of our children (and, to a certain extent, into doing the same for the lives of our husbands). We are then left trying to balance all our hard-earned skills of submerging ourselves for the family with having no one at home to worry about.

"No wonder Rebecca felt bad when her daughter Susan left for school. During the same season, her husband split for South America with a younger woman," Sunny snorts. For a rising number of women, the empty nest syndrome is brought on by husbands who, feeling that they have discharged their duty to mate by bringing home the "seeds and worms" for several decades, soar off to bluer skies.

Children growing up and leaving home, a temporary but agonizing disruption of a marriage, or the divorce or death of a mate (especially if it occurs when a woman is 35 to 50) causes a shift in thinking from "time filled since birth," to thinking of "time left till death," which does not have to be morbid. To some, new opportunities are daily unveiling themselves. Exciting decisions must be made, projects and relationships started or furthered. Feelings of freedom and freshness prevail. "Section II of my life is launching," Sarah says. "I'm experiencing *now* what my *men* friends say they experienced right after college."

To others, all is over, all is lost. The only things ahead are old age and meeting the maker. "I never wanted anything beyond marriage and the family, and I still don't," Cindy sighs. "I'm not prepared for anything else. I don't have the energy to go out into the job world."

Confusion typifies a third group of women. Is this liberation I feel or loneliness? It makes some women content to see their young move up and out. To others, definitely the minority, this natural happening becomes a crisis. Probably a number of factors are involved.

If you feel you've been a good mother, your feeling now is of a job well done. You've experienced the warm, elating feelings of competence, which breed confidence. You may be looking for the next thing to throw yourself into with equal competence. Most likely, you're approaching the whole new era with contentment and eager anticipation. Better yet, a project you're already involved in and itching to give more time to is now going to get more of your energies. A job? A different job? You're going back to school to get a degree? A higher degree? Is it the love-of-your-life volunteer work that you're scarcely restraining yourself from flying away with? Music, painting or dance lessons? A new man?

"Know what I'm doing?" Sunny asks rhetorically, "I'm selectively shedding all the leftovers that aren't rewarding any more. Then I'll have room to do new things." When the youngest child leaves home, he takes the mother's role with him. Thus a role change is required.

"I'm afraid I don't know what you're talking about," Mary says. "*I'm* suffering the *opposite* of a post-childrearing depression. I loved being a mother. For 25 years, I did. But my children are out of college, and I'm pining to travel, frantic to get my master's in management, do a ton of stuff, and yet these grown "kids" are always coming or going with more and more friends and possessions and revolving life partners and dogs, needing constant welcome home and goodbye dinners. I love it that they *want* to come home so much, but frankly, I feel most of it is a nonstop series of interruptions in my life. They left. The waters of my life have flowed in, there is no hole. When *they* show up, they displace the water I'm contentedly swimming in. I feel guilty, but I *resent* these intrusions. I want time for the *next* part of my life now, before I'm an old woman."

With four of my five in their 20s, I relate to what she says. Just about all of my friends and acquaintances say the same thing, but lovingly, with pride in their children, and delight that friendship with these adult babies is deep and forever.

A woman who doesn't feel she's been a good mother may be left dragging along a lot of unfinished business, an unfulfilled self-image as a proper mother, so she may lack confidence about tackling the next task. What she views as "nurturing deficits," may flood her with guilt. This is likely to be all the more true if there have been serious interpersonal disputes between her and her severing children.

Joan experiences this. "But we went to family therapy, and you'd be amazed how forgiving grown kids can be! The therapist emphasized, 'What's a good mother, anyway? Who can define one? How do you know you haven't been a good mother?' You know, I fought the divorce for 14 years, pitted the kids against their dad, was always tired and distracted and didn't do a good job with my own family once I remarried. The therapist talked about the good points of myself and each 'child,' and encouraged us to move on, become good friends as grownups in the here and now."

Professional help, available on a short-term

basis, will very likely and quickly free you of "deficiency mother" empty nest syndrome.

"Part of what it is," muses Joan, "is keeping your 'self' hanging in mid-air till you land a husband, and then letting it gel in his image. If you divorce, that 'self' is blown apart, and you have to lick your wounds while growing a *new* one. When the last kid leaves home, lo, it happens again."

How do you feel about yourself in other ways than mothering? If you've taken risks and landed on your feet before, you're in a better position when the children grow up than if you've fallen on your face in serious ways; or worse, if you've never taken big risks at all. You may have to free yourself of a dependency complex. If it hasn't occured earlier, one of the shocks that strikes women in mid-life, perhaps brought on by the departure of the last child, is that the myth of the Cinderella self who is waiting to be rescued by a knight on a white horse, must yield to this observation: one must save oneself.

It's September. Sandy phones at 2 a.m. Greg left for college during the day. Sandy has been drinking. "Know what I just realized?" she sobs. "I'm never going to be the woman of my girlhood dreams."

"Probably not," I mumble sleepily. "Who is? Maybe you can be some other terrific person. Not now, though, become one in the morning." Facing the realistic limits of your potential, or the limited time you are allowed on earth to do anything about it is part of the mid-years pain, too. But the grown children don't do it to us, nature does.

It's not just that the children are leaving, it's that an era is ending. It's that most of us are at 40 or more when our children leave home, which is also when (1) more marriages break up; (2) we may be mourning the fact that our childbearing years are over; or (3) going through the heavy decision of whether or not to have one more child. (4) Possibly we're dealing with some man who's driving us crazy with his "male menopause" erratics and erotics. (5) We may have depressed, depressing, deteriorating or dying parents (one or both may be significantly upwards of 65 by now). (6) We look in the mirror and realize we can no longer influence with cuteness and charm, and that even finding a new formula for a facial quickie, a morning makeover, learning to cope with a fading tan, won't bring back the breezy body we used to know so well. All this is quite a bit to contend with. It may well lead to occasional emotional overload. Maybe even a six-week short circuit.

"It's really depressing. It really is. You lose your children, sometimes your man, and your body, all at once. My body wasn't bad. I was attached to it the way it was," Mary moans. "But the worst of the worst," she complains, "is that if you're unattractively ambivalent, resentful and depressed on and off for a few months while you work your way through all this, you're seen as a shrew, a doomsday sayer, or some other awful thing. The most frustrating thing about this period of life is that everyone in your support system—most of all your growing children—are down on you for not being perfectly adjusted or for being perfectly adjusted, and wanting them to go away so you can get on with your life! A great Catch 22."

Maria says that for her, the loss of identity via the loss of a familiar and attractive young body, is the easiest aspect of this time in her life to handle. "With my self-sacrificing nature," she giggles, "I felt great going on 800 calories a day for eight weeks—1600 on Sundays—depriving myself to death, and dropping lots of lard. I'm coming up quite improved! Women are judged by looks much more than men. I decided to look better. I never had cared before. Now it matters to me because my emotions aren't invested in family life as much, and they're floating around looking for things to care about. I'm replacing my children with short-order shape ups and all those snappy looks they sell."

Nancy adds a sobering perspective. "I've been having empty nest syndrome, and I've never even married or had children. It's not the chicks in the nest, it's the eggs in the ovaries. I have a fantastic career, but it's just hitting home that it's too late for me ever to have a child. I feel fatigued, frigid, frozen. I fidget. I feel terribly irritable." All symptoms of depression, a clinically recognized condition from which 42 million people in the United States, two-thirds of them women, suffer. Feelings of sadness, helplessness, hopelessness, brooding, being rundown, having difficulty making even the most minor decisions, loss of pleasure, popping awake at night or being groggy with sleep all day, sudden changes in eating habits, are all signs that a person's positive energies are being detoured and drained into a problem perceived as overwhelming. And innumerable studies show that never-married and childless women are included in this statistic in as large numbers are those staring at their empty nests!

Why are so many more women than men depressed? The psychiatric world tends to think it's because more women risk, wrap and invest a great amount of their emotional resources in intimate relationships than men do. Therefore, they're more vulnerable when people leave the family in the natural course of growing into adults, or when they leave because something has gone wrong. If women's emotional attachments to loved ones are deeper than men's, it hurts more to drastically loosen them.

However, in my opinion, there's more to it. Women are taught not to try to determine the specific course of their lives while men *are* urged to. Yet we know the ability to predict and somewhat determine one's "destiny" is a key to helping children mature and adults achieve good mental health. An essential ingredient of mental health for all people is feeling that they can guide their own lives. Conversely, the chief feature of depression is a feeling of powerlessness. I believe that a central ingredient in emotional depression for women is a feeling of "ego diffusion" (the necessity, as Joan explained, of keeping the self "jello-like" until a husband and his lifestyle have been "adopted"—and maybe a second husband and yet another lifestyle later on) and "ego shattering" (the necessity of giving up part of self from time to time due to death or divorce of a mate or departure of a child).

It's hard to feel whole when immense chunks of your life's involvements and investments are apt to fly away, and directions switch so swiftly. It's at these confused times that our wings as well as our hearts miss a few beats, the air currents we count on fail to hold us aloft, and we dip and flap a bit. It's called depression. Barring other problems, the women who do best are the women with the greatest ego strength; those with clear, self-determined directions, those whose "life themes" remain constant through thick and thin and family members who come and go.

Women have so many causes in midlife to pause, ponder, plan and re-group the pieces of their identities. But is the problem that the kids are grown that the nest is empty? For all birds, animals and human beings, the filling of the nest with young is followed by the emptying of the nest because of the maturing and floundering forth of the babies. Is this nest-emptying a crisis? Is it a *syndrome?*

Research strongly suggests that when events are "one time"—children leaving home, menopause, death of a mate—they're not usually experienced as crises. Departure, illness, death of loved ones of course cause great grief and sadness, as does the prospect of one's own death. But when things occur at times and in ways consistent with the normal, well-known and expected life cycle, most people suffer through without lasting trauma. Responsive friends and professional support services are, of course, central in helping a person get through these strenuous experiences.

Watching children go out into the world independently, as we have been grooming them to do, does not cause most women grief. On the contrary, most commonly, women are proud of the work they've done, of the people they've created. They welcome a chance to do for *themselves* for once, and are, to tell the truth (but please *don't* tell the kids!) weary of childrearing and ready to be as free as children themselves.

Personal experience has become more and more categorized by psychiatrists and allied professionals seeking subjects to "treat" and theories to stamp their names on; the normal, pleasurable growing up and going away of wonderful young adults became a psychiatric disorder, elegantly entitled "the empty nest syndrome." However, hang on to your hats—and your empty nest syndrome, too, if you want it, for now the researchers are coming. Unlike the medical community, they aren't looking for diseases. It's just that after half-a-century of studying children, they've discovered that adults, too, have psychology.

39

THE KIDS WHO WON'T LEAVE HOME

Audrey C. Foote

Along with all the other miseries of the modern woman's middle years there is a predicament which has been a favorite motif of syndicated psychologists in the last few years. They call it the Empty Nest Syndrome. Just in case there is anyone out there who hasn't heard about it, this quaintly labeled malady is the devastating depression of the mother whose children have all grown up and left home. But current sociology is now questioning this dilemma. Delia Ephron, in *Esquire,* writes that three national surveys have exposed the Empty Nest Syndrome as a pious fiction. And Patricia Williams, in the New York *Times,* asserts, "Women whose children have grown up and gone are found to be happier than women of the same age who are still mothering on a daily basis." "The Empty Nest Syndrome," she says, "is for the birds."

While I read these findings with interest, I am suspicious of those neat categories "children who have grown up and left home" and "mothering on a daily basis." There is a universe of nuances between those two extremes. *Whose* empty nest? I thought with only a twinge of irony as I looked up from the *Times* to see two of my children playing Mastermind at the coffee table, another slouched by the stereo replacing Vivaldi with James Taylor, and the fourth bent over his math at the dining room table. A traditional heartwarming family vignette,

except for the fact that apart from the youngest, age eleven, not one will ever again celebrate his or her twenty-first birthday. And yet for a considerable portion of this past year, as in the years before, they have all been, both *de jure* and *de facto,* resident at home.

Like parents of the past, my husband and I assumed when our children went off to college that it was an irrevocable break. It has turned out that entry into college was not the final flight from home but merely a four-year intermission.

Eight years ago, when our oldest left for Harvard, I produced an elaborate dinner at which I lachrymosely observed that this might well be the last time, at least as part of daily routine, that we six would dine together. We have had quite a number of such valedictory dinners since, but they have become mere pretexts for a party since we all now know that the youth leaving today may be back in a month and departing again the next, equally inconclusively. Had I foreseen this state of affairs, say ten years ago, I might well have assumed that it would brand me as a Philip Wylie-style Mom, and my children as emotional and social retards. Fortunately, in the intervening years I've had the benefit of the experience of friends with slightly older children. From observing them I've learned that to have grown children living at home is not necessarily a Freudian failing or an ethnic joke but rather a new "life-style" of the 1970s. As we stood with bulging grocery bags on the porch of Sewards Market in Menemsha this summer, a friend observed, "In the fifties the kids went to college and

---

Audrey C. Foote, "The Kids Who Won't Leave Home," *Atlantic Monthly,* Vol. 241, No. 3 (March 1978), pp. 357–63. Copyright © 1978 by the Atlantic Monthly Company, Boston, Massachusetts. Reprinted by permission of the author.

got married when they graduated or else took an apartment with a pal of the same sex; in the sixties they dropped out, made leather sandals, and lived in communes. But now, why, they aren't even *living together!*"

The first hint of this peculiar change in youthful mores came to me a few years ago when I had tea with a friend in the library of her five-story Washington town house. Sally had always been a kind of bellwether for me as she progressed through the maternal miseries and splendors of the 1960s. She had accepted her children's idealistic but often dangerous involvements with awesome equanimity. But that day she mentioned that her oldest son had come home for an apparently indefinite stay, and remarked, "I simply don't understand it. He has a lovely girl with a nice little apartment in Georgetown who I know would be delighted to share it with him." Not long afterward I learned that they had sold their handsome mansion and moved into a chic but minuscule apartment nearby. The big house kept being broken into and robbed when they were traveling, Sally first explained. This was indeed true, but she later confessed it was also to elude all their postgraduate children who simply *would* keep coming back to camp in their old bedrooms, appearing hopefully at mealtimes and helplessly with armloads of dirty shirts.

Now in Sally's case this congregation of the young may well have been a deserved personal tribute, but in the following years I saw this bizarre exception become a trend and then finally a whole new alternative life-style. My neighbor has a twenty-eight-year-old son living at home and commuting to New York to his job in public relations; a friend of a friend in Monsey has two post-college daughters at home, one going to law school, the other a cocktail waitress. (The other innovation now is, I think, the diversity of occupations. Our children are as likely to be mechanics, carpenters, butchers, and policemen as doctors or lawyers; often there are both extremes in a family. My friend in Croton has one son who is a newspaper writer, another who is a moving man. The latter's girlfriend is a doctor and her sister is going to clown school. Their friends have produced a geologist, a magazine editor, and a short-order cook. Of my own grown children, the oldest is a postal clerk, one sister is in publishing, and the other is studying to become a costume designer. This does make life interesting, for the parents as well. Former routine inquiries at large cocktail parties concerning the offspring of acquaintances are answered no longer with prideful accounts of progress at the Chase Manhattan but often with piquant incongruities. I encountered one the other night: the older boy was already a famous rock star—*really* famous; even I had heard him on the radio—while the younger son was a nurse.) But however original and various their *métiers,* a great many of the young people we know are living in the family home.

We mothers quite often ask ourselves how and why this has happened. Except in classic cliché cases of flagrant Oedipal attachment or literal incompetence, the primary motive appears to be quite simple—to save money. Nothing is ever quite that simple, however. The young have always needed to save money, but in the past they would have sold themselves piece by piece—in futurity—to medical schools rather than move back home. This phenomenon must be related to another trend, the tendency to postpone marriage or even the commitment of living together. Like the costume of dirty jeans and unisex haircuts, it may be one of Nature's sneaky ways of exerting population control. But in any case, it is made feasible surely by the fact that home is an easier place to return to now that mother and father aren't so punctilious about schedules, dress codes, and table manners. The children drift in and out with often maddening insouciance.

I hardly ever know just how many places to lay on the table, be it breakfast or dinner, or whose socks are whirling around in the dryer. The dog starts to wag her tail and grin at no matter what hour the front door creaks open. Nor have I figured out an appropriate answer to phone calls for the children, even the 3 A.M. ones, other than to mumble, "Well I don't know whether she's here, I suppose I might find her." A yet older generation might think this feckless, but one would feel just *silly,* I think, expressing concern for the safety or doubt about the resourcefulness of the son or daughter who has hitchhiked through Nigeria or backpacked in Nepal.

And as for the inconvenience, one brings that

on oneself, of course, if one can't get the knack of being "laid back," of "hanging loose"; the kids don't care if they go without supper, miss phone calls and buses, have to wear the same shirt four days in a row. Other than employing the *force majeure* of "for *my* sake, then," which one needs to keep in reserve to forestall schemes like weekend parachute jumping, there is nothing a parent can say or do short of expulsion. Occasionally we sulk a little, but mostly we come to take it all in stride, with only a stumble now and then. Therefore it is obvious that the modern home offers a number of conveniences, even pleasures, and only a manageable number of "hassles." So it is after all no mystery that the children keep coming home. The real question is, Why do we let them in?

For the parents the situation can be a trying one. The first thing one notices is the matter of diminishing physical space. A house which once comfortably contained two adults and three to five children, with rooms and furniture adequate to their size, has to accommodate five to seven big people, all adults at least in physique. These new grown-ups need large beds in place of cots, cribs, or convertibles, large closets, extra showers, and cupboards for their curling irons. Moreover, returning from their colleges and apartments, they import the funky furnishings of those temporary digs. Our basement and attic, once repositories for tools, storm windows, Christmas decorations, and old love letters, now bulge and buckle with Coca-Cola cartons filled with books and records, electric hot plates, mini-fridges, toaster-ovens, fans, rolls of posters and remnant rugs, two guitars, four sets of skis, and a canoe. What a garage sale! I think wistfully; the proceeds could easily pay off the mortgage. But alas, not one item of this vast commercial cornucopia can be sold or even given away, since the time will come when it will all be shoehorned back into the weary station wagon or U-Haul and driven off many miles away to adorn yet another room.

Sometimes muttering "Om" and standing in that basement, which looks like a Green Stamp warehouse or backstage at a giveaway quiz show, I reflect that despite their jeans and rubber sandals, and their proudly proletarian occupations (my son was shocked when my husband once said to him, "Working in the post office isn't proletarian—it's petty bourgeois"), our children live in some ways on a more elevated economic scale than we do—at least in terms of material acquisition. Even as I type here I am tapping, gratefully, on Victoria's Smith-Corona electric with power return instead of on my $65 portable. I am wearing Valerie's Bulova Accutron, which she passed on to me when she got a watch she liked better. Beside me is our oldest's tape recorder, borrowed and not returned since he has a more elaborate model upstairs. In the next room is his Zenith color TV; our own Sears black and white portable with its wobbly rabbit ears now lives in the attic. Stereos, ten-speed bikes, Japanese cameras, calculators, hair-dryers, they have them all, often in duplicate.

But then I remind myself that (1) many of these baubles were given by us as Christmas or birthday presents or awards for academic achievements; (2) the rest, the kids bought for themselves with money earned at jobs we would not have endured at their age; (3) the children are generous in sharing them or even giving them away, hand-me-ups, as they replace them with newer models; and (4) there is nothing much really to keep me from going out and buying at least some of these gadgets for *myself*—except for the fact that like most of my generation I did not grow up with these electronic marvels. We went off to college on *trains*—with *suitcases*. So we don't quite regard these things as necessities, and sometimes we can hardly master the intricacies of their operation. No, I begrudge the children not their possession of these tools and playthings but rather the space that they monopolize. The house swells and sags as they are moved in, is stripped and stark as they are moved out; one must be constantly making room or filling cavities.

After space, the major problem is transportation. Grown children living at home either still haven't learned to drive and must be chauffeured about or entrusted to their peers; *do* know how to drive but have no cars of their own and are thus invariably cruising in the parents' vehicle; do have a car/cars of their own so the driveway looks like a used-car lot and it requires the skill and recklessness of a parking attendant to get out of the garage. Actually, all these combinations have their inherent compensations. The nondrivers can be marooned at home occasionally to answer phones, welcome plumbers, or make yogurt. The carless drivers can often be bribed into collecting cat food or dry cleaning on their way to *Star Wars.* Those with multiple cars can serve as the family's private Hertz company when the station wagon—hernia'd from all that moving—is in hospital. Our son, while not precisely forthcoming with his silver Mercedes or even his Volkswagen bug for petty chores like taking the golden retriever to the vet, carting costumes to our local amateur theater, or collecting his younger brother who, the school nurse says, feels he's about to throw up, rises to the occasion when it is a question of a big mission. He is good for about one major moving job a season, and positively saintly about delivering and collecting his sisters at the airport. (Money saved roughing it at home can be diverted into holidays.) This free limousine service is no small contribution to my own leisure time and peace of mind.

One last problem for the mother with resident grown children is the extra housework involved, most of which invariably falls upon her *if she is at home.* Many of us have discovered that proviso and have renounced gardening and gourmet dinners for two and begun stampeding offices, boutiques, and graduate schools, which in their mercy often let us in. All statistics show that more middle-aged women are entering the work force; it has been naively assumed that a large segment are trying to escape the doldrums of an empty nest. *Au contraire!* Lots I know have abandoned housewifery to make room in that nest for all the returnees and to help pay for the extra wheat germ and long-distance phone calls. (Characteristic episode: Phone rings. Our son, age twenty-six, picks it up. Operator asks, "Is this Mr. Foote?" Short pause. Judicious answer. "That depends.") But above all, the mother's flight from home is a means of decently ducking the dishes and the dusting, which somehow manage to get done by someone else in her absence but *never* in her presence. Or, if not, who notices after dark and a long day in the office?

In spite of the crowding, chauffeuring, and extra housework, there are rewards in having the children home again: they help with engine rattles, making rum cake, and pinning up hems, and they provide company for afternoon tea and Scrabble. What's more, one learns so much. After all those years of teaching them skills—shoelace tying, New Math, soufflé baking, and parallel parking—how satisfying to learn a few from them, like putting on mascara, raising a spinnaker, and basic yoga.

My husband, who relishes having all the children under our roof, cherishes illusions, which periodically soar into ambitions, of making this arrangement not merely a sometime pleasure but also an economic asset like the traditional farm family. He visualizes us turning our collective talents to some sort of cottage industry. The girls have always made ingenious family gifts from various *objets trouvés,* flotsam and jetsam of the Hudson River or our neighbors' curbside offerings to Goodwill. Valerie once got a citation "Worthy" at a county fair for her apple pie, her first try, too. And as an assistant den mother I have helped make medieval castles from milk cartons, egg boxes, and beer-can tabs. So the children's father dreams of us all clustered, chortling, in a revamped corner of our dank and crowded basement, turning out boudoir wastebaskets covered with flocked wallpaper, pickled picture frames, jars of jam from our dying quince tree, velvet-covered jewel cases created from cigar boxes, scissors-holders from sequined tennis-ball cans, and decoupage umbrella stands from transmogrified plastic Clorox bottles. Our attic groans under the weight of empty but promising coffee tins, wooden cheese cartons, oatmeal boxes, and samples of tweed suit materials received in the mail. We will sell our creations in the local boutiques or antique shops—on consignment, if necessary—or perhaps peddle them door-to-door. (Actually, our only entrepreneurial success is Andrew, who at age seven borrowed a pound of peat moss from our neighbors, put two level tablespoons in each of a stack of plastic Baggies, and sold them to the other neighbors for a quarter a shot.) Or better still, we will market them by mail order. My husband is quite prepared to leave his editorial job in the city to help Victoria, who has studied Chinese calligraphy, and Valerie, who does etchings, concoct a catalogue. When these fits come upon him, usually during snowstorms, torrential rains, or heat waves, and at breakfast just before train time, the children and I pat him fondly on the arm and hand him his briefcase. After all, he has all those mouths to feed.

40

POLYGYNY AFTER 60

Victor Kassel

During the past fifteen years in the private practice of geriatrics, I have noticed a change in the attitude of many aged patients. Earlier in my career, these people felt a greater personal responsibility for working out the solutions to their own problems. Although they recognized the need for guidance to help effect a solution, they tended to assume a more active role in solving these problems. The aged have changed. Now, they have become passive, except to challenge everybody else to improve their lot. Their disabilities have become status symbols, a means whereby they can obtain attention and control their families. Years ago, these people considered old age a disadvantage and preferred that the nation ignore their chronological age. Now the aged are asking for special advantages because they are elderly. The emphasis has changed from what the aged can do to help themselves to what America can do to help the aged. Today, the needs of the aged are a major concern of our nation.

In considering these needs, it is best to categorize them into three main groups: medical-surgical, psychiatric-psychological, and social. The aged concentrate mostly on their medical-surgical and psychiatric-psychological needs. But in the private practice of geriatrics the greatest frustrations arise when trying to fill their social necessities. This would include needs caused by the death of a spouse, economic limitations due to inflation, decline of prestige, loss of status, compulsory retirement from business, and, most of all, inability to find fully satisfying activities. Unlike the treatment directed against a medical illness, where the physician participates actively in helping the patient, the acceptance or modification of the social problems must be done by the patient. More and more the aged have become unwilling to try to change their lot. Rather, they look to society to modify itself to suit their needs. They seek to regain the way they lived in earlier adulthood. They would resurrect their dead spouses; they would undo the industrial advances of today. Many seem to say: "You've done this to me, now fix it!" I even have had patients blame me because they've lived so long: now they claim that it is my responsibility to make them happy.

What can be done about it? The aged are with us and, in increasing numbers, they shall continue to be with us. If the aged find it so difficult to change, perhaps society might change so that the aged may be reintegrated and live comfortably.

During the past two hundred years, we have seen a gradual change in political, economic, and social philosophy in this country. Of the unfilled social needs of the aged which the social scientists have identified, there is a set which a certain change in our present social philosophy or ethic might fill. Many might consider this change radical, but it is a return to a practice which at one time was considered proper in the Judeo-Christian ethic. I mean a change to polygyny—a limited polygyny—*polygyny after 60.*

Victor Kassel, "Polygyny After 60," *Geriatrics*, Vol. 21, No. 4 (1966), pp. 214–18. Copyright © 1966 The New York Times Media Company, Inc. Reprinted with permission of *Geriatrics*.

ADVANTAGES OFFERED BY POLYGYNY AFTER 60

Greater Ratio of Older Women to Older Men

With the American concept of equal rights and opportunities, not only all older men but also all older women should have the chance to marry or remarry following the death of a spouse. The average wife can expect to outlive her husband five to fifteen years so that, after the age of 60, the women outnumber the men. Thus, the need for polygyny is obvious: there just are not enough men. Therefore, any man over age 60 could marry 2, 3, 4, or 5 women over 60. Were the situation reversed and the men outnumbered the women, then polyandry would be the answer. Thus, there is a chance that polygyny would offer to the excess women the opportunity to obtain a husband. The inability of many older widows to remarry because of the limited number of available men represents an unfilled need which polygyny could help to alleviate.

The Family Constellation

Besides the opportunity to remarry, polygyny offers to these women the opportunity to reestablish a meaningful family group. Sociologists have stressed the importance of the family in American life. Our urban living has limited the size of the modern family in contrast to the size of the rural family during the last century. And likewise, our homes are large enough only for the parents and children of the modern family. There just is not enough room in the average modern home for 3 generations. In addition, changing ideas about child raising often bring conflict between parents and grandparents. Consequently, except as baby-sitters, grandparents cannot play a meaningful role in the modern family circle. They are not intimates in the family constellation; they are outsiders. With polygyny, there would be a return to the married state for the many lonely widows as well as a chance to establish a genuine, intrarelated family group composed of these married women and their spouse.

Diet

Studies have demonstrated that married couples subsist on a more adequate diet than do widows and widowers. The lonely women, who were once excellent cooks, have no one for whom to prepare a complete meal. There is no incentive to cook. Many men never could cook well so they, too, exist on a limited, unbalanced diet. On the other hand, where there is a group of people living together as a family, eating in the company of one another, the story is different. Mealtime regains its social atmosphere: appetites return. Each wife can take her turn at cooking so that the task does not become too great, and menu planning becomes a source of pride. This can lead only to better and more adequate meals.

Living Conditions

Another cause for the inadequate diet of aged men and women, besides the loneliness described above, is their limited income. And limited income contributes to the inadequate living conditions found among many aged. The polygynous marriage offers the opportunity to pool funds so that there is enough money for all. The family can live more graciously.

Illness

Added to the opportunities to maintain good health, another advantage of polygyny relates to illness. Many aged persons would not need nursing home care if responsible people at home were available to nurse the infirm person. In addition, many aged are hospitalized because they live alone and are unable to obtain adequate home nursing care. Polygyny solves this difficulty, for the husband and wives would take turns nursing the sick. Also, the care does not become too great a burden for one person as so often happens in monogamous marriages; the responsibility is shared. Added to these advantages is the fact that the ill person remains within the familiar surroundings of his or her own home.

Housework

Many aged find it impossible to keep their homes in order because of the fatigue produced by the physical labor of housework. Two or more women in a polygynous marriage, working together to keep the house in order, lighten the burden for one another. They also have an opportunity to display their abilities as fine homemakers without overworking themselves. In addition, when one of the wives finds her physical infirmity activated, she need not strain herself. She can rest, knowing full well that the other wives will continue the homemaking until she is capable again.

Sex

Now we come to the most delicate and the most controversial aspect. Studies at various geriatric centers have disproved the misconception that older people are not interested in sexual activity. Marriage sanctions sexual activity, and the polygynous marriage enables the unmarried older woman to find a partner. Most widows refrain from sex because they lack this partner; society has taught women to remain chaste when not married.

To many people it is abhorrent to visualize grandparents or even parents past the childbearing stage enjoying the pleasures of sexual intercourse. Older women, recognizing this attitude, repress their sexual desires and develop psychological conflicts and consequent guilt. Studies have demonstrated, however, that most women have an increase in libido after the menopause simply because they lose the fear of pregnancy. A polygynous marriage enables them to express this desire, instead of remaining repressed through a continent widowhood.

As for the men, sexologists claim that the male is polygynous by nature. The development of impotency and decreased libido in older men need not represent a senile change. The existence of a climacteric in the male has never been positively established. It seems that most impotency in the aged male represents boredom and many times an unattractive, uninterested partner. With variety, greater interest is sparked and many men can come back to life sexually. Also, the problem of the frigid wife is eliminated; other partners are available. Polygynous marriage offers a solution to a number of sexual problems of the aged.

Grooming

Where you have many women competing for the attention of the lone male, both the women and the man would show an increased interest in better grooming. Many aged persons are uninterested in their appearance, change their undergarments infrequently, bathe inadequately, and seldom cleanse their external excretory organs. Polygyny offers to the woman someone for whom to compete. The man, on the other hand, is interested in being courted. Each person will do his or her best to upgrade appearances, each will be alert to the advantages gained by the competitor, and each will learn the tricks of becoming more attractive. The end result must be finer-appearing older citizens.

It can be argued that the jealousy aroused as the result of the competition would be carried to an extreme by the women and would disrupt the quiet, peaceful home. This may occur. But when there is a choice between uninterested, dowdy, foul-smelling hags and alert, interested, smartly dressed ladies, the selection is obvious. Troubles might arise, but what marriage—monogamous or polygynous—is without troubles? The strained competition between the women does represent an obvious disadvantage of this married state, but the advantages compensate for this one difficulty.

Depression and Loneliness

In the practice of geriatrics, one of the major psychiatric problems encountered is depression. As mentioned above, the aged no longer find themselves members of a family. The result is loneliness and a feeling of uselessness on the part of the aged parent. Depression results from this loneliness and uselessness. These people always ask, "What is the point of my existence?" There is no answer that seems to satisfy them: they find no reason to continue living. In our youth-centered, family-oriented society, the aged find their own youth gone and their family grown. Depression results. Their children may try to make work for them in order to reestablish the parents' importance and feeling of being needed, but the contrivance is obvious. The sham only produces a deeper depression.

Although the polygynous family group is not the same as the youthful, monogamous family, at least it is the closest thing to it. In contrast to the monogamous marriage, polygyny frees a larger percentage of older women from the loneliness and depression of widowhood.

Since this is polygyny after the age of 60, the married partners will be close in age, with a greater likelihood of similar interests. This would spur a more intimate socialization between members of the family so that they could attend community activities and programs together. When living alone, the aged are reluctant to participate in activities outside their home. When living with others, however, interests are more likely to become contagious. The married partners can engage in activities as a family. It is knowing that one is a member of a distinct group that produces a feeling of belonging, with a consequent reason to live.

In addition, polygyny enables a number of people to live together intimately. Each one has lived his unique life, and each one enters the marriage with a different set of experiences. There is then the chance for each member of the marriage to grow further by his close contact with the other members of the family. Each can learn from the experiences of the others, and in that way deepen his insight into life. Living alone seldom offers this opportunity.

Thus, a polygynous marriage in old age is capable of dispelling depression and loneliness, as well as enabling the participant to grow in depth.

Health Insurance

The final advantage of a polygynous marriage in the later years has to do with health insurance. Recent years have seen the growth of group health insurance. Membership in it offers advantages over individual policies. For example, Utah Blue Cross and Blue Shield is less expensive and more inclusive when the insuree is part of a group plan. Older persons who, upon retirement, elect to continue their health insurance find their premiums more expensive, and they are excluded from psychiatric benefits. There is no reason why group insurance should not consider the polygynous family within its coverage and charge less expensive premiums.

SUMMARY

Polygyny after 60 is offered for consideration as a solution to a number of the social problems of the aged. This modification of marriage is not unique in the history of our culture. At one time, it was a socially acceptable way of life. Today, too many aged persons find it impossible to adjust to the social changes that occur in their senescence. Less and less are they able to establish a meaningful role for themselves in American society, and much unhappiness has been the result. They have become less aggressive and more passive while waiting for solutions to be effected for them, and they seem contented in allowing the nation to grant them special privileges merely because they are elderly. Therefore, it would seem that society should attempt to find solutions to these problems. Polygyny after 60 could insure the elimination of a certain set of the aged's social problems, even though it meant a total change in certain aspects of the structure of marriage. The writer fully recognizes that the introduction of polygyny after 60 entails many complications, but he feels certain that the advantages gained for the aged would more than compensate for the trouble necessary to work through these difficulties. Thus, if the aged refuse to solve these problems for themselves, then, rather than allow the aged to continue in their miserable, unhappy state, society must change.

vs. John B. Hamilton, 1508 Maiden Lane; divorce action, gross neglect of duty and extreme cruelty charged.

84-CIV-1365 — Janet G. Adams, 2135 Stowe Dr., and Roy K. Adams, 1530 Koa Dr.; petition for dissolution of marriage.

Photographs by Alan McEvoy

Part Six

TRANSITIONS

The subtitle of this anthology is *Coping with Change,* and we have been discussing transitions in every area of marriage and the family. The transitions that we will discuss in part six are those major departures from the dominant marital lifestyle that are becoming so common today: divorce, widowhood, and remarriage. The final chapter sums up this idea of transition by looking at changes we can expect in the future.

How one views the rapidly rising divorce rate depends on how one views the role of the marriage and family institution in our society. Those who see the nuclear family as the norm perceive the rising divorce rate as an indicator of the breakdown of the social structure. Those who believe in the marriage vow of "until death do us part" see the rising divorce rate as a sign of moral decay. Those who see marriage as a choice for personal fulfillment regard the higher divorce rate as a sign that this goal is being accomplished (Shultz, 1982, p. 228). It is expectations, then, that define what is acceptable and desirable in marriage, and these expectations, as noted in chapter 1, are changing toward an emphasis on self-fulfillment, personal happiness, personal growth, and sexual satisfaction. When we add to these changing perceptions our immense romantic expectations of marriage, along with our lack of preparation for it, it is not surprising that few anticipate the conflicts that occur or know how to resolve them. Perhaps, then, the divorce rate is high not because we regard marriage so little, but rather because we expect so much of it—affection, companionship, empathy, and self-actualization.

Social change has added to the acceptability of divorce and made getting a divorce easier. There has been greater social and religious acceptance of divorce as our society has moved from predominantly sacred to predominantly secular values. Smaller families have become the norm, and a more permissive attitude toward individual behavior has developed, including acceptance of more subjective criteria in selecting a mate. There has been a movement toward greater equalitarianism, along with greater social and economic independence for women through education, work, and civil rights. When social change is added to longer life spans, it can be seen that the longer duration of marriage may mean more difficulties. Another, final factor of instability is, as we saw, the marriage gradient—pairings based on a mutually agreed-to unequal relationship of older, more-educated, higher-salaried, higher-status husbands to younger, less-educated, lower-salaried, lower-status wives (Stiehm, 1975).

Some or all of these factors make divorce a viable option when marriage deteriorates. Whether they actually lead to divorce depends upon a balancing of the costs and rewards of the relationship. In the first article of chapter 15, Stan Albrecht and Phillip Kunz describe this exchange procedure. The process may begin with an initial stress-provoking event, such as infidelity, a financial problem, physical abuse, misuse of alcohol, or a sexual problem. If the problem continues, attempted remedies may only exacerbate the situation by compounding the initial stress. The result is a withdrawal of emotions to limit being hurt further, but this in turn leads to withdrawals from shared activities and a consequent decrease in overall marital satisfaction. However, there may still be barriers to choosing divorce as the way out of a difficult situation. These barriers may include personal religious beliefs, the presence of children, lack of financial resources or wage-earning abilities, negative counsel from family, friends, or religious leaders, fear of the unknown, or difficult divorce laws in one's state.

As can be seen, it is almost never easy for the individuals involved in a marriage to make the decision to terminate that marriage. Yet the rise in divorce rates has led to the development of a romantic view of divorce. Complementing the myth of romantic love and marriage, the myth of romantic divorce leads to the expectation that with divorce will come less stress and conflict, the joys of freedom, and the delights of self-discovery. The result of this myth is a lack of preparedness for the traumas and stresses that actually follow (Hetherington, Cox, and Cox, 1977).

In sum, divorce may resolve a number of dissatisfactions with a marriage, but the process itself produces stress and requires a number of adjustments. In the second article, Paul Bohannan notes the need to adjust to a new style of life and states that there are really six divorces: an emotional divorce, involving the bitterness of the breakup; the legal divorce, involving causes and complaints; the financial divorce, dealing with property settlement, child support, and, perhaps, alimony; the coparental divorce, involving decisions regarding the children, such as custody and visitation; the community divorce, involving the recognition of new friends and participation in community activities; and the psychic divorce, involving the transition to being an autonomous social individual. Studies have shown that social participation is the most influential variable in alleviating postdivorce stress. Other factors aiding adjustment are being more sexually permissive, being economically independent of one's former spouse, and having a high "orientation to change" (Raschke, 1978).

Divorce is, of course, not the only means of losing a mate. In fact, until the 1960s more marriages were ended by death than by divorce. But since that time, the number of marriages ended by death has remained fairly steady or actually declined, whereas the divorce rate has doubled. It may be for this reason that most marriage and family texts overlook death as a worthy subject. That is to say, "unlike divorce, death does not seem to be defined as a crisis by family sociologists" (Dickinson and Fritz, 1981, p. 379).

Another reason for this lack of concern may be a misconception of the emotional and social adjustments that must be made by the widowed as compared to the divorced. This misconception may be due to the fact that being widowed is considered a tragedy and evokes sympathy, whereas being divorced is considered a failure (Pickhardt, 1982). Nonetheless, problems exist for the widowed, and adjustments must be made; in fact, they "must make a total emotional, financial, and social reorganization of their lives at a time when their resources for such a task are generally inadequate" (Hiltz, 1978). In the final article of chapter 15, Carolyn Balkwell sums up these difficulties and describes some successful means of adaptation: keeping busy, making use of helping programs, developing new roles.

The higher divorce rate and large number of widows does not mean, however, that people do not want to be married. In fact, one of the most telling reminders of the importance of marriage in our society is the remarriage rate: most of the divorced will remarry. The figures tell us that it is not marriage that is being rejected, but particular mates. The remarriage figures are somewhat lower for the widowed due to differences in the number of available potential mates and such personal factors as age and income.

Remarriage does not mean that the problems of being divorced or widowed are over; they are just different. As the two authors in chapter 16 indicate, there are numerous adjustments to be made in the new state. In the first article, Ann Goetting likens these adjustments to those that must be made to a divorce; that is, there are also six developmental tasks in adjusting to remarriage. She summarizes these as reestablishing trust and commitment; reinstating an identity as a couple; establishing a couple relationship with friends and in community endeavors; making decisions regarding roles with children; dealing with the financial needs and obligations of a dual household; and adjusting to the legal and social factors involved in dealing with ex-spouses and in-laws. It would appear that premarital contracts would be as helpful in remarriage as in marriage, or at least discussions of the above issues. Specifically, this would mean discussions revolving around the division of labor, responsibilities, views of childrearing, financial arrangements, and relations with ex-spouses, relatives, and partner's children.

These adjustment difficulties are complicated by the fact that remarriage is an incomplete institution. The remarriage, as Andrew Cherlin notes in the second article, is a complex family structure with problems unknown to other types of families and without realistic social guidelines. That is to say, "there are no sets of beliefs, no language, and no rules for a family form that has more than two parents" (Furstenberg, 1980, p. 443). Perhaps this explains why about 40 percent of the remarried will redivorce. For those who manage to make the adjustment despite these difficulties, the second marriage will be happier than the first (Glenn, 1981).

Most family life takes place in the context of institutionally defined norms. But as we have seen, divorce and remarriage are aspects of family life that lack clearly defined norms. Other areas examined in this anthology also revealed this absence of normative guides. There is, for example, the lack of standards regarding gender-role socialization in an era demanding equality between the sexes (chapter 4). The result, as DeFrain noted in chapter 13, is a plea for help by androgynous parents. Also noted in chapter 4 was the lack of knowledge and guidance regarding sexual behavior, an experience involving younger and younger participants. And yet Americans seem shocked over the large increase in teenage sex and pregnancy. Couples still get married without any training in such important skills as constructive communication or conflict resolution (chapter 9), and then we wonder about the growth of divorce and the future of the family (chapter 1). Bergman wants to license parents as a means of insuring that couples will have the knowledge to enable their children to grow to their full potential—knowledge they lack today, as reflected in statistics on physical and emotional child abuse (chapter 11). It seems illogical that such major life stages and transitions as marriage, family, divorce, and remarriage, with their far-reaching social and psychological consequences, lack institutional guidelines.

In sum, the profile of the American family has changed, but the institutions interacting with the family have not kept pace. The important question, then, is not where we have been, but where we go from here—that is, what will be done about this lack of institutional guidelines? In the first article of chapter 17, David Knox sums up the changes described in this book and notes that these trends have a behavioral implication for family life educators—to stay informed. Myths regarding marriage and family may die out, and norms regarding such practices as parental training may be instituted; it is important for counselors and educators to be aware of these trends.

Like previous changes, these changes will be the result of four revolutions that have occurred in this country: the demographic revolution revealing longer life spans; the biological revolution that has allowed women to gain control over their own bodies and biology; the economic revolution that has led to the replacement of the family as the basic unit in society with the individual, whether male or female; and the revolution of technological development and instantaneous communication that have sped up the rate of change. (Ramey, 1978, pp. 3–4). As these new technologies continue to come into use, social customs and laws will gradually change, bringing with them alterations in life-styles. One of these alterations is discussed by Rosabeth Moss Kanter in the second article of chapter 17. She indicates that the new family forms are a reflection of "a movement toward the 'post-biological family' "—a family where biological imperatives will no longer define intimacy and household composition. She believes that it may be the role of the commune to make "people feel close and committed to one another when biological givens no longer seem sufficient to sustain a group." It is not change, then, that will destroy us both as individuals and as a social system, but the inability to change (Otto, 1970).

STUDY QUESTIONS

Chapter 15

Albrecht and Kunz
1. What are some of the rewards of the decision to divorce?
2. What are some of the costs?

Bohannon
1. Explain the six stations of divorce.
2. Which of the six stations would seem to be the most difficult? Why?

Balkwell
1. What are the major problems facing a widow?
2. Indicate several successful adaptations.

Chapter 16

Goetting
1. Note several reasons for the high rate of remarriage.
2. Describe the six stations of remarriage.

Cherlin
1. Why does Cherlin say that remarriage is an incomplete institution?
2. Specifically, what are the problems for the remarried associated with family law?

Chapter 17

Knox
1. Describe several of the trends in marriage and the family.
2. Why does the author say that the trends have a behavioral implication for family life educators and counselors?

Kanter
1. What does the author mean when she refers to a movement toward a "post-biological family"?
2. Describe several of the challenges to the traditional family form.

References for Part Six

Dickinson, George, and Judy L. Fritz. 1981. Death in the family. *Journal of Social Issues,* September, pp. 379–84.

Furstenberg, Frank F. 1980. Reflections on remarriage. *Journal of Family Issues,* December, pp. 443–53.

Glenn, Norval D. 1981. The well-being of persons remarried after divorce. *Journal of Family Issues,* March, pp. 61–75.

Hetherington, E. Mavis, Martha Cox, and Roger Cox. 1977. Divorced fathers. *Psychiatry Today,* April, pp. 42–46.

Hiltz, Starr Roxanne. 1978. Widowhood: A roleless role. *Marriage and Family Review,* November/December, pp. 3–10.

Otto, Herbert A. 1970. The era of the innovative society. In *The Family in Search of a Future.* Englewood Cliffs, N.J.: Prentice-Hall.

Pickhardt, Carl E. 1981. Working it out. *The Single Parent,* January/February, pp. 26–27.

Ramey, James. 1978. Experimental family forms—The family of the future. *Family Review,* January/February, pp. 1,3–9.

Raschke, Helen. 1977. The role of social participation in separation and postdivorce adjustment. *Journal of Divorce,* Winter, pp. 129–39.

Schultz, David A. 1982. *The changing family.* Englewood Cliffs, N.J.: Prentice-Hall.

Stiehm, Judith. 1975. Inequality between the sexes. *The New York Times,* July 2, p. 33.

XV

DIVORCE AND WIDOWHOOD

41

THE DECISION TO DIVORCE: A SOCIAL EXCHANGE PERSPECTIVE

Stan L. Albrecht and Phillip R. Kunz

THE DECISION TO DIVORCE: CONSIDERATIONS OF REWARD-COST OUTCOMES

In assessing the decision to divorce, it is important to recognize that the relationship that exists between satisfaction and happiness in a marriage and the stability of that relationship is never a simple or direct one. As Lenthall (1977: 25) has noted, "happy" marriages often end in divorce and "unhappy" marriages often endure. Or, as Hicks and Platt (1970) conclude after their comprehensive review of the marital satisfaction literature, the factors that make a marriage stable or unstable are much more complicated than just "being happy." Understanding the complexity of these relationships even evades the experts and leads to erroneous and often untested assertions, as Kunz and Albrecht (1977) point out.

Many researchers, in their efforts to explain the decision to divorce and, more particularly, to clarify the relationship that exists between satisfaction and stability, have adopted a scheme developed a number of years ago by Thibaut and Kelley (1959). Using a social exchange framework similar to that employed by Homans (1958, 1974) and others, Thibaut and Kelley explain outcomes in social relationships in terms of costs and rewards. More specifically, they propose that the amount of happiness or satisfaction that one attributes to a relationship will be based on the extent to which that relationship measures up to a specified standard that is referred to as the comparison level (CL). Individual comparison levels develop on the basis of personal past experience, observance of the experience of others, and so on. If an individual feels that a relationship he or she is involved with is "better than" the standard (CL), then the individual is likely to feel relative happiness or satisfaction with that relationship.

However, a relationship that is more rewarding to the individual than the comparison level does not have to be a stable relationship. To handle this situation, Thibaut and Kelley (1959) introduce what they refer to as a comparison level for alternatives (CL alt). While an existing relationship may be satisfactory on the comparison level criteria, an al-

---

Stan L. Albrecht and Phillip R. Kunz, "The Decision to Divorce: A Social Exchange Perspective," *Journal of Divorce*, Vol. 3, No. 4 (Summer 1980), pp. 319–37. Copyright © 1980 by The Haworth Press, Inc. Reprinted by permission.

ternative relationship may become available that is even more attractive. In such a circumstance, the "happy" relationship may become an unstable relationship. On the other hand, a relationship that does not measure up to the comparison level standard may nevertheless remain a stable relationship if only because the alternatives available (CL alt) are even less attractive to the individual involved. These relationships are summarized in Table 1 which compares individual outcomes from present relationships (0) with the comparison level (CL) and the comparison level for alternatives (CL alt).

TABLE 1
RELATIONSHIPS BETWEEN STABILITY AND HAPPINESS IN MARITAL RELATIONSHIPS

Happiness	Stability	
	Stable	Unstable
Happy	1 $0 \rightarrow CL$ $0 \rightarrow CL_{alt}$	2 $0 \rightarrow CL$ $0 \leftarrow CL_{alt}$
Unhappy	3 $0 \leftarrow CL$ $0 \rightarrow CL_{alt}$	4 $0 \leftarrow CL$ $0 \leftarrow CL_{alt}$

0 = *Present Outcomes* associated with one's marriage
CL = Comparison Level
CL_{alt} = Comparison Level for Alternatives
$\rightarrow$ = Better Than
$\leftarrow$ = Worse Than

Relationships that fall within the first cell are both stable and happy relationships because their outcomes are higher than either the comparison level or the comparison level for alternatives. Cell 2 relationships, though happy, are unstable because alternatives are available that are more attractive than present outcomes—even though those present outcomes are better than the individual would expect on the basis of the comparison level. Cell 3 summarizes stable but unhappy relationships. In this instance, the individual finds himself or herself in a relationship that just doesn't measure up to what had been expected of it and doesn't measure up to what the individual sees others experiencing in their relationships. However, the outcomes from that relationship are still greater than what could be expected from other alternative relationships that are available. In such an instance, a person will stay with a bad relationship rather than opt for what is defined as an even more negative alternative. Finally, Cell 4 relationships are both unhappy and unstable. They measure up neither to the standard established by the comparison level nor to the available alternatives. One would not expect such relationships to last very long.

This cost-reward framework implies that the decision to divorce will be made only after it is determined that the alternative to sustaining a marital relationship is either more rewarding or less costly than the decision to remain with the relationship. It implies the ability on the part of the individual actor to compare the outcomes of his or her own marital relationship with some internal standard as well as with other options that are available or that are made available in the actor's environment. Such comparisons are highly dependent upon individual *sui generis* judgment of reward and cost. The reward-cost framework also recognizes changes that may occur in a relationship over time. The termination of an intimate relationship with another may often occur only after drastic shifts have occurred in reward-cost outcomes. That is, relationships that may once have compared favorably both with the comparison level and with comparison levels for alternatives may have taken a downward turn to the point that they now fall well below either or both of these standards.

Levinger (1965, 1976) has used somewhat of a different approach to that adopted by exchange theorists. However, his analysis of the process through which individuals reach the decision to divorce still contains important reward-cost considerations. Levinger, however, prefers to call these *attractions* and *barriers* that exist in any dyadic relationship. According to Levinger, inducements to remain in a relationship include the attractiveness of that relationship to the individual actor and the restraints or barriers against breaking up that relationship. Attractions include perceived rewards such as the receipt of love, status, goods, services, support, security, and physical attributes of one's partner. Attractions might also include joint possessions such as a home, joint accomplishments associated with the bearing and rearing of children, and sexual enjoyment.

Barriers to the dissolution of a relationship, on the other hand, include feelings of obligation to each other, concerns about effects of divorce on the children, fears about group and community reactions, religious prohibitions, abstract moral values, concerns about financial costs associated with divorce, and so on. The implication, again, is that as attractions in a relationship decrease or as barriers to the dissolution of that relationship are eroded, the probability of divorce increases.

We will draw from both of these orientations in assessing the decision reached by our respondents to terminate their marriage. Many of the variables used in the analysis fit clearly within the reward-cost attraction-barrier frameworks. Others are less directly related to these theoretical orientations but fall within similar traditions in the divorce literature.

RESEARCH PROCEDURES

A frequently encountered problem for those interested in studying divorced persons is that of developing a sampling frame from which respondents can be selected. It is because of this problem that studies of divorce have often used small and unrepresentative samples. In an attempt to overcome this and to develop a sample that would be both large enough for detailed analysis and generally representative of some larger universe of divorced persons, a two-page screening questionnaire was sent to a sample of 11,014 households that were randomly selected from a compilation of telephone directories for eight western states (Arizona, Colorado, Idaho, Montana, New Mexico, Nevada, Utah, and Wyoming). Households were chosen by selecting a random starting point and using a systematic "skip" interval thereafter. Businesses were deleted. The screening questionnaire obtained information on selected demographic characteristics of the respondent and also included items to determine if either the respondent or his or her spouse had ever been divorced. The number of questionnaires initially sent to each state was proportional to the population of that state according to the 1970 census and ranged from a high of 2,958 in Colorado to a low of 472 in Wyoming. From the initial sample, 1,245 questionnaires were undeliverable because the addressee had either moved or was deceased. Forty-nine percent or 4,827 of the remaining households returned questionnaires in response to the initial mailing and one follow-up letter. Response rates were generally consistent from state to state though somewhat higher than average in Utah and somewhat lower than average in Nevada.

A total of 1,265 of the 4,827 persons who returned the screening questionnaire reported that they or their spouse were or had been divorced. A more detailed questionnaire was then sent to these individuals. The second questionnaire was designed to obtain rather extensive information on the divorce experience and the individual's adjustment to that experience. The pool of 1,265 ever-divorced was reduced to 843 because 267 questionnaires were undeliverable (usually the prospective respondent had moved or died), and an additional 157 persons reported that they had not been divorced. Apparently in many of these instances the person filling out the initial screening questionnaire had reported that they were married to someone who had been divorced though they, themselves, had not been. Rather than passing the second questionnaire on to the previously divorced spouse, they sent it back with the notation that they did not fulfill the criteria of having been divorced. Five hundred (59%) of the remaining 843 persons returned completed questionnaires. Of this number 293 (59%) were females and 207 (41%) were males. Most of the analysis which follows will focus on these 500 ever-divorced who completed the questionnaire.

FINDINGS

Falling Below the Comparison Level: Marital Satisfaction Compared with Others and with Prior Expectations

Married couples frequently assess the happiness and satisfaction of their own marriages by comparing them with those of other couples they know. If they perceive their own relationships to be better than those of others, they are more likely to be satisfied with those relationships. In this sense, then, their marriage measures up on the comparison level scale.

There are some important inherent dangers in this process that few individuals recognize, however. For example, almost all persons have a tendency to put on their best front when in public and not reveal those important negative things that occur in their private relationships. Thus, the comparison level that many couples use when they compare their own relationship is an artificially created comparison level. They measure themselves against the public mask of others. Each person knows his or her private life and the problems that exist there but tends to see only the better side of others. This same situation may induce unrealistically high cultural standards of marital performance against which couples judge their own marriage or by which one spouse judges the other. Using Goffman's (1959) terms, individual back regions, with all of their problems, are compared against the carefully contrived front regions of other people. It is not very likely that the reality of the former will measure up to the artificiality of the latter.

To whatever extent people judge themselves in a context of front-back behavior of others, our sample of divorced respondents felt that their marriages fared very poorly when compared with the marriages of others. Each respondent was asked the following question: "Compared with other couples you have known, how would you rate the degree of overall satisfaction that you felt with your marriage?" Responses to this question are summarized in Table 2.

Almost three-fifths of the respondents felt that their marriage which had been terminated through divorce had been somewhat or much less satisfying than were the marriages of other couples they knew. However, this was much more true of females; 65% of the females compared with 49% of the males rated their former marriage as less satisfying than other couples while 20% of the males and 12% of the females rated their former marriage as more satisfying. In terms of the comparison level concepts discussed above, a clear majority of the marriages would have been "unhappy" marriages. However, the remainder of the table affirms the point made earlier that even "happy" marriages are not necessarily stable marriages.

Comparison levels are developed not only by observing the relationships of others but also by determining whether or not a relationship is what we expected it to be when we entered into it. To see how the marriages of our respondents had fared on this second criteria, each individual was asked the following question: "Compared with your expectations of marriage before you were married, how did the marriage turn out?" Table 3 summarizes these results.

As Table 3 indicates, over half of all respondents stated that their marriage had been much worse than they had expected it to be. An additional 29% felt that it had been somewhat worse than they had anticipated. Again, this tended to be more true of women in the sample than of men. Fully 84% of the female respondents felt their marriage had failed to live up to their expectations for it.

Of course, most persons do not enter into a marital relationship assuming that it will not work.

TABLE 2
SATISFACTION WITH FORMER MARRIAGE COMPARED WITH PERCEIVED
SATISFACTION OF OTHER COUPLES

Satisfaction Compared with Others	Total Sample N	Total Sample %	Males N	Males %	Females N	Females %
Much less satisfied	180	37	61	30	119	42
Somewhat less satisfied	104	21	39	19	65	23
About the same	127	26	61	30	66	23
Somewhat more satisfied	49	10	23	11	26	9
Much more satisfied	26	5	18	9	8	3

TABLE 3
SATISFACTION WITH FORMER MARRIAGE COMPARED WITH EXPECTATIONS PRIOR TO ENTERING THE MARRIAGE

Satisfaction Compared with Prior Expectations	Total Sample N	Total Sample %	Males N	Males %	Females N	Females %
Much worse than expected	251	51	85	41	166	57
Somewhat worse than expected	145	29	68	33	77	27
About as expected	73	15	41	20	32	11
Somewhat better than expected	19	4	7	3	12	4
Much better than expected	7	1	4	2	3	1

The fact that the first marriages of all of these persons failed would be reason enough to assume that they had not measured up to the expectations held about them by those entering the relationship. However, the overwhelming failure of the marriages to measure up to this "prior expectations" comparison level is interesting. For a very small minority (five %), the marriage that had been terminated was rated as better than it had been expected to be. One can only assume that these individuals entered the marriage initially with very low expectations or that the divorce had been initiated by a spouse toward whom they still felt positive affection.

Problems in the Marriage

Many of the things that the exchange theorists like Thibaut and Kelley (1959) would refer to as costs in a relationship can be identified by asking individuals to define the major problems that occurred between them. The divorce literature is filled with hypotheses concerning the nature and types of problems that are likely to lead to divorce between spouses. In our survey, each respondent was asked to identify the major reasons why he or she felt that the marriage had failed. Respondents could list as many reasons as they desired but were asked to rank each reason listed in terms of its overall importance. Table 4 provides a summary of these responses. The first half of the table lists all of those reasons that were identified by the respondents as the most important reasons for marital failure by rank order and then lists the total number of times that each of the reasons was listed by all of the respondents. The second half shows a breakdown by sex.

A total of 490 of the 500 ever-divorced respondents listed one or more reasons why they felt that their marriage had failed, and of these 490, 168 listed infidelity on the part of the spouse as the most important reason. These figures are almost identical to those generally reported in the literature which indicate that adultery on the part of one's spouse is defined as the key reason for divorce in about one-third of the instances of marital failure. Somewhat surprisingly, when we compute a percentage based on the total number of reasons given, more males than females identified infidelity on the part of spouse (37% compared with 33%) as an important cause for divorce. An additional 103 of the subjects stated that the major reason for marital dissolution was that they and their spouse no longer loved each other. These two factors account for fully 55% of the first-listed reasons for marriage failure. Other frequently listed reasons were emotional problems, financial problems, and physical abuse.

Turning to the question of the total number of times each reason was listed, the order of the first four items does not change. These four most important reasons include: (1) infidelity, (2) loss of love for each other, (3) emotional problems, and (4) financial problems. Sexual problems comes in fifth in the overall ranking though this was listed as the most important reason for marital failure by only 4% of the respondents.

TABLE 4
MAJOR REASONS WHY MARRIAGE FAILED

Reason	Listed First by All Respondents (N)	(Order)	Total Number of Times Listed by All Respondents	(Order)	Listed First by Male Respondents	(Order)	Listed First by Female Respondents	(Order)
Infidelity	168	(1)	255	(1)	74	(1)	94	(1)
No Longer Loved Each Other	103	(2)	188	(2)	47	(2)	56	(2)
Emotional Problems	53	(3)	185	(3)	24	(3)	29	(3)
Financial Problems	30	(4)	135	(4)	16	(4)	14	(5)
Physical Abuse	29	(5)	72	(8)	0	(9)	29	(3)
Alcohol	25	(6)	47	(9)	5	(7)	20	(4)
Sexual Problems	22	(7)	115	(5)	13	(5)	9	(6)
Problems with In-Laws	16	(8)	81	(6)	10	(6)	6	(8)
Neglect of Children	11	(9)	74	(7)	2	(9)	9	(6)
Communication Problems	10	(10)	18	(11)	3	(8)	7	(7)
Married Too Young	9	(11)	14	(12)	3	(8)	6	(8)
Job Conflicts	7	(12)	20	(10)	3	(8)	4	(9)
Other	7		19		2		5	

Sample N = 500

Some important sex differences are obvious from the data. For example, 10% of the female respondents identified physical abuse as an important reason for failure in their marriage; none of the males saw this as a problem. Females were also more likely to cite alcohol-related problems as important while males were more likely to cite loss of love and sexual problems.

Each of these factors can be viewed as costs in a marriage. As such, they can cause the satisfaction that one feels with that relationship to fall below either or both the comparison level and the comparison level for alternatives. When infidelity enters into a relationship, the costs for the injured party may far outweigh the rewards that have otherwise been associated with the marriage. In the overall balance, the individual may feel that he or she is no longer interested in maintaining the relationship. The same holds true for the other factors as well. For example, one of the primary attractions associated with a marriage is the emotional feelings of love that one feels for a spouse. When that love is gone, reasons for continuing the relationship are diminished.

Barriers to Divorce

Even though problems develop in a marriage, there are still strong forces toward keeping that relationship intact. As noted earlier, Levinger (1965, 1976) refers to these forces as barriers. "Barriers lessen the effect of temporary fluctuations in interpersonal attraction; even if attraction becomes negative, barriers act to continue the relationship" (1976:26). Levinger identifies a number of different types of barriers to divorce, including: (1) material barriers such as the expenses associated with filing a divorce application, paying legal fees, maintaining two places of residence, and so on; (2) symbolic barriers, including feelings of obligation to keep a relationship together even when there are obvious and major problems with that relationship; religious constraints, pressures from primary groups, and pressures that result from fears of community disapproval; and (3) affectional barriers that are linked primarily to concerns about what the divorce will mean for dependent children.

We have noted that many of the traditional barriers to obtaining a divorce have eroded over the past few years. Most states have greatly liberalized their divorce laws and some have moved toward establishing "no fault" standards. The traditional legal hassles associated with marital dissolution are therefore no longer a major consideration in most instances, although there has not been a concomitant diminution in the financial cost of divorce. Equally as important have been the changes in public attitudes and perceptions relating to divorce. In the past, to have been divorced meant that one had to bear a major social stigma. In fact, divorce not only brought shame and discredit to the individual parties involved but also to their extended families. Divorce no longer bears this degree of stigma and at least a part of the public accepts it as a rather normal, everyday occurrence.

While these traditional barriers are no longer as important as they once were, there remain some hurdles that must be overcome as the individual makes the decision to end an unsatisfactory relationship. To determine the relative importance of these, each respondent in the study was asked to identify what they considered the major barriers that had to be overcome as they reached the decision to obtain a divorce. Table 5 summarizes the responses to this question.

The single most important concern that our respondents faced overall in making their decision was financial. However, this was clearly a much more important problem for females than for males. Of all the barriers to divorce noted by females, 36% dealt with financial constraints; this was true of only 10% of those noted by males. For the women, particularly those with young children, a major fear was that of how they would be able to support themselves and their families without a husband. One can assume on the basis of the frequency with which this factor was mentioned that there are probably a great many wives that put up with unsatisfactory marriages because the alternatives associated with having to provide for themselves and their children are even less satisfactory.

On the other hand, males were more likely than females to cite their children as an important barrier. This seems to reflect the fact that in di-

TABLE 5
PERCEIVED BARRIERS TO OBTAINING A DIVORCE

Barrier	Frequency of Mention Overall	Male Respondents	Female Respondents
No Financial Support	156	20	136
Children	102	54	48
Personal Religious Beliefs	102	29	73
Difficulty of Divorce Laws	64	34	30
Parents	56	23	33
Friends	36	17	19
Negative Counsel from Religious Leaders	25	11	14
Fear of Unknown	14	3	11
Spouse Didn't Want Divorce	8	2	6
Neighbors	4	1	3
Other	16	7	9

vorce settlements, women are much more likely to gain custody of the children and this is an important concern for many of the male respondents.

Religious constraints to divorce, like legal and attitudinal constraints, are probably less significant today than they have been in the past. Most religious organizations now recognize divorce as a means for terminating an unsatisfactory relationship. This has not always been the case. In addition, there is less religious stigma associated with divorce than has been true in the past. Nevertheless, a great many people have internalized beliefs which say that divorce is bad and is indicative of failure or even of personal sinfulness; this is indicated in our findings by the fact that personal religious beliefs are cited second most frequently (tied with concern for children) as a barrier to obtaining a divorce.

While significant changes have occurred in many states in recent years that have led to the liberalization of divorce laws, the fourth most frequently mentioned barrier to divorce overall was the difficulty of divorce laws. Males cited this more often than females. It is not possible for us to say whether these legal barriers were real or perceived barriers for the respondents. If one is unaware that the divorce laws in one's state have been greatly liberalized, then one may perceive legal constraints as being a much greater barrier than they really are. On the other hand, some states do have much tougher divorce laws than do others and for some, the realization of this may cause the individual to think that in a comparative sense, the difficulty of their state's divorce laws constitute a very real barrier to obtaining a divorce.

The one other factor that received fairly frequent mention as a barrier to divorce was concern about one's parents. In some instances, parents may have actively opposed the decision. In others, the person may have been hesitant because of the embarrassment that they felt that their decision would cause for their family. While this is probably not as significant a factor as it may have been in the past because less stigma is now attached to divorce, for some of the respondents it was an important concern.

Making the Decision to Divorce: Overcoming the Barriers

Because we are dealing with a sample of divorced persons, it is obvious that each of the individuals involved successfully overcame the barriers that had to be overcome before the divorce could be obtained. Going back to the social exchange framework discussed above, what this implies is that being "unmarried" was perceived as being less costly or more rewarding than being married. Most of the subjects rightly perceived that there would be important costs associated with their decisions. However, not to pursue the divorce was seen as even more costly. Using Thibaut and Kelley's (1959) terms, the comparison level for alternatives was higher than present outcomes. Or, as Levinger (1976: 40) has stated it, "even if internal attractions are low and barriers offer minimal restraint, a relationship will not be terminated unless an alternative seems more attractive." Of course, the alternative need not be another man or another woman. In many instances, it can be singlehood or simply escape from a bad relationship.

These alternatives can be viewed as factors that facilitate or ease the divorce decision. However, other factors such as social support from family and friends might also ease the decision to divorce even though they cannot be considered as alternatives to the marital state. To identify things that helped individuals overcome the barriers noted earlier or otherwise provided a positive impetus to obtain the divorce, each respondent was asked to identify factors that influenced them in actually seeking a divorce. Table 6 summarizes responses to this question.

The numbers in Table 6 suggest that the most important factors involved in the decision to go ahead with the divorce were individual personal unhappiness and the desire to escape a bad situation. As we have noted, feelings of personal unhappiness are often of a comparative nature. That is, individuals compare their own relationships with those of other couples around them and, as a consequence of such comparisons, feel relatively deprived or satisfied. Most of our sample of divorced persons perceived their former marriages to be much less satisfying than were the marriages of other couples they knew. Thus, not only were they unhappy but they also perceived that many others with whom they could compare their relationships were much happier with their marriages. This feeling of relative deprivation probably made their situation even more unbearable.

It was noted above that the most frequent bar-

TABLE 6
FACTORS INFLUENCING DECISION TO OBTAIN DIVORCE

Factor	Frequency of Mention Overall	Male Respondents	Female Respondents
Personal Unhappiness	77	18	59
Own Desires to Get Out of Bad Situation	58	19	39
Opportunities for Alternative Financial Support	50	11	39
Became Involved with Someone Else	42	19	23
Ease of Divorce Laws	39	18	21
Children's Desires	36	4	32
Parents' Desires	33	14	19
Spouse Made the Decision	32	18	14
Never Loved Each Other	23	9	14
Approval of Religious Leader	18	2	16
Children Grew Up and Left Home	17	9	8
Divorced Friends	15	10	5
Desertion	13	5	8
Non-Divorced Friends	8	3	5
Other	12	2	10

rier to seeking a divorce among our female respondents was financial concerns. The removal of these financial constraints was tied for second in importance as a factor influencing women to obtain the divorce. In many instances financial alternatives probably included the obtaining of a job. In fact, some commentators have argued that increased financial independence created by a large number of women entering the labor force is a prime factor that has contributed to high divorce rates in recent years. In addition, some state laws have augmented the women's access to property once controlled mainly by men. Other financial alternatives may have included establishing relationships with others or otherwise determining that separate existences were manageable. As we would expect, financial concerns were less important for men.

A fairly large number of the members of our sample reported that the key factor in their decision to divorce was advice received from someone else. If we combine all of the factors in Table 6 that involve receiving advice from someone else to complete the divorce process, we find that of the 376 persons who listed specific persons or events that played a major role in their decision, 152 of these or 40% made reference to advice or influence from someone else.

One other factor from Table 6 that probably deserves some special mention is the fact that 39 respondents reported that the key factor in influencing them to finally go ahead with the decision to divorce was the ease of the divorce laws. It will be remembered that a much larger number reported that the difficulty of divorce laws was a prime barrier that they had to overcome in their reaching the decision they did. Thus, it appears that the degree of liberality of a state's divorce laws can be seen both as a help and a hindrance in couples making the decision they do to terminate their marriage. However, it is probably a relatively safe conclusion that when a marriage gets bad enough, one or the other or both of the individuals involved are likely to begin to consider other alternatives whatever the constraints that are imposed by the law.

In summary, what the data in Table 6 imply is that the decision to divorce among the members of our sample was more influenced by their consideration of the costs of the present relationship than by the alternatives that were available to them. Thus, personal unhappiness was perceived as more important than the availability of alternative financial support or involvement with some other person. Present costs, then, seem more important than alternative rewards.

FAMILY AND FRIENDS: EXPLICIT AND IMPLICIT APPROVAL OF DIVORCE

Often before the person makes the final decision to terminate what has been defined as a bad marriage, there is some assessment of the degree to which significant others, such as parents and friends, would concur with and support that decision. Miller (1970: 74) has noted that "friends are often consulted when one or both partners are considering a divorce. They can shift the balance toward decision to divorce or continuation of the marriage." Miller also notes that the reaction of friends often determines the form the divorce takes and the behavior of the divorcees after it is finalized. Since divorce involves a great deal of trauma and stress and since very few individuals are able to cope with that alone, they frequently look to others who are important to them for guidance and, once the decision has been made, for support of that decision. Two types of approval can be noted. Explicit approval is given when family and friends make it known to the individual that they agree that they should go ahead with the decision to obtain a divorce. In fact, such a decision may only be made in many instances after such explicit approval has been granted. In a sense, this involves the other party saying that what the individual is doing, though difficult, is right and given the same circumstances, the other party would probably make the same decision.

Implicit approval may be considered as more behavioral. For example, have parents and friends themselves gone through a divorce? While such individuals may not come right out and say that they approve of such an action, the fact that they have experienced a divorce in their own lives says to the person that they define divorce as an acceptable alternative to a bad relationship.

A clear majority of our respondents felt that

close friends and family gave explicit approval to their decision to obtain a divorce. When asked to indicate what percentage of their friends and family approved of their decision, two-fifths of the respondents said that "all of them" did. For 69% of the sample, more than half of close friends and family members were perceived as supporting the action. On the other hand, 12% reported that none of their close friends and family supported their decision. Given the difficulty associated with divorce in the best of circumstances, it is hard to imagine how it would be if one received no social support for the decision from those whose opinions would mean most. While these instances are uncommon, one can only anticipate that such divorces are especially traumatic.

Turning to a form of more implicit approval, the data indicated that 83% of the sample report that they have some close friends who have gotten divorces. The most common response is for the subject to report that "a few" of their close friends are divorced (70%). While just 13% report that "most" or "all" of their close friends are divorced, the fact is that a large majority of the respondents have been or are acquainted with divorce through the experience of friends.

While there is some evidence in the literature that divorce tends to run in families in the sense that parents who divorce are more likely to have children who will divorce, our respondents were more likely to have divorced friends than divorced family members. Twenty-four percent report that their parents have been divorced and almost the same number (25%) report that spouse's parents have been divorced. Three-fourths of the respondents and their spouses come from homes in which their parents' marriage has remained intact. This finding is not unlike the population of the United States as a whole.

On the other hand, almost half of the respondents report that one or more of their own brothers or sisters have obtained a divorce and somewhat fewer (41%) report that one or more of their ex-spouse's brothers or sisters have obtained a divorce. A majority in both instances have brothers and sisters with stable marriages but many have experienced divorce within the context of their families. Sixteen percent reported that two or more of their own brothers and sisters have divorced and 14% report this to be the case for the ex-spouse's brothers and sisters.

To a great extent, then, those in our study who are divorced define their action as having received a stamp of approval from family members or other significant persons for them. Many others have witnessed divorces among parents, siblings, or close friends. Very few of our respondents stood alone without approval from significant others or without knowing something of the experience of others with whom they had somewhat of a close relationship. No doubt this feeling of understanding and support from significant others plays an important role in the decision that is reached.

A FINAL EFFORT TO SAVE THE MARRIAGE: THE EFFECT AND POTENTIAL EFFECT OF MARITAL COUNSELING

In many deteriorating marriages, there are points at which some form of counseling or other professional aid might be critical in helping to put the marriage back on more even ground. More and more individuals, particularly among the middle and upper classes, are seeking such professional help in improving the quality of their relationships. While the admission that professional help is needed is still a difficult one to make for most people, it does not carry the negative stigma that it once did. In addition, such help is more readily available now than it has been at any other time and while the potential financial costs entailed may act as a barrier for some couples, the low or no-cost services provided by many public and church-related agencies now puts marriage and family counseling within the reach of practically anyone who is willing to seek it.

Even when counseling is obtained, however, it may not resolve the problems involved. There are many reasons why this is the case. For example, for some couples the marital relationship may have deteriorated so far before they ever seek outside help that little can be done to resolve their problems. In other cases, one of the pair may seek counseling reluctantly and only at the insistance of the other partner or some other outside person or agency. In other cases, neither of the partners may be willing to pay the price that the professional feels would be required to make some improvement in the relationship. Counseling may be started but then terminated before observable progress has been made.

Given all of these considerations, we decided to determine the proportion of our sample of divorced persons who had some form of professional marriage counseling and their evaluations of the effectiveness of this counseling in aiding them in resolving their problems. It must be recognized, of course, that we are dealing with a biased sample from the perspective of the marriage counselor in that we are dealing exclusively with what could be referred to as cases of failure. Adequate comparisons would require including samples of still-married persons who have also received counseling in order to assess the role that counseling may have played in helping them to improve their marriages.

A total of 491 of the subjects responded to the question of marital counseling and of this number, 127 reported that they had received professional help of some type. Eighty percent, or 101 of these 127 persons who reported having received counseling reported that it did not help. The remaining 26 observed that the help came primarily in the form of easing the divorce process rather than making the marriage better. For those who had received counseling, then, the evaluation of its effectiveness was overwhelmingly negative.

Almost as many persons as had received counseling reported that while they had not received professional help, it was their feeling that such help might have saved their marriage or otherwise improved their relationship with their spouse. However, a much larger number of the sample (51% of the total) reported that they had received no counseling and that it would have made no difference anyway. Again, while these figures give a rather negative impression of the utility of marriage counseling in improving the quality of deteriorating marriages, it must be recognized that we are dealing with only one side of the picture. There may be a great number of strong marriages that have become such through the aid of professional counseling. None of these would be tapped by our data because we are dealing, by definition, with cases of failure.

SUMMARY

Even when marriages have gone bad, it is almost never easy for the individuals involved to make the decision to terminate those marriages through divorce. Breaking close ties with others with whom we have shared strong emotional and other attachments is always a painful experience both within and outside the marital bond. It is especially difficult within the marital relationship because of the range of things and activities that married couples have usually shared.

Based on self-report data, the marriages of our respondents that had ended in divorce had not been nearly as good as were the marriages of other couples they had known nor had the marriage met the expectations that they had held for it prior to entering into the relationship. The most frequent problem identified in the marriages that was important in leading to marital failure was infidelity or unfaithfulness on the part of one's spouse. About one-third of the divorced members of the sample reported that their spouse had been unfaithful. Also important were loss of love, financial difficulties, emotional problems, and, especially for wives, physical abuse. Since all of these are important costs associated with the effort to maintain a relationship, they can be considered crucial in adversely affecting the reward-cost balance that is often rather precarious in most marriage situations.

Even though the costs associated with trying to maintain a marriage may be very high, there remain important barriers that operate to inhibit a decision in favor of divorce. The respondents indicated the most important barriers included such things as financial concerns (especially for women), concerns for the children (especially for men), and implications of such an action on personal religious beliefs.

All of the respondents were, of course, successful in overcoming these barriers and the primary reasons included their high degree of personal unhappiness and the strong desire to end what had become a very bad relationship. The availability of alternatives was also important for many of the respondents. For example, the opportunities for alternative financial support was especially important for female respondents and involvement with someone else as an alternative source of emotional and sexual gratification was important for some members of both sexes.

Once the marriages of our respondents had deteriorated to the point that one or both spouses were considering divorce action, professional counseling was of little help in righting the situation. While many of the respondents had received professional counseling, the overwhelming majority of these reported that the counseling was of little help in improving their marriages. Among those who had not received such professional assistance, a majority were of the opinion that it would not have helped anyway. Apparently we are describing a sample of people for whom the costs associated with maintaining a relationship had risen so high that there was little likelihood of saving the relationship.

REFERENCES

Bernard, J. 1970. No news, but new ideas. In Paul Bohannan (ed.), *Divorce and after*, pp. 3–25. Garden City, N.Y.: Doubleday.

Goffman, E. 1959. *The presentation of self in everyday life*. Garden City, N.Y.: Doubleday.

Hicks, Mary W., and M. Platt. Marital happiness and stability: A review of the research in the sixties. *Journal of Marriage and the Family* 32:553–74.

Homans, G. C. Social behavior as exchange. *American Journal of Sociology* 63:597–606.

———. 1974. *Social behavior: Its elementary forms*. New York: Harcourt, Brace, Jovanovich.

Kunz, P., and S. L. Albrecht. 1977. Religion, marital happiness and divorce. *International Journal of Sociology of the Family* 7:227–32.

Lenthall, G. 1977. Marital satisfaction and marital stability. *Journal of Marriage and Family Counseling* (October): 25–32.

Levinger, G. 1965. Marital cohesiveness and dissolution: An integrative review. *Journal of Marriage and the Family* (February), 19–28.

Levinger, G. A. 1976. A social psychological perspective on marital dissolution. *Journal of Social Issues* 32:21–47.

Miller, A. 1970. Reactions of friends to divorce. In Paul Bohannan (ed.), *Divorce and after*, pp. 56–77. Garden City, N.Y.: Doubleday.

Thibaut, J. W., and H. H. Kelley. 1959. *The social psychology of groups*. New York: Wiley.

42

THE SIX STATIONS OF DIVORCE

Paul Bohannan

Divorce is a complex social phenomenon as well as a complex personal experience. Because most of us are ignorant of what it requires of us, divorce is likely to be traumatic; emotional stimulation is so great that accustomed ways of acting are inadequate. The usual way for the healthy mind to deal with trauma is to block it out, then let it reappear slowly, so it is easier to manage. The blocking may appear as memory lapses or as general apathy.

On a social level we do something analogous, not allowing ourselves to think fully about divorce as a social problem. Our personal distrust of the emotions that surround it leads us to consider it only with traditional cultural defenses. Our ignorance masquerades as approval or disapproval, as enlightenment or moral conviction.

The complexity of divorce arises because at least six things are happening at once. They may come in a different order and with varying intensities but there are at least these six different experiences of separation. They are the more painful and puzzling as personal experiences because society is not yet equipped to handle any of them well, and some of them we do not handle at all.

I have called these six overlapping experiences (1) the emotional divorce, which centers around the problem of the deteriorating marriage; (2) the legal divorce, based on grounds; (3) the economic divorce, which deals with money and property; (4) the coparental divorce, which deals with custody, single-parent homes, and visitation; (5) the community divorce, surrounding the changes of friends and community that every divorcee experiences; and (6) the psychic divorce, with the problem of regaining individual autonomy.

The first visible stage of a deteriorating marriage is likely to be what psychiatrists call emotional divorce. This occurs when the spouses withhold emotion from their relationship because they dislike the intensity or ambivalence of their feelings. They may continue to work together as a social team, but their attraction and trust for one another have disappeared. The self-regard of each is no longer reinforced by love for the other. The emotional divorce is experienced as an unsavory choice between giving in and hating oneself and domineering and hating oneself. The natural and healthy "growing apart" of a married couple is very different. As marriages mature, the partners grow in new directions, but also establish bonds of ever greater interdependence. With emotional divorce, people do not grow together as they grow apart—they become, instead, mutually antagonistic and imprisoned, hating the vestiges of their dependence. Two people in emotional divorce grate on each other because each is disappointed.

In American society, we have turned over to the courts the responsibility for formalizing the dissolution of such a marriage. The legislature (which in early English law usurped the responsibility from the church, and then in the American colonies turned it over to the courts) makes the

---

"The Six Stations of Divorce," from *Divorce and After* by Paul Bohannan. Copyright © 1968, 1970 by Paul Bohannan. Reprinted by permission of Doubleday & Company, Inc.

statutes and defines the categories into which every marital dispute must be thrust if legal divorce is possible. Divorce is not "legalized" in many societies but may be done by a church or even by contract. Even in our own society, there is only one thing that a divorce court can do that cannot be done more effectively some other way—establish the right to remarry.

The economic divorce must occur because in Western countries husband and wife are an economic unit. Their unity is recognized by the law. They can—and in some states must—own property as a single "legal person." While technically the couple is not a corporation, they certainly have many of the characteristics of a legal corporation. At the time the household is broken up by divorce, an economic settlement must be made, separating the assets of the "corporation" into two sets of assets, each belonging to one person. This is the property settlement.

All divorced persons suffer more or less because their community is altered. Friends necessarily take a different view of a person during and after divorce—he ceases to be a part of a couple. Their own inadequacies, therefore, will be projected in a new way. Their fantasies are likely to change as they focus on the changing situation. In many cases, the change in community attitude—and perhaps people too—is experienced by a divorcee as ostracism and disapproval. For many divorcing people, the divorce from community may make it seem that nothing in the world is stable.

Finally comes the psychic divorce. It is almost always last, and always the most difficult. Indeed, I have not found a word strong or precise enough to describe the difficulty or the process. Each partner to the ex-marriage, either before or after the legal divorce—usually after, and sometimes years after—must turn himself or herself again into an autonomous social individual. People who have been long married tend to have become socially part of a couple or a family; they lose the habit of seeing themselves as individuals. This is worse for people who married in order to avoid becoming autonomous individuals in the first place.

To become an individual again, at the center of a new community, requires developing new facets of character. Some people have forgotten how to do it—some never learned. The most potent argument against teen-age marriages is that they are likely to occur between people who are searching for independence but avoiding autonomy. The most potent argument against hurried remarriage is the same: avoidance of the responsibilities of autonomy.

Divorce is an institution that nobody enters without great trepidation. In the emotional divorce, people are likely to feel hurt and angry. In the legal divorce, people often feel bewildered—they have lost control, and events sweep them along. In the economic divorce, the reassignment of property and the division of money (there is *never* enough) may make them feel cheated. In the parental divorce they worry about what is going to happen to the children; they feel guilty for what they have done. With the community divorce, they may get angry with their friends and perhaps suffer despair because there seems to be no fidelity in friendship. In the psychic divorce, in which they have to become autonomous again, they are probably afraid and are certainly lonely. However, the resolution of any or all of these various six divorces may provide an elation of victory that comes from having accomplished something that had to be done and having done it well. There may be ultimate satisfactions in it. . . .

43

TRANSITION TO WIDOWHOOD: A REVIEW OF THE LITERATURE

Carolyn Balkwell

Becoming widowed—the difficult and sometimes devastating life transition associated with losing one's spouse to death—is a process which is being undertaken by an increasing proportion of the American population. In 1960 there were nine million widowed persons in this country; this number had increased to 12 million by 1975—and of these 11 million were women. Three out of every four American wives may expect to become widows at some point in their lives. The median age at which this event occurs is now 56 years, with 80% of all currently widowed women being over the age of 65 (Lewis & Berns, 1975). Therefore, it tends to be middle-aged females who are most often required to embark on the life passage associated with widowhood and elderly women who are required to hold to the courses charted for surviving spouses.

Even when unmarried persons over the age of 65 are relatively incapacitated, they are more likely to live alone than in any other type of household (Stehouwer, 1968; Streib, 1970). This tendency is even more marked among women than among men—even greater now than earlier in this century. Twenty percent of American widows lived alone in 1940; this figure had increased to 50% by 1970 (Arling, 1976b). Whether this situation is desirable or undesirable is open to question. It has been argued that the existence of harmonious three-generation households in the past is probably a myth because so few people reached old age. Also, there is no evidence that such living arrangements would improve the lot of older persons (Treas, 1975). However, those older persons who do live with one of their children now tend to play a dependent role in the household of a married daughter. This is in contrast to the situation which existed at the turn of the century when a married son would stay on at the *parent*'s farm to help out (Nimkoff, 1962). It has been suggested that older persons, whether widowed or not, find the dependent role unpleasant, perhaps because they must be compliant in the relationship with the child (Dowd, 1975), and do not wish to impose a burden on their offspring (Field, 1972).

The sex ratio among widowed persons has undergone a great change in recent years. Two out of every three widowed persons were women in 1940; in 1968 the ratio was four out of every five (Berardo, 1968). Changes in the magnitude and sex composition of the widowed population are affected by such factors as the age-specific mortality rates of successive cohorts, marriage and remarriage rates, and the difference in age at marriage between husbands and wives (Townsend, 1968). Predictions regarding the distribution of the American population by marital status in the future are

---

Carolyn Balkwell, "Transition to Widowhood: A Review of the Literature," *Family Relations,* January 1981, pp. 117–27. Copyrighted © 1981 by the National Council on Family Relations; 1219 University Avenue Southeast, Minneapolis, Minnesota 55414. Reprinted by permission.

somewhat contradictory. Those models which focus on the increasing proportion of elderly persons in the population and on differential mortality rates for men and women in the advanced years forecast an increasing proportion of widowed persons (Townsend, 1968). Those which give primary emphasis to the tendency for women to marry husbands closer to their own age than was true in the past argue that the proportion of widows among the elderly population may decline in the future (Parke & Glick, 1967), although the actual number of widows might increase.

Composition of the general and widowed populations clearly affects the probability of remarriage among those who are widowed. Age specific remarriage rates are higher than the marriage rates of single persons, but the widowed have a lesser chance of remarriage than the divorced of the same age. While the probability of remarriage for both sexes declines with age, this decline is more rapid for women than for men (Bernard, 1956). Among those 65 and over, 1.7% of the currently single men married, as compared to 0.3% of the currently single women—these figures having remained stable since 1960 (Treas & VanHilst, 1976). People seem to prefer a spouse with a marital history similar to their own. Hence, the pool of eligible mates is smaller for widowed women than it is for widowed men. In addition to being more likely to remarry, men are able to do so after a relatively shorter interval following the death of a spouse (Cleveland & Gianturco, 1976).

ECONOMIC PROBLEMS ASSOCIATED WITH WIDOWHOOD

One area of difficulty frequently faced by widowed persons is related to economic subsistence and the management of resources. Berardo (1968) reported that in 1965 the median income for the widowed aged was less than half that for the married aged. Pihlblad, Adams, and Rosencranz (1972) found a similar relationship between the incomes of widowers and aged married persons; however, widows in their sample had only 75% as much income as the widowers. Widows tended to adjust to their income situation by seeking employment—even if they were very old. Men were more apt to try to reduce expenditures (especially those for medical care) in order to adjust to reduced income levels. While current estimates of financial hardship vary, it has been suggested that one-half of all widows live on or below the income adequacy level determined by the Social Security Administration (Lopata, 1978b).

A proportionate decrease in present income relative to previous economic level (i.e., relative deprivation) may have as great an impact on some widows as actual poverty does upon others. In the sample studied by Lewis & Berns (1975), an average reduction of 44% from previous income levels occurred in the first two years of widowhood. Six out of every 10 widows had their incomes reduced so much that they were not able to maintain their former standards of living. Two years after the deaths of their husbands 56% of these women were employed and 18% of this group started working after being widowed. Although employment seems to be associated with a successful adjustment to widowhood, widows who seek employment face many obstacles because they likely have been absent from the labor force for some time—thus their marketable skills may be rusty, obsolete, or absent. Age and sex probably further handicap these women in the job market, in spite of laws prohibiting discriminatory practices. If the widow does obtain a job, all too often it is a low paying one with little chance of advancement. Compounding these problems is the fact that the current cohort of widows (having been socialized into dependent roles in youth) have few skills in matters related to the handling of real estate, titles, contracts, mortgages, stocks, bonds, and property (Berardo, 1968; Lewis & Berns, 1975). Thus, these women are especially vulnerable to those who would take advantage of them.

HEALTH PROBLEMS ASSOCIATED WITH WIDOWHOOD

Non-economic problems are also associated with widowhood. The widowed typically have higher death rates (especially the young widowed) than their married counterparts (Berardo, 1968). A large sample of widowers over the age of 55 was followed for nine years after the spouse's death (Parkes,

Benjamin, & Fitzgerald, 1969). The greatest excess over expected age-specific mortality rates occurred during the first six months of bereavement. Diseases related to degeneration of the heart and/or arteries (rather than conjoint accidents or infectious diseases that might have been shared with the spouse) were responsible for most of the supernumerary deaths. Psychological stress was believed to precipitate many of these deaths by altering biochemical processes. Analyses of vital statistics (Gove, 1973) also demonstrate higher mortality rates for the widowed when compared to married persons. These differences were greatest for those causes of death for which psychological states may influence life chances—i.e., homicides, accidents, and diseases (such as cirrhosis of the liver) which are related to the use of legal narcotics. Marital status had a greater impact on the mortality rates of men than of women, suggesting that marital roles are more beneficial to males with respect to the sheer ability to survive. However, widowed women are more likely to have chronic, disabling illnesses than are widowed men; and, both have elevated morbidity rates when compared with their married counterparts (Verbrugge, 1979).

Anomie, a condition associated with the absence of social norms to guide behavior, has long been believed to be associated with suicide (Durkheim, 1951). In modern societies, the role of the widowed person tends to be a "roleless" role—that is, it lacks norms or prescriptions for behavior (Arling, 1976a; Hiltz, 1978; Lopata, 1975a) and tends to be somewhat flexible and ambiguous (Cowgill & Holmes, 1972). Thus, one would expect suicide rates to be higher among the widowed than among their married counterparts. Such is, indeed, the case; the discrepancy between the two marital categories being greater for men than for women (Gove, 1972a; Kraft & Babigan, 1976; Rico-Velasco & Mynko, 1973). However, other social ties (i.e., membership in formal organizations or living near one's relatives) may mitigate some of the isolation associated with widowhood and may provide partial protection against the forces which impel individuals toward suicide (Bock, 1972; Bock & Webber, 1972).

Mental illness also afflicts the widowed to a greater extent than it does married persons. Depression is so often experienced by the widowed that it may be viewed as a normal reaction to the loss of one's spouse. Elevated rates of depressive symptoms were noted for the widowed (Clayton, 1974) and they persisted even when age, race, and sex were controlled (Pearlin & Johnson, 1977). In modern Western societies women typically have higher rates of mental illness than men. This excess, however, seems to be due to sex differences in the mental health of married persons. Among the widowed it is the *men* who exhibit higher rates of mental illness (Gove, 1972b).

The road to recovery from psychiatric symptoms may take different turns depending on the patient's marital status. Persons previously diagnosed as delirious are less apt to recover if they become widowed during the course of treatment than if their marriages remain intact (Gabriel, 1975). Hospitalized schizophrenics are more often widowed than married. There is, however, some evidence that this may be due partly to differential utilization of hospital facilities by the widowed (who tend to live alone) and by persons whose spouses can serve as caregivers (Eaton, 1975). Whether all of the difference in rates of hospitalization may be attributed to this factor is open to question. Elderly men who were admitted to a hospital for acute medical and surgical problems were evaluated for psychiatric symptoms. Unrecognized mental illness was found more frequently among the widowed than among the married (Schuckit, Miller, & Hahlbohm, 1975), indicating that factors other than differential utilization of psychiatric services also contributed to the excess of mental illness among the widowed.

GRIEF: A HEALING PROCESS

From the foregoing it is clear that the widowed run a relatively high risk of experiencing a number of problems. The degree of risk (as well as the widowed person's feelings and reactions to his/her loss) changes as the process of grieving moves forward. The initial stage in this developmental process is a state of shock or bewilderment in which the newly widowed person feels numb and may refuse to believe that the spouse is dead. Restlessness and purposeless activity may alternate with numbed stupor during this period, which tends to last from one day to two months (Parkes, 1970, 1975a, 1975b). At the end of this stage the level of affect rises sharply. Feelings include intense pining for the dead person, anger, and guilt as the second stage of grief is entered. During this period, which tends to occur somewhere between the first month and the first year of widowhood (Silverman, 1972; Golan, 1975), the widowed person may behave in a hostile manner toward family and friends (Epstein, Weitz, Roback, & McKee, 1976) and may disengage from social relationships as loneliness for the companionship of the spouse is experienced (Lopata, 1969) Next comes a limbo-like exploratory phase in which new roles are tried out. Decisive action may be troublesome even for those who are unusually able and competent. Purposeless action which may lead to despair or to regret over unwise decisions may occur at this point (Walters, 1980). Dependency on others and depression are frequent concomitants of this stage of grief. Finally, upon completion of grief work, the wounds of being widowed start to heal and either acceptance of one's status or reengagement with new roles and relationships is achieved (Lopata, 1969, 1972; Loge, 1977).

In a poignant account of her personal passage through the healing process of grief, one widow stated:

I am convinced that if I had known the facts of grief before I had to experience them, it would not have made my grief less intense, not lessened my misery, minimized my loss or quietened by anger. No, none of these things. But it would have allowed me hope. It would have given me courage, I would have known that once my grief was worked through, I would be joyful again. Not my old self, I am another woman now. And I like this woman better (Caine, 1974, p. 92).

PREDICTORS OF SUCCESSFUL ADAPTATION TO WIDOWHOOD

Sex

Some widowed persons reach this final stage of grief more rapidly than others. Indeed, some bereaved persons never resolve their grief work adequately. Numerous authors have tried to identify reliable predictors of successful adaptation to widowhood. Factors which have been investigated include the sex of the widowed person. These analyses have yielded contradictory results. For example, it has been suggested that the impact of widowhood is greater on women because more of their identity is tied up in the spousal role (Caine, 1974). Also, the greater ease of remarriage which men experience has been cited as a reason for the less drastic role shifts—and, hence, life changes—which widowhood brings to men in most societies (Lopata, 1972). An empirical study found widowers to be better adjusted than widows even when income, education, age, and amount of forewarning of the death were controlled (Carcy, 1977). However, the scale of adjustment which was used was worded in such a way that it might have tapped a culturally induced reticence to agree to the items among men rather than actual levels of adjustment.

On the other hand, it has been suggested that widowed men are more vulnerable because: (a) they find taking the initiative in the dating process awkward after being married; (b) retirement (an event which isolates one from former friends) *may* occur at about the same time; (c) men are less apt to openly express grief; (d) same-sex friends who are also widowed are not apt to exist; (e) men lack familiarity with household chores; and (f) ties with the extended family tend to be maintained through women (Balswick & Averett, 1977; Berardo, 1970; Kennedy, 1978; Pihlblad & McNamara, 1965; Vinick, 1978; Walters, 1980). Greater elevation of the suicide, mental illness, and mortality rates among widowers also suggests that they may be more severely affected than widows by the loss of a spouse. Level of interaction with friends, however, was not found to be lower for widowed men in a community which had a large proportion of widowed persons. Indeed, the widowed of both sexes interacted more with friends than married persons did—suggesting that the composition by martial status of the larger population may affect the impact of widowhood on the individual (Petrowsky, 1976).

Although consistent evidence that one sex is more adversely affected by bereavement than the other does not exist, it is known that the morale of women seems to be influenced more by the quality of the marital relationship. Men seem to be more sensitive to the mere presence of a spouse (Glenn,

1975; Lee, 1978). It might be argued that women experience more stress or satisfaction from marriage than men depending on the quality of the marital relationship. Therefore, the impact of the loss of a spouse might be expected to be related to marital happiness, at least among women. Empirical studies, however, do not support this notion. Happiness in marriage, by itself, was not related to the physical or mental health of widows (Maddison, 1968); nor was it related to adjustment to widowhood when both sexes were studied (Carey, 1977; Clayton, Halikas, & Maurice, 1972).

Age

Age is another variable which has been explored in terms of its impact on adjustment to widowhood. Older widowed persons tend to be better adjusted than young persons (Ball, 1977; Carey, 1977; Morgan, 1976). Those under 45 years who have dependent children seem to have the worst outcome (Maddison, 1968). By ages 65 to 74 the morale of widows was actually higher than that of their married counterparts (Tallmer & Kutner, 1970). A longitudinal study of people over 60 indicated that most of them adapted rather well to widowhood, with only mild increases in depressive feelings among some women (Heyman & Gianturco, 1973). The greater likelihood of being widowed at advanced ages may make acceptance of this event easier than at earlier stages of life.

Forewarning of Spouse's Death

The effect of anticipatory grief, or forewarning of the spouse's death, has also been studied in terms of its relationship to the ability to adapt to widowhood—with mixed results. In a set of longitudinal studies of widowed persons, all of whom were under the age of 45, sudden death of the spouse (defined as an illness of less than two weeks duration with a terminal decline of less than three days) was associated with more severe grief reactions and slower completion of grief work than were more lingering fatal illnesses (Glick, Weiss, & Parkes, 1974; Parkes, 1975; Sheskin & Wallace, 1976–77). This difference in levels of grief was apparent even a year after bereavement.

However, another set of studies (which investigated the impact of widowhood on persons aged 20 to 90) indicated that those individuals whose spouses had a terminal illness of less than five days were not more depressed than others at intervals of 30 days and 13 months after bereavement (Bornstein, Clayton, Halikas, Maurice, & Robins, 1973; Clayton, Halikas, & Maurice, 1972). Nor did persons whose spouses had experienced terminal illnesses of six months or more differ in the tendency to be depressed from those whose spouses had illnesses which lasted from five days to six months (Clayton, Halikas, Maurice, & Robins, 1973).

An interaction effect between age and the consequence of being forewarned of the death has been observed and may explain this apparent contradiction in findings. Young widows (under age 46) whose husbands died suddenly (in less than five days) and middle aged widows (47 to 59 years) whose husbands' final illnesses lasted more than six days showed the greatest degree of irritability six to nine months after bereavement (Ball, 1977). Elderly persons whose spouses died of long-term chronic illnesses (six months or more) fared worse in terms of medical adjustment than those whose spouses' deaths resulted from illnesses of shorter duration (Gerber, Rusalem, Hannon, Battin, & Arkin, 1975). In addition, it has been noted that a period of two weeks forewarning led to better adjustment to widowhood—but only for women whose marriages had been somewhat unhappy and whose husbands suffered seriously in the final illness (Carey, 1977).

Thus, it appears that forewarning is important when the likelihood of being widowed is very small (i.e., among the young) and when the bereaved individual may have had some reason to wish to "make peace" with the spouse before his death. Among the elderly, lengthy illness of the spouse may lead to disruption of interactions with others, to a great deal of investment of the self into the role of caregiver, and to physical exhaustion from the demands of caregiving—thereby making adjustment to widowhood and re-engagement with new roles more difficult at a point in life when the number of available new roles may be limited by societal and/or physical constraints.

OVERCOMING LONELINESS AS A DEVELOPMENTAL TASK

In modern societies, in which there is voluntary mate selection and neolocal marriage, it is often not the early period of grieving which presents the most severe problems to the widowed person. Rather, it is the later periods when ritualized support for the survivor is removed and the person is left to carve out a new identity on his/her own. Women socialized to traditional, dependent sex-roles are especially vulnerable to loneliness at this stage of widowhood (Lopata, 1975b). Such loneliness is not due simply to living without a spouse—it is greater among the widowed than among the never married (Gubrium, 1974). Urban widows were found to perceive their situations in terms of loneliness and of low status. Same-sex friendship groups were viewed as less prestigeful than mixed-sex groups. Many widows simply refused to interact in a "society of widows" in which all of the members shared their own stigmatized condition. Loneliness, experienced in a number of forms, was a major problem for 48% of these widows. The forms included:

1. a desire to carry on interactions with a particular person who is no longer available;
2. feelings that one is no longer an object of love;
3. feelings that one no longer has anyone *to* love;
4. a desire for a deep companionate relationship;
5. a desire for the presence of another person in the dwelling unit;
6. unhappiness over the absence of anyone to share the workload;
7. homesickness for a past style of life;
8. alienation due to a drop in status;
9. anger at past friends due to decreased frequency of interaction. Such anger may result from (a) differing definitions of the appropriate form and time for expressing grief, (b) a gradual withering away of associates if a long-illness preceded the husband's death, (c) awkwardness in interactions when grief is expressed, (d) a desire not to associate with others who have been close to death on the part of persons who fear their own death, (e) the complications involved in including an extra single woman in mixed-sex activities, (f) jealousy on the part of former couple friends, (g) the wife having relied on the husband to make social contacts in the past, and/or financial considerations which may make past activities unavailable, or;
10. a composite of the above, which may be compounded by the inability to make new friends (Lopata, 1969, 1972).

Effective means of overcoming loneliness appear to consist of keeping busy, developing new roles, and/or focusing one's life on a preexistent social role (perhaps that of grandmother). Well-educated women of the middle and upper classes tended to ease their loneliness through one or both of the first two means (Lopata, 1969). These women are apt to have experienced the greatest disorganization in their lives at widowhood, to have felt the deepest loneliness for the late husband as a person, and to have had multidimensional relationships with the spouse when he was alive. However, they also have the skills and personality traits to develop new self-identities after being widowed—many of them reporting that they changed in such positive ways as being more independent and freer than they had been before—and to mitigate their loneliness. Those who remained very lonely tended to have been socialized to be dependent and passive and, thus, had the most trouble in establishing new role relationships after years of relying on the husband (Lopata, 1970; 1973a; 1973c). They also tended to be of the working class and, thus, to be more apt to have inadequate incomes—a factor which would restrict social participation (Atchley, 1975).

Rural widows may be even more vulnerable to loneliness because of their greater distance from neighbors and services. In one sample of elderly rural widows (aged 65 to 99) 75% were found to be lonely some portion of the time. Compared to the never lonely, the sometimes lonely were more apt to visit frequently with friends, to have a confidante, to be better educated, and to talk on the telephone frequently; but tended to be less satisfied with life, less satisfied with the visits they did receive, and to have lower morale. Thus, emotional isolation appeared to be the factor which separated these two groups. However, physical isolation appeared to be the factor which differentiated the frequently lonely from the never lonely. Poor health, frequent problems with transportation, less physical mobility, lack of a confidante, and less satisfaction with the sheer frequency of interactions with others were associated with often experiencing loneliness (Kivett, 1978).

The importance of the quality of familial interactions for widowed women has been demonstrated. Arling (1976a, 1976b) found that elderly widows tended to have frequent contacts with their families, but that these contacts made little, if any, difference in the women's experience of loneliness. Only contacts with relatives other than one's children eased forlornness. Neighbors or friends (i.e., persons who shared the interests and values of the widows and who did not make them feel dependent) seemed to be more important than offspring in promoting a positive outlook on life.

Widows and widowers who lived in one of their children's homes thought of themselves as guests and the women tended to complain about being expected to babysit (Cosneck, 1970), reinforcing the idea that frequent contacts with offspring may not be entirely beneficial to the elderly widowed person. Older people seem to prefer to "do without" rather than to be dependent on their offspring (Field, 1972) and do live independently unless factors such as extreme old age or ill health make them unable to do so (Watson & Kivett, 1976).

Middle class widows appear to have less interaction with their sons than do their married counterparts; however, they have more interactions with their daughters. Relationships with sons tend to be characterized by dependency on the offspring, while interactions with daughters tend to include social companionship as well as the giving and receiving of assistance (Adams, 1968). It has been suggested that positive attitudes toward aging and a satisfactory living environment are the factors which contribute directly to good relationships between elderly mothers (many of whom were widowed) and their daughters (Johnson, 1978).

Men widowed more than five years, possibly because they are older and more apt to be retired and/or dependent, appear to be less satisfied with life if they have frequent contacts with their children. Life satisfaction of men widowed less than five years does not appear to be related to frequency of contact with children (Pihlblad & Adams, 1972). The nature of the relationship between these two variables for elderly widows has been explored by several authors. Pihlblad & Adams (1972) found increased life satisfaction among those who regularly saw their children. Similar results were reported by Morgan (1976), with the relationship between family interaction and morale being especially strong among Mexican-American widows. VanCoevering (1973) found no relationship between the morale of elderly widows and regular, frequent interaction with family members—including children. Rosen's (1973) data indicated that morale was lower for those who frequently saw their children and was lowest of all for those who lived with their children. These data were collected from both women and men, but one may infer that the vast majority of the respondents were women.

Younger widows who have dependent children tend to believe that their offspring give meaning to their lives, although the children's needs may exacerbate the economic problems which the widows experience. Some of the offspring were perceived as having special emotional needs because they feared that they would lose the remaining parent, because they took over the roles played by the dead spouse in an exaggerated manner, or because they became rebellious (Silverman & Englander, 1975). Interactions with children will clearly have a different impact on the widow depending on whether they are dependent on her or she is dependent on them.

Traditional women in the urban sample studied by Lopata (1973c; 1978a; 1979) were apt to turn to the family as the sole provider of service and emotional support. But for most of these widows, the extended family did not appear to be much of a mainstay. There was some exchange of services with adult children, but (as was noted earlier) the efficacy of these exchanges as a means of overcoming loneliness or improving morale is questionable. Lower class women were apt to see at least one of their children frequently and conflict which was openly expressed was common in these relationships. Women who were less traditional in their outlook were more likely to have contacts with *all* of their children, but to have a relatively low level of contact with any one of them.

The degree of isolation from other contacts (i.e., neighbors, siblings, and organizations) did not differ between black and white widows in this urban environment (Lopata, 1973b). However, in small southern towns elderly black widows were more apt to know neighbors with whom they could visit (Arling, 1976a). Friends were called upon infrequently by the urban widows and did not seem to serve the role of confidante (Lopata, 1979). The importance of having someone with whom to share one's feelings as a means of overcoming loneliness cannot be overemphasized. Weekly contacts with a confidante are concomitant with high morale in widowhood (VanCoevering, 1974). Permissive support from others (especially that which allows the widowed person to express grief) seems crucial in overcoming loneliness and re-engaging in society (Maddison, 1968).

In comparison to the docile ladies who continued to feel lonely, widowed persons of both sexes who possessed instrumental skills were more apt to adjust satisfactorily to widowhood (Rux, 1977). Since the ability to earn one's living is an important instrumental skill, it may be that economic factors alone account for the lower morale of the widowed. Harvey and Bahr (1974) suggest that the long-term consequences of widowhood are, indeed, due to economic deprivation. However, among lower-income elderly persons either abject poverty *or* widowhood was associated with low morale (Hutchison, 1975). It appears that once a minimal existence is assured marital status makes an independent contribution to morale. Middle-class widows who possess instrumental skills are able to re-engage voluntarily in new roles and relations (Lopata, 1979). Others may need help in developing these skills so that they may overcome the problems associated with their low income and loneliness. The absence of service networks (including the inefficacy of such helping professionals as the clergy) which would assist those who do not have them in developing these skills has been noted. Neighborhood service networks were suggested as one means of providing support for urban widows until they are able to re-engage in society (Lopata, 1978b).

HELPING THE WIDOWED: A COMPARISON OF PROGRAMS

Among the service programs which are available to widowed persons in some areas, perhaps the most widely known is the Widow-to-Widow Program. Volunteers who have been widowed maintain phone hotlines and make home visits to newly widowed persons. The phone hotlines serve to provide listeners to the lonely, to help widowed persons make new friends, and to provide some specific piece of information (Abrahams, 1972). The primary aim of the entire program is to help the widowed person progress through the developmental stages involved in the transition from married life to widowed life. Aids provide support and serve as role models of what it is to be widowed (Silverman, 1972). Another program, which in addition to the hotline and home visits also provided social gatherings and community seminars, has also been developed. Interest of widowed persons in the group events was difficult to sustain. Nonetheless, 85% of those questioned said that the program had been of some assistance to them (McCourt, Barnett, Brennen, & Becker, 1976).

Discussion groups of widowed persons have also been used as a means of helping individuals handle "grief work," deal with any other emotional problems which are brought to the surface with the death of the spouse, and build new lives. Weekly sessions were held for periods ranging from four months to one year. A professional counselor served as the leader of each group, the effectiveness of this person seeming to be crucial in making the group a success. Homogeneity of group members in terms of such background factors as age and social class facilitated the identification of these individuals with each other. When successful, the groups motivated the members to go on with life in a new direction; when unsuccessful, they tended to depress the participants further (Hiltz, 1975).

Barrett (1978) has assessed the relative effectiveness of three types of group treatments for urban widows. Self-help groups, confidante groups, consciousness raising groups and control groups were compared. All of the widows, even those in the control condition, had higher self-esteem and a greater intensity of grief at the end of the testing period. Follow-up studies indicated that the consciousness-raising treatment, which would have the clearest relationship to the development of instrumental skills, seemed to have the most positive impact on the life changes of the widows.

There is a need for service programs which will help widows make progress in their transitions to new lives and, most importantly, in the development of instrumental skills. The programs which were discussed above seem to make positive impacts on widowed persons in most cases; however, their existence is not widespread. Those programs which do exist tend to be located in urban areas. Geographically isolated widowed persons in rural areas may be even more in need of these services than are their urban counterparts.

SUMMARY AND CONCLUSIONS

The death of one's spouse brings with it trauma, grief, and the necessity of restructuring one's life. Some widowed persons experience severe economic hardships. Others need face only the emotional and social problems associated with adapting to their new social status—but these alone may be substantial enough to lead to ill health or even suicide. Help in overcoming the problems associated with widowhood is frequently inadequate and all too often is non-existent. When aid is offered, it may be by adult children—thus making the widowed person feel dependent on offspring. This role-reversal may exacerbate any feelings of inadequacy or powerlessness which may be experienced by the surviving spouse. It is imperative that help be offered to widowed persons in such a way that they are not made to feel dependent if they are to be assisted in overcoming loneliness and in building new lives for themselves. Counselors and educators might provide useful services to these individuals by explaining the grief process, by providing an accepting atmosphere in which the individuals can come to terms with their needs for intimacy and sexual expression, and by assisting widowed persons to acquire instrumental skills.

REFERENCES

Abrahams, R. B. 1972. Mutual help for the widowed. *Social Work* 17:54–61.

Adams, B. N. 1968. The middle-class adult and his widowed or still-married mother. *Social Problems* 18:50–59.

Arling, G. 1976a. Resistance to isolation among elderly widows. *International Journal of Aging and Human Development* 7:67–86.

———. 1976b. The elderly widow and her family, neighbors, and friends. *Journal of Marriage and the Family* 38:757–68.

Atchley, R. C. 1975. Dimensions of widowhood in later life. *Gerontologist* 15:176–78.

Ball, J. F. 1976–77. Widow's grief: The impact of age and mode of death. *Omega* 7:307–33.

Balswick, J. O., and C. P. Averett. 1977. Differences in expressiveness: Gender, interpersonal orientation and perceived parental expressiveness as factors. *Journal of Marriage and the Family* 39:121–27.

Barrett, C. J. 1978. Effectiveness of widows' groups in facilitating change. *Journal of Consulting and Clinical Psychology* 48:20–31.

Berardo, F. M. 1970. Survivorship and social isolation: The case of the aged widower. *The Family Coordinator* 19:11–25.

———. 1968. Widowhood status in the United States; Perspective on a neglected aspect of the family life-cycle. *The Family Coordinator* 17:191–203.

Bernard, J. 1956. *Remarriage—A study of marriage*. New York: Dryden Press.

Bock, E. W. 1972. Aging and suicide: The significance of marital, kinship, and alternative relations. *The Family Coordinator* 21:71–79.

———, and I. L. Webber. 1972. Suicide among the elderly: Isolating widowhood and mitigating alternatives. *Journal of Marriage and the Family* 34:24–31.

Bornstein, P. E., P. J. Clayton, J. A. Halikas, W. L. Maurice, and E. Robins. 1973. The depression of widowhood after thirteen months. *British Journal of Psychiatry* 122:561–66.

Caine, L. 1974. *Widow*. New York: William Morrow.

Carey, R. G. 1977. The widowed: A year later. *Journal of Consulting Psychology* 24:125–31.

Clayton, P. J. 1974. Mortality and morbidity in the first year of widowhood. *Archives of General Psychiatry* 30:747–50.

Clayton, P. J., J. A. Halikas, and W. Maurice. 1972. The depression of widowhood. *British Journal of Psychiatry* 120:71–77.

Clayton, P. J., J. A. Halikas, W. L. Maurice, and E. Robins. 1973. Anticipatory grief and widowhood. *British Journal of Psychiatry* 122:47–51.

Cleveland, W. P., and D. T. Gianturco. 1976. Remarriage probability after widowhood: A retrospective method. *Journal of Gerontology* 31:99–103.

Cosneck, B. J. 1970. Family patterns of older widowed Jewish people. *The Family Coordinator* 19:368–73.

Cowgill, D. O., and L. D. Holmes. 1972. Summary and conclusions: The theory in review. In D. O. Cowgill and L. D. Holmes (eds.), *Aging and modernization*. New York: Appleton-Century-Crofts.

Dowd, J. J. 1975. Aging as exchange: A preface to theory. *Journal of Gerontology* 30:584–94.

Durkheim, E. 1951. *Suicide: A study in sociology*. Ed. and trans. by J. A. Spaulding and G. Simpson. New York: The Free Press.

Eaton, W. W. 1975. Marital status and schizophrenia. *Acta Psychiatrica Scandinavia* 52:320–29.

Epstein, G., L. Weitz, H. Roback, and E. McKee. 1976. Research on bereavement: A selective and critical review. *Comprehensive Psychiatry* 16:537–46.

Field, M. 1972. *The aged, the family, and the community*. New York: Columbia University Press.

Gabriel, E. 1975. Délire chronique et sociogénèse. *Annales Medico-Psychologiques* 133:128–35.

Gerber, I., R. Rusalem, N. Hannon, D. Battin, and A. Arkin. 1975. Anticipatory grief and aged widows and widowers. *Journal of Gerontology* 30:225–29.

Glenn, N. D. 1975. The contribution of marriage to the psychological well-being of males and females. *Journal of Marriage and the Family* 37:594–600.

Glick, I. O., R. Weiss, and C. M. Parkes. 1974. *The first year of bereavement*. New York: Wiley.

Golan, N. 1975. Wife to widow to woman. *Social Work*, 20:369–74.

Gove, W. R. 1973. Sex, marital status, and mortality. *American Journal of Sociology* 79:45–67.

———. 1972a. Sex, marital status, and suicide. *Journal of Health and Social Behavior* 13:204–13.

———. 1972b. The relationship between sex roles, marital status, and mental illness. *Social Forces* 51:34–44.

Gubrium, J. F. 1974. Marital desolation and the evaluation of everyday life in old age. *Journal of Marriage and the Family* 36:107–13.

Harvey, C. D., and H. M. Bahr. 1974. Widowhood, morale, and affiliation. *Journal of Marriage and the Family* 36:97–106.

Heyman, D. K., and D. T. Gianturco. 1973. Long-term adaptation by the elderly to bereavement. *Journal of Gerontology* 28:359–62.

Hiltz, S. R. 1975. Helping widows: Group discussions as a therapeutic technique. *The Family Coordinator* 24:331–36.

———. 1978. Widowhood: A roleless role. *Marriage and Family Review*, 1:2–10.

Hutchison, I. W., III. 1975. The significance of marital status for morale and life satisfaction among lower-income elderly. *Journal of Marriage and the Family* 37:287–93.

Johnson, E. S. 1978. "Good" relationships between older mothers and their daughters: A causal model. *Gerontologist* 18:301–06.

Kennedy, C. E. 1978. *Human Development: The adult years and aging*. New York: Macmillan.

Kivett, V. R. 1978. Loneliness and the rural widow. *The Family Coordinator* 27:389–94.

Kraft, D. P., and H. M. Babigan. 1976. Suicide by persons with and without psychiatric contacts. *Archives of General Psychiatry* 33:209–16.

Lee, G. R. 1978. Marriage and morale in later life. *Journal of Marriage and the Family* 40:131–39.

Lewis, A. A., and B. Berns. 1975. *Three out of four wives: Widowhood in America*. New York: Macmillan.

Loge, B. J. 1977. Role adjustments to single parenthood: A study of divorced and widowed men and women. *Dissertation Abstracts International* 37:4647A.

Lopata, H. Z. 1969. Loneliness: Forms and components. *Social Problems* 17:248–62.

———. 1970. The social involvement of American widows. *American Behavioral Scientist* 14:41–57.

———. 1972. Role changes in widowhood: A world perspective. In D. O. Cowgill and L. D. Holmes (eds.), *Aging and modernization*. New York: Appleton-Century-Crofts.

———. 1973a. Self-identity in marriage and widowhood. *Sociological Quarterly* 14:407–18.

———. 1973b. Social relations of black and white widowed women in a Northern metropolis. *American Journal of Sociology* 78:1003–10.

———. 1973c. *Widowhood in an American city*. Cambridge, Mass.: Schenkman.

———. 1975a. On widowhood: Grief work and identity reconstruction. *Journal of Geriatric Psychiatry* 8:47–55.

———. 1975b. Widowhood: Societal factors in life-span disruptions and alternatives. In N. Datan and L. E. Ginsberg (eds.), *Life-span developmental psychology: Normative life crises*. New York: Academic Press.

———. 1978a. Contributions of extended families to the support systems of metropolitan area widows: Limitations of the modified kin network. *Journal of Marriage and the Family* 40:355–64.

———. 1978b. The absence of community resources in support systems of urban widows. *The Family Coordinator* 27:383–88.

———. 1979. *Women as widows: Support systems*. New York: Eisener.

Maddison, D. 1968. The relevance of conjugal bereavement for preventive psychiatry. *British Journal of Medical Psychology* 41:223–33.

McCourt, W. F., R. D. Barnett, J. Brennen, and A. Becker. 1976. We help each other: Primary prevention for the widowed. *American Journal of Psychiatry* 133:98–100.

Morgan, L. A. 1976. A re-examination of widowhood and morale. *Journal of Gerontology* 31:687–95.

Nimkoff, M. F. 1962. Changing family relationships of older people in the United States during the last fifty years. In C. Tibbits and W. Donahue (eds.), *Social and psychological aspects of aging*. New York: Columbia University Press.

Parke, R., Jr., and P. C. Glick. 1967. Prospective changes in marriage and the family. *Journal of Marriage and the Family* 29:249–56.

Parkes, C. M. 1970. The first year of bereavement—A longitudinal study of the reaction of London widows to the death of their husbands. *Psychiatry* 33:444–67.

———. 1975. Determinants of outcome following bereavement. *Omega* 6:303–23.

———. 1975b. Psycho-social transitions: Comparison between reactions to loss of a limb and loss of a spouse. *The British Journal of Psychiatry* 127:204–10.

———, B. Benjamin, and R. G. Fitzgerald. 1969. Broken heart: A statistical study of increased mortality among widowers. *British Medical Journal* 1:740–43.

Pearlin, L. I., and J. S. Johnson. 1977. Marital status, life-strains and depression. *American Sociological Review* 42:704–15.

Petrowsky, M. 1976. Marital status, sex, and the social networks of the elderly. *Journal of Marriage and the Family* 38:749–56.

Pihlblad, C. T., and D. L. Adams. 1972. Widowhood, social participation and life satisfaction. *Aging and Human Development* 3:323–30.

Pihlblad, C. T., D. L. Adams, and H. A. Rosencranz. 1972. Socioeconomic adjustment to widowhood. *Omega* 3:295–305.

Pihlblad, C. T., and R. L. McNamara. 1965. Social adjustment of elderly people in three small towns. In A. M. Rose and W. A. Peterson (eds.), *Older people and their social worlds*. Philadelphia: F. A. David Company.

Rico-Velasco, J., and L. Mynko. 1973. Suicide and marital status: A changing relationship? *Journal of Marriage and the Family* 35:239–44.

Rosen, D. H. 1973. Social relationships and successful aging among the widowed aged. *Dissertation Abstracts International* 34:2029A.

Rux, J. M. 1977. Widows and widowers: Instrumental skills, socio-economic status, and life satisfaction. *Dissertation Abstracts International* 37:7352A.

Schuckit, M. A., P. L. Miller, and D. Hahlbohm. 1975. Unrecognized psychiatric illness in elderly medical patients. *Journal of Gerontology* 30:655–60.

Sheskin, A., and S. E. Wallace. 1976–77. Differing bereavements: Suicide, natural, and accidental death. *Omega* 7:229–42.

Silverman, P. 1972. Widowhood and preventive intervention. *The Family Coordinator* 21:95–102.

———, and S. Englander. 1975. The widow's view of her dependent children. *Omega* 8:3–20.

Stehouwer, J. 1968. The household and family relations of old people. In E. Shanas, P. Townsend, D. Wedderburn, H. Friis, P. Milhoj, and J. Stehouwer (eds.), *Old people in three industrial societies*. New York: Atherton.

Streib, G. F. 1970. Old age and the family—Facts and forecasts. *American Behavioral Scientist* 14:25–39.

Tallmer, M., and B. Kutner. 1970. Disengagement and morale. *Gerontologist* 10:317–20.

Townsend, P. 1968. The structure of the family. In E. Shanss, P. Townsend, D. Wedderburn, H. Friis, P. Milhoj, and J. Stehouwer (eds.), *Old people in three industrial societies*. New York: Atherton.

Treas, J. 1975. Aging and the family. In D. S. Woodruff and J. Birren (eds.), *Aging: Scientific perspectives and social issues*. New York: D. VanNostrand.

———, and A. VanHiist. 1976. Marriage and remarriage rates among older Americans. *Gerontologist* 18:132–36.

VanCoevering, V. G. R. 1974. An exploratory study of middle-aged and older widows to investigate those variables which differentiate high and low life satisfaction. *Dissertation Abstracts International* 34:3895A.

Verbrugge, L. M. 1979. Marital status and health. *Journal of Marriage and the Family* 41:267–85.

Vinick, B. H. 1978. Remarriage in old age. *The Family Coordinator* 27:359–63.

Walters, J. 1980. Widowhood: The clapping of one hand. In J. E. Montgomery (ed.), *Handbook on aging*. Washington, D.C.: American Home Economics Association.

Watson, J. A. and V. R. Kivett. 1976. Influences on the life satisfaction of older fathers. *The Family Coordinator* 25:482–88.

XVI

REMARRIAGE

44

THE SIX STATIONS OF REMARRIAGE: DEVELOPMENTAL TASKS OF REMARRIAGE AFTER DIVORCE

Ann Goetting

Remarriage is emerging as a common form of marriage. Currently, remarriages represent 32% of all marriages in the United States (Price-Bonham & Balswick, 1980). As the divorce rate continues to rise and the rate of remarriage remains high—it recently has been estimated that 80% of Americans who are currently obtaining divorces will eventually remarry (Glick, 1975a)—an increasing number of people are finding themselves immersed in a marital structure quite different from the one with which they are familiar. As Schlesinger (1970) pointed out, a remarriage "possesses its own constructs, characteristics, and possibilities" (p. 101). Some of the most important differences between a first marriage and a remarriage are based on the ties each partner has to the previous marriage

Ann Goetting, "The Six Stations of Remarriage: Developmental Tasks of Remarriage After Divorce," *Family Relations*, April 1982, pp. 213–22. Copyrighted © by the National Council on Family Relations, 1219 University Avenue Southeast, Minneapolis, Minnesota 55414. Reprinted by permission.

through children, through financial and custodial settlement, through the family and friends of the former spouse, and through continued commitment and/or attachment to the former spouse. It is probably true that the single visible factor which most differentiates a remarriage from a first marriage is the presence of children from a former marriage. Cherlin (1978) indicated that when neither spouse had a child from a previous marriage, the family of remarriage closely resembled families of first marriage and most of the norms for first marriages applied.

Though it has been suggested that remarriages are happier and more successful than first marriages (Rollin, 1971), the best available evidence has consistently indicated over the last two decades that while most remarriages do remain intact until death, the risk of marital dissatisfaction and divorce is somewhat greater than that associated with first marriages (Cherlin, 1978; McCarthy, 1978). It is estimated that one third of first marriages will end in divorce while close to one half of remarriages will do so (U.S. Bureau of the Census, 1976).

Furstenberg (1979) pointed out that the rate of conjugal stability in remarriage is only slightly lower than that in first marriage and might well be accounted for, not by greater difficulties inherent in the structure of remarriage, but by the fact that remarriages include a disproportionately greater number of individuals who accept divorce as a solution to an unsatisfactory marital situation. While this may be true, while remarriage may not require a *more difficult* lifestyle or adjustment process than first marriage, it can be assumed to require one that is *different* and therefore worthy of consideration because of the unique nature of remarriage.

The main purpose of this paper is to examine remarriage as a process. More specifically, the concern is to explore the various developmental tasks associated with the status passage from divorced to remarried. The question addressed here is: what are the situations which a person may expect to encounter upon entering and participating in remarried life? Furstenberg introduced the concept "normative schedule" to describe demographic processes that become relatively constant over time. As marriage, divorce and subsequent remarriage become routinized, they become part of a normative schedule, part of the life course. While the processes of marriage and divorce have been charted (Berger & Kellner, 1964; Bohannan, 1970; Vaughan, 1978), the final component of this marital normative schedule, that is remarriage, virtually has been overlooked in the family literature. A descriptive model of this status passage from divorced to remarried could aid the practitioner in guiding clients through the developmental tasks associated with their transition into remarriage after divorce.

Before addressing the developmental tasks of remarriage, attention is turned to the divorce and remarriage trends which are the sources of this emerging marital form. The concern here is with why divorce and subsequent remarriage have become increasingly common. Why are more and more people accepting divorce as a solution to an unsatisfactory marriage? And why do so many, though the proportion is declining (Norton & Glick, 1976), find their way back into the marriage market and eventually recommitted to matrimony?

EXPLANATIONS FOR DIVORCE AND REMARRIAGE

Divorce

The divorce rate in the United States has been rising almost continuously since data were first collected by the United States Census Bureau. It is estimated that about 37% of first marriages currently being contracted will end in divorce if the present conditions affecting divorce continue (Glick, 1973). In the past when divorce was relatively rare it was blamed on individual deficiencies. With the dramatic increase during the middle 1960's when divorce was chosen as a solution to marital problems by a broader spectrum of the population, however, emphasis has turned away from the deviance perspective and toward societal-level explanations. One recent analysis blamed the long term divorce increase on five components of our social structure: (1) the doctrine of individualism; (2) the trend toward equality of sexes; (3) the trend toward a general acceptance of divorce; (4) growing systemness; and, (5) affluence (Goetting, 1979). While this analysis is quite comprehensive, other components could be added to constitute a long list of factors fostering divorce. For example, Glick (1975b, p. 8) suggested that the following factors contibute to marital disruption: (1) social disruption such as the Vietnam war and inflation; (2) the secularization of life which dilutes the influence of organized religion in discouraging divorce; (3) education for marriage and family life in churches, schools and colleges which fosters more objective evaluation of marriage and divorce; and, (4) marriage and divorce counseling which assist incompatible couples in dissolving intolerable marriages. Also, divorce has been blamed on the socialization process which teaches men and women to have different and even opposing interests and social orientations. The result is that they have difficulty as adults becoming the companions required by the modern marriage ethic (Goetting, 1981).

Remarriage

Unlike divorce, little attention has been devoted to the high rate of remarriage after divorce. While single isolated explanations are scattered throughout the family literature, no attempt has been made to integrate these ideas into a comprehensive set of societallevel explanations. An attempt here to do so yields four: (1) the value of romantic love; (2) social exchange—satiation and alternatives; (3) social norms; and, (4) norm ambiguity and role instability.

Romantic Love. Romantic love was conceptualized by Goode (1959) to mean a strong emotional attachment between adolescents or adults, consisting of at least the components of sex desire and tenderness. In American society it has been taught that being romantically in love and having this love reciprocated is a major goal in life. The individual who "has no one" is pitied or at least considered to be in this way unfulfilled. Furthermore it has been taught that appropriate fulfillment of the need for romantic love is found within the institution of marriage. Biegel (1951) and Goode (1959) suggested that while romantic love serves important functions for social stability, it is based on temporary personal need satisfaction, and therefore is unstable. A marriage based on such fragile ground is conducive to divorce. Biegel stated that the "burning craving" of romantic love cannot last. Goode agreed that the passion of romantic love dies in the marital relationship. He stated that the "antithesis of romantic love is 'conjugal' love, the love between a settled couple" (Goode, 1959, p. 39). Synthesizing this series of ideas on romantic love, it is suggested here that romantic love leads to marriage, which in turn leads to conjugal love, a nonromantic form of love. If this simple process is extended, some implications for remarriage can be suggested. The individual is taught to strive for romantic love and seek satisfaction within marriage. But then marriage destroys the romantic elements of the relationship and replaces them with a relationship based on responsibility. Therefore, married individuals who are no longer romantically involved with each other would be left unfulfilled and once again in pursuit of romantic love. Extramarital romantic love relationships or at least desires or fantasies of such would then stimulate divorce and ultimately result in remarriage.

Benson (Note 1) suggested that most married individuals avoid this cycle of remarriage probably because of a lack of ambition in the continuing search for love. Because they are influenced by various social controls (for example, norms disapproving extramarital romantic involvements), they in fact remain unfulfilled romantically.

Social Exchange—Satiation and Alternatives. Exchange theory offers another cyclical scheme explaining serial monogamy. Theories of social exchange view humans as reward-seeking, punishment-avoiding creatures. The theories perceive human interaction to be analogous to economic markets, though humans can exchange things which are not measured by money. People are motivated toward profit—that is, an excess of reward (something valuable) over cost (something punishing or loss of reward). From the perspectives of Homans (1961) and Thibaut and Kelley (1959) divorce and subsequent remarriage can be viewed as the exchange between marital partners, and explained in the following way: A and B choose to interact with one another (marry) because each obtains the highest profit (such as companionship, romantic love or whatever is valuable) relative to interacting with alternative persons in that kind of relationship. But eventually satiation will weaken that relationship. This is based on the assumption that the more of a rewarding activity a person receives from another, the less valuable the further units of that activity ("diminishing returns"). At the same time that the relationship is becoming weakened due to satiation, it is becoming further weakened because of the increase in alternative marriage partners resulting from social changes including industrialization, urbanization, the doctrine of individualism, and the increased proportion of women in the labor force. The many alternative spouses raise what Thibaut and Kelley refer to as the "comparison level for alternatives." Therefore, because of the satiation of marital rewards and the increase in alternative spouses, A and B will divorce and both find new partners who will again offer them the best profit (remarriage) until once again satiation sets in and a better alternative presents itself.

While under the principle of satiation it is assumed that the individual seeks rewards from interacting with a variety of people, a person *may* get such variety of interaction while being married. The need for variety may be satisfied by interacting with family, friends, colleagues or an extramarital lover. This is how exchange theorists would explain the marriages that last. If the spouses do not limit themselves to interacting with each other, that is, if they spend time together as well as time with others, satiation does not occur and so alternatives are less attractive. Thibaut and Kelley (1959) devoted a chapter to nonvoluntary relationships. They suggested that some below-comparison-level relationships (relationships that are below the person's standards of satisfaction) are maintained because alternatives are unacceptable. In other words, the marriage may provide too little reward, but the costs of divorce (one alternative) outweigh its rewards.

Social Norms. Another explanation for remarriage after divorce is that it represents an adaptation to social norms. One such norm is Farber's (1964) "permanent availability." Like romantic love, permanent availability is useful in explaining divorce and remarriage. According to Farber the norm of permanent marriage is being replaced by the norm of permanent availability. This notion implies that divorce can be explained by greater attractions to new spouses. It implies an expectation to better one's lot in society by progressing on to more attractive marital partners in somewhat the same way that one would move to a new position that offered a higher salary or better working conditions.

Another norm which has implications for remarriage is that of success in marriage. To the extent that divorce represents some kind of failure, marriage represents success. While there is social pressure on both sexes for success in marriage, such pressure is greater for women because the marriage and family have traditionally been her primary domain of responsibility. Whether a marriage is a "success" or "failure" is commonly largely attributed to the wife's "expressive" skills in maintaining the marriage. After an individual becomes divorced, the sense of failure can often be relieved by success within subsequent remarriage. In this sense, divorce carries within it the seeds of remarriage. Remarriage is an attempt to alleviate feelings of failure.

The third and final norm to be considered here which is conducive to remarriage after divorce is that of marriage itself. Marriage is the "normal" life-style, and society tends to organize social life on the basis of couples and families. Duberman (1974) stated: "Ours is a two-by-two world, and there is little room in it for the unaccompanied individual. . . . To justify their own state, married people think of marriage as 'natural' and anyone who does not conform to this point of view is challenging the social values" (p. 115). Being without a spouse places one in an awkward position often resulting in a truncated social life. Single persons may be excluded from social affairs because of their proverbial "fifth wheel" status. Adult singleness, not necessarily the divorced status, represents deviance from the norm, and in that way exerts social pressure toward marriage.

The pressure to become "normal" in terms of becoming a partner in marriage may be greater for parents than for other categories of singles because there are more individuals involved in the striving for a normal family life. Single parents may feel added pressure in terms of accomplishing normal lives not for only themselves but for their children.

Norm Ambiguity and Role Instability. In contrast to the view that remarriage after divorce is an adaptation to social norms is Goode's argument that such remarriage represents adaptation to norm ambiguity associated with the status of divorce. In his classic volume *Women in Divorce,* Goode (1956) suggested that the lack of norms associated with the status of being divorced created pressures toward remarriage, and in this way minimized social disruption caused by divorce. It was his contention that such norm ambiguity provided institutional pressures conducive to remarriage which allowed a high divorce rate to exist while kinship institutions were maintained and major societal disruption was avoided. Goode (1956) described the following four areas of norm ambiguity associated with the divorced status:

1. There are no ethical imperatives for relatives or friends to furnish needed material or emotional support during and after the crisis to divorcees *as* divorcees.

2. Issues are unclear concerning the readmission of divorcees into their former kinship structure or into a new one. We are not at all clear

as to where members of the divorcing family ought to go. Families of orientation are under no obligation to take them back, nor are former in-laws, even though in the case of the woman, they all have surnames in common.

3. There are no clear avenues for the formation of new families. It is unclear as to what constitutes appropriate behavior in terms of finding a second husband or wife. Such norm ambiguity permeates the relationships of the divorcees with parents, friends and children.

4. There is no clear definition concerning the general proper behavior and emotional attitudes of the divorced. They don't know whether they should be grieved or relieved. Lacking specification of behavior expectations, divorcees are subject to criticism by some regardless what they do.

It was Goode's assumption that the norm ambiguity associated with divorce places sufficient stress on most divorcees to pressure them back into the comfortably norm-regulated state of marriage. He believed that the lack of institutionalization of postdivorce adjustment functions to create pressures toward new marriages, which in turn maintain the kinship structures necessary for the survival of society. It should be noted that while such norm ambiguity could create pressure toward remarriage, it could instead lead to the development of clear norms for the divorced.

Bernard (1956) argued along the same general lines as Goode in her explanation of the high rate of remarriage after divorce. She referred to the inherent instability in the status of "divorced" and the resulting drive toward remarriage. She contended that even if divorced persons have no children, they cannot resume the status of being single because marriage has fundamentally altered their self-images, daily habits and leisure activities, relations with friends and family and even their identities.

Dissolution of marriage disrupts a complex integration of role, which requires a corresponding role to be played by someone in the outside world . . . his need for a partner who will play a complementary role and thus render functional a longstanding role of one's own is undoubtedly a strong motivational drive toward remarriage. (p. 125)

THE STATIONS OF REMARRIAGE

While there are clear factors favoring remarriage after divorce such as experience and maturity, it remains a trying experience for most who pursue it. As suggested earlier, a great portion of the problems associated with remarriage are related to the complexities introduced by children from former marriages. The complexity of an institution in itself need not present problems, but if society fails to provide guidelines for the relationships involved, the outcome may be one of chaos and conflict. For lack of such guidelines in Western culture, the remarried pair is often expected to function in the same way as does a first married pair, despite the fact that in addition to the new husband and wife there may be two former spouses, two sets of children, four sets of grandparents, and numerous other relatives and friends associated with a former marriage. In addition, there may be many unresolved feelings carried over into the new marriage.

Undoubtedly, remarriage after divorce is a complex process with several interrelated components. That process is described here through use of Bohannan's (1970) model outlining developmental tasks of divorce. His six "stations" of divorce consist of those tasks which must be mastered in order to exit successfully from an existing marriage. They include the emotional, legal, economic, coparental, community and psychic divorces. Those stations are revisited here in the course of moving from divorce to remarriage. As Furstenberg (1979) pointed out, a successful remarriage must involve undoing or refashioning many of the adaptations made to a successful divorce. As is true of the divorce stations, all six stations or remarriage need not necessarily occur to all remarrying people with the same intensity and in the same order. In fact, some individuals may avoid some stations altogether. The six stations of remarriage are ordered here in such a way that the first three can occur independent of the existence of children from a former marriage, while the last three assume the involvement of such children.

Emotional Remarriage

Typically the remarriage process begins with the emotional remarriage. This is the often slow process by which a divorced person reestablishes a bond of attraction, commitment and trust with a member of the opposite sex. After having experienced severe disappointment in a previous relationship, the divorcee learns to release emotions in an effort to once again secure comfort and love. Often this process is wrought with the fear that this emotional investment will lead to loss and rejection. Such fears may justifiably be intense because an additional failure at relationships threatens not only to leave the individual once again disappointed and alone, but also to damage identity and self-concept. Another divorce could strongly suggest to others as well as self a deficiency in those skills, whatever they may be, which are necessary to sustain a marriage. While there is always ambiguity in terms of cause and fault with one divorce—possibly it was at least partially the fault of the other spouse, or maybe the divorce could be blamed on a situation which surrounded that particular marriage—additional failures begin to single out an individual as a "loser." Due to the loss, rejection and failure that are typically associated with divorce, the emotional remarriage is a unique and often arduous and volatile process which is not satisfactorily completed by all who attempt it.

Psychic Remarriage

Psychic remarriage is the process of changing one's conjugal identity from individual to couple. It involves relinquishing the personal freedom and autonomy established by the psychic divorce, and resuming a lifestyle in which a person is expected to be viewed as one component of a partnership.

The psychic remarriage affects different individuals in different ways. For example, men and women are likely to differ in the amount of stress experienced in their respective transitions in conjugal identity. In general the psychic remarriage may represent less change for men than for women, and therefore mean less potential for difficulties in adjustment. Since the role of adult male in our society dictates a primary identity with occupational status thereby deemphasizing conjugal identity, men are likely to experience a relatively mild identity shift as they pass from the status of single person to that of mate. In other words, since the social status and therefore personal identity of a man is relatively independent of his marital status, a shift in his marital status would not represent an extreme alteration in personal identity. But the situation may be very different for women, who in accordance with traditional gender roles, identify strongly with their marital status. While the occupational sphere tends to be the domain of the man, the conjugal sphere is seen as the domain of the woman. It is the woman, then, who is faced with the more extreme identity shift when there is an alteration in marital status.

But the shift is not of equal intensity among all women. Changes in marital status would seemingly have a greater affect on women who hold traditional gender role attitudes than on those who hold non-traditional attitudes. The traditional women would suffer a great loss with psychic divorce, a true identity crisis. But upon remarriage these women would adjust easily in the psychic realm. For them psychic remarriage represents the recovery of their valued identity as wife. Non-traditional women, on the other hand, are likely to view the psychic divorce in positive terms as a period of growth into autonomous identity, an opportunity to do away with the restraints of couple identity. It is these women who are likely to have adjustment problems associated with psychic remarriage. To them the wife role is less important, and psychic remarriage represents loss of the more highly valued independence and freedom. It is interesting to note that the suggestion presented here that non-traditional women, when compared with traditional women, are likely to discover satisfaction in psychic divorce and severe stress in psychic remarriage has some empirical support in 1970 census statistics. Those data indicate that women with five or more years of college education (an index of non-traditional attitude) are divorcing more often than other divorced men and women (Glick, 1975b).

It becomes clear that psychic remarriage represents a different kind of process for different categories of people, but it safely can be assumed that in most, if not all, cases it represents some disruption and the consequent need for adjustment.

Community Remarriage

The community remarriage like the community divorce represents an alteration which a person often must make in relationships with a community of friends. Where the community divorce involves breaking away from the world of couples, entering what Hunt (1966) called "the world of the formerly married," the community remarriage involves re-entrance into the couple's world. Like the community divorce, the community remarriage may be a turbulent process. Unmarried friends are typically lost for lack of a common lifestyle, especially friends of the opposite sex. These friends are replaced by married couples, often remarried couples with whom remarrieds share important aspects of biography.

In some ways the process of community remarriage has potential for being more strenuous than does the process of community divorce because it can result in the loss of closer friends. With the community divorce one must give up couples, that is *pairs* of friends who were shared with a spouse. Often the friendships had not been intimate. Instead, they were secondary to, convenient to, and dependent upon, the marital relationship. They were not one's own friends, selected as a reflection of one's interests and needs. They were relationships based on the combined interests and needs of the spouses. But with the community remarriage, one may be put in a position of severing the close personally-tailored ties established while divorced, and replacing them with less intimate, couple-oriented relationships. Furthermore, those bonds of friendship established during that period of time when one was divorced may be particularly valuable because they lent support at a time of personal crisis. These were the friends who were there to help the individual through the typically devastating experiences associated with the divorce process.

So the community remarriage, while representing re-entrance into the "normality" of the couples' world, also may mean the eventual loss of valuable friendship bonds. Married life is often intolerant of relationships with unmarried friends. Its structure discourages those connections with the past, those ties with the world of the formerly married.

Parental Remarriage

The parental remarriage is necessary if there are children. It is the union of an individual with the children of this new spouse. Parental remarriage may be the most difficult developmental task of remarriage as suggested by one recent study (Messinger, 1976). It is certainly the one that has received the most attention in the literature as is indicated by the fact that a series of bibliographies on steprelationships, the product of parental remarriage, is periodically compiled and distributed for the use of social scientists (Sell, 1977). Unprecedented numbers of people find themselves living with other peoples' children, and many view the process of combining with them to form a family unit as challenging at best.

Fast and Cain (1966) suggested that the problems of stepparenthood are based on the fact that the role definition of stepparent in this society is poorly articulated, and implies contradictory expectations as "parent," "stepparent" and "nonparent." The stepparent cannot fully assume any of these roles, and therefore must individually work out behavior patterns for interacting with one's spouse's children. Folk tradition describes the stepmother as wicked and cruel—in a word, unparentlike—so to enact that role would be socially unacceptable. Instead, the stepparent is encouraged to assume the role of parent, for which there is legal support in the explication of the rights and duties entailed by the "in loco parentis" relationship. But the stepparent cannot totally assume the role of father or mother. The natural parent is typically still active in the parental role, which requires that the stepparent gracefully accede to the parental rights of another and behave as nonparent. The stepparent and the natural parent are placed in a position of sharing the residential, educational, financial, health, and moral decisions incumbent on the parental role. Society provides no guidelines for this sharing of rights and responsibilities which can easily lead to confusion, frustration, and resentment.

Another explanation for the difficulties associated with parental remarriage and the associated steprelationships is that marital role expectations between husband and wife are not worked out prior to the assumption of parental roles. Spouses are not allowed the opportunity to develop workable and comfortable marital relationships and to establish a primary husband-wife bond prior to the birth of children. Marital and parental adjustment must be confronted simultaneously which could encourage the inappropriate involvement of children in marital dissention. Marital and parental problems could easily confound one another. The natural parent's prior relationship to his child can serve as a threat to the establishment of a primary husband-wife bond. In that way it may detract from the integration of the new family unit.

One problem relating to stepparenthood that appears often in the literature is discipline. The stepparent is often reluctant to provide discipline because the clear authority vested in a natural parent is lacking. If the stepparent does actually attempt to discipline, such action may not be well-received by the child or may not be interpreted as acceptable by the spouse. This problem of discipline would seemingly be more common for stepfathers than stepmothers, since children typically stay with their mothers after divorce. It is the stepfather who most often enters a formerly single-parent family unit and who, therefore, actually experiences daily interaction with his stepchildren. The stepmother, on the other hand, usually spends limited time with her visiting stepchildren.

Another specific problem associated with parental remarriage concerns children as a link to the former marriage, and was expressed by Messinger's (1976) subjects. Some felt that continued ties through the children with previous family members made it more difficult for the new spouse to integrate into the new family unit. In this way they saw the children as a source of marital disruption. New mates frequently felt that such continued ties made them feel as though they were outsiders.

Economic Remarriage

The economic remarriage is the reestablishment after divorce of a marital household as a unit of economic productivity and consumption. Like the parental remarriage, it is a particularly difficult developmental task of remarriage, as evidenced by the Messinger study, which suggested that the problem of finances in remarriage was surpassed in severity only by problems associated with children. The economic remarriage as a developmental task can be considered as being an extension of the parental remarriage in that its main difficulties stem from the existence of children from a former marriage. When there are such children involved, the economic remarriage becomes complex in that it emerges as an open system, dependent on or at least interrelated with the economic behavior of individuals other than the two spouses.

Typically the standard of living increases at remarriage due to the simple fact that financial resources which had formerly maintained two residences are combined to support only one. So the problem is not so much one of insufficient funds as it is one of financial instability and resource distribution. One source of instability stems from the sporadic nature of incoming child support payments, especially after the mother has remarried. Many reconstituted families are simply unable to predict how much money will be available from month to month because of the uncertainty associated with the arrival of child support payment. Information (Note 2) collected in 1978 from a sample of United States women indicates that continuity of support payments declined somewhat with the remarriage of the mother; only 43% of the remarried wives reported having received their payments always, as opposed to 51% of the divorced but not remarried. Not knowing whether that next payment will arrive can introduce significant inconvenience into the remarriage household. A second source of economic instability lies in the unpredictable nature of the needs of the husband's children, who typically reside with their mother. While outgoing child support payments may be constant, the possibility of unexpected needs requiring extra financial cost (medical, educational, etc.) can loom as a dark cloud over the remarriage. It can bring the same kind of uncertainty and consequent inconvenience into the remarriage household as lack of continuity associated with incoming child support payments.

The problem of resource distribution refers to the issue of how the money should be spent; who should get how much of what is available? For example, if *his* daughter is given ballet lessons, should not *her* son be allowed tennis lessons, even though the sources of support for the two children are quite different? If the resources available to her son from her ex-spouse preclude such tennis lessons, should the stepfather finance such lessons for the sake of equity? Messinger (1976) reported frequent statements of discomfort and embarrassment on the part of mothers over the financial cost incurred for her new husband on behalf of her children. Society fails to provide guidelines for these kinds of situations, which can lead to stress in the remarital relationship.

The economic remarriage unites individuals from two different family systems and two different generations who have learned different and possibly opposing earning and spending habits. The problems involved in integrating such persons into a smooth functioning economic unit may provide a true challenge for all involved.

Legal Remarriage

Remarriage as a form of marriage is a creature of the law. Since it is such a relatively newly recognized way of life, its legal ramifications are only beginning to be explored. By the time a remarriage takes place, alimony, child support, and the division of property have already been set regarding the former marriage. The new marriage may cause additional legal considerations concerning responsibility toward relationships from the former marriage. The complexity of what Bohannan (1970) referred to as the pseudokinship system created by remarriage after divorce requires decisions regarding his and her financial resources, his and her former spouses, and his, her, and their children. In consideration of all of these, people need to evaluate their legal responsibilities and to decide how they want their resources distributed. Remarriage after divorce does not mean that a person exchanges one family for another; instead it means that the individual takes on an additional family. Since legal responsibilities associated with this action have not been clearly charted, individuals are left to base legal decisions on their own moral guidelines. For some this can be a difficult process because it involves assigning weights of importance to members of their complicated pseudokinship networks. Such questions arise as to which wife deserves the life and accident insurance, medical coverage, retirement benefits, pension rights and property rights. Is it the former wife who played a major role in building the estate or is it the current wife who has contributed less but is currently in his "good graces"? Also, to which children should he lend support for college education—his children, her children or their children? Since state inheritance laws typically favor a person's current spouse and natural children, inheritance rights need to be clearly defined at the point of legal remarriage if the person wishes to will benefits to a former spouse or to stepchildren.

Until the time that state legal codes respond to the needs of the remarried, individuals will continue to be left to work out the legal problems and decisions of remarriage after divorce. The imposition of structure by the state in this area not only would make the legal remarriage logistically simpler, but might contribute to increased affability for the relationships involved. The implementation of a standard procedure for the distribution of resources, for example, would eliminate the sense of competition and jealousy which is now encouraged by the lack of guidelines. If, for example, it was predetermined by the state that the resources of remarried persons would be divided among all of their surviving spouses in proportions corresponding to the length of each marriage, bitterness on the part of any of those spouses toward one another before or after death regarding equity in inheritance rights might be reduced. The burden of responsibility for distribution of resources would have been lifted from the individual by the state. Such legal structure could relieve tension among spouses, former spouses, parent-child relationships and steprelationships, and therefore contribute to the maintenance of the complex pseudokinship structure created by remarriage after divorce.

CONCLUDING STATEMENT

As divorce and subsequent remarriage become increasingly common, adjustment to their developmental tasks becomes a greater concern for family practitioners. While individuals face different tasks in varying orders, it has been suggested here that the six developmental tasks of divorce outlined by Bohannan are also important developmental tasks of remarriage. Remarriage can be a complex process, and its adjustment accordingly difficult. The problems associated with remarital adjustment are often heightened by the fact that partners in remarriage may still be adjusting to their divorces. At remarriage, a person may be compelled to commence the stations of remarriage while having not yet completed the stations of divorce. For example, as an individual struggles with establishing bonds of affection, commitment and trust with a new partner, he or she may still be contending with the severance of emotional ties with the former spouse. In order to be able to provide guidance and support to individuals in the throes of remarital adjustment, the practitioner needs to be familiar, first, with the general complexity of remarriage after divorce and, second, with the specific developmental tasks which can be anticipated as part of the adjustment process.

NOTES

[1] Benson, L. Personal communication. 1969.

[2] These data were obtained from a combination of the March and April 1979 Current Population Surveys conducted by the United States Bureau of the Census. Although the information has not been published by the Bureau, it has been made available on computer tapes.

REFERENCES

Berger, P. L. and H. Kellner, 1964. Marriage and the construction of reality. *Diogenes* 46:1–23.

Bernard, J. 1956. *Remarriage: A study of marriage.* New York: Dryden Press.

Biegel, H. 1951. Romantic love. *American Sociological Review* 16:326–34.

Bohannan, P. 1970. The six stations of divorce. In P. Bohannan (ed.), *Divorce and after.* New York: Doubleday.

Cherlin, A. 1978. Remarriage as an incomplete institution. *American Journal of Sociology* 84:634–50.

Duberman, L. 1974. *Remarriage and its alternatives.* New York: Praeger.

Farber, B. 1964. *Family: Organization and interaction.* San Francisco: Chandler.

Fast, I., and A. C. Cain. 1966. The stepparent role: Potential for disturbances in family functioning. *American Journal of Orthopsychiatry* 36:485–91.

Furstenberg, F. F. 1979. Recycling the family. *Marriage and Family Review* 2 (3), 1:12–22.

Glick, P. C. 1973. Dissolution of marriage by divorce and its demographic consequences. *International Population Conference* 2:65–69. Liege, Belgium: International Union for the Scientific Study of Population.

———. 1975a. A demographer looks at American families. *Journal of Marriage and the Family* 31:15–26.

———. 1975b. Some recent changes in American families. *Current Population Reports: Special Studies,* Series P-23, No. 52. Washington, D.C.: Government Printing Office.

Goetting, A. 1979. Some societal-level explanations for the rising divorce rate. *Family Therapy* VI (2):71–87.

———. 1981. Divorce outcome research: Issues and perspectives. *Journal of Family Issues* 2:350–78.

Goode, W. J. 1956. *Women in divorce.* New York: Free Press.

———. 1959. The theoretical importance of love. *American Sociological Review* 24:38–47.

Homans, G. C. 1961. *Social behavior: Its elementary forms.* New York: Harcourt, Brace and World.

Hunt, M. M. 1966. *The world of the formerly married.* New York: McGraw-Hill.

McCarthy, J. 1978. A comparison of the probability of the dissolution of first and second marriages. *Demography* 15 (3): 345–59.

Messinger, L. 1976. Remarriage between divorced people with children from previous marriages: A proposal for preparation for remarriage. *Journal of Marriage and Family Counseling* 38:193–200.

Norton, A. J., and P. C. Glick. 1976. Marital instability: Past, present and future. *Journal of Social Issues* 32:5–20.

Price-Bonham, S. and J. O. Balswick. 1980. The noninstitutions: Divorce, desertion and remarriage. *Journal of Marriage and the Family* 42:959–72.

Rollin, B. 1971. The American way of marriage: Remarriage. *Look,* September 21, pp. 62–67.

Schlesinger, B. 1970. Remarriage as family reorganization for divorced persons: A Canadian study. *Journal of Comparative Family Studies,* 1 (1):101–18.

Sell, K. D. 1977. *Divorce in the 1970's*. Salisbury, N.C.: Department of Sociology, Catawba College.

Thibaut, J. W. and H. H. Kelley. 1959. *The social psychology of groups*. New York: Wiley.

U.S. Bureau of the Census. 1976. Number, timing and duration of marriages and divorces in the United States: June, 1975. *Current Population Reports,* Series P-20, No. 297. Washington, D.C.: Government Printing Office.

Vaughan, D. 1978. Uncoupling: The social construction of divorce. In H. Robboy, S. L. Greenblatt, and C. Clark (eds.), *Social Interaction: Introductory readings in sociology*. New York: St. Martins.

45

REMARRIAGE AS AN INCOMPLETE INSTITUTION

Andrew Cherlin

Sociologists believe that social institutions shape people's behavior in important ways. Gerth and Mills (1953, p. 173) wrote that institutions are organizations of social roles which "imprint their stamps upon the individual, modifying his external conduct as well as his inner life." More recently, Berger and Luckmann (1966) argued that institutions define not only acceptable behavior, as Gerth and Mills believed, but also objective reality itself. Social institutions range from political and economic systems to religion and language. And displayed prominently in any sociologist's catalogue of institutions is a fundamental form of social organization, the family.

The institution of the family provides social control of reproduction and child rearing. It also provides family members with guidelines for proper behavior in everyday family life, and, presumably, these guidelines contribute to the unity and stability of families. But in recent years, sociologists have de-emphasized the institutional basis of family unity in the United States. According to many scholars, contemporary families are held together more by consensus and mutual affection than by formal, institutional controls.

The main source of this viewpoint is an influential text by Ernest Burgess and Harvey Locke which appeared in 1945. They wrote:

The central thesis of this volume is that the family in historical times has been, and at present is, in transition from an institution to a companionship. In the past, the important factors unifying the family have been external, formal, and authoritarian, as the law, the mores, public opinion, tradition, the authority of the family head, rigid discipline, and elaborate ritual. At present, in the new emerging form of the companionship family, its unity inheres less and less in community pressures and more and more in such interpersonal relationships as the mutual affection, the sympathetic understanding, and the comradeship of its members. [P. vii]

In the institutional family, Burgess and Locke stated, unity derived from the unchallenged authority of

Andrew Cherlin, "Remarriage as an Incomplete Institution," *American Journal of Sociology,* Vol. 84, No. 3 (1978), pp. 634–50. Copyright ©1978 by the University of Chicago. Reprinted by permission.

the patriarch, who was supported by strong social pressure. But, they argued, with urbanization and the decline of patriarchal authority, a democratic family has emerged which creates its own unity from interpersonal relations.

Many subsequent studies have retained the idea of the companionship family in some form, such as the equalitarian family of Blood and Wolfe (1960) or the symmetrical family of Young and Wilmott (1973). Common to all is the notion that patriarchal authority has declined and sex roles have become less segregated. Historical studies of family life demonstrate that the authority of the husband was indeed stronger in the preindustrial West than it is now (see, e.g., Aries 1962; Shorter 1975). As for today, numerous studies of "family power" have attempted to show that authority and power are shared more equally between spouses (see Blood and Wolfe 1960). Although these studies have been criticized (Safilios-Rothschild 1970), no one has claimed that patriarchal authority is as strong now as the historical record indicates it once was. Even if we believe that husbands still have more authority than wives, we can nevertheless agree that patriarchal authority seems to have declined in the United States in this century.

But it does not follow that institutional sources of family unity have declined also. Burgess and Locke reached this conclusion in part because of their assumption that the patriarch was the transmitter of social norms and values to his family. With the decline of the patriarch, so they believed, a vital institutional link between family and society was broken. This argument is similar to the perspective of Gerth and Mills, who wrote that a set of social roles becomes an institution when it is stabilized by a "head" who wields authority over the members. It follows from his premise that if the head loses his authority, the institutional nature of family life will become problematic.

Yet institutionalized patterns of behavior clearly persist in family life, despite the trend away from patriarchy and segregated sex roles. As others have noted (Dyer and Urban 1958; Nye and Berardo 1973), the equalitarian pattern may be as firmly institutionalized now as the traditional pattern was in the past. In the terms of Berger and Luckmann, most family behavior today is habitualized action which is accepted as typical by all members—that is, it is institutionalized behavior. In most everyday situations, parents and children base their behavior on social norms: parents know how harshly to discipline their children, and children learn from parents and friends which parental rules are fair and which to protest. These sources of institutionalization in the contemporary American family have received little attention from students of family unity, just as family members themselves pay little attention to them.

The presence of these habitualized patterns directly affects family unity. "Habitualization," Berger and Luckmann wrote, "carries with it the important psychological gain that choices are narrowed" (1966, p. 53). With choices narrowed, family members face fewer decisions which will cause disagreements and, correspondingly, have less difficulty maintaining family unity. Thus, institutional support for family unity exists through the routinization of everyday behavior even though the husband is no longer the unchallenged agent of social control.

Nowhere in contemporary family life is the psychological gain from habitualization more evident than in the families of remarried spouses and their children, where, paradoxically, habitualized behavior is often absent. We know that the unity of families of remarriages which follow a divorce is often precarious—as evidenced by the higher divorce rate for these families than for families of first marriages (U.S. Bureau of the Census 1976). And in the last few decades, remarriage after divorce—as opposed to remarriage after widowhood—has become the predominant form of remarriage. In this paper, I will argue that the higher divorce rate for remarriages after divorce is a consequence of the incomplete institutionalization of remarriage after divorce in our society. The institution of the family in the United States has developed in response to the needs of families of first marriages and families of remarriages after widowhood. But because of their complex structure, families of remarriages after divorce that include children from previous marriages must solve problems unknown to other types of families. For many of these problems, such as proper kinship terms, authority to discipline stepchildren, and legal relationships, no institutionalized solutions have emerged. As a result, there is more opportunity for disagreements and divisions among family members and more strain in many remarriages after divorce.

The incomplete institutionalization of remarriage after divorce reveals, by way of contrast, the high degree of institutionalization still present in first marriages. Family members, especially those in first marriages, rely on a wide range of habitualized behaviors to assist them in solving the common problems of family life. We take these behavioral patterns for granted until their absence forces us to create solutions on our own. Only then do we see the continuing importance of institutionalized patterns of family behavior for maintaining family unity.

I cannot provide definitive proof of the hypothesis linking the higher divorce rate for remarriages after divorce to incomplete institutionalization. There is very little quantitative information concerning remarriages. In fact, we do not even know how many stepparents and stepchildren there are in the United States. Nor has there ever been a large, random-sample survey designed with families of remarriages in mind. (Bernard's 1956 book on remarriage, for example, was based on information supplied nonrandomly by third parties.) There are, nevertheless, several studies which do provide valuable information, and there is much indirect evidence bearing on the plausibility of this hypothesis and of alternative explanations. I will review this evidence, and I will also refer occasionally to information I collected through personal interviews with a small, nonrandom sample of remarried couples and family counselors in the northeast. Despite the lack of data, I believe that the problems of families of remarriages are worth examining, especially given the recent increases in divorce and remarriage rates. In the hope that this article will stimulate further investigations, I will also present suggestions for future research. . . .

PREVIOUS EXPLANATIONS

One explanation, favored until recently by many psychiatrists, is that the problems of remarried people arise from personality disorders which preceded their marriages (see Bergler 1948). People in troubled marriages, according to this view, have unresolved personal conflicts which must be treated before a successful marriage can be achieved. Their problems lead them to marry second spouses who may be superficially quite different from their first spouse but are characterologically quite similar. As a result, this theory states, remarried people repeat the problems of their first marriages.

If this explanation were correct, one would expect that people in remarriages would show higher levels of psychiatric symptomatology than people in first marriages. But there is little evidence of this. On the contrary, Overall (1971) reported that in a sample of 2,000 clients seeking help for psychiatric problems, currently remarried people showed lower levels of psychopathology on a general rating scale than persons in first marriages and currently divorced persons. These findings, of course, apply only to people who sought psychiatric help. And it may be, as Overall noted, that the differences emerged because remarried people are more likely to seek help for less serious problems. The findings, nevertheless, weaken the psychoanalytic interpretation of the problems of remarried life.

On the other hand, Monahan (1958) and Cherlin (1977) reported that the divorce rate was considerably higher for people in their third marriages who had divorced twice than for people in their second marriages. Perhaps personality disorders among some of those who marry several times prevent them from achieving a successful marriage. But even with the currently high rates of divorce and remarriage, only a small proportion of all adults marry more than twice. About 10% of all adults in 1975 had married twice, but less than 2% had married three or more times (U.S. Bureau of the Census 1976).

Most remarried people, then, are in a second marriage. And the large number of people now divorcing and entering a second marriage also undercuts the psychoanalytic interpretation. If current rates hold, about one-third of all young married people will become divorced, and about four-fifths of these will remarry. It is hard to believe that the recent increases in divorce and remarriage are due to the sudden spread of marriage-threatening personality disorders to a large part of the young adult population. I conclude, instead, that the psychoanalytic explanation for the rise in divorce and the difficulties of remarried spouses and their children is at best incomplete.[1]

A second possible explanation is that once a person has divorced he or she is less hesitant to do so again. Having divorced once, a person knows how to get divorced and what to expect from family members, friends, and the courts. This explanation is plausible and probably accounts for some of the difference in divorce rates. But it does not account for all of the research findings on remarriage, such as the finding of Becker et al. (1976) that the presence of children from a previous marriage increased the probability of divorce for women in remarriages, while the presence of children from the new marriage reduced the probability of divorce. I will discuss the implications of this study below, but let me note here that a general decrease in the reluctance of remarried persons to divorce would not explain this finding. Moreover, the previously divorced may be more hesitant to divorce again because of the stigma attached to divorcing twice. Several remarried people I interviewed expressed great reluctance to divorce a second time. They reasoned that friends and relatives excused one divorce but would judge them incompetent at marriage after two divorces.

Yet another explanation for the higher divorce rate is the belief that many remarried men are deficient at fulfilling their economic responsibilities. We know that divorce is more likely in families where the husband has low earnings (Goode 1956). Some remarried men, therefore, may be unable to earn a sufficient amount of money to support a family. It is conceivable that this inability to be a successful breadwinner could account for all of the divorce rate differential, but statistical studies of divorce suggest otherwise. Three recent multivariate analyses of survey data on divorce have shown that remarried persons still had a higher probability of divorce or separation, independent of controls for such socioeconomic variables as husband's earnings (Becker et al. 1976), husband's educational attainment (Bumpass and Sweet 1972), and husband's and wife's earnings, employment status, and savings (Cherlin 1977). These analyses show that controlling for low earnings can reduce the difference in divorce probabilities, but they also show that low earnings cannot fully explain the difference. It is possible, nevertheless, that a given amount of income must be spread thinner in many remarriages, because of child-support or alimony payments (although the remarried couple also may be receiving these payments). But this type of financial strain must be distinguished from the questionable notion that many remarried husbands are inherently unable to provide for a wife and children.

INSTITUTIONAL SUPPORT

The unsatisfactory nature of all these explanations leads us to consider one more interpretation. I hypothesize that the difficulties of couples in remarriages after divorce stem from a lack of institutionalized guidelines for solving many common problems of their remarried life. The lack of institutional support is less serious when neither spouse has a child from a previous marriage. In this case, the family of remarriage closely resembles families of first marriages, and most of the norms for first marriages apply. But when at least one spouse has children from a previous marriage, family life often differs sharply from first marriages. Frequently, as I will show, family members face problems quite unlike those in first marriages—problems for which institutionalized solutions do not exist. And without accepted solutions to their problems, families of remarriages must resolve difficult issues by themselves. As a result, solving everyday problems is sometimes impossible without engendering conflict and confusion among family members.

The complex structure of families of remarriages after divorce which include children from a previous marriage has been noted by others (Bernard 1956; Bohannan 1970; Duberman 1975). These families are expanded in the number of social roles and relationships they possess and also are expanded in space over more than one household. The additional social roles include stepparents, stepchildren, stepsiblings, and the new spouses of noncustodial parents, among others. And the links between the households are the children of previous marriages. These children are commonly in the custody of one parent—usually the mother—but they normally visit the noncustodial parent regularly. Thus they promote communication among the divorced parents, the new stepparent, and the noncustodial parent's new spouse.

Family relationships can be quite complex, because the new kin in a remarriage after divorce do not, in general, replace the kin from the first marriage as they do in a remarriage after widowhood. Rather, they add to the existing kin (Fast and Cain 1966). But this complexity alone does not necessarily imply that problems of family unity will develop. While families of remarriages may appear complicated to Americans, there are many societies in which complicated kinship rules and family patterns coexist with a functioning, stable family system (Bohannan 1963; Fox 1967).

In most of these societies, however, familial roles and relationships are well defined. Family life may seem complex to Westerners, but activity is regulated by established patterns of behavior. The central difference, then, between families of remarriages in the United States and complicated family situations in other societies is the lack of institutionalized social regulation of remarried life in this country. Our society, oriented toward first marriages, provides little guidance on problems peculiar to remarriages, especially remarriages after divorce.

In order to illustrate the incomplete institutionalization of remarriage and its consequences for family life, let us examine two of the major institutions in society: language and the law. "Language," Gerth and Mills (1953, p. 305) wrote, "is necessary to the operations of institutions. For the symbols used in institutions coordinate the roles that compose them, and justify the enactment of these roles by the members of the institution." Where no adequate terms exist for an important social role, the institutional support for this role is deficient, and general acceptance of the role as a legitimate pattern of activity is questionable.

Consider English terms for the roles peculiar to remarriage after divorce. The term "stepparent," as Bohannan (1970) has observed, originally meant a person who replaced a dead parent, not a person who was an additional parent. And the negative connotations of the "stepparent," especially the "stepmother," are well known (Bernard 1956; Smith 1953). Yet there are no other terms in use. In some situations, no term exists for a child to use in addressing a stepparent. If the child calls her mother "mom," for example, what should she call her stepmother? This lack of appropriate terms for parents in remarriages after divorce can have negative consequences for family functioning. In one family I interviewed, the wife's children wanted to call their stepfather "dad," but the stepfather's own children, who also lived in the household, refused to allow this usage. To them, sharing the term "dad" represented a threat to their claim on their father's attention and affection. The dispute caused bad feelings, and it impaired the father's ability to act as a parent to all the children in the household.

For more extended relationships, the lack of appropriate terms is even more acute. At least the word "stepparent," however inadequate, has a widely accepted meaning. But there is no term a child living with his mother can use to describe his relationship to the woman his father remarried after he divorced the child's mother. And, not surprisingly, the rights and duties of the child and this woman toward each other are unclear. Nor is the problem limited to kinship terms. Suppose a child's parents both remarry and he alternates between their households under a joint custody arrangement. Where, then, is his "home"? And who are the members of his "family"? These linguistic inadequacies correspond to the absence of widely accepted definitions for many of the roles and relationships in families of remarriage. The absence of proper terms is both a symptom and a cause of some of the problems of remarried life.

As for the law, it is both a means of social control and an indicator of accepted patterns of behavior. It was to the law, for instance, that Durkheim turned for evidence on the forms of social solidarity. When we examine family law, we find a set of traditional guidelines, based on precedent, which define the rights and duties of family members. But as Weitzman (1974) has shown, implicit in the precedents is the assumption that the marriage in question is a first marriage. For example, Weitzman found no provisions for several problems of remarriage, such as balancing the financial obligations of husbands to their spouses and children from current and previous marriages, defining the wife's obligations to husbands and children from the new and the old marriages, and reconciling the competing claims of current and ex-spouses for shares of the estate of a deceased spouse.

Legal regulations concerning incest and consanguineal marriage are also inadequate for families of remarriages. In all states marriage and sexual relations are prohibited between persons closely related by blood, but in many states these restrictions do not cover sexual relations or marriage between other family members in a remarriage—between a stepmother and a stepson, for example, or between two stepchildren (Goldstein and Katz 1965). Mead (1970), among others, has argued that incest taboos serve the important function of allowing children to develop affection for and identification with other family members without the risk of sexual exploitation. She suggested that current beliefs about incest—as embodied in law and social norms—fail to provide adequate security and protection for children in households of remarriage.[2]

The law, then, ignores the special problems of families of remarriages after divorce. It assumes, for the most part, that remarriages are similar to first marriages. Families of remarriages after divorce, consequently, often must deal with problems such as financial obligations or sexual relations without legal regulations or clear legal precedent. The law, like the language, offers incomplete institutional support to families of remarriages.

In addition, other customs and conventions of family life are deficient when applied to remarriages after divorce. Stepparents, for example, have difficulty determining their proper disciplinary relationship to stepchildren. One woman I interviewed, determined not to show favoritism toward her own children, disciplined them more harshly than her stepchildren. Other couples who had children from the wife's previous marriage reported that the stepfather had difficulty establishing himself as a disciplinarian in the household. Fast and Cain (1966), in a study of about 50 case records from child-guidance settings, noted many uncertainties among stepparents about appropriate role behavior. They theorized that the uncertainties derived from the sharing of the role of parent between the stepparent and the noncustodial, biological parent. Years ago, when most remarriages took place after widowhood, this sharing did not exist. Now, even though most remarriages follow divorce, generally accepted guidelines for sharing parenthood still have not emerged.

There is other evidence consistent with the idea that the incomplete institutionalization of remarriage after divorce may underlie the difficulties of families of remarriages. Becker et al. (1976) analyzed the Survey of Economic Opportunity, a nationwide study of approximately 30,000 households. As I mentioned above, they found that the presence of children from a previous marriage increased the probability of divorce for women in remarriages, while the presence of children from the new marriage reduced the probability of divorce. This is as we would expect, since children from a previous marriage expand the family across households and complicate the structure of family roles and relationships. But children born into the new marriage bring none of these complications. Consequently, only children from a previous marriage should add to the special problems of families of remarriages.[3]

In addition, Goetting (1978a, 1978b) studied the attitudes of remarried people toward relationships among adults who are associated by broken marital ties, such as ex-spouses and the people ex-spouses remarry. Bohannan (1970) has called these people "quasi-kin." Goetting presented hypothetical situations involving the behavior of quasi-kin to 90 remarried men and 90 remarried women who were white, previously divorced, and who had children from previous marriages. The subjects were asked to approve, disapprove, or express indifference about the behavior in each situation. Goetting then arbitrarily decided that the respondents reached "consensus" on a given situation if any of the three possible response categories received more than half of all responses. But even by this lenient definition, consensus was not reached on the proper behavior in most of the hypothetical situations. For example, in situations involving conversations between a person's present spouse and his or her ex-spouse, the only consensus of the respondents was that the pair should say "hello." Beyond that, there was no consensus on whether they should engage in polite conversation in public places or on the telephone or whether the ex-spouse should be invited into the new spouse's home while waiting to pick up his or her children. Since meetings of various quasi-kin must occur regularly in the lives of most respondents, their disagreement is indicative of their own confusion about how to act in common family situations.

Still, there are many aspects of remarried life which are similar to life in first marriages, and these are subject to established rules of behavior. Even some of the unique aspects of remarriage may be regulated by social norms—such as the norms concerning the size and nature of wedding cermonies in remarriages (Hollingshead 1952). Furthermore, as Goode (1956) noted, remarriage is itself an institutional solution to the ambiguous status of the divorced (and not remarried) parent. But the day-to-day life of remarried adults and their children also includes many problems for which there are no institutionalized solutions. And since members of a household of remarriage often have competing or conflicting interests (Bernard 1956), the lack of consensual solutions can make these problems more serious than they otherwise would be. One anthropologist, noting the lack of relevant social norms, wrote, "the present situation approaches chaos, with each individual set of families having to work out its own destiny without any realistic guidelines" (Bohannan 1970, p. 137). . . .

NOTES

[1] Despite the lack of convincing evidence, I am reluctant to discount this explanation completely. Clinical psychologists and psychiatrists with whom I have talked insist that many troubled married persons they have treated had made the same mistakes twice and were in need of therapy to resolve long-standing problems. Their clinical experience should not be ignored, but this "divorce-proneness" syndrome seems inadequate as a complete explanation for the greater problems of remarried people.

[2] Bernard (1956) noted this problem in the preface to the reprinted edition of her book on remarriage. "Institutional patterns," she wrote, "are needed to help remarried parents establish relationships with one another conducive to the protection of their children."

[3] In an earlier paper (Cherlin 1977), I found that children affected the probability that a woman in a first marriage or remarriage would divorce only when the children were of preschool age. But the National Longitudinal Surveys of Mature Women, from which this analysis was drawn, contained no information about whether the children of remarried wives were from the woman's previous or current marriage. Since the Becker et al. (1976) results showed that this distinction is crucial, we cannot draw any relevant inferences about children and remarriage from my earlier study.

REFERENCES

Ariès, Philippe. 1962. *Centuries of childhood*. New York: Knopf.

Becker, G., E. Landes, and R. Michael. 1976. Economics of marital instability. Working Paper no. 153. Stanford, Calif.: National Bureau of Economic Research.

Berger, Peter L., and Thomas Luckmann. 1966. *The social construction of reality*. New York: Doubleday.

Bergler, Edmund. 1948. *Divorce won't help*. New York: Harper & Bros.

Bernard, Jessie. 1956. *Remarriage*. New York: Dryden.

Blood, Robert O., and Donald M. Wolfe. 1960. *Husbands and wives*. New York: Free Press.

Bohannan, Paul. 1963. *Social anthropology*. New York: Holt, Rinehart & Winston.

———. 1970. Divorce chains, households of remarriage, and multiple divorces. Pp. 127–39 in *Divorce and after*, edited by Paul Bohannan. New York: Doubleday.

Bumpass, L. L., and A. Sweet. 1972. Differentials in marital instability: 1970. *American Sociological Review* 37 (December): 754–66.

Burgess, Ernest W., and Harvey J. Locke. 1945. *The family: From institution to companionship*. New York: American.

Cherlin, A. 1977. The effects of children on marital dissolution. *Demography* 14 (August): 265–72.

Duberman, Lucile. 1975. *The reconstituted family*. Chicago: Nelson-Hall.

Dyer, W. G., and D. Urban. 1958. The institutionalization of equalitarian family norms. *Journal of Marriage and Family Living* 20 (February): 53–58.

Fast, I., and A. C. Cain. 1966. The stepparent role: Potential for disturbances in family functioning. *American Journal of Orthopsychiatry* 36 (April): 485–91.

Fox, Robin. 1967. *Kinship and marriage.* Baltimore: Penguin.

Gerth, Hans, and C. Wright Mills. 1953. *Character and social structure.* New York: Harcourt, Brace & Co.

Goetting, Ann. 1978*a*. The normative integration of the former spouse relationship. Paper presented at the annual meeting of the American Sociological Association, San Francisco, September 4–8.

———. 1978*b*. The normative integration of two divorce chain relationships. Paper presented at the annual meeting of the Southwestern Sociological Association, Houston, April 12–15.

Goldstein, Joseph, and Jay Katz. 1965. *The family and the law.* New York: Free Press.

Goode, William J. 1956. *Women in divorce.* New York: Free Press.

Hollingshead, A. B. 1952. Marital status and wedding behavior. *Marriage and Family Living* (November), pp. 308–11.

Locke, Harvey J. 1951. *Predicting adjustment in marriage: A comparison of a divorced and a happily married group.* New York: Holt.

Mead, M. 1970. Anomalies in American postdivorce relationships. Pp. 107–25 in *Divorce and After,* edited by Paul Bohannan. New York: Doubleday.

Monahan, T. P. 1958. The changing nature and instability of remarriages. *Eugenics Quarterly* 5:73–85.

Nye, F. Ivan, and Felix M. Berardo. 1973. *The family: Its structure and interaction.* New York: Macmillan.

Overall, J. E. 1971. Associations between marital history and the nature of manifest psychopathology. *Journal of Abnormal Psychology* 78 (2):213–21.

Safilios-Rothschild, Constantina. 1970. The study of family power structure: A review 1960–1969. *Journal of Marriage and the Family* 32 (November): 539–52.

Shorter, Edward. 1975. *The making of the modern family.* New York: Basic.

Smith, William C. 1953. *The stepchild.* Chicago: University of Chicago Press.

U.S. Bureau of the Census. 1973. *U.S. census of the population: 1970. Persons by family characteristics.* Final Report PC(2)-4B. Washington, D.C.: Government Printing Office.

———. 1976. *Number, timing, and duration of marriages and divorces in the United States: June 1975.* Current Population Reports, Series P-20, No. 297. Washington, D.C.: Government Printing Office.

U.S. National Center for Health Statistics. 1953. *Vital statistics of the United States, 1950.* Vol. 2. *Marriage, divorce, natality, fetal mortality, and infant mortality data.* Washington, D.C.: Government Printing Office.

———. 1977. *Vital statistics report. Advance report. Final marriage statistics, 1975.* Washington, D.C.: Government Printing Office.

Weitzman, L. J. 1974. Legal regulation of marriage: Tradition and change. *California Law Review* 62:1169–1288.

Young, Michael, and Peter Wilmott. 1973. *The symmetrical family.* New York: Pantheon.

XVII

THE FUTURE

46

TRENDS IN MARRIAGE AND THE FAMILY—THE 1980'S

David Knox

"New" is the most frequently used word in the advertising industry. It alerts interested buyers to the latest fashion, product, or advancement. Such interest in "what's new?" is also true of educators/counselors in marriage and the family. We are concerned not only about "what's new" but "what's next" in our field.

This paper is an attempt to identify the latest trends in marriage and the family. It is based on a comprehensive review of the literature as part of the research for a textbook—*Exploring Marriage and the Family* (Knox, 1979).[1] While some of the trends are firmly established, others are more tenuous or predictive.

GENERAL TRENDS

Increased governmental interest is a general trend in marriage and the family. President Carter said in his inaugural address, "I join in the hope that when my time as your President has ended, people might say this about our nation . . . that we had strengthened the American Family, which is the basis of our society." Although the White House Conference on Families has been postponed, it is scheduled for 1981.

Another general trend in marriage and the family is the accumulation of more sophisticated data. General Mills recently sponsored a study conducted by Yankelovich, Skelly and White, Inc. of 23 million American families with children under 13. The report was based on a national probability sample of 1,230 families and a total of 2,102 interviews including parents and children (General Mills, 1977). In addition, the National Opinion Research Center in Chicago annually collects data from a random sample of non-institutionalized adults 18 years and over in the United States. Questions relevant to marriage and the family are always included in this study. Furthermore, as the competition for journal space increases, the quality of research improves. A review of articles published in *The Journal of Marriage and the Family* will verify this trend.

David Knox, "Trends in Marriage and the Family—The 1980's," *Family Relations,* April 1980, pp. 145–50. Copyrighted ©1980 by the National Council on Family Relations, 1219 University Avenue Southeast, Minneapolis, Minnesota 55414. Reprinted by permission.

SEX ROLES

Trends in sex roles include fewer barriers to women, fewer workaholic men, and more androgynous people. In the past ten years, a number of barriers to women have been removed. Opportunities now exist for women to become judges, business executives, doctors, and generals where recently there was little if any chance of doing so. And, while inequities still exist in the economic and political arenas, advances are being made on both fronts.

In addition to women gaining greater access to the positions in society they desire, more men are beginning to question the value of devoting their lives to chasing money. Personnel managers in private industry now speak of a "new breed" who are less willing to take a promotion if it would mean moving their families or greater personal stress (Filene, 1976).

As pressures to perform traditional female or male roles are lessened, an increasing number of people will be regarded as androgynous—they will have both feminine and masculine characteristics. In a study of 2,000 undergraduates, one-third were classified as androgynous (Bem, 1977). Such androgynous individuals feel freer to follow their own interests independent of stereotyped sex-role expectations (Bem & Lenney, 1976).

LOVE RELATIONSHIPS

Just as the sexes will become more similar, love relationships will include less romanticism. A central belief of the romantic is that there is only one person with whom one can "truly" fall in love. This belief had its basis in the past. "Men and women most often loved only once in their lives partly because their life expectancy was much shorter and partly because, in most cases, their lifestyle did not allow them to meet a great variety of people" (Safilios-Rothschild, 1977, p. 9). But female children born in 1977 have a life expectancy of 81, and male children can expect to live until 72. During this span, each sex will doubtless encounter an array of love relationships and will less likely maintain the belief that there is "only one true love."

One researcher emphasized that the decline in romantic love has already begun (Wilkinson, 1978). Such a decline is related to greater sexual permissiveness, the lessening of the double standard, and the increasing popularity of cohabitation. In essence, as the obstacles to spending more time together in intimate interaction are removed, the reality of the woman-man relationship will replace romantic notions.

SEX: BEHAVIOR AND EDUCATION

With increasing acceptance of the permissiveness-with-affection sexual value (Reiss, 1976), a greater percentage of unmarried individuals will engage in sexual intercourse at earlier ages. Between 1971 and 1976 the prevalence of sexual intercourse among never married women in the United States (ages 15–19) increased 30 percent (Zelnik and Kanter, 1977). And the median age for their first intercourse experience declined about four months during this period. The median ages for 1971 and 1976 were, respectively, 16.5 and 16.2 (p. 61). Both trends will continue.

Consistent with the trends just noted, our society will increasingly recognize that sexual behavior among youth is already occurring, that parents do not provide adequate sex education, and that the school system must. The Supreme Court's decision allowing contraceptives to be made available to all children forecasts the trend away from pretending that what the young don't know won't hurt them. Instead, the trend will be toward insuring that individuals in our society have accurate information about their own bodies, reproduction, and the place of sexual behavior in human relationships.

MARRIAGE/COHABITATION

Although marriage will continue to be the dominant life-style choice for most Americans, the age at marriage will increase. This trend is already established. Of those who married in 1977, both sexes were one year older than those married in 1960. In 1977, the median age at marriage for men was 24.0 and for women, 21.6, in contrast to 22.8 and 20.3 respectively in 1960 (U.S. Bureau of the Census, 1978).

Just as the age at marriage is increasing, the

prevalence of cohabitation is increasing. After reviewing a variety of data, Macklin (1978) wrote, "... one is tempted to project that, across the country as a whole, probably about 25% of the undergraduate population has cohabited; 50% would if they were to find themselves in an appropriate relationship and in a situation where they could; and 25% feel they probably would not do so even if it were possible (more of these being females and underclassmen)" (p. 209).

But those who live together are likely to be more cautious about the legal implications of their relationship, particularly if they live together for a considerable period of time. In the case of Michelle Triola Marvin and Lee Marvin who lived together for almost seven years, the California Supreme Court held that "the mere fact that a couple have not participated in a valid marriage ceremony cannot serve as a basis for a court's inference that the couple intended to keep their earnings and property separate and independent" (Bernstein, 1977, p. 365). The fact that Marvin was ordered to pay $104,000 for the "rehabilitation" of Ms. Marvin suggests implied agreements between cohabitants may be enforceable. Rod Stewart, Nicke Nolte, Alice Cooper, and Flip Wilson, like Lee Marvin are being sued by the women they lived with. The caution light is on for cohabitants.

MATE SELECTION/ENGAGEMENT

The pattern by which women and men meet is also changing. The traditional pattern in which the man calls the woman for a "date" is being replaced by the contemporary pattern of "hanging out" and "getting together" (Libby, 1977). In this pattern, individuals go where they can meet members of the opposite sex in informal ways without an introduction. The women's movement has been instrumental in increasing the acceptance of women going to singles' bars and initiating relationships.

But since role relationships are changing, the person they meet may not have the role values they anticipate. While the women's movement has sensitized women to seek equalitarian relationships with men, socialization of men to perceive women in other than traditional roles has been less extensive. As a result, there may be more confusion during first encounters when the "new" woman and the traditional man meet. And, since the women's movement has not influenced all women and since some men are nontraditional, the woman seeking a traditional relationship may be surprised to find a nontraditional man.

Once a decision to marry is made, an increasing number of couples will try alternatives to the traditional formal engagement. While the engagement ring and announcement of the impending wedding will remain the script for most people, a growing number, particularly those who have cohabited, will bypass the formality of the engagement (and honeymoon) period.

DUAL-CAREER MARRIAGE

The trend toward married women working outside the home will continue. The proportion of employed married women in the labor force increased from 30% in 1960 to 40% in 1970. By 1977, 46.6% of the labor force were employed wives (Department of Labor, 1977). The women's movement and a decreased birth rate are primary factors influencing the continued trend toward increased employment among married women.

An increased commitment by wives to paid employment will result in fewer mothers with small children remaining at home. To encourage young mothers to continue working, more companies will offer "flexitime." This system permits a worker to select the eight hours he or she will work between 7:30 a.m. and 6:30 p.m. By 1976, over 300,000 Americans were enjoying flexitime in over one thousand companies and government agencies (Stein, Cohen & Gadon, 1976).

In addition to more young mothers in the work force enjoying flexitime schedules, there will be an increase in commuter marriages. Also referred to as "weekend" or "long distance" marriages, commuter marriages refer to spouses who live apart because the demands of their respective careers require that they live in different cities (New York Times News Service, 1977).

SEXUAL FULFILLMENT

Greater availability of information on factors that contribute to sexual fulfillment, increased willingness to seek help for sexual dysfunctions, and a larger supply of trained professionals to meet the demand for therapy are among the current trends that promise more widespread sexual fulfillment in the future. Magazines such as *Redbook, Ladies Home Journal, McCall's* and *Family Circle* regularly feature articles on sexual aspects of the woman-man relationship. Masters and Johnson are names no longer known by professionals alone since their research is available to every person who stands in line to pay for groceries.

Reading about sex therapy alerts individuals to the causes and potential cures of sexual dysfunctions they may be experiencing in their own relationships. And becoming aware that others have consulted professionals to assist them in achieving various sexual goals increases the chance that they will do likewise.

To meet the increasing demand for sex therapy, more professionals are being trained. A beginning point is to provide physicians with more training in sexuality. In the early 1960s, only three schools offered any instruction in sexuality. In the mid-1970s, 106 of the country's 112 medical schools offered sex courses (Holden, 1976, p. 99). In addition, the American Association of Sex Educators accredits trained experts in sex education. As standards for sex therapists are raised, more will seek the appropriate training that will insure better service to couples. In essence, Americans will become more sophisticated about sexual matters and will expect more help with their sexual problems from the professional community.

PLANNING CHILDREN

The future of family planning will involve increased tolerance for the childfree alternative. Current research suggests that childfree couples are similar to couples who have children in life satisfaction, maturity, and self esteem (Silka & Kiesler, 1977). Whether the number of couples who choose the childfree lifestyle will increase significantly is unknown. The key seems to be the availability of rewarding career opportunities for young women. If low-status, low-paying jobs remain the predominant employment opportunity, motherhood will continue to be viewed as the more rewarding alternative (Silka & Kiesler, 1977).

It is likely that the one-child family will also become more acceptable (Hawke & Knox, 1977). Current concerns about inflation, population growth, and the wife's career will influence young couples to question whether the two-child family is indeed "ideal." And, as more parents examine the myths about only children, fewer will have a second child "to save the first."

Test tube conception will also increase. In the summer of 1978, the world's first "test tube" baby was born to Lesley Brown, a thirty-year-old British woman. The procedure of uniting a sperm and egg in the laboratory and implanting the fertilized egg in the uterus was developed by Drs. Pat Steptoe and Robert Edwards. Both predicted an increase in the use of this procedure by the estimated 2 million American couples whose infertility stems from problems related to blocked or damaged fallopian tubes. A study supported by *Parents Magazine* revealed that 85% of American women believed that the test-tube method of conception should be made available to married couples unable to conceive naturally (Yarrow, 1978).

HAVING CHILDREN

The future of parenthood will include a greater awareness of what the role involves, increased sharing by both spouses in the birth of their child/children, and more emphasis on fatherhood. Proponents of the National Alliance for Optional Parenthood and authors of such books as *A Baby . . . Maybe?* (Whelan, 1976) sensitize would-be parents to the realities of parenthood. Although most couples opt for having children regardless of the childfree media, they are more likely to enter parenthood with a more realistic awareness of the positive and negative aspects of that role. And the increased availability of and enrollment in preparation for parenthood classes suggests that spouses will be more informed about parenthood when their children are born.

Among the preparation for parenthood classes available to potential parents is the Lamaze class which emphasizes active involvement of the father in the delivery process (Phillips & Anzalone, 1978).

Some hospitals are adapting to this trend toward couple participation in childbirth and permit the father to observe and participate (cut the umbilical cord) during the delivery. At Family Hospital in Milwaukee, fathers are not considered visitors but can spend as much time as they like with the mother and baby.

In addition to more sophisticated parents who share the birth experience, the role of the father will be increasingly emphasized. "Far from being irrelevant or insignificant, fathers are salient figures in the lives of their infants from early life" (Lamb & Lamb, 1976, p. 383). Books such as *Father Power* (Biller & Meredith, 1975) and *Fathering* (Green, 1976) provide a guide to fathering in much the same way the Spock books have been a guide for millions of mothers.

REARING CHILDREN

Trends in child rearing include more single parent families, more single parent fathers, and less authoritative disciplining procedures. In addition to single parent families created out of divorce, more never-married individuals are seeking to adopt children (Kopecky, 1977) or to have them though they are not married (Ashdown-Sharp, 1977). And, while there will be an overall increase in the number of single parent families (and less stigmatization), more fathers will seek custody of their children in divorce settlements (Mendes, 1976). Dr. Ken Lewis, a divorced father of two daughters, won custody of his children on the grounds that the word "mother" is a verb and that he had demonstrated better "mothering skills" than the biological mother.

A new trend in child discipline may also be in the offing. One psychologist observed that regular spankings and phrases like "Because I said so" will be replaced with positive rewards, parent-child contracts, and family councils (Dodson, 1978).

THE LATER YEARS

Gerontology will continue to be an expanding field, not only because there is an interest in discovering causes of the aging process (with the hope of slowing it), but because there will be an increasing number of older people in our society. The number of elderly will double in the next fifty years. Such a rapid growth is due to the "graying" of those born in the post-World War II baby boom.

Governmental interest in the elderly will also continue. The raising of mandatory retirement age, the growth of Social Security benefits, and the plans for a White House Conference on Aging in 1981 all reflect the growing political power of the elderly. Further gains can be expected.

Attitudes toward aging in our society will also become more positive as the elderly increase in number and visibility and become more normative and politically powerful. Increased political clout can be used to ensure benefits for them. The "Gray Revolution" has begun.

DIVORCE

Trends in marital dissolution include an increasing divorce rate, new divorce laws, and the suggestion of a National Center for the Study of Divorce. Regarding the frequency of divorce, "If the current trends continue, over one-half of America's populous will have been directly touched by divorce before the turn of the century" (Johnson, 1977, p. 263). And these divorces are not limited to those in the early years of marriage. Increasingly, spouses who have been married over 20 years are terminating their marriages.

In addition to an escalating divorce rate, there are several trends in divorce legislation. These include an increasing number of states switching from fault grounds for divorce to no-fault divorce, the granting of alimony payments to either sex (e.g., Maryland), the granting of child custody to both parents, (e.g., Arizona), and the inclusion in divorce settlements that grandparents will have visitation rights (e.g., Wisconsin).

One researcher has suggested the establishment of a National Center for the Study of Divorce (Johnson, 1977). Such a center would go "beyond the traditional legalistic approach to divorce, making use of that vast body of knowledge and resources available with the social sciences to institute a comprehensive program directed at understanding marital breakdown" (p. 265).

IMPLICATIONS

The various trends in marriage and the family have a behavioral implication—to stay informed. What was once a relatively infrequent occurrence (living together, childless marriages, working wives) now happens with increasing frequency and/or greater visibility (cohabitation, childfree marriages, dual-career marriages). And traditional values regarding virginity, authoritarian parenthood, and uninvolved fatherhood are experiencing increased competition with those of permissiveness-with-affection, democratic parenthood and Lamaze deliveries. In addition, new phenomena keep emerging—test tube conceptions, no-fault divorce, and commuter marriages. As family life educators, we are responsible to provide our students with the most current information available to assist them in making their own decisions about marriage and parenthood.

Marriage and family counselors might also increase their awareness of trends in marriage and family living. The counselor who knows that sex roles (androgyny) and marriage roles (dual-career/commuter marriages) are changing will bring a different cognitive set to the counseling experience than the counselor who assumes that traditional patterns are firmly established. In essence, as family life educators and counselors, we have the same charge—to do our homework so as to provide the best possible service to our students and clients.

NOTE

[1] Lewis, Ken. *The tender years doctrine.* Unpublished manuscript, 1977. (Available from the author, Department of Social Work and Corrections, East Carolina University.)

REFERENCES

Ashdown-Sharp, P. 1977. *A guide to pregnancy & parenthood for women on their own.* New York: Vintage.

Bem, S. L. 1977. Beyond androgyny: Some presumptuous prescriptions for a liberated sexual identity. In A. S. Skolnick and J. H. Skolnick (eds.), *Family in transition.* Boston: Little, Brown.

———, and E. Lenney, 1976. Sex typing and the avoidance of cross-sex behavior. *Journal of Personality and Social Psychology* 33: 48–54.

Bernstein, B. E. 1977. Legal problems of cohabitation. *The Family Coordinator* 26: 361–66.

Biller, H., and D. Meredith. 1975. *Father power.* New York: Anchor.

Dodson, F. 1978. *How to discipline with love, from crib to college.* New York: Rawson.

Filene, P. 1976. Him/her/self. In J. Blankenship (ed.), *Scenes from life: Family, marriage and intimacy.* Boston: Little, Brown.

General Mills American family report: Raising children in a changing society. 1977. Minneapolis: General Mills, Inc.

Green, M. 1976. *Fathering.* New York: McGraw-Hill.

Hawke, S., and D. Knox, 1977. *One child by choice.* Englewood Cliffs, N.J.: Prentice-Hall.

Holden, C. 1976. Sex therapy: Making it as a science and an industry. In A. Kilbride (ed.), *Focus: Human sexuality.* Guilford, Conn.: Dushkin.

Johnson, W. D. 1977. Establishing a national center for the study of divorce. *The Family Coordinator* 26: 331–36.

Knox, D. 1979. *Exploring marriage and the family.* Glenview, Ill.: Scott, Foresman.

Kopecky, G. 1977. What is it like for singles who adopt: Four family stories. *Ms.,* June, p. 45.

Lamb, M., and J. E. Lamb. 1976. The nature and importance of the father-infant relationship. *The Family Coordinator* 25: 379–85.

Libby, R. W. 1977. Creative singlehood as a sexual life style: Beyond marriage as a rite of passage. In R. Libby and R. Whitehurst (eds.), *Marriage and alternatives: Exploring intimate relationships.* Glenview, Ill.: Scott, Foresman.

Macklin, E. D. 1978. Review of research on nonmarital cohabitation in the United States. In B. Murstein (ed.), *Exploring intimate life styles.* New York: Springer.

Mendes, H. A. 1976. Single fatherhood. *Social Work* 21: 308–12.

New York Times News Service. 1977. Commuter marriages on rise. *Raleigh News and Observer,* October 31.

Phillips, C. R., and J. T. Anzalone. 1978. *Fathering: Participation in labor and birth.* St. Louis: Mosby.

Reiss, I. L. 1976. The effect of changing trends, attitudes, and values on premarital sexual behavior in the United States. In S. Gordon and R. Libby (eds.), *Sexuality today and tomorrow.* North Scituate, Mass.: Duxbury.

Safilios-Rothschild, C. 1977. *Love, sex, and sex roles.* Englewood Cliffs, N.J.: Prentice-Hall.

Silka, L., and S. Kiesler. 1977. Couples who choose to remain childless. *Family Planning Perspectives* 9: 16–25.

Stein, B., A. Cohen, and H. Gadon. 1976. Flexitime: Work when you want to. *Psychology Today.* July, pp. 40–44.

U.S. Bureau of the Census. 1978. Marital status and living arrangements, March, 1977. *Current Population Reports.* (Series P-20, No. 323). Washington, D.C.: Government Printing Office.

U.S. Department of Labor. 1977. *Single men and married women show unusually large labor force gains.* (News Release 77-792). Washington, D.C.: Government Printing Office.

Whelan, E. 1976. *A baby . . . maybe?* New York: Bobbs-Merrill.

Wilkinson, M. L. 1978. Romantic love and sexual expression. *The Family Coordinator* 27: 141–48.

Yarrow, L. 1978. Test-tube babies: For or against? *Parents Magazine,* November, p. 83.

Zelnik, M., and J. F. Kanter. 1977. Sexual and contraceptive experience of young unmarried women in the United States 1976 and 1971. *Family Planning Perspectives* 9: 55–71.

47

THE NEW UTOPIAN VISION? BRINGING COMMUNITY TO THE FAMILY

Rosabeth Moss Kanter

I

The recent search for intimate community was a revival, not a discovery. Communal movements are as old as American history. In the mid-1800s Ralph Waldo Emerson remarked that every other person seemed to carry in his vest pocket a plan for the "perfect society." Indeed, Emerson's friends had gone back-to-the-land at Brook Farm; New York newspapers were running columns for people interested in forming communal associations; the Shakers, a sturdy network of communal villages already decades old, were reaching a population peak of several thousand members; Louisa May Alcott was observing with amusement her father's abortive attempt to create an organic Garden of Eden called Fruitlands; and guardians of conventional morality were condemning the radical "free lovers" at the Oneida community.

The United States, with its promise of endless land and abundant resources, has provided fertile soil for the full flowering of the urge to utopia. Believing that the world is not fully given but that people fashion it, pioneers have periodically set out to find the right place for a Fresh Start. If only we could be free to reshape social institutions, utopians argue, then inherent human goodness will flourish.

In the past a large number of American utopian visions have been imported: immigrants such as the Puritans, the Shakers, and a variety of German religious sects came to the New World to establish their ideal communities. European thinkers such as Robert Owen and Charles Fourier inspired

---

Rosabeth Moss Kanter, "The New Utopian Vision? Bringing Community to the Family," *Journal of Current Social Issues.* Used by permission.

ventures in the States rather than in their own countries, just as Eastern gurus today flock to America to find a following. A new nation founded in liberal optimism supports utopian experimentation.

At the same time, America's very newness and emphasis on progress (psychologically internalized as the need to achieve) has left many Americans feeling rootless and isolated. From the nineteenth century to today, American critics have decried a "loss of community" with the growth of distancing, impersonal, achievement-pressuring industrial institutions. Out of criticisms of the present quality of life coupled with faith in human perfectibility have come the communal alternatives, disengaged from the urban-industrial mainstream. Communal movements have been prominent at times of social ferment like the 1840–50s and the late 1960s, and they tend to occur along with other radical movements: feminism, black liberation, mysticism and pastoralism.[1]

The first American communes were predominantly religious, basing their common work, joint property ownership and distaste for private families on Biblical or spiritual precepts, often conveyed by a charismatic leader perceived to be directly inspired by God. A second theme stressing socialist economics as an antidote to industrial capitalism developed with Owen's New Town of New Harmony, Indiana, in the 1820s (a disaster) and the Associationist movement of the 1840s. The recent communal movements contributed still a third theme, an image of a personal utopia the size of family, more often inspired by psychology than theology. Despite differences in rhetoric, most American utopian visions always stressed the personal, spiritual growth of the individual in a climate of close, loving relationships. From the Shakers' concern with salvation to Synanon's present sense of itself as a therapeutic community, personal growth has always been embodied in the distinctively American search for community.

What difference has American communalism made? Until now, very little. The mainstream society has conducted business as usual. But in the 1970s the idea of communal living spread from hippie farms and isolated spiritual retreats into the cities, where urban dwellers took over rambling old houses and established communal households. Six or eight adults renting a house together, sharing chores, working out cooperative child care and helping each other through transitions like school to job, divorce, or early days in a new city—all this may seem a long way from Utopia. But such small steps, suddenly manageable for vast numbers of people, may have more long-range meaning to American society than all of the unattainable grand visions of the past.

II

The impact of new family forms is not in their numbers or the degree to which they become widespread throughout the society, but rather that the forms themselves are indicators of a shifting basis for relationships in all families, conventional as well as unconventional. New family forms indicate a movement towards what I term the "post-biological family." In *The Coming of Post-Industrial Society,* Daniel Bell lists a large number of words prefixed by "post" to indicate the character of the emerging future: "post-bourgeoise," "post-modern," "post-civilized," "post-Puritan," "post-literate," as well as Bell's own "post-industrial."[2] "The use of the hyphenated prefix 'post' indicates," says Bell, "that sense of living in interstitial time." We may not know where we are going as a society, but we certainly know where we have been, and we may also sense that the past is not an appropriate guide to the society of the future.

There are two traditional meanings of "family": as an actual set of biologically defined relationships; and as a metaphor for a quality of relationships. I believe that there is a growing separation of these two meanings of "family." Even families that resemble in all structural and formal respects the conventional nuclear family model of the past are increasingly basing their relations on the second meaning of the family, *family as quality of feeling* rather than family as biological ties. Families of the past have derived their strength and stability from relationships of commitment based on an implied biological base. Families of the future may gain their strength and stability because of their ability intentionally to create family feeling, whether or not biological ties and biological imperatives are present. Thus, I mean by the term post-biological family a situation in which biological imperatives no longer define intimacy and household composition.

There are many indications that family relationships are already changing, that the shift away from the biological imperative as the prime definer of family relationships is already occurring. The biological imperatives behind traditional family life assume that families are incomplete without one man and one woman in a sexual relationship and one child attached to both of them, and that families are essentially complete with such members; that mutual connections to a bloodline through the childbirth process define rights, obligations and residence; that family feeling derives from the given of blood-relatedness and intimate connection through prolonged sexual contact (for the parents) and through early childhood (for the child); that fidelity and loyalty, possessiveness and jealousy are natural and necessary; that biologically-defined differences (age and sex) lead to role differentiation and mutual dependence; that ties created by childbirth and prolonged sexual contact are unique and not replaceable; and that generational differences define and make legitimate parental authority. Such assumed biological imperatives have been challenged today by a variety of new forms competing for the definition "family." These include single parents, reconstituted families in which the biological link with children is broken through divorce, egalitarian marriages in which sex-typed division of labor is minimized, homosexual marriages and the creation of artificial kin relations and households of unrelated adults such as communes, cooperatives and family clusters. In addition to the existence of new family forms, a number of other developments also indicate a movement toward the transcendence of biology in building intimate relationships, including limited fertility; high divorce rates; the separation of sex from procreation; an increasing assumption promoted in part by encounter groups and the encounter group culture of interchangeability among people with respect to intimacy; a long secular trend of decline in parental authority; an assumption that what is idealized with respect to the family can be intentionally created; and criteria of self-fulfillment and emotional satisfaction rather than commitment and legal responsibility as bases for relationships.

The family may be "here to stay," then, as Mary Jo Bane indicates in her new book by that title,[3] but what people want and expect from their close relationships may be different. The contemporary utopian urge is close to home; it involves bringing the spirit of community to a family setting. In this sense, there is something important to be learned from communal movements despite the transiency and difficulties of communes as a social form. Communes are a social laboratory, a place for experimentation, rather than a replacement for the family. The difficulties and problems are undeniable; contemporary communal groups are highly fragile and vulnerable to a number of characteristic stresses. The initial enthusiasm for the potentials represented by communes has declined as openness to social experimentation itself has waned in the 1970s. What was once a popular—and publicly visible—movement has dwindled to a handful of groups. Cooperative households, where they still exist, are now scaled down in size and aspirations, with looser and more utilitarian commitments (low-cost housing and housemates for companionship). Group living is clearly temporary, and turnover in membership is high. Couples and parents with children generally prefer the sanctity of their own territory to the strains of including others.[4] It is single people, those on their way out of marriages, or those moving through life transitions that seek the support of the artificial and intentional "family" in a communal group.

But communal households are an arena in which new assumptions about intimate relationships are worked out and lived daily. Those biological families that wish to enrich the quality of their relationships can examine how communes go about intentionally creating a spirit of community. The new urban communes that sprung up since 1969 can be viewed as repositories of traditional family virtues and values—but in a collective context and without biological basis. While nurturant services are increasingly available for purchase from secondary institutions outside the home (the *New York Times* recently reported that 60 percent of the meals consumed inside the American home were purchased outside of the home), communal households make such services the central focus of their joint existence. Home-centeredness and participation in nurturant functions are characteristic of men as well as women in urban communes, for example. Thus, communes can be seen as laboratories for the family, as indicating ways in which family feeling can be created and made meaningful in the absence of biological ties.

III

Some communal groups have succeeded in this mission better than others and from examination of their experiences we can learn about developing the spirit of community. My own research uncovered some of the things that distinguished successful communities of the past. I compared thirty nineteenth-century American utopian communities—nine that lasted thirty-three years or more (called "successful") with twenty-one that existed less than sixteen years and on the average about four years ("unsuccessful"). Among the communes in the study were the Shakers, Oneida, Amana, Harmony, New Harmony and Brook Farm. The study asked over 120 questions about the presence or absence of certain social arrangements that build commitment and create strong group feeling.[5]

Successful nineteenth-century communities built strong commitment to their group through the kinds of sacrifices and investments members made for and in the community, through discouraging extra-group ties and building strong family feeling within the community, through identity change processes for members and through value and belief systems that gave meaning and direction to the community.

Long-lived communities tended to require some sacrifices of their members and an austere life of struggle, as well as full investment of money and property, so that participants had a stake in the fate of the community. They tended to ensure the concentration of loyalty within the community by geographical separation and by discouraging contact with the outside. They spread affection throughout the whole community by discouraging exclusive relationships based on two person attraction or biological family—through either free love (in which sexual contact with all others was required) or celibacy (in which no one had sexual contact) and separation of biological families with communal child-rearing. These mechanisms aimed at creating an equal share in man-woman and adult-child relationships for everyone. Family feeling was enhanced by selection of a homogeneous group of members; by full communistic sharing of property; by collective labor in which no jobs were paid in money, everyone shared equally in community benefits, jobs were rotated through the membership, and some work was done by the whole community by regular group contact through meetings (routine decision-making ones and T-group-like sessions); and by rituals emphasizing the communion of the whole. Identity change processes in long-lived communes tended to consist of T-group-like mutual criticism sessions in which issues of commitment and deviance and meeting of community standards were examined, and through stratification systems that accorded deference to those best living up to community norms. Finally, long-lived communes tended to have elaborate beliefs and values providing purpose and meaning for community life and an ultimate guide and justification for decisions. There tended to be strong central figures, charismatic leaders who symbolized the community's values and provided inspiration for decisions. While routine decisions might be made by assemblies of the whole or committees with special responsibilities, and while administrative and other work assignments might be rotated and shared, the charismatic leader, as value bearer, still was an ultimate source of authority. In some cases charisma came not from a single leader but from participation in meaningful historic traditions. In general, daily life was defined by, and stemmed from coherent and explicit values.

What I found, then, was that successful nineteenth-century utopias developed a number of ways of dealing with group relations, property, work, values and leadership—all of which created an enduring commitment, involving motivation to work, will to continue, fellowship and cohesion as a group. At the same time that this enabled the successful communities to survive in terms of longevity, such practices also created strong communities in the utopian sense and fulfilled many of the desires impelling people toward community today. The successful groups provided for their members strong feelings of participation, involvement and belonging to a family group. They built a world centered around sharing—of property, of work, of living space, of feelings, of values. They offered identity and meaning, a value-oriented life of direction and purpose.

IV

Many practices of these traditional communities strike us today as authoritarian or unduly restricting of individual freedom and choice—although contemporary spiritual movements (from Zen monasteries to Jesus communes to Arica) are organized in remarkably similar ways. But in milder, more engaging, less demanding ways, the practices that enhance commitment and feelings of closeness can be translated to modern life. We can note the importance of sacrifice and shared struggle in building togetherness—working hard to create something jointly, rather than having it without effort. (How many parents forget that their own closeness is based on the material struggles of their early years when they try to give their children everything?) We can see that developing some boundaries around a relationship, some things that are special inside it, helps its cohesiveness. The value of joint projects, of rotating and sharing chores, of whole group work efforts, becomes clear. And also relevant to contemporary life are the rituals and celebrations, the open communication and honest expression of feelings, and the interest in traditions and recording shared history that make people feel bound together. Some examples from contemporary communal households show how the spirit of community can be translated to a family setting.

Dinner and meal preparation in general play a central role in a communal household. Meals tend to be the one activity common to every group defining itself in communal terms. An ad on the bulletin board of a Boston referral service indicated the two most central functions that at least one person saw in communal living; "Share food and self." For many members of communal households, the sharing of food is seen to be an aspect of sharing of self. Meals, particularly dinner, are often to be spiritual as well as physical events. Many groups begin the meal with songs or grace or a moment of silence when all present at the table hold hands with one another. Meal preparation is the one chore that is universally shared across communal households, with every member of the group generally cooking once a week. The act of cooking for the group is sometimes seen as a gift, an offering, a way of taking responsibility for the nurturance of another. Meals are often feasts with several courses and elaborate desserts. (It is much easier to prepare a feast if one does so only once a week.)

The kitchen, thus, becomes the ritual center of the household as it is in many families, a place where the most important activities of the group take place. Since meals are one of the few routine times at which the whole group gathers to enjoy itself, people often linger around the dinner table well after the dishes are cleared in order to continue the banter or good conversation. The kitchen functions as communication center in other ways also. The refrigerator is often the place where notices and announcements are posted, where the cooking and cleaning schedule is to be found, and where people post requests for services from one another. It is likely that a person coming home will stop by the refrigerator before going to his or her own quarters. In asking people to draw psychological maps of their houses in which they put the spaces in which they felt most connected in the center, the kitchen was often next to the person's own room as a place of comfort and connection. Meals and kitchens are but symbols of a larger value in communal households; the imbuing of domestic events from cleaning to garbage collection with political and spiritual significance. Among the counter-cultures of the 1960s were many that stressed ecology, nutrition, and caretaking as important and valued aspects of concern. Thus the most mundane and even obnoxious domestic chores tend to be seen as important and shared by members of the household. In one commune, for example, the man who was responsible for sorting garbage and trash and recycling cans and bottles glorified his job with the title "Ecology Man."

For many members of communal households

the immediate environment is a locus of creative efforts. Crafts, decorating, construction and remodeling are all signs of the interest people take in the home. In this realm in particular, members of communal households can be seen as acting out traditional family virtues and values in a very direct way; it is interesting to note that they are merely living out the direction for domesticity embedded in women's supermarket magazines and the American home handyman penchant for "do-it-yourself."

Open communication and consensual decision-making, along with sharing and rotation of chores, help create an egalitarian atmosphere in communal households. Weekly or bi-weekly house meetings are nearly universal features of communal life, and attendance is considered one of the most important parts of a member's commitment. Such meetings serve multiple functions: decision-making about household business (should we buy a dishwasher? whom should we take in as new members? how will we mobilize to reshingle the house?); task allocation (who's cooking and cleaning this week? who wants to buy the Christmas tree?); announcement and information about events and activities (I'm having two guests for the weekend, my musical group is playing here next week . . .); and the airing of grievances and concerns. Perhaps the latter is one of the most important functions of meetings, for they offer the opportunity for members to work out their relationships, to give each other feedback, to learn about what pleases and annoys each other and to communicate openly about how to achieve that delicate balance of personal prerogative and responsibility toward others that permits any two or more people to live together in harmony and satisfaction. It is also helpful for people to know that there is a structured time to air grievances, when other people will listen, when action may be taken. Emotional support and personal problem-solving may also occur at house meetings, one member soliciting the help of others. Emotional renewal can occur routinely in households where it is built into the weekly schedule.

Woven through the fabric of life in these new household arrangements are a variety of rituals and celebrations that honor the shared life. Communal households are notable tradition-keepers; the energy of a large group, like the energy of a large family, provides the impetus for feasts and festivals. Urban communes continue many religious traditions and invent their own, sometimes a mix of rituals representing the mix of people in the group. A number of groups begin meals with a silent grace with hands held around the table. A five-year-old group celebrated four house holidays each year: Epiphany, twelve days after Christmas, to celebrate Christmas, Chanukah, and the winter solstice; Omega Day in the spring, a remembrance of the beginnings of the anti-war and draft resistance movements, Easter, and Passover, complete with an ecumenical Seder; Founders' Day, their own anniversary, in the summer; and a fall harvest holiday that might include a trip to the country to pick apples. The importance of such events as rituals is not only in the value of each activity but that they *recur,* they can be anticipated, they reflect the cycle of seasons and the rhythm of life. They are more meaningful because they can be looked forward to with excitement.

V

In a variety of ways, then, communal households keep alive a very traditional set of family virtues; the centrality of meals, concern with the beauty of the environment, open communication and emotional support, and rituals and celebration. To talk of the virtues should not minimize the problems of creating new family forms; interpersonal difficulties are perhaps most responsible for the high turnover and transiency in communes. Some people have very unsatisfying experiences living communally. (I have documented the problems and drawbacks elsewhere.) But my concern here is not with evaluating communal households *per se;* rather I want to point out their relevance for a direction in which all families need to move in the future; toward nourishing in the home those ways of being together with other people most likely to create the warm glow of "family feeling."

The "post-biological family" of the future may borrow from communes—from non-biological intentional families—those experiences which make a set of people feel close and committed to one another when biological givens no longer seem sufficient to sustain a group. And as high mobility continues to undercut kin networks as source of family support, people may increasingly turn to non-blood but intentional and chosen "kin" inside and outside of shared households to provide the relatedness that we associate with "family."

Even real families have to work at *feeling* like a family.

NOTES

[1] Rosabeth Moss Kanter, *Commitment and Community* (Cambridge, Mass.: Harvard University Press, 1972). See also Rosabeth Moss Kanter (ed.), *Communes: Creating and Managing the Collective Life* (New York: Harper and Row, 1973).

[2] Daniel Bell, *The Coming of Post-Industrial Society* (New York: Basic Books, 1973).

[3] Mary Jo Bane, *Here to Stay: American Families in the Twentieth Century* (New York: Basic Books, 1976).

[4] Rosabeth Moss Kanter, Dennis T. Jaffe, and D. Kelly Weisberg, "Coupling, Parenting, and the Presence of Others: Intimate Relationships in Communal Households," *The Family Coordinator* 24 (1975): 433–52. See also Dennis T. Jaffe and Rosabeth Moss Kanter, "Couple Strains in Communal Households: A Four-Factor Model of the Separation Process," *Journal of Social Issues* 32 (1976): 169–91.

[5] Kanter, *Commitment and Community*.

APPENDICES: SOME GUIDES

The appendices of this anthology are designed to provide practical information in two areas related to marriage and family. The article presented in Appendix A carries us forward into the probable second stage of the adult life cycle—marriage—and the issue of budgeting income(s) not only to make ends meet but also to obtain desired items, prepare for children, and possibly lessen family arguments over money. Sylvia Porter briefly and simply notes the importance of a budget and how to make one that will work.

The article in Appendix B deals with a growing occurrence among marriages and remarriages—divorce. This is another area full of legal problems, despite the increase in no-fault divorce. Consumer Reports has outlined the legal implications of divorce to assist people involved in this traumatic experience.

APPENDIX A

Why Budget?

Sylvia Porter

As the previous analysis surely hinted, it's a virtual certainty that if you're a young couple in our country today you quarrel about money. How to finance not only your day-to-day needs but also your aspirations—that's the objective of people everywhere, in every income group, in every circumstance. And many of you are seeking help because you have an uncomfortable feeling that you ought to be able to manage better than you do.

You may be the rare one who does not need a budget at all, for you may have an instinctive sense of money management within the limits of your regular income. Or you may manage comfortably with only a loose outline of your living expenses and anticipated earnings.

But for the first time in a full generation, budget-keeping is coming back into style—as a result of the oppressively rapid rate of rise in living costs during the early 1970s and skyrocketing prices of many necessities and semi-luxuries. If, therefore, you feel you want or need a budget, you should have one. And if this is you, get this fundamental point straight now: your family's budget almost certainly will be radically different from that of families living near you. And it will without question differ in many key respects from any "average" spending-saving pattern of any "average" American family. The average family exists only on paper and its average budget is a fiction, invented by statisticians for the convenience of statisticians.

The shape of your own budget will depend directly on your own or your family's individual goals and priorities. Would you prefer to spend $4,000 on a new car or on a year of postgraduate education? Would $500 worth of color television mean more, or less, to you than $500 worth of, say, guitar lessons? There is no sense in attempting to fit into a ready-to-wear financial pattern which ignores your own personal wants and desires.

The budget you draw also will depend heavily on the composition of your family. A young working couple without children may have relatively low housing costs, relatively high entertainment and clothes costs, and a good opportunity to save substantial amounts toward future family goals. Drastically different will be the spending-savings blueprint of the young couple with growing children and a heavily mortgaged house.

In essence, there is no such thing as an average budget and you should not even look for a standardized format. Search instead for a simple, flexible financial outline to help you achieve the goals you truly want.

Which System of Money Management for You?

You can get your first basic guidance from the experience and methods of others. The shopkeeper on your corner has part of the answer in the way he handles his store's income and outgo and fits the two together with a margin left for "reserve." Your parents had part of the answer in the way they measured their earnings and their prospects

---

"Why Budget?" from *Sylvia Porter's Money Book*, Copyright © 1975 by Sylvia Porter. Reprinted by permission of Doubleday & Company, Inc.

for earnings, then divided their spending into so much for essentials, so much for savings, so much for luxuries. The giant corporation has much of the answer in the ways it keeps its books, prepares for bad as well as good times, and provides a cushion for the unexpected and unpredictable.

You may now be handling all your income and outgo on a basis of "Here's what's in my pocket, here's what has been spent." Income, in short, is what you actually have in your hands; outgo is what you are paying to other people. What's coming to you later isn't important this minute. What you owe later isn't important either. The big thing is what you have and what you spend now. Accountants call that operating on a "cash basis"—but, as millions discover, it doesn't go far enough.

It is obvious that what most people need is a system of money management which will:

1. tell you what money is coming in during the next several weeks or months;
2. tell you what has to be put aside today for future security and independence and for those big unavoidable bills due in the next several weeks or months;
3. tell you what is left over for the day-to-day expenses, ranging from food to a new household gadget;
4. tell you too how much is left, if any, for luxuries and semiluxuries;
5. relate your income and expenses to a reasonably long period of time so that you can avoid fumbling along from minute to minute and day to day;
6. show you how to run your personal affairs the way most successful businessmen run their affairs;
7. achieve your financial priorities.

This system, incidentally, is what accountants call operating on an "accrual" basis, but dismiss that fancy-sounding word right here. The important point is that no business can get anywhere unless it knows what money is coming in tomorrow as well as today and unless it knows also what is to be done with tomorrow's as well as today's cash.

A family or person cannot get far without this type of planning either.

Money is earned to be spent. When you spend, you buy more than material things such as bread or shoes; you make decisions which determine your whole way of life. Your decisions bring you closer to—or perhaps send you further away from—your ambitions, your aspirations, the things and nonthings which are really most worth while to you.

Money never remains just coins and pieces of paper. It is constantly changing into the comforts of daily life. Money can be translated into the beauty of living, a support in misfortune, an education, or future security. It also can be translated into a source of bitterness.

It may seem that so many of your decisions are forced by circumstances that you have very little chance to control your own money. Perhaps, however, your income appears too small to go around only because you did not take into account the "nibblers"—the little items that nibble away at your income until there is nothing left. Perhaps you have debts left at the end of the year only because you ignored the "bouncers"—the big expenses that turn up a couple of times a year and make giant dents in your income. Or perhaps you're in trouble only because you haven't considered the "sluggers"—the unexpected expenses, such as sickness and major household repairs, that can throw even a good spending plan way off balance.

Start from the premise that no income you will earn will ever be large enough to cover *all* your wants. Accept the theory that the more income you have the greater will be your desires. Make up your mind that if you want something badly enough you will sacrifice other things for it.

Take the trouble to think out your own philosophy of living and your ambitions for the future. Develop a plan of control over your spending. Then you will make progress toward the kind of living which means most to you.

Three Preliminary Notes on Budgeting

Although no system in itself can completely eliminate your money problems the following preliminary notes will certainly help:

1. You must work together if you are married. Your plan must be a joint project and you must

talk about a wide variety of things before trying to put down a single figure about income or outgo.
2. You must provide for personal allowances in your plan—and let each person decide what to do with his or her own allotment. None of you should have to account for every cent of your allowance; that is a personal matter. Similarly, if you're a wife at home, you should not be asked to submit an item-by-item explanation of what happened to the food money. Never permit a budget to become a strait jacket—or it will surely fail. And most important, I repeat, do not try to fit yourself into other people's budgets or try to make the spending averages of other families solve your own problems.
3. You must keep your records simple. Then they will be fun to maintain as well as helpful. All that is required from your records is a blueprint for each month's spending, a history of where money goes each month, and an overall picture to help you whenever a financial emergency arises. You can get vital information from simple records, and the simpler the records, the more they will reveal.

FOUR SIMPLE FORMS TO CREATE A PERSONAL MONEY MANAGER

You are about to create a personal money manager that, no matter what your income, will do four things:

1. tell you where your money is coming from—and when it is coming;
2. provide for the necessities first, then the comforts and self-improvements, then the luxuries—when you have the money to spend for them;
3. give you a means for saving—a plan to pay off debts or to keep out of debt;
4. build good habits for spending—for today and tomorrow.

You can do this job very successfully if you, as a family, will learn to complete four simple forms.

Form I. Here is how I get my income.

Form II. Here is what I must put aside to cover my unavoidable expenses and my savings.

Form III. Here is where I find how much I have available for my day-to-day expenses.

Form IV. Here is how I will spend the money available for my day-to-day expenses during this period.

Form I—Family Income

The mistake most people make in beginning a money management plan is that they don't start at the beginning. The *beginning* surely is to find out how much money you have coming in to spend for all purposes during the year.

To reach this vital figure, take a sheet of paper and write down every item of income you expect during the year. Convert each total to a monthly basis. If you are a husband-and-wife working couple or are just living together under one roof, include the earnings of both.

1. List not only the amounts of your regular take-home pay, translated into equal monthly totals, but also any income you anticipate from stock dividends, commissions, interest on bonds or savings accounts, yearly cash gifts from relatives, rent, bonuses, tax refunds due you, amounts owed to you by others. Also include profits from any sales of securities, your car, real estate, your home, assuming, of course, you sell any of these at a profit. Anything else? List it.
2. Estimate each item of income as accurately and realistically as you can. When in doubt, put down the *minimum*.
3. List only the net amounts of your regular pay checks—after subtracting withheld income taxes, your Social Security contributions, union dues, company pension plan payments you make, any group insurance or other payments which your company automatically deducts from your pay check, etc.
4. If your income is irregular—as it well may be if you are an artist, writer, teacher, small businessman, work part time or on a commission basis—divide the total you expect for the year by 12. Always keep your estimates low.

5. If you are not certain how much your income will be for the entire year, list only the amounts you can accurately predict for a shorter period—again, converted to a monthly basis.
6. If your income increases, don't get carried away: a pay raise always looks bigger than it really is. Before you start even to touch your raise, revise your budget income sheet to place the addition in accurate perspective. Add only the extra *net* (take-home) total—not the amount before taxes and other deductions.
7. By the same token, if your income takes an unexpected dive, revise all your monthly totals downward as soon as the drop occurs. Remember, the amounts of money you'll have to spend will be based on the amounts actually coming in at any given time.

Your inventory of income must reflect *facts*. On this sheet, there is little room for flexibility and *none* for fuzziness.

You have now broken down your income into 12 spending periods. You have taken the first step away from the "feast or famine" cash basis.

Knowing what you have available to spend each month, you will know how your expenses must be divided to match that real monthly income. When you have set up this kind of money manager, you'll be amazed how different your over-all income-expense picture will appear!

Form II—Fixed Expenses

Now let's consider expenses.

There are three classes of outgo: (1) the unavoidable expenses—the big items such as insurance premiums, repayment of personal debts, real estate taxes—which must be paid no matter what the inconvenience; (2) savings and rainy-day reserves; and (3) day-to-day living expenses.

The key to a good system of money management lies in spreading your big expenses and your savings so that each month bears a share of them. When you put aside $20 every month to meet a $240 yearly insurance premium, for instance, you will not risk spending that insurance money on an unnecessary luxury.

Take a second sheet of paper. On it list all of your fixed expenses during the coming year and convert each of these to a monthly basis.

Among the more obvious fixed expenses to include on your monthly list are:

1. Rent or mortgage payments.
2. Predictable, regular household bills for such items as electricity, gas, fuel, telephone, water, garbage collection, cable TV, lawn mowing.
3. Installment payments you make regularly for your car, washing machine, Christmas or Hanukkah Club, charge or credit card accounts, personal or education loan, etc.
4. Big once- or twice-a-year obligations such as real estate taxes, payments for tuition and fees, auto, life, and homeowners insurance premiums, dues to your professional society, pledged contributions.
5. Medical and dental expenses which can be accurately pinpointed for the year (e.g., costs of annual checkups, eye exams, orthodontia); health insurance premiums; predictable drug and vitamin bills.
6. Federal and state income taxes which have not been withheld.
7. Automobile and commuting expenses which you can accurately estimate, such as commuter train tickets and car pool costs, monthly parking bills, car registration and inspection, average gas and oil bills for your car or cars.
8. Membership dues—e.g., union, club, or professional association.

Among the less obvious fixed expenses to include are your monthly personal allowances for each family member. The amount of allowances you allot to each will depend partly on what expenses each person is expected to meet out of the allowance. Is the allowance supposed to pay for gifts? Lunches? Clothes? Music lessons? Charitable contributions?

Without a money management plan, if you have to pay a life insurance premium of $240, a property tax bill of $96, and a personal loan of $600—all in January—you would have to dig up $936 somewhere. And that might be tough indeed. But you probably know beforehand that in January you must meet those payments. When your money management plan is in full effect, you would set

Form I Family Income

WHAT WE WILL GET FROM	JAN.	FEB.	MAR.	APR.	MAY	JUNE	JULY	AUG.	SEPT.	OCT.	NOV.	DEC.	YEARLY TOTALS	NOTES
Husband's job														
Wife's job														
Business interests														
Interest														
Dividends														
Rent														
Gifts														
Company bonus or bonuses														
Tax refunds														
Moonlighting or jobs														
Profits from sales														
Allimony														
?														
?														
?														
Totals for the month														

aside $78 out of each month's income and then you would be able to take the financial blows in stride.

Of course, when you start your plan, you might find it impossible to provide for those big expenses. For example, let's assume that the $936 is due in January and it is now November. You might have to get a loan or make the November, December, and January income bear the full brunt. But once that hurdle has been passed, you would divide the expenses by 12 to find out how much of the burden each month's income should bear.

Some of your large debts, such as loans from a member of the family, may be past due. Try to pay these as soon as possible and clear your slate.

Include Your Savings!

At this point, let me back up and assure you that item (2) under the above "classes of outgo" was not a misprint. Rather a savings reserve is the least obvious—but still vital—expense you must include in your monthly list.

Put down a total you can reasonably expect to save each month. *Treat savings as an expense and budget for savings as you budget for rent or mortgage payments, and you will discipline yourself into building a nest egg.* "Pay yourself" first—as soon as you get your pay check—and your small monthly totals will become big totals over a period of time.

Include in your savings total an emergency fund equal to at least two months' income, to cover you should you be hit by big unforeseen expenses such as illness, unexpected home repairs, moving expenses. Note: The emergency part of your savings fund should be kept in a readily accessible ("liquid") form—for instance, a savings account.

As a starter, earmark 5 per cent of your total monthly income for savings, and boost the percentage from there if you can swing it.

If you have already saved the recommended equivalent of two months' income, freeze this amount as your emergency reserve. While you may want more or less than two months' income in reserve, be guided on this basically by the size of your other financial cushions: the amount of unemployment compensation for which you are eligible in the event that you are laid off or fired from your job and cannot find another one; the amount of your disability benefits which would be paid under Social Security or by your employer or through your health insurance policies; other health insurance benefits due you in the event of a medical crisis; your non-working wife's ability to take a job if an emergency arises or, if she has a job, to carry the family for a period; your credit-worthiness.

If you haven't the fund on hand now, figure how much more you will have to save before you reach the total. Then decide how long a time you'll need to save the amount necessary to lift your fund to the proper level. Don't try to save the extra amount too fast. Decide what you can put aside each month until the fund is assured and enter that amount on Form II as a fixed expense until your emergency fund is equal to the suggested level. Once it is there, keep it at that comfortable mark.

As for *how* you will save, you have many alternatives today.

1. An automatic deduction plan from your checking account is offered by many banks. Under this plan, you authorize the bank to transfer to a simple savings account your specified sum at fixed intervals. You will receive the bank's stated interest rate on the amounts you accumulate in your savings account.
2. Payroll savings plans are offered by many corporations under which a portion of your pay check is automatically deducted (by your authorization) and also is deposited in a savings account.
3. Under other corporate employee savings plans now available to millions, a corporation may add its own contribution to the amount you authorize to be deducted regularly from your pay check. Your savings then may be in-

Form II Fixed Expenses—Including Savings

WHAT WE MUST SPEND AND SAVE	JAN.	FEB.	MAR.	APR.	MAY	JUNE	JULY	AUG.	SEPT.	OCT.	NOV.	DEC.	YEAR'S TOTAL	NOTES
Rent or mortgage														
Fuel bills														
Telephone														
Electricity, gas														
Water														
Installment payment A														
Installment payment B														
Education (or other) payment														
Real estate taxes														
Income taxes														
Home and life insurance														
Auto insurance														
Medical, dental														
What we must set aside for savings alone														
Other														
Totals for the Month														

vested in U.S. savings bonds, mutual funds, or company stock.

Whatever method you choose, these fundamentals will remain unaltered:

The "secret" to saving is to put aside little amounts regularly and let the little amounts mount up to big totals.

The great value of your emergency reserve is protection for you against the unexpected and thus preservation of your peace of mind when the unexpected comes.

Form III—What You Have Left for Day-to-Day Expenses

Now that you have taken care of your inflexible expenses—which you must regard as already spent from each pay check—you are ready to begin work on budgeting for day-to-day expenses.

Take a third sheet of paper for Form III. As illustrated, put down your total income divided into 12 equal parts. Put down your unavoidable expenses and your savings, divided into 12 equal parts. The difference is what you have available for day-to-day living expenses.

This much is easy.

Form IV—Budgeting Your Day-to-Day Expenses

Form IV will show you whether you will have to do some major juggling to make ends meet. You can't argue with the fixed figures on Form II, but you can juggle the items you will list on Form IV.

This is important: on Form IV, don't try to figure ahead for a full year. That's too difficult. Simply plan your regular day-to-day living expenses for a month or two ahead.

These will vary considerably but they are a substantial and crucial part of your budget. They also are expenses over which you have the most control.

Because you probably won't even be able to remember many of the little items when you begin your list, keep a detailed record of *all* your living expenses just for a couple of weeks. From this, you'll get an accurate idea of how much you're spending and for what. After you've obtained this guide, stop keeping records in such stultifying detail.

Here are the main categories of day-to-day expenses:

1. *Food and related items:* the amounts of your regular grocery bills; what you spend to eat out in restaurants (including tips); candy and snacks from vending machines; soft drinks, beer, wine, and liquor; cigarettes; pet foods and supplies; personal and household items such as toothpaste and cosmetics which you buy at the supermarket.
2. *Household services and expenses:* home repairs and improvements; any maintenance costs not counted in your fixed expenses; cleaning supplies; household help.
3. *Furnishings and equipment:* what you buy outright for cash and down payments for large and small appliances, glass, china, silver-

Form III Day-to-Day Expenses

		JAN.	FEB.	MAR.	APR.	MAY	JUNE	JULY	AUG.	SEPT.	OCT.	NOV.	DEC.
From Form I, your monthly income	$												
From Form II, the total of your unavoidable expenses and savings for the year, divided by 12.	$												
What you have available for your day-to-day living expenses	$												

ware, curtains, rugs, upholstering, accessories, other items.
4. *Clothes:* everything, ranging from repairs and alterations through laundry and dry cleaning to the seemingly insignificant accessories which can mount up to alarming totals.
5. *Transportation:* car repairs, tune-ups, oil changes, new tires; bus, train, taxi, and air fares, parking charges; bridge tolls.
6. *Medical care:* doctor and dentist bills not listed under your fixed expenses; drugs; eyeglasses; hospital and nursing expenses not covered by medical insurance; veterinary bills for your pets.
7. *Personal care:* the barber and hairdresser; toilet articles; cosmetics and other items not paid for by each family member's personal allowance and *not* in your supermarket bills.
8. *Education and recreation:* books; theater, movie, and concert tickets; entertaining friends; newspaper and magazine subscriptions; musical instruments and music lessons; hobby equipment; vacation and holiday expenses; the upkeep of your pleasure boat, swimming pool, or riding horse; tuition and fees not included on Form II.
9. *Gifts and contributions:* what is not paid out of personal allowances.
10. *Other things and non-things:* Only you can fill out this item.

Don'ts to Guide You

Just a glance at the list on Form IV shows why it is futile to attempt a precise budget at the start. Unless you are the exception who always has kept exact records of your spending, you will have to estimate the totals. Later it will be possible to be more accurate.

Don't set spending limits which are impossible to meet. It may be hard to fix a range until you've tried this money management system for a few months. That's expected. You'll learn by experience what the limits are and what they should be.

Form IV Budgeting Day-to-Day Expenses

WHAT WE WILL SPEND FOR DAY-TO-DAY LIVING THIS MONTH	JAN.	FEB.	MAR.	APR.	MAY	JUNE	JULY	AUG.	SEPT.	OCT.	NOV.	DEC.	NOTES
For food and related items	$	$	$	$	$	$	$	$	$	$	$	$	
For household services and expenses													
For furnishings and equipment													
For clothes													
For transportation													
For medical care													
For personal care													
For education and recreation													
For gifts and contributions													
For other things and non-things													
TOTAL													
Total available for the month (from last line of form III)	$	$	$	$	$	$	$	$	$	$	$	$	

APPENDIX A

Don't start out by slashing one classification arbitrarily, "on paper." A major expense category cannot be cut just because the figure appears so big when listed. "Food" is the category that most of you will try to slash first. But if you cut this too low, you'll discover you've set an impossible limit.

Don't forget that the big expenses are on Form II. The classifications on Form IV cover only the usual day-to-day expenses. Major costs, such as orthodontia for your child, may be spread over a whole year of income periods. If "spreading" is easier for you, transfer other big items from Form IV to Form II.

Don't ignore your wants and don't try to kid yourself. When you're setting your allocations, be realistic. If your menu says steak, don't put down a figure for stew.

Don't fail to leave room for unexpected expenses. These are certain to arise and you never know in advance what they will be. They may range from a flat tire to an office contribution for a wedding gift.

Don't underestimate the importance of detailed records during the first month of your money management plan. When the next period rolls around and it turns out that your guesses weren't right, cross out the inaccurate estimates and put down what was really spent for each item.

With these hints to help, you can fill out Form IV, marking down your estimates, adding them up for each month, and comparing them with the total amount available. The result easily could be a big minus, indicating that you're spending or planning to spend more than your projected income. If your expense total, including savings, comes out way above your income total and the tally indicates you're heading into a flood of red ink, some items here must be cut.

But you can't cut unless you vow to make the cuts good. This money management plan is more than a pencil-pushing game.

APPENDIX B

What You Should Know About Divorce Today

Consumer Reports

Attitudes toward divorce have changed radically in recent years. So have the divorce laws. All but two states—Illinois and South Dakota—have authorized some form of "no fault" divorce, which means it's not necessary to establish that one party is to blame for the marriage breakdown. Consequently, the procedures for getting a divorce are much simpler than they used to be.

The fault idea has existed in European countries for several hundred years. With the rise of Christianity, marriage had become a religious matter rather than a civil one, and therefore subject to rigorous ecclesiastical law. By the time of the Protestant Reformation, about four centuries ago, divorce was extremely rare, and legal separation was permitted only if one partner was guilty of serious misconduct.

In England, for example, if you could prove your spouse's adultery, cruelty, or predilection for unnatural acts, you might have been able to get a divorce *a mensa et thoro*—"from table and bed." But that only meant you were free to live apart; you couldn't legally remarry.

With the Matrimonial Causes Act of 1857, the King's Courts assumed jurisdiction over divorce, but adultery was the only recognized ground. American divorce laws followed the English pattern, though certain other grounds were added, and annulments were occasionally substituted for divorce. The fault system survived virtually intact until about 10 years ago.

Copyright © 1981 by Consumers Union of the United States, Inc., Mount Vernon, N.Y. 10553. Reprinted by permission from *Consumer Reports*, June 1981. Some state provisions may have changed since the preparation of this report.

NO-FAULT BEGINS

In 1968, England and Canada recognized the breakdown of a marriage as a ground for divorce. And in 1970, California became the first state in this country to do so. California's Family Law Act modified the terminology and the process of divorce. The official forms now refer to "dissolution of marriage" rather than divorce, and the legal act of dissolution is no longer an "adversary proceeding"—that is, the parties aren't considered opponents. The main requirement is to satisfy the court that "irreconcilable differences" have led to an "irremediable breakdown" of the marriage. As a practical matter, there are now no defenses against divorce in California, and it is available at the request of either party.

Although nearly all states permit some form of no-fault divorce, the grounds vary considerably. Irremediable breakdown is the sole ground for divorce in 16 states (some also accept insanity as a ground, but it's rarely used). In another 17 states, the irremediable-breakdown ground is available along with the traditional fault grounds of adultery, cruelty, and desertion.

In the remaining states, the primary no-fault grounds are incompatibility, living apart for a specified period of time (sometimes beginning from the date of a court-issued separation decree), and mutual consent (sometimes established by a separation agreement or by living apart).

It's not clear what effect the new no-fault laws have had on the divorce rate. In the 1920's, the U.S. had roughly 10 marriages and 1.5 divorces per 1000 population per year. The rates have gradually converged since then. Today the respective rates are roughly 10 and 5. Where there was one divorce for every seven marriages before, there is now one divorce for every two marriages.

Since the divorce rate has been rising gradually for more than half a century, we can't attribute the rise to the no-fault laws. But the no-fault laws may have accelerated the change in the rate in recent years.

TRENDS IN FAMILY LAW

Although no-fault divorce is the most conspicuous of recent changes in family law—which includes not only divorce but also such things as custody, alimony, and adoption—several other changes are worth noting. Doris Jonas Freed, a leading authority on family law, summarizes them this way: "I see a trend toward equality and equity. Most states now consider marriage a partnership of economic as well as social equals, and divorcing partners must get a fair share of all the property acquired during the marriage, regardless of who holds title. Alimony has been de-emphasized and de-sexed. And increasingly, the parents are sharing both custody and financial support of their children."

Here is the current situation on the various elements in a divorce:

Dividing property. State laws differ substantially on this point. The principle of "community property" prevails in eight states—Arizona, California, Idaho, Louisiana, Nevada, New Mexico, Texas, and Washington. It's assumed that the marital community—the couple—owns all the property acquired during the marriage, sometimes excepting individual gifts and inheritances. California, Louisiana, and New Mexico ordinarily require a 50-50 split of the community property when the marriage is dissolved. Other community-property states require an equitable division but may tip the balance in favor of one party if the other has been guilty of marital misconduct.

Three states—Mississippi, Virginia, and West Virginia—follow "common law," a collection of rules and principles based on custom and precedent rather than statutes. In those states, the spouse who holds title to the property is generally allowed to keep it.

Although the rest of the states and the District of Columbia follow common-law rules in most matters, the courts have the power to require "equitable distribution" in divorces, without regard to who actually holds title to the property. That doesn't necessarily mean a 50-50 split. The division may favor one spouse or the other, depending on the circumstances.

In the states without community-property laws, a judge might consider such factors as: the length of the marriage; how employable each spouse is; each spouse's relative age, health, income, wealth, and liabilities; and how much each spouse contributed—by taking care of the home and children, for example, or by holding a job while the other attended school or college.

A couple's property may include not only such obvious things as a house and a car but also financial property or "intangibles." For example, if the couple acquired life insurance, bank accounts, pension funds, or a small business during the marriage, that property may also be divided, depending on state law.

The couple usually decides how the property is to be divided prior to the divorce, but the actual division may occur much later. For example, if they own a house and there are minor children in the family, the couple might agree that whoever has custody of the children should live in the house until the children are no longer dependent. Then the house can be sold and the proceeds divided according to a formula specifed at the time of the divorce.

Alimony. "Alimony" is from the Latin "alimonia," meaning nourishment or sustenance. The term is linked to the ancient idea that, in return for her services in the home, a wife is entitled to be supported by her husband. Traditionally, alimony has been awarded only to wives, but the U.S. Supreme Court recently ruled that alimony statutes have to be gender-neutral. Before the no-fault laws, alimony was awarded to the wife almost automatically. But, as women have become more financially independent and as the equitable-distribution rule has spread, alimony has become a less important element in divorce settlements. In many states, alimony has come to be known as "maintenance," and its function is to give the dependent partner a

GROUNDS FOR DIVORCE

State	Irremediable Breakdown Only	Fault Grounds* Plus Irremediable Breakdown	Fault Grounds* Plus Incompatibility	Fault Grounds* Plus Living Apart	Fault Grounds* Plus Mutual Consent	Fault Grounds Only*
Alabama		•	•	•		
Alaska		•	•		•	
Arizona	•					
Arkansas				•		
California	•					
Colorado	•					
Connecticut		•	•	•		
Delaware	•					
District of Columbia				•		
Florida	•					
Georgia		•				
Hawaii		•		•		
Idaho		•		•		
Illinois						•
Indiana		•				
Iowa	•					
Kansas			•			
Kentucky	•					
Louisiana				•		
Maine		•				
Maryland				•		
Massachusetts		•				
Michigan	•					
Minnesota						
Mississippi		•			•	
Missouri	•					
Montana	•					
Nebraska	•					
Nevada			•	•		
New Hampshire		•		•		
New Jersey				•		
New Mexico			•			
New York				•	•	
New Carolina				•		
North Dakota		•		•		
Ohio		•		•	•	
Oklahoma			•			
Oregon	•					
Pennsylvania		•		•	•	
Rhode Island		•		•		
South Carolina				•		
South Dakota						•
Tennessee		•		•	•	
Texas		•		•		
Utah				•		
Vermont				•		
Virginia				•		
Washington	•					
West Virginia				•		
Wisconsin	•			•		
Wyoming	•					

*Major fault grounds are adultery, mental or physical cruelty, and desertion.

APPENDIX B

kind of unemployment compensation until he or she may be self-supporting.

Alimony payments consequently depend on the size of the property settlement and on each spouse's earning capacity. For example, a young woman who has a good job probably can't expect to receive alimony. But a middle-aged woman who has never worked can probably expect to receive alimony at least temporarily—permanently if she can't find a way to support herself. Alimony usually stops if the recipient remarries or if either party dies.

Child custody. Under old English common law, the father of a child born in wedlock had the sole right to custody. That right eroded over the centuries and was replaced by the "tender years presumption," which is that very young children are better off living with their mother than with their father.

Today, courts take the view that married parents are joint guardians of their children and have equal rights and responsibilities for raising them. When the parents are divorced, courts may award custody to either or both parents. In practice, however, most courts still tend to award custody to the mother.

A court's primary objective is to do what's best for the children. In making custody decisions, courts consider such factors as the child's age and sex, which parent the child would prefer to live with, and the mental and physical health of everyone concerned.

Although it has been customary to assign custody to one parent or the other, "joint custody" is more and more common. The underlying assumption is that it's beneficial for the children to continue to have the guidance and companionship of both parents.

Joint custody requires the divorced parents to share the responsibility for raising the children and making decisions about their education, religious training, leisure time, and so on. The parents are also required to divide the time spent with the children, though not necessarily equally. The children may live with their parents alternately over a period of time, but that arrangement isn't essential.

Of course, joint custody works best when the parents are friendly. If the parents are openly hostile to each other, it may make more sense to assign custody to one parent.

Visiting rights. Visiting rights also depend on the court's view of what would be in the best interest of the child. Generally, unless there's strong evidence that the arrangement would be detrimental to the child, a court will enforce the agreement made by the divorcing couple.

Child support. It used to be up to the father to support the children after divorce, but now practically all states require both parents to contribute to child support. Courts consider the parents' relative financial positions in deciding how much each is to contribute.

SOME TAX CONSEQUENCES

Decisions about alimony, child support, and property division may have serious income-tax consequences. As far as the Internal Revenue Service is concerned, alimony is deductible but child support is not. Alimony is considered part of the recipient's income. (The IRS requires that the payments be periodic and made according to a written court decree or separation agreement.)

For example, if a husband pays his ex-wife $10,000 a year in alimony, he can reduce his taxable income by that amount, and she has to increase her taxable income by the same amount. But if the $10,000 is given as child support, the husband can't deduct it and the wife doesn't have to add it to her income.

Another factor to consider is the tax exemption for dependents. Generally, the parent who contributes more than half of a child's support is entitled to the dependent's exemption.

Then there's the matter of capital gains. For example, suppose the couple jointly own a house purchased for $50,000 but now worth $100,000. And suppose, as part of the settlement, the husband agrees to turn the house over to the wife. A $50,000 capital gain would result—$25,000 each. But only the husband's gain would be taxable at that point. The wife's gain would be taxable, along with any additional gain, when she sells the house.

Of course, these are only a few of the tax consequences to consider when substantial amounts of property and money are divided.

SIMPLIFIED FILING PROCEDURES

Along with changes in the divorce laws themselves have come simpler filing procedures, which facilitate do-it-yourself divorce. In California, the state that led the way in reform, getting a divorce is mainly a matter of filling out several forms and waiting a few months.

Most of the California forms are fairly brief—one or two pages long. You can get them at the County Clerk's Office, and you return them to that office when they're completed. The forms are also available in books and kits sold by commercial publishers and public-interest organizations.

A few states have authorized "summary dissolution," an extremely simple procedure for couples who have been married a short time and have no children and little property. In California, for example, a couple may apply for a summary dissolution if they meet these requirements:

- The couple have been married for less than two years.

- They have no children from that marriage and no adopted children under 18.

- The wife isn't pregnant.

- The couple own no real estate.

- Their community property (not counting cars) isn't worth more than $5000.

- Neither has separately owned property worth more than $5000.

- Their joint debts (not counting any car loans) amount to no more than $2000.

- At least one of them has lived in the state for six months.

The dissolution is accomplished in three stages: The couple file a petition for summary dissolution and an agreement describing how their property will be divided. They wait six months. Then they file a form confirming that they want to go through with the dissolution. The whole thing can be done by mail.

SEPARATION AGREEMENTS

Now that most states' procedural barriers have been lowered, the main obstacle to splitting up—and the main expense—may be preparing a "separation agreement." That's a contract between the spouses covering all the issues that have to be settled before the divorce is granted.

In some cases, the law requires a written agreement. For example, as noted earlier, if you apply for a summary dissolution in California, you'll have to submit a statement about how the property is to be divided. But written agreements are usually optional.

In any case, it's advantageous to both parties to put the terms of their agreement on paper. That will make it easier for the court to see whether the settlement is fair. It will also reduce the chance of a dispute later on.

When a separation agreement is submitted to the court, the judge will usually accept it as written, unless the terms are clearly unfair to one of the parties. In most states, judges have the power to modify those terms that create serious hardship. In other states, judges are empowered to change only those terms that apply to the couple's children. The children are considered wards of the state, so it's up to the judge to see that their rights are protected.

That, incidentally, is a continuing obligation. For example, if the mother has custody of the children and she later thinks that the child-support payments from the father are inadequate, she may petition the court for an increase. However, unless circumstances have changed drastically, the court will generally avoid interfering with the original agreement.

There's a sample agreement on pages 372–373. It's a fairly simple one, and it ignores many variations in state laws. But it will give some sense of the basic points to be covered.

A more complex agreement might include paragraphs on such things as insurance, pension funds, cost-of-living adjustments for alimony and child support, formulas for increasing alimony and child-support payments as the payer's income increases, selling the family home in the distant future, and special trusts for minor children.

A separation agreement can be constructed in many ways. What matters is that every important question about the separation be answered clearly and in as much detail as necessary. For example, if the agreement covers alimony payments from the husband to the wife, it should specify exactly how much is to be paid, when it is to be paid, and under what conditions the payments will stop.

DO YOU NEED A LAWYER?

The range of legal costs involved in a divorce is wide. If you hire a lawyer who specializes in divorce problems, the fee may amount to a few thousand dollars or more. If you hire a general practitioner, the fee may be lower. Many legal clinics advertise they will handle a simple divorce for as little as $150 plus court costs. It's also possible to buy do-it-yourself books and kits at prices ranging from a few dollars to a hundred or more. The question is, then, how much and what kind of legal help do you need?

To answer that, let's first divide divorces into those that are "contested" and those that are "uncontested." Less than 10 percent of all divorces are contested. In a contested divorce, the parties have serious differences that they can't settle amicably, and they're willing to go to court to have a judge settle them.

Although you have the right to participate in such a case without a lawyer, it would be foolish to do so. And you probably have a much better chance of getting what you want if you engage a lawyer who is very experienced in contested-divorce work.

But what if you're involved in an uncontested divorce? That's not quite as simple as it sounds, since you're confronted with two different problems: You have to deal with the state, and you have to deal with your spouse.

Dealing with the state is usually fairly easy. As noted earlier, you'll probably have to fill out several forms, submit them to the right office, and wait the required amount of time between steps.

Dealing with your spouse may be a lot more difficult—and a lot more expensive; you need to know what your rights and options are. You may have trouble agreeing about alimony and child-support payments. Or you may disagree about how your property should be divided. Of course, the more property you have, the greater the opportunity for disagreement and the greater the opportunity for serious error.

The problem will be compounded if some of your property is not easily evaluated or divided—a small business, let's say. If you and your spouse own a store, and you agree that one of you should continue to run it, you'll have to decide who will keep the business and how much the other should be paid to give up his or her share.

Obviously, when you're uncertain about property, custody, and various financial arrangements, it will pay to hire an expert to represent you. Contrary to the impression created by television, your lawyer's most important job is not to defeat another lawyer in a courtroom but to work out the details of an agreement you can live with. (You should also encourage your spouse to get legal advice, to make sure the agreement won't be challenged as unfair in the future.)

As Henry Foster, professor emeritus of New York University, puts it: "The lawyer is primarily a negotiator, and the essence of law is compromise—settling disputes, getting your client to give a little, and trying to get the other side to give more. A good settlement of a divorce case is one that pleases neither party but is workable."

On the other hand, not everyone needs a lawyer in a divorce proceeding. For example, if you can meet the criteria listed above for a summary dissolution in California, you can probably proceed without legal help.

How about kits? Are they worth the price? Like most products and services, they vary a lot in quality, and the quality isn't necessarily proportional to the price. If a kit costs more than $50, you would probably be better off going to a low-fee legal clinic or to a lawyer who charges a low hourly rate.

Michael Atkins, a lawyer in Garden City, N.Y., summed up the situation this way: "If there's not much property and no children, then any intelligent person can compile the necessary forms.

Of course, kits and books are available. And why not? The public is entitled to have legal service at the lowest possible price. But once you get beyond the simplest area of divorce, you get into problems of finance—certainly where children are involved—and the role of the lawyer becomes much more significant. Even a do-it-yourself kit will say, 'Be careful. If you have any complications, consult a lawyer.' That's good advice.''

FURTHER REFORM

Although most divorce laws have improved substantially in the last 10 years or so, some states have been slow to make useful changes. To ease the process for those who wish to divorce, here are the primary reforms that should be established in all states:

No-fault. This is the most important of recent changes. All but two states now have some form of no-fault divorce.

Equitable distribution. If marriage is an economic partnership—as most state laws now assume—the material gain should be divided fairly between the parties when the partnership is dissolved.

Summary dissolution. This procedure, described earlier, applies to brief marriages involving little property and no children. The idea is to simplify the dissolution of such marriages.

Child custody. Until fairly recently, one state could ignore another's custody decrees. (This isn't true of other kinds of court judgments.) For example, suppose the mother is awarded custody of the child, and the father moves to another state. Suppose also that, during one of the child's visits to the father's home, the father decides to keep the child with him permanently. The father might eventually be able to persuade a court in his state to assign him custody, in disregard of the original custody decree. The National Conference of Commissioners on Uniform State Laws proposed the Uniform Child Custody Jurisdiction Act in 1968 to avoid such conflicts and abductions. So far, 44 states have adopted the act.

Protection of children's rights. When there are children in the family, there are at least three parties to a divorce proceeding—the wife, the husband, and the children. The trouble is that, while the husband and wife may each have a lawyer, the children are left without legal representation. What's urgently needed is some procedure for insuring that the financial and psychological needs of the children are considered.

Sample Separation Agreement

The following agreement is a fairly simple one. It shows the kinds of issues that must be considered, but it shouldn't be used as a model for writing your own agreement. Each case is unique, and each agreement must be constructed to deal with a different set of problems.

This agreement is between a man and a woman who have been married nearly 11 years and who have an eight-year-old son. They've agreed that the wife will have custody of the son and that the husband will contribute $6000 a year for the son's support. The husband will also pay for the son's college education and will record the son as a dependent for tax purposes. The wife will receive $6000 a year for three years for maintenance while she goes back to college. They've agreed to sell their house and split the proceeds equally.

We, Ann Jones and Paul Jones, made this agreement on March 30, 1981.

We were married on June 1, 1970, and our only child, Robert, was born September 27, 1972. Because our marriage is seriously damaged beyond repair, we have separated and intend to live apart for the rest of our lives. We want to divide our property and make whatever legal and financial arrangements are necessary under the circumstances. The purpose of this document is to record the terms we have agreed on:

1. Independence. Except as noted below, each of us will live completely independent of the other, as if we were unmarried. We will not interfere with each other in any way.

2. Custody of our child. Ann will have sole custody of our child as long as he is a minor, and he will live with her.

3. The child's visits. The child will visit Paul at these times: every other weekend, from 6 P.M. Friday to 6 P.M. Sunday; during the Christmas and Easter school holidays, from 6 P.M. the last day of school before the holiday to 6 P.M. the day before school starts again; at least 30 days during the summer recess. Paul will pick the child up at home at the beginning of the visiting period and take him home at the end of the period. If we agree to do so, this schedule may be changed for any particular visit.

During the child's visits, Paul will pay for the child's food, transportation, housing, and any other expenses connected with the visit. If Paul and Ann ever live permanently or temporarily at places more than 50 miles apart, the schedule for the child's visits with his father will be rearranged so it is equivalent to the present schedule.

4. Payments for child support. As basic child support, Paul will pay Ann $6000 a year in $500 installments payable on the first day of each month. The first installment will be due on the first month after the date of this agreement. These payments will terminate under any of these conditions: if either parent or the child dies; if the child marries; if the child becomes fully self-supporting; if the child reaches his 21st birthday; if the child stops living permanently with his mother (excluding periods away at school or college); if the father assumes custody by written agreement or by court order.

5. Payments for college. If the child goes to college, and if he remains a student in good standing, Paul will pay for room and board, textbooks, tuition, laboratory fees, and any other charges billed by the college. These college payments will be in addition to the support payments described in section 4. Paul's obligation to make these payments will terminate under any of these conditions: if either parent dies; if the child receives his bachelor's degree; if the child reaches his 23rd birthday.

6. Payments for maintenance. Paul will pay Ann $6000 a year in $500 installments payable on the first day of each month. The first installment will be due the first month after the date of this agreement. These payments will terminate under any of these conditions: after the 36th monthly payment; if either Paul or Ann dies; if Ann remarries; if Ann chooses to live with another male not related by blood or marriage.

7. Personal property. We have divided all the property acquired during our marriage. The list appended to this agreement shows the items each of us will own separately from now on. We are satisfied with this division, and neither will later ask the other for any of the property divided according to this agreement.

8. Real estate. We jointly own the house and land at 100 Ridge Road, Saltmine, Ohio. We will try to sell this property as soon as possible. After the sale, we will pay off the mortgage and divide the net proceeds equally. In the interim, Paul will pay 70 percent of the carrying costs (mortgage payments, property taxes, and homeowners insurance premiums) and Ann will pay 30 percent.

9. Taxes. The maintenance payments described in section 6 will be considered part of Ann's taxable income and will be deducted from Paul's taxable income. If those payments are affected by a subsequent change in the tax laws, the payments will be adjusted so Ann will end up with an after-tax maintenance income equal to the amount resulting from the present arrangement.

As in the past, we will file a joint income-tax return this year. If there are any refunds, we will share them equally. If there are any taxes, assessments, or penalties due, each of us will pay half.

Next year, the child will be listed as a dependent on Paul's tax returns.

10. Debts. A list of debts is appended to this agreement, indicating which debts will be paid by Paul and which by Ann. Our understanding is that there are no other debts for which we are jointly liable, and we agree not to incur any such debts in the future.

11. Cooperation in handling documents. We will promptly sign and deliver any papers necessary to carry out the terms of this agreement.

12. Entire agreement. We have made no agreements about separation other than those detailed in this document. If we choose to make any changes later on, the changes must be in writing and signed and dated by both of us.

13. Governing laws. We made this agreement in Ohio, and it is covered by the laws of that state.

14. Partial invalidity. If we find that part of this agreement isn't valid for some reason, the rest of the agreement will remain in effect.

15. Subsequent divorce. If we are divorced later, we will ask the court to append this agreement to the divorce decree.

16. Waiver of estate claims. Except with respect to the terms already stated in this agreement, each of us agrees not to make any claims against the other's estate. We also waive all such rights that exist now or may exist in the future.

17. Release from other obligations. Except as noted in this agreement, and except for any obligations in connection with a subsequent divorce decree, each of us releases the other from all past, present, and future obligations.

18. Change of status or address. If one of us remarries, he or she will notify the other of the date and the name of the new spouse. Also, each will notify the other of any change of address.

19. Binding effect. This agreement will be binding on our heirs, representatives, and assignees.

Signed: _____ Signed: _____
Ann Jones   Paul Jones
100 Ridge Road   4 Valley Road
Saltmine, Ohio   Saltmine, Ohio
Notarized: On _____, 1981, Ann and Paul Jones signed this document in my presence.
Signed: _____, Notary Public